Lecture Notes in Artificial Intelligence  2373

Subseries of Lecture Notes in Computer Science
Edited by J. G. Carbonell, and J. Siekmann

Lecture Notes in Computer Science
Edited by G. Goos, J. Hartmanis, and J. van Leeuwen

Springer
Berlin
Heidelberg
New York
Barcelona
Hong Kong
London
Milan
Paris
Tokyo

Jyrki Kivinen   Robert H. Sloan (Eds.)

Computational Learning Theory

15th Annual Conference on Computational Learning Theory,
COLT 2002
Sydney, Australia, July 8-10, 2002
Proceedings

 Springer

Series Editors

Jaime G. Carbonell,Carnegie Mellon University, Pittsburgh, PA, USA
Jörg Siekmann, University of Saarland, Saarbrücken, Germany

Volume Editors

Jyrki Kivinen
Australian National University
Research School of Information Sciences and Engineering
Canberra ACT 0200, Australia
E-mail: Jyrki.Kivinen@anu.edu au

Robert H. Sloan
University of Illinois at Chicago, Computer Science Department
851 S. Morgan St., Chicago, IL 60607, USA
E-mail: sloan@cs.uic.edu

Cataloging-in-Publication Data applied for

Die Deutsche Bibliothek - CIP-Einheitsaufnahme

Computational learning theory : proceedings / 15th Annual Conference on
Computational Learning Theory, COLT 2002, Sydney, Australia, July 8 - 10,
2002. Jyrki Kivinen ; Robert H. Sloan (ed.). - Berlin ; Heidelberg ; New
York ; Barcelona ; Hong Kong ; London ; Milan ; Paris ; Tokyo : Springer,
2002
    (Lecture notes in computer science ; Vol. 2375 : Lecture notes in
    artificial intelligence)
    ISBN 3-540-43836-X

CR Subject Classification (1998): I.2.6, I.2.3, F.4.1, F.1.1, F.2

ISSN 0302-9743
ISBN 3-540-43836-X Springer-Verlag Berlin Heidelberg New York

Springer-Verlag Berlin Heidelberg New York
a member of BertelsmannSpringer Science+Business Media GmbH

http://www.springer.de

© Springer-Verlag Berlin Heidelberg 2002
Printed in Germany

Typesetting: Camera-ready by author, data conversion by DA-TeX Gerd Blumenstein
Printed on acid-free paper   SPIN 10870415   06/3142   5 4 3 2 1 0

Preface

This volume contains papers presented at the Fifteenth Annual Conference on Computational Learning Theory (COLT 2002) held on the main campus of the University of New South Wales in Sydney, Australia from July 8 to 10, 2002. Naturally, these are papers in the field of computational learning theory, a research field devoted to studying the design and analysis of algorithms for making predictions about the future based on past experiences, with an emphasis on rigorous mathematical analysis.

COLT 2002 was co-located with the Nineteenth International Conference on Machine Learning (ICML 2002) and with the Twelfth International Conference on Inductive Logic Programming (ILP 2002).

Note that COLT 2002 was the first conference to take place after the full merger of the Annual Conference on Computational Learning Theory with the European Conference on Computational Learning Theory. (In 2001 a joint conference consisting of the 5th European Conference on Computational Learning Theory and the 14th Annual Conference on Computational Learning Theory was held; the last independent European Conference on Computational Learning Theory was held in 1999.)

The technical program of COLT 2002 contained 26 papers selected from 55 submissions. In addition, Christos Papadimitriou (University of California at Berkeley) was invited to give a keynote lecture and to contribute an abstract of his lecture to these proceedings.

The Mark Fulk Award is presented annually for the best paper coauthored by a student. This year's award was won by Sandra Zilles for the paper "Merging Uniform Inductive Learners."

April 2002

Jyrki Kivinen
Robert H. Sloan

Thanks and Acknowledgments

We gratefully thank all the individuals and organizations responsible for the success of the conference.

Program Committee

We especially want to thank the program committee: Dana Angluin (Yale), Javed Aslam (Dartmouth), Peter Bartlett (BIOwulf Technologies), Shai Ben-David (Technion), John Case (Univ. of Delaware), Peter Grünwald (CWI), Ralf Herbrich (Microsoft Research), Mark Herbster (University College London), Gábor Lugosi (Pompeu Fabra University), Ron Meir (Technion), Shahar Mendelson (Australian National Univ.), Michael Schmitt (Ruhr-Universität Bochum), Rocco Servedio (Harvard), and Santosh Vempala (MIT).

We also acknowledge the creators of the CyberChair software for making a software package that helped the committee do its work.

Local Arrangements, Co-located Conferences Support

Special thanks go to our conference chair Arun Sharma and local arrangements chair Eric Martin (both at Univ. of New South Wales) for setting up COLT 2002 in Sydney. Rochelle McDonald and Sue Lewis provided administrative support. Claude Sammut in his role as conference chair of ICML and program co-chair of ILP ensured smooth coordination with the two co-located conferences.

COLT Community

For keeping the COLT series going, we thank the COLT steering committee, and especially Chair John Shawe-Taylor and Treasurer John Case for all their hard work. We also thank Stephen Kwek for maintaining the COLT web site at http://www.learningtheory.org.

Sponsoring Institution

School of Computer Science and Engineering, University of New South Wales, Australia

Referees

Peter Auer	Lisa Hellerstein	Alain Pajor
Andrew Barto	Daniel Herrmann	Gunnar Rätsch
Stephane Boucheron	Colin de la Higuera	Robert Schapire
Olivier Bousquet	Sean Holden	John Shawe-Taylor
Nicolò Cesa-Bianchi	Marcus Hutter	Takeshi Shinohara
Tapio Elomaa	Sanjay Jain	David Shmoys
Ran El-Yaniv	Yuri Kalnishkan	Yoram Singer
Allan Erskine	Makoto Kanazawa	Carl Smith
Henning Fernau	Satoshi Kobayashi	Frank Stephan
Jürgen Forster	Vladimir Koltchinskii	György Turán
Dean Foster	Matti Kääriäinen	Paul Vitányi
Claudio Gentile	Wee Sun Lee	Manfred Warmuth
Judy Goldsmith	Shie Mannor	Jon A. Wellner
Thore Graepel	Ryan O'Donnell	Robert C. Williamson

Table of Contents

PAC Learning

Boosting

Other Learning Paradigms

Invited Talk

Agnostic Learning Nonconvex Function Classes

Shahar Mendelson and Robert C. Williamson

Research School of Information Sciences and Engineering
Australian National University
Canberra, ACT 0200, Australia
{shahar.mendelson,Bob.Williamson}@anu.edu.au

Abstract. We consider the sample complexity of agnostic learning with respect to squared loss. It is known that if the function class F used for learning is convex then one can obtain better sample complexity bounds than usual. It has been claimed that there is a lower bound that showed there was an essential gap in the rate. In this paper we show that the lower bound proof has a gap in it. Although we do not provide a definitive answer to its validity. More positively, we show one can obtain "fast" sample complexity bounds for nonconvex F for "most" target conditional expectations. The new bounds depend on the detailed geometry of F, in particular the distance in a certain sense of the target's conditional expectation from the set of nonuniqueness points of the class F.

1 Introduction

The agnostic learning model [6] is a generalization of the PAC learning model that does not presume the target function lies within the space of functions (hypotheses) used for learning. There are now a number of results concerning the sample complexity of agnostic learning, especially with respect to the squared loss functional. In particular, in [9] it was shown that if ε is the required accuracy, then the sample complexity (ignoring log factors and the confidence terms) of agnostic learning from a closed class of functions F with squared loss is $O(d/\varepsilon)$ if F is convex, where d is an appropriate complexity parameter (e.g. the empirical metric entropy of the class). This result was extended and improved in [10].

It was claimed in [9] that if F is not convex, there exists a lower bound of $\Omega(1/\varepsilon^2)$ on the sample complexity. Thus, whether or not F is convex seemed important for the sample complexity of agnostic learning with squared loss.

However, these are deceptive results. The claimed lower bound relies on a random construction and the fact that for nonconvex F, one can always find a target "function" (actually a target conditional expectation) f^* which has two best approximations in the class F. Unfortunately, as we show here, the random construction has a gap in the proof.

It *is* the case though that sample complexity of agnostic learning does depend on the closeness of f^* to a point with a nonunique best approximation. In this paper we will develop some *nonuniform* results which hold for "most" target conditional expectations in the agnostic learning scenario from a nonconvex class F and obtain sharper sample complexity upper bounds. The proof

J. Kivinen and R. H. Sloan (Eds.): COLT 2002, LNAI 2375, pp. 1–13, 2002.

we present here is based on recently developed methods which can be used for complexity estimates. It was shown in [10] that the complexity of a learning problem can be governed by two properties. The first is the Rademacher complexity of the class, which is a parameter that indicates "how large" the class is (see [11,1]). The other property is the ability to control the mean square value of each loss function using its expectation. We will show that indeed the mean square value can be bounded in terms of the expectation as long as as one knows the distance of the target from the set of points which have more than a unique best approximation in the class.

In the next section we present some basic definitions, notation, and some general complexity estimates. Then, we present our nonuniform upper bound. Finally, we briefly present the proof of the lower bound claimed in [9] and show where there is a gap in the argument.

Thus the present paper does not completely resolve the question of sample complexity for agnostic learning for squared loss. The lower bound proof of [9] may be patchable: $O(1/\varepsilon^2)$ may be the best *uniform* lower bound one can achieve. What is clear from the present paper is the crucial role the set of nonuniqueness points of F plays in the sample complexity of agnostic learning with squared loss.

2   Definitions, Notation and Background Results

If $(\mathcal{X}, d)$ is a metric space, and $U \subseteq \mathcal{X}$, then for $\varepsilon > 0$, we say that $C \subseteq \mathcal{X}$ is an ε-*cover* of U with respect to d if for all $v \in U$, there exists $w \in C$ such that $d(v, w) \leq \varepsilon$. The ε-*covering number* with respect to d, $N(\varepsilon, U, d)$, is the cardinality of the smallest ε-cover of U with respect to d. If the metric d is obvious, we will simply say ε-cover etc.

The closed ball centered at c of radius r is denoted by $B(c, r) := \{x \in \mathcal{X}: \|x - c\| \leq r\}$. Its boundary is $\partial B(c, r) := \{x \in \mathcal{X}: \|x - c\| = r\}$. If $x \in \mathcal{X}$, and $A \subset \mathcal{X}$, let the distance between A and x be defined as $d_A(x) := \inf\{d(x, a): a \in A\}$. The *metric projection* of x onto A is $P_A(x) := \{a \in A: \|x - a\| = d_A(x)\}$. Hence, elements of $P_A(x)$ are all *best approximations* of x in A.

Denote by $L_\infty(\mathcal{X})$ the space of bounded functions on $\mathcal{X}$ with respect to the sup norm and set $B(L_\infty(\mathcal{X}))$ to be its unit ball. Let μ be a probability measure on $\mathcal{X}$ and put $L_2(\mu)$ to be the Hilbert space of functions from $\mathcal{X}$ to $\mathbb{R}$ with the norm endowed by the inner product $\langle f, g \rangle = \int f(x)g(x)\mathrm{d}\mu(x)$. Let $\mathcal{Y} \subset [-1, 1]$, and set F to be a class of functions from $\mathcal{X}$ to $\mathcal{Y}$, and thus a subset of $L_2(\mu)$. Assumptions we will make throughout are that F is a closed subset of $L_2(\mu)$ and that it satisfies a measurability condition called "admissibility" (see [4,5,15]) for details.

Definition 1. *Let $F \subset L_2(\mu)$. A point $f \in L_2(\mu)$ is said to be a nup point (nonunique projection) of F with respect to (w.r.t.) $L_2(\mu)$ if it has two or more best approximations in F with respect to the $L_2(\mu)$ norm. Define*

$$\mathrm{nup}(F, \mu) := \{f \in L_2(\mu) : f \text{ is a nup point of } F \text{ w.r.t. } L_2(\mu)\}.$$

It is possible to show that in order to solve the agnostic learning problem of approximating a random variable Y with values in $\mathcal{Y}$ by elements in F, it suffices to learn the function $f^* = \mathbb{E}(Y|X = x)$. Indeed, for every $f \in F$,

$$\mathbb{E}\big(f(X) - Y\big)^2 = \mathbb{E}\big(\mathbb{E}(Y|X) - f(X)\big)^2 + \mathbb{E}\big(\mathbb{E}(Y|X) - Y\big)^2$$
$$= \mathbb{E}\big(f^*(X) - f(X)\big)^2 + \mathbb{E}\big(f^*(X) - Y\big)^2.$$

Thus, a minimizer of the distance between $f(X)$ and Y will depend only on finding a minimizer for $\mathbb{E}\big(f^*(X) - f(X)\big)^2$, that is, solving the function learning problem of approximating f^* by members of F with respect to the $L_2(\mu)$ norm.

Assume that we have fixed the target f^*. We denote by f_a its best approximation in F with respect to the given $L_2(\mu)$ norm. (Of course f_a is unique only if $f^* \notin \text{nup}(F, \mu)$.) For any function $f \in F$, let the squared loss function associated with f^* and f be

$$g_{f,f^*} : x \mapsto (f(x) - f^*(x))^2 - (f_a(x) - f^*(x))^2,$$

and set $\mathcal{L}(f^*) = \mathcal{L} := \{g_{f,f^*} : f \in F\}$.

Interestingly, although a "randomly chosen" $f^* \in L_2(\mu)$ is very unlikely[1] to be in $\text{nup}(F, \mu)$, as we shall see below, $\text{nup}(F, \mu)$ nevertheless controls the sample complexity of learning f^* for all $f^* \in L_2(\mu) \setminus F$.

Definition 2. *For any set $\{x_1, \ldots, x_n\} \subset \mathcal{X}$, let μ_n be the empirical measure supported on the set; i.e. $\mu_n = \frac{1}{n} \sum_{i=1}^n \delta_{x_i}$. Given a class of functions F, a random variable Y taking values in $\mathcal{Y}$, and parameters $0 < \varepsilon, \delta < 1$ let $C_F(\varepsilon, \delta, Y)$ be the smallest integer such that for any probability measure μ*

$$\Pr\{\exists g_{f,f^*} \in \mathcal{L}(f^*) : \mathbb{E}_{\mu_n} g_{f,f^*} < \varepsilon, \mathbb{E}_\mu g_{f,f^*} \geq 2\varepsilon\} < \delta, \tag{1}$$

where $f^* = \mathbb{E}(Y|X = x)$.

The quantity $C_F(\varepsilon, \delta, Y)$ is known as the *sample complexity of learning a target Y with the function class F*. The definition means that if one draws a sample of size greater than $C_F(\varepsilon, \delta, Y)$ then with probability greater than $1 - \delta$, if one "almost minimizes" the empirical loss (less than ε) then the expected loss will not be greater than 2ε. Typically, the sample complexity of a class is defined as the "worst" sample complexity when going over all possible selections of Y.

Recent results have yielded good estimates on the probability of the set in (1). These estimates are based on the Rademacher averages as a way of measuring the complexity of a class of functions. The averages are better suited to proving sample complexity results than classical techniques using the union bound over an ε-cover, mainly because of the "functional Bennett inequality" due to Talagrand [14].

---

[1] Since Hilbert spaces are uniformly convex it follows from a theorem of Stechkin [13] (see [17, page 9] or [3, page 29]) that $L_2(\mu) \setminus \text{nup}(F, \mu)$ is a countable intersection of open dense sets. This implies that if one puts a reasonable probability measure ν on $L_2(\mu)$, then $\nu(\{f \in L_2(\mu) : f \notin \text{nup}(F, \mu)\}) = 1$.

Definition 3. *Let μ be a probability measure on $\mathcal{X}$ and suppose F is a class of uniformly bounded functions. For every integer n, set*

$$R_n(F) := \mathbb{E}_\mu \mathbb{E}_\varepsilon \frac{1}{\sqrt{n}} \sup_{f \in F} \left| \sum_{i=1}^{n} \varepsilon_i f(X_i) \right|$$

where $(X_i)_{i=1}^n$ are independent random variables distributed according to μ and $(\varepsilon_i)_{i=1}^n$ are independent Rademacher random variables.

Various relationships between Rademacher averages and classical measures of complexity are shown in [11,12]. It turns out that the best sample complexity bounds to date are in terms of *local* Rademacher averages. Before presenting these bounds, we require the next definition.

Definition 4. *We say that $F \subset L_2(\mu)$ is star-shaped with centre f if for every $g \in F$, the interval $[f, g] = \{tf + (1-t)g : 0 \le t \le 1\} \subset F$. Given F and f, let*

$$\operatorname{star}(F, f) := \bigcup_{g \in F} [f, g].$$

Theorem 1. *Let $F \subset B\big(L_\infty(\mathcal{X})\big)$, fix some f^* bounded by 1 and set $\mathcal{L}(f^*)$ to be the squared loss class associated with F and f^*. Assume that there is a constant B such that for every $g \in \mathcal{L}(f^*)$, $\mathbb{E}g^2 \le B\mathbb{E}g$.*

Let $\mathcal{G} := \operatorname{star}(\mathcal{L}, 0)$ and for every $\varepsilon > 0$ set $\mathcal{G}_\varepsilon = \mathcal{G} \cap \{h : \mathbb{E}h^2 \le \varepsilon\}$. Then for every $0 < \varepsilon, \delta < 1$,

$$\Pr\left\{ \exists g \in \mathcal{L}, \mathbb{E}_{\mu_n} g \le \varepsilon/2, \mathbb{E}g \ge \varepsilon \right\} \le \delta$$

provided that

$$n \ge C \max\left\{ \frac{R_n^2(\mathcal{G}_\varepsilon)}{\varepsilon^2}, \frac{B \log \frac{2}{\delta}}{\varepsilon} \right\},$$

where C is an absolute constant.

Using this result one can determine an upper bound on the sample complexity in various cases. The one we present here is a bound in terms of the metric entropy of the class.

Theorem 2 ([12]). *Let Y be a random variable on $\mathcal{Y}$ and put $f^* = \mathbb{E}(Y|X = x)$. Let $F, \mathcal{L}, \mathcal{G}$ and B be as in theorem 1.*

1. *If there are $\gamma, p, d \ge 1$ such that for every $\varepsilon > 0$,*

$$\sup_n \sup_{\mu_n} \log N(\varepsilon, F, L_2(\mu_n)) < d \log^p\left(\frac{\gamma}{\varepsilon}\right),$$

then for every $0 < \varepsilon, \delta < 1$,

$$C(\varepsilon, \delta, Y) \le \frac{C_{p,\gamma}}{\varepsilon} \max\left\{ d \log^p \frac{1}{\varepsilon}, B \log \frac{2}{\delta} \right\},$$

where $C_{p,\gamma}$ depends only on p and γ.

2. *If there are $0 < p < 2$ and $\gamma \geq 1$ such that for every $\varepsilon > 0$,*

$$\sup_{n} \sup_{\mu_n} \log N(\varepsilon, F, L_2(\mu_n)) < \gamma \varepsilon^{-p}$$

then

$$C(\varepsilon, \delta, Y) \leq C_{p,\gamma} \max\left\{ \left(\frac{1}{\varepsilon}\right)^{1+\frac{p}{2}}, B \log \frac{2}{\delta} \right\},$$

where $C_{p,\gamma}$ depends only on p and γ.

From this result it follows that if the original class F is "small enough", one can establish good generalization bounds, if, of course, the mean-square value of each member of the loss class can be uniformly controlled by its expectation. This is trivially the case in the proper learning scenario, since each loss function is nonnegative. It was known to be true if F is convex in the squared loss case [9] and was later extended in the more general case of p-loss classes for $2 \leq p < \infty$ [10].

Our aim is to investigate this condition and to see what assumptions must be imposed on f^* to ensure such a uniform control of the mean square value in terms of the expectation.

3 Nonuniform Agnostic Learnability of Nonconvex Classes

We will now study agnostic learning using nonconvex hypothesis classes. The key observation is that whilst in the absence of convexity one can not control $\mathbb{E}[g_{f,f^*}^2]$ in terms of $\mathbb{E}[g_{f,f^*}]$ *uniformly* in f^*, one can control it *nonuniformly* in f^* by exploiting the geometry of F. The main result is corollary 1.

The following result is a generalization of [8, lemma 14] (cf. [7, lemma A.12]).

Lemma 1. *Let F be a class of functions from $\mathcal{X}$ to $\mathcal{Y}$. Put $\alpha \in [0, 1)$, set $f^* \in L_2(\mu)$ and suppose f^* has range contained in $[0, 1]$. If for every $f \in F$*

$$\langle f_a - f^*, f_a - f \rangle \leq \frac{\alpha}{2} \|f_a - f\|^2, \tag{2}$$

then for every $g_{f,f^*} \in \mathcal{L}(f^*)$,

$$\mathbb{E}[g_{f,f^*}^2] \leq \frac{16}{1-\alpha} \mathbb{E}[g_{f,f^*}].$$

Proof. For the sake of simplicity, we denote each loss function by g_f. Observe that

$$\begin{aligned}
\mathbb{E}[g_f^2] &= \mathbb{E}[((f^*(X) - f(X))^2 - (f^*(X) - f_a(X))^2)^2] \\
&= \mathbb{E}[((2f^*(X) - f(X) - f_a(X))(f_a(X) - f(X)))^2] \\
&\leq 16\mathbb{E}[(f(X) - f_a(X))^2] \\
&= 16\|f_a - f\|^2. \tag{3}
\end{aligned}$$

Furthermore,

$$
\begin{aligned}
\mathbb{E}[g_f] &= \mathbb{E}[(f^*(X) - f(X))^2 - (f^*(X) - f_a(X))^2] \\
&= \mathbb{E}[(f^*(X) - f_a(X))^2 + (f_a(X) - f(X))^2 \\
&\quad + 2(f^*(X) - f_a(X))(f_a(X) - f(X)) - (f^*(X) - f_a(X))^2] \\
&= \mathbb{E}[(f_a(X) - f(X))^2 + 2(f^*(X) - f_a(X))(f_a(X) - f(X))] \\
&= \mathbb{E}[(f_a(X) - f(X))^2] + 2\mathbb{E}[(f^*(X) - f_a(X))(f_a(X) - f(X))] \\
&= \|f_a - f\|^2 + 2\langle f^* - f_a, f_a - f\rangle \\
&= \|f_a - f\|^2 - 2\langle f_a - f^*, f_a - f\rangle \\
&\geq \|f_a - f\|^2 - \alpha\|f_a - f\|^2 \\
&= (1 - \alpha)\|f_a - f\|^2 \\
&= \frac{1 - \alpha}{16}\mathbb{E}[g_f^2].
\end{aligned}
$$

□

Lemma 2. *Fix $f^* \in L_2(\mu)$. Then, $f \in L_2(\mu)$ satisfies (2) if and only if f is not contained in*

$$
B^{(\alpha)} := B\left(\frac{1}{\alpha}(f^* - f_a) + f_a, \frac{1}{\alpha}\|f^* - f_a\|\right),
$$

which is the closed ball in $L_2(\mu)$ centered at $\frac{1}{\alpha}(f^* - f_a) + f_a$ with radius $\frac{1}{\alpha}\|f^* - f_a\|$.

Proof. Note that $\langle f^* - f_a, f - f_a\rangle \leq \frac{\alpha}{2}\|f_a - f\|^2$ if and only if $\|f_a - f\|^2 - \frac{2}{\alpha}\langle f^* - f_a, f - f_a\rangle \geq 0$. Clearly, the latter is equivalent to

$$
\langle f_a - f, f_a - f\rangle + \langle\frac{1}{\alpha}(f^* - f_a), \frac{1}{\alpha}(f^* - f_a)\rangle - \langle\frac{1}{\alpha}(f^* - f_a), \frac{1}{\alpha}(f^* - f_a)\rangle
$$
$$
+ \frac{2}{\alpha}\langle f^* - f_a, f_a - f\rangle \geq 0.
$$

Thus,

$$
\langle f_a - f + \frac{1}{\alpha}(f^* - f_a), f_a - f + \frac{1}{\alpha}(f^* - f_a)\rangle \geq \langle\frac{1}{\alpha}(f^* - f_a), \frac{1}{\alpha}(f^* - f_a)\rangle. \quad (4)
$$

Clearly, f satisfies (4) if and only if $\|f - (f_a + \frac{1}{\alpha}(f^* - f_a))\| \geq \frac{1}{\alpha}\|f^* - f_a\|$; hence it belongs to the region outside of $B^{(\alpha)}$.   □

In the limit as $\alpha \to 0$, ∂B_α approaches a hyperplane. Then by the unique supporting hyperplane characterization of convex sets [16, theorem 4.1] this implies F is convex.

We will use lemma 2 as indicated in figure 1. The key factor in bounding B is the closeness of f^* to $\mathrm{nup}(F, \mu)$ in a particular sense. Suppose $f^* \in L_2(\mu) \setminus (F \cup \mathrm{nup}(F, \mu))$, and let

$$
r_{F,\mu}(f^*) := \inf\{\|f - P_F(f^*)\| : f \in \{\lambda(f^* - P_F(f^*)) : \lambda > 0\} \cap \mathrm{nup}(F, \mu)\}.
$$

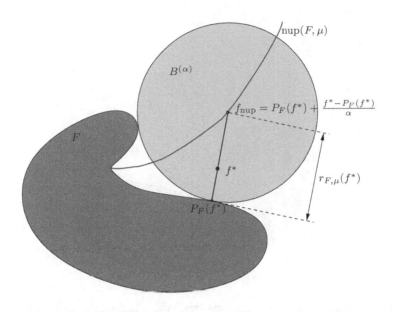

Fig. 1. Illustration of lemma 2 and the definition of $r_{F,\mu}(f^*)$

Observe that $r_{F,\mu}(f^*) = \|f_{\mathrm{nup}} - P_F(f^*)\|$ where f_{nup} is the point in $\mathrm{nup}(F, \mu)$ found by extending a ray ρ from $P_F(f^*)$ through f^* until reaching $\mathrm{nup}(F, \mu)$ (see Figure 1). Let

$$\alpha_{F,\mu}(f^*) := \frac{\|f^* - P_F(f^*)\|}{r_{F,\mu}(f^*)} = \frac{\|f^* - P_F(f^*)\|}{\|f_{\mathrm{nup}} - P_F(f^*)\|}$$

and observe that $\alpha_{F,\mu}(f^*) \in [0, 1]$ is the largest α such that $B_F^{(\alpha)}(f^*)$ only intersects F at $P_F(f^*)$ and as f^* "approaches" $\mathrm{nup}(F, \mu)$ along ρ, $\alpha_{F,\mu}(f^*) \to 1$.

Note that if F is convex then $\mathrm{nup}(F, \mu)$ is the empty set; hence for all $f^* \in L_2(\mu)$, $r_{F,\mu}(f^*) = \infty$ and $\alpha_{F,\mu}(f^*) = 0$.

Combining theorem 2 with lemmas 1 and 2 leads to our main positive result:

Corollary 1. *Let $F \subset L_2(\mu)$ be a class of functions into $[0, 1]$, set Y to be a random variable taking its values in $[0, 1]$, and assume that $f^* = \mathbb{E}(Y|X) \notin \mathrm{nup}(F, \mu)$. Assume further that there are constants $d, \gamma, p \geq 1$ such that for every empirical measure μ_n, $\log N(\varepsilon, F, L_2(\mu_n)) \leq d \log^p(\gamma/\varepsilon)$. Then, there exists a constant $C_{p,\gamma}$, which depends only on p and γ, such that for every $0 < \varepsilon, \delta < 1$,*

$$C_F(\varepsilon, \delta, Y) \leq \frac{C_{p,\gamma}}{\varepsilon} \max\left\{ d \log^p \frac{1}{\varepsilon}, \frac{\log \frac{2}{\delta}}{1 - \alpha_{F,\mu}(f^*)} \right\}.$$

Note that this result is *non-uniform* in the target Y because some functions f^* are harder to learn than others. For all $f^* \in F^\alpha := \{f \in H : \alpha_{F,\mu}(f) \geq \alpha\}$, one

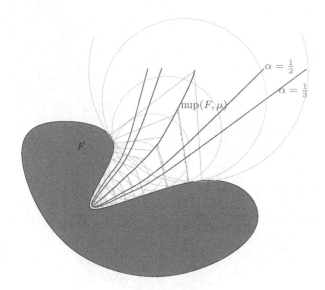

Fig. 2. Illustration of the sets F^α. The lines marked $\alpha = \frac{1}{3}$ and $\alpha = \frac{1}{2}$ are the boundaries of $F^{1/2}$ and $F^{1/3}$ respectively

obtains a uniform bound in terms of α. Figure 2 illustrates the boundaries of F^α for a given F and two different values of α. If F is convex, then $\alpha_{F,\mu}(f^*) = 0$ always and one recovers a completely uniform result.

4   The Lower Bound

In this section we present the geometric construction which led to the claimed lower bound presented in [9]. We then show where there is a gap in the proof and the bound can not be true for function learning. In our discussion we shall use several geometric results, the first of which is the following standard lemma, whose proof we omit.

Lemma 3. *Let X be a Hilbert space and set $x \in X$ and $r > 0$. Put $B_1 = B(x, r)$ and let $y \in \partial B_1$. For any $0 < t < 1$ let $z_t = tx + (1 - t)y$ and set $B_2 = B(z_t, \|z_t - y\|)$. Then $B_2 \subset B_1$ and $\partial B_1 \cap \partial B_2 = \{x\}$.*

Using lemma 3 it is possible to show that even if x has several best approximations in G, then any point on the interval connecting x and any one of the best approximations of x has a unique best approximation.

Corollary 2. *Let $x \in X$, set $y \in P_G(x)$ and for every $0 < t < 1$ let $z_t = tx + (1 - t)y$. Then, $P_G(z_t) = y$.*

Proof. We begin by showing that $P_G(z_t) \subset P_G(x)$. To that end, note that $d_G(z_t) = \|z_t - y\| = (1 - t)\|x - y\|$. Indeed, $d_G(z_t) \leq \|z_t - y\|$. If there is

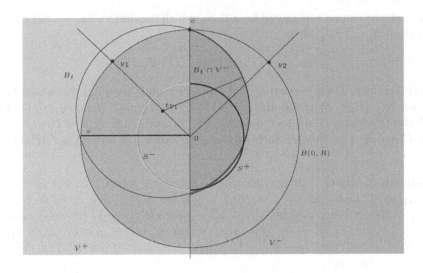

Fig. 3. Illustration for lemma 4

some $y' \in G$ such that $\|y' - z_t\| < (1 - t)\|x - y\|$ then by the triangle inequality $\|y' - x\| \le \|y' - z_t\| + \|z_t - x\| < \|x - y\|$, which is impossible. In fact, the same argument shows that if $y' \in P_G(z_t)$ then $\|x - y'\| = d_G(x)$, implying that $y' \in P_G(x)$. Therefore,

$$P_G(z_t) \subset \partial B\big(x, d_G(x)\big) \cap \partial B\big(z_t, d_G(z_t)\big),$$

and thus, by lemma 3, $P_G(z_t)$ contains a single element — which has to be y. ⊔

In the next two results we deal with the following scenario: let $R > 0$ and let $B = B(0, R)$. Fix any $y_1, y_2 \in \partial B$ which are linearly independent, and put $U \subset X$ to be the space spanned by y_1 and y_2. Let $c = R(y_1 + y_2)/\|y_1 + y_2\|$ and set $v \in U$ to be a unit vector orthogonal to c, such that $\langle v, y_1 \rangle > 0$. Denote $V_- = \{x : \langle x, v \rangle \le 0\}$ and $S_- = V_- \cap S_X$, where S_X is the unit sphere $S_X = \{x \in X : \|x\| = 1\}$. In a similar fashion, let $V_+ = \{x : \langle x, v \rangle > 0\}$ and set $S_+ = V_+ \cap S_X$.

Lemma 4. *For every $0 < t < 1$, $d(ty_1, RS_-) = \|ty_1 - c\|$ and c is the unique minimum.*

The lemma has the following geometric interpretation: for every $0 < t < 1$, let B_t be the ball centered in ty_1 which passes through c. Then, by the lemma, any point in the intersection of B_t with V_- other than c is contained in the interior of $B(0, R)$. (See Figure 3.)

Proof. For any $Rs \in RS_-$,

$$\|ty_1 - Rs\|^2 = \|ty_1\|^2 + R^2 - 2tR\langle y_1, s \rangle,$$

hence, the minimum is attained for $s \in S_-$ which maximizes $\langle y_1, s \rangle$. Set $U = v^\perp$, and since $X = V \oplus U$ then

$$\langle y_1, s \rangle = \langle P_v y_1, P_v s \rangle + \langle P_U y_1, P_U s \rangle,$$

where P_U (resp. P_v) is the orthogonal projection on U (resp. v). Note that for every $s \in S_-$, $\langle P_v y_1, P_v s \rangle \leq 0$ and $\langle P_U y_1, P_U s \rangle \leq \|P_U y_1\|$. Thus, $\langle y_1, s \rangle \leq \|P_U y\|$ and the maximum is attained only by $s \in S_-$ such that $P_U s = P_U y_1 / \|P_U y_1\|$ and $P_v s = 0$. The only s which satisfies the criteria is $s = P_U y_1 / \|P_U y\|$, and $Rs = c$. □

Theorem 3. *Let $G \subset X$ be a compact set and $x \in \mathrm{nup}(G, \mu)$. Set $R = d_G(x)$, put $y_1, y_2 \in P_G x$ and set $c = R(y_1 + y_2)/\|y_1 + y_2\|$. For every $0 < t < 1$ let $z_t^1 = y_1 + tR(x - y_1)/\|x - y_1\|$, $z_t^2 = y_1 + tR(x - y_2)/\|x - y_2\|$ and $\varepsilon_t = \|z_t^1 - c\| - \|z_t^1 - y_1\|$. Then, if ρ satisfies that $d_G(z_t^1) \leq \rho < d_G(z_t^1) + \varepsilon_t$, and $g \in B(z_t^1, \rho) \cap G$ then $\|g - y_1\| < \|g - y_2\|$. Similarly, if $g \in B(z_t^2, \rho) \cap G$ then $\|g - y_2\| < \|g - y_1\|$.*

Proof. Clearly we may assume that $x = 0$, thus $z_t^1 = ty_1$ and $z_t^2 = ty_2$. Also, note that $\varepsilon_t = \|z_t^2 - c\| - \|z_t^2 - y_2\|$, hence the second part of the claim follows by an identical argument to the first part. By corollary 2, y_1 is the unique best approximation to z_t^1, hence $\varepsilon_t > 0$. If y_1 and y_2 are linearly dependent then $y_2 = -y_1$ and the result is immediate, thus, we may assume that y_1, y_2 are independent. Let U be the space spanned by $\{y_1, y_2\}$, and let $v \in U$ be a unit vector orthogonal to c such that $\langle v, y_1 \rangle > 0$. By lemma 4 and using the notation of that lemma,

$$B(ty_1, \rho) \cap V_- \subset \mathrm{int}B(ty_1, \|ty_1 - c\|) \cap V_- \subset \mathrm{int}B(0, R).$$

Thus $G \cap (B(ty_1, \rho) \cap V_-) \subset G \cap \mathrm{int}B(0, R) = \emptyset$, implying that

$$G \cap B(ty_1, \rho) \subset V_+.$$

Clearly, for every $g \in V_+$, $\|g - y_1\| < \|g - y_2\|$, as claimed. □

Remark 1. It is easy to see that there is a constant $C_{d,R}$ such that for every $0 < t < 1$, $\|z_t^i - c\| - \|z_t^i - y_i\| \geq C_{d,R}t$, where $R = d_G(x)$ and $d = \|y_1 - y_2\|$.

Theorem 3 was the key idea behind the argument in [9] for the lower bound. What was claimed by the authors is the following:

Theorem 4 (Unproven). *Let $G \subset L_2(\mu) \cap bB(L_\infty(\mu))$ be compact and non-convex. For any $\varepsilon > 0$ there exists a random variable W_ε such that $C_G(\varepsilon, \delta, W_\varepsilon) = \Omega(1/\varepsilon^2)$.*

Note that even this claim does not guarantee that there is a target concept for which the sample complexity is $O(\varepsilon^{-2})$. Rather, its actual claim is that it is impossible to obtain an upper bound which is better than the GC limit in the nonconvex case. The targets W_ε will be constructed in such a way that for smaller values of ε, the conditional expectation of W_ε is closer to $\mathrm{nup}(F, \mu)$. It does *not* (as incorrectly claimed in [9]) imply that $C_G(\varepsilon, \delta, Y) = \Omega(1/\varepsilon^2)$ for some random variable Y. Below we shall present the outline of the incomplete proof.

"Proof". Set $x \in \mathrm{nup}(G, \mu)$ and put $d = \mathrm{diam} P_G(x)$ and $R = d_G(x)$. Let $y_1, y_2 \in P_G(x)$ such that $\|y_1 - y_2\| = d$ and for every $0 \le t \le 1$ and $i = 1, 2$ let $z_t^i = ty_i + (1-t)x$. Assume that y_1 and y_2 are linearly independent (the other case follows from a similar argument) and let $U = \mathrm{span}\{y_1, y_2\}$. As in theorem 3, set $c = R(y_1 + y_2)/ \|y_1 + y_2\|$ and choose $v \in U$ to be a unit vector orthogonal to c such that $\langle v, y_1 \rangle > 0$. Since $v = (y_1 - y_2)/ \|y_1 - y_2\|$ then $\|v\|_\infty \le 2b/d$. Also, recall that by remark 1, there is a constant $C_{d,r}$ such that for $0 \le t \le 1$ and $i = 1, 2$, $\rho_t = \left\| z_t^i - c \right\| - \left\| z_t^i - y_i \right\| \ge C_{d,R} t$. For every $0 < \varepsilon < 1$ define the following $\{0, 1\}$-valued random sequence: let ξ_i be i.i.d Bernoulli random variables such that

$$\Delta = \left| \mathbb{E}\xi_i - \frac{1}{2} \right| = \frac{\varepsilon}{2}.$$

By a result stated as lemma 3 in [9] and originally proved in [2], there is an absolute constant C such that one needs a sample of at least $C(\log(1/\delta)\varepsilon^{-2})$ points to identify whether $\Delta = \varepsilon/2$ or $\Delta = -\varepsilon/2$ with probability $1 - \delta$. The idea is to assume that there is an efficient algorithm for agnostic learning, and to use this algorithm to identify the value of Δ with high confidence.

Let $c_\varepsilon = (1 - \varepsilon)x + \varepsilon(y_1 + y_2)/2$, and for every integer n set

$$W_\varepsilon^n = \begin{cases} dv + c_\varepsilon & \text{if } \xi_n = 1, \\ -dv + c_\varepsilon & \text{if } \xi_n = 0. \end{cases}$$

Note that the $\mathbb{E}W_\varepsilon^n = dv/2 + c_\varepsilon = z_\varepsilon^1$ if $\Delta = \varepsilon/2$, and $\mathbb{E}W_\varepsilon = z_\varepsilon^2$ if $\Delta = -\varepsilon/2$. Also, for every $0 < \varepsilon < 1$, $\|W_\varepsilon^n\|_\infty < 3b$. By remark 1, there is a constant $C_{d,R}$ such that for every $0 < t < 1$, $\left\| z_t^i - c \right\| - \left\| z_t^i - y_i \right\| \ge C_{d,R} t$. Let $\varepsilon < 1/2$ and set $\varepsilon' = \frac{R}{2}C_{d,R}\varepsilon$. Assume that $h \in G$ is such that

$$\left\| z_\varepsilon^1 - h \right\|^2 - \left\| z_\varepsilon^1 - y_1 \right\|^2 < \varepsilon'.$$

Since $\left\| z_\varepsilon^1 - h \right\| > \left\| z_\varepsilon^1 - y_1 \right\|$ then

$$\left\| z_\varepsilon^1 - h \right\| - \left\| z_\varepsilon^1 - y_1 \right\| < \frac{\varepsilon'}{\left\| z_\varepsilon^1 - h \right\| + \left\| z_\varepsilon^1 - y_1 \right\|} \le \frac{\varepsilon'}{2 \left\| z_\varepsilon^1 - y \right\|} < \frac{C_{d,r}\varepsilon}{2}.$$

Therefore, $h \in \mathrm{int} B(z_\varepsilon^1, \left\| z_\varepsilon^1 - c \right\|)$, implying that $\|h - y_1\| < \|h - y_2\|$.

Now, assume that one had an efficient algorithm to learn W_ε at the scale ε'. Since the conditional expectation of W_ε is either z_ε^1 or z_ε^2 depending on Δ, then the learning rule would produce a function h which satisfies either $\left\| z_\varepsilon^1 - h \right\|^2 - \left\| z_\varepsilon^1 - y_1 \right\|^2 < \varepsilon'$ or $\left\| z_\varepsilon^2 - h \right\|^2 - \left\| z_\varepsilon^2 - y_1 \right\|^2 < \varepsilon'$. We can identify which one it was according to the distances $\|h - y_1\|$ and $\|h - y_2\|$. We predict that $\Delta = \varepsilon/2$ if h is closer to y_1 and that $\Delta = -\varepsilon/2$ if h is closer to y_2.

By the lower bound on the sample complexity of estimating Δ, it was claimed that the agnostic sample complexity

$$C_G(\varepsilon', \delta, W_\varepsilon) \geq \frac{K}{\varepsilon'^2} \log \frac{1}{\delta},$$

where K is an absolute constant. To conclude, if this were the case, one could find constants K_1, K_2 (which depend only on R and on d) such that for every $0 < \varepsilon < 1/2$ there is a random variable Y, such that $\mathbb{E}(Y|X) = z_\varepsilon^1$ and

$$C_G(K_1\varepsilon, \delta, Y) \geq \frac{K_2}{\varepsilon^2} \log \frac{1}{\delta}.$$

The gap in the proof is due to the different probability spaces used. The first is the space defined by the Bernoulli random variables, and the second is the one associated with the learning problem. The transition between the two algorithms corresponds to a map between the two probability spaces. The problem arises because this map does not have to be measure preserving (it is certainly not proven to be measure preserving in [9]. Hence, a "large" subset in one space could be mapped to a very small set in the other.

Thus, just because with probability $1 - \delta$ (over the Bernoulli random variables) one can not identify which of the two values W_ε^n takes on, one can not conclude that with probability $1 - \delta$ (over the random variables X, Y) one can not agnostically learn $\mathbb{E}(Y|X)$.   □

5   Conclusion

We have shown that a previously presented lower bound on the sample complexity of agnostically learning nonconvex classes of functions F with squared loss has a gap in its proof. We have also presented an improved upper bound on that sample complexity in terms of the geometry of F and $\text{nup}(F, \mu)$. The new bound holds for "most" target conditional expectations (recall footnote 1). The interesting thing about the upper bound is that it is intrinsically nonuniform — functions closer to $\text{nup}(F, \mu)$ are harder to learn.

The nonuniform upper bound does not, by itself, contradict the lower bound the validity of which still remains in some doubt. The upper bound only holds for $f^* \notin \text{nup}(F, \mu)$ and, crucially, is *nonuniform*. The lower bound argument relies on the construction of a series of targets f^* approaching $\text{nup}(F, \mu)$.

Finally, we stress that although the nonuniform upper bounds are obviously of no use in the direct sense (in that the bound depends on a parameter that depends on f^* and thus can not be known), they do provide some guidance: if a priori one knows something about the target function, and one wants to use a nonconvex F, then the bound suggests it may be wise to try and choose an F such that $\text{nup}(F, \mu)$ is very distant from f^*.

Acknowledgement

This work was supported by the Australian Research Council. Thanks to Wee Sun Lee for pointing out a substantial error in the submitted version of the paper.

References

1. Peter L. Bartlett, Olivier Bousquet, Shahar Mendelson, "Localized Rademacher averages", in COLT2002 (these proceedings). 2
2. Shai Ben-David and Michael Lindenbaum, "Learning Distributions by their Density Levels — A Paradigm for Learning without a Teacher," in *Computational Learning Theory — EUROCOLT'95*, pages 53-68 (1995). 11
3. Dietrich Braess, *Nonlinear Approximation Theory*, Springer-Verlag, Berlin, 1986. 3
4. Richard M. Dudley, *Uniform Central Limit Theorems*, Cambridge Studies in Advanced Mathematics 63, Cambridge University Press 1999. 2
5. David Haussler, "Decision Theoretic Generalizations of the PAC Model for Neural Net and Other Learning Applications," *Information and Computation*, **100**, 78–150 (1992). 2
6. Michael J. Kearns, Robert E. Schapire and Linda M. Sellie, "Toward Efficient Agnostic Learning," pages 341–352 in *Proceedings of the 5th Annual Workshop on Computational Learning Theory*, ACM press, New York, 1992. 1
7. Wee Sun Lee, *Agnostic Learning and Single Hidden Layer Neural Networks*, Ph.D. Thesis, Australian National University, 1996. 5
8. Wee Sun Lee, Peter L. Bartlett and Robert C. Williamson, "Efficient Agnostic Learning of Neural Networks with Bounded Fan-in," *IEEE Trans. on Information Theory*, **42**(6), 2118–2132 (1996). 5
9. Wee Sun Lee, Peter L. Bartlett and Robert C. Williamson, "The Importance of Convexity in Learning with Squared Loss" *IEEE Transactions on Information Theory* **44**(5), 1974–1980, 1998 (earlier version in *Proceedings of the 9th Annual Conference on Computational Learning Theory*, pages 140–146, 1996.) 1, 2, 5, 8, 10, 11, 12
10. Shahar Mendelson, "Improving the sample complexity using global data," *IEEE transactions on Information Theory*, to appear. http://axiom.anu.edu.au/~shahar 1, 2, 5
11. Shahar Mendelson "Rademacher averages and phase transitions in Glivenko-Cantelli classes" *IEEE transactions on Information Theory*, **48**(1), 251–263, (2002). 2, 4
12. Shahar Mendelson "A few remarks on Statistical Learning Theory", preprint. http://axiom.anu.edu.au/~shahar 4
13. S. B. Stechkin, "Approximation Properties of Sets in Normed Linear Spaces," *Revue de mathematiques pures et appliquees*, **8**, 5–18, (1963) [in Russian]. 3
14. M. Talagrand, "Sharper bounds for Gaussian and empirical processes", *Annals of Probability*, **22**(1), 28–76, (1994). 3
15. Aad W. van der Vaart and Jon A. Wellner, *Weak Convergence and Empirical Processes*, Springer, New York, 1996. 2
16. Frederick A. Valentine, *Convex Sets*, McGraw-Hill, San Francisco, 1964. 6
17. L. P. Vlasov, "Approximative Properties of Sets in Normed Linear Spaces," *Russian Mathematical Surveys*, **28**(6), 1–66, (1973). 3

Entropy, Combinatorial Dimensions and Random Averages

Shahar Mendelson[1] and Roman Vershynin[2]

[1] RSISE, The Australian National University
Canberra, ACT 0200, Australia
shahar.mendelson@anu.edu.au
[2] Department of Mathematical Sciences, University of Alberta
Edmonton, Alberta T6G 2G1, Canada
Vershynin@yahoo.com

Abstract. In this article we introduce a new combinatorial parameter which generalizes the VC dimension and the fat-shattering dimension, and extends beyond the function-class setup. Using this parameter we establish entropy bounds for subsets of the n-dimensional unit cube, and in particular, we present new bounds on the empirical covering numbers and gaussian averages associated with classes of functions in terms of the fat-shattering dimension.

1 Introduction

Empirical entropy estimates play an important role in Machine Learning since they are one of the only ways in which one can control the "size" of the function class one is interested in, and thus obtain sample complexity estimates.

Thanks to the development of the theory of empirical processes in recent years, entropy bounds are no longer the best way to obtain sample complexity estimates. Rather, the notion of random averages (such as the Rademacher or gaussain complexities) seems to be a better way to obtain generalization results. However, entropy bounds are still extremely important, since they are almost the only way in which one can establish bounds on the random complexities. Thus, finding ways to control the empirical entropy of function classes remains an interesting problem.

In an attempt to tackle this issue, several combinatorial parameters were introduced, in the hope that using them, one would be able to bound the entropy.

This approach was pioneered by the work of Vapnik and Chervonenkis [17] who introduced the VC dimension to obtain bounds on the L_∞ empirical entropy of Boolean classes of functions. Other results regarding the empirical entropy of Boolean classes with respect to empirical L_p norms for $1 \leq p < \infty$ were established by Dudley (see [8]) and then improved by Haussler [6].

Extending these results to classes of real-valued, uniformly bounded functions is very difficult. To that end, the notion of the *fat-shattering dimension*

J. Kivinen and R. H. Sloan (Eds.): COLT 2002, LNAI 2375, pp. 14–28, 2002.
© Springer-Verlag Berlin Heidelberg 2002

was introduced and in [1] the authors presented empirical L_∞ bounds and generalization results using this parameter. Only recently, in [9], improved empirical entropy bounds were established for L_p spaces, when $1 \leq p < \infty$.

The motivation for this article is the fact that the combinatorial parameters used in Machine Learning literature were also used to tackle problems in Convex Geometry [13]. Our original aim was to study a new combinatorial parameter which would be suitable for the analysis of convex bodies in $\mathbb{R}^n$, but our methods yield improved entropy bounds in terms of the fat-shattering dimension as well.

All the results presented here are based on new entropy estimates for subsets of the unit cube in $\mathbb{R}^n$, which is denoted by B_∞^n. For example, we show that if $K \subset B_\infty^n$ is convex, then its controlled by its *generalized Vapnik-Chervonenkis dimension*. This parameter, denoted by $VC(A, t)$, is defined for every $0 < t < 1$ as the maximal size of a subset σ of $\{1, \ldots, n\}$, such that the coordinate projection of K onto $\mathbb{R}^\sigma$ contains a coordinate cube of the form $x + [0, t]^\sigma$. This notion carries over to convexity the "classical" concept of the VC dimension, denoted by $VC(A)$, and defined for subsets A of the discrete cube $\{0, 1\}^n$ as the maximal size of the subset σ of $\{1, \ldots, n\}$ such that $P_\sigma A = \{0, 1\}^\sigma$, where P_σ is the coordinate projection onto the coordinates in σ (see [8] §14.3).

To see how this relates to function classes, assume that F consists of functions which are all bounded by 1. For every sample $s_n = \{x_1, \ldots, x_n\}$ let $\mu_n = n^{-1} \sum_{i=1}^n \delta_{x_i}$, where δ_x is the point evaluation functional at x. Set $F/s_n = \{(f(x_i))_{i=1}^n | f \in F\}$ and note that $F/s_n \subset B_\infty^n$. One can see that the $L_p(\mu_n)$ covering numbers of F at scale t are simply the number of translates of $t n^{1/p} B_p^n$ needed to cover F/s_n, where $B_p^n = \{(a_i)_{i=1}^n | \sum_{i=1}^n |a_i|^p \leq 1\}$. Thus, by investigating the structure of the sets F/s_n, the problem of estimating the empirical entropy numbers is reduced to the analysis of the entropy of subsets of B_∞^n.

If K is a convex body then a volumetric bound on the entropy shows that for every $0 < t \leq 1$,

$$\log N(K, n^{1/p} B_p^n, t) \leq \log(5/t) \cdot n,$$

where $N(K, B, t)$ is the covering number of K at scale t, that is, the number of translates of tB needed to cover K.

One question is whether it is possible to replace the dimension n on the right-hand side of this estimate by the VC dimension $VC(K, ct)$, which is generally smaller? This is perfectly true for the *Boolean* cube: the known theorem of R. Dudley that lead to a characterization of the uniform central limit property in the Boolean case states that if $A \subset \{0, 1\}^n$ then

$$\log N(A, n^{1/2} B_2^n, t) \leq C \log(2/t) \cdot VC(A).$$

This estimate follows by a random choice of coordinates and an application of the Sauer-Shelah Lemma (see [8] Theorem 14.12). The same problem for convex bodies is considerably more difficult, since in that case, one needs to find a cube in $P_\sigma K$ with well separated faces, not merely disjoint. The same difficulty occurs in the case of classes of real-valued functions. We prove the following theorem.

Theorem 1. *There are absolute constants $C, c > 0$ such that for every convex body $K \subset B^n_\infty$, every $1 \leq p < \infty$ and any $0 < t < 1$,*

$$\log N(K, n^{1/p} B^n_p, t) \leq C p^2 v \log^2(2/t), \tag{1}$$

and

$$\log N(K, B^n_\infty, t) \leq C v \log^2\left(\frac{n}{tv}\right), \tag{2}$$

where $v = \mathrm{VC}(K, ct)$.

Observe that (2) is best complemented by the lower bound $\log N(K, B^n_\infty, t) \geq \mathrm{VC}(K, ct)$, for some absolute constant $c > 0$, which follows from the definition of the generalized VC dimension and a comparison of volumes.

A very similar theorem can be formulated for general subsets of the unit cube, which leads to this next result regarding function classes.

Theorem 2. *There are absolute constants c and C such that for every $0 < t < 1$, every $1 \leq p < \infty$ and every empirical measure μ_n,*

$$\log N(F, L_p(\mu_n), t) \leq C p^2 v \log^2(2/t) \tag{3}$$

and

$$\log N(F, L_\infty(s_n), t) \leq C v \log^2\left(\frac{n}{tv}\right), \tag{4}$$

where $v = \mathrm{fat}_{ct}(F)$ and s_n is the sample on which μ_n is supported.

The main difference between (3) and (4) is that the first is dimension free, in the sense that is does not depend on the cardinality of the set on which the sample is supported. Note that (3) is linear in the fat-shattering dimension. One can also show that both these bounds are optimal up to the power of the logarithmic factor. For example, a volumetric bound show that for (3) one needs at least a factor of $\log(2/t)$.

These two theorems show that the $\|\cdot\|_\infty$-entropy of a subset of B^n_∞ is governed by the appropriate combinatorial parameter, up to a logarithmic factor in $1/t$.

The other main result we present, deals with estimating the gaussian averages associated with a class of functions. Given a class F and a sample $s_n = \{x_1, ..., x_n\}$, let $E(s_n) = \mathbb{E} \sup_{f \in F} |\sum_{i=1}^n g_i f(x_i)|$, where $(g_i)_{i=1}^n$ are independent standard gaussian random variables.

There are many results which show that the gaussian averages (and likewise, the Rademacher averages) play an important part in the quest for generalization bounds [10,11], hence their importance in the Machine Learning context.

It is easy to see that $E(s_n) = \mathbb{E} \sup_{f \in F} |\langle f/s_n, \sum_{i=1}^n g_i e_i \rangle|$, where $f/s_n = (f(x_1), ...f(x_n))$ and $(e_i)_{i=1}^n$ is the standard basis in the n-dimensional inner product space ℓ_2^n.

This naturally leads to the use of the polar of a subset of ℓ_2^n; if F is a bounded subset of ℓ_2^n, let the *polar* of F be $F^\circ = \{x \in \ell_2^n | \sup_{f \in F} |\langle f, x \rangle| \leq 1\}$. Let K be the symmetric convex hull of F. As a convex and symmetric set, it is the unit ball of a norm denoted by $\| \ \|_K$. It is easy to see that F° is the unit ball of the norm dual to $\| \ \|_K$, and for every $x \in \mathbb{R}^n$, $\|x\|_{F^\circ} = \sup_{f \in F} \langle f, x \rangle$. Thus, $E(s_n) = \mathbb{E}\| \sum_{i=1}^n g_i e_i \|_{(F/s_n)^\circ}$.

We shall present bounds on $E = \mathbb{E}\| \sum_{i=1}^n g_i e_i \|_{F^\circ}$ for arbitrary subsets $F \subset B_\infty^n$ in terms of their generalized VC dimension or their fat-shattering dimension.

Both are relatively easy once we know (1) or (3). Indeed, replacing the entropy by the VC dimension in Dudley's entropy inequality it follows that there are absolute constants C and c such that

$$E \leq C \int_{cE/\sqrt{n}}^{\infty} \sqrt{\log N(K, B_2^n, t)} \, dt \leq C\sqrt{n} \int_{cE/n}^{1} \sqrt{\mathrm{VC}(K, ct)} \log(2/t) \, dt. \quad (5)$$

and

$$E(s_n) \leq C\sqrt{n} \int_{cE(s_n)/n}^{\sigma_F(s_n)} \sqrt{\mathrm{fat}_{ct}(F)} \log(2/t) \, dt, \quad (6)$$

where $\sigma_F^2(s_n) = \sup_{f \in F} n^{-1} \sum_{i=1}^n f^2(x_i)$.

Inequality (5) improves the main theorem of M. Talagrand in [15]. An additional application which follows from (3) is that if F is a class of uniformly bounded functions which has a relatively small fat-shattering dimension, then it satisfies the uniform central limit theorem. This extends Dudley's characterization for VC classes to the real-valued case.

The paper is organized as follows; in Section 2 we prove the bound for the B_p^n-entropy in abstract finite product spaces, and then derive (1) by approximation. In Section 3 we apply (1) to prove (3) and obtain the uniform CLT result. In Section 4 we obtain the bounds on the gaussian complexities of a class. Finally, in Section 5 we prove (2) for the B_∞^n-entropy by reducing it to (1) through an independent lemma that compares the B_p^n-entropy to the B_∞^n-entropy.

Throughout this article, positive absolute constants are denoted by C and c. Their values may change from line to line, or even within the same line.

2 B_p^n-Entropy in Abstract Product Spaces

We will introduce and work with the notion of the VC dimension in an abstract setting that encompasses the classes considered in the introduction.

We call a map $d : T \times T \to \mathbb{R}_+$ a *quasi-metric* if d is symmetric and reflexive (that is, $\forall x, y$, $d(x, y) = d(y, x)$ and $d(x, x) = 0$). We say that points x and y in T are separated if $d(x, y) > 0$. Thus, d does not necessarily separate points or satisfy the triangle inequality.

Definition 1. *Let (T, d) be a quasi-metric space and let n be a positive integer. For a set $A \subset T^n$ and $t > 0$, the VC-dimension $\mathrm{VC}(A, t)$ is the maximal cardinality of a subset $\sigma \subset \{1, \dots, n\}$ such that the inclusion*

$$P_\sigma A \supseteq \prod_{i \in \sigma} \{a_i, b_i\} \quad (7)$$

holds for some points $a_i, b_i \in T$, $i \in \sigma$ with $d(a_i, b_i) \geq t$. If no such σ exists, we set $\mathrm{VC}(A, t) = 0$. When there is a need to specify the underlying metric, we denote the VC dimension by $\mathrm{VC}_d(A, t)$.

Since $\text{VC}(A, t)$ is decreasing in t and is bounded by n, which is the "usual" dimension of the product space, the limit $\text{VC}(A) := \lim_{t \to 0_+} \text{VC}(A, t)$ always exists. Equivalently, $\text{VC}(A)$ is the maximal cardinality of a subset $\sigma \subset \{1, \ldots, n\}$ such that (7) holds for some pairs (a_i, b_i) of separated points in T.

This definition is an extension of the "classical" VC dimension for subsets of the discrete cube $\{0, 1\}^n$, where we think of $\{0, 1\}$ as a metric space with the $0-1$ metric. Clearly, for any set $A \subset \{0, 1\}^n$ the quantity $\text{VC}(A, t)$ does not depend on $0 < t < 1$, and hence $\text{VC}(A) = \max\Big\{|\sigma| : \sigma \subset \{1, \ldots, n\}, \ P_\sigma A = \{0, 1\}^\sigma\Big\}$, which is precisely the "classical" definition of the VC dimension.

The other example discussed in the introduction was the VC dimension of convex bodies. Here $T = \mathbb{R}$ or, more frequently, $T = [-1, 1]$, both with respect to the usual metric. If $K \subset T^n$ is a convex body, then $\text{VC}(K, t)$ is the maximal cardinality of a subset $\sigma \subset \{1, \ldots, n\}$ for which the inclusion $P_\sigma K \supseteq x + (t/2)B_\infty^\sigma$ holds for some vector $x \in \mathbb{R}^\sigma$ (which automatically lies in $P_\sigma K$). It is easy to see that if K is symmetric, we can set $x = 0$. Also note that for every convex body (that is a convex, symmetric subset of $\mathbb{R}^n$ with a nonempty interior) $\text{VC}(K) = n$.

The generalized VC dimension may be controlled by the fat-shattering dimension, in the following sense. Assume that F is a subset of the unit ball in $L_\infty(\Omega)$, which is denoted by $B\big(L_\infty(\Omega)\big)$. Let $s_n = \{x_1, \ldots, x_n\}$ be a subset of Ω and set $F/s_n = \big\{ (f(x_1), \ldots, f(x_n)) \big| f \in F \big\} \subset \mathbb{R}^n$. If $\text{VC}(F/s_n, t) = m$, there is a subset $\sigma \subset \{1, \ldots, n\}$ of cardinality m such that $P_\sigma F/s_n \supset \prod_{i \in \sigma} \{a_i, b_i\}$ where $|b_i - a_i| \geq t$. By selecting $s(x_i) = (b_i + a_i)/2$ as the witness to the shattering (see [2]), it is clear that $(x_i)_{i \in \sigma}$ is $t/2$-shattered by F, and thus $VC(F/s_n, t) \leq \text{fat}_{t/2}(F)$.

The main results of this article rely on (and are easily reduced to) a discrete problem: to estimate the generalized VC-dimension of a set in a product space T^n, where (T, d) is a *finite* quasi-metric space. T^n is usually endowed with the normalized Hamming quasi-metric $d_n(x, y) = n^{-1} \sum_{i=1}^n d(x(i), y(i))$ for $x, y \in T^n$.

In this section we bound the entropy of a set $A \subset T^n$ with respect to d_n in terms of $\text{VC}(A)$.

Theorem 3. *Let (T, d) be a finite quasi-metric space with $\text{diam}(T) \leq 1$, and set n to be a positive integer. Then, for every set $A \subset T^n$ and every $0 < \varepsilon < 1$,*

$$\log N(A, d_n, \varepsilon) \leq C \log^2(|T|/\varepsilon) \cdot \text{VC}(A),$$

where C is an absolute constant.

Before presenting the proof, let us make two standard observations. We say that points $x, y \in T^n$ are separated on the coordinate i_0 if $x(i_0)$ and $y(i_0)$ are separated. Points x and y are called ε-separated if $d_n(x, y) \geq \varepsilon$.

Clearly, if A' is a maximal ε-separated subset of A then $|A'| \geq N(A, d_n, \varepsilon)$. Moreover, the definition of d_n and the fact that $\text{diam}(T) \leq 1$ imply that every two distinct points in A' are separated on at least εn coordinates. This shows that Theorem 3 is a consequence of the following statement.

Theorem 4. *Let (T, d) be a quasi-metric space for which* $\text{diam}(T) \leq 1$. *Let* $0 < \varepsilon < 1$ *and consider a set* $A \subset T^n$ *such that every two distinct points in* A *are separated on at least* εn *coordinates. Then*

$$\log |A| \leq C \log^2(|T|/\varepsilon) \cdot \text{VC}(A). \tag{8}$$

The first step in the proof of Theorem 4 is a probabilistic extraction principle, which allows one to reduce the number of coordinates without changing the separation assumption by much. Its proof is based on a simple discrepancy bound for a set system.

Lemma 1. *There exists an absolute constant* $c > 0$ *for which the following holds. Let* $\varepsilon > 0$ *and assume that* $\mathcal{S}$ *is a system of subsets of* $\{1, \ldots, n\}$ *which satisfies that each* $S \in \mathcal{S}$ *contains at least* εn *elements. Let* $k \leq n$ *be an integer such that* $\log |\mathcal{S}| \leq c\varepsilon k$. *Then there exists a subset* $I \subset \{1, \ldots, n\}$ *of cardinality* $|I| = k$, *such that*

$$|I \cap S| \geq \varepsilon k/4 \quad \text{for all } S \in \mathcal{S}.$$

Proof. If $|\mathcal{S}| = 1$ the lemma is trivially true, hence we may assume that $|\mathcal{S}| \geq 2$. Let $0 < \delta < 1/2$ and set $\delta_1, \ldots, \delta_n$ to be $\{0, 1\}$-valued independent random variables with $\mathbb{E}\delta_i = \delta$ for all i. By the classical bounds on the tails of the binomial law (see [7], or [8] 6.3 for more general inequalities), there is an absolute constant $c_0 > 0$ for which

$$\mathbb{P}\left\{ \left| \sum_{i=1}^{n} (\delta_i - \delta) \right| > \frac{1}{2}\delta n \right\} \leq 2\exp(-c_0\delta n). \tag{9}$$

Let $\delta = k/2n$ and consider the random set $I = \{i : \delta_i = 1\}$. For any set $B \subset \{1, \ldots, n\}$, $|I \cap B| = \sum_{i \in B} \delta_i$. Then (9) implies that

$$\mathbb{P}\{|I \cap B| \geq \delta|B|/2\} \geq 1 - 2\exp(-c_0\delta|B|).$$

Since for every $S \in \mathcal{S}$, $|S| > \varepsilon n$, then $\mathbb{P}\{|I \cap S| \geq \varepsilon k/4\} \geq 1 - 2\exp(-c_0\varepsilon k/2)$. Therefore, $\mathbb{P}\{\forall S \in \mathcal{S}, \ |I \cap S| \geq \varepsilon k/4\} \geq 1 - 2|\mathcal{S}|\exp(-c_0\varepsilon k/2)$. By the assumption on k, this quantity is larger than $1/2$ (with an appropriately chosen absolute constant c). Moreover, by a similar argument, $|I| \leq k$ with probability larger than $1/2$. This proves the existence of a set I satisfying the assumptions of the lemma.   □

Proof of Theorem 4. We may assume that $|T| \geq 2$, $\varepsilon \leq 1/2$, $n \geq 2$ and $\max(4, \exp(4c)) \leq |A| \leq |T|^n$, where $0 < c < 1$ is the constant in Lemma 1. The first step in the proof is to use previous lemma, which enables one to make the additional assumption that $\log |A| \geq c\varepsilon n/4$. Indeed, assume that the converse inequality holds, and for every pair of distinct points $x, y \in A$, let $S(x, y) \subset \{1, \ldots, n\}$ be the set of coordinates on which x and y are separated. Put $\mathcal{S}$ to be the collection of the sets $S(x, y)$ and let k be the minimal positive integer for which $\log |\mathcal{S}| \leq c\varepsilon k$. Since $|A| \leq |\mathcal{S}| \leq |A|^2$, then

$$c\varepsilon(k-1) \leq \log |\mathcal{S}| \leq 2\log |A| \leq \frac{1}{2}c\varepsilon n,$$

which implies that $1 \leq k \leq n$. Thus, by Lemma 1 there is a set $I \subset \{1, \ldots, n\}$, $|I| = k$, with the property that every pair of distinct points $x, y \in A$ is separated on at least $\varepsilon |I|/4$ coordinates in I. Also, since $4c \leq \log |A| \leq \log |\mathcal{S}| \leq c\varepsilon k$, then $\varepsilon |I|/4 \geq 1$ and thus $|P_I A| = |A|$. Clearly, to prove the assertion of the theorem for the set $A \subset T^n$, it is sufficient to prove it for the set $P_I A \subset T^I$ (with $|I|$ instead of n), whose cardinality already satisfies $\log |P_I A| = \log |A| \geq c\varepsilon(k-1)/2 \geq c\varepsilon |I|/4$. Therefore, we can assume that $|A| = \exp(\alpha n)$ with $\alpha > c\varepsilon$ for some absolute constant c.

The next step in the proof is a counting argument, which is based on the proof of Lemma 3.3 in [1] (see also [3]).

A set is called a *cube* if it is of the form $D_\sigma = \prod_{i \in \sigma} \{a_i, b_i\}$, where σ is a subset of $\{1, \ldots, n\}$ and $a_i, b_i \in T$. We will be interested only in *large cubes*, which are the cubes in which a_i and b_i are separated for all $i \in \sigma$. Given a set $B \subset T^n$, we say that a cube D_σ *embeds* into B if $D_\sigma \subset P_\sigma B$. Note that if a large cube D_σ with $|\sigma| \geq v$ embeds into B then $\mathrm{VC}(B) \geq v$.

For all $m \geq 2$, $n \geq 1$ and $0 < \varepsilon \leq 1/2$, let $t_\varepsilon(m, n)$ denote the maximal number t such that for every set $B \subset T^n$, $|B| = m$, which satisfies the separation condition we imposed (that is, every distinct points $x, y \in B$ are separated on at least εn coordinates), there exist t large cubes that embed into B. If no such B exists, we set $t_\varepsilon(m, n)$ to be infinite. The number of possible large cubes D_σ for $|\sigma| \leq v$ is smaller than $\sum_{k=1}^{v} \binom{n}{k} |T|^{2k}$, as for every σ of cardinality k there are less than $|T|^{2k}$ possibilities to choose D_σ. Therefore, if $t_\varepsilon(|A|, n) \geq \sum_{k=1}^{v} \binom{n}{k} |T|^{2k}$, there exists a large cube D_σ for some $|\sigma| \geq v$ that embeds into A, implying that $\mathrm{VC}(A) \geq v$. Thus, to prove the theorem, it suffices to estimate $t_\varepsilon(m, n)$ from below. To that end, we will show that for every $n \geq 2$, $m \geq 1$ and $0 < \varepsilon \leq 1/2$,

$$t_\varepsilon(2m \cdot |T|^2/\varepsilon, n) \geq 2t_\varepsilon(2m, n-1). \tag{10}$$

Indeed, fix any set $B \subset T^n$ of cardinality $|B| = 2m \cdot |T|^2/\varepsilon$, which satisfies the separation condition above. If no such B exists then $t_\varepsilon(2m \cdot |T|^2/\varepsilon, n) = \infty$, and (10) holds trivially. Split B arbitrarily into $m \cdot |T|^2/\varepsilon$ pairs, and denote the set of the pairs by $\mathcal{P}$. For each pair $(x, y) \in \mathcal{P}$ let $I(x, y) \subset \{1, \ldots, n\}$ be the set of the coordinates on which x and y are separated, and note that by the separation condition, $|I(x, y)| \geq \varepsilon n$.

Let i_0 be the random coordinate, that is, a random variable uniformly distributed in $\{1, \ldots, n\}$. The expected number of the pairs $(x, y) \in \mathcal{P}$ for which $i_0 \in I(x, y)$ is

$$\mathbb{E} \sum_{(x,y) \in \mathcal{P}} \mathbf{1}_{\{i_0 \in I(x,y)\}} = \sum_{(x,y) \in \mathcal{P}} \mathbb{P}\{i_0 \in I(x,y)\} \geq |\mathcal{P}| \cdot \varepsilon = m|T|^2.$$

Hence, there is a coordinate i_0 on which at least $m|T|^2$ pairs $(x, y) \in \mathcal{P}$ are separated. By the pigeonhole principle, there are at least $m|T|^2/\binom{|T|}{2} \geq 2m$ pairs $(x, y) \in \mathcal{P}$ for which the (unordered) set $\{x(i_0), y(i_0)\}$ is the same.

Let $I = \{1, \ldots, n\} \setminus \{i_0\}$. It follows that there are two subsets of B, denoted by B_1 and B_2, such that $|B_1| = |B_2| = 2m$ and

$$B_1 \subset \{b_1\} \times T^I, \quad B_2 \subset \{b_2\} \times T^I$$

for some separated points $b_1, b_2 \in T$. Clearly, the set B_1 satisfies the separation condition and so does B_2. It is also clear that if a large cube D_σ embeds into B_1, then it also embeds into B, and the same holds for B_2. Moreover, if the same cube D_σ embeds into both B_1 and B_2, then the large cube $\{b_1, b_2\} \times D_\sigma$ embeds into B (since $\{b_1, b_2\} \times D_\sigma \subset P_{\{i_0\} \cup \sigma} B$). Therefore, $t_\varepsilon(|B|, n) \geq 2t_{\frac{\varepsilon n}{n-1}}(|B_1|, n-1) \geq 2t_\varepsilon(|B_1|, n-1)$, establishing (10).

Since $t_\varepsilon(2, n) \geq 1$, an induction argument yields that $t_\varepsilon(2(|T|^2/\varepsilon)^r, n) \geq 2^r$ for every $r \geq 1$. Thus, for every $m \geq 4$

$$t_\varepsilon(m, n) \geq m^{\frac{1}{2 \log(|T|^2/\varepsilon)}}.$$

(It is remarkable that the right hand side does not depend on n). Therefore, $\mathrm{VC}(A) \geq v$ provided that v satisfies

$$t_\varepsilon(|A|, n) \geq \exp\left(\frac{\alpha n}{2 \log(|T|^2/\varepsilon)}\right) \geq \sum_{k=1}^{v} \binom{n}{k} |T|^{2k}. \tag{11}$$

To estimate v, one can bound the right-hand side of (11) using Stirling's approximation $\sum_{k=1}^{v} \binom{n}{k} \leq [\gamma^\gamma (1-\gamma)^{1-\gamma}]^{-n}$, where $\gamma = v/n \leq 1/2$. It follows that for $v \leq n/2$, $\sum_{k=1}^{v} \binom{n}{k} |T|^{2k} < (\frac{|T|n}{v})^{2v}$. Taking logarithms in (11), we seek integers $v \leq n/2$ satisfying that

$$\frac{\alpha n}{2 \log(|T|^2/\varepsilon)} \geq 2v \log\left(\frac{|T|n}{v}\right).$$

This holds if

$$v \leq \cdot \left(\frac{\alpha n}{\log(|T|^2/\varepsilon)}\right) \Big/ 8 \log\left(\frac{4|T| \log(|T|^2/\varepsilon)}{\alpha}\right),$$

proving our assertion since $\alpha > c\varepsilon$.   □

Corollary 1. *Let $n > 2$ and $p \geq 2$ be integers, set $0 < \varepsilon < 1$ and $q > 0$. Consider a set $A \subset \{1, \ldots, p\}^n$ such that for every two distinct points $x, y \in A$, $|x(i) - y(i)| \geq q$ for at least εn coordinates i. Then*

$$\log |A| \leq C \log^2(p/\varepsilon) \cdot \mathrm{VC}(A, q).$$

Proof. We can assume that $q \geq 1$. Define the following quasi-metric on $T = \{1, \ldots, p\}$:

$$d(a, b) = \begin{cases} 0 & \text{if } |a - b| < q, \\ 1 & \text{otherwise.} \end{cases}$$

Then $N(A, d_n, \varepsilon) = |A|$. By Theorem 3, $\log |A| \leq C \log^2(p/\varepsilon) \cdot \mathrm{VC}_d(A)$, which completes the proof by the definition of the metric d.   □

Now we pass from the discrete setting to the "continuous" one - namely, we study subsets of B_∞^n. Recall that the Minkowski sum of two convex bodies $A, B \subset \mathbb{R}^n$ is defined as $A + B = \{a + b|\ a \in A,\ b \in B\}$.

Corollary 2. *For every $A \subset B_\infty^n$, $0 < t < 1$ and $0 < \varepsilon < 1$,*

$$\log N(A, \sqrt{n}B_2^n, t) \le C \log^2(2/t\varepsilon) \cdot \mathrm{VC}(A + \varepsilon B_\infty^n, t/2).$$

Proof. Clearly, we may assume that $\varepsilon \le t/4$. Put $p = \frac{1}{2\varepsilon}$ and let

$$T = \{-2\varepsilon p, -2\varepsilon(p-1), \ldots, -2\varepsilon, 0, 2\varepsilon, \ldots, 2\varepsilon(p-1), 2\varepsilon p\}.$$

Since $t - \varepsilon > 3t/4$, then by approximation one can find a subset $A_1 \subset T^n$ for which $A_1 \subset A + \varepsilon B_\infty^n$ and $N(A_1, \sqrt{n}B_2^n, t-\varepsilon) \ge N(A, \sqrt{n}B_2^n, t)$. Therefore, there exists a subset $A_2 \subset A_1$ of cardinality $|A_2| \ge N(A, \sqrt{n}B_2^n, t)$, which is $\frac{3t}{4}\sqrt{n}$-separated with respect to the $\|\cdot\|_2$-norm. Note that every two distinct points $x, y \in A_2$ satisfy that $\sum_{i=1}^n |x(i) - y(i)|^2 \ge (9t^2/16)n \ge t^2n/2$ and that $|x(i) - y(i)|^2 \le 4$ for all i. Hence $|x(i) - y(i)| \ge t/2$ on at least $t^2n/16$ coordinates i. By corollary 1 applied to A_2, $\log|A_2| \le C \log^2(2/t\varepsilon) \cdot \mathrm{VC}(A_2, t/2)$, and since $A_2 \subset A_1 \subset A + \varepsilon B_\infty^n$, our claim follows. □

From this we derive the entropy estimate (1).

Corollary 3. *There exists an absolute constant C such that for any convex body $K \subset B_\infty^n$ and every $0 < t < 1$,*

$$\log N(K, \sqrt{n}B_2^n, t) \le C \log^2(2/t) \cdot \mathrm{VC}(K, t/4).$$

Proof. This estimate follows from Corollary 2 by selecting $\varepsilon = t/4$ and recalling the fact that for every convex body $K \subset \mathbb{R}^n$ and every $0 < b < a$,

$$\mathrm{VC}(K + bB_\infty^n, a) \le \mathrm{VC}(K, a - b).$$

The latter inequality is a consequence of the definition of the VC-dimension and the observation that if $0 < b < a$ are such that $aB_\infty^n \subset K + bB_\infty^n$, then $(a - b)B_\infty^n \subset K$. □

Note that Corollary 2 and Corollary 3 can be extended to the case where the covering numbers are computed with respect to $n^{1/p}B_p^n$ for $1 < p < \infty$, thus establishing the complete claim in (1).

3   Fat-Shattering Dimension and Entropy

Turning to the case of function classes, we will show that one can obtain empirical entropy bounds in terms of the fat-shattering dimension.

Let $F \subset B(L_\infty(\Omega))$ and fix a set $s_n \in \Omega$. For every $f \in F$ let $f/s_n = \sum_{i=1}^n f(x_i)e_i \in F/s_n$. Recall that, $\|f-g\|_{L_2(\mu_n)} = \|f/s_n - g/s_n\|_{\sqrt{n}B_2^n}$, implying that for every $t > 0$, $N(F, L_2(\mu_n), t) = N(F/s_n, \sqrt{n}B_2^n, t)$. Also, observe that for any $t > 0$,

$$\mathrm{VC}\Big(F/s_n + \frac{t}{8}B_\infty^n, \frac{t}{2}\Big) \le \mathrm{fat}_{\frac{t}{4}}\Big(F/s_n + \frac{t}{8}B_\infty^n\Big) \le \mathrm{fat}_{\frac{t}{8}}(F/s_n) \le \mathrm{fat}_{\frac{t}{8}}(F). \quad (12)$$

Theorem 5. *There is an absolute constant C such that for any class $F \subset B\big(L_\infty(\Omega)\big)$, any integer n, every empirical measure μ_n and every $t > 0$,*

$$\log N\big(F, L_2(\mu_n), t\big) \le C\mathrm{fat}_{t/8}(F) \log^2(2/t).$$

Proof. Let $s_n = \{x_1, ..., x_n\}$ be the points on which μ_n is supported, and apply corollary 2 for the set F/s_n. We obtain that

$$\log N(F/s_n, \sqrt{n}B_2^n, t) \le C \log^2(2/t) \cdot \mathrm{VC}(F/s_n + \frac{t}{8}B_\infty^n, t/2)$$

and our claim follows from (12). □

Remark. It is possible to show that this bound is essentially tight. Indeed, fix a class $F \subset B\big(L_\infty(\Omega)\big)$ and put $H(t) = \sup_n \sup_{\mu_n} \log N\big(F, L_2(\mu_n), t\big)$ (that is, the supremum is taken with respect to all the empirical measures supported on a finite set). By theorem 5, $H(t) \le C\mathrm{fat}_{\frac{t}{8}}(F) \log^2(2/t)$. On the other hand it was shown in [9] that $H(t) \ge c\mathrm{fat}_{16t}(F, \Omega)$ for some absolute constant c.

This uniform entropy estimate gives us the opportunity to prove a result which is important in the context of empirical processes.

Empirical covering numbers play a central role in the theory of empirical processes. They can be used to characterize classes which satisfy the *uniform law of large numbers* (see [4] or [18] for a detailed discussion). Indeed, if $F \subset B\big(L_\infty(\Omega)\big)$ then F satisfies the uniform law of large numbers if and only if $\sup_{\mu_n} \log N\big(F, L_2(\mu_n), \varepsilon\big) = o(n)$ for every $\varepsilon > 0$, where the supremum is taken with respect to all empirical measures supported on at most n elements of Ω. In [1] it was shown that $F \subset B\big(L_\infty(\Omega)\big)$ satisfies the uniform law of large numbers if and only if $\mathrm{fat}_\varepsilon(F) < \infty$ for every $\varepsilon > 0$.

Another important application of covering numbers estimates is the analysis of the *uniform central limit property*.

Definition 2. *Let $F \subset B\big(L_\infty(\Omega)\big)$, set P to be a probability measure on Ω and assume G_P to be a gaussian process indexed by F, which has mean 0 and covariance*

$$\mathbb{E}G_P(f)G_P(g) = \int fg\,dP \quad \int f\,dP \int g\,dP.$$

A class F is called a universal Donsker class if for any probability measure P the law G_P is tight in $\ell_\infty(F)$ and $\nu_n^P = n^{1/2}(P_n - P) \in \ell_\infty(F)$ converges in law to G_P in $\ell_\infty(F)$.

A property stronger than the universal Donsker property is the uniform Donsker property. For such classes, ν_n^P converges to G_P uniformly in P in some sense. A detailed discussion on uniform Donsker classes is beyond the scope of this article. We refer the reader to [5] or [4] for additional information.

It is possible to show that the uniform Donsker property is connected to estimates on covering numbers [4].

Theorem 6. *Let* $F \subset B\big(L_\infty(\Omega)\big)$. *If*

$$\int_0^\infty \sup_n \sup_{\mu_n} \sqrt{\log N\big(F, L_2(\mu_n), \varepsilon\big)}\ d\varepsilon < \infty,$$

then F *is a uniform Donsker class.*

Having this entropy condition in mind, it is natural to try to find covering numbers estimates which are "dimension free", that is, do not depend on the size of the sample. In the Boolean case, such bounds where first obtained by Dudley (see [8] Theorem 14.13), and then improved by Haussler [6,18] who showed that for any empirical measure μ_n and any Boolean class F,

$$N(F, L_2(\mu), \varepsilon) \leq Cd(4e)^d \varepsilon^{-2d},$$

where C is an absolute constant and $d = \mathrm{VC}(F)$. In particular this shows that every VC class is a uniform Donsker class.

We can extend Dudley's result from VC classes to the real valued case.

Corollary 4. *If* $F \subset B(L_\infty(\Omega))$ *and* $\int_0^1 \sqrt{\mathrm{fat}_{t/8}(F)} \log \frac{2}{t}\ dt$ *converges then* F *is a uniform Donsker class.*

In particular this shows that if $\mathrm{fat}_\varepsilon(F)$ is "slightly better" than $1/\varepsilon^2$, then F is a uniform Donsker class.

4   Gaussian Complexities

The result we present below improves the main result of M. Talagrand from [15].

Theorem 7. *There are absolute constants* $C, c > 0$ *such that for every convex body* $K \subset B_\infty^n$

$$E \leq C\sqrt{n} \int_{cE/n}^1 \sqrt{\mathrm{VC}(K, ct)} \log(2/t) dt,$$

where $E = \mathbb{E}\| \sum_{i=1}^n g_i e_i \|_{K^\circ}$, *and* $(e_i)_{i=1}^n$ *is the canonical vector basis in* $\mathbb{R}^n$.

For the proof, we need a few standard definitions and facts from the local theory of Banach spaces, which may be found in [12].

Given an integer n, let S^{n-1} be the unit Euclidean sphere with the normalized Lebesgue measure σ_n, and for every measurable set $A \subset \mathbb{R}^n$ denote by $\mathrm{vol}(A)$ its Lebesgue measure in $\mathbb{R}^n$. For a convex body K in $\mathbb{R}^n$, put $M_K = \int_{S^{n-1}} \|x\|_K\ d\sigma_n(x)$ and let M_K^* denote M_{K°, where K° is the polar of K. Recall that for any two convex bodies K and L, $M_{K+L}^* \leq M_K^* + M_L^*$. Urysohn's inequality states that $\left(\frac{\mathrm{vol}(K)}{\mathrm{vol}(B_2^n)}\right)^{1/n} \leq M_K^*$.

Next, put $\ell(K) = \mathbb{E}\| \sum_{i=1}^n g_i e_i \|_K$, where $(g_i)_{i=1}^n$ are independent standard gaussian random variables and $(e_i)_{i=1}^n$ is the canonical basis of $\mathbb{R}^n$. It is well known that $\ell(K) = c_n\sqrt{n}M_K$, where $c_n < 1$ and $c_n \to 1$ as $n \to \infty$. Recall that by Dudley's inequality (see [14]) there is an absolute constant C_0 such that for every convex body K,

$$\ell(K^\circ) \le C_1 \int_0^\infty \sqrt{\log N(K, B_2^n, \varepsilon)}\, d\varepsilon.$$

It is possible to slightly improve Dudley's inequality using an additional volumetric argument. This observation is due to A. Pajor, and we omit its proof.

Lemma 2. *There exist absolute constants C and c such that for any set $K \subset \mathbb{R}^n$*

$$\ell(K^\circ) \le C \int_{cM_K^*}^\infty \sqrt{\log N(K, B_2^n, \varepsilon)}\, d\varepsilon.$$

Proof of Theorem 7. By Lemma 2, there exist absolute constants C and c such that

$$E = \ell(K^\circ) \le C \int_{cE/\sqrt{n}}^\infty \sqrt{\log N(K, B_2^n, t)}\, dt.$$

Since $K \subset B_\infty^n \subset \sqrt{n}B_2^n$, the integrand vanishes for all $t \ge \sqrt{n}$. Therefore, changing the integration variable and using Corollary 3,

$$E \le C \int_{cE/\sqrt{n}}^{\sqrt{n}} \sqrt{\log N(K, B_2^n, t)}\, dt = C\sqrt{n} \int_{cE/n}^1 \sqrt{\log N(K, n^{1/2}B_2^n, t)}\, dt$$

$$\le C\sqrt{n} \int_{cE/n}^1 \sqrt{VC(K, ct)\log(2/t)}\, dt,$$

as claimed. $\square$

In a similar way to theorem 7 one can obtain the following:

Theorem 8. *There are absolute constants C and c for which the following holds. Let F be a class of functions which are all bounded by 1, set $s_n = \{x_1, ..., x_n\}$ to be a sample and let $G_n = n^{-1/2} \sup_{f \in F} |\sum_{i=1}^n g_i f(x_i)|$. Then,*

$$G_n \le C \int_{cG/\sqrt{n}}^{\sigma_F(s_n)} \sqrt{\mathrm{fat}_{ct}(F)}\log(2/t)\, dt, \tag{13}$$

where $\sigma_F^2(s_n) = n^{-1}\sum_{i=1}^n f^2(x_i)$ and μ_n is the empirical measure supported on s_n.

To complement this result, let us mention another one of Talagrand's results, which enables one to estimate the expectation of σ_F^2 when s_n is selected randomly according to an underlying probability measure.

Lemma 3. *[16] There is an absolute constant C such that for any class F of functions bounded by 1,*

$$\mathbb{E}_\mu \sup_{f \in F} \sum_{i=1}^n f^2(X_i) \le n\tau^2 + C\mathbb{E} \sup_{f \in F} \Big|\sum_{i=1}^n g_i f(X_i)\Big|,$$

where (X_i) are independent, distributed according to μ and $\tau^2 = \sup_{f \in F} \mathbb{E}_\mu f^2$.

Results of the nature of theorem 8 combined with lemma 3 were used to obtain estimates or the "localized" gaussian averages in [10,11] to obtain improved complexity estimates for various learning problems.

5   Application: B_∞^n-Entropy

In this section we prove estimate (2), which improves the main combinatorial result in [1]. Our result can be equivalently stated as follows.

Theorem 9. *Let $K \subset B_\infty^n$ be a convex body, set $t > 0$ and put $v = \mathrm{VC}(K, t/8)$. Then,*

$$\log N(K, B_\infty^n, t) \leq Cv \cdot \log^2(n/tv), \tag{14}$$

where C is an absolute constant.

This estimate should be compared with the Sauer-Shelah lemma for subsets of the Boolean cube $\{0,1\}^n$. It says that if $A \subset \{0,1\}^n$ then for $v = \mathrm{VC}(K)$ we have $|A| \leq \binom{n}{0} + \binom{n}{1} + \ldots + \binom{n}{v}$, so that

$$\log |A| \leq 2v \cdot \log(n/v)$$

(and note that, of course, $|A| = N(K, B_\infty^n, t)$ for all $0 < t < 1/2$).

We reduce the proof of (14) to an application of the B_p^n-entropy estimate (1). As a start, note that for $p = \log n$, $B_\infty^n \subset n^{1/p} B_p^n \subset e B_\infty^n$. Therefore, an application of (1) for this value of p yields

$$\log N(K, B_\infty^n, t) \leq Cv \cdot \log^2(n/t),$$

which is slightly worse than (14).

To deduce (14) we need a result that compares the B_∞^n-entropy to the B_p^n-entropy, and which may be useful in other applications as well.

Lemma 4. *There is an absolute constant $c > 0$ such that the following holds. Let A be a subset of B_∞^n such that every two distinct points $x, y \in A$ satisfy $\|x - y\|_\infty \geq t$. Then, for every integer $1 \leq k \leq n/2$, there exists a subset $A' \subset A$ of cardinality*

$$|A'| \geq \binom{n}{k}^{-1} (ct)^k |A|,$$

with the property that every two distinct points in A' satisfy that $|x(i) - y(i)| \geq t/2$ for at least k coordinates i.

Proof. We can assume that $0 < t < 1/8$. Set $s = t/2$. The separation assumption imply that $N(A, B_\infty^n, s) \geq |A|$. Denote by D_k the set of all points x in $\mathbb{R}^n$ for which $|x(i)| \geq 1$ on at most k coordinates i. One can see that $N(A, D_k, s) = N(A, sD_k, 1) = N(A, sD_k \cap 3B_\infty^n, 1)$. Then, by the submultiplicative property of the covering numbers,

$$N(A, B_\infty^n, s) \leq N(A, sD_k \cap 3B_\infty^n, 1) \cdot N(sD_k \cap 3B_\infty^n, B_\infty^n, s)$$
$$\leq N(A, sD_k, 1) \cdot N(sD_k \cap 3B_\infty^n, B_\infty^n, s). \tag{15}$$

To bound the second term, write D_k as

$$D_k = \bigcup_{|\sigma|=k} \left(\mathbb{R}^\sigma + (-1,1)^{\sigma^c} \right),$$

where the union is taken with respect to all subsets $\sigma \subset \{1, \ldots, n\}$ and σ^c is the complement of σ. Thus,

$$sD_k \cap 3B_\infty^n = \bigcup_{|\sigma|=k} \left(3B_\infty^\sigma + (-s,s)^{\sigma^c} \right).$$

Denote by $N'(A, B, t)$ the number of translates of tB by vectors in A needed to cover A. Therefore,

$$N\left(sD_k \cap 3B_\infty^n, B_\infty^n, s\right) \le \sum_{|\sigma|=k} N\left(3B_\infty^\sigma + (-s,s)^{\sigma^c}, B_\infty^n, s\right)$$

$$\le \sum_{|\sigma|=k} N'(3B_\infty^\sigma, B_\infty^n, s).$$

The latter inequality holds because any cover of $3B_\infty^\sigma$ by translates of sB_∞^n automatically covers $3B_\infty^\sigma + (-s,s)^{\sigma^c}$. Hence, for some absolute constant C,

$$N\left(sD_k \cap 3B_\infty^n, B_\infty^n, s\right) \le \binom{n}{k} N'(3B_\infty^k, B_\infty^k, s)$$

$$\le \binom{n}{k} (C/s)^k$$

by a comparison of the volumes, and by (15) we obtain

$$N(A, D_k, s) \ge \binom{n}{k}^{-1} (cs)^k N(A, B_\infty^n, s) > \binom{n}{k}^{-1} (ct)^k |A|,$$

from which the statement of the lemma follows by the definition of D_k.   □

Proof of Theorem 9. Fix $0 < t < 1$, and define α by $\log N(K, B_\infty^n, t) = \exp(\alpha n)$. Hence, there exists a set $A \subset K$ of cardinality $|A| = \exp(\alpha n)$, where every two distinct points $x, y \in A$ satisfy that $\|x - y\|_\infty \ge t$. Applying Lemma 4 we obtain a subset $A' \subset A \subset K$ of cardinality

$$|A'| \ge \binom{n}{k}^{-1} (ct)^k e^{\alpha n},$$

such that for every two distinct points in A', $|x(i) - y(i)| \ge t/2$ on at least k coordinates i. Selecting $k = \frac{c\alpha n}{\log(2/t\alpha)}$ we see that $|A'| \ge e^{\alpha n/2}$.

The proof is completed by discretizing A' and applying Corollary 1 with $p = 4/t$ and $\varepsilon = k/n$ in the same manner as we did in the previous section. Therefore

$$\alpha n/2 = \log |A'| \le C \log^2 \left(\frac{4n}{tk}\right) \cdot \mathrm{VC}(A' + (t/4)B_\infty^n, t/2)$$

$$\le C \log^2(1/t\alpha) \cdot \mathrm{VC}(K, t/4),$$

and thus $\alpha n \le c \log^2(n/tv) \cdot v$, as claimed.   □

Remark. As the proof shows, only a slight modification is needed to obtain the analogous result for function classes. Due to the lack of space, we omit the formulation and the proof of this assertion.

References

1. N. Alon, S. Ben-David, N. Cesa-Bianchi, D. Hausser, *Scale sensitive dimensions, uniform convergence and learnability*, Journal of the ACM 44 (1997), 615–631. 15, 20, 23, 26
2. M. Anthony, P. L. Bartlett, *Neural Network Learning, Theoretical Foundations*, Cambridge University Press, 1999. 18
3. P. Bartlett, P. Long, *Prediction, learning, uniform convergence, and scale-sensitive dimensions*, J. Comput. System Sci. 56 (1998), 174–190. 20
4. R. M. Dudley, *Uniform central limit theorems*, Cambridge University Press, 1999. 23
5. E. Giné, J. Zinn, *Gaussian charachterization of uniform Donsker classes of functions*, Annals of Probability, 19 (1991), 758–782. 23
6. D. Haussler, *Sphere packing numbers for subsets of Boolean n-cube with bounded Vapnik-Chervonenkis dimension*, Journal of Combinatorial Theory A 69 (1995), 217–232. 14, 24
7. W. Hoeffding, *Probability inequalities for sums of bounded random variables*, J. Amer. Statist. Assoc. 58 (1963), 13–30. 19
8. M. Ledoux and M. Talagrand, *Probability in Banach spaces*, Springer, 1991. 14, 15, 19, 24
9. S. Mendelson, *Rademacher averages and phase transitions in Glivenko-Cantelli classes*, IEEE transactions on Information Thery, Jan 2002. 15, 23
10. S. Mendelson, *Improving the sample complexity using global data* To appear, IEEE transactions on Information Theory. 16, 26
11. S. Mendelson, *Geometric parameters of Kernel Machines*, These proceedings. 16, 26
12. V. Milman, G. Schechtman, *Asymptotic theory of finite dimensional normed spaces*, Lecture Notes in Math., vol. 1200, Springer Verlag, 1986. 24
13. A. Pajor, *Sous espaces ℓ_1^n des espaces de Banach*, Hermann, Paris, 1985. 15
14. G. Pisier, *The volume of convex bodies and Banach space geometry*, Cambridge University Press, 1989. 25
15. M. Talagrand, *Type, infratype, and Elton-Pajor Theorem*, Inventiones Math. 107 (1992), 41–59. 17, 24
16. M. Talagrand, *Sharper bounds for Gaussian and empirical processes*, Annals of Probability, 22(1), 28–76, 1994. 25
17. V. Vapnik, A. Chervonenkis, *Necessary and sufficient conditions for uniform convergence of means to mathematical expectations*, Theory Prob. Applic. 26(3), 532-553, 1971. 14
18. A. W. Van–der–Vaart, J. A. Wellner, *Weak convergence and Empirical Processes*, Springer-Verlag, 1996. 23, 24

Geometric Parameters of Kernel Machines

Shahar Mendelson

Computer Sciences Laboratory, RSISE, The Australian National University
Canberra, ACT 0200, Australia
shahar.mendelson@anu.edu.au

Abstract. We investigate the fat-shattering dimension and the localized
Rademacher averages of kernel machines and their connection to the
eigenvalues associated with the kernel.

1 Introduction

In this article we investigate two parameters which may be used to obtain error bounds for various kernel machines - the fat-shattering dimension and the
Rademacher averages[1].

Using the reproducing kernel property, the problem of estimating the fat-
shattering dimension becomes a problem in convex geometry. The approach we
introduce uses estimates on the volume of convex bodies which are naturally associated with kernel machines. We show that from this viewpoint, the most important quantity is the volume of the symmetric convex hull of $\{\Phi(x_1), ..., \Phi(x_n)\}$,
where Φ is the kernel feature map and $\{x_1, ..., x_n\}$ is the shattered set (see section 3). The bound we present is given in terms of eigenvalues of Gram matrices,
and we show that in some cases the bound is optimal. We then impose a "global"
assumption on the kernel, namely, that the eigenfunctions of the integral operator are uniformly bounded. In that case, it is possible to bound the volume
of the symmetric convex hull of $\{\Phi(x_1), ..., \Phi(x_n)\}$ using the eigenvalues of the
integral operator, which yields a bound on the fat-shattering dimension of the
class.

The second result we present deals with the Rademacher averages of kernel
machines. Let μ be a probability measure on Ω and set $(X_i)_{i=1}^n$ to be independent random variables distributed according to μ. One can show that the
function $H_F^n(\sigma) = n^{-1/2} \mathbb{E} \sup_{f \in F, \; \mathbb{E}_\mu f^2 \le \sigma^2} |\sum_{i=1}^n \varepsilon_i f(X_i)|$, where $(\varepsilon_i)_{i=1}^n$ are in-
dependent Rademacher random variables, plays an important role in the perfor-
mance of the class F (see appendix A).

We establish tight bounds on H_F^n for kernel classes defined by an integral
operator, in terms of the eigenvalues of the integral operator.

An observation which follows from our analysis is that any attempt to obtain
tight generalization bounds using spectral methods (assumptions on either the
eigenvalues of the integral operator associated with the kernel K or on those of

---

[1] I would like to thank Gideon Schechtman and Vladimir Koltchinskii for many stimulating discussions. This work was supported by the Australian Research Council.

J. Kivinen and R. H. Sloan (Eds.): COLT 2002, LNAI 2375, pp. 29–43, 2002.

the Gram matrices) is bound to fail. Indeed, since the spectrum of the integral operator might change dramatically when the measure changes, such spectral bounds are useless without an a-priori information on the underlying measure μ, which is unavailable in the usual formulation of a learning problem. Furthermore, we show that the fat-shattering dimension depends on the set $(\Phi(x_i))$ and not just on the spectrum of the Gram matrix, thus, a purely spectral-based bound would always be suboptimal.

In this work all absolute constants are denoted by C or c. Their values may change from line to line, or even within the same line.

1.1   Kernel Machines

A kernel is a bounded positive definite continuous function $K : \Omega \times \Omega \to \mathbb{R}$ for a compact domain Ω. For every fixed set $\{y_1, ..., y_r\}$ (r may be infinite) we are interested the class $F = \{\sum_{i=1}^{r} \alpha_i K(y_i, -) | (\alpha_i)_{i=1}^{r} \in \Lambda\}$, where Λ is a constraint. For example, the most commonly used constraint is to assume that each $(\alpha_i)_{i=1}^{\infty} \in \Lambda$ if and only if it satisfies that $\sum_{i,j=1}^{\infty} \alpha_i \alpha_j K(y_i, y_j) \leq 1$. Another example is the case of the so-called ℓ_p machines, where the constraint is given by $\sum_{i=1}^{r} |\alpha_i|^p \leq 1$, $r \in \mathbb{N}$.

Recall that if μ is a Borel measure on Ω then each positive definite kernel K is associated with an integral operator $T_K : L_2(\mu) \to L_2(\mu)$, defined by $T_K f = \int_Y K(x, y) f(y) d\mu(y)$. There are many results connecting the performance of kernel machines and the eigenvalues of the integral operator defined by K [3]. All the results are based on two fundamental ideas. Firstly, one may apply the notion of reproducing kernel Hilbert spaces to show that each class F is embedded in a Hilbert space. To that end, note that every $y \in \Omega$ may be embedded in ℓ_2 using the *feature map* $\Phi : \Omega \to \ell_2$. Indeed, by Mercer's Theorem, there is a complete orthonormal basis of $L_2(\mu)$ consisting of eigenfunctions of the integral operator T_K, such that $K(y_1, y_2) = \sum_{i=1}^{\infty} \lambda_i \phi_i(y_1) \phi_i(y_2)$ for every $y_1, y_2 \in \Omega$, where $(\phi_i)_{i=1}^{\infty}$ are the eigenfunctions and $(\lambda_i)_{i=1}^{\infty}$ are the corresponding eigenvalues of the integral operator T_K. For every $y \in \Omega$, let $\Phi(y) = \left(\sqrt{\lambda_i} \phi_i(y)\right)_{i=1}^{\infty}$. Moreover, each $f \in F$ may be embedded in ℓ_2, by mapping $\sum_{i=1}^{r} \alpha_i K(y_i, -)$ to $\sum_{i=1}^{r} \alpha_i \Phi(y_i) \equiv \Phi(f)$. It is easy to see that for every $f \in F$ and every $y \in \Omega$, $f(y) = \langle \Phi(f), \Phi(y) \rangle$.

The second observation is that the "size" of $\Phi(F)$ and $\Phi(\Omega)$ may be controlled. For example, in [14] the authors used estimates on the entropy numbers of diagonal operators to bound the empirical L_∞ covering numbers of several families of kernel machines, under an assumption that the eigenfunctions of the kernel are uniformly bounded. The argument is based on the fact that the image of the feature map $\Phi(\Omega)$ is contained in an ellipsoid in ℓ_2, for which the lengths of the principle axes have a similar behaviour to the eigenvalues of the integral operator associated with the kernel. In the volumetric approach presented here we investigate the volume of sections of $\Phi(F)$ and $\Phi(\Omega)$, since these quantities may be used to control the fat-shattering dimension of F.

We focus on $F_K = \{\sum_{i=1}^{\infty} \alpha_i K(y_i, x) | \sum_{i,j=1}^{\infty} \alpha_i \alpha_j K(y_i, y_j) \leq 1\}$, and on $F^p(y_1, ..., y_m) = \{\sum_{i=1}^{m} \alpha_i K(y_i, x) | \sum_{i=1}^{m} |\alpha_i|^p \leq 1, \ \|f\|_{\infty} \leq 1\}$. Recall that $\Phi(F_K)$ is the unit ball in the reproducing kernel Hilbert space.

Let us turn to a few standard definitions and notation which will be needed in the sequel. From here on we sometimes abuse notation and identify a class with its image in the reproducing kernel Hilbert space under the feature map.

Denote by $\text{fat}_\varepsilon(F, \Omega)$ the fat-shattering dimension of the F at scale ε. For every integer n, let fat_n^{-1} be the largest ε such that there exists a set of cardinality n which is ε-shattered by F. Hence, fat_n^{-1} is the formal inverse of the fat-shattering dimension.

Given a metric space (X, d), let $N(\varepsilon, X, d)$ be the covering numbers of the set X by balls (with respect to the metric d) of radius ε. One metric we shall be interested in is the empirical L_2 metric: if $\{x_1, ..., x_n\} \subset \Omega$, let δ_{x_i} be the point evaluation functional at x_i and put $\mu_n = n^{-1} \sum_{i=1}^{n} \delta_{x_i}$. Then, $\|f\|_{L_2(\mu_n)} = \left(n^{-1} \sum_{i=1}^{n} f^2(x_i)\right)^{1/2}$.

The following is tightest known bound on the $L_2(\mu_n)$ covering numbers in terms of the fat-shattering dimension [8].

Theorem 11 *There is an absolute constant C such that for every class F of functions bounded by 1, every empirical measure μ_n and every $\varepsilon > 0$,*

$$\log N\big(\varepsilon, F, L_2(\mu_n)\big) \leq C\text{fat}_{\varepsilon/8}(F) \log^2(2/\varepsilon).$$

The results regarding the fat-shattering dimension we establish will enable us to bound the covering numbers of kernel classes, and this provides an alternative way to estimate the *localized Rademacher averages* (see definition below) as in [7].

One of the main difficulties in the way performance bounds depend on the fat-shattering dimension is the fact that the fat-shattering dimension is a "worst case parameter" and does not take into account the measure according to which the sampling is done. A parameter which serves as a powerful alternative to the fat-shattering dimension is a "localized" version of the Rademacher averages.

Definition 12 *For every class of functions F on (Ω, μ), every integer n and every $\sigma > 0$, let $H_F^n(\sigma) = n^{-1/2} \mathbb{E} \sup_{f \in F, \mathbb{E}_\mu f^2 < \sigma^2} |\sum_{i=1}^{n} \varepsilon_i f(X_i)|$ where $(\varepsilon_i)_{i=1}^{n}$ are independent, Rademacher random variables and (X_i) are independent, distributed according to μ.*

Since the way in which the localized Rademacher averages may be used to control the generalization performance of the class is not the main topic of this article, we will not present such results in the body of the text. Results which describes how H_F^n can be used to establish error bounds will be briefly discussed in appendix A.

1.2   Background in Convex Geometry

Given a real Banach space X, let B_X (or $B(X)$) be its unit ball and set X^* to be the dual space. For every integer n, we fix the Euclidean structure $\langle \, , \, \rangle$ on $\mathbb{R}^n$ with an orthonormal basis denoted by $(e_i)_{i=1}^{n}$.

A set K is called symmetric if the fact that $x \in K$ implies that $-x \in K$. The symmetric convex hull of K, denoted by absconv(K), is the convex hull of $K \cup -K$.

If $K \subset \mathbb{R}^n$ is bounded, convex and symmetric with a nonempty interior, then K is a unit ball of a norm denoted by $\| \; \|_K$. It is possible to show that the *polar* of K, defined as $K^\circ = \{x \in \mathbb{R}^n | \sup_{k \in K} \langle k, x \rangle \leq 1\}$ is the unit ball of the dual space of $(\mathbb{R}^n, \| \; \|_K)$. In the sequel we shall abuse notation and denote by K the normed space whose unit ball is K. From here on, a ball will be a bounded, convex and symmetric subset of $\mathbb{R}^n$, with a nonempty interior.

If $1 \leq p < \infty$, let ℓ_p^n be $\mathbb{R}^n$ endowed with the norm $\|\sum_{i=1}^n a_i e_i\|_p = (\sum_{i=1}^n |a_i|^p)^{1/p}$. ℓ_∞^n is $\mathbb{R}^n$ endowed with the norm $\|\sum_{i=1}^n a_i e_i\|_\infty = \sup_i |a_i|$. B_p^n is the unit ball of ℓ_p^n, and for every $1 \leq p \leq \infty$, $(B_p^n)^\circ = B_{p'}^n$, where $1/p + 1/p' = 1$. In this case, p' is called the conjugate index of p.

If Ω is a set, let $L_\infty(\Omega)$ be the space of bounded functions on Ω with respect to the norm $\|f\| = \sup_{\omega \in \Omega} |f(\omega)|$.

As stated above, we can identify ℓ_2^n with $\mathbb{R}^n$. Hence, ℓ_2^n is endowed with the n-dimensional Lebesgue measure, denoted by $|\;|$. Let GL_n be the set of invertible operators $T : \mathbb{R}^n \to \mathbb{R}^n$. It is easy to see that for every measurable set $A \subset \mathbb{R}^n$ and every $T \in GL_n$, $|TA| = |\det(T)| \, |A|$. We say that a set $A \subset \mathbb{R}^n$ is an ellipsoid if there is some $T \in GL_n$, such that $A = TB_2^n$.

It will be useful to determine the volume of the balls B_p^n and the volume of their sections. First, let us mention the following well known fact.

Theorem 13 *[11] There are absolute constants C and c such that for every integer n and every $1 \leq p \leq \infty$, $cn^{-1/p} \leq \left|B_p^n\right|^{1/n} \leq Cn^{-1/p}$.*

Unlike the clear structure of sections of B_2^n, the geometry of sections of B_p^n is far less obvious. The following result, due to Meyer and Pajor [9], bounds the volume of k-dimensional sections of B_p^n.

Theorem 14 *For every k-dimensional subspace $E \subset \mathbb{R}^n$ and every $1 \leq p \leq q \leq \infty$, $\frac{|B_p^n \cap E|}{|B_p^k|} \leq \frac{|B_q^n \cap E|}{|B_q^k|}$.*

By selecting $q = 2$ it follows that for $1 \leq p \leq 2$, the volume of any k-dimensional section of B_p^n is smaller than the volume of B_p^k. Similarly, by taking $p = 2$, the volume of any k-dimensional section of B_q^n for $2 \leq q \leq \infty$ is larger than the volume of B_q^k.

An important fact about the volume of balls are the Santaló and inverse Santaló inequalities.

Theorem 15 *There is an absolute constant c such that for every integer n and every ball $K \subset \mathbb{R}^n$, $c \leq \left(\frac{|K||K^\circ|}{|B_2^n|^2}\right)^{1/n} \leq 1$.*

The upper bound was established by Santaló, while the lower bound is due to Bourgain and Milman. The proof to both parts may be found in [11].

One of the tools used in modern convex geometry is the notion of volume ratios. The idea is to compare the volume of a given ball with the "best" possible volume of an ellipsoid contained in it, since this may be used to understand "how close" the norm induced by the ball is to a Euclidean structure.

Definition 16 *For every ball $K \subset \mathbb{R}^n$, the volume ratio of K is $\mathrm{vr}(K) = \sup\left(\frac{|K|}{|TB_2^n|}\right)^{1/n}$, where the supremum is taken with respect to all $T \in GL_n$ such that $TB_2^n \subset K$. The external volume ratio is defined as $\mathrm{evr}(K) = \inf\left(\frac{|TB_2^n|}{|K|}\right)^{1/n}$, where the infimum is with respect to all $T \in GL_n$ such that $K \subset TB_2^n$.*

It is possible to show [11] that both the supremum and the infimum in the definition above are uniquely attained. Hence, for every ball $K \subset \mathbb{R}^n$ there is an ellipsoid of maximal volume contained in K and an ellipsoid of minimal volume containing K. The ellipsoid of maximal volume contained in K is denoted by $\mathcal{E}_K$, and the ellipsoid of minimal volume containing K is denoted by $\tilde{\mathcal{E}}_K$. It is evident that for every ball K, $\mathcal{E}_K^\circ = \tilde{\mathcal{E}}_{K^\circ}$.

If K is an ellipsoid then $\mathrm{vr}(K) = \mathrm{evr}(K) = 1$. Moreover, one can show that for every ball $K \subset \mathbb{R}^n$, $\mathrm{vr}(K) \le \sqrt{n}$. A significant fact is that the volume ratio of ℓ_∞^n is asymptotically the worst possible, and is of the order of $\sqrt{n}$ (see [1]). In fact, For every integer n, $\mathrm{vr}(B_\infty^n) = 4/|B_2^n|^{1/n}$.

A different notion of volume ratios is the *cubic ratios* which was introduced by Keith Ball. For every ball $K \subset \mathbb{R}^n$ let $\mathrm{cr}(K) = \inf_{T \in GL_n, \ K \subset TB_\infty^n} \left(\frac{|TB_\infty^n|}{|K|}\right)^{1/n}$.

Lemma 17 *[1] There are absolute constants c and C such that for every integer n and every ball $K \subset \mathbb{R}^n$, $c\sqrt{n} \le \mathrm{vr}(K)\mathrm{cr}(K) \le C\sqrt{n}$.*

2   Linear Fat-Shattering Dimension

The goal of this section is to bound the fat-shattering dimension in a scenario which is more general than just kernel machines. To that end, we present a geometric interpretation of the fat-shattering dimension in the linear case, when $\Omega \subset X$ and $F = B_{X^*}$.

Lemma 21 *Let X be a Banach space. Assume that $\{x_1, ..., x_n\} \subset X$, let A be the symmetric convex hull of $\{x_1, ..., x_n\}$ and set $E = \mathrm{span}\{x_1, ..., x_n\}$. Then $\{x_1, ..., x_n\}$ is ε-shattered by B_{X^*} if and only if $\{x_1, ..., x_n\}$ are linearly independent and $\varepsilon(B_X \cap E) \subset A$.*

We present a proof only to the "if" part. The "only if" is a modification of a result from [7] and we omit its proof.

(Partial) Proof: Define $T : \ell_1^n \to \ell_2^n$ by $Te_i = x_i$. For every $I \subset \{1, ..., n\}$ there is some $v \in B_\infty^n$ such that $\langle v, e_i \rangle = 1$ if $i \in I$ and $\langle v, e_j \rangle = -1$ otherwise. Note that $\langle v, e_i \rangle = \langle v, T^{-1}Te_i \rangle = \langle T^{-1^*}v, Te_i \rangle$ and that $A^\circ = (TB_1^n)^\circ = T^{-1^*}B_\infty^n$, implying that $T^{-1^*}v \in A^\circ$. If $\varepsilon(B_X \cap E) \subset A$ then $A^\circ \subset \varepsilon^{-1}(B_X \cap E)^\circ = \varepsilon^{-1}P_E B_{X^*}$, where P_E is the orthogonal projection onto E. Thus, there is some $x^* \in B_{X^*}$ such that $T^{-1^*}v = tP_E x^*$ for some $0 < t \le \varepsilon^{-1}$. Hence,

$\langle x^*, x_i \rangle = \langle x^*, Te_i \rangle = \langle P_E x^*, Te_i \rangle = t^{-1}\langle T^{-1*}v, Te_i \rangle \geq \varepsilon$ if $i \in I$. By a similar argument, $\langle x^*, Te_j \rangle \leq -\varepsilon$ if $j \notin I$, which shows that $\{x_1, ..., x_n\}$ is ε-shattered by B_{X^*}.

□

Using this geometric interpretation, the question we investigate can be formulated in the following manner:

Question 22 *Let K and L be two convex and symmetric subsets of $\mathbb{R}^d$. For every $\varepsilon > 0$, what is the largest integer n such that the following holds: there exists a set $\{x_1, ..., x_n\} \subset K$ of linearly independent vectors, such that $\varepsilon L \subset \text{absconv}\{x_1, ..., x_n\}$?*

The next theorem provides a partial solution to this problem, based on the volumetric approach.

Theorem 23 *There is an absolute constant C such that for every integers $n \leq m$ and every convex and symmetric sets $K, L \subset \mathbb{R}^m$ the following holds: if $\{x_1, ..., x_n\} \subset K$ is ε-shattered by L^o then*

$$\sqrt{n} \leq \frac{C}{\varepsilon}\text{vr}((K \cap E)^o)\left(\frac{|K \cap E|}{|L \cap E|}\right)^{\frac{1}{n}}.$$

Proof: Assume that $\{x_1, ..., x_n\} \subset K$ is ε-shattered by L^o. By Lemma 21, $\varepsilon(L \cap E) \subset A \subset K \cap E$, where A is the symmetric convex hull of $\{x_1, ..., x_n\}$, and thus, $(K \cap E)^o \subset A^o$. By Lemma 17

$$c\sqrt{n} \leq \text{vr}((K \cap E)^o)\text{cr}((K \cap E)^o) \leq \text{vr}((K \cap E)^o)\left(\frac{|A^o|}{|(K \cap E)^o|}\right)^{\frac{1}{n}}$$
$$\leq \frac{1}{\varepsilon}\text{vr}((K \cap E)^o)\left(\frac{|(L \cap E)^o|}{|(K \cap E)^o|}\right)^{\frac{1}{n}} \leq \frac{C}{\varepsilon}\text{vr}((K \cap E)^o)\left(\frac{|K \cap E|}{|L \cap E|}\right)^{\frac{1}{n}},$$

where the last inequality follows from the Santaló and inverse Santaló inequalities.

□

Let us mention a few facts we require. Firstly, the assumption that K and L are finite dimensional bodies is merely for convenience. It suffices to assume that they are both bounded subsets of ℓ_2. Secondly, using Santaló's inequality, $\text{vr}((K \cap E)^o)|K \cap E|^{\frac{1}{n}} \leq |\tilde{\mathcal{E}}_{K \cap E}|^{\frac{1}{n}}$. Therefore, from the volumetric point of view, all that matters is the volume of the ellipsoid of minimal volume containing the section of K spanned by $\{x_1, ..., x_n\}$.

Finally, if one is interested in fat_n^{-1} of a given of set $\{x_1, ..., x_n\}$, one can take K to be the symmetric convex hull of the given set. Thus $K = TB_1^n$, where $T : \ell_1^n \to \ell_2$ is defined by $Te_i = x_i$. In this case, we are interested in the volume of the ellipsoid of minimal volume containing TB_1^n. Observe that $|\tilde{\mathcal{E}}_{TB_1^n}|^{1/n}$ is equivalent to $n^{-1/2}\left(\prod_{i=1}^n \lambda_i\right)^{1/n}$, where $(\lambda_i)_{i=1}^n$ are the singular values of the operator T, that is, the eigenvalues of $\sqrt{T^*T}$. Also note that if $\mathcal{E} \subset \ell_2$ is an ellipsoid and if $TB_1^n \subset \mathcal{E}$ then $|\tilde{\mathcal{E}}_{TB_1^n}| \leq \prod_{i=1}^\infty a_i$, where $(a_i)_{i=1}^\infty$ are the lengths of the principle axes of $\mathcal{E}$ arranged in a non-increasing order. Indeed, the n-dimensional section of $\mathcal{E}$ spanned by TB_1^n is an ellipsoid containing TB_1^n, therefore, its volume must be larger than that of $\tilde{\mathcal{E}}_{TB_1^n}$.

3   The Fat-Shattering Dimension of Kernel Machines

Applying the volumetric approach, one can investigate the fat-shattering dimension of kernel machines. In most cases, the bounds we present will be given in terms of the geometric mean of the eigenvalues of Gram matrices. The difficulty arises since the bounds will be in a "worst case scenario" - the supremum with respect to all Gram matrices of a given dimension, making it difficult to compute. Therefore, we will present some bounds which depend on the eigenvalues of the integral operator, under an additional assumption on the kernel. Throughout this section, we denote by ℓ_2 the reproducing kernel Hilbert space.

3.1   The Fat-Shattering Dimension of F_K

Assume that $S = \{x_1, ..., x_n\} \subset \Omega$. We wish to estimate $\mathrm{fat}_n^{-1}(F_K, S)$ in terms of the eigenvalues of the Gram matrix $(K(x_i, x_j))$.

For every $S = \{x_1, ..., x_n\}$ let P_S be the orthogonal projection in the reproducing kernel Hilbert space onto the space spanned by $\{\Phi(x_1), ..., \Phi(x_n)\}$. Clearly, S is ε-shattered by F_K if and only if it is ε-shattered by $P_S(F_K)$. Moreover, since F_K is the unit ball in the reproducing kernel Hilbert space then $P_S(F_K) \subset F_K$, and thus, $\mathrm{fat}_n^{-1}(F_K, S) = \mathrm{fat}_n^{-1}(P_S(F_K), S)$. Recall that $P_S(F_K) \subset \ell_2$ is an n-dimensional Euclidean ball B_2^n. Let $T_S : \ell_1^n \to \ell_2^n$ be given by $T_S e_i = \Phi(x_i)$. Hence, $\mathrm{fat}_n^{-1}(F_K, S) = \mathrm{fat}_n^{-1}(B_2^n, \{T_S e_1, ..., T_S e_n\})$, implying that $\mathrm{fat}_n^{-1}(F_K, \Omega) = \sup_{T_S} \mathrm{fat}_n^{-1}(B_2^n, \{T_S e_1, ..., T_S e_n\})$, and the supremum is taken with respect to all the injective operators which map the formal unit vector basis in $\mathbb{R}^n$, $(e_i)_{i=1}^n$, into $\Phi(\Omega)$.

Using the volumetric approach (Theorem 23), we may take $K = TB_1^n$ and $L^o = B_2^n$. Hence, if $\{x_1, ..., x_n\}$ is ε-shattered by F_K then $n \leq C\varepsilon^{-2}(\prod_{i=1}^n \lambda_i^2)^{1/n}$, where (λ_i) are the singular values of T_S. However, in this case one can use a more direct approach, which yields the optimal bound in terms of the singular values of the operator T_S.

Given a set of singular values (arranged in a non-increasing order) $\Lambda = \{\lambda_1, ..., \lambda_n\}$, let $\mathbb{T}_\Lambda$ be the subset of GL_n consisting of matrices which have Λ as singular values and set $\alpha_n(T) = \mathrm{fat}_n^{-1}(B_2^n, \{Te_1, ..., Te_n\})$.

Theorem 31 *For every set Λ of singular values, $\inf_{T \in \mathbb{T}_\Lambda} \alpha_n(T) = \lambda_n/\sqrt{n}$ and $\sup_{T \in \mathbb{T}_\Lambda} \alpha_n(T) = \left(\sum_{i=1}^n \lambda_i^{-2}\right)^{-1/2}$. This implies that for every $\lambda_n/\sqrt{n} \leq t \leq \left(\sum_{i=1}^n \lambda_i^{-2}\right)^{-1/2}$, there is some $T \in T_\Lambda$ such that $\mathrm{fat}_n^{-1}(B_2^n, \{Te_1, ..., Te_n\}) = t$.*

A consequence of this result is that the geometry of $\Phi(\Omega)$ is as important as the spectral properties in determining the fat-shattering dimension. Indeed, the geometry of $\Phi(\Omega)$ is the constraint which determines which values of $\lambda_n/\sqrt{n} \leq t \leq \left(\sum_{i=1}^{n} \lambda_i^{-2}\right)^{-1/2}$ can be obtained.

Proof: By lemma 21, for every $T \in GL_n$,

$$\alpha_n(T) = \sup\{\varepsilon | \varepsilon B_2^n \subset TB_1^n\} = \left(\max_{\|x\|_2=1} \|x\|_{TB_1^n}\right)^{-1}.$$

Thus, $\sup_{T\in\mathbb{T}_A} \alpha_n(T) = \left(\inf_{T\in\mathbb{T}_A} \max_{\|x\|_2=1} \|x\|_{TB_1^n}\right)^{-1}$, while $\inf_{T\in\mathbb{T}_A} \alpha_n(T) = \left(\sup_{T\in\mathbb{T}_A} \max_{\|x\|_2=1} \|x\|_{TB_1^n}\right)^{-1}$.

Since $(TB_1^n)^\circ = T^{-1^*}B_\infty^n$, then for every x,

$$\|x\|_{TB_1^n} = \sup_{y\in(TB_1^n)^\circ} \langle x, y \rangle = \sup_{y\in B_\infty^n} \langle x, T^{-1^*}y \rangle = \sup_{(\varepsilon_i)_{i=1}^n\in\{-1,1\}^n} \langle T^{-1}x, \sum_{i=1}^n \varepsilon_i e_i \rangle,$$

and $\max_{\|x\|_2=1} \|x\|_{TB_1^n} = \sup_{(\varepsilon_i)_{i=1}^n\in\{-1,1\}^n} \sup_{\|x\|_2=1}\langle T^{-1}x, \sum_{i=1}^n \varepsilon_i e_i \rangle$. By the polar decomposition, $T^{-1} = ODU$ where U and O are orthogonal and D is diagonal, and since the Euclidean ball is invariant under orthogonal transformations,

$$\inf_{T\in\mathbb{T}_A} \max_{\|x\|_2=1} \|x\|_{TB_1^n} = \inf_{O\in O(n)} \sup_{(\varepsilon_i)_{i=1}^n\in\{-1,1\}^n} \sup_{\|x\|_2=1} \langle ODx, \sum_{i=1}^n \varepsilon_i e_i \rangle$$

$$\sup_{T\in\mathbb{T}_A} \max_{\|x\|_2=1} \|x\|_{TB_1^n} = \sup_{O\in O(n)} \sup_{(\varepsilon_i)_{i=1}^n\in\{-1,1\}^n} \sup_{\|x\|_2=1} \langle ODx, \sum_{i=1}^n \varepsilon_i e_i \rangle.$$

where D is the diagonal matrix with the set of eigenvalues λ_i^{-1} and $O(n)$ is the set of orthogonal matrices on $\mathbb{R}^n$. Set (μ_i) to be the eigenvalues of D^{-1} arranged in a non-increasing order. That is, $\mu_1 = \lambda_n^{-1} \leq ... \leq \mu_n = \lambda_1^{-1}$.

Let $f(O) = \sup_{(\varepsilon_i)_{i=1}^n\in\{-1,1\}^n} \sup_{\|x\|_2=1}\langle ODx, \sum_{i=1}^n \varepsilon_i e_i \rangle$.

To compute $\inf_{O\in O(n)} f(O)$, fix any orthogonal matrix $O = (O_{ij})$ and any vector $(\varepsilon_i)_{i=1}^n \in \{-1,1\}^n$. A straightforward use of Lagrange multipliers shows that

$$\sup_{\|x\|_2=1} \langle ODx, \sum_{i=1}^n \varepsilon_i e_i \rangle = \left(\sum_{j=1}^n \mu_j^2 \left(\sum_{i=1}^n \varepsilon_i O_{ij}\right)^2\right)^{\frac{1}{2}}. \tag{3.1}$$

Set $H(\varepsilon_1, ..., \varepsilon_n) = \sum_{j=1}^n \mu_j^2 \left(\sum_{i=1}^n \varepsilon_i O_{ij}\right)^2$. Taking the expectation of H with respect to the Rademacher random variables $(\varepsilon_i)_{i=1}^n$,

$$\mathbb{E}_\varepsilon H = \sum_{j=1}^n \mu_j^2 \mathbb{E}_\varepsilon \left(\sum_{i=1}^n \varepsilon_i O_{ij}\right)^2 = \sum_{j=1}^n \mu_j^2 \sum_{i=1}^n O_{ij}^2 = \sum_{j=1}^n \mu_j^2.$$

Thus, there is a realization $(\varepsilon_i)_{i=1}^n \in \{-1,1\}^n$ such that $H(\varepsilon_1, ..., \varepsilon_n) \geq \sum_{j=1}^n \mu_j^2$, implying that $\inf_{T\in\mathbb{T}_A} \max_{\|x\|_2=1} \|x\|_{TB_1^n} \geq \left(\sum_{i=1}^n \lambda_i^{-2}\right)^{1/2}$, as claimed.

To show that we actually have an equality, take T to be the diagonal operator and observe that $f(I) = \left(\sum_{i=1}^n \mu_j^2\right)^{1/2}$, proving that the upper bound is optimal.

Finally, by (3.1),

$$\sup_{O \in O(n)} f(O) = \sup_{\|z\|_2 = \sqrt{n}} \Big(\sum_{i=1}^{n} \mu_j^2 z_j^2\Big)^{1/2} = \sqrt{n}\mu_1,$$

which yields the lower bound on the fat-shattering dimension.

$\square$

It is easy to see that if $Te_i = \phi(x_i)$ then $T^*T = \big(K(x_i, x_j)\big)$. Thus, we obtain the following

Corollary 32 *Let K be a kernel. Then, for every $\varepsilon > 0$*

$$\mathrm{fat}_\varepsilon(F_K, \Omega) \le \sup\Big\{n \big| \exists s_n = \{x_1, ..., x_n\} \ \Big(\frac{1}{\sum_{i=1}^{n} \theta_i^{-1}(s_n)}\Big)^{\frac{1}{2}} \ge \varepsilon\Big\},$$

where $(\theta_i(s_n))$ are the eigenvalues of the Gram matrix $\big(K(x_i, x_j)\big)$.

Since the harmonic mean of $\big(\theta_i(s_n)\big)$ is bounded by the geometric mean, this bound is better than the bound established via the volumetric approach.

3.2   The Fat-Shattering Dimension of ℓ_p Machines

Next, we prove an estimate on the fat-shattering dimension of ℓ_p machines. Unlike the previous case, we will see that the number of the basis functions which form the class influences the fat-shattering dimension.

Theorem 33 *Let K be a kernel and let $1 \le p \le 2$. If $\{x_1, ..., x_n\}$ is ε-shattered by $F^p(y_1, ..., y_m)$ then $n \le C\varepsilon^{-p}\big(\prod_{i=1}^{n} \theta_i^{(1)}\theta_i^{(2)}\big)^{p/2n}$, where $(\theta_i^{(1)})$ are the eigenvalues of $\big(K(x_i, x_j)\big)$, $(\theta_i^{(2)})$ are the n largest eigenvalues of $\big(K(y_i, y_j)\big)$ and C is an absolute constant.*

Proof: Fix an integer m and a set $\{y_1, ..., y_m\}$. By the reproducing kernel property, if $s_n = \{x_1, ..., x_n\}$ is ε-shattered by $\mathcal{H} = F^p(y_1, ..., y_m)$ then the same holds for $\{\Phi(x_1), ..., \Phi(x_n)\}$. Define $T_1 : \ell_1^n \to \ell_2$ by $T_1 e_i = \Phi(x_i)$ and $T_2 : \ell_2^m \to \ell_2$ by $T_2 e_i = \Phi(y_i)$. Set $Q = T_2 id_{\ell_p^m \to \ell_2^m}$ and note that $\mathcal{H} = QB_p^m$. Therefore,

$$\mathrm{fat}_\varepsilon(\mathcal{H}, s_n) = \mathrm{fat}_\varepsilon\big(QB_p^m, \{T_1 e_1, ..., T_1 e_n\}\big) = \mathrm{fat}_\varepsilon\big(B_p^m, \{Q^*T_1 e_1, ..., Q^*T_1 e_n\}\big).$$

Let $T = Q^*T_1 : \ell_1^n \to \ell_{p'}^m$ and set E to be $T\ell_1^n$. Using the notation of theorem 23, $K = TB_1^n$ and $L^o = B_p^m$. Thus, $\sqrt{n} \le C\varepsilon^{-1}\big(|\tilde{\mathcal{E}}_K| / |L \cap E|\big)^{1/n}$. Denote by Q_E^* the restriction of Q^* to E. Since $\tilde{\mathcal{E}}_K = Q_E^*T_1 B_2^n$ then $|\tilde{\mathcal{E}}_K|^{1/n} \le cn^{-1/2}\big(\prod_{i=1}^{n} \lambda_i^1 \lambda_i^2\big)^{1/n}$, where $(\lambda_i^j)_{i=1}^n$, $j = 1, 2$ are the singular values of T_j. By the Meyer-Pajor Theorem, $\big|B_{p'}^m \cap E\big| \ge \big|B_{p'}^n\big|$. Thus, $n \le C\varepsilon^{-p}\big(\prod_{i=1}^{n} \theta_i^{(1)}\theta_i^{(2)}\big)^{\frac{p}{2n}}$, where $(\theta_i^{(1)})$ are the eigenvalues of $\big(K(x_i, x_j)\big)$ and $(\theta_i^{(2)})$ are the n largest eigenvalues of $\big(K(y_i, y_j)\big)$.

$\square$

3.3   Global Assumptions

As we mentioned in previous sections, one important aspect in the volumetric approach is to bound on the volume of the ellipsoid of minimal volume containing TB_1^n, where $T : \ell_1^n \to \ell_2$ maps e_i to $\Phi(x_i)$. Our aim is to replace the eigenvalues of the Gram matrix by a "global" quantity. To that end, we assume that the eigenfunctions of the integral operator are uniformly bounded, which implies that there is a relatively small ellipsoid $\mathcal{E} \subset \ell_2$ such that $\Phi(\Omega) \subset \mathcal{E}$.

Lemma 34 *[3,14] Assume that $K(x,y) = \sum_{i=1}^{\infty} \lambda_i \phi_i(x) \phi_i(y)$ for every $x, y \in \Omega$ and that the eigenvalues $(\phi_i)_{i=1}^{\infty}$ of T_K are all bounded by 1. Set $(a_n)_{n=1}^{\infty} \in \ell_2$ to be such that $(b_n)_{n=1}^{\infty} = (\sqrt{\lambda_n}/a_n)_{n=1}^{\infty} \in \ell_2$ and put $R = \|(b_n)\|_{\ell_2}$. If $A : \ell_2 \to \ell_2$ is defined by $Ae_i = Ra_i e_i \equiv d_i e_i$, and if $\mathcal{E} = A(B(\ell_2))$, then for every $x \in \Omega$, $\Phi(x) \in \mathcal{E}$.*

As an example, we can apply our results (using the notation of the previous results) and obtain the following estimates on the fat-shattering dimension

Theorem 35 *There is an absolute constant C such that the following holds: for every kernel which satisfies the assumption of lemma 34 and any sample s_n which is ε-shattered by F_K, $\varepsilon \leq C \left(\prod_{i=1}^{n} d_i \right)^{1/n} / \sqrt{n}$. If s_n is ε-shattered by $F^1(y_1, ..., y_m)$ then $\varepsilon \leq C \left(\prod_{i=1}^{n} d_i^2 \right)^{1/n} / \sqrt{n}$.*

Proof: In both cases we shall use theorem 23. Let $\mathcal{E} \subset \ell_2$ be the ellipsoid containing $\Phi(\Omega)$ with $(d_i)_{i=1}^{\infty}$ as axes. Then, $\mathrm{fat}_\varepsilon(F_K, \Omega) \leq \mathrm{fat}_\varepsilon(B_2, \mathcal{E})$ for every $\varepsilon > 0$. Take $K = \mathcal{E}$ and $L^o = B_2$. Since K is an ellipsoid then for every subspace E, $K \cap E$ is also an ellipsoid and thus $\mathrm{vr}\left((K \cap E)^o \right) = 1$. Moreover, if $\dim(E) = n$ then $|\mathcal{E} \cap E|^{1/n} \leq Cn^{-1/2} \left(\prod_{i=1}^{n} d_i \right)^{1/n}$ and the first part of our claim follows. As for the second, by convexity $F^1(y_1, ..., y_m) \subset \mathrm{conv}\Phi(\Omega) \subset \mathcal{E}$. Hence, $\mathrm{fat}_\varepsilon(F_1, \Omega) \leq \mathrm{fat}_\varepsilon(\mathcal{E}, \mathcal{E})$. As an ellipsoid, $|(\mathcal{E}^o \cap E)|^{-\frac{1}{n}} = |P_E \mathcal{E}|^{\frac{1}{n}} / |B_2^n|^{\frac{2}{n}}$, where P_E is the orthogonal projection on E, and the latter is smaller than $C\sqrt{n} \left(\prod_{i=1}^{n} d_i \right)^{1/n}$ for an absolute constant C. Our claim now follows from theorem 23.

$\square$

4   Localized Averages of Kernel Classes

Here we present a direct tight bound on the localized Rademacher averages $H_F^n(\sigma)$ of the class F_K in terms of the eigenvalues of the integral operator T_K. It is important to note that the underlying measures in the definitions of H_F^n and of T_K have to be the same, which stresses the problem one faces in the learning scenario; the eigenvalues can not be computed since the underlying measure is unknown.

Fix a probability measure μ on Ω, let $T_K f = \int K(x,y) f(y) d\mu(y)$ and put F_K to be the reproducing kernel Hilbert space associated with T_K. Set $(\lambda_i)_{i=1}^{\infty}$ to be the eigenvalues of T_K arranged in a non increasing order, and let $(X_i)_{i=1}^{\infty}$ to be independent random variables distributed according to μ.

Theorem 41 *There are absolute constants C and c such that if $\lambda_1 \geq 1/n$, then for every $\sigma^2 \geq 1/n$,*

$$c\Big(\sum_{j=1}^{\infty} \min\{\lambda_i, \sigma^2\}\Big)^{\frac{1}{2}} \leq H_{F_K}^n(\sigma) \leq C\Big(\sum_{j=1}^{\infty} \min\{\lambda_i, \sigma^2\}\Big)^{\frac{1}{2}}.$$

Remark 1. As will be evident from the proof, the upper bound is true even without the assumption of λ_1, and holds for every $\sigma > 0$. The additional assumptions are needed only to handle the lower bound.

Our proof is divided into two parts. We begin by showing that the estimate above is true not for H_F^n but for $n^{-1/2}\big(\mathbb{E}\sup_{f \in F_K,\, \mathbb{E}_\mu f^2 \leq \sigma^2} \big|\sum_{i=1}^{n} \varepsilon_i f(X_i)\big|^2\big)^{1/2}$. Then, we prove that all the L_p norms are equivalent for functions of the form $R_\sigma = n^{-1/2}\sup_{f \in F,\, \mathbb{E}_\mu f^2 \leq \sigma^2} \big|\sum_{i=1}^{n} \varepsilon_i f(X_i)\big|$.

Lemma 42 *There are absolute constants C and c which satisfy that for every $\sigma > 0$,*

$$c\Big(\sum_{j=1}^{\infty} \min\{\lambda_i, \sigma^2\}\Big)^{\frac{1}{2}} \leq (\mathbb{E}R_\sigma^2(F_K))^{\frac{1}{2}} \leq C\Big(\sum_{j=1}^{\infty} \min\{\lambda_i, \sigma^2\}\Big)^{\frac{1}{2}}.$$

Proof: Let ℓ_2 be the reproducing kernel Hilbert space and recall that $F_K = \{f(\cdot) = \langle \beta, \Phi(\cdot) \rangle \mid \|\beta\|_2 \leq 1\}$. By Setting $B(\sigma) = \{f \mid \mathbb{E}_\mu f^2 \leq \sigma^2\}$ it follows that $f \in F_K$ is also in $B(\sigma)$ if and only if its representing vector β satisfies that $\sum_{i=1}^{\infty} \beta_i^2 \lambda_i \leq \sigma^2$. Hence, in ℓ_2, $F_K \cap B(\sigma) = \{\beta \mid \sum_{i=1}^{\infty} \beta_i^2 \leq 1, \sum_{i=1}^{\infty} \beta_i^2 \lambda_i \leq \sigma^2\}$. Let $\mathcal{E} \subset \ell_2$ be defined as $\{\beta \mid \sum_{i=1}^{\infty} \mu_i \beta_i^2 \leq 1\}$, where $\mu_i = (\min\{1, \sigma^2/\lambda_i\})^{-1}$. It is easy to see that $\mathcal{E} \subset F_K \cap B_\sigma \subset \sqrt{2}\mathcal{E}$. Therefore, one can replace $F_K \cap B(\sigma)$ by $\mathcal{E}$ in the computation of the Rademacher complexities, losing a factor of $\sqrt{2}$ at the most. Finally,

$$\mathbb{E}\sup_{\beta \in \mathcal{E}} |\langle \beta, \sum_{j=1}^{n} \varepsilon_j \Phi(X_j) \rangle|^2 = \mathbb{E}\sup_{\beta \in \mathcal{E}} |\langle \sum_{i=1}^{\infty} \sqrt{\mu_i}\beta_i e_i, \sum_{i=1}^{\infty} \sqrt{\frac{\lambda_i}{\mu_i}}\Big(\sum_{j=1}^{n} \varepsilon_j \phi_i(X_j)\Big)e_i \rangle|^2$$

$$= \mathbb{E}\sum_{i=1}^{\infty} \frac{\lambda_i}{\mu_i}\Big(\sum_{j=1}^{\infty} \varepsilon_j \phi_i(X_j)\Big)^2 = \mathbb{E}_\mu \sum_{i,j} \frac{\lambda_i}{\mu_i} \phi_i^2(X_j) = n \sum_{i=1}^{\infty} \frac{\lambda_i}{\mu_i},$$

which proves our claim.

$\square$

The next step is to prove that all the L_p norms of R_σ equivalent, as long as σ is not "too small".

Theorem 43 *For every $1 < p < \infty$ there is an absolute constant c_p for which the following holds. Let F be a class of functions bounded by 1, set μ to be a probability measure on Ω and put $\sigma_F^2 = \sup_{f \in F} \mathbb{E}_\mu f^2$. If n satisfies that $\sigma_F^2 \geq 1/n$ then*

$$c_p\big(\mathbb{E}\sup_{f \in F} |\sum_{i=1}^{n} \varepsilon_i f(X_i)|^p\big)^{\frac{1}{p}} \leq \mathbb{E}\sup_{f \in F} |\sum_{i=1}^{n} \varepsilon_i f(X_i)| \leq \big(\mathbb{E}\sup_{f \in F} |\sum_{i=1}^{n} \varepsilon_i f(X_i)|^p\big)^{\frac{1}{p}},$$

where $(X_i)_{i=1}^n$ are independent random variables distributed according to μ and $(\varepsilon_i)_{i=1}^n$ are independent Rademacher random variables.

The proof of this theorem is based on the fact that $\sup_{f \in F} |\sum_{i=1}^n \varepsilon_i f(X_i)|$ is highly concentrated around its mean value, with an exponential tail. The first step in the proof is to show that if one can establish such an exponential tail for a class of functions, then all the L_p norms are equivalent on the class. In fact, we show a little more:

Lemma 44 *Let G be a class of nonnegative functions which satisfies that there is some absolute constant c such that for every $g \in G$ and every integer m, $Pr\{|g - \mathbb{E}g| \geq m\mathbb{E}g\} \leq 2e^{-cm}$. Then, for every $0 < p < \infty$ there is are constants c_p and C_p which depends only on p and c, such that for every $g \in G$,*

$$c_p(\mathbb{E}g^p)^{\frac{1}{p}} \leq \mathbb{E}g \leq C_p(\mathbb{E}g^p)^{\frac{1}{p}}.$$

Proof: Fix some $0 < p < \infty$ and $g \in G$. Set $a = \mathbb{E}g$ and for a set A denote by χ_A its characteristic function. Clearly,

$$\mathbb{E}g^p = \mathbb{E}g^p \chi_{\{g < a\}} + \sum_{m=0}^{\infty} \mathbb{E}g^p \chi_{\{(m+1)a \leq g < (m+2)a\}}.$$

By the exponential tail of g, $Pr\{g \geq (m+1)a\} \leq 2e^{-cm}$, and thus $\mathbb{E}g^p \leq a^p + 2a^p \sum_{m=0}^{\infty}(m+2)^p e^{-cm}$, proving that $c_p(\mathbb{E}g^p)^{1/p} \leq \mathbb{E}g$.

To prove the upper bound, set $h_m = \mathbb{E}g\chi_{\{g \geq ma\}}$. We will show that there is an absolute constant $C \geq 1$ such that for every $m \geq C$, $h_m \leq (\mathbb{E}g)/2$. Indeed,

$$h_m = \sum_{n=m}^{\infty} \mathbb{E}g\chi_{\{na \leq g < (n+1)a\}} \leq 2a \sum_{n=m}^{\infty}(n+1)e^{-cn} = 2ab_m.$$

b_m is a tail of a converging series that does not depend on the choice of g, hence for a sufficiently large m and every $g \in G$, $h_m \leq (\mathbb{E}g)/2$.

Set $A = \{g \leq a/4\}$ and observe that

$$\frac{a}{2} \leq \mathbb{E}g\chi_{\{g \leq Ca\}} = \mathbb{E}g\chi_A + \mathbb{E}g\chi_{\{a/4 < g \leq Ca\}} \leq \frac{a}{4}Pr(A) + Ca(1 - Pr(A)).$$

Hence, $Pr(A^c) \geq 1/(4C - 1)$ and $\mathbb{E}g^p \geq \mathbb{E}g^p \chi_{A^c} \geq \left(\frac{a}{4}\right)^p \cdot \frac{1}{4C-1} = C_p a^p$, as claimed.

$\square$

Before we continue with our discussion, let us observe that the exponential tail assumption can be slightly relaxed. In fact, all that one needs is that the probability that g is much larger than its expectation decays rapidly, uniformly in g.

For any class F let $R_n(F) = n^{-1/2}\mathbb{E}\sup_{f \in F}|\sum_{i=1}^n \varepsilon_i f(X_i)|$. We show that $R_n(F)$ may be bounded below by $\sigma_F = \sup_{f \in F} \mathbb{E}_\mu f^2$.

Lemma 45 *There is an absolute constant c such that if $F \subset B(L_\infty(\Omega))$ and if μ is a probability measure for which $\sigma_F^2 \geq 1/n$ then $R_n(F) \geq c\sigma_F$.*

Proof: By the assumption on σ_F, there is some $f \in F$ for which $\sigma_f^2 = \mathbb{E}_\mu f^2 \geq 1/n$. Applying the Kahane-Khintchine inequality [10], there is an absolute constant c such that for every $\{x_1, ..., x_n\}$

$$\mathbb{E}_\varepsilon \sup_{f \in F} \left| \sum_{i=1}^n \varepsilon_i f(x_i) \right| \geq c \left(\mathbb{E}_\varepsilon \sup_{f \in F} \left| \sum_{i=1}^n \varepsilon_i f(x_i) \right|^2 \right)^{\frac{1}{2}} = c \left(\sum_{i=1}^n f^2(x_i) \right)^{\frac{1}{2}}.$$

Hence, $R_n(F) \geq c \mathbb{E}_\mu \left(n^{-1} \sum_{i=1}^n f^2(x_i) \right)^{\frac{1}{2}}$.

Define $g(X_1, ..., X_n) = n^{-1} \sum_{i=1}^n f^2(X_i)$ and since f is bounded by 1 then $\mathbb{E}g^2 \leq \sigma_f^2$. By Bernstein's inequality ([13]),

$$Pr\{|g - \mathbb{E}_\mu g| \geq m\mathbb{E}_\mu g\} \leq 2e^{-c \frac{n^2 m^2 (\mathbb{E}_\mu g)^2}{\sigma_f^2 n + nm\mathbb{E}_\mu g}}.$$

But since $\mathbb{E}_\mu g = \sigma_f^2$ then the exponent is of the order of $nm\sigma_f^2$, and because $n\sigma_f^2 \geq 1$, there is an absolute constant c such that $Pr\{|g - \mathbb{E}_\mu g| \geq m\mathbb{E}_\mu g\} \leq 2e^{-cm}$. Using the previous lemma for $p = 1/2$ it follows that there are absolute constants c and C such that $c(\mathbb{E}_\mu g^{1/2})^2 \leq \mathbb{E}_\mu g \leq C(\mathbb{E}_\mu g^{1/2})^2$. Thus,

$$(\mathbb{E}_\mu g^{\frac{1}{2}}) \geq c(\mathbb{E}_\mu g)^{\frac{1}{2}} = c \left(\frac{1}{n} \mathbb{E}_\mu \sum_{i=1}^n f^2(X_i) \right)^{\frac{1}{2}} = c\sigma_f,$$

as claimed.

□

To prove theorem 43 we require the "functional" version of Bernstein's inequality. This result is originally due to Talagrand [12], but we shall use it in the following version, established by Massart [5].

Theorem 46 *Let ν be a probability measure on Ω, set $F \subset B(L_\infty(\Omega))$ and put $\sigma^2 = \sup_{f \in F} \sum_{i=1}^n \text{var}(f(X_i))$, where (X_i) are independent random variables distributed according to ν. Then, there is an absolute constant $C \geq 1$ such that for every $x > 0$, there is a set of probability larger than $1 - e^{-x}$ on which*

$$\sup_{f \in F} \left| \frac{1}{n} \sum_{i=1}^n f(X_i) - \mathbb{E}_\mu f \right| \leq \frac{2R_n(F)}{\sqrt{n}} + \frac{C}{n}(\sigma\sqrt{x} + x). \tag{4.1}$$

proof of theorem 43: Denote by $\mathbb{E}$ the expectation with respect to the product measure $\nu^n = (\varepsilon \otimes \mu)^n$ and set $R = n^{-1/2} \sup_{f \in F} |\sum_{i=1}^n \varepsilon_i f(X_i)|$. We apply (4.1), for the random variable

$$Z = \sup_{f \in F} \left| \sum_{i=1}^n \varepsilon_i f(X_i) - \mathbb{E} \sum_{i=1}^n \varepsilon_i f(X_i) \right| = \sqrt{n}R.$$

Using the notation of theorem 46, $\sigma^2 = n\sigma_F^2$, and with probability larger than $1 - e^{-x}$,

$$\frac{1}{\sqrt{n}} \sup_{f \in F} \left| \sum_{i=1}^n \varepsilon_i f(X_i) \right| \leq 2\mathbb{E} \frac{1}{\sqrt{n}} \sup_{f \in F} \left| \sum_{i=1}^n \varepsilon_i f(X_i) \right| + C \left(\sigma_F \sqrt{x} + \frac{x}{\sqrt{n}} \right),$$

for some absolute constant C. By our assumption, $\sigma_F \geq 1/\sqrt{n}$, and by lemma 45, $c\sigma_F \leq n^{-1/2}\mathbb{E}\sup_{f \in F}|\sum_{i=1}^n \varepsilon_i f(X_i)|$. Thus, selecting $x = m$ for some integer m, it follows that there is an absolute constant C such that with probability larger that $1 - e^{-m}$, $R \leq Cm\mathbb{E}R$. Hence, $Pr\{R \geq m\mathbb{E}R\} \leq e^{-cm}$, for an appropriate absolute constant c. Using the same argument as in lemma 44, it follows that all the L_p norms of R are equivalent, which proves our assertion.

$\square$

Remark 47 *It is possible to prove theorem 43 in an alternative way, using the Hoffmann-Jørgenson inequality (see [4] theorem 1.2.5 and lemma 1.2.6) combined with the Marcinkiewicz inequalities ([4] lemma 1.4.13). This argument was pointed out to us by V. Koltchiinskii.*

Proof of theorem 41: The upper estimate follows since for any probability measure ν and every $\sigma > 0$, $\|R_\sigma\|_{L_1(\nu)} \leq \|R_\sigma\|_{L_2(\nu)}$. For the lower one, we have to show there is some $h \in F_\sigma = \{f \in F_K | \mathbb{E}_\mu f^2 \leq \sigma^2\}$, for which $\mathbb{E}_\mu h^2 \geq 1/n$.

Indeed, let ϕ_1 be the eigenfunction of T_K associated with the largest eigenvalue λ_1, and set $g = \sqrt{T_K}\phi_1 = \lambda_1\phi_1$. Then, $g \in F_K$ and $\mathbb{E}_\mu g^2 = \lambda_1 \geq 1/n$. Put $h = tg$ for an appropriate selection of $0 < t \leq 1$. Then, $h \in F_K$ as a convex combination of g and 0, $E_\mu h^2 \geq \sigma^2$, and thus, $\sup_{f \in F_\sigma} \mathbb{E}_\mu f^2 \geq 1/n$. Our assertion follows from lemma 42 and theorem 41.

$\square$

This result yields bounds in the case when the sampling is conducted according to the same probability measure for which one has the Mercer decomposition. This reveals the fundamental weakness in the attempt to characterize error bounds of kernel machines using only the spectral properties of the integral operator - since those might change dramatically when the measure changes, and the learner does not have a-priori information on that measure.

A H_F^n and Error Bounds

Before presenting the error bound we require, we need to define random variables associated with the class F. Let $V_r = \sup_{f \in F, \ \mathbb{E}_\mu f^2 < r} |\mathbb{E}_\mu f - \frac{1}{n}\sum_{i=1}^n f(X_i)|$, and put $W_r = \sup_{f \in F, \ \mathbb{E}_\mu f \geq r, \ \mathbb{E}_\mu f^2 \geq r} \frac{r}{\mathbb{E}_\mu f}|\mathbb{E}_\mu f - \frac{1}{n}\sum_{i=1}^n f(X_i)|$. Below we define two properties of sets which will be essential in our discussion.

Definition A1 *We say that a class F on (Ω, μ) is a Bernstein class with constant B (B class), if for every $f \in F$, $\mathbb{E}_\mu f^2 \leq B\mathbb{E}_\mu f$.*

The reason for the name of Bernstein class is that the ability to uniformly control the variance of class members in terms of their expectations is very significant when trying to apply "functional Bernstein" inequalities.

Definition A2 *A set A is called star-shaped with x as a center, if for every $a \in A$ and every $0 \leq t \leq 1$, $tx + (1 - t)a \in A$.*

Important examples of B-classes are p-loss classes in the proper learning scenario (which are actually 1-classes, since each function in nonnegative) and 2-loss classes in the improper setup (see [7]). Now, we can present error bounds for bounded B-classes of functions.

Theorem A3   *[2] Let F be a B-class of functions bounded by 1. If s_n is a sample for which $W_r(s_n) < r$ then for every $f \in F$,*

$$\mathbb{E}_\mu f \leq \max\left\{r, \frac{1}{n}\sum_{i=1}^n f(X_i) + V_r, \frac{n^{-1}\sum_{i=1}^n f(X_i)}{1 - W_r/r}\right\}.$$

Moreover, there is an absolute constant C such that for any star-shaped class F with 0 as a center and every $x > 0$, there is a set of measure larger than $1 - 2e^{-x}$, on which

$$\max\{V_r, W_r\} \leq C\left(\frac{1}{\sqrt{n}}H_F^n(\sqrt{Br}) + \sqrt{\frac{Brx}{n}} + \frac{x}{n}\right). \tag{A.1}$$

References

1. K. Ball: Volumes of sections on cubes and related problems, in *Lecture Notes in Mathematics 1470*, 36-47, Springer-Berlin. 33
2. P. L. Bartlett, O. Bousquet, S. Mendelson: Localized Rademacher Averages, these proceedings. 43
3. F. Cucker, S. Smale: On the mathematical foundations of learning, preprint. 30, 38
4. V. De la Peña, E. Giné: *Decoupling: from dependence to independence*, Springer, 1999. 42
5. P. Massart: About the constants in Talagrand's concentration inequality for empirical processes, Annals of Probability, 28(2) 863-884, 2000. 41
6. S. Mendelson: Rademacher averages and phase transitions in Glivenko-Cantelli classes, IEEE transactions on Information Theory, Jan, 2002.
7. S. Mendelson: Improving the sample complexity using global data, to appear, IEEE transactions on Information Theory. 31, 33, 43
8. S. Mendelson, R. Vershynin: Entropy, Combinatorial Dimensions and Random Averages, these proceedings. 31
9. M. Meyer, A. Pajor: Sections of the unit ball of ℓ_p^n, Journal of Functional Analysis 80 (1), 109-123, 1988. 32
10. V. D. Milman, G. Schechtman: *Asymptotic theory of finite dimensional normed spaces*, Lecture Notes in Mathematics 1200, Springer 1986. 41
11. G. Pisier: *The volume of convex bodies and Banach space geometry*, Cambridge University Press, 1989. 32, 33
12. M. Talagrand: Sharper bounds for Gaussian and empirical processes, Annals of Probability, 22(1), 28-76, 1994. 41
13. A. W. Van der Vaart, J.A. Wellner: *Weak convergence and Empirical Processes*, Springer-Verlag, 1996. 41
14. R. C. Williamson, B. Scheolkopf, A. Smola: Generalization performance of regularization networks and support vector machines via entropy numbers of compact networks, IEEE transactions on Information Theory. 30, 38

Localized Rademacher Complexities

Peter L. Bartlett[1,3], Olivier Bousquet[1,2], and Shahar Mendelson[3]

[1] BIOwulf Technologies
Berkeley, CA, USA
Peter.Bartlett@anu.edu.au
[2] Centre de Mathématiques Appliquées, Ecole Polytechnique
91128 Palaiseau, France
bousquet@cmapx.polytechnique.fr
[3] Research School of Information Sciences and Engineering
The Australian National University
Canberra, ACT 0200, Australia
shahar.mendelson@anu.edu.au

Abstract. We investigate the behaviour of global and local Rademacher averages. We present new error bounds which are based on the local averages and indicate how data-dependent local averages can be estimated without *a priori* knowledge of the class at hand.

1 Introduction

In this article we investigate the role that Rademacher averages have in formulating error bounds. Given a class $\mathcal{F}$ of functions on a probability space $(\mathcal{X}, P)$, the (global) Rademacher averages associated with the class and with P are

$$\mathbb{E}\left[\frac{1}{n} \sup_{f \in F} \left| \sum_{i=1}^{n} \sigma_i f(X_i) \right| \right],$$

where $(X_i)_{i=1}^n$ are independent random variables distributed according to P and $(\sigma_i)_{i=1}^n$ are independent Rademacher (that is, symmetric $\{-1, 1\}$-valued) random variables. The expectation is taken with respect to both (X_i) and (σ_i). Recent results have shown [5,1,6,9,2] that the Rademacher averages can be used to measure the sample complexity of a learning problem or as a complexity term in error bounds.

At the heart of our discussion is a concentration inequality which estimates the deviation of $\sup_{f \in \mathcal{F}} |\sum_{i=1}^{n} f(X_i)|$ (or $\mathbb{E}_\sigma \left[\frac{1}{n} \left| \sum_{i=1}^{n} \sigma_i f(X_i) \right| \right]$) from its mean value. The result we use is a version of Talagrand's concentration inequality for empirical processes [4]. The benefit of this result is that it enables one to control the deviation in terms of the Rademacher averages and the largest variance of a class member.

As an application of this result we obtain error bounds for loss classes using the Rademacher averages of the entire class (see Section 5). Moreover, we show that the important quantity is not the Rademacher averages associated with the

J. Kivinen and R. H. Sloan (Eds.): COLT 2002, LNAI 2375, pp. 44–58, 2002.

entire class, but rather, the local Rademacher averages, which are defined for every $r > 0$ as

$$\mathbb{E}\left[\frac{1}{n}\sup_{f\in\mathcal{F},\ Pf^2\leq r}|\sum_{i=1}^{n}\sigma_i f(X_i)|\right],$$

where Pf^2 denotes the expectation of f^2 with respect to P.

Thus, instead of computing the supremum over the entire class, the supremum is taken with respect to the intersection of the class and a ball in $L_2(P)$ of radius $\sqrt{r}$, which leads to significantly better bounds.

Our results are based on two structural assumptions on the class. The first one is that the class consists of uniformly bounded functions. The other assumption is that for every member of the class, it is possible to control its variance using its expectation. In other words, we assume that there is some constant B such that for every $f \in \mathcal{F}$, $Pf^2 \leq BPf$. The classes we are interested in are loss classes naturally appearing in learning theory. Although this structural assumption seems restrictive, in the learning setup it is satisfied by many loss classes. For example, in proper learning, where the target is assumed to be a member of the class, each loss function is nonnegative and uniformly bounded. Thus, $Pf^2 \leq BPf$ for every loss function. The case of improper learning is less trivial. It is possible to show that if the original class is convex and $\mathcal{F}$ is the class of excess squared loss (so that each $f \in \mathcal{F}$ is the difference between expected squared loss and minimal expected squared loss), then for every $f \in \mathcal{F}$, $Pf^2 \leq 16Pf$ [7]. Related results are known for other loss classes, such as those defined using p-norms with $p > 2$ [9], and for certain non-convex classes [10].

This article is organized as follows; first, we present some definitions and notation. Then, we present the basic properties of the Rademacher (both local and global) complexities. In Section 4 we recall the basic concentration result and prove a deviation bound based on the Rademacher complexities of the class. Then, in Section 5 we present error bounds using the global averages. The error bounds based on the local Rademacher complexities are presented in Section 6. Finally, we establish several results which can enable one to compute the Rademacher complexities using empirical data.

2   Definitions and Notation

Let $\mathcal{X}$ be the input space and $\mathcal{Y} \subset \mathbb{R}$. Fix a probability measure P on the product space $\mathcal{X} \times \mathcal{Y}$ and consider n independent random pairs $(X_1, Y_1), \ldots, (X_n, Y_n)$ distributed according to P. Denote by $\mathcal{G}$ a class of functions mapping $\mathcal{X}$ into $\mathcal{Y}$, and by D_n the data $(X_i, Y_i)_{i=1}^n$. We use P to denote both the probability distribution on $\mathcal{X} \times \mathcal{Y}$ and the marginal distribution on $\mathcal{X}$. The distinction should always be clear from the context.

Let ℓ be a loss function and define the loss class

$$\mathcal{F} = \{f(x,y) = \ell(g(x), y) : g \in \mathcal{G}\}. \tag{1}$$

For every $f \in \mathcal{F}$, denote by Pf the expectation of f, $\mathbb{E}\left[f(X, Y)\right]$, and in our case, this would be called the expected loss. Given a sample D_n, set $P_n f = n^{-1} \sum_{i=1}^{n} f(X_i, Y_i)$ to be the empirical loss.

For every $f \in \mathcal{F}$, let $R_n f = n^{-1} \sum_{i=1}^{n} \sigma_i f(X_i, Y_i)$. Hence, $R_n f$ is a function of both the Rademacher random variables and the sample D_n, and the expectation of its magnitude is the Rademacher average of $\mathcal{F}$. We use $\mathbb{E}_\sigma \left[R_n f\right]$ to denote $\mathbb{E}\left[R_n f | D_n\right]$.

A class $\mathcal{F}$ is called *star-shaped* around f_0 if for every $f \in \mathcal{F}$ and every $0 \leq t \leq 1$, $tf + (1-t)f_0 \in \mathcal{F}$. We denote by $\mathrm{star}(\mathcal{F}, f_0)$ the set of all functions $tf + (1-t)f_0$, with $0 \leq t \leq 1$ and $f \in \mathcal{F}$. We call this set the *star hull* of $\mathcal{F}$ around f_0.

Finally, recall that $a \vee b = \max(a, b)$ and $a \wedge b = \min(a, b)$.

3 Measuring the Complexity Locally

We are interested in the local Rademacher average, defined for some $r > 0$ as

$$\mathbb{E}\left[\sup_{f \in \mathcal{F}: Pf^2 \leq r} |R_n f|\right].$$

This is a function of r which measures the so-called Rademacher complexity of subspaces of the function class defined by a bound on the variance. In order to see why this is important for bounding the generalization error, suppose that the function chosen by a learning algorithm has small expected error. For classes where there is a relationship between the variance and the expectation, this function also has small variance. In this case, the algorithm chooses elements with small variance and the generalization error bound should thus take into account the complexity of the subclass of elements with small variance only.

However, since the local Rademacher average is a function of r, we have to specify some r_0 at which we compute it. We shall see in Section 6 that the complexity term (the only term in the bound that depends on the 'size' of the class of functions) is proportional to the value r_0 of r which satisifies the following fixed point equation,

$$\psi(r) = r,$$

where $\psi(r)$ is an upper bound on the local Rademacher average at radius r.

Of course, in order for this fixed point equation to have a (unique) solution, ψ should satisfy certain regularity conditions (which may not be satisfied by the local Rademacher average itself).

The relevance of the quantity r_0 defined above has been pointed out by Koltchinskii and Panchenko [6] and Massart [8]. Typically one upper bounds the local Rademacher average by an entropy integral [6]

$$\mathbb{E}\left[\sup_{f \in \mathcal{F}: Pf^2 \leq r} |R_n f|\right] \leq \mathbb{E}\left[\frac{K}{\sqrt{n}} \int_0^{\sqrt{r}} \sqrt{\log N(\mathcal{F}, u, d_n)}\, du\right],$$

where $N(\mathcal{F}, u, d_n)$ is the covering number of $\mathcal{F}$ at radius u for the empirical L_2 metric. Another possibility is to upper bound it using VC-dimension or VC-entropies as in [8].

Both of these approaches are rather indirect, and introduce some looseness. Here we show that it is possible, by slightly enlarging the class on which the local Rademacher average is computed, to ensure that this average satisfies the required conditions for the existence of a (unique) fixed point r_0.

Lemma 1. *Let $\mathcal{F}$ be a class of functions. We have*

$$\mathbb{E}\left[\sup_{f \in star(\mathcal{F}, 0)} |R_n f|\right] = \mathbb{E}\left[\sup_{f \in \mathcal{F}} |R_n f|\right],$$

and defining for all $r > 0$,

$$F(r) = \mathbb{E}\left[\sup_{f \in star(\mathcal{F}, 0): Pf^2 \le r} |R_n f|\right],$$

then $F(r)$ is an upper bound on the local Rademacher average of $\mathcal{F}$ at radius r and $F(r)/\sqrt{r}$ is non-increasing.

Proof. The first claim is true since the averages of a class and of its symmetric convex hull coincide. Therefore, they both equal the averages of $star(\mathcal{F}, 0)$ because the latter contains $\mathcal{F}$ and is contained in the symmetric convex hull of $\mathcal{F}$.

For the second claim, we will show that for any $r_1 \le r_2$, $F(r_1) \ge \sqrt{r_1/r_2} \cdot F(r_2)$. Indeed, fix any sample and any realization of the Rademacher random variables, and set f to be a function for which $\sup_{f \in F,\ Pf^2 \le r_2} |\sum_{i=1}^n \sigma_i f(x_i)|$ is attained (if the supremum is not attained only a slight modification is required). Since $Pf^2 \le r_2$, we have $P(\sqrt{r_1/r_2} \cdot f)^2 \le r_1$. Furthermore, the function $\sqrt{r_1/r_2} f$ is in $\mathcal{F}$ because $\mathcal{F}$ is star-shaped around zero, and satisfies $P(\sqrt{r_1/r_2} f)^2 \le r_1$. Hence,

$$\sup_{f \in F: Pf^2 \le r_1} \left|\sum_{i=1}^n \sigma_i f(x_i)\right| \ge \left|\sum_{i=1}^n \sigma_i \sqrt{\frac{r_1}{r_2}} \cdot f(x_i)\right| = \sqrt{\frac{r_1}{r_2}} \sup_{f \in F: Pf^2 \le r_2} \left|\sum_{i=1}^n \sigma_i f(x_i)\right|,$$

and the proof follows by taking expectations with respect to the Rademacher random variables. □

We observe that the global Rademacher average is not affected by taking the star hull of a class, while the local Rademacher average *is* affected.

Also, we notice that taking the star hull makes the complexity uniform over the balls $\{f : Pf^2 \le r\}$, in a sense. In other words, computing a local average in a star-shaped class corresponds to taking into account the complexity of the whole class, scaled appropriately. One could think that we thus lose the interest of looking locally, but this is not the case since we gain the fact that we have a scaling parameter (the radius of the ball) to adjust.

To see why this is interesting, consider again the entropy bound. Assume that we have a Vapnik-Chervonenkis class of functions of VC dimension V. Then it is well known [12] that one has the bound $N(\mathcal{F}, \epsilon, d_n) \leq K\epsilon^{-V}$. Moreover, taking the star hull of the class does not affect significantly the covering numbers (see e.g. [9]) and we obtain

$$N(\text{star}(\mathcal{F}, 0), \epsilon, d_n) \leq K\epsilon^{-V-1}.$$

As a result, we obtain by the entropy bound

$$\mathbb{E}\left[\sup_{f \in \text{star}(\mathcal{F}, 0): Pf^2 \leq r} |R_n f|\right] \leq K\sqrt{\frac{Vr}{n} \log \frac{n}{r}},$$

so that the complexity r_0 of the class (or its star-hull) will be of order

$$r_0 = O\left(\frac{V}{n} \log \frac{n}{V}\right),$$

which is optimal for such classes. It is possible to check that, for other rates of growth of the covering numbers, the value of r_0 obtained by this computation gives the optimal rate of convergence of the generalization error (see [6]).

Thus, in considering upper bounds F on the local Rademacher average of the class, we can say that taking the local Rademacher average of the star-hull gives the smallest (at least, in order of magnitude) upper bound that satisfies the condition that $F(r)/\sqrt{r}$ is non-increasing.

4   Concentration Results

This section is devoted to the main concentration results we require. The following is an improvement of Rio's [11] version of Talagrand's concentration inequality and is due to Bousquet [4].

Theorem 1. *Assume the X_i are identically distributed according to P. Let $\mathcal{F}$ be a countable set of functions from $\mathcal{X}$ to $\mathbb{R}$ and assume that all the functions in $\mathcal{F}$ are P-measurable, square-integrable and satisfy $\mathbb{E}[f] = 0$. If $\sup_{f \in \mathcal{F}} \text{ess sup} f \leq 1$, denote $Z = \sup_{f \in \mathcal{F}} \sum_{i=1}^{n} f(X_i)$ and if $\sup_{f \in \mathcal{F}} \|f\|_\infty \leq 1$ denote $Z = \sup_{f \in \mathcal{F}} |\sum_{i=1}^{n} f(X_i)|$.*

Let σ be a positive real number such that $\sigma^2 \geq \sup_{f \in \mathcal{F}} \text{Var}[f(X_1)]$. Then, for any $x \geq 0$, we have

$$\mathbb{P}[Z \geq \mathbb{E}[Z] + x] \leq \exp\left(-vh\left(\frac{x}{v}\right)\right),$$

where $h(x) = (1+x)\log(1+x) - x$ and $v = n\sigma^2 + 2\mathbb{E}[Z]$. Also,

$$\mathbb{P}\left[Z \geq \mathbb{E}[Z] + \sqrt{2xv} + \frac{x}{3}\right] \leq e^{-x}.$$

In a similar way one can obtain a concentration result for the Rademacher averages of a class (see e.g. [3]).

Theorem 2. *Assume* $|f(x)| \leq 1$. *Let*

$$Z := \mathbb{E}_\sigma \left[\sup_{f \in \mathcal{F}} \sum_{i=1}^n \sigma_i f(X_i) \right] \quad or \quad Z := \mathbb{E}_\sigma \left[\sup_{f \in \mathcal{F}} \left| \sum_{i=1}^n \sigma_i f(X_i) \right| \right],$$

then for all $x \geq 0$,

$$\mathbb{P} \left[Z \geq \mathbb{E}[Z] + \sqrt{2x\mathbb{E}[Z]} + \frac{x}{3} \right] \leq e^{-x}.$$

and

$$\mathbb{P} \left[Z \leq \mathbb{E}[Z] - \sqrt{2x\mathbb{E}[Z]} \right] \leq e^{-x}.$$

A standard fact we shall use is that the expected deviation of the empirical means from the actual ones can be controlled by the Rademacher averages of the class.

Lemma 2. *[12] For any class of functions* $\mathcal{F}$,

$$\mathbb{E} \left[\sup_{f \in \mathcal{F}} Pf - P_n f \right] \leq \mathbb{E} \left[\sup_{f \in \mathcal{F}} |Pf - P_n f| \right] \leq 2\mathbb{E} \left[\sup_{f \in \mathcal{F}} |R_n f| \right].$$

Using the concentration results and the symmetrization lemma one can estimate the probability of the deviation of the empirical means from the actual ones in terms of the Rademacher averages. Note that the bound in the following result improves as the largest variance of a class member decreases.

Corollary 1. *Let* $\mathcal{F}$ *be a class of functions which maps* $\mathcal{X} \times \mathcal{Y}$ *into* $[a, a+1]$ *for some* $a \in \mathbb{R}$. *Assume that there is some* $r > 0$ *such that for every* $f \in \mathcal{F}$, $\mathsf{Var}[f(X_i)] \leq r$ *and set*

$$V = \sup_{f \in \mathcal{F}} |Pf - P_n f|.$$

Then, for every $x > 0$ *and every* $\alpha > 0$ *there is a set of probability larger than* $1 - e^{-x}$ *on which*

$$V \leq (1 + \alpha)\mathbb{E}[V] + \sqrt{\frac{2rx}{n}} + \left(\frac{1}{3} + \frac{1}{\alpha} \right) \frac{x}{n}.$$

Moreover, for all $0 < \alpha < 1$, *with probability at least* $1 - 2e^{-x}$,

$$V \leq 2\frac{1 + \alpha}{1 - \alpha} \mathbb{E}_\sigma \left[\sup_{f \in F} |R_n f| \right] + \sqrt{\frac{2rx}{n}} + \left(\frac{1}{3} + \frac{1}{\alpha} + \frac{1}{2\alpha(1 - \alpha)} \right) \frac{x}{n}.$$

The proof requires two additional preliminary results. The first is easy to verify.

Lemma 3. *For $u, v \geq 0$,*

$$\sqrt{u+v} \leq \sqrt{u} + \sqrt{v},$$

and for any $\alpha > 0$,

$$2\sqrt{uv} \leq \alpha u + \frac{v}{\alpha}$$

Lemma 4. *Using the notation of Corollary 1, with probability at least $1 - e^{-x}$,*

$$\mathbb{E}\left[\sup_{f \in \mathcal{F}} |R_n f|\right] \leq \frac{1}{1-\alpha} \mathbb{E}_\sigma\left[\sup_{f \in F} |R_n f|\right] + \frac{x}{2n\alpha(1-\alpha)}.$$

Proof. The last inequality of Theorem 2 and Lemma 3 imply that

$$\mathbb{E}\left[\sup_{f \in F} |R_n f|\right] \leq \mathbb{E}_\sigma\left[\sup_{f \in F} |R_n f|\right] + \sqrt{\frac{2x}{n}\mathbb{E}\left[\sup_{f \in F} |R_n f|\right]}$$

$$\leq \mathbb{E}_\sigma\left[\sup_{f \in F} |R_n f|\right] + \alpha\mathbb{E}\left[\sup_{f \in F} |R_n f|\right] + \frac{x}{2n\alpha},$$

hence, our claim follows.   □

Proof. (of Corollary 1) The proof of the first part follows from Theorem 1. Using its notation,

$$\sigma^2 = \sup_{f \in \mathcal{F}} \mathsf{Var}[f(X_i)] \leq r.$$

Thus, with probability at least $1 - e^{-x}$, we have

$$V \leq \mathbb{E}[V] + \sqrt{\frac{2xr}{n} + \frac{4x\mathbb{E}[V]}{n}} + \frac{x}{3n}.$$

The first part of the corollary follows from Lemma 3. The second part follows by combining this inequality with Lemmas 2 and 4.   □

5   Error Bounds and Global Averages

Using the various concentration results presented in the previous section, we are now ready to present the error bounds we promised. The bounds are based on the Rademacher averages of the entire class.

Simply applying uniform convergence results to the entire class leads to unsatisfactory error bounds. Better results can be obtained by using various normalization or scaling schemes, in which more weight is assigned to functions that are likely to be the best ones in the class (that is, closer to 0), thus allowing one to "zoom in" on the best region of the space.

When the functions in the class are nonnegative and bounded one can normalize by dividing class members by Pf. Otherwise one normalizes by dividing by Pf^2. In both cases, one needs to be careful when getting too close to zero. Hence, the normalization is conducted only for functions which are "sufficiently far" from 0.

5.1   Normalizing by Pf

Let us introduce some additional notation. Given the class $\mathcal{F}$ and some $r > 0$ set

$$\mathcal{G}_r = \left\{ \frac{r}{r \vee Pf} f : f \in \mathcal{F} \right\}.$$

It is easy to see that $\mathcal{G}_r \subset \{\alpha f : f \in \mathcal{F}, \ \alpha \in [0,1]\} \subset \mathrm{star}(\mathcal{F}, 0)$. It is also easy to check that every $g \in \mathcal{G}_r$ satisfies $Pg \leq r$. Define

$$V_r = \sup_{g \in \mathcal{G}_r} Pg - P_n g.$$

Lemma 5. *For any $r > 0$ and $K > 1$, if $V_r \leq \frac{r}{K}$ then every $f \in \mathcal{F}$ satisfies*

$$Pf \leq \frac{K}{K-1} P_n f + \frac{r}{K}.$$

Proof. Observe that for any $g \in \mathcal{G}_r$, $Pg \leq P_n g + V_r$. Let $f \in \mathcal{F}$ and thus $g = rf/(r \vee Pf)$.

First, assume that $Pf \leq r$. By the definition of $\mathcal{G}_r$, $g = f$, hence $Pf \leq P_n f + V_r \leq (K/(K-1)) P_n f + r/K$.

Otherwise, if $Pf > r$, then $g = rf/Pf$. Therefore, since $Pg \leq P_n g + V_r$ then

$$r \leq r \frac{P_n f}{Pf} + V_r.$$

In that case, if $V_r \leq r/K < r$, we obtain

$$Pf \leq \frac{P_n f}{1 - V_r/r} \leq \frac{K}{K-1} P_n f \leq \frac{K}{K-1} P_n f + \frac{r}{K}.$$

$\square$

Combining this deterministic result and the probabilistic estimates of the previous section gives the main result of this section.

Lemma 6. *Let $\mathcal{F}$ be a class of nonnegative functions which are bounded by 1. For any $K > 1$ and $x > 0$ there is a set of probability larger than $1 - 2e^{-x}$, such that for any $f \in \mathcal{F}$,*

$$Pf \leq \frac{K}{K-1} P_n f + 12 \mathbb{E}_\sigma \left[\sup_{f \in \mathcal{F}} |R_n f| \right] + \frac{(2K + 17)x}{n}.$$

Although this result suggests that the error decreases at the rate $1/n$, this is misleading because one can show that if $\mathcal{F}$ has even a single function for which $Pf^2 \geq c$ then $\mathbb{E}_\sigma \left[\sup_{f \in \mathcal{F}} |R_n f| \right] \geq c'/\sqrt{n}$, where c' depends only on c. Thus, when applied to the whole class, this bound will typically be dominated by the Rademacher term. However, when we consider subsets of the class, this result will enable us to obtain error bounds using local averages.

Proof. We begin with the observation that functions in $\mathcal{G}_r$ satisfy that $Pg^2 \leq r$. Indeed, if $Pf \leq r$ then $g = f$ and $Pg^2 = Pf^2 \leq Pf \leq r$ (where we used the fact that f maps to $[0, 1]$, and hence $f^2 \leq f$). Otherwise, if $Pf > r$ then $g = rf/Pf$ and $Pg^2 = r^2 Pf^2/(Pf)^2 < rPf^2/Pf \leq r$.

Applying Corollary 1 and Lemma 2 to V_r it follows that for any $0 < \alpha < 1$,

$$V_r \leq 2(1 + \alpha)\mathbb{E}\left[\sup_{g \in \mathcal{G}}|R_n g|\right] + \sqrt{\frac{2rx}{n}} + \left(\frac{1}{3} + \frac{1}{\alpha}\right)\frac{x}{n}$$

with probability larger than $1 - e^{-x}$.

Since $\mathcal{G}_r \subset \text{star}(\mathcal{F}, 0)$ and by Lemma 1,

$$\mathbb{E}\left[\sup_{g \in \mathcal{G}}|R_n g|\right] \leq \mathbb{E}\left[\sup_{f \in \text{star}(\mathcal{F}, 0)}|R_n f|\right] = \mathbb{E}\left[\sup_{f \in \mathcal{F}}|R_n f|\right].$$

Therefore, with probability at least $1 - e^{-x}$,

$$V_r \leq 2(1 + \alpha)\mathbb{E}\left[\sup_{f \in \mathcal{F}}|R_n f|\right] + \sqrt{\frac{2rx}{n}} + \left(\frac{1}{3} + \frac{1}{\alpha}\right)\frac{x}{n}.$$

Now, we can select a specific value of r (which is denoted by r^*). Fix some $K > 1$ and set r to be such that the term on the right hand side is equal to r/K. (Such an r always exists, since the right hand side is of the form $C + A\sqrt{r}$.) Note that if $r/K = C + A\sqrt{r}$ then $r \leq K^2 A^2 + 2KC$, and thus r^* may be selected as

$$r^* \leq 4K(1 + \alpha)\mathbb{E}\left[\sup_{f \in \mathcal{F}}|R_n f|\right] + \left(2K^2 + 2K\left(\frac{1}{3} + \frac{1}{\alpha}\right)\right)\frac{x}{n}$$

$$\leq 4K\frac{1 + \alpha}{1 - \alpha}\mathbb{E}_\sigma\left[\sup_{f \in \mathcal{F}}|R_n f|\right] + \frac{2K(1 + \alpha)x}{n\alpha(1 - \alpha)} + \left(2K^2 + 2K\left(\frac{1}{3} + \frac{1}{\alpha}\right)\right)\frac{x}{n},$$

where the second inequality holds with probability of at least $1 - e^{-x}$ by Lemma 4. By Lemma 5 there is a set of probability at least $1 - 2e^{-x}$ such that for every $f \in \mathcal{F}$,

$$Pf \leq \frac{K}{K - 1}P_n f + 4\frac{1 + \alpha}{1 - \alpha}\mathbb{E}_\sigma\left[\sup_{f \in \mathcal{F}}|R_n f|\right] + \frac{2(1 + \alpha)x}{n\alpha(1 - \alpha)} + 2\left(K + \left(\frac{1}{3} + \frac{1}{\alpha}\right)\right)\frac{x}{n},$$

and our result follows by taking $\alpha = 1/2$.   □

5.2 Normalizing by Pf^2

In this section, we present error bounds in the more general case, where the elements of $\mathcal{F}$ are not assumed to be nonnegative. The results are analogous to those of the previous section, but here we must impose the assumption that the variance of class members is small if their expectation is small. In particular, we assume that there is some $B > 0$ such that for every $f \in \mathcal{F}$, $Pf^2 \leq BPf$.

Given a class $\mathcal{F}$ let

$$\mathcal{G}_r = \left\{ \frac{r}{r \vee Pf^2} f : f \in \mathcal{F} \right\},$$

and note that $\mathcal{G}_r \subset \{\alpha f : f \in \mathcal{F}, \ \alpha \in [0,1]\} \subset \text{star}(\mathcal{F}, 0)$. Define

$$V_r = \sup_{g \in \mathcal{G}_r} Pg - P_n g.$$

Lemma 7. *Let $\mathcal{F}$ be a class of functions with ranges in $[-1, 1]$. Assume that there is a constant $B > 0$ such that for every $f \in \mathcal{F}$, $Pf^2 \leq BPf$. For every $r > 0$ and $K > 1$ which satisfy that $V_r \leq \frac{r}{BK}$, and any $f \in \mathcal{F}$,*

$$Pf \leq \frac{K}{K-1} P_n f + \frac{r}{BK}.$$

The proof is similar to that of Lemma 5, we omit it due to lack of space.

Lemma 8. *Let $\mathcal{F}$ be a class of functions with ranges in $[-1, 1]$. Assume that there is a constant $B > 0$ such that for every $f \in \mathcal{F}$, $Pf^2 \leq BPf$. For any $K > 1$ and $x > 0$ there is a set of probability larger than $1 - 2e^{-x}$, on which for any $f \in \mathcal{F}$,*

$$Pf \leq \frac{K}{K-1} P_n f + 12 \mathbb{E}_\sigma \left[\sup_{f \in \mathcal{F}} |R_n f| \right] + \frac{(2BK + 22)x}{n}.$$

Again, the proof is similar to the one used in the previous section, and we omit it.

6   Error Bounds and Local Averages

Thus far, the Rademacher averages of the entire class were used as the complexity measure in the error bounds. In this section our aim is to show that the *local* Rademacher averages can serve as a complexity measure. The advantage in using the local version of the averages is that they can be considerably smaller than the global ones.

6.1   Distribution Dependent Complexity

Our analysis is connected to the idea of *peeling* and was inspired by the work of Massart [8].

Theorem 3. *Let $\mathcal{F}$ be a class of functions with ranges in $[0,1]$. Let ψ be a function such that $\psi(r)/\sqrt{r}$ is non-increasing for $r > 0$ and for all $r \geq 0$*

$$\mathbb{E}\left[\sup_{f\in\mathcal{F}, Pf\leq r}|R_n(f)|\right] \leq \psi(r).$$

For any $K > 1$ and every $x > 0$, there is a set of probability larger than $1 - e^{-x}$, on which every $f \in \mathcal{F}$ satisfies

$$Pf \leq \frac{K}{K-1}P_n f + 300Kr_0 + \frac{x(5+4K)}{n},$$

where r_0 is the largest solution of the equation $r_0 = \psi(r_0)$.

Proof. Let $\mathcal{G}_r$ be defined as in section 5.1. Fix any $r > 0$ and recall that for all $x > 0$, with probability $1 - e^{-x}$,

$$V_r \leq 2(1+\alpha)\mathbb{E}\left[\sup_{g\in\mathcal{G}_r}|R_n g|\right] + \sqrt{\frac{2rx}{n}} + \left(\frac{1}{3} + \frac{1}{\alpha}\right)\frac{x}{n}.$$

Let $\mathcal{F}(x,y) := \{f : x \leq Pf \leq y, f \in \mathcal{F}\}$. Let $\lambda > 1$ and let k be the smallest integer such that $r\lambda^{k+1} \geq 1$. We have

$$\mathbb{E}\left[\sup_{g\in\mathcal{G}_r}|R_n g|\right] \leq \mathbb{E}\left[\sup_{\mathcal{F}(0,r)}|R_n f|\right] + \mathbb{E}\left[\sup_{\mathcal{F}(r,1)}\frac{r}{Pf^2}|R_n f|\right]$$

$$\leq \mathbb{E}\left[\sup_{\mathcal{F}(0,r)}|R_n f|\right] + \sum_{j=0}^{k}\mathbb{E}\left[\sup_{\mathcal{F}(r\lambda^j, r\lambda^{j+1})}\frac{r}{Pf^2}|R_n f|\right]$$

$$\leq \mathbb{E}\left[\sup_{\mathcal{F}(0,r)}|R_n f|\right] + \sum_{j=0}^{k}\lambda^{-j}\mathbb{E}\left[\sup_{\mathcal{F}(r\lambda^j, r\lambda^{j+1})}|R_n f|\right]$$

$$\leq \psi(r) + \sum_{j=0}^{k}\lambda^{-j}\psi(r\lambda^{j+1}).$$

By our assumption it follows that for $\alpha \geq 1$

$$\psi(\alpha r) \leq \sqrt{\alpha}\psi(r),$$

so that

$$\mathbb{E}\left[\sup_{g\in\mathcal{G}_r}|R_n g|\right] \leq \psi(r)\left(1 + \sqrt{\lambda}\sum_{j=0}^{k}\lambda^{-j/2}\right),$$

and taking $\lambda = 4$, the right-hand side is upper bounded by $5\psi(r)$. Moreover, for $r \geq r_0$, we have $\psi(r) \leq \sqrt{r/r_0}\psi(r_0) = \sqrt{rr_0}$, and thus

$$V_r \leq 10(1+\alpha)\sqrt{rr_0} + \sqrt{\frac{2rx}{n}} + \left(\frac{1}{3} + \frac{1}{\alpha}\right)\frac{x}{n}.$$

Let r^* be the value of r for which the right hand side is equal to r^*/K. It follows that

$$r^* \leq K^2 \left(10(1+\alpha)\sqrt{r_0} + \sqrt{\frac{2x}{n}} \right)^2 + 2K \left(\frac{1}{3} + \frac{1}{\alpha} \right) \frac{x}{n},$$

(we use the fact that $r/K = C + A\sqrt{r}$ implies $r \leq K^2 A^2 + 2KC$). The same reasoning as in previous proofs gives the result. $\square$

We now derive a similar result for general classes of functions.

Theorem 4. *Let $\mathcal{F}$ be a class of functions with ranges in $[-1,1]$ and assume that there is some B such that for every $f \in \mathcal{F}$, $Pf^2 \leq BPf$. Let ϕ be a function such that $\phi(r)/\sqrt{r}$ is non-increasing for $r > 0$ and*

$$\mathbb{E}\left[\sup_{f \in \mathcal{F}, Pf^2 \leq r} |R_n(f)| \right] \leq \phi(r).$$

For any $K > 1$ and every $x > 0$, there is a set of probability larger than $1 - e^{-x}$, on which every $f \in \mathcal{F}$ satisfies

$$Pf \leq \frac{K}{K-1} P_n f + 300 K r_0 + \frac{x(10 + 4BK)}{n},$$

where r_0 is the largest solution of the equation $r_0 = \phi(r_0)$.

Notice that by Lemma 1, when $\mathcal{F}$ is star-shaped around 0, one can choose

$$\phi(r) = \mathbb{E}\left[\sup_{f \in \mathcal{F}, Pf^2 \leq r} |R_n(f)| \right].$$

Proof. Let $\mathcal{G}_r$ be defined as in section 5.2. As before we have with probability $1 - e^{-x}$,

$$V_r \leq 2(1+\alpha)\mathbb{E}\left[\sup_{g \in \mathcal{G}_r} |R_n g| \right] + \sqrt{\frac{2rx}{n}} + 2 \left(\frac{1}{3} + \frac{1}{\alpha} \right) \frac{x}{n}.$$

Also we can prove as in the previous proof,

$$\mathbb{E}\left[\sup_{g \in \mathcal{G}_r} |R_n g| \right] \leq \phi(r) + \sum_{j=0}^{k} \lambda^{-j} \phi(r\lambda^{j+1})).$$

By our assumption it follows that for $\alpha \geq 1$

$$\phi(\alpha r) \leq \sqrt{\alpha}\phi(r),$$

so that we can get as before

$$V_r \leq 10(1+\alpha)\sqrt{rr_0} + \sqrt{\frac{2rx}{n}} + 2 \left(\frac{1}{3} + \frac{1}{\alpha} \right) \frac{x}{n}.$$

Choosing r^* such that the right-hand side is equal to r^*/BK and using the same reasoning as in the previous proof gives the result. $\square$

6.2   Applications

As an application of Theorem 4 we present oracle inequalities for the empirical risk minimization procedure, i.e. inequalities that relate the performance of minimizer of the empirical risk to that of the best possible function in the class.

For a class $\mathcal{G}$ of functions, we consider the class $\mathcal{F}$ defined as in (1) and we define
$$\bar{\mathcal{F}} = \{f - f^* : f \in \mathcal{F}\},$$

where $f^* = \arg\min_{f \in \mathcal{F}} Pf$ is the function achieving minimal error in the class $\mathcal{F}$. We want to apply Theorem 4 to $\bar{\mathcal{F}}$, we thus have to check that there exists some $B > 0$ such that

$$\forall f \in \mathcal{F}, \ P(f - f^*)^2 \leq B(Pf - Pf^*). \tag{2}$$

Corollary 2. *Let $\mathcal{F}$ be a class of functions with range in $[0, 1]$, satisfying (2) for some B. Let f_n be a function in $\mathcal{F}$ such that*

$$P_n f_n = \inf_{f \in \mathcal{F}} P_n f.$$

Let ϕ and r_0 be defined as in Theorem 4 for the class $\bar{\mathcal{F}}$. Then for every $x > 0$, there is a set of probability larger than $1 - e^{-x}$ on which we have

$$Pf_n - Pf^* \leq 300r_0 + \frac{x(10 + 4B)}{n}.$$

As mentioned before, condition (2) is satisfied by the class of quadratic loss functions associated with a convex function class [7]. It is also satisfied for discrete loss in pattern classification under specific circumstances. For example, suppose that some function in the class has conditional error probability uniformly bounded over x, that is, for some $0 \leq \eta < 1/2$, there is a function $g^* \in \mathcal{G}$ satisfying

$$\forall x, \ \Pr(Y \neq g^*(X) | X = x) \leq \eta.$$

Then if f^* is the corresponding loss function ($f^*(x, y) = \ell(g^*(x), y)$), then it is straightforward to show that, for any $f \in \mathcal{F}$, $P(f - f^*)^2 \leq (Pf - Pf^*)/(1 - 2\eta)$.

6.3   Data Dependent Complexity

In this section we present a *computable* iterative procedure that gives error bounds, at least in the proper case, without having *a priori* knowledge regarding the global structure of the given class.

We present a result due to Koltchinskii and Panchenko [6] which gives an upper bound on the generalization error of the minimizer of the empirical risk in terms of local Rademacher averages computed on empirical balls.

Theorem 5 ([6]). *Let* $x > 0$, N *be a positive integer and define*

$$r_0 = 1 \quad and \quad r_{k+1} = 1 \wedge \left(K_1 \mathbb{E}_\sigma \left[\sup_{f \in \mathcal{F}: P_n f < 2r_k} |R_n f| \right] + K_2 \sqrt{\frac{2r_k x}{n}} + K_3 \frac{x}{n} \right),$$

Then for some appropriate choice of the constants K_i *we have that for any integer* $k \leq N$ *there is a set of probability larger than* $1 - N e^{-x}$ *on which*

$$P f_n \leq r_k.$$

This result only applies to classes of nonnegative functions that contain 0 (proper learning or zero-error case) and the result is valid for empirical risk minimization only, which limits its applications.

As proved in [6], it turns out that if there exists a non-decreasing concave function ψ such that

$$\mathbb{E}_\sigma \left[\sup_{f \in \mathcal{F}, P_n f \leq r} R_n(f) \right] \leq \psi(\sqrt{r}),$$

then the solution $\hat{r}$ of the equation $r = \psi(\sqrt{r})$, is, with high probability, and up to a constant, an upper bound on r_N for a some large enough N (roughly of the order of $\log \log 1/\hat{r}$).

In order to use the result of Theorem 5, one has to compute, from the training sample, the quantity $\mathbb{E}_\sigma \left[\sup_{f \in \mathcal{F}, P_n f \leq r} R_n(f) \right]$. In the classification case, we consider a class $\mathcal{G}$ of $\{-1, 1\}$-valued functions and $\ell(x, y) = \frac{1}{2}|x - y|$. As noticed in [1], we have

$$\mathbb{E}_\sigma \left[\sup_{f \in \mathcal{F}} R_n(f) \right] = \frac{1}{2} - \mathbb{E}_\sigma \left[\inf_{g \in \mathcal{G}} \frac{1}{n} \sum_{i=1}^n \ell(g(x_i), \sigma_i y_i) \right].$$

This shows that computing the global Rademacher average is equivalent to minimizing the empirical error on a sample where the labels have been randomly switched.

For the local Rademacher averages, we have an extra constraint on $P_n f$ which can be handled, for example, by modifying the functional to optimize. Indeed, one can prove that for all $r > 0$, and all fixed σ, there is a λ such that

$$\sup_{f \in \mathcal{F}, P_n f \leq r} R_n(f) = \frac{1 - \lambda}{2} - \inf_{g \in G} \frac{1}{n} \sum_{i=1}^n (1 - \sigma_i \lambda) \ell(g(x_i), \sigma_i y_i).$$

This amounts to minimizing a weighted empirical error after switching of the labels. However, the value of λ which satisfies this equality may depend on σ and r. Since we need to compute the local Rademacher average for various values of r (in order to find r_0), this corresponds to solving the above minimization problem for various values of λ. It remains to be investigated whether this can be done efficiently for real-world data.

Acknowledgements

We are grateful to Gábor Lugosi and Pascal Massart for many inspiring discussions.

References

1. P. L. Bartlett, S. Boucheron and G. Lugosi. Model selection and error estimation. *Machine Learning*, 48, 85–113, 2002. 44, 57
2. P. L. Bartlett and S. Mendelson. Rademacher and Gaussian Complexities: Risk Bounds and Structural Results. Proceedings of the Fourteenth Annual Conference on Computational Learning Theory, pp. 224–240, 2001. 44
3. S. Boucheron, G. Lugosi and P. Massart. Concentration inequalities using the entropy method. *Preprint*, CNRS-Université Paris-Sud. 2002. 49
4. O. Bousquet. A Bennett concentration inequality and its application to empirical processes. *C. R. Acad. Sci. Paris*, Ser. I, 334, pp. 495-500, 2002. 44, 48
5. V. I. Koltchinskii. Rademacher penalties and structural risk minimization. Technical report, University of New Mexico, 2000. 44
6. V. I. Koltchinskii and D. Panchenko. Rademacher processes and bounding the risk of function learning. In *High Dimensional Probability II*, Eds. E. Gine, D. Mason and J. Wellner, pp. 443 - 459, 2000. 44, 46, 48, 56, 57
7. W. S. Lee, P. L. Bartlett and R. C. Williamson. Efficient agnostic learning of neural networks with bounded fan-in. IEEE Transactions on Information Theory, **42**(6), 2118–2132, 1996. 45, 56
8. P. Massart. Some applications of concentration inequalities to statistics. *Annales de la Faculté des Sciences de Toulouse*, IX:245-303, 2000. 46, 47, 53
9. S. Mendelson. Improving the sample complexity using global data. *IEEE Transactions on Information Theory*, 2002. 44, 45, 48
10. S. Mendelson and R. C. Williamson Agnostic learning nonconvex classes of function. To appear in Proceedings of the Fifteenth Annual Conference on Computational Learning Theory, 2002. 45
11. E. Rio Une inegalité de Bennett pour les maxima de processus empiriques. Colloque en l'honneur de J. Bretagnolle, D. Dacunha-Castelle et I. Ibragimov, 2001. 48
12. A. W. van der Vaart and J. A. Wellner. Weak Convergence and Empirical Processes. Springer, 1996. 48, 49

Some Local Measures of Complexity of Convex Hulls and Generalization Bounds

Olivier Bousquet[1], Vladimir Koltchinskii[2*], and Dmitriy Panchenko[2]

[1] Centre de Mathématiques Appliquées, Ecole Polytechnique
91128 Palaiseau, FRANCE
`bousquet@cmapx.polytechnique.fr`
[2] Department of Mathematics and Statistics, The University of New Mexico
Albuquerque, NM 87131-1141, U.S.A.
`{vlad,panchenk}@math.unm.edu`

Abstract. We investigate measures of complexity of function classes based on continuity moduli of Gaussian and Rademacher processes. For Gaussian processes, we obtain bounds on the continuity modulus on the convex hull of a function class in terms of the same quantity for the class itself. We also obtain new bounds on generalization error in terms of localized Rademacher complexities. This allows us to prove new results about generalization performance for convex hulls in terms of characteristics of the base class. As a byproduct, we obtain a simple proof of some of the known bounds on the entropy of convex hulls.

1 Introduction

Convex hulls of function classes have become of great interest in Machine Learning since the introduction of AdaBoost and other methods of combining classifiers. Working with convex combinations of simple functions allows to enhance the approximation properties of the learning algorithm with a small increase of computational cost. However, since the convex hull of the class is typically much larger than the class itself, the learning complexity gets also increased. It is thus of importance to assess the complexity of a convex hull in terms of the complexity of the base class.

The most commonly used measure of complexity of convex hulls is based on covering numbers (or metric entropies). The first bound on the entropy of the convex hull of a set in a Hilbert space was obtained by Dudley [9] and later refined by Ball and Pajor [1] and a different proof was given independently by van der Vaart and Wellner [21]. These authors considered the case of polynomial growth of the covering numbers of the base class. Sharp bounds in the case of exponential growth of the covering numbers of the base class as well as extension of previously konwn results to the case of Banach spaces were obtained later [7,19,16,11,8].

In Machine Learning, however, the quantities of primary importance for determining the generalization performance are not the entropies themselves but

* Partially supported by NSA Grant MDA904-99-1-0031

J. Kivinen and R. H. Sloan (Eds.): COLT 2002, LNAI 2375, pp. 59–73, 2002.
© Springer-Verlag Berlin Heidelberg 2002

rather the so-called Gaussian or Rademacher complexities of function classes [3]. It turns out that there is a direct relationship between such quantities measured on the convex hull and measured on the class itself as pointed out in [14].

More recently, it has been proven that it is possible to obtain refined generalization bounds by considering localized Gaussian or Rademacher complexities of the function classes [13,2]. These quantities are closely related to continuity moduli of the corresponding stochastic processes.

Our main purpose in this paper is to study such quantities defined on convex hulls of function classes. In section 2, we provide a bound on the continuity modulus of a Gaussian process on the convex hull of a class in terms of the continuity modulus on the class itself.

Then, in section 3, we combine this result with some new bounds on the generalization error in function learning problems based on localized Rademacher complexities. This allows us to bound the generalization error in a convex hull in terms of characteristics of the base class.

Finally, we use the bounds on continuity moduli on convex hulls to give very simple proofs of some previously known results on the entropy of such classes.

2   Continuity Modulus on Convex Hulls

Let $\mathcal{F}$ be a subset of a Hilbert space $\mathcal{H}$ and W denote an isonormal Gaussian process defined on $\mathcal{H}$, that is a collection $(W(h))_{h\in\mathcal{H}}$ of Gaussian random variables indexed by $\mathcal{H}$ such that

$$\forall h \in \mathcal{H}, \; \mathbb{E}\left[W(h)\right] = 0 \quad \text{and} \quad \forall h, h' \in \mathcal{H}, \; \mathbb{E}\left[W(h)W(h')\right] = \langle h, h'\rangle_{\mathcal{H}} \; .$$

We define the modulus of continuity of the process W as

$$\omega(\mathcal{F}, \delta) := \omega_{\mathcal{H}}(\mathcal{F}, \delta) = \mathbb{E}\left[\sup_{\substack{f,g\in\mathcal{F} \\ \|f-g\|\leq\delta}} |W(f) - W(g)|\right] \; .$$

Since we are in a Hilbert space, we use the natural metric induced by the inner product $d(f,g) = \|f - g\| = \sqrt{\langle f - g, f - g\rangle}$ to define balls in $\mathcal{H}$. Let $\mathcal{F}_\varepsilon$ denote a minimal ε-net of $\mathcal{F}$, i.e. a subset of $\mathcal{F}$ of minimal cardinality such that $\mathcal{F}$ is contained in the union of the balls of radius ε with centers in $\mathcal{F}_\varepsilon$. Let $\mathcal{F}^\varepsilon$ denote a maximal ε-separated subset of $\mathcal{F}$, i.e. a subset of $\mathcal{F}$ of maximal cardinality such that the distance between any two points in this subset is larger than or equal to ε. The ε-covering number of $\mathcal{F}$ is then defined as

$$N(\mathcal{F}, \varepsilon) := N_{\mathcal{H}}(\mathcal{F}, \varepsilon, d) = |\mathcal{F}_\varepsilon| \; ,$$

and the ε-entropy is defined as $H(\mathcal{F}, \varepsilon) = \log N(\mathcal{F}, \varepsilon)$ (this quantity is usually referred to as the metric entropy of $\mathcal{F}$).

In the remainder, K will denote a non-negative constant. Its value may change from one line to another.

2.1   Main Result

Our main result relates the continuity modulus of an isonormal Gaussian process defined on the convex hull of a set $\mathcal{F}$ to the continuity modulus of the same process on this set.

Theorem 1. *We have for all $\delta \geq 0$*

$$\omega(conv(\mathcal{F}), \delta) \leq \inf_{\varepsilon} \left(2\omega(\mathcal{F}, \varepsilon) + \delta\sqrt{N(\mathcal{F}, \varepsilon)} \right).$$

Proof. Let $\varepsilon > 0$, and let L be the linear span of $\mathcal{F}_\varepsilon$. We denote by Π_L the orthogonal projection on L. We have for all $f \in \mathcal{F}$,

$$f = \Pi_L(f) + \Pi_{L^\perp}(f),$$

so that

$$\omega(conv(\mathcal{F}), \delta) \leq \mathbb{E}\left[\sup_{\substack{f, g \in conv(\mathcal{F}) \\ \|f-g\| \leq \delta}} |W(\Pi_L f) - W(\Pi_L g)| \right]$$

$$+ \mathbb{E}\left[\sup_{\substack{f, g \in conv(\mathcal{F}) \\ \|f-g\| \leq \delta}} |W(\Pi_{L^\perp} f) - W(\Pi_{L^\perp} g)| \right].$$

Now since for any orthogonal projection Π, $\|\Pi(f) - \Pi(g)\| \leq \|f - g\|$ we have

$$\omega(conv(\mathcal{F}), \delta) \leq \omega(\Pi_L conv(\mathcal{F}), \delta) + \omega(\Pi_{L^\perp} conv(\mathcal{F}), \delta). \tag{1}$$

We will upper bound both terms in the right hand side separately. For the first term, since $\Pi_L(conv(\mathcal{F})) \subset L$, we have

$$\omega(\Pi_L conv(\mathcal{F}), \delta) \leq \omega(L, \delta),$$

and by linearity of W and the fact that L is a vector space,

$$\omega(L, \delta) = \mathbb{E}\left[\sup_{\substack{f \in L \\ \|f\| \leq \delta}} |W(f)| \right] \leq \delta\mathbb{E}\left[\sup_{\substack{\|y\|_{\mathbb{R}^d} \leq 1 \\ y \in \mathbb{R}^d}} \langle Z, y \rangle \right],$$

where Z is a standard normal vector in $\mathbb{R}^d$ (with $d = \dim L$ and $\|\cdot\|_{\mathbb{R}^d}$ the euclidean norm in $\mathbb{R}^d$). This gives

$$\omega(L, \delta) \leq \delta\mathbb{E}\left[\|Z\|_{\mathbb{R}^d} \right] \leq \delta\sqrt{\mathbb{E}\left[\|Z\|_{\mathbb{R}^d}^2 \right]} \leq \delta\sqrt{d}.$$

Since L is the linear span of $\mathcal{F}_\varepsilon$ which is a finite set of size $N(\mathcal{F}, \varepsilon)$ we have $d \leq N(\mathcal{F}, \varepsilon)$ so that

$$\omega(L, \delta) \leq \delta\sqrt{N(\mathcal{F}, \varepsilon)}.$$

Now let's consider the second term of (1). We crudely upper bound it as follows

$$\omega(\Pi_{L^\perp} conv(\mathcal{F}), \delta) \le 2\mathbb{E}\left[\sup_{f \in conv(\mathcal{F})} |W(\Pi_{L^\perp} f)|\right].$$

Since $\Pi_{L^\perp}$ is linear, the supremum is attained at extreme points of the convex hull which are elements of $\mathcal{F}$, that is

$$\omega(\Pi_{L^\perp} conv(\mathcal{F}), \delta) \le 2\mathbb{E}\left[\sup_{f \in \mathcal{F}} |W(\Pi_{L^\perp} f)|\right].$$

Now for each $f \in \mathcal{F}$, let g be the closest point to f in $\mathcal{F}_\varepsilon$. By definition we have $\|f - g\| \le \varepsilon$ and $g \in L \cap \mathcal{F}$ so that $\Pi_{L^\perp} g = 0$ and thus

$$\omega(\Pi_{L^\perp} conv(\mathcal{F}), \delta) \le 2\mathbb{E}\left[\sup_{\substack{f,g \in \mathcal{F} \\ \|f-g\| \le \varepsilon}} |W(\Pi_{L^\perp} f) - W(\Pi_{L^\perp} g)|\right].$$

Now since $\Pi_{L^\perp}$ is a contraction, using Slepian's lemma (see [15], Theorem 3.15 page 78) we get

$$\omega(\Pi_{L^\perp} conv(\mathcal{F}), \delta) \le 2\mathbb{E}\left[\sup_{\substack{f,g \in \mathcal{F} \\ \|f-g\| \le \varepsilon}} |W(f) - W(g)|\right] = 2\omega(\mathcal{F}, \varepsilon).$$

This concludes the proof.   □

Note that Theorem 1 allows us to give a positive answer to a question raised by Giné and Zinn in [12]. Indeed, we can prove that the convex hull of a uniformly Donsker class is uniformly Donsker. Due to lack of space, we do not give the details here.

2.2   Examples

As an application of Theorem 1, we will derive bounds on the continuity modulus of convex hulls of classes for which we know the rate of growth of the metric entropy.

Let's first recall a well-known relationship between the modulus of continuity of a Gaussian process defined on a class and the metric entropy of that class[1]. By Dudley's entropy bound (see [15], Theorem 11.17, page 321) we have

$$\omega(\mathcal{F}, \varepsilon) \le K \int_0^\varepsilon H^{1/2}(\mathcal{F}, u)\, du.$$

---

[1] with respect to the natural metric associated to the process, which in the case of the isonormal Gaussian process is simply the metric induced by the inner product.

It is well known (and easy to check by inspection of the proof of the above result) that when the class is δ-separated, the integral can start at δ, so that for a maximal δ-separated subset $\mathcal{F}^\delta$ of $\mathcal{F}$ we have

$$w(\mathcal{F}^\delta, \varepsilon) \leq K \int_\delta^\varepsilon H^{1/2}(\mathcal{F}^\delta, u)\, du \,,$$

for all $\varepsilon > \delta$.

We first consider the case when the entropy of the base class grows logarithmically (e.g. classes of functions with finite Vapnik-Chervonenkis dimension V).

Example 1. If for all $\varepsilon > 0$,

$$N(\mathcal{F}, \varepsilon) \leq K\varepsilon^{-V} \,,$$

then for all $\delta > 0$,

$$w(conv(\mathcal{F}), \delta) \leq K\delta^{2/(2+V)} \log^{V/(2+V)} \delta^{-1} \,.$$

Proof. We have from Theorem 1,

$$w(conv(\mathcal{F}), \delta) \leq \inf_\varepsilon \left(K \int_0^\varepsilon \log^{1/2} u^{-1} du + \delta\varepsilon^{-V/2} \right)$$

$$\leq \inf_\varepsilon \left(K\varepsilon \log^{1/2} \varepsilon^{-1} + \delta\varepsilon^{-V/2} \right) \,.$$

Choosing

$$\varepsilon = \delta^{2V/(2+V)} \log^{2V/(2+V)} \delta^{-1} \,,$$

we obtain for $\delta \leq 1$,

$$w(conv(\mathcal{F}), \delta) \leq K\delta^{2/(2+V)} \log^{V/(2+V)} \delta^{-1} \,.$$

$\square$

Although the main term in the above bound is correct, we obtain a superfluous logarithm. This logarithm can be removed if one uses directly the entropy integral in combination with results on the entropy of the convex hull of such classes [1,21,19]. At the moment of this writing, we do not know a simple proof of this fact that does not rely upon the bounds on the entropy of convex hulls.

Now we consider the case when the entropy of the base class has polynomial growth. In this case, we shall distinguish several situations: when the exponent is larger than 2, the class is no longer pre-Gaussian which means that the continuity modulus is unbounded. However, it is possible to study the continuity modulus of a restricted class. Here we consider the convex hull of a δ-separated subset of the base class, for which the continuity modulus is bounded when computed at a scale proportional to δ.

Example 2. If for all $\varepsilon > 0$,

$$H(\mathcal{F}, \varepsilon) \leq K\varepsilon^{-V},$$

then for all $\delta > 0$, for $0 < V < 2$,

$$\omega(conv(\mathcal{F}), \delta) \leq K \log^{1/2 - 1/V} \delta^{-1},$$

for $V = 2$,

$$\omega(conv(\mathcal{F}^{\delta/4}), \delta) \leq K \log \delta^{-1},$$

and for $V > 2$,

$$\omega(conv(\mathcal{F}^{\delta/4}), \delta) \leq K\delta^{1 - V/2}.$$

Proof. We have from Theorem 1, for $\varepsilon > \delta/4$,

$$\omega(conv(\mathcal{F}^{\delta/4}), \delta) \leq \inf_{\varepsilon} \left(K \int_{\delta/4}^{\varepsilon} u^{-V/2} du + \delta \exp(K\varepsilon^{-V}/2) \right).$$

For $0 < V < 2$, this gives

$$\omega(conv(\mathcal{F}), \delta) \leq \inf_{\varepsilon} \left(K\varepsilon^{(2-V)/2} + \delta \exp(K\varepsilon^{-V}/2) \right).$$

Choosing

$$\varepsilon = K^{1/V} \log^{-1/V} \delta^{-1},$$

we obtain for δ small enough

$$\omega(conv(\mathcal{F}), \delta) \leq K \log^{(V-2)/2V} \delta^{-1}.$$

For $V = 2$, we get

$$\omega(conv(\mathcal{F}^{\delta/4}), \delta) \leq \inf_{\varepsilon} \left(K \log \frac{4\varepsilon}{\delta} + \delta \exp(K\varepsilon^{-2}/2) \right).$$

Taking $\varepsilon = 1/4$ we get for δ small enough

$$\omega(conv(\mathcal{F}^{\delta/4}), \delta) \leq K \log \delta^{-1}.$$

For $V > 2$, we get

$$\omega(conv(\mathcal{F}^{\delta/4}), \delta) \leq \inf_{\varepsilon} \left(K\delta^{(2-V)/2} - \varepsilon^{(2-V)/2} + \delta \exp(K\varepsilon^{-2}/2) \right).$$

Taking $\varepsilon \to \infty$, we obtain

$$\omega(conv(\mathcal{F}^{\delta/4}), \delta) \leq K\delta^{(2-V)/2}.$$

$\square$

3   Generalization Error Bounds

3.1   Results

We begin this section with a general bound that relates the error of the function minimizing the empirical risk to a local measure of complexity of the class which is the same in spirit as the bound in [13].

Let $(S, \mathcal{A})$ be a measurable space and let $X_1, \ldots, X_n$ be n i.i.d. random variables in this space with common distribution P. P_n will denote the empirical measure based on the sample

$$P_n = \frac{1}{n} \sum_{i=1}^{n} \delta_{X_i}.$$

In what follows, we choose[2] $\mathcal{H} = L_2(P_n)$ and we are using the notations of Section 2.

We consider a class $\mathcal{F}$ of measurable functions defined on S with values in $[0, 1]$. We assume in what follows that $\mathcal{F}$ also satisfies standard measurability conditions used in the theory of empirical processes as in [10,21].

We define

$$R_n(f) := \frac{1}{n} \sum_{i=1}^{n} \varepsilon_i f(X_i),$$

and let ψ_n be an increasing concave (possibly data-dependent random) function with $\psi_n(0) = 0$ such that

$$\mathbb{E}_\varepsilon \left[\sup_{P_n f \leq r} |R_n(f)| \right] \leq \psi_n(\sqrt{r}), \ \forall r \geq 0.$$

Let $\hat{r}_n$ be the largest solution of the equation

$$r = \psi_n(\sqrt{r}). \tag{2}$$

The solution $\hat{r}_n$ of (2) gives what is usually called zero error rate for the class $\mathcal{F}$[13], i.e. the bound for Pf given that $P_n f = 0$.

The bounds we obtain below are data-dependent and they do not require any structural assumptions on the class (such as VC conditions or entropy conditions). Note that $\hat{r}_n$ is determined only by the restriction of the class $\mathcal{F}$ to the sample $(X_1, \ldots, X_n)$.

Theorem 2. *If ψ_n is a non-decreasing concave function and $\psi_n(0) = 0$ then there exists $K > 0$ such that with probability at least $1 - e^{-t}$ for all $f \in \mathcal{F}$*

$$Pf \leq K \left(P_n f + \hat{r}_n + \frac{t + \log \log n}{n} \right). \tag{3}$$

---

[2] This choice implies that we work with the random metric induced by the training data. In other words, we measure the distance between two functions f and g by $d(f, g) = (\sum (f(X_i) - g(X_i))^2)^{1/2}$.

It is most common to estimate the expectation of Rademacher processes via an entropy integral (Theorem 2.2.4 in [21]):

$$\mathbb{E}_{\varepsilon}\left[\sup_{P_n f \le \delta} |R_n(f)|\right] \le \frac{4\sqrt{3}}{\sqrt{n}} \int_0^{\sqrt{\delta}/2} H^{1/2}(\mathcal{F}, u) du \,,$$

which means one can choose $\psi_n(\delta)$ as the right hand side of the above bound. This approach was used for instance in [13].

If the (empirical L_2) covering numbers of the base class grow polynomially, e.g. the base class is a Vapnik-Chervonenkis class of VC dimension $V > 0$, then

$$N(\mathcal{G}, \varepsilon) \le K\varepsilon^{-V} \,,$$

and thus using results in [19]

$$\log N(conv(\mathcal{G}), \varepsilon) \le K\varepsilon^{-2V/(2+V)} \,,$$

so that the entropy integral is upper bounded by $Kn^{-1/2}\delta^{1/(2+V)}$ and thus we obtain $\hat{r}_n$ of the order of

$$n^{-\frac{1}{2}\frac{2+V}{1+V}} \,.$$

If the metric entropy is polynomial with exponent $0 < V < 2$, the same reasoning gives $\hat{r}_n$ of the order of

$$n^{-\frac{1}{2}} \log^{1/2 - 1/V} n \,.$$

These results are optimal in the sense that there are classes with such entropy growth for which they cannot be improved. However, our goal is to avoid using entropies as measures of the complexity of the classes and to rather use localized Rademacher or Gaussian complexities.

We will thus apply the bound of Theorem 2 to the function learning problem in the convex hull of a given class.

Let $\mathcal{G}$ be a class of measurable functions from S into $[0, 1]$. Let $g_0 \in conv(\mathcal{G})$ be an unknown target function. The goal is to learn g_0 based on the data $(X_1, g_0(X_1)), \ldots, (X_n, g_0(X_n))$. We introduce $\hat{g}_n$ defined as

$$\hat{g}_n := \arg\min_{g \in conv(\mathcal{G})} P_n |g - g_0| \,,$$

which in principle can be computed from the data.

We introduce the function $\psi_n(\mathcal{G}, \delta)$ defined as

$$\psi_n(\mathcal{G}, \delta) := \sqrt{\frac{\pi}{2n}} \inf_{\varepsilon > 0} \left(\omega(\mathcal{G}, \varepsilon) + \delta\sqrt{N(\mathcal{G}, \varepsilon)}\right) \,.$$

Corollary 1. *Let $\hat{r}_n(\mathcal{G})$ be the largest solution of the equation*

$$r = \psi_n(\mathcal{G}, \sqrt{r}) \,.$$

Then there exists $K > 0$ such that for all $g_0 \in conv(\mathcal{G})$ the following inequality holds with probability at least $1 - e^{-t}$

$$P|\hat{g}_n - g_0| \le K\left(\hat{r}_n(\mathcal{G}) + \frac{t + \log\log n}{n}\right) \,.$$

Proof. Let $\mathcal{F} = \{|g - g_0| : g \in conv(\mathcal{G})\}$. Note that $\psi_n(\mathcal{G}, \delta)$ is concave non-decreasing (as the infimum of linear functions) and $\psi_n(\mathcal{G}, 0) = 0$, it can thus be used in Theorem 2. We obtain (using bound (4.8) on page 97 of [15])

$$\mathbb{E}\left[\sup_{\substack{f \in \mathcal{F} \\ P_n f \leq r}} |R_n(f)|\right] \leq \sqrt{\frac{\pi}{2n}} \mathbb{E}\left[\sup_{\substack{f \in \mathcal{F} \\ P_n f \leq r}} |W_{P_n}(f)|\right]$$

$$\leq \sqrt{\frac{\pi}{2n}} \mathbb{E}\left[\sup_{\substack{f \in \mathcal{F} \\ (P_n f^2)^{1/2} \leq \sqrt{r}}} |W_{P_n}(f)|\right]$$

$$\leq \sqrt{\frac{\pi}{2n}} \omega(conv\mathcal{G}, \sqrt{r}) \leq \psi_n(\mathcal{G}, \sqrt{r}),$$

where in the last step we used Theorem 1. To complete the proof, it is enough to notice that $P_n|\hat{g}_n - g_0| = 0$ (since $g_0 \in conv(\mathcal{G})$) and to use the bound of Theorem 2. □

A simple application of the above corollary in combination with the bounds of examples 1 and 2 give, for instance, the following rates. If the covering numbers of the base class grow polynomially, i.e.

$$N(\mathcal{G}, \varepsilon) \leq K\varepsilon^{-V},$$

we obtain $\hat{r}_n$ of the order of (up to logarithmic factors)

$$n^{-\frac{1}{2}\frac{2+V}{1+V}}.$$

If the random metric entropy is polynomial with exponent $0 < V < 2$, $\hat{r}_n$ is of the order of

$$n^{-\frac{1}{2}} \log^{1/2 - 1/V} n.$$

Notice that in both cases we obtain the same results as with a direct application of the entropy bound of the convex hull.

However the bound of corollary 1 contains only terms that can be computed from the data and that depend on the base class. This means that if one actually computes $\psi_n(\mathcal{G}, \delta)$ (without using an entropy upper bound), one can only obtain better results.

3.2 Proof of Theorem 2

STEP 1: Concentration. We define $\delta_k = 2^{-k}$ for $k \geq 0$, and consider a sequence of classes

$$\mathcal{F}_k = \{f \in \mathcal{F} : \delta_{k+1} < Pf \leq \delta_k\}.$$

If we denote

$$R_k = \mathbb{E}_\varepsilon\left[\sup_{\mathcal{F}_k} |R_n(f)|\right],$$

then the symmetrization inequality implies that

$$\mathbb{E}\left[\sup_{\mathcal{F}_k}|P_n f - P f|\right] \le 2\mathbb{E}\left[R_k\right] .$$

Note that for $f \in \mathcal{F}_k$, $P(f - Pf)^2 \le Pf^2 \le Pf \le \delta_k$, so that Theorem 3 in [5] implies that with probability at least $1 - e^{-t}$ for all $f \in \mathcal{F}_k$

$$|P_n f - P f| \le 4\mathbb{E}\left[R_k\right] + \left(\frac{2\delta_k t}{n}\right)^{1/2} + \frac{4t}{3n} .$$

Now, Theorem 16 in [4] gives that with probability at least $1 - e^{-t}$

$$\mathbb{E}\left[R_k\right] \le \frac{2t}{n} + 2R_k .$$

Therefore, with probability at least $1 - 2e^{-t}$ for all $f \in \mathcal{F}_k$

$$|P_n f - P f| \le 8R_k + \left(\frac{2\delta_k t}{n}\right)^{1/2} + \frac{10t}{n} . \tag{4}$$

STEP 2: Union Bound. Now we apply an union bound over $k = 0, 1, \ldots$. We define

$$l(\delta) = 2\log\left(\frac{\pi}{\sqrt{3}}\log_2 \frac{2}{\delta}\right) .$$

We have

$$\sum_{k \ge 0} e^{-l(\delta_k)} = \frac{\pi^2}{3}\sum_{k \ge 0}\frac{1}{(k+1)^2} = \frac{1}{2} .$$

Therefore, replacing t by $t + l(\delta_k)$ in Inequality (4) and applying the union bound we get that with probability at least $1 - e^{-t}$ for all $k \ge 0$ and for all $f \in \mathcal{F}_k$

$$|P_n f - P f| \le 8R_k + \left(\frac{2\delta_k(t + l(\delta_k))}{n}\right)^{1/2} + \frac{10(t + l(\delta_k))}{n} . \tag{5}$$

Now we reason on the event where this inequality holds.

STEP 3: Empirical Complexity. If we denote

$$U_k = \delta_k + 8R_k + \left(\frac{2\delta_k(t + l(\delta_k))}{n}\right)^{1/2} + \frac{10(t + l(\delta_k))}{n} ,$$

then on this event for any k and for all $f \in \mathcal{F}_k$, $P_n f \le U_k$ so that

$$R_k \le \mathbb{E}_\varepsilon\left[\sup_{P_n f \le U_k}|R_n(f)|\right] \le \psi_n(\sqrt{U_k}) ,$$

and thus

$$U_k \le \delta_k + 8\psi_n(\sqrt{U_k}) + \left(\frac{2\delta_k(t + l(\delta_k))}{n}\right)^{1/2} + \frac{10(t + l(\delta_k))}{n}.$$

Notice that for $k \ge \log_2 n$, we have for $f \in \mathcal{F}_k$, $Pf \le \delta_k \le 1/n$ so that the result holds trivially for such functions. We thus have to prove the result for the other values of k. For $k \le \log_2 n$, $\delta_k \ge 1/n$ so that we have

$$U_k \le \delta_k + 8\psi_n(\sqrt{U_k}) + \sqrt{2\delta_k r_0} + 10r_0 \le 8\psi_n(\sqrt{U_k}) + 2\delta_k + 11r_0,$$

with $r_0 = (t + K\log\log n)/n$ for some large enough K (we used the fact that $2\sqrt{ab} \le a + b$).

STEP 4: Solving. Let's denote by $f(\sqrt{U_k})$ the right hand side of the above inequality. f is a non-decreasing concave function so that the above inequality implies that U_k is upper bounded by the largest solution x^* of $f(\sqrt{x}) = x$. Moreover, any non-negative real number z such that $f(\sqrt{z}) \le z$ is an upper bound for x^* and thus for U_k. Let's prove that $z = K(\hat{r}_n + \delta_k + r_0)$ satisfies such a condition (for some large enough K).

Since ψ_n is concave and $\psi_n(0) = 0$, we have for $x > 0$, $\psi_n(\sqrt{Kx}) \le \sqrt{K}\psi_n(\sqrt{x})$. Also, for $x > 0$, $\psi_n(\sqrt{\hat{r}_n + x}) \le \hat{r}_n + x$ since $\hat{r}_n + x$ upper bounds the solution of $\psi_n(\sqrt{r}) = r$. We thus have

$$f(\sqrt{K(\hat{r}_n + \delta_k + r_0)}) \le 8\sqrt{K}(\hat{r}_n + \delta_k + r_0) + 2\delta_k + 11r_0,$$

and this is less than $K(\hat{r}_n + \delta_k + r_0)$ for a large enough K.

We thus get $U_k \le K(\hat{r}_n + \delta_k + r_0)$. Finally, (5) implies that for all $k \le \log_2 n$ and $f \in \mathcal{F}_k$

$$Pf \le P_n f + 8\psi_n(\sqrt{K(\hat{r}_n + \delta_k + r_0)}) + \sqrt{2\delta_k r_0} + 10r_0.$$

If $f \in \mathcal{F}_k$ then $\delta_k \le 2Pf$, which proves

$$Pf \le P_n f + 8\psi_n(\sqrt{K(\hat{r}_n + 2Pf + r_0)}) + \sqrt{4r_0 Pf} + 10r_0.$$

Now the same reasoning as above proves that there exists a constant K such that Pf is upper bounded by $K(P_n f + \hat{r}_n + r_0)$ which concludes the proof. □

4   Entropy of Convex Hulls

4.1   Relating Entropy With Continuity Modulus

By Sudakov's minoration (see [15], Theorem 3.18, page 80) we have

$$\sup_{\varepsilon > 0} \varepsilon H^{1/2}(\mathcal{F}, \varepsilon) \le K\mathbb{E}\left[\sup_{f \in \mathcal{F}} |W(f)|\right].$$

Let $B(f, \delta)$ be the ball centered in f of radius δ. We define

$$H(\mathcal{F}, \delta, \varepsilon) := \sup_{f \in \mathcal{F}} H(B(f, \delta) \cap \mathcal{F}, \varepsilon).$$

The following lemma relates the entropy of $\mathcal{F}$ with the modulus of continuity of the process W. This type of bound is well known (see e.g. [17]) but we give the proof for completeness.

Lemma 1. *Assume $\mathcal{F}$ is of diameter 1. For all integer k we have*

$$H^{1/2}(\mathcal{F}, 2^{-k}) \leq K \sum_{i=0}^{k} 2^i \omega(\mathcal{F}, 2^{1-i}).$$

This can also be written

$$H^{1/2}(\mathcal{F}, \delta) \leq K \int_{\delta}^{1} u^{-2} \omega(\mathcal{F}, u) \, du.$$

Proof. We have

$$\omega(\mathcal{F}, \delta) = \mathbb{E} \left[\sup_{\substack{f, g \in \mathcal{F} \\ \|f - g\| \leq \delta}} |W(f) - W(g)| \right]$$

$$\geq \sup_{f \in \mathcal{F}} \mathbb{E} \left[\sup_{g \in B(f, \delta) \cap \mathcal{F}} |W(f) - W(g)| \right]$$

$$\geq \sup_{f \in \mathcal{F}} \sup_{\varepsilon > 0} \varepsilon H^{1/2}(B(f, \delta) \cap \mathcal{F}, \varepsilon),$$

so that we obtain

$$\frac{\delta}{2} H^{1/2}(\mathcal{F}, \delta, \frac{\delta}{2}) \leq K \omega(\mathcal{F}, \delta).$$

Notice that we can construct a 2^{-k} covering of $\mathcal{F}$ by covering $\mathcal{F}$ by $N(\mathcal{F}, 1)$ balls of radius 1 and then covering the intersection of each of these balls with $\mathcal{F}$ with $N(B(f, 1) \cap \mathcal{F}, 1/2)$ balls of radius $1/2$ and so on. We thus have

$$N(\mathcal{F}, 2^{-k}) \leq \prod_{i=0}^{k} \sup_{f \in \mathcal{F}} N(B(f, 2^{1-i}) \cap \mathcal{F}, 2^{-i}).$$

Hence

$$H(\mathcal{F}, 2^{-k}) \leq \sum_{i=0}^{k} H(\mathcal{F}, 2^{1-i}, 2^{-i}).$$

We thus have

$$H^{1/2}(\mathcal{F}, 2^{-k}) \leq \sum_{i=0}^{k} H^{1/2}(\mathcal{F}, 2^{1-i}, 2^{-i}) \leq K \sum_{i=0}^{k} 2^i \omega(\mathcal{F}, 2^{1-i}),$$

which concludes the proof. $\square$

Next we present a modification of the previous lemma that can be applied to δ-separated subsets.

Lemma 2. *Assume $\mathcal{F}$ is of diameter 1. For all integer k we have*

$$H^{1/2}(\mathcal{F}, 2^{-k}) \leq K \sum_{i=0}^{k} 2^i \omega(\mathcal{F}^{2^{-i-1}}, 2^{2-i}).$$

Proof. Notice that for $f \in \mathcal{F}$, there exists $f' \in \mathcal{F}^{\delta/4}$ such that

$$B(f, \delta) \cap \mathcal{F} \subset B(f', \delta + \delta/4) \cap \mathcal{F}.$$

Moreover, since a maximal δ-separated set is a δ-net,

$$N(\mathcal{F}, \delta) \leq |N^\delta| = N(\mathcal{F}^\delta, \delta/2),$$

since for a δ-separated set A we have $N(A, \delta/2) = |A|$.

Let's prove that we have for any γ,

$$\left|(B(f, \gamma) \cup \mathcal{F})^{\delta/2}\right| \leq \left|B(f, \gamma + \delta/4) \cup \mathcal{F}^{\delta/4}\right|.$$

Indeed, since the points in $\mathcal{F}^{\delta/4}$ form a $\delta/4$ cover of $\mathcal{F}$, all the points in $(B(f, \gamma) \cup \mathcal{F})^{\delta/2}$ are at distance less than $\delta/4$ of one and only one point of $\mathcal{F}^{\delta/4}$ (the unicity comes from the fact that they are $\delta/2$ separated). We can thus establish an injection from points in $(B(f, \gamma) \cup \mathcal{F})^{\delta/2}$ to corresponding points in $\mathcal{F}^{\delta/4}$ and the image of this injection is included in $B(f, \gamma + \delta/4)$ since the image points are within distance $\delta/4$ of points in $B(f, \gamma)$.

Now we obtain

$$N((B(f', \delta + \delta/4) \cup \mathcal{F})^{\delta/2}, \delta/4) \leq N(B(f', 3\delta/2) \cup \mathcal{F}^{\delta/4}, \delta/8).$$

We thus have

$$\begin{aligned} N(B(f, \delta) \cup \mathcal{F}, \delta/2) &\leq N(B(f', \delta + \delta/4) \cup \mathcal{F}, \delta/2) \\ &\leq N((B(f', \delta + \delta/4) \cup \mathcal{F})^{\delta/2}, \delta/4) \\ &\leq N(B(f', 3\delta/2) \cup \mathcal{F}^{\delta/4}, \delta/8). \end{aligned}$$

This gives

$$\sup_{f \in \mathcal{F}} N(B(f, \delta) \cap \mathcal{F}, \delta/2) \leq \sup_{f \in \mathcal{F}^{\delta/4}} N(B(f, 3\delta/2) \cap \mathcal{F}^{\delta/4}, \delta/8)$$

$$= N(\mathcal{F}^{\delta/4}, 3\delta/2, \delta/8).$$

Hence

$$H(\mathcal{F}, \delta, \delta/2) \leq H(\mathcal{F}^{\delta/4}, 3\delta/2, \delta/8).$$

By the same argument as in previous Lemma we obtain

$$\frac{\delta}{8} H^{1/2}(\mathcal{F}^{\delta/4}, 3\delta/2, \delta/8) \leq K \omega(\mathcal{F}^{\delta/4}, 3\delta/2).$$

$\square$

4.2   Applications

Example 3. If for all $\varepsilon > 0$,

$$N(\mathcal{F}, \varepsilon) \leq \varepsilon^{-V} \, ,$$

then for all $\varepsilon > 0$,

$$H(conv(\mathcal{F}), \varepsilon) \leq \varepsilon^{-2V/(2+V)} \log^{2V/(2+V)} \varepsilon^{-1} \, .$$

Proof. Recall from Example 1 that

$$\omega(conv(\mathcal{F}), \delta) \leq K\delta^{2/(2+V)} \log^{V/(2+V)} \delta^{-1} \, .$$

Now, using Lemma 1 we get

$$H^{1/2}(conv(\mathcal{F}), 2^{-k}) \leq K \sum_{i=0}^{k} 2^{i} 2^{2(1-i)/(2+V)} (i-1)^{V/(2+V)}$$

$$= K \sum_{i=0}^{k} (2^{V/(2+V)})^{i} (i-1)^{V/(2+V)} \, .$$

We check that in the above sum, the i-th term is always larger than twice the $i-1$-th term (for $i \geq 2$) so that we can upper bound the sum by the last term,

$$H^{1/2}(\mathcal{F}, 2^{-k}) \leq K(2^{V/(2+V)})^{k} (k-1)^{V/(2+V)} \, ,$$

hence, using $\varepsilon = 2^{-k}$, we get the result.   □

Note that the result we obtain contains an extra logarithmic factor compared to the optimal bound [21,19].

Example 4. If for all $\varepsilon > 0$,

$$H(\mathcal{F}, \varepsilon) \leq \varepsilon^{-V} \, ,$$

then for all $\varepsilon > 0$, for $0 < V < 2$,

$$H(conv(\mathcal{F}), \varepsilon) \leq \varepsilon^{-2} \log^{1-V/2} \varepsilon^{-1} \, ,$$

for $V = 2$,

$$H(conv(\mathcal{F}), \varepsilon) \leq \varepsilon^{-2} \log^{2} \varepsilon^{-1} \, ,$$

and for $V > 2$,

$$H(conv(\mathcal{F}), \varepsilon) \leq \varepsilon^{-V} \, .$$

Proof. The proof is similar to the previous one.   □

In this example, all the bounds are known to be sharp [7,11].

References

1. K. Ball and A. Pajor. The entropy of convex bodies with "few" extreme points. *London MAth. Soc. Lectrure Note Ser.* 158, pages 25–32, 1990. 59, 63
2. P. Bartlett, O. Bousquet and S. Mendelson. Localized Rademacher Complexity. *Preprint*, 2002. 60
3. P. Bartlett, S. Mendelson. Rademacher and Gaussian complexities: risk bounds and structural results. In *Proceeding of the 14th Annual Conference on Computational Learning Theory*, Srpinger, 2001. 60
4. S. Boucheron, G. Lugosi and P. Massart. Concentration inequalities using the entropy method. *Preprint*, 2002. 68
5. O. Bousquet. A Bennett concentration inequality and its application to empirical processes. *C. R. Acad. Sci. Paris, Ser. I* 334, pages 495-500, 2002. 68
6. B. Carl. Metric entropy of convex hulls in Hilbert spaces. *Bulletin of the London Mathematical Society*, 29, pages 452-458, 1997.
7. B. Carl, I. Kyrezi and A. Pajor. Metric entropy of convex hulls in Banach spaces. *Journal of the London Mathematical Society*, 2001. 59, 72
8. J. Creutzig and I. Steinwart. Metric entropy of convex hulls in type p spaces – the critical case. 2001. 59
9. R. Dudley. Universal Donsker classes and metric entropy. *Annals of Probability*, 15, pages 1306-1326, 1987. 59
10. R. Dudley. Uniform central limit theorems. Cambridge University Press, 2000. 65
11. F. Gao. Metric entropy of convex hulls. *Israel Journal of Mathematics*, 123, pages 359-364, 2001. 59, 72
12. E. Giné and J. Zinn. Gaussian characterization of uniform Donsker classes of functions. *Annals of Probability*, 19, pages 758-782, 1991. 62
13. V. I. Koltchinskii and D. Panchenko. Rademacher processes and bounding the risk of function learning. In *High Dimensional Probability II*, Eds. E. Gine, D. Mason and J. Wellner, pp. 443-459, 2000. 60, 65, 66
14. V. I. Koltchinskii and D. Panchenko. Empirical margin distributions and bounding the generalization error of combined classifiers. *Annals of Statistics*, 30(1), 2002. 60
15. M. Ledoux and M. Talagrand Probability in Banach spaces. Springer-Verlag, 1991. 62, 67, 69
16. W. Li and W. Linde. Metric entropy of convex hulls in Hilbert spaces. *Preprint*, 2001. 59
17. M. Lifshits. Gaussian random functions. Kluwer, 1995. 70
18. P. Massart. Some applications of concentration inequalities to statistics. *Annales de la Faculté des Sciences de Toulouse*, IX, pages 245-303, 2000.
19. S. Mendelson. On the size of convex hulls of small sets. *Preprint*, 2001. 59, 63, 66, 72
20. S. Mendelson. Improving the sample complexity using global data. *Preprint*, 2001.
21. A. van der Vaart and J. Wellner. Weak convergence and empirical processes with applications to statistics. John Wiley & Sons, New York, 1996. 59, 63, 65, 66, 72

Path Kernels and Multiplicative Updates

Eiji Takimoto[1]* and Manfred K. Warmuth[2]**

[1] Graduate School of Information Sciences,Tohoku University
Sendai, 980-8579, Japan
[2] Computer Science Department, University of California
Santa Cruz, CA 95064, U.S.A.

Abstract. We consider a natural convolution kernel defined by a directed graph. Each edge contributes an input. The inputs along a path form a product and the products for all paths are summed. We also have a set of probabilities on the edges so that the outflow from each node is one. We then discuss multiplicative updates on these graphs where the prediction is essentially a kernel computation and the update contributes a factor to each edge. Now the total outflow out of each node is not one any more. However some clever algorithms re-normalize the weights on the paths so that the total outflow out of each node is one again. Finally we discuss the use of regular expressions for speeding up the kernel and re-normalization computation. In particular we rewrite the multiplicative algorithms that predict as well as the best pruning of a series parallel graph in terms of efficient kernel computations.

1 Introduction

Assume we have a directed graph with a source and a sink node. A weight v_e is associated with each edge e of the graph so that the total outflow from each non-sink node is one. The weighting on the edges extends to a weighting on the source-to-sink paths: $w_P = \prod_{e \in P} v_e$. Each such path contributes a feature w_P to a feature vector $\boldsymbol{w} = \Phi(\boldsymbol{v})$ (see Figure 1) and in this paper we focus on the kernel associated with the path features of directed graphs. The predictions of the algorithms are often determined by kernel computations, i.e. there is a second weighting x_e on the edges and the prediction of the algorithm is based on:

$$K(\boldsymbol{v}, \boldsymbol{x}) = \Phi(\boldsymbol{v}) \cdot \Phi(\boldsymbol{x}) = \sum_P \prod_{e \in P} v_e x_e.$$

Similar related kernels that are built from regular expressions or pair-HMMs were introduced in [Hau99, Wat99] for the purpose of characterizing the similarity between strings. Any path kernel can easily be used for additive algorithms such as the Perceptron algorithm and Support Vector Machines. Such algorithms compute a linear model in a feature space, i.e. the weight vector $\boldsymbol{w}_t$ at trial t is

---

* Part of this work was done while the author visited University of California, Santa Cruz.
** Supported by NSF grant CCR 9821087

J. Kivinen and R. H. Sloan (Eds.): COLT 2002, LNAI 2375, pp. 74–89, 2002.

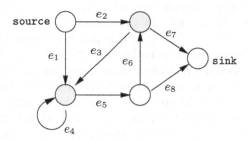

Fig. 1. An example of a digraph. If the weight of e_i is v_i, then its feature vector is $\Phi(v) = \{v_2v_7, v_1v_5v_8, v_2v_3v_5v_8, v_1v_4v_5v_8, v_1v_5v_6v_7, v_2v_3v_4v_5v_8, v_2v_3v_5v_6v_7, v_1v_4v_4v_5v_8, v_1v_5v_6v_3v_5v_8, \dots\}$

a linear combination of the expanded past inputs $\Phi(x_q)$ $(1 \leq q \leq t-1)$. The linear predictions $w_t \cdot x_t$ can be computed via the dot products $\Phi(x_q) \cdot \Phi(x_t)$.

In this paper we are particularly concerned with multiplicative update algorithms where each path is an expert or a feature. Typically there are exponentially (sometimes infinitely) many features and maintaining one weight per feature is prohibitive. However in this paper we manipulate the exponentially many path weights via efficient kernel computations. A key requirement for our methods is that the loss of a path P decomposes into a sum of the losses over its edges. Except for a normalization, the updates multiply each path weight w_P by an exponential factor whose exponent decomposes into a sum over the edges of P. Thus the path weights are multiplied by a product containing a factor per edge of the path. Viewed differently, the updates multiply each edge by a factor.

We want three properties for the weightings on the paths.

1. The weighting should be in *product form*, i.e. $w_P = \prod_{e \in P} v_e$.
2. The outflow from each node u should be one, i.e. $\sum_{u':(u,u')\in E(G)} v_{(u,u')} = 1$, where $E(G)$ denotes the set of edges of G.
3. The total path weight is one, i.e. $\sum_P w_P = 1$.

The three properties make it trivial to generate random paths: Start at the source and iteratively pick an outgoing edge from the current node according to the prescribed edge probabilities until the sink is reached.

The additional factors on the edges that are introduced by the multiplicative update mess up these properties. However there is an algorithm that rearranges the weights on the edges so that the weights on the path remain unchanged but again have the three properties. This algorithm is called the *Weight Pushing algorithm*. It was developed by Mehryar Mohri in the context of speech recognition [Moh98].

One of the goals of this paper is to show that multiplicative updates nicely mesh with path kernels. The algorithms can easily be described by "direct" algorithms that maintain exponentially many path-weights. The algorithms are then simulated by "indirect" algorithms that maintain only polynomially many edge-weights. There is a lot of precedents for this type of research [HS97, MW98, HPW02, TW99]. In this paper we hope to give a unifying view and make the connection to path kernels. We will also re-express many of the previously developed indirect algorithms using our methods.

In the next section we review the Weight Pushing algorithm which reestablishes the properties of the edge weights after each edge received a factor. We also give the properties of the update that we need so that the updated weights contribute a factor to each edge. We then apply our methods to a dynamic routing problem (Section 3) and to an on-line shortest path problem (Section 4). We prove bounds for the algorithm that decay with the length of the longest path in the graph. However we also give an example graph where the length of the longest path does not enter into the bound. The set of paths associated with this graph can be concisely presented as a regular expression and was implicitly used in the BEG algorithm for learning disjunctions [HPW02]. In Section 5 we introduce path sets defined as regular expressions and give an efficient implementation for the Weight Pushing algorithm in this case. Finally we rewrite the algorithms for predicting as well as the best pruning of Series Parallel graph using the methods just introduced (Section 5.2).

2   Preliminaries

Let G be a directed graph with a source and a sink node. Assume that the edge weights v_e and the path weights w_P fulfill the three properties given in the introduction.

Now each edge receives a factor b_e and the new weights of the paths become

$$\tilde{w}_P = \frac{w_P \prod_{e \in P} b_e}{\sum_P w_P \prod_{e \in P} b_e} = \frac{\prod_{e \in P} v_e b_e}{\sum_P \prod_{e \in P} v_e b_e}. \tag{1}$$

The normalization needs to be non-zero, i.e. we need the following property:

4. The edge factors b_e are non-negative and for some path P, $\prod_{e \in P} v_e b_e > 0$.

Our goal is to find new edge weights $\tilde{v}_e$ such that the first two properties are maintained. Note that Property 3 is maintained because the path weights in (1) are normalized.

We begin by introducing a kernel. For any node u, let $\mathcal{P}(u)$ denote the set of paths from the node u to the sink. Assume that input vectors v and x to edges are given. For any node u, let

$$K_u(v, x) = \sum_{P \in \mathcal{P}(u)} \prod_{e \in P} v_e \prod_{e \in P} x_e = \sum_{P \in \mathcal{P}(u)} \prod_{e \in P} v_e x_e.$$

Clearly $K_{\text{source}}(v, x)$ gives the dot product $\Phi(v) \cdot \Phi(x)$ given in the introduction that is associated with the whole graph G.

The computation of K depends on the complexity of the graph G. If G is acyclic, then the functions $K_u(v, x)$ can be recursively calculated as

$$K_{\text{sink}}(v, x) = 1$$

and in the bottom up order

$$K_u(v, x) = \sum_{u':(u,u')\in E(G)} v_{(u,u')} x_{(u,u')} K_{u'}(v, x).$$

Clearly this takes time linear in the number of edges.

In the case when G is an arbitrary digraph then K_u can be computed using a matrix inversion or via dynamic programming using essentially the Floyd-Warshal all-pairs shortest path algorithm [Moh98]. The cost of these algorithms is essentially cubic in the number of vertices of G. Speedups are possible for sparse graphs.

A straight-forward way to normalize the edge weights would be to divide the weights of the edges leaving a vertex by the total weight of all edges leaving the vertex. However this usually does not give the correct path weights (1) because the product of the normalization factors along different paths is not the same. Instead, the Weight Pushing algorithm [Moh98] assigns the following new weight to the edge $e = (u, u')$:

$$\tilde{v}_e = \frac{v_e b_e K_{u'}(v, b)}{K_u(v, b)}. \tag{2}$$

It is easy to see that the new weights $\tilde{v}_e$ are normalized, i.e.

$$\sum_{u':(u,u')\in E(G)} \tilde{v}_{(u,u')} = 1.$$

Property 1 is proven as follows: Let $P = \{(u_0, u_1), (u_2, u_3), \ldots, (u_{k-1}, u_k)\}$ be any path from the source u_0 to the sink u_k. Then

$$\prod_{e\in P} \tilde{v}_e = \prod_{i=1}^{k} \frac{v_{(u_{i-1},u_i)} b_{(u_{i-1},u_i)} K_{u_i}(v, b)}{K_{u_{i-1}}(v, b)}$$

$$= \frac{\prod_{e\in P} v_e b_e K_{\text{sink}}(v, b)}{K_{\text{source}}(v, b)}$$

$$= \frac{w_P \prod_{e\in P} b_e}{K_{\text{source}}(v, b)}$$

$$= \frac{w_P \prod_{e\in P} b_e}{\sum_P w_P \prod_{e\in P} b_e}.$$

The last expression equals $\tilde{w}_P$ (See (1)).

Typically the multiplicative weights updates have the form

$$\tilde{w}_P = \frac{w_P \exp(-\eta L(P))}{\sum_P w_P \exp(-\eta L(P))} \quad \text{or} \quad \tilde{w}_P = \frac{w_P \exp(-\eta \frac{\partial L(P)}{\partial w_P})}{\sum_P w_P \exp(-\eta \frac{\partial L(P)}{\partial w_P})},$$

where $L(P)$ is the loss of path P. So if the loss $L(P)$ can be decomposed into a sum over the edges of P, i.e. $L(P) = \sum_{e \in P} l(e)$, then these update rules have the form of (1) and so they can be efficiently simulated by the edge updates using the Weight Pushing algorithm. Property 4 is also easily satisfied. In most cases, however, the loss is given by

$$L(P) = L(y, \Phi(x)_P) = L(y, \prod_{e \in P} x_e)$$

for some loss function L, which cannot be decomposed into a sum over the edges in general. Actually, Khardon, Roth and Servedio show that simulating Winnow (a multiplicative update algorithm) with the monomial kernel (which is a path kernel) is #P-hard [KRS01]. Still certain problems can be solved using multiplicative updates of the form of (1). In the subsequent sections we will give some examples. In the full paper we will also discuss in more detail how the efficient disjunction learning algorithm (such as Winnow with one weight per variable) may be seen as examples of the same method.

3   A Dynamic Routing Problem

In this section we regard the digraph G as a probabilistic automaton and consider a dynamic routing problem based on G. At trial $t = 1, 2, \ldots$ we want to send a packet X_t from the source to the sink and assign transition probabilities $v_{t,e}$ to the edges that define a probabilistic routing. Starting from the source we choose a random path to the sink according to the transition probabilities and try to send the packet along the path. But some edges may reject the request with a certain probability that is given by nature and the current trial may fail. The goal is make the success probability as large as possible. Below we give the problem formally.

In each trial $t = 1, 2, \ldots, T$, the following happens:

1. The algorithm assigns transition probabilities $v_{t,e} \in [0, 1]$ to all edges e.
2. Real numbers $d_{t,e} \in [0, 1]$ for all edges are given. The number $d_{t,e}$ is interpreted as the probability that the edge e "accepts" the packet X_t. A path P "accepts" X_t if all the edges e of P accept X_t and the probability of this is

$$\Pr(X_t \mid P) = \prod_{e \in P} d_{t,e}.$$

   We assume that $\Pr(X_t \mid P) > 0$ for at least one path P, so that Property 4 holds. Moreover, this probability is independent for all trials.
3. The probability that the current probabilistic automaton accepts X_t is

$$A_t = \sum_P w_{t,P} \Pr(X_t \mid P),$$

   where $w_{t,P} = \prod_{e \in P} v_{t,e}$ is the probability that the path P is chosen.

The goal is to make the total success probability $\prod_{t=1}^{T} A_t$ as large as possible.

In the feature space we can employ the Bayes algorithm. The initial weight $w_{1,P}$ is a prior of path P. Then the Bayes algorithm sets the weight $w_{t+1,P}$ as a posterior of P given the input packets $X_1, \ldots, X_t$ observed so far. Specifically the Bayes algorithm updates weights so that

$$
\begin{aligned}
w_{t+1,P} &= \Pr(P \mid X_1, \ldots, X_t) \\
&= \frac{w_{1,P} \Pr(X_1, \ldots, X_t \mid P)}{\sum_P w_{1,P} \Pr(X_1, \ldots, X_t \mid P)} \\
&= \frac{w_{t,P} \Pr(X_t \mid P)}{\sum_P w_{t,P} \Pr(X_t \mid P)} \\
&= \frac{w_{t,P} \prod_{e \in P} d_{t,e}}{\sum_P w_{t,P} \prod_{e \in P} d_{t,e}}.
\end{aligned}
\tag{3}
$$

It is well known that the Bayes algorithm guarantees that

$$
\prod_{t=1}^{T} A_t = \sum_P w_{1,P} \Pr(X_1, \ldots, X_T \mid P) \geq \max_P w_{1,P} \Pr(X_1, \ldots, X_T \mid P).
$$

This implies that the probability that the Bayes algorithm succeeds to send the all packets $X_1, \ldots, X_T$ is at least the probability for the path P that attains the maximum of the success probability.

It is easy to check that the Bayes update rule (3) has the multiplicative form (1). So we can run the Bayes algorithm efficiently using the Weight Pushing algorithm.

4   On-Line Shortest Path Problem

We consider an on-line version of the shortest path problem. The problem is similar to the previous one, but now $d_{t,e}$ is the distance of the edge e at trial t. Furthermore we assume that the given graph G is acyclic, so that any path has a bounded length.

In each trial $t = 1, 2, \ldots, T$, the following happens:

1. The algorithm assigns transition probabilities $v_{t,e} \in [0, 1]$ to all edges e.
2. Then distances $d_{t,e} \in [0, 1]$ for all edges are given.
3. The algorithm incurs a loss L_t which is defined as the expected length of path of G. That is,

$$
L_t = \sum_{P \in \mathcal{P}(G)} w_{t,P} l_{t,P},
$$

where

$$
l_{t,P} = \sum_{e \in P} d_{t,e}
\tag{4}
$$

is the length of the path P, which is interpreted as the loss of P.

Note that the length $l_{t,P}$ of path P at each trial is upper bounded by the number of edges in P. Letting D denote the depth (maximum number of edges of P) of G, we have $l_{t,P} \in [0, D]$. Note that the path P minimizing the total length

$$\sum_{t=1}^{T} l_{t,P} = \sum_{t=1}^{T} \sum_{e \in P} d_{t,e} = \sum_{e \in P} \sum_{t=1}^{T} d_{t,e}$$

can be interpreted as the shortest path based on the cumulative distances of edges: $\sum_{t=1}^{T} d_{t,e}$. The goal of the algorithm is to make its total loss $\sum_{t=1}^{T} L_t$ not much larger than the length of the shortest path.

Considering each path P as an expert, we can view the problem above as a dynamic resource allocation problem [FS97] introduced by Freund and Schapire. So we can apply their *Hedge algorithm* which is a reformulation of the *Weighted Majority algorithm* (see WMC and WMR of [LW94]). The Hedge algorithm works over the feature space. Let $w_{1,P}$ be initial weights for paths/experts that sum to 1. At each trial t, when given losses $l_{t,P} \in [0, D]$ for paths/experts, the algorithm incurs loss

$$L_t = \sum_P w_{t,P} l_{t,P}$$

and updates weights according to

$$w_{t+1,P} = \frac{w_{t,P} \beta^{l_{t,P}/D}}{\sum_{P'} w_{t,P'} \beta^{l_{t,P'}/D}}, \tag{5}$$

where $0 \le \beta < 1$ is a parameter. It is shown in [LW94, FS97] that for any sequence of loss vectors for experts, the Hedge algorithm guarantees[1] that

$$\sum_{t=1}^{T} L_t \le \min_P \left(\frac{\ln(1/\beta)}{1 - \beta} \sum_{t=1}^{T} l_{t,P} + \frac{D}{1 - \beta} \ln \frac{1}{w_{1,P}} \right). \tag{6}$$

Since $l_{t,P} = \sum_{e \in P} d_{t,e}$, the update rule (5) is the multiplicative form of (1). So we can employ the Weight Pushing algorithm to run the Hedge algorithm efficiently. Below we give a proof of (6).

Let $W_t = \sum_P w_{1,P} \beta^{l_{1..t-1,P}/D}$, where $l_{1..t-1,P}$ is shorthand for $\sum_{q=1}^{t-1} l_{q,P}$. Note that $W_1 = 1$. It is not hard to see that the update rule (5) implies $w_{t,P} = w_{1,P} \beta^{l_{1..t-1,P}/D}/W_t$. So

$$\ln \frac{W_{t+1}}{W_t} = \ln \left(\frac{\sum_P w_{1,P} \beta^{l_{1..t,P}/D}}{W_t} \right)$$

$$= \ln \sum_P \left(\frac{w_{1,P} \beta^{l_{1..t-1,P}/D}}{W_t} \right) \beta^{l_{t,P}/D}$$

$$= \ln \sum_P w_{t,P} \beta^{l_{t,P}/D}.$$

---

[1] In [FS97] losses of experts are upper bounded by 1 at each trial, while in our case they are upper bounded by D. So the second term of the loss bound in (6) has the factor D.

Since $l_{t,P}/D \in [0,1]$ and $0 \leq \beta < 1$, we have $\beta^{l_{t,P}/D} \leq 1 - (1 - \beta)l_{t,P}/D$. Plugging this inequality into the above formula, we have

$$\ln \frac{W_{t+1}}{W_t} \leq \ln \sum_P w_{t,P}\left(1 - (1 - \beta)l_{t,P}/D\right)$$
$$= \ln\left(1 - (1 - \beta)L_t/D\right)$$
$$\leq -(1 - \beta)L_t/D.$$

Summing the both sides over all t's, we get

$$\sum_{t=1}^{T} L_t \leq \frac{D(\ln W_1 - \ln W_{T+1})}{1 - \beta}$$
$$= -\frac{D \ln \sum_P w_{1,P}\beta^{l_{1..T,P}/D}}{1 - \beta}$$
$$\leq -\frac{D \ln\left(w_{1,P*}\beta^{l_{1..T,P*}/D}\right)}{1 - \beta}$$
$$= \frac{\ln 1/\beta}{1 - \beta}l_{1..T,P*} + \frac{D}{1 - \beta}\ln\frac{1}{w_{1,P*}},$$

where P^* is any path. This proves (6).

Unfortunately, the loss bound in (6) depends on the depth D of G. Thus the graphs of large depth or for cyclic graphs the bound is vacuous. In some cases, however, we have a bound where D does not appear in the bound although the depth can be arbitrarily large. We give an example of such graphs in Figure 2. The graph has $n+1$ nodes and each node i ($1 \leq i \leq n$) has two outgoing edges e_i and e_i' to node $i + 1$. Let $v_{t,i}$ and $1 - v_{t,i}$ denote the weights of these edges at trial t, respectively. Let $d_{t,i}$ and $d_{t,i}'$ be the distances assigned to these edges at trial t. Note that the depth of the graph is n.

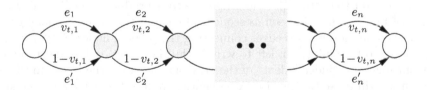

Fig. 2. An example graph whose depth D does not appear in the loss bound

Now we give a loss bound of the Hedge algorithm when applied to this graph. In this case we use the following update rule

$$w_{t+1,P} = \frac{w_{t,P}\beta^{l_{t,P}}}{\sum_{P'} w_{t,P'}\beta^{l_{t,P'}}} \tag{7}$$

instead of (5). The key property we use in the analysis is that $\ln(W_{t+1}/W_t)$ is decomposed into n independent sums:

$$\ln \frac{W_{t+1}}{W_t} = \ln \sum_P w_{t,P} \beta^{l_{t,P}}$$

$$= \ln \sum_{A \subseteq \{1,\ldots,n\}} \left(\prod_{i \in A} (v_{t,i} \beta^{d_{t,i}}) \prod_{i \notin A} (1 - v_{t,i}) \beta^{d'_{t,i}} \right)$$

$$= \ln \prod_{i=1}^{n} \left(v_{t,i} \beta^{d_{t,i}} + (1 - v_{t,i}) \beta^{d'_{t,i}} \right)$$

$$= \sum_{i=1}^{n} \ln \left(v_{t,i} \beta^{d_{t,i}} + (1 - v_{t,i}) \beta^{d'_{t,i}} \right).$$

Here we used the following formula: $\sum_A \prod_{i \in A} a_i \prod_{i \notin A} b_i = \prod_i (a_i + b_i)$. Using the approximation $\beta^x \leq 1 - (1 - \beta)x$ for $x \in [0, 1]$ as before, we have

$$\ln \frac{W_{t+1}}{W_t} \leq \sum_{i=1}^{n} \ln \left(1 - (1 - \beta)(v_{t,i}d_{t,i} + (1 - v_{t,i})d'_{t,i}) \right)$$

$$\leq -(1 - \beta) \sum_{i=1}^{n} (v_{t,i}d_{t,i} + (1 - v_{t,i})d'_{t,i})$$

$$= -(1 - \beta) \sum_{i=1}^{n} L_t,$$

which ends up in the following tighter bound

$$\sum_{t=1}^{T} L_t \leq \min_P \left(\frac{\ln(1/\beta)}{1 - \beta} \sum_{t=1}^{T} l_{t,P} + \frac{1}{1 - \beta} \ln \frac{1}{w_{1,P}} \right).$$

So why did the ratio $\frac{W_{t+1}}{W_t}$ decompose into a product? This is because the graph of Figure 2 may be seen as sequential composition of n two-node graphs, where there are always two edges connecting the pairs of nodes. As you go from the source to the sink (from left to write), the choices at each node (top versus bottom edge) are "independent" of the previous choices of the edges. In the next section we will make this precise. A sequential composition will cause the kernel computation to decompose into a product (And conveniently logs of products become sums of logs). The graph of Figure 2 represents n sequential binary choices, i.e. a product of Bernoulli variables and this was used to model the BEG algorithm for learning disjunctions [HPW02] (A literal in the disjunction is either on or off). The direct algorithm maintains one weight per disjunction (subset of $\{0, 1, \ldots, n\}$). If the loss of a disjunction is measured with the attribute loss then the loss of a disjunction is the sum of the losses of its literals. We obtain an efficient indirect algorithm by maintaining only one weight per

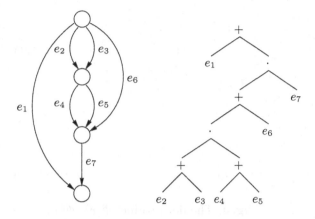

Fig. 3. An example of an SP digraph and its syntax tree

literal and the analysis decomposes as shown above. In this case the Weigh-Pushing algorithm converts the update (7) for the path weights to an update for the edge/literal weights, resulting in the standard BEG algorithm for learning disjunctions [HPW02].

5   Regular Expressions for Digraphs

In this section we consider a digraph as an automaton by identifying the source and the sink with the start and the accept state, respectively. The set of all source-sink paths is a regular language and can be expressed as a regular expression. For example the set of paths of the digraph given in Figure 1 is expressed as

$$e_2e_7 + (e_1 + e_2e_3)e_4^*e_5(e_6e_3e_4^*e_5)^*(e_8 + e_6e_7).$$

The convolution kernel based on regular expressions is introduced by Haussler [Hau99] and is used to measure the similarity between strings. Here we show that the kernel computation gives an efficient implementation for the Weight Pushing algorithm. For the sake of simplicity we assume that the source has no incoming and the sink no outgoing edges, respectively.

5.1   Series Parallel Digraphs

First let us consider the simple case where regular expressions do not have the ∗-operation. In this case the prescribed graphs are series parallel digraphs (SP digraphs, for short). See an example of SP digraphs with its regular expression (in terms of the syntax tree) in Figure 3. Note that any edge symbol e_i appears exactly once in the regular expression that represents an SP digraph. The syntax tree is used to compute the dot product $\Phi(v) \cdot \Phi(x)$: Replace the leaves labeled edge e_i by the input product $v_i x_i$ and + by plus (+) and ∘ by times (·) (See

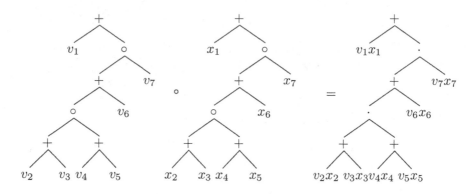

Fig. 4. The dot product $\Phi(v) \cdot \Phi(x)$

Fig. 4). Now the value of the dot product is computed by a postorder traversal of the tree. This takes time linear in the size of the tree (number of edges).

Although SP digraphs seem a very restricted class of acyclic digraphs, they can define some important kernels such as the polynomial kernel: $\Phi(z) \cdot \Phi(x) = (1 + z \cdot x)^k$, for some degree k. This is essentially the path kernel defined by the regular expression

$$(\epsilon + e_{1,1} + \cdots + e_{1,n})(\epsilon + e_{2,1} + \cdots + e_{2,n}) \cdots (\epsilon + e_{k,1} + \cdots + e_{k,n}),$$

where any set of k edges $e_{1,i}, \ldots e_{k,i}$ happen to receive the same input values z_i and x_i and the edges labeled with ϵ always receive one as input. Note that z does not necessarily represent edge weights that define a probability distribution over the paths. But if all z_i's are non-negative, then the Weight Pushing algorithm when applied to the weights z_i produces the edge weights $v_{j,i} = z_i/(1+z_1+\cdots+z_n)$ for the edges $e_{j,i}$ and and $v_{0,i} = 1/(1+z_1+\cdots+z_n)$ for all ϵ edges. The edge weights v of resulting kernel now satisfy Property 1 and 2, and $\Phi(v) \cdot \Phi(x) = \Phi(z) \cdot \Phi(x)/(1 + z_1 + \cdots + z_n)^k$. This kernel (without the ϵ edges) is the path kernel underlying the Normalized Winnow algorithm [HPW02]. Also the case $k = 2$ (related to the kernel associated with Figure 2) is perhaps the simplest kernel of this type:

$$\Phi(z) \cdot \Phi(x) = \sum_{A \subseteq \{1,\ldots,n\}} \prod_{i \in A} z_i x_i = \prod_{i=1}^{n} (1 + z_i x_i).$$

This is the "subset kernel" introduced in [KW97] (also the "monomial kernel" of [KRS01]) which was the initial focal point of this research.

Now we give an efficient implementation for the Weight Pushing algorithm that guarantees normalized updates (1), namely,

$$\prod_{e \in P} \tilde{v}_e = \frac{\prod_{e \in P} v_e b_e}{\sum_{P'} \prod_{e \in P'} v_e b_e} = \frac{\prod_{e \in P} v_e b_e}{\Phi(v) \cdot \Phi(b)} \tag{8}$$

for any path P. Each node of the syntax tree corresponds to a regular expression which represents a component of the given SP digraph G. Note that the root of the tree corresponds to the entire graph G. For any component regular expression H of G, let $\mathcal{P}(H)$ denote the set of all paths that H generates. For values $\boldsymbol{x}$ on the edges of H, let $\Phi^H(\boldsymbol{x}) = \sum_{P \in \mathcal{P}(H)} \prod_{e \in P} x_e$. Furthermore, we define the kernel associated with H as

$$K^H(\boldsymbol{v}, \boldsymbol{b}) = \Phi^H(\boldsymbol{v}) \cdot \Phi^H(\boldsymbol{b}) = \sum_{P \in \mathcal{P}(H)} \prod_{e \in P} v_e b_e.$$

As stated in the beginning of this section, this is recursively calculated as follows.

$$K^H(\boldsymbol{v}, \boldsymbol{b}) = \begin{cases} v_e b_e & \text{if } H = e \text{ for some single edge } e, \\ \prod_{i=1}^k K^{H_i}(\boldsymbol{v}, \boldsymbol{b}) & \text{if } H = H_1 \circ \cdots \circ H_k, \\ \sum_{i=1}^k K^{H_i}(\boldsymbol{v}, \boldsymbol{b}) & \text{if } H = H_1 + \cdots + H_k. \end{cases}$$

Now we give an update rule for $\boldsymbol{v}$. For any edge e in H, let $\tilde{v}_e^H$ be defined recursively as

$$\tilde{v}_e^H = \begin{cases} 1 & \text{if } H = e \text{ for some single edge } e, \\ \frac{K^{H_i}(\boldsymbol{v},\boldsymbol{b})}{K^H(\boldsymbol{v},\boldsymbol{b})} \tilde{v}_e^{H_i} & \text{if } H = H_1 + \cdots + H_k \text{ and } e \text{ is the prefix of some path} \\ & P \in \mathcal{P}(H_i), \\ \tilde{v}_e^{H_i} & \text{otherwise, where } H_i \text{ is a child node of } H \text{ for which} \\ & e \in P \text{ for some path } P \in \mathcal{P}(H_i). \end{cases}$$

Finally the weights on the edges are given by $\tilde{v}_e = \tilde{v}_e^G$. The next theorem shows that this update assures (8).

Theorem 1. *For any component graph H of G and any path $P \in \mathcal{P}(H)$,*

$$\prod_{e \in P} \tilde{v}_e^H = \frac{\prod_{e \in P} v_e b_e}{K^H(\boldsymbol{v}, \boldsymbol{b})}.$$

Proof. We show the theorem by an induction on the depth of the syntax tree.
   In the case where H consists of a single edge, the theorem trivially holds.
   Consider the case where $H = H_1 \circ \cdots \circ H_k$. In this case any path $P \in \mathcal{P}(H)$ is a union $P = P_1 \cup \cdots \cup P_k$ for some $P_i \in \mathcal{P}(H_i)$ for $1 \le i \le k$. So

$$\prod_{e \in P} \tilde{v}_e^H = \prod_{i=1}^k \prod_{e \in P_i} \tilde{v}_e^H$$

$$= \prod_{i=1}^k \prod_{e \in P_i} \tilde{v}_e^{H_i} \qquad \text{by the definition of } \tilde{v}_e^H$$

$$= \prod_{i=1}^k \frac{\prod_{e \in P_i} v_e b_e}{K^{H_i}(\boldsymbol{v}, \boldsymbol{b})} \qquad \text{by the induction hypothesis}$$

$$= \frac{\prod_{e \in P} v_e b_e}{K^H(\boldsymbol{v}, \boldsymbol{b})}.$$

Finally for the case where $H = H_1 + \cdots + H_k$, any path $P \in \mathcal{P}(H)$ is a path in some $\mathcal{P}(H_i)$. Moreover only the prefix edge of P changes its weight. Therefore,

$$
\begin{aligned}
\prod_{e \in P} \tilde{v}_e^H &= \frac{K^{H_i}(\boldsymbol{v}, \boldsymbol{b})}{K^H(\boldsymbol{v}, \boldsymbol{b})} \prod_{e \in P} \tilde{v}_e^{H_i} \\
&= \frac{K^{H_i}(\boldsymbol{v}, \boldsymbol{b})}{K^H(\boldsymbol{v}, \boldsymbol{b})} \frac{\prod_{e \in P} v_e b_e}{K^{H_i}(\boldsymbol{v}, \boldsymbol{b})} \quad \text{by the induction hypothesis} \\
&= \frac{\prod_{e \in P} v_e b_e}{K^H(\boldsymbol{v}, \boldsymbol{b})},
\end{aligned}
$$

which completes the proof. □

It is not hard to see that the weights $\tilde{\boldsymbol{v}}$ can be calculated in linear time.

5.2   Predicting Nearly as Well as the Best Pruning

One of the main representations of Machine Learning is decision trees. Frequently a large tree is produced initially and then this tree is pruned for the purpose of obtaining a better predictor. A pruning is produced by deleting some nodes in the tree and with them all their successors. Although there are exponentially many prunings, a recent method developed in coding theory and machine learning makes it possible to maintain one weight per pruning. In particular, Helmbold and Schapire [HS97] use this method to design an elegant multiplicative algorithm that is guaranteed to predict nearly as well as the best pruning of a decision tree in the on-line prediction setting. Recently, the authors [TW99] generalizes the pruning problem to the much more general class of acyclic planar digraphs. In this section we restate this result in terms of path kernels on SP digraphs.

A pruning of an SP digraph G is a minimal set of edges (a cut) that interrupts all paths from the source to the sink. In the example of Fig. 3, all the prunings of the graph are $\{e_1, e_2, e_3, e_6\}$, $\{e_1, e_4, e_5, e_6\}$, $\{e_1, e_7\}$. The key property we use below is that for any path P and pruning R, the intersection always consists of exactly one edge. Let $P \cap R$ denote the edge.

First we describe an algorithm working on the feature space that performs nearly as well as the best pruning of a given SP digraph. The algorithm maintains a weight $w_{t,R}$ per pruning R. Previously an input vector $\boldsymbol{x}_t$ at trial t is given to all edges. Now an input vector $\boldsymbol{x}_t$ is given only to the edges of a single path P_t. In the decision tree example this path is produced by some decision process that passes down the tree. We do not need to be concerned with how the path P_t at trial t is produced. Each pruning R predicts as the edge that cuts the path P_t, i.e. the prediction of R is $x_{t,R} = x_{t,P_t \cap R}$. The algorithm predicts with the weighted average of predictions of prunings, i.e. $\hat{y}_t = \sum_R w_{t,R} x_{t,R}$. Then an outcome y_t is given and the algorithm suffers loss $L_t = L(y_t, \hat{y}_t)$ for a previously fixed loss function L, say, $L(y_t, \hat{y}_t) = (y_t - \hat{y}_t)^2$. Similarly pruning R suffers loss

$L(y_t, x_{t,R})$. Finally the algorithm updates weights so that

$$w_{t+1,R} = \frac{w_{t,R}\exp(-\eta L(y_t, x_{t,R}))}{\sum_R w_{t,R}\exp(-\eta L(y_t, x_{t,R}))}$$

holds for all R.

Now we express this algorithm in terms of path kernels and weight updates on the edges. Consider the dual SP digraph G^D which is defined by swapping the $+$ and $\circ$ operations in the syntax tree. Note that prunings and paths in G are swapped in G^D, namely, a pruning R in G is a path in G^D and the path P_t in G is a pruning in G^D. The algorithm works on the dual graph G^D and maintains weights v_t on the edges of G^D that represent the weight of path R as $w_{t,R} = \prod_{e \in R} v_{t,e}$. At trial t the input vector x_t is assigned to the edges of a pruning P_t. The $x_{t,e}$ for which $e \notin P_t$ are set to one. Let $\Phi^D(x_t)$ denote the vector of all feature values corresponding to the paths in G^D. Then the value of feature/path R is

$$\Phi^D(x_t)_R = \prod_{e \in R} x_{t,e} = x_{t, P_t \cap R} = x_{t,R}.$$

So the prediction $\hat{y}_t$ of the algorithm is expressed as $\hat{y}_t = \Phi^D(v_t) \cdot \Phi^D(x_t)$, which is efficiently computed by a path kernel.

Moreover, since the loss of path R at trial t is $L(y_t, x_{t,R}) = L(y_t, x_{t,P_t \cap R})$, letting

$$b_{t,e} = \begin{cases} \exp(-\eta L(y_t, x_{t,e})) & \text{if } e \in P_t, \\ 1 & \text{otherwise,} \end{cases}$$

we have

$$\prod_{e \in R} v_{t+1,e} = \frac{\prod_{e \in R} v_{t,e} b_{t,e}}{\sum_R \prod_{e \in R} v_{t,e} b_{t,e}}.$$

This is the same form as (8) and hence can be efficiently calculated as shown in the previous section.

Note that in each trial t only the edges in the input path P_t are "relevant" to computing the prediction value $\hat{y}_t$ and the new edge weights v_{t+1}. Maintaining $K^H(v_t, b_t)$ for each component expression H, we can compute $\hat{y}_t$ and v_{t+1} in time linear in the size of P_t [TW99], which can be much smaller than the number of all edges. So when the given graph is series-parallel, the implementation we give in this section can be exponentially faster than the original Weight Pushing algorithm.

5.3   Allowing $*$-Operations

Now we consider the general case where regular expressions have $*$-operations. First let us clarify how the digraph is defined by $*$-operations. Let H_1 be any digraph that is defined by a regular expression. Then we define the digraph for $H = H_1^*$ as in Figure 5: add a new source with an ϵ-edge from it to the old

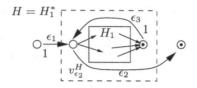

Fig. 5. The digraph defined by H_1^*. The solid box represents H_1, where its source and sink are designated as $\bigcirc$ and $\odot$, respectively

source, add a new sink with an ϵ-edge from the old source to the new sink, and add an ϵ-edge from the old sink back to the old source. For convenience we call them ϵ_1, ϵ_2 and ϵ_3, respectively. All ϵ-edges are assumed to always receive one as input, namely, $b_{\epsilon_i} = 1$. Let $v_{\epsilon_i}^H$ denote the weight for the edge ϵ_i. Clearly it always holds that $v_{\epsilon_3}^H = 1$.

The kernel $K^H(\boldsymbol{v}, \boldsymbol{b}) = \sum_{P \in \mathcal{P}(H)} \prod_{e \in P} v_e b_e$ can be calculated in the same way as stated in Section 5.1 when H is a concatenation or a union. When $H = H_1^*$ for some regular expression H_1, it is not hard to see that

$$K^H(\boldsymbol{v}, \boldsymbol{b}) = v_{\epsilon_1}^H \sum_{k=0}^{\infty} \left(K^{H_1}(\boldsymbol{v}, \boldsymbol{b}) \right)^k v_{\epsilon_2}^H = v_{\epsilon_1}^H v_{\epsilon_2}^H / \left(1 - K^{H_1}(\boldsymbol{v}, \boldsymbol{b}) \right)$$

if $K^{H_1}(\boldsymbol{v}, \boldsymbol{b}) < 1$ and $K^H(\boldsymbol{v}, \boldsymbol{b}) = \infty$ otherwise.

Similarly the update rule for $\boldsymbol{v}$ is computed through $\tilde{v}_e^H$. The definition of $\tilde{v}_e^H$ is the same as in Section 5.1 when H is a concatenation or a union. When $H = H_1^*$

$$\tilde{v}_e^H = \begin{cases} v_{\epsilon_1}^H & \text{if } e = \epsilon_1, \\ K^{H_1}(\boldsymbol{v}, \boldsymbol{b}) \tilde{v}_e^{H_1} & \text{if } e \text{ is the prefix of some path } P \in \mathcal{P}(H_1), \\ v_{\epsilon_2}^H / \left(1 - K^{H_1}(\boldsymbol{v}, \boldsymbol{b}) \right) & \text{if } e = \epsilon_2 \\ \tilde{v}_e^{H_1} & \text{otherwise.} \end{cases}$$

Then we can show that the weights $\tilde{v}_e^H$ satisfy

$$\prod_{e \in P} \tilde{v}_e^H = \frac{\prod_{e \in P} v_e b_e}{K^H(\boldsymbol{v}, \boldsymbol{b})}$$

for any path $P \in \mathcal{P}(H)$.

6   Conclusion

In this paper we showed that path kernels can be used to indirectly maintain exponentially many path weights. Multiplicative updates give factors to the edges and the Weight Pushing algorithm renormalizes the edge weights so that the outflow out of each vertex is one. We also showed that it is often convenient to express the path sets as regular expressions, leading to efficient implementations of path kernels and the Weight Pushing algorithm. We gave the path kernels that interpret BEG and normalized Winnow as direct algorithms over exponentially many paths. A similar interpretation for Winnow is unknown [HPW02].

Acknowledgment

We thank Fernando Pereira for pointing out that we rediscovered the Weight Pushing algorithm of Mehryar Mohri and Sandra Panizza for fruitful discussions.

References

[FS97]   Yoav Freund and Robert E. Schapire. A decision-theoretic generalization of on-line learning and an application to boosting. *Journal of Computer and System Sciences*, 55(1):119–139, August 1997. 80

[Hau99]   David Haussler. Convolution kernels on discrete structures. Technical Report UCSC-CRL-99-10, Univ. of Calif. Computer Research Lab, Santa Cruz, CA, 1999. 74, 83

[HPW02]   D. P. Helmbold, S. Panizza, and M. K. Warmuth. Direct and indirect algorithms for on-line learning of disjunctions. *Theoretical Computer Science*, 2002. To appear. 76, 82, 83, 84, 89

[HS97]   D. P. Helmbold and R. E. Schapire. Predicting nearly as well as the best pruning of a decision tree. *Machine Learning*, 27(01):51–68, 1997. 76, 86

[KRS01]   Roni Khardon, Dan Roth, and Rocco Servedio. Efficiency versus convergence of Boolean kernels for on-line learning algorithms. In *Advances in Neural Information Processing Systems 14*, 2001. 78, 84

[KW97]   J. Kivinen and M. K. Warmuth. Additive versus exponentiated gradient updates for linear prediction. *Information and Computation*, 132(1):1–64, January 1997. 84

[LW94]   N. Littlestone and M. K. Warmuth. The weighted majority algorithm. *Inform. Comput.*, 108(2):212–261, 1994. 80

[Moh98]   Mehryar Mohri. General algebraic frameworks and algorithms for shortest distance problems. Technical Report 981219-10TM, AT&T Labs-Research, 1998. 75, 77

[MW98]   M. Maass and M. K. Warmuth. Efficient learning with virtual threshold gates. *Information and Computation*, 141(1):66–83, February 1998. 76

[TW99]   Eiji Takimoto and Manfred K. Warmuth. Predicting nearly as well as the best pruning of a planar decision graph. In *10th ALT*, volume 1720 of *Lecture Notes in Artificial Intelligence*, pages 335–346, 1999. To appear in *Theoretical Computer Science*. 76, 86, 87

[Wat99]   Chris Watkins. Dynamic alignment kernels. Technical Report CSD-TR-98-11, Royal Holloway, University of London, 1999. 74

Predictive Complexity and Information

Michael V. Vyugin[1] and Vladimir V. V'yugin[2,3]

[1] Department of Computer Science, Royal Holloway, University of London
Egham, Surrey TW20 0EX, England
misha@cs.rhul.ac.uk
[2] Institute for Information Transmission Problems, Russian Academy of Sciences
Bol'shoi Karetnyi per. 19, Moscow GSP-4, 101447, Russia
[3] Computer Learning Research Centre, Royal Holloway, University of London
Egham, Surrey TW20 0EX, England
vld@vyugin.mccme.ru

Abstract. A new notion of predictive complexity and corresponding amount of information are considered. Predictive complexity is a generalization of Kolmogorov complexity which bounds the ability of any algorithm to predict elements of a sequence of outcomes. We consider predictive complexity for a wide class of bounded loss functions which are generalizations of square-loss function. Relations between unconditional $KG(x)$ and conditional $KG(x|y)$ predictive complexities are studied. We define an algorithm which has some "expanding property". It transforms with positive probability sequences of given predictive complexity into sequences of essentially bigger predictive complexity. A concept of amount of predictive information $IG(y : x)$ is studied. We show that this information is non-commutative in a very strong sense and present asymptotic relations between values $IG(y : x)$, $IG(x : y)$, $KG(x)$ and $KG(y)$.

1   Introduction

Machine learning (and statistics) considers a problem of predicting a future event x_n from past observations $x_1 x_2 \ldots x_{n-1}$, where $n = 1, 2 \ldots$. A prediction algorithm makes its prediction in a form of a real number between 0 and 1. The quality of prediction is measured by a loss function $\lambda(\sigma, p)$, where σ is an outcome and $0 \le p \le 1$ is a prediction. Various loss functions are considered in literature on machine learning and prediction with expert advice [8,10,2,14,1]. The logarithmic loss function, where $\lambda(\sigma, p) = -\log p$ if $\sigma = 1$ and $\lambda(\sigma, p) = -\log(1-p)$ otherwise, is important in probability theory and generates the log-likelihood function. The square-loss function $\lambda(\sigma, p) = (\sigma - p)^2$ is important for applications.

The main goal of on-line prediction is to find a method of prediction which minimizes the total loss suffered on a sequence $x = x_1 x_2 \ldots x_n$ for $n = 1, 2 \ldots$. This idea of "minimal" possible total loss was formalized by Vovk [10] in a notion of predictive complexity. Intuitively, it is the loss of an optimal idealized prediction strategy ("idealized" means that this strategy is allowed to work infinitely long). This loss gives a natural lower bound to ability of any algorithm

J. Kivinen and R. H. Sloan (Eds.): COLT 2002, LNAI 2375, pp. 90–105, 2002.

to predict elements of a sequence of outcomes. For the exact definition of predictive complexity see Section 2. Since predictive complexity is defined only up to an additive constant, it cannot have direct applications in practice. However it allows us to give a very general formal representation to our intuitions about prediction. It provides a tool to determine the limits of effectiveness of prediction algorithms. An example of an application of this tool is the statement and the solution of the snooping problem published in [11]: given a bit of information about a data set, how much better can elements of this data set be predicted?

The situation is similar to that with Kolmogorov complexity, which formalizes our intuitions about the shortest description of an object. Results of the theory of predictive complexity are expressed in the same asymptotic fashion as the results about Kolmogorov complexity. In fact, Kolmogorov complexity coincides with predictive complexity for a particular loss function.

In this paper we present results for a class of bounded loss functions which are generalizations of the squared difference. We study relations between unconditional and conditional predictive complexities. The motivation for this study can be provided by the following practical problem. Suppose we have to predict a sequence of data $y = \{y_1, y_2, y_3, \ldots\}$ (say, prices of houses) given another sequence on-line $z = \{z_1, z_2, z_3, \ldots\}$ (say, a set of attributes of these houses) and there is third sequence $x = \{x_1, x_2, x_3, \ldots\}$ (which contains some other attribute). The question is: given sequences z and x on-line, how much better can sequence y be predicted than in the situation when only z is given? The sequence z can be considered as an oracle and all further results can be rewritten for the oracle case. Thus we will not mention z below. This problem justifies our interest in the comparison of minimal losses on y and on y given x, or in other words $KG(y)$ and $KG(y|x)$. The value $KG(x)$ is also important. A difference between $KG(y)$ and $KG(y|x)$ can be considered as an amount of information in x about y. We denote it as $IG(x : y)$ and call *amount of predictive information*.

At first, we prove a variant of triangle inequality (Proposition 4) to obtain an upper bound on $K(y)$. The main result of the paper, Theorem 2, implies that the upper bound is reached in a wide range of cases. In order to prove it, we describe an algorithm Φ (Theorem 1) which has some "expanding property": this algorithm transforms with positive probability a sequence x of given predictive complexity k into a sequence $\Phi(x)$ with predictive complexity $KG(\Phi(x)) \geq ck \log \frac{n}{k}$, where n is the length of x, c is a constant. This is impossible for Kolmogorov complexity $K(x)$, since for any computable mapping Φ, it satisfies the inequality $K(\Phi(x)) \leq K(x) + O(1)$. Theorem 3 is an interesting reformulation of the main result showing that pair can be can be predicted easier than its element.

The second group of results concerning predictive information is given in Section 4. We explore relations between four important values $IG(y : x)$, $IG(x : y)$, $KG(x)$ and $KG(y)$ in a limit form (Theorems 5, 6, 7). In particular, we prove that $IG(y : x)$ is non-commutative in a very strong sense.

2   Predictive Complexity

We consider only simplest case, where events are simple binary outcomes from $\{0,1\}$. Let us denote $\Xi_n = \{0,1\}^n$ and $\Xi = \cup_{n=0}^{\infty} \Xi_n$. We denote by $l(x)$ the length of a finite sequence $x \in \Xi$, $x^n = x_1 \dots x_n$ is its initial prefix of length n. By $\square$ we denote the empty sequence from Ξ. We write $x \subseteq y$ if $x = y^n$ for some $n \le l(y)$. We also will identify elements of Ξ and positive integer numbers in a natural fashion. It is important to consider the case when some *a priori* information is used in performing predictions. We consider a set of *signals* Δ. For simplicity we will consider the case $\Delta = \Xi$.

It is natural to suppose that all predictions are given according to a *prediction strategy* (or *prediction algorithm*) S. When performing prediction p_i the strategy S uses two input sequences, a sequence $x^{i-1} = x_1, x_2, \dots x_{i-1}$ of previous outcomes, and a sequence $y^i = y_1, y_2, \dots, y_i$ of signals, i.e. $p_i = S(x^{i-1}, y^i)$. The total loss suffered by S on a sequence x^n is represented

$$\text{Loss}_S(x^n|y^n) = \sum_{i=1}^{n} \lambda(x_i, S(x^{i-1}, y^i)).$$

The value $y^n = 0^n$, $n = 0, 1, \dots$, corresponds to the case when *a priori* information does not used (here by 0^n we denote the sequence of n zeros).

The value $\text{Loss}_S(x^n|y^n)$ can be interpreted as predictive complexity of x^n given y^n. This value, however, depends on S and it is unclear which S to choose. Levin [13], developing ideas of Kolmogorov and Solomonoff, suggested (for the logarithmic loss function) a very natural solution to the problem of existence of a smallest measure of predictive complexity. Vovk [9] extended these ideas in a more general setting for a class of mixable loss functions.

Let us fix $\eta > 0$ (the *learning rate*) and put $\beta = e^{-\eta} \in (0,1)$. A loss function (game) $\lambda(\sigma, \gamma)$ is called η-mixable if for any sequence of predictions $\gamma_1, \gamma_2, \dots$ and for any sequence of nonnegative weights $p_1, p_2, \dots$ with sum ≤ 1 a prediction $\hat{\gamma}$ exists such that

$$\lambda(\sigma, \hat{\gamma}) \le \log_\beta \sum_i p_i \beta^{\lambda(\sigma, \gamma_i)} \tag{1}$$

for all σ. The log-loss function is η-mixable for any $0 < \eta \le \ln 2$, and square loss function is also η-mixable for any $0 < \eta \le 2$ (see [8]).

A function $KG(x|y)$ is a *measure of predictive complexity* if the following two conditions hold:

- (i) $KG(\square|\square) = 0$ and for every x and y of equal length and each extension γ of y there exists a prediction p depending on x and $y\gamma$ such that inequality

$$KG(x\sigma|y\gamma) \ge KG(x|y) + \lambda(\sigma, p) \tag{2}$$

  holds for each σ.
- (ii) KG is *semicomputable from above*, which means that there exists a computable nondecreasing by t sequence of simple functions KG^t such that for every x and y it holds $KG(x|y) = \inf_t KG^t(x|y)$.

By a simple function we mean a function which takes rational values or $+\infty$ and equals $+\infty$ for almost all $x \in \Xi$.

Requirement (i) means that the measure of predictive complexity must be valid: there exists a prediction strategy that achieves it. Notice that if $\geq$ is replaced by $=$ in (2), the definition of a total loss function will be obtained. Requirement (ii) means that $KG(x|y)$ must be "computable in the limit".

The main advantage of such definition is that a semicomputable from above sequence $KG_i(x|y)$ of all measures of predictive complexity can be constructed. More precise, there exists a computable from i, t, x, y sequence $KG_i^t(x|y)$ of simple functions such that

- (iii) $KG_i^{t+1}(x|y) \leq KG_i^t(x|y)$ for all i, t, x;
- (iv) $KG_i(x|y) = \inf_t KG_i^t(x|y)$ for all i, x;
- (v) for each measure of predictive complexity $KG(x|y)$ there exists an i such that $KG(x|y) = KG_i(x|y)$ for all x and y. In particular, for any computable prediction strategy S there exists an i such that $\mathrm{Loss}_S(x|y) = KG_i(x|y)$ for all x and y.

Let us consider some analogy with Kolmogorov complexity which used computable methods of decoding of finite binary sequences. By this method F of decoding we can reconstruct any finite sequence x using its binary program p and some parameter y: $x = F(p, y)$. Each method of decoding F defines some measure of conditional complexity $K_F(x|y) = \min\{l(p) : F(p, y) = x\}$ of finite sequences x. It is easy to verify that this function is semicomputable from above. Kolmogorov's idea was to "mix" all these measures of complexity in a "universal" measure. A computable sequence F_i of all methods of decoding can be constructed by the methods of the theory of algorithms [6]. A universal method of decoding can be defined $U(\langle i, p, y \rangle) = F_i(p, y)$, where i is a program computing F_i and $\langle i, p, y \rangle$ is a suitable code of a triple (i, p, y). Then for any method of decoding F semicomputable from above it holds $K_U(x|y) \leq K_F(x|y) + O(1)$ for each x and y, where a constant $O(1)$ depends on F. We fix some $K_U(x|y)$, denote it $K(x|y)$, and call the conditional Kolmogorov complexity of a finite sequence x given a finite sequence y. Unconditional complexity is defined $K(x) = K(x|\square)$. For technical reason we consider prefix-free methods of decoding: for any (p, y) and (p', y') from the domain of F if $p \neq p'$ then $p \not\subseteq p'$ and $p' \not\subseteq p$. Then $\sum 2^{-K(x)} \leq 1$. In prefix-free case Kolmogorov complexity can be also defined analytically (see [5]).

$$KU(x|y) = \log_{1/2} \sum_{i=1}^{\infty} r_i 2^{-K_{F_i}(x|y)},$$

where $r_1, r_2, \ldots$ is a computable sequence of nonnegative weights with sum ≤ 1. For example, we can take $r_i = 2^{-i}$, $i = 1, 2, \ldots$.

Analogously the mixture of all measures of predictive complexity $KG_i(x|y)$ in the case of η-mixable loss function is defined

$$KG(x|y) = \log_\beta \sum_{i=1}^{\infty} r_i \beta^{KG_i(x|y)}, \tag{3}$$

where $r_i = 2^{-K(i)}$, $i = 1, 2, \ldots$. The following proposition asserts that the function $KG(x|y)$ is a measure of predictive complexity minimal up to an additive constant.

Proposition 1. *Let a loss function $\lambda(\omega, p)$ be computable and η-mixable for some $\eta > 0$. Then there exists a measure of predictive complexity $KG(x|y)$ such that for each measure of predictive complexity $KG_i(x|y)$*

$$KG(x|y) \leq KG_i(x|y) + (\ln 2/\eta)K(i) \qquad (4)$$

holds for all x, y, where $K(i)$ is the Kolmogorov prefix complexity of the program i enumerating KG_i from above, besides, a constant c exists such that $KG(x|y) \leq \mathrm{Loss}_S(x|y) + (\ln 2/\eta)(K(S) + c)$ holds for each computable prediction strategy S and each x, y [1].

In Vovk [10] (Section 7.6) it is proved that $KG(x|y)$ defined by (3) is a measure of predictive complexity. Inequality (4) is an easy consequence of (3). To prove the rest part of this proposition note that there exists a computable function $f(p)$ which transform any program p computing S into an enumerating program $i = f(p)$ such that $\mathrm{Loss}_S(x|y) = KG_i(x|y)$. We have also $K(i) = K(f(p)) \leq K(p) + c$, where c is a constant.

Let some η-mixable loss function $\lambda(\sigma, p)$ be given. Put

$$b = \inf_p \sup_\sigma \lambda(\sigma, p). \qquad (5)$$

We suppose that $b > 0$. We suppose also that the loss function is computable, and hence, it is continuous in p in the interval $[0, 1]$. We also suppose that the infimum in (5) is attained for some computable real number $\hat{p}$. For log-loss function $b = 1$, $\hat{p} = 1/2$ and $b = \frac{1}{4}$, $\hat{p} = 1/2$ in the case of squared difference.

We impose a very natural condition

$$\lambda(0, 0) = \lambda(1, 1) = 0, \qquad (6)$$

which holds in both cases of log-loss and square-loss functions. We also consider additional requirements on loss function by which square-loss function differs from log-loss function:

$$\lambda(0, 1) = \lambda(1, 0) = a. \qquad (7)$$

Now, when restrictions on a loss function were specified let us fix some $KG(x|y)$ satisfying conditions of Proposition 1 and call its value the conditional *predictive complexity* of x given y. In the case when y is trivial, i.e. consists only from zeros we consider (unconditional) predictive complexity $KG(x)$ of a sequence x.

Let us consider a set

$$A_{n,k} = \{y | l(y) = n, KG(y) \leq k\}. \qquad (8)$$

---

[1] We suppose that some universal programming language is fixed. Let p be any program which given x and a degree of accuracy ϵ computes a rational approximation of $S(x)$ with this accuracy. We denote by $K(S)$ the length of the shortest such p.

We denote by $\#A$ the cardinality of a finite set A. Tight upper and lower bounds of the number $\#A_{n,k}$ of all sequences of length n having predictive complexity $\leq k$ were obtained in [12]. Relations between Kolmogorov and predictive complexities also were obtained in that paper. Here we present simplified versions of these results which will be used in this paper.

Proposition 2. *There exists a constant c such that for all n and k*

$$\sum_{i\leq(k-c)/a}\binom{n}{i} \leq \#A_{n,k} \leq \sum_{i\leq k/b}\binom{n}{i}. \tag{9}$$

Proof. Let a sequence x of length n have no more than m ones. Consider prediction strategy $S(z) = 0$ for all z. Then by (6) and (7) there are at least $\sum_{i\leq m}\binom{n}{i}$ of x such that $KG(x) \leq \mathrm{Loss}_S(x)+c \leq am+c \leq k$, where c is a constant. Then $m \leq (k-c)/a$ and we obtain the left-hand side of the inequality (9).

To prove the right-hand side of the inequality (9) consider the (possibly incomputable) *universal* prediction strategy $\Lambda(x) = p$, where $p = p(x)$ is the prediction from the item (i) of definition of the measure of predictive complexity. By definition $\mathrm{Loss}_\Lambda(x) \leq KG(x)$ for each x. We consider a binary tree defined by the set Ξ of vertices with edges $(x, x0)$ and $(x, x1)$ for all $x \in \Xi$. By (5) for any x we have $\lambda(0, \Lambda(x)) > b$ or $\lambda(1, \Lambda(x)) \geq b$. By this property we assign new labelling to edges of the binary tree using letters A and B. We assign A to $(x, x0)$ and B to $(x, x1)$ if $\lambda(0, \Lambda(x)) \geq b$, and assign B to $(x, x0)$ and A to $(x, x1)$ otherwise. Evidently, two different sequences of length n have different labellings. For each edge $(x, x\sigma)$ labelled by A it holds $\lambda(\sigma, \Lambda(x)) \geq b$ and, hence, for any sequence x of length n having more than m As it holds $KG(x) \geq \mathrm{Loss}_\Lambda(x) \geq bm$. Therefore, $\#A_{n,k} \leq \sum_{i\leq k/b}\binom{n}{i}$. $\square$

Remember, that $K(x)$ is the Kolmogorov prefix complexity of x.

Proposition 3. *A positive constant c exists such that for all n and k such that $6b \leq k \leq \frac{bn}{2}$ inequality*

$$K(x) \leq \left(\frac{k}{b}+3\right)\log n - \frac{k}{b}\log\frac{k}{4b} + c \tag{10}$$

holds for all x of the length n satisfying $KG(x) \leq k$.

Proof. To prove inequality (10) let us consider the recursively enumerable set (8). We can specify any $x \in A_{n,k}$ by n, k and the ordinal number of x in the natural enumeration of $A_{n,k}$. Let $k \leq bn/2$. Then using an appropriate encoding of all triples of positive integer numbers we obtain for all $x \in A_{n,k}$

$$K(x) \leq \log\#A_{n,k} + 3\log n + \log k + c_1 \leq \tag{11}$$

$$\log\frac{k}{b}\binom{n}{k/b} + 3\log n + \log k + c \leq \tag{12}$$

$$\log\frac{k}{b}\left(\frac{en}{k/b}\right)^{k/b} + 3\log n + \log k + c \leq \tag{13}$$

$$\left(\frac{k}{b} + 3\right) \log n - \left(1 - \frac{2}{\log(k/b)}\right) \frac{k}{b} \log \frac{k}{b} + c' = \tag{14}$$

$$\left(\frac{k}{b} + 3\right) \log n - \frac{k}{b} \log \frac{k}{4b} + c', \tag{15}$$

where c and c' are positive constants and $k \geq 6b$.   □

3   Expanding Property

The following Proposition 4 is an analogue of the corresponding result for the prefix Kolmogorov complexity $K(x) \leq K(x|y) + K(y) + O(1)$ [5].

Proposition 4. *Positive constants c_1 and c_2 exist such that for all x and y of length n*

$$KG(x) \leq KG(x|y) + (\ln 2/\eta)K(y) + c_1 \leq \tag{16}$$

$$KG(x|y) + c_2 KG(y) \log \left(\frac{n}{KG(y)}\right). \tag{17}$$

Inequality (17) holds if $6b \leq KG(y) \leq bn/2$.

Proof. This proposition is a direct corollary of Proposition 1. For any finite sequence y define $\bar{y} = y0^\infty$. The measure of predictive complexity $S(x) = KG(x|\bar{y}^{l(x)})$ can be enumerated from below by a program depending from y. Then by (4) for any x such that $l(x) = l(y)$ it holds $KG(x) \leq KG(x|y) + (\ln 2/\eta)K(y) + c_1$, where c_1 is a positive constant. Applying the upper bound on $K(y)$ from Proposition 3 we obtain the needed result.   □

The following theorem shows that inequality (17) cannot be improved. We construct a computable mapping having some "expanding property": it transforms sequences of given predictive complexity into sequences of essentially bigger predictive complexity.

Let $C_{n,k}$ be a set of sequences y of the length n having k changes from 0 to 1 or from 1 to 0 (occurrences of combinations 01 and 10 in y); it is also convenient to consider a case $y_1 = 1$ (i.e. a case when y starts from 1) as a change.

Let us consider a computable predictive strategy S such that $S(\square) = 0$ and $S(x1) = 1$, $S(x0) = 0$ for all x. By (7) we have $\text{Loss}_S(y) \leq a(k+1)$ for each $y \in C_{n,k}$. Therefore, $KG(y) \leq ak + O(1)$ for each $y \in C_{n,k}$. Let $\lceil r \rceil$ be the least integer number s such that $s \geq r$.

Theorem 1. *For any n and $k \leq \frac{n}{2}$ a computable mapping Φ from $C_{n,k}$ to a subtree $\{x|l(x) = n, 0^{n-m} \subseteq x\}$, where $m = \lceil \log 4^k \binom{n}{k} \rceil$, exists such that for a portion $\geq 1/2$ of all $y \in C_{n,k}$ the output $x = \Phi(y)$ satisfies*

$$KG(x) \geq \frac{b}{20} \log \binom{n}{k}, KG(x|y) = O(\log n). \tag{18}$$

We have also $KG(y) \leq ak + O(1)$ for each $y \in C_{n,k}$. In the case $k = k(n) = o(n)$ the factor $b/20$ in (18) can be replaced on $b/2$.

Sketch of the proof. We construct a mapping Φ which compresses the set $C_{n,k}$ into the set $\{x|l(x) = n, 0^{n-m} \subseteq x\}$, where $m = \lceil \log 4^k \binom{n}{k} \rceil$, such that the density of of the image of Φ in this set is sufficiently large, namely, 4^{-k}. We prove also a variant of "incompressibility lemma", from which follows that the large portion of this image consists of elements x of predictive complexity $KG(x)$ satisfying (18) (see Section 5.1 for a detailed construction). $\qquad\square$

In the following theorems we present results of Proposition 4 and Theorem 1 in an asymptotic form. For any functions $\alpha(n)$ and $\beta(n)$ the expression $\alpha(n) = \Theta(\beta(n))$ means that there exist constants c_1 and c_2 such that $c_1\beta(n) \le \alpha(n) \le c_2\beta(n)$ holds for all n. The expression $\alpha(n) = \Omega(\beta(n))$ means that there exists a constant c_1 such that $\alpha(n) \ge c_1\beta(n)$ for all n.

Theorem 2. *Let a function $k(n)$ be unbounded, $\nu(n) = \Omega(\log n)$, and $k(n) = O(n)$, $\nu(n) = O(n)$. Then*

$$\sup_{x:\exists y(KG(y)\le k(n), KG(x|y)\le\nu(n))} KG(x) = \Theta\left(\nu(n) + k(n)\log\left(\frac{n}{k(n)}\right)\right) \quad (19)$$

Proof. The part $\le$ follows from Propositions 3 and 4. In case $\nu(n) \ge k(n)\log\left(\frac{n}{k(n)}\right)$ the part $\ge$ of (19) is evident. Otherwise, the statement follows from Theorem 1. $\qquad\square$

For any $x = x_1\ldots x_n$ and $y = y_1\ldots y_n$ we consider "a pair" $[y, x] = y_1x_1\ldots y_nx_n$.

Theorem 3. *Let $k(n) = \Omega(\log n)$, $\nu(n) = \Omega(k(n))$, $k(n) = O(n)$ and $\nu(n) = O(n)$. Then*

$$\sup_{x:\exists y(KG(y)\le k(n), KG([y,x])\le\nu(n))} KG(x) = \Theta\left(\nu(n) + k(n)\log\left(\frac{n}{k(n)}\right)\right). \quad (20)$$

Proof. In case $\nu(n) \ge k(n)\log\left(\frac{n}{k(n)}\right)$ the part $\ge$ of (20) is evident. Otherwise, we use Theorem 1 and its proof. Let us consider the mapping Φ from the proof of Theorem 1 (see Section 5.1) and the sequences y and $x = \Phi(y)$ satisfying the conditions of this proposition. Define a computable prediction strategy S by $S(y_1x_1\ldots y_{i-1}x_{i-1}y_i) = \Phi(y^i)_i = x_i$, (see also the end of the proof of Theorem 1 in Section 5.1), and $S(y_1x_1\ldots y_ix_i) = 0$. This strategy predicts each even bit precisely and outputs 0 as prediction for any odd bit. Then by (7) we have $\mathrm{Loss}_S([y, x]) \le ak(n)$ and, therefore,

$$KG([y, x]) \le ak(n) + (\ln 2/\eta)K(S) \le ak(n) + (2\ln 2/\eta)\log n \le c_1\nu(n) \quad (21)$$

for some constant c_1. By Theorem 1 it holds $KG(y) \le c_2\log n \le c_3k(n)$ for all y, where c_2, c_3 are constants. The part $\ge$ of (20) follows from these inequalities after normalizing of $k(n)$ and $\nu(n)$.

The $\le$ part of (20) follows from Proposition 4 and an obvious inequality $KG(x|y) \le KG([y, x]) + c$, where c is a positive constant. $\qquad\square$

4 Predictive Information

The *amount of predictive information* in a sequence y about a sequence x of the same length in the process of on-line prediction was defined by Vovk [10]

$$IG(y : x) = KG(x) - KG(x|y). \tag{22}$$

In this section we explore relations between four important values $IG(y : x)$, $IG(x : y)$, $KG(x)$ and $KG(y)$ in a limit form. These results are mainly based on the construction of Theorem 1.

The next Theorem 4 implies that predictive information is non-commutative in a strongest possible sense. Define

$$g_1(n) = \sup_{l(x)=l(y)=n} (IG(x : y) - IG(y : x)). \tag{23}$$

Theorem 4. *It holds* $g_1(n) = bn + O(1)$.

Proof. For any sequence $x = x_1 \ldots x_n$ define its left shift $Tx = x_2 \ldots x_n 0$. The proof of theorem is based on the following simple lemma.

Lemma 1. *It holds*

$$KG(x|Tx) = O(1), KG(Tx) = KG(Tx|x) + O(1) \tag{24}$$

The proof of this lemma is given in Section 5.2.

To prove the right-hand side inequality of Theorem 4 take $y = Tx$. Then by Lemma 1 a positive constant c exists such that

$$IG(Tx : x) = KG(x) - KG(x|Tx) \geq KG(x) - c$$
$$IG(x : Tx) = KG(Tx) - KG(Tx|x) \leq c$$

for all x. Using the definition (5) of b and the diagonal argument it easy to construct a sequence x of length n such that $KG(x) \geq bn$. From this the right-hand side of Theorem 4 follows. The left-hand side inequality of Theorem 4 follows from inequalities $IG(x : y) - IG(y : x) \leq KG(y) \leq bl(y) + c$ for all x and y, where c is a positive constant. The last inequality can be easily proved using a computable prediction strategy which always predicts $\hat{p}$, where $\hat{p}$ minimizes the condition (5). $\square$

Let us define

$$g_2(n) = \sup_{l(x)=l(y)=n, 6b \leq KG(y)} \frac{IG(y : x)}{KG(y)}. \tag{25}$$

Main results of Section 3 can be summarized in the following theorem.

Theorem 5. *It holds* $g_2(n) = \Theta(\log n)$.

Proof. The right-hand inequality follows directly from (17). The left-hand inequality can be derived from Theorem 1. Its enough to let $k = \sqrt{n}$.   □

Let us define also

$$g_3(n) = \sup_{l(x)=l(y)=n, 0<KG(x)} \frac{IG(y:x)}{KG(x)}. \tag{26}$$

Theorem 6. *It holds* $\lim_{n\to\infty} g_3(n) = 1$.

Proof. This relation follows from representation

$$g_3(n) = \sup_{l(x)=l(y)=n, 0<KG(x)} \left(1 - \frac{KG(x|y)}{KG(x)}\right)$$

and from Theorem 1, where we let $k = n/4$.   □

Theorem 7. *Let $k(n) \le bn$ for all n. Then a constant c exists such that*

$$\sup_{(x,y):l(x)=l(y)=n, KG(y)\le k(n)} IG(y:x) = \Theta\left(k(n)\log\left(\frac{n}{k(n)}\right)\right) \tag{27}$$

$$\sup_{(x,y):l(x)=l(y)=n, KG(x)\le k(n)} IG(y:x) = k(n) + O(1) \tag{28}$$

$$\sup_{(x,y):l(x)=l(y)=n, IG(x:y)\le c} IG(y:x) = \Theta(n) \tag{29}$$

Proof. The right-hand part of (27) follows from Proposition 4. The left-hand part of (27) follows from Theorem 1. To prove (28) put $x = y$ and note that $KG(x|x) = O(1)$. Relation (29) follows from the proof of Theorem 4.   □

Acknowledgements

Authors are grateful to Volodya Vovk for useful discussions and for his suggestions about formulating of main results of the paper. The first author was supported by the EPSRC grant GR/R46670/01. The second author was supported by RFBR grant 01-01-01028.

5   Appendix

5.1   Proof of Theorem 1

For any n and any sequence z of the length $\le n$ by a subtree $\Xi_n(z)$ we mean a set

$$\Xi_n(z) = \{y | l(y) = n, z \subseteq y\}.$$

The height of the subtree is the number $m = n - l(z)$.

The main technical result of this paper is a construction of a mapping Φ from $C_{n,k}$ into a subtree $\Xi_n(0^l)$ of height $m = \lceil \log 4^k \binom{n}{k} \rceil$, where $l = n - m$.

Let $y * y'$ denotes the maximal joint prefix of y and y', i.e. a sequence z of maximal length such that $z \subseteq y$ and $z \subseteq y'$. The main requirement to Φ is that

$$l(\Phi(y) * \Phi(y')) \geq l(y * y') \tag{30}$$

for all $y, y' \in C_{n,k}$.

We construct the mapping Φ as a result of a recursive procedure COMP(n, k, σ), where n and k be positive integer numbers and $\sigma = 0$ or 1.

Procedure COMP(n, k, σ).

For any n the procedure COMP$(n, 0, 0)$ returns the identical mapping Φ on the set $\{0^n\}$, the procedures COMP$(n, 1, 1)$ and COMP$(n, 0, 1)$ return the identical mapping Φ on the set $\{1^n\}$.

Let $C_{n,k}^\sigma$ be the set of all sequences from $C_{n,k}$ starting from σ ($\sigma = 0, 1$).

If $k > 0$ the procedure returns a mapping Φ from $C_{n,k}^\sigma$ into a subtree $\Xi_n(\sigma^l)$ for some l. Without loss of generality we suppose that $\sigma = 0$.

In the following we will construct this mapping Φ by series of subsequent reassignments of the values of Φ. We start with the mapping Φ identical on $C_{n,k}^0$. We will do also a series of subsequent transformations of subtrees of the initial tree Ξ_n.

Consider the *base* which is a sequence of n zeros 0^n (in the case $\sigma = 1$ the base is a sequence of n ones 1^n). There are $n - 1$ subtrees $\Xi_n(0^i 1)$ on the base, $i = 1, \ldots, n - 1$. Each sequence $x \in C_{n,k}^0$ of length n belongs to one of such trees $\Xi_n(0^i 1)$. We call them *basic subtrees*.

For each $i = 1, \ldots, n - 1$ we apply the procedure COMP$(n - i, k - 1, 1)$. For each i the procedure returns a subtree $\Xi_{n-i}(1^{k_i})$ and a mapping Φ_i from $C_{n-i,k-1}^1$ into this subtree.

Induction hypothesis: for each i the set $\Phi_i(C_{n-i,k-1}^1) \cap \Xi_{n-i}(1^{k_i})$ occupies at least $4^{-(k-1)}$ portion of all sequences of basic subtree $\Xi_{n-i}(1^{k_i})$. In other words,

$$\#\Phi_i(C_{n-i,k-1}^1 \cap \Xi_{n-i}(1^{k_i})) \geq 4^{-(k-1)} \#\Xi_{n-i}(1^{k_i}).$$

There is a natural one-to-one correspondence between sequences $0^i 1x \in C_{n,k}^0$ and sequences $x \in C_{n-i,k-1}^1$. Then we can redefine Φ on $C_{n,k}^0$ such that for each i and for each $1x \in C_{n-i,k-1}^1$ it holds $\Phi(0^i 1x) = 0^i \Phi_i(1x)$.

Denote $A_i = \Xi_n(0^i 1^{k_i})$ and call it the compressed basic subtree. By the induction hypothesis we obtain that $\Phi(C_{n,k}^0) \cap (\cup_i A_i)$ occupies at least $4^{-(k-1)}$ portion of all sequences from $\cup_i A_i$.

At the current step of induction we will change this assignment of Φ according instructions given below.

Each initial basic subtree $\Xi_n(0^i 1)$, $1 \leq i \leq n-1$ contains (before applying the procedure COMP) a subtree $T = \Xi_n(0^i 11)$ isomorphic to its upper neighbour $\Xi_n(0^{i+1} 1)$. This subtree T will be transformed by the procedure COMP as a part of $\Xi_n(0^i 1)$ on the previous inductive step into a subtree T' of corresponding resulting basic subtree $A_i = \Xi_n(0^i 1^{k_i})$. The height of A_i is equal to $h_i = n - i - k_i$.

For each i if $h_i < h_{i+1}$ then replace A_{i+1} on the corresponding subtree T' of A_i. Doing these replacements we simultaneously changing corresponding assignments of the values of Φ. This process provides us that $h_i \geq h_{i+1}$ for all i.

Now we will transform all compressed basic subtrees A_i into a resulting compressed subtree $\Xi_n(0^l)$ and will change the corresponding assignments of Φ such that the density of the image of Φ in the resulting subtree $\Xi_n(0^l)$ will be at least 4^{-k}. The reconstruction consists of subsequent application of the following two operations on subtrees of a binary tree.

1) *Joining to the nearest upper neighbour.* Suppose that there are at least two basic subtrees of type $\Xi_n(0^i1^{3+s_i})$ and $\Xi_n(0^{i+1}1^{2+s_i})$ of the same height h, where $s_i \geq 0$. We transform each assignment of type $\Phi(y) = 0^i1^{3+s_i}u$ to $\Phi(y) = 0^{i+1}1^{1+s_i}0u$, i.e. move subtree $\Xi_n(0^i1^{3+s_i})$ to $\Xi_n(0^{i+1}1^{1+s_i}0)$. We will apply this transformation only to the first (left) pair of the basic subtrees of height h. Then the height of the resulting subtree will be $h+1$ and will not exceed the height of the previous basic subtree.

2) *Moving up to the nearest upper free vertex on the base.* Suppose that there is a basic subtree $\Xi_n(0^i1^2)$ and there is no basic subtree of type $\Xi_n(0^{i+1}1)$. In this case we change each assignment $\Phi(y) = 0^i1^2u$ to $\Phi(y) = 0^{i+1}1u$, i.e. we move basic subtree $\Xi_n(0^i1^2u)$ to $\Xi_n(0^{i+1}1u)$.

By definition, after these transformations, the image of Φ still occupies at least $4^{-(k-1)}$ portion of all sequences from each transformed basic subtree.

Given initial compressed basic subtrees we transform them by applying these two operations as many times as possible. Suppose that among final basic subtrees there is a basic subtree of type $\Xi(0^i1^{j+3})$, where $j \geq 0$. Then there are only two possibilities. The first one is that there is no basic subtree of type $\Xi_n(0^{i+1}1^s)$, where $s \geq 1$, and then the operation 2) must be applied. The second one is that there is a subtree $\Xi_n(0^{i+1}1^{2+s_i})$ (and there is no subtree $\Xi_n(0^{i+1}10)$). In this case the operation 1) must be applied. No basic subtree of type $\Xi_n(0^{i+1}1)$ exists, since otherwise the property $h_i \geq h_{i+1}$ for heights of basic subtrees will be failed. The contradiction obtained shows that there is no basic subtree of type $\Xi(0^i1^{j+3})$ after all transformations.

As a result we obtain the base 0^n and a sequence of the new basic subtrees on it of the type $\Xi_n(0^i1^j)$, where $i \geq 1$ and $j = 1$ or $j = 2$. We obtained also a new assignment to values of Φ.

Consider the first basic subtree B of maximal height. Since, the operations 1) and 2) cannot be applied to B, it is of the form $\Xi_n(0^l1)$ or $\Xi_n(0^l11)$, where $l \geq 1$. Then the portion of sequences of B among all sequences of $\Xi_n(0^l)$ is at least $\frac{1}{4}$. Therefore, the portion of sequences in $\Xi_n(0^l)$ which are of a form $\Phi(y)$, where $y \in C^0_{n,k}$, can decrease no more than in 4 times, and so it is $\geq \frac{1}{4}4^{-(k-1)} = 4^{-k}$.

We declare the mapping Φ and the subtree $\Xi_n(0^l)$ as the results returning by procedure COMP$(n, k, 0)$. We also proved that the induction hypothesis holds for these results.

End of the procedure COMP.

Let Φ and $\Xi_n(0^l)$ be outputs of COMP$(n, k, 0)$. Since the image $\Phi(C_{n,k})$ contains $\binom{n}{k}$ sequences in the binary tree $\Xi_n(0^l)$ by density condition this tree have $\leq 4^k\binom{n}{k}$ sequences.

The following lemma will be used to prove the existence of elements of big predictive complexity in a set of given cardinality.

Lemma 2. *For any n let $m < n$ and z be a sequence of the length $n - m$. Then for any set $W \subseteq \{x | l(x) = n, z \subseteq x\}$ for at least $1/2$ portion of all $x \in W$ it holds*

$$KG(x) \geq bl_{max},$$

where l_{max} is the maximal integer number l such that $l \leq \frac{m}{2}$ and

$$H\left(\frac{l}{m}\right) \leq \frac{\log \#W}{m} - \frac{\log m}{m} - \frac{1}{m}, \tag{31}$$

where $H(p) = -p \log p - (1 - p) \log(1 - p)$ is the Shannon entropy.

Proof. Let $\Lambda(x)$ be the universal predictive strategy as in the proof of Proposition 2 such that $\text{Loss}_\Lambda(x) \leq KG(x)$ for all x. By definition of b (see (5)) for any x we have $\lambda(0, \Lambda(x)) \geq b$ or $\lambda(1, \Lambda(x)) \geq b$. Using this property we assign the labelling to edges using letters A and B as in the proof of Proposition 2. Then for any sequence x of the length m having more than k As it holds $\text{Loss}_\Lambda(x) \geq bk$.

Now, to estimate from below the maximal total loss of Λ on sequences from W we must estimate from below the maximal number of As occurring in sequences from W. This estimate l satisfies inequality

$$\sum_{i=1}^{l} \binom{m}{i} < \frac{1}{2} \#W. \tag{32}$$

The inequality (32) follows from $l\binom{m}{l} < \frac{1}{2}\#W$. Since the elementary inequality

$$\binom{m}{l} \leq 2^{mH(\frac{l}{m})}$$

holds (see [3], Section 6.1), the inequality (32) also follows from

$$l2^{mH(\frac{l}{m})} \leq \frac{1}{2}\#W. \tag{33}$$

This inequality follows from

$$H\left(\frac{l}{m}\right) \leq \frac{\log \#W}{m} - \frac{\log m}{m} - \frac{1}{m}. \tag{34}$$

Hence, we have $KG(x) \geq bl$ for at least $1/2$ portion of all $x \in W$, where l is the maximal number satisfying (34). $\square$

To apply Lemma 2 get

$$m = \lceil \log 4^k \binom{n}{k} \rceil,$$

$$W = \Phi(C_{n,k}).$$

We have $\#W = \binom{n}{k}$. We must find maximal l such that the inequality

$$H\left(\frac{l}{m}\right) \leq \frac{\log \binom{n}{k}}{2k + \log \binom{n}{k}} - \frac{\log m}{m} - \frac{1}{m} \tag{35}$$

holds. It holds $\binom{n}{k} \geq 2^k$ if $k \leq \frac{n}{2}$. Then since $\log \binom{n}{k} \geq k$, the first term of (35) is bigger than $\frac{1}{3}$. Hence, for m sufficiently large it is sufficient to find l such that

$$H\left(\frac{l}{m}\right) \leq \frac{3}{10}. \tag{36}$$

It is easy to verify by table values of Shannon entropy that the inequality (36) wittingly holds if

$$\frac{l}{m} \leq \frac{1}{20}$$

and so, we can take estimate

$$l_{max} = \frac{m}{20}.$$

By Lemma 2 an x of the length n exists such that

$$KG(x) \geq \frac{b}{20}\left(2k + \log \binom{n}{k}\right) \geq \frac{b}{20} \log \binom{n}{k}.$$

Let $\Phi(y) = x$. By the prefix property (30) of mapping Φ each prefix x^i of length i can be recovered from a prefix y^i of length i. Hence, a prediction strategy S exists which computes the i-th member of x given $y^i = y_1 \ldots y_i$. By definition we have $\text{Loss}_S(x|y) = 0$. This predictive strategy S is trivially defined by the mapping Φ given n and k as parameters. Hence, by (4) we have $KG(x|y) \leq (2\ln 2/\eta)\log n$ for all sufficiently large n. The proof of the theorem is completed.

5.2 Proof of Lemma 1

To prove the first part of (24) consider a computable prediction strategy S such that for any sequences x and y of length $n \geq 2$ it holds $S(x|y) = y_{n-1}$ (for $n = 1$ define $S(x|y) = 0$). Then $\text{Loss}_S(x|Tx) \leq b$ for each x, and by definition $KG(x|Tx) \leq b + c$ hold for all x, where c is a positive constant c.

Let us prove the second part of (24). $KG(Tx|x) \leq KG(Tx) + O(1)$ by definition. To prove the converse inequality define a function $S(u)$ using an idea of Vovk's $[8]$ aggregating algorithm.

$$S(u) = \log_\beta(2^{-1}\beta^{KG(u|0u)} + 2^{-1}\beta^{KG(u|1u)}). \tag{37}$$

We show that $S(u)$ is a measure of predictive complexity. Indeed, for any σ

$$S(u\sigma) - S(u) = \log_\beta \sum_{i=0}^{1} 2^{-1}\beta^{KG(u\sigma|iu)} - \log_\beta \sum_{i=0}^{1} 2^{-1}\beta^{KG(u|iu)} =$$

$$\log_\beta \sum_{i=0}^{1} q_i \beta^{KG(u\sigma|iu)-KG(u|iu)} \geq \log_\beta \sum_{i=0}^{1} 2^{-1}\beta^{\lambda(\sigma,\hat{p}(iu))} \geq \lambda(\sigma, \hat{p}(u)),$$

where

$$q_i = \frac{2^{-1}\beta^{KG(u|iu)}}{\sum_{j=0}^{1} 2^{-1}\beta^{KG(u|ju)}},$$

$i = 0, 1$, and predictions $\hat{p}(iu)$ and $\hat{p}(u)$ exist by η-mixability property of the loss function $\lambda(\sigma, p)$. By definition (37) of $S(u)$ we have for $i = 0, 1$

$$S(u) \leq KG(u|iu) + (\ln 2/\eta)$$

for all u. Hence, by definition

$$KG(Tx) \leq KG(Tx|x) + c$$

for all x, where c is a positive constant.

References

1. Haussler, D., Kivinen, J., Warmuth, M. K. (1994) Tight worst-case loss bounds for predicting with expert advice. Technical Report UCSC-CRL-94-36, University of California at Santa Cruz, revised December 1994. Short version in P. Vitányi, editor, *Computational Learning Theory*, Lecture Notes in Computer Science, volume 904, pages 69–83, Springer, Berlin, 1995. 90

2. Cesa-Bianchi, N., Freund, Y., Helmbold, D. P., Haussler, D., Schapire, R. E., Warmuth, M. K. (1997) How to use expert advice. *Journal of the ACM*, 44, 427–485 90

3. Cormen, H., Leiserson, E., Rivest, R (1990) *Introduction to Algorithms*. New York: McGraw Hill. 102

4. Kalnishkan, Y. (1999) General linear relations among different types of predictive complexity. In. *Proc. 10th international Conference on Algorithmic Learning Theory–ALT '99, v. 1720 of Lecture Notes in Artificial Intelligence*, pp. 323–334, Springer–Verlag.

5. Li, M., Vitányi, P. (1997) *An Introduction to Kolmogorov Complexity and Its Applications*. Springer, New York, 2nd edition. 93, 96

6. Rogers, H. (1967) Theory of recursive functions and effective computability, New York: McGraw Hill. 93

7. Vovk, V. (1990) Aggregating strategies. In M. Fulk and J. Case, editors, *Proceedings of the 3rd Annual Workshop on Computational Learning Theory*, pages 371–383, San Mateo, CA, 1990. Morgan Kaufmann.

8. Vovk, V. (1998) A game of prediction with expert advice. *J. Comput. Syst. Sci.*, 56:153–173. 90, 92, 103

9. Vovk, V., Gammerman, A. (1999) Complexity estimation principle, *The Computer Journal, 42:4*, 318–322. 92

10. Vovk, V., Watkins, C. J. H. C. (1998) Universal portfolio selection, *Proceedings of the 11th Annual Conference on Computational Learning Theory*, 12–23. 90, 94, 98

11. V'yugin, V. V. (1999) Does snooping help? Technical report No CLRC-TR-99-06, December 1999, Computer Learning Research Centre, Royal Holloway, University of London. 91

12. Vyugin, M. V., V'yugin, V. V. (2001) Non-linear inequalities between Kolmogorov and predictive complexities, In Proc. Twelfth International Conference on Algorithmic Learning Theory–ALT '01, 190-204. 95

13. Zvonkin, A. K., Levin, L. A. (1970) The complexity of finite objects and the algorithmic concepts of information and randomness, *Russ. Math. Surv.* **25**, 83–124. 92

14. Yamanishi, K. (1995) Randomized approximate aggregating strategies and their applications to prediction and discrimination, in *Proceedings, 8th Annual ACM Conference on Computational Learning Theory*, 83–90, Assoc. Comput. Mach., New York. 90

Mixability and the Existence
of Weak Complexities

Yuri Kalnishkan and Michael V. Vyugin

Department of Computer Science, Royal Holloway, University of London
Egham, Surrey, TW20 0EX, United Kingdom
{yura,misha}@cs.rhul.ac.uk

Abstract. This paper investigates the behaviour of the constant $c(\beta)$ from the Aggregating Algorithm. Some conditions for mixability are derived and it is shown that for many non-mixable games $c(\beta)$ still converges to 1. The condition $c(\beta) \to 1$ is shown to imply the existence of weak predictive complexity and it is proved that many games specify complexity up to $\sqrt{n}$.

1   Introduction

In this paper we consider on-line prediction protocols. An on-line prediction algorithm $\mathfrak{A}$ receives elements of a sequence one by one and tries to predict each element before it actually sees it. The discrepancy between the prediction and the outcome is measured by a loss function and loss over several trials sums up to the total loss $\text{Loss}_{\mathfrak{A}}$. A particular environment of this kind is called a game.

Prediction with expert advice (see [CBFH+97, HKW98, LW94]) is an important problem in this prediction model. Suppose that there are N experts $\mathcal{E}^{(1)}, \mathcal{E}^{(2)}, \ldots, \mathcal{E}^{(N)}$ working according to the same on-line protocol. Their predictions are available to $\mathfrak{A}$, which observes them each time before making its own prediction. The problem is to suggest a method for $\mathfrak{A}$ to achieve loss comparable to that of the best expert. The Aggregating Algorithm (AA) described in [Vov90, Vov98] provides a fairly general solution to this problem. If $\mathfrak{A}$ follows the AA, its loss satisfies

$$\text{Loss}_{\mathfrak{A}} \leq c(\beta) \, \text{Loss}_{\mathcal{E}_{\text{best}}} + \frac{c(\beta)}{\ln(1/\beta)} \ln N \;,$$

where $\text{Loss}_{\mathcal{E}_{\text{best}}}$ is the loss of the best expert and $c(\beta)$ is some constant depending on the parameter $\beta \in (0, 1)$ accepted by the AA. It can be shown that the AA is optimal in some sense.

The constant $c(\beta)$ plays a very important role since it determines the asymptotic behaviour of the cumulative loss $\text{Loss}_{\mathfrak{A}}$. Our goal is to investigate the dependence between the prediction environment and properties of $c(\beta)$, i.e., to describe how the loss function determines $c(\beta)$.

If $c(\beta) = 1$ for some $\beta \in (0, 1)$, the learning algorithm predicts nearly as well as the best expert. Games with this property are called mixable. In this paper

J. Kivinen and R. H. Sloan (Eds.): COLT 2002, LNAI 2375, pp. 105–120, 2002.
© Springer-Verlag Berlin Heidelberg 2002

we formulate a criterion of mixability for games with smooth loss functions. If the loss function is bounded, our criterion leads to a series of simple and natural conditions. If the game is not mixable, i.e., $c(\beta)$ does not take the value 1, it is still often possible to conclude that $c(\beta) \to 1$ as $\beta \to 1-$, e.g., this is true for all games with bounded loss functions and convex sets of superpredictions. If $\mathfrak{G}$ satisfies certain conditions, the rate of convergence can be estimated. We show that for a wide class of games $c(\beta) = 1 + O(\ln(1/\beta))$ as $\beta \to 1-$.

Mixable games have an interesting property. They define predictive complexities. The concept of predictive complexity introduced in [VW98] is a natural development of the theory of prediction with expert advice. Predictive complexity bounds the loss of every algorithm from below. Generally this bound does not correspond to the loss of an algorithm but it is optimal 'in the limit'. Thus it is an intrinsic measure of 'learnability' of a finite sequence. It is similar to Kolmogorov complexity, which is a measure of the descriptive complexity of a string independent of a particular description method.

The result about the convergence of $c(\beta)$ allows us to construct weaker predictive complexities for non-mixable games. Unlike standard predictive complexity, which is defined up to a constant, these complexities are defined up to the term of the order $\sqrt{|x|}$, where $|x|$ is the length of a string x. If $c(\beta) = 1 + O(\ln(1/\beta))$ as $\beta \to 1-$, then the game has complexity defined up to $\sqrt{n}$.

We also discuss the situation for unbounded games. Some of our results can be extended to unbounded games but the straightforward generalisation fails. We show that for a wide class of unbounded games with smooth loss functions and convex sets of superpredictions $c(\beta) \equiv +\infty$.

2   Preliminaries

2.1   On-Line Prediction

A *game* $\mathfrak{G}$ is a triple $(\mathbb{B}, [0,1], \lambda)$, where $\mathbb{B} = \{0,1\}$ is an *outcome space*[1], $[0,1]$ is a *prediction space*, and $\lambda : \mathbb{B} \times [0,1] \to [0,+\infty]$ is a *loss function*. We suppose that λ is continuous w.r.t. the extended topology of $[-\infty, +\infty]$ and computable. The *square-loss* game with $\lambda(\omega, \gamma) = (\omega - \gamma)^2$ and the *logarithmic* game with

$$\lambda(\omega, \gamma) = \begin{cases} -\log(1-\gamma) & \text{if } \omega = 0 \\ -\log \gamma & \text{if } \omega = 1 \end{cases}$$

are examples of games.

A prediction algorithm $\mathfrak{A}$ works according to the following protocol:

```
FOR t = 1, 2, ...
    (1) 𝔄 chooses a prediction γₜ ∈ Γ
    (2) 𝔄 observes the actual outcome ωₜ ∈ Ω
    (3) 𝔄 suffers loss λ(ωₜ, γₜ)
END FOR.
```

---

[1] In this paper we restrict ourselves to binary games of this kind. A more general definition is possible.

Over the first T trials, $\mathfrak{A}$ suffers the total loss

$$\mathrm{Loss}_{\mathfrak{A}}^{\mathfrak{G}}(\omega_1, \omega_2, \ldots, \omega_T) = \sum_{t=1}^{T} \lambda(\omega_t, \gamma_t) \ .$$

By definition, put $\mathrm{Loss}_{\mathfrak{A}}(\Lambda) = 0$, where Λ denotes the empty string.

In the problem of prediction with expert advice we have a pool of N experts $\mathcal{E}^{(1)}, \mathcal{E}^{(2)}, \ldots, \mathcal{E}^{(N)}$ working according to the same protocol. No other assumptions is made about them, e.g., they do not have to be computable or independent. On trial t they output predictions $\gamma_t^{(1)}, \gamma_t^{(2)}, \ldots, \gamma_t^{(N)}$ and these predictions become available to $\mathfrak{A}$.

The Aggregating Algorithm (AA) is a method of merging experts' predictions. It accepts a parameter $\beta \in (0, 1)$ and its behaviour is determined by the value $c(\beta)$ specified by the game. By definition, let $c(\beta)$ be the infimum of all c satisfying the following condition: for every finite array of predictions $\gamma^{(1)}, \gamma^{(2)}, \ldots, \gamma^{(n)} \in [0, 1]$ and weights $p_1, p_2, \ldots, p_n \in [0, 1]$ such that $p_1 + p_2 + \ldots + p_n = 1$, there exists $\gamma^* \in [0, 1]$ such that $\lambda(0, \gamma^*) \leq c \log_\beta \sum_{i=1}^{n} p_i \beta^{\lambda(0, \gamma^{(i)})}$ and $\lambda(1, \gamma^*) \leq c \log_\beta \sum_{i=1}^{n} p_i \beta^{\lambda(1, \gamma^{(i)})}$. The work of AA is described in [Vov98]. The following theorem assesses its performance.

Proposition 1 ([Vov90, Vov98]). *Let* $\mathfrak{G} = (\mathbb{B}, [0, 1], \lambda)$ *be a game where* $\lambda :$ $\mathbb{B} \times [0, 1] \to [0, +\infty]$ *is a continuous function such that*

- *there is* $\gamma \in [0, 1]$ *such that* $\lambda(0, \gamma), \lambda(1, \gamma) < +\infty$ *and*
- *there is no* $\gamma \in [0, 1]$ *such that such that* $\lambda(0, \gamma) = \lambda(1, \gamma) = 0$.

Then

(i) *For every* $\beta \in (0, 1)$, *every finite set of experts* $\mathcal{E}^{(1)}, \mathcal{E}^{(2)}, \ldots, \mathcal{E}^{(N)}$, *and every finite sequence* $\omega_1, \omega_2, \ldots, \omega_n \in \mathbb{B}$ *we have*

$$\mathrm{Loss}_{\mathfrak{A}}^{\mathfrak{G}}(\omega_1, \omega_2, \ldots, \omega_n) \leq c(\beta) \, \mathrm{Loss}_{\mathcal{E}_i}(\omega_1, \omega_2, \ldots, \omega_n) + \frac{c(\beta)}{\ln(1/\beta)} \ln N$$

for every $i = 1, 2, \ldots, N$, *provided* $\mathfrak{A}$ *has access to experts' predictions and uses the AA with the parameter* β.

(ii) *If there is a method of merging experts predictions and positive constants* c, a *such that by following this method* $\mathfrak{A}$ *achieves*

$$\mathrm{Loss}_{\mathfrak{A}}^{\mathfrak{G}}(\omega_1, \omega_2, \ldots, \omega_n) \leq c \, \mathrm{Loss}_{\mathcal{E}_i}(\omega_1, \omega_2, \ldots, \omega_n) + a \ln N$$

for all $i = 1, 2, \ldots, N$, *every finite set of experts* $\mathcal{E}^{(1)}, \mathcal{E}^{(2)}, \ldots, \mathcal{E}^{(N)}$, *and every finite sequence* $\omega_1, \omega_2, \ldots, \omega_n \in \mathbb{B}$, *then* $c \geq c(\beta)$ *and* $a \geq c(\beta)/\ln(1/\beta)$ *for some* $\beta \in (0, 1)$.

It is easy to see that $c(\beta) \geq 1$. A game is called β-*mixable* if $c(\beta) = 1$. A game is *mixable* if it is β-mixable for some $\beta \in (0, 1)$. The square-loss game and the logarithmic game introduced above are mixable (see [Vov90]).

2.2   Predictive Complexities

The theory of the AA suggests the following idea. If we merge all computable prediction algorithms that work according to the protocol described above, we end up with a universal algorithm that performs little worse than any computable algorithm. However this straightforward approach fails. It follows from a simple diagonalizational argument that every computable algorithm is greatly outperformed by some other algorithm on some inputs.

This problem may be avoided if we extend the class. We will be looking for a universal element in the class of all so called superloss processes.

Consider a game $\mathfrak{G} = (\mathbb{B}, [0,1], \lambda)$. We say that a pair $(s_0, s_1) \in [-\infty, +\infty]^2$ is a *superprediction* w.r.t. $\mathfrak{G}$ if there exists a prediction $\gamma \in [0,1]$ such that $s_0 \geq \lambda(0, \gamma)$ and $s_1 \geq \lambda(1, \gamma)$. If we let $P = \{(p_0, p_1) \in [-\infty, +\infty]^2 \mid \exists \gamma \in [0,1] : p_0 = \lambda(0, \gamma)$ and $p_1 = \lambda(1, \gamma)\}$ (cf. the canonical form of a game in [Vov98]), the set S of all superpredictions is the set of points that lie 'north-east' of P.

A function $L : \mathbb{B}^* \to \mathbb{R} \cup \{+\infty\}$ is called a *superloss process* w.r.t. $\mathfrak{G}$ (see [VW98]) if $L(\Lambda) = 0$, for every $x \in \mathbb{B}^*$, the pair $(L(x0) - L(x), L(x1) - L(x))$ is a superprediction w.r.t. $\mathfrak{G}$, and L is semicomputable from above. It is shown in [VW98] that the set of all superloss processes is enumerable.

Now we can define different variants of predictive complexity. A superloss process $\mathcal{K}$ w.r.t. a game $\mathfrak{G} = \langle \mathbb{B}, [0,1], \lambda \rangle$ is called *(simple) predictive complexity* w.r.t. $\mathfrak{G}$ if for every other superloss process L w.r.t. $\mathfrak{G}$ there is a constant C such that the inequality $\mathcal{K}(x) \leq L(x) + C$ holds for every $x \in \mathbb{B}^*$.

Proposition 2 ([VW98]). *If a game $\mathfrak{G}$ is mixable, then there exists simple predictive complexity $\mathcal{K}^{\mathfrak{G}}$ w.r.t. $\mathfrak{G}$.*

The definition can be relaxed as follows. A superloss process $\mathcal{K}$ is *predictive complexity up to* $f(n)$, where $f : \mathbb{N} \to [0, +\infty)$, if for every other superloss process L there is a constant C such that the inequality $\mathcal{K}(x) \leq L(x) + Cf(|x|)$ holds for every $x \in \mathbb{B}^*$ ($|x|$ denotes the length of a string x). The definition makes sense if $f(n) = o(n)$ as $n \to +\infty$.

The square-loss and the logarithmic games are mixable and thus they specify predictive complexities. The logarithmic complexity coincides with Levin's a priori semimeasure (see [VW98]).

2.3   Geometric Interpretations of the Constant $c(\beta)$ and Mixability

Within the approach of this paper two games with the same set of superpredictions are indistinguishable. Different loss functions are mere parametrisations of the same geometrical object.

The value $c(\beta)$ has the following geometric meaning (see [Vov98]). Let S be the set of superpredictions for a game $\mathfrak{G}$. Consider the homeomorphism from $[0, +\infty]$ onto $[0,1]^2$ given by the equation $\mathfrak{B}_\beta(x, y) = (\beta^x, \beta^y)$. For every $A \subseteq [0, +\infty]^2$ and $\theta \in [0, 2\pi)$ put

$$\mathrm{osc}_\theta \, A = \frac{\sup\{t \geq 0 \mid (t\cos\theta, t\sin\theta) \in A\}}{\inf\{t \geq 0 \mid (t\cos\theta, t\sin\theta) \in A\}} \,, \tag{1}$$

where we assume that $\sup \varnothing = 0, \inf \varnothing = +\infty$ and $(+\infty)/(+\infty) = 1$. This function represents the 'thickness' of a section of A by the half-line $\{(t \cos \theta, t \sin \theta) \mid t \geq 0\}$. Put $\operatorname{osc} A = \sup_{\theta \in [0, 2\pi)} \operatorname{osc}_\theta A$. If S is the set of superpredictions for $\mathfrak{G}$, then $c(\beta) = \operatorname{osc} \left(\mathfrak{B}_\beta^{-1} \left(\mathfrak{C} \left(\mathfrak{B}_\beta(S) \right) \right) \setminus S \right)$, where $\mathfrak{C}(A)$ denotes the convex hull of a set A. Sometimes we will write $c(\mathfrak{G}, \beta)$ to refer to a particular game; the notation $c_\theta(\mathfrak{G}, \beta) = \operatorname{osc}_\theta \left(\mathfrak{B}_\beta^{-1} \left(\mathfrak{C} \left(\mathfrak{B}_\beta(S) \right) \right) \setminus S \right)$ will also be used.

Note that $\mathfrak{G}$ is mixable if and only if the set $\mathfrak{B}_\beta(S)$ is convex for some $\beta \in (0, 1)$.

Remark 1. It is easy to visualise the set $S' = \mathfrak{B}_\beta^{-1} \left(\mathfrak{C} \left(\mathfrak{B}_\beta(S) \right) \right)$. Just as the convex hull of a set is a union of all line segments connecting the points from the set, so the set S' consists of segments of the curve $\beta^x + \beta^y = 1$. If two points from S can be connected by a shift of a segment of the curve, the segment is a subset of S'. Since the curve $\beta^x + \beta^y = 1$ is convex, the set S' contains the convex hull of $S \cap \mathbb{R}^2$. This observation implies that if $S \cap \mathbb{R}^2$ is not convex, there is $\varepsilon > 0$ such that $c(\beta) > 1 + \varepsilon$ for each $\beta \in (0, 1)$.

The paper [KVV01] proves that if $S \cap \mathbb{R}^2$ is not convex, there is no simple predictive complexity w.r.t. $\mathfrak{G}$. The proof can be easily modified to show that in this case there is no predictive complexity up to $f(n)$ for every f such that $f(n) = o(n)$ as $n \to +\infty$.

3   Differential Criteria of Mixability

In this section we derive a number of criteria and conditions for mixability. Here is an informal overview of our results. Let $\mathfrak{G}$ be a game with the set of superpredictions S. For simplicity, assume for a while that the loss function $\lambda(\omega, \gamma)$ is monotone in the second argument. If λ is bounded and smooth, so is the curve $P = \{(\lambda(0, \gamma), \lambda(1, \gamma)) \mid \gamma \in [0, 1]\}$, which forms a part of the boundary of S. If $S \cap \mathbb{R}^2$ is not convex, the game is not mixable so let $S \cap \mathbb{R}^2$ be convex. The theorems state the following. If the curvature of P never vanishes, the game is mixable. If it vanishes at an interior point, the game is not mixable; if it vanishes at an endpoint and the tangent is neither horizontal nor vertical there, the game is not mixable either. However if certain regularity conditions hold and the curvature only vanishes at points where the tangent is either horizontal or vertical, the game is mixable. Some conditions are formulated in Theorem 2 and Corollary 2. They are quite natural so most interesting cases satisfy them.

We start with a lemma, which is, in fact, a restatement of a theorem from [HKW98].

Lemma 1. *Let $\mathfrak{G}$ be a game with the set of superpredictions S. Suppose that there are twice differentiable functions $x, y : I \to \mathbb{R}$, where $I \subseteq \mathbb{R}$ is an open (perhaps infinite) interval, such that $x' > 0$ and $y' < 0$ on I and S is the closure of the set $\{(u, v) \in \mathbb{R}^2 \mid \exists t \in I : x(t) \leq u, y(t) \leq v\}$ w.r.t. the extended topology* of $[-\infty, +\infty]^2$. Then, for every $\beta \in (0,1)$, the game $\mathfrak{G}$ is β-mixable if and only if

$$\ln \frac{1}{\beta} \leq \frac{y''(t)x'(t) - x''(t)y'(t)}{x'(t)y'(t)(y'(t) - x'(t))} \tag{2}$$

holds for every $t \in I$. The game $\mathfrak{G}$ is mixable if and only if the fraction $(y''x' - x''y')/x'y'(y' - x')$ is separated from the zero, i.e., there is $\varepsilon > 0$ such that $\frac{y''x' - x''y'}{x'y'(y' - x')} \geq \varepsilon$ holds on I.

Proof. Convexity of $\mathfrak{B}_\beta(S)$ is equivalent to concavity of the function with the graph $\{\mathfrak{B}_\beta(x(t), y(t)) \mid t \in I\}$. Since the functions $x(t)$ and $y(t)$ are smooth, this curve is concave if and only if the inequality

$$\frac{d^2 \beta^{y(t)}}{d \left(\beta^{x(t)}\right)^2} \leq 0 \tag{3}$$

holds on I. Differentiation yields

$$\frac{d\beta^{y(t)}}{d\beta^{x(t)}} = \beta^{y(t) - x(t)} \frac{y'(t)}{x'(t)}, \tag{4}$$

$$\frac{d^2 \beta^{y(t)}}{d \left(\beta^{x(t)}\right)^2} = \frac{\beta^{y(t) - 2x(t)}}{\ln \beta \cdot (x'(t))^2} \left((y'(t) - x'(t))y'(t) \ln \beta + \frac{y''(t)x'(t) - y'(t)x''(t)}{x'(t)} \right). \tag{5}$$

The theorem follows.   □

The theorem holds for all smooth parametrisations of S. We need one particularly convenient method of parametrisation. We will say that $f : I \to \mathbb{R}$, where $I = (a, b) \subseteq \mathbb{R}$ is an open (perhaps infinite) nonempty interval, is a *canonical representation* of a game $\mathfrak{G}$ with the set of superpredictions S, if

- f is monotone,
- f is semi-continuous from the right,
- f is not constant on every non-void interval $(a', b) \subseteq I$, and
- S is a closure w.r.t. the extended topology of the set $\{(x, y) \in \mathbb{R}^2 \mid \exists \tilde{x} \leq x : f(\tilde{x}) \leq y\}$.

The following theorem shows that most games have a canonical representation.

Lemma 2. *Let $\mathfrak{G}$ be a game with the set of superpredictions $S \subseteq [0, +\infty]^2$. Then S satisfies the conditions*

- $S \cap \mathbb{R}^2 \neq \varnothing$ *and*
- S *is the closure of its final part $S \cap \mathbb{R}^2$ w.r.t. the extended topology of $[-\infty, +\infty]^2$*

if and only if either $S = [c, +\infty] \times [d, +\infty]$ for some $c, d \in \mathbb{R}$ or $\mathfrak{G}$ has a canonical representation. If under the above conditions there is a canonical representation, it is unique.

If we consider the parametrisation $(x, f(x))$ in Lemma 1, we get the following corollary.

Corollary 1. *Let $\mathfrak{G}$ be a game with the set of superpredictions $S \subseteq [0, +\infty]^2$ and the canonical representation $f : I \to \mathbb{R}$. Suppose that f is twice differentiable on I. Then, for every $\beta \in (0,1)$, the game $\mathfrak{G}$ is β-mixable if and only if*

$$\ln \frac{1}{\beta} \le \frac{f''(x)}{f'(x)(f'(x) - 1)} \tag{6}$$

holds for every $x \in I$. The game $\mathfrak{G}$ is mixable if and only if there is $\varepsilon > 0$ such that $\frac{f''}{f'(f'-1)} \ge \varepsilon$ holds on I.

The following lemma allows us to split S into parts and to study the parts separately.

Lemma 3. *Let $\mathfrak{G}$ be a game with the canonical representation $f : (a,b) \to \mathbb{R}$ and the set of superpredictions S. Let $d \in (a,b)$ and let $f|_{(a,d)}$ and $f|_{(d,b)}$ be the canonical representations of the games $\mathfrak{G}_1$ and $\mathfrak{G}_2$, respectively. Then $\mathfrak{G}$ is mixable if and only if $\mathfrak{G}_1$ and $\mathfrak{G}_2$ are mixable and the set $S \cap \mathbb{R}^2$ is convex.*

Proof. The 'only if' part is trivial. Let us prove the 'if' part.

Let $\mathfrak{G}_1$ be β_1-mixable, $\mathfrak{G}_2$ be β_2-mixable, and $\beta = \max(\beta_1, \beta_2)$. The both curves $\{\mathfrak{B}_\beta(x, f(x)) \mid x \in (a,d)\}$ and $\{\mathfrak{B}_\beta(x, f(x)) \mid x \in (d,b)\}$ are graphs of concave functions. Their union is the graph of a function g. Since $S \cap \mathbb{R}^2$ is convex, the inequality $f'_-(d) \le f'_+(d)$ holds for the one-sided derivatives of f. Eq. (2) implies that $g'_-(\beta^d) \ge g'_+(\beta^d)$ and thus g is concave. $\qquad\square$

Let $\mathfrak{G}$ be a game with the set of superpredictions S and the canonical representation $f : (a,b) \to \mathbb{R}$. If there is $d < b$ such that the game with the set of superpredictions $S \cap ([d, +\infty] \times (-\infty, +\infty])$ is mixable, we say that $\mathfrak{G}$ has a *mixable 0-edge*. If the game with the set of superpredictions obtained by reflecting S in the straight line $x = y$ has a mixable 0-edge, we say that $\mathfrak{G}$ has a *mixable 1-edge*.

Now we can formulate the following criterion.

Theorem 1. *Let $\mathfrak{G}$ be a game and let $f : (a,b) \to \mathbb{R}$ be the canonical representation of the set of superpredictions S. Let f have a continuous second derivative on (a,b). Then $\mathfrak{G}$ is mixable if and only if f'' is positive on (a,b) and $\mathfrak{G}$ has mixable 0- and 1-edges.*

The game $\mathfrak{G}$ has a mixable 0-edge if and only if $\liminf_{x \to b-} -f''(x)/f'(x) > 0$. If b is finite, we can formulate the following statements.

Theorem 2. *Let $\mathfrak{G}$ be a game with the canonical representation $f : (a,b) \to \mathbb{R}$ and the set of superpredictions S. Let $b < +\infty$ and $\bar{f} : (a,b] \to \mathbb{R}$ be the function coinciding with f on (a,b) and defined by $\bar{f}(b) = \lim_{x \to b-} f(x)$ at b. If $\bar{f}$ has a continuous second derivative[2] in a vicinity of b, the following statements hold:*

---

[2] From here on the derivatives $\bar{f}'(b)$ and $\bar{f}''(b)$ are the left derivatives $\bar{f}'(b)_-$ and $\bar{f}''(b)_-$.

(i) if $\bar{f}'(b) < 0$, then $\mathfrak{G}$ has a mixable 0-edge if and only if $f''(b) > 0$;
(ii) if $\bar{f}'(b) = 0$ and f'' is positive and monotone in a punctured vicinity of b, then $\mathfrak{G}$ has a mixable 0-edge.

Note that if $\bar{f}''(b) < 0$, the set $S \cap ([d, +\infty) \times (-\infty, +\infty))$ is not convex for any $d > 0$ and thus $\mathfrak{G}$ does not have a mixable 0-edge.

Proof. The theorem follows from Corollary 1.

If $\bar{f}'(b) < 0$ or $\bar{f}''(b) > 0$, the theorem trivialises. Consider the case $\bar{f}'(b) = \bar{f}''(b) = 0$. We will show now that under the conditions of (ii) the fraction $-f''(x)/f'(x)$ tends to $+\infty$ as $x \to b-$. Indeed, the classical first mean value theorem for integrals implies that for every x from a punctured vicinity of b we have

$$f'(x) = -\int_x^b f''(t)dt = -(b-x)f''(\xi(x)) , \qquad (7)$$

where $\xi(x) \in [x, b]$. Since f'' is monotone, we get

$$-\frac{f''(x)}{f'(x)} = \frac{f''(x)}{(b-x)f''(\xi(x))} \geq \frac{1}{b-x} .$$

$\square$

The following corollary describes the situation where $\bar{f}$ has a finite order touch with the horizontal line.

Corollary 2. *Let $\mathfrak{G}$ be a game with the canonical representation $f : (a, b) \to \mathbb{R}$ and the set of superpredictions S. Let $S \cap \mathbb{R}^2$ be convex, $b < +\infty$, and $\bar{f} : (a, b] \to \mathbb{R}$ be as defined in Theorem 2. If there is an integer $k \geq 2$ such that $\bar{f}(x)$ has derivatives up to the order k at b and $f^{(m)}(b) = 0$ for every $m = 1, 2, \ldots, k-1$, but $f^{(k)}(b) = a \neq 0$, then $\mathfrak{G}$ has a mixable 0-edge.*

Proof. Under the conditions of the corollary either $\bar{f}''(b) > 0$ or $f^{(3)}(x)$ is negative in a vicinity of b and thus $f''(x)$ is monotone. We can apply Theorem 2. $\square$

It is possible to give a simple independent proof. If $k > 2$, Taylor's theorem implies that

$$f''(x) = \frac{(x-b)^{k-2}}{(k-2)!}a + o\left((x-b)^{(k-2)}\right) \qquad \text{as } x \to b-,$$

$$f'(x) = \frac{(x-b)^{k-1}}{(k-1)!}a + o\left((x-b)^{(k-1)}\right) \qquad \text{as } x \to b-$$

and thus $-f''(x)/f'(x) \to +\infty$ as $x \to b-$.

The conditions we have formulated cannot be essentially relaxed. For example, it is not sufficient to assume the existence of a continuous second derivative for f. Indeed, let us construct a convex g with a continuous second derivative

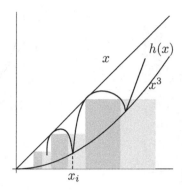

Fig. 1. Construction of the counterexample

such that $g''(x)/g'(x) \to 0$ as $x \to 0+$. Moreover, it will be strictly positive for $x > 0$. Such an example can be easily turned into an example of a game.

Let us construct $h = g''$. By definition, put $g'(x) = \int_0^x h(t)dt$ and $g(x) = \int_0^x g'(t)dt$. The function h is constructed as follows. Consider the sequence of squares with sides $1/2^i$ and left bottom corner at points $1/2^i$, $i = 1, 2, \ldots$ (see Fig. 1). We split each square into two halves. Consider the graph of the function x^3. Let us draw the graph of h inside the 'angle' between the graphs of x and x^3 in such a way that left half of each square lies below the graph but h touches x^3 inside the right half. Let x_i be the point inside the right half of the i-th square where the touch occurs. The value $g'(x_i)$ is greater than the area of the right half of the i-th square, i.e., $g'(x_i) > (x_i/2)^2$. On the other hand $g''(x_i) = h(x_i) = x_i^3$ and thus $g''(x_i)/g'(x_i) \to 0$ as $i \to +\infty$.

4   Convergence of $c(\beta)$

In this section we show that for a wide class of games $c(\beta) \to 1$ as $\beta \to 1-$.

Theorem 3. *Let $\mathfrak{G}$ be a game with the canonical representation $f : (a, b) \to \mathbb{R}$ and the set of superpredictions S. If $S \cap \mathbb{R}^2$ is convex and the following conditions hold:*

- *$\mathfrak{G}$ has a mixable 1-edge or there is $T < +\infty$ such that $f'_- > -T$ on (a, b), and*
- *$\mathfrak{G}$ has a mixable 0-edge or there is $\varepsilon > 0$ such that $f'_+ < -\varepsilon$ on (a, b),*

then $c(\beta) = 1 + O(\ln(1/\beta))$ as $\beta \to 1-$.

Proof. We start with a lemma for one particular type of games. Let $\mathfrak{G}^{A,B}_{abs}$ be the game with the set of superpredictions $S^{A,B}_{abs} = \{(x, y) \in [0, +\infty]^2 \mid Bx + Ay > AB\}$. A special case of this game, $\mathfrak{G}^{1,1}_{abs}$, is the absolute loss game with the loss function $|\omega - \gamma|$.

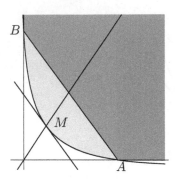

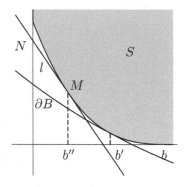

Fig. 2. The set of superpredictions for the game $G_{\text{abs}}^{A,B}$

Fig. 3. The case of a mixable 0-edge

Lemma 4. *For all $A, B > 0$, we have*

$$c(\mathfrak{G}_{\text{abs}}^{A,B}, \beta) = \frac{AB \ln \beta}{A \ln \frac{A(1-\beta^{A+B})}{(A+B)(1-\beta^A)} + B \ln \frac{B(1-\beta^{A+B})}{(A+B)(1-\beta^B)}} \, . \tag{8}$$

Proof. Consider a shift of $\beta^x + \beta^y = 1$ passing through $(A, 0)$ and $(0, B)$. Let M be the point where the tangent to this shift is parallel to the line $Bx + Ay = AB$. It follows from the Thales theorem that the maximum value of $c_\theta(\mathfrak{G}, \beta)$ is achieved on θ corresponding to the half-line passing through M (see Fig. 2; the set $S_{\text{abs}}^{A,B}$ is shaded darker and the set $\mathfrak{B}_\beta^{-1}(\mathfrak{C}(\mathfrak{B}_\beta(S))) \setminus S$ lighter). $\square$

We will show that there is $C \in \mathbb{R}$ such that the inequality $c_\theta(\mathfrak{G}, \beta) \leq C_1 + \ln(1/\beta)$ holds for every $\theta \in [0, \pi/2]$.

If the half-line $l_\theta = \{(t \cos \theta, t \sin \theta) \mid t \geq 0\}$ does not intersect S, then $c_\theta(\mathfrak{G}, \beta) = 1$ for all $\beta \in (0, 1)$. Otherwise let $(x_\theta, y_\theta) \in [0, +\infty]$ be the point where l_θ first meets S, i.e., $(x_\theta, y_\theta) = (t_0 \cos \theta, t_0 \sin \theta)$, where $t_0 = \inf\{t \geq 0 \mid (t \cos \theta, t \sin \theta) \in S\}$. If $x_\theta \notin [a, b]$, we have $c_\theta(\mathfrak{G}, \beta) = 1$ for all β as well.

The convex set $S \cap \mathbb{R}^2$ has a hyper-plane (i.e., a straight line) of support at (x_θ, y_θ). Let $(c_\theta, 0)$ and $(0, d_\theta)$ be the points where this line intersects the coordinate axes. We have $S \subseteq S_{\text{abs}}^{c_\theta, d_\theta} = \{(x, y) \in [0, +\infty] \mid qx + ry > s\}$, where the latter set is the set of superpredictions for the game $\mathfrak{G}_{\text{abs}}^{c_\theta, d_\theta}$. We have $1 \leq c_\theta(\mathfrak{G}, \beta) \leq c_\theta(\mathfrak{G}_{\text{abs}}^{c_\theta, d_\theta}, \beta) \leq c(\mathfrak{G}_{\text{abs}}^{c_\theta, d_\theta}, \beta)$ hold.

Suppose that there are $0 < \varepsilon < T < +\infty$ such that $-T \leq f'_-(x) \leq f'_+(x) \leq -\varepsilon$ for every (a, b) (this implies that $b < +\infty$ and f is bounded on (a, b)). The slopes of lines of support constructed above are negative and separated from both $-\infty$ and 0. This yields that there are $\underline{c}, \underline{d} > 0$ and $\bar{c}, \bar{d} < +\infty$ such that $\underline{c} \leq c_\theta \leq \bar{c}$ and $\underline{d} \leq d_\theta \leq \bar{d}$ for every $\theta \in [\underline{\theta}, \bar{\theta}]$.

It remains to show the following. If

$$g(t, c, d) = -\frac{cdt}{c \ln \frac{c(1-e^{-t(c+d)})}{(c+d)(1-e^{-tc})} + d \ln \frac{d(1-e^{-t(c+d)})}{(c+d)(1-e^{-td})}}$$

then $g(t, c, d) \leq 1 + Ct$ for some C, small t, and $(c, d) \in [\underline{c}, \bar{c}] \times [\underline{d}, \bar{d}]$. It is easy to see that for every $t > 0$ we have $g(t, c, d) = 1 + \frac{c+d}{8}t + t^2 r_2(t, c, d)$, where $r_2(t, c, d) = \frac{1}{2}\frac{\partial^2 g}{\partial t^2}(\xi, c, d)$, for some $\xi = \xi(t) \in [0, t]$. Since the derivative $\partial^2 g/\partial t^2$ is uniformly bounded when $(c, d) \in [\underline{c}, \bar{c}] \times [\underline{d}, \bar{d}]$ and $0 \leq t \leq t_0$, we get the desired result.

The remaining cases can be reduced to the one we have considered. Suppose that $\mathfrak{G}$ has, say, a mixable 0-edge. We will find $b' \in (a, b)$ and $\beta' \in (0, 1)$ such that for every θ, if $x_\theta \geq b'$, then $c_\theta(\mathfrak{G}, \beta) = 1$ for every $\beta \in [\beta', 1)$.

It follows from the definition of a mixable 0-edge that there is $b'' \in (a, b)$ such that the game with the canonical representation $f|_{(b'', b)}$ is mixable. Suppose that it is β_1–mixable. Let l be a support hyper-plane to $S \cap \mathbb{R}^2$ passing through $M = (b'', f(b''))$ and let N be the intersection of l with the coordinate axis $x = 0$ (see Fig. 3).

Pick $b' \in (b'', b)$. For every $\beta \in [\beta_1, 1)$ there is a shift B of the set $\{(x, y) \in [-\infty, +\infty]^2 \mid \beta^x + \beta^y \leq 1\}$ such that $S \subseteq B$ and $(b', f(b')) \in \partial B$. For every sufficiently large $\beta \in [\beta_1, 1)$, the points M and N belong to B. Indeed, consider a shift of the curve $\beta^x + \beta^y = 1$ passing through the origin. If at the origin it touches the line $y = -tx$, where $t > 0$, then its equation is

$$y(x) = \frac{\ln(1 + t(1 - \beta^x))}{\ln \beta}.$$

(This can be checked by direct calculation.) Let us analyse this expression. It decreases in t and tends to $-tx$ as $\beta \to 1$ and t, x are fixed. It remains to notice that $f'_+(b'') \leq f'_-(b')$.

Pick some $\beta \in (\beta_1, 1)$ such that M and N are inside B. Consider the game with the set of superpredictions

$$S' = (S \cap [b', +\infty] \times [0, +\infty]) \cup (B \cap [0, b'] \times [0, +\infty]).$$

It follows from Lemma 3 that this game is mixable, say, β'-mixable. This implies that for every point $P \in \partial(S' \cap \mathbb{R}^2)$ there is a shift B of the curve $(\beta')^x + (\beta')^y = 1$ such that $P \in \partial B$ and $S \subseteq S' \subseteq B$.

□

Remark 2. Consider an arbitrary game $\mathfrak{G}$ with a bounded loss function λ. Suppose that the set of superpredictions S is such that $S \cap \mathbb{R}^2$ is convex. Let $f : (a, b) \to \mathbb{R}$ be the canonical representation of $\mathfrak{G}$. For every θ such that $x_\theta \neq a, b$ we still have the estimate on $c_\theta(\beta)$ from the theorem. This is sufficient to conclude that $c(\beta) \to 1$ as $\beta \to 1-$.

5   The Existence of Weak Complexity

The results of the previous section imply the existence of weak complexity. The following theorem generalises a result from [V'y00] about the absolute-loss game. The idea of the proof goes back to [CBFH$^+$97].

Theorem 4. *Let $\mathfrak{G} = (\mathbb{B}, [0, 1], \lambda)$ be a game such that λ is bounded and $c(\beta) \to 1$ as $\beta \to 1$. Then there exists predictive complexity w.r.t. $\mathfrak{G}$ up to $f(n)$, where*

$$f(n) = \sqrt{n} + \sum_{k=1}^{n} \left(1 - \frac{1}{c(e^{-1/\sqrt{k}})} \right) = o(n)$$

as $n \to +\infty$.

Proof. There is $l > 0$ such that $\lambda(\omega, \gamma) \leq l$ for every $\omega \in \Omega$ and $\gamma \in \Gamma$.

Put $\beta_n = e^{-1/\sqrt{n}}$, $n = 1, 2, \ldots$. Let L_i, $i = 1, 2, \ldots$, be an effective enumeration of all superloss processes w.r.t. $\mathfrak{G}$. Let the sequence L_i^* be defined by

$$L_i^*(\boldsymbol{x}) = L_i(\boldsymbol{x}) + l \sum_{k=1}^{|\boldsymbol{x}|-1} \left(1 - \frac{1}{c(\beta_k)} \right) ,$$

for every $\boldsymbol{x} \in \mathbb{B}^*$. Pick a sequence $p_i > 0$, $i = 1, 2, \ldots$, such that $\sum_{i=1}^{+\infty} p_i = 1$ and consider the function defined by the formula $\mathcal{K}(\boldsymbol{x}) = \log_{\beta_n} \sum_{i=1}^{+\infty} p_i \beta_n^{L_i^*(\boldsymbol{x})}$ for every $\boldsymbol{x}$ of length n, $n = 1, 2, \ldots$.

Let us check that $\mathcal{K}$ is a superloss process w.r.t. $\mathfrak{G}$. Fix some arbitrary positive integer n and $\boldsymbol{x}$ of length n. We have $\beta_n^{\mathcal{K}(\boldsymbol{x})} = \sum_{i=1}^{+\infty} p_i \beta_n^{L_i^*(\boldsymbol{x})}$ and $\beta_{n+1}^{\mathcal{K}(\boldsymbol{x}\omega)} = \sum_{i=1}^{+\infty} p_i \beta_{n+1}^{L_i^*(\boldsymbol{x})}$ for each $\omega = 0, 1$. We cannot manipulate with these formulae because they include different bases β_n and β_{n+1}. This obstacle can be overcome with the following trick. Since the function $y = x^a$ is convex on $[0, +\infty)$ for every $a \geq 1$, the inequality $(\sum_i p_i t_i)^a \leq \sum_i p_i t_i^a$ holds for every $t_1, t_2, \ldots \geq 0$ and every sequence $p_1, p_2, \ldots \geq 0$ that sums up to 1. This implies

$$\beta_n^{\mathcal{K}(\boldsymbol{x}\omega)} = \left(\beta_{n+1}^{\mathcal{K}(\boldsymbol{x}\omega)} \right)^{\log_{\beta_{n+1}} \beta_n} \leq \sum_{i=1}^{+\infty} p_i \left(\beta_{n+1}^{L_i^*(\boldsymbol{x})} \right)^{\log_{\beta_{n+1}} \beta_n} = \sum_{i=1}^{+\infty} p_i \beta_n^{L_i^*(\boldsymbol{x}\omega)}$$

for each $\omega = 0, 1$. We get

$$\beta_n^{\mathcal{K}(\boldsymbol{x}\omega) - \mathcal{K}(\boldsymbol{x})} \leq \sum_{i=1}^{+\infty} q_i \beta_n^{L_i^*(\boldsymbol{x}\omega) - L_i^*(\boldsymbol{x})} \tag{9}$$

for each $\omega = 0, 1$, where $q_i = p_i \beta_n^{L_i^*(\boldsymbol{x})} / \sum_{k=1}^{+\infty} p_k \beta_n^{L_k^*(\boldsymbol{x})}$.

Since all L_i are superloss processes, there exists a sequence of superpredictions $(s_1^{(0)}, s_1^{(1)}), (s_2^{(0)}, s_2^{(1)}), \ldots \in S$ such that for every $i = 1, 2, \ldots$ and each

$\omega = 0, 1$ we have

$$L_i^*(\boldsymbol{x}\omega) - L_i^*(\boldsymbol{x}) = L_i(\boldsymbol{x}\omega) - L_i(\boldsymbol{x}) + l\left(1 - \frac{1}{c(\beta_n)}\right) \geq s_i^{(\omega)} + l\left(1 - \frac{1}{c(\beta_n)}\right) .$$
(10)

It can be assumed that $s_i^{(\omega)} \leq l$ for all i and ω.

If we combine (9) with (10) and take into account the definition of $c(\beta)$, we obtain

$$\beta_n^{\mathcal{K}(\boldsymbol{x}\omega) - \mathcal{K}(\boldsymbol{x})} \leq \beta_n^{l\left(1 - \frac{1}{c(\beta_n)}\right)} \sum_{i=1}^{+\infty} q_i \beta_n^{s_i^{(\omega)}} \leq \beta_n^{l\left(1 - \frac{1}{c(\beta_n)}\right) + \frac{s^{(\omega)}}{c(\beta_n)}}$$

$$= \beta_n^{s^{(\omega)} + (l - s^{(\omega)})\left(1 - \frac{1}{c(\beta_n)}\right)} \leq \beta_n^{s^{(\omega)}}$$

for each $\omega = 0, 1$, where $(s^{(0)}, s^{(1)})$ is a superprediction. This implies the inequalities $\mathcal{K}(\boldsymbol{x}0) - \mathcal{K}(\boldsymbol{x}) \geq s^{(0)}$ and $\mathcal{K}(\boldsymbol{x}1) - \mathcal{K}(\boldsymbol{x}) \geq s^{(1)}$. Thus $\mathcal{K}$ is a superloss process.

It follows from our definition of $\mathcal{K}$ that for every $\boldsymbol{x}$ of length n and every $i = 1, 2, \ldots$ we get

$$\mathcal{K}(\boldsymbol{x}) \leq L_i^*(\boldsymbol{x}) + \log_{\beta_n} p_i = L_i(\boldsymbol{x}) + \sum_{k=1}^{n-1}\left(1 - \frac{1}{c(\beta_k)}\right) + \sqrt{n}\ln\frac{1}{p_i} .$$

A simple lemma from calculus completes the proof.

Lemma 5. *Let $a_n \geq 0$, $n = 1, 2, \ldots$ be such that $a_n = o(1)$ as $n \to +\infty$. Then $\sum_{k=1}^{n} a_k = o(n)$ as $n \to +\infty$.*

□

Corollary 3. *If a game $\mathfrak{G}$ has a bounded loss function, there is a function $f(n) = o(n)$ such that there is predictive complexity w.r.t. $\mathfrak{G}$ up to $f(n)$.*

Corollary 4. *Let $\mathfrak{G}$ be a game with a bounded loss function, the canonical representation $f : (a, b) \to \mathbb{R}$, and the set of superpredictions S. If $S \cap \mathbb{R}^2$ is convex and both the following conditions hold:*

- *$\mathfrak{G}$ has a mixable 1-edge or there is $T < +\infty$ such that $f'_- > -T$ on (a, b)*
- *$\mathfrak{G}$ has a mixable 0-edge or there is $\varepsilon > 0$ such that $f'_+ < -\varepsilon$ on (a, b)*

then there is complexity w.r.t. $\mathfrak{G}$ up to $\sqrt{n}$.

6   Unbounded Loss Functions

The result of Theorem 1 still holds for games with unbounded loss functions. However other results do not generalise to this case.

The following theorem shows that $c(\beta)$ equals $+\infty$ for a large class of games. Consider a game with the smooth canonical representation $f : (a, +\infty) \to \mathbb{R}$.

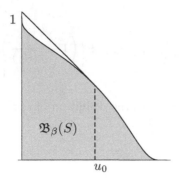

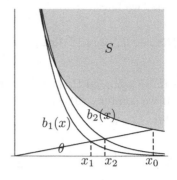

Fig. 4. The drawing of $\mathfrak{B}_\beta(S)$ for Theorem 5

Fig. 5. The drawing of S, $C_1\beta_1^x$, and $C_1\beta_1^x$ for Theorem 5

If the fraction $f''(x)/f'(x)$ is separated from 0 as $x \to +\infty$ then so is the fraction $f''(x)/f'(x)(f'(x) - 1)$ and the game has a mixable 0-edge. The case $f''(x)/f'(x) \to 0$ is completely different. We cannot guarantee the convergence of $c(\beta)$ to 1.

Theorem 5. *Let $\mathfrak{G}$ be a game with the canonical representation $f : (a, +\infty) \to \mathbb{R}$ and the set of superpredictions S. Let f be twice differentiable on $(a, +\infty)$. If $\lim_{x \to +\infty} f(x) = 0$ and $\lim_{x \to +\infty} \frac{f''(x)}{f'(x)} = 0$ then $c(\beta) = +\infty$ for every $\beta \in (0, 1)$.*

Proof. Pick $\beta \in (0, 1)$ and consider the image of S under $\mathfrak{B}_\beta$. It is easy to check by evaluating the second derivative (cf. (5)) that the boundary of $\mathfrak{B}_\beta(S)$ in a vicinity of the point $(0, 1)$ is the graph of a convex function. There exists $u_0 > 0$ such that the line segment connecting the points $(0, 1)$ and $(u_0, \beta^{f(\log_\beta(u_0))})$ lies above the arc of the boundary of $\mathfrak{B}_\beta(S)$ between these points (see Fig. 4). The inverse image of the corresponding straight line is a shift $y = b(x)$ of the curve $\beta^x + \beta^y = 1$ such that $b(x) \to 0$ as $x \to +\infty$ but $b(x) < f(x)$ for every $x \in (\log_\beta(u_0), +\infty)$. It is easy to see that $b(x) \sim C\beta^x$ for some constant C as $x \to +\infty$.

Now let us pick an arbitrary $\beta_1 \in (0, 1)$ and show that $c_\theta(\beta_1) \to +\infty$ as $\theta \to 0$. Consider some $\beta_2 \in (\beta_1, 1)$. There are functions $b_1(x) \sim C_1\beta_1^x$ and $b_2(x) \sim C_2\beta_2^x$ (as $x \to +\infty$) such that $b_1(x) < b_2(x) < f(x)$ for all sufficiently large $x \in \mathbb{R}$. Let x_1 and x_2 be such that

$$\frac{C_1\beta_1^{x_1}}{x_1} = \frac{C_2\beta_2^{x_2}}{x_2} = \tan\theta \tag{11}$$

(see Fig. 5). Suppose that θ is sufficiently small for $b_1(x) < b_2(x) < f(x)$ to hold for x_1 and x_2.

We get $c_\theta(\beta_1) \geq x_0/x_1$, where x_0 is such that $f(x_0)/x_0 = \tan\theta$. It follows from $b_1(x) < b_2(x) < f(x)$ that $x_0 > x_2$ so it suffices to evaluate the relation x_2/x_1. Taking the logarithm of (11) yields

$$\ln \tan \theta = \ln C_1 + x_1 \ln \beta_1 - \ln x_1 = x_1 \ln \beta_1 + o(x_1) = x_1 \ln \beta_1 (1 + o(1))$$

as $\theta \to 0$ and, respectively, $x_1 \to +\infty$. Likewise we have $\ln \tan \theta = x_2 \ln \beta_2 (1 + o(1))$ and thus $\frac{x_2}{x_1} = \frac{\ln \beta_1}{\ln \beta_2}(1 + o(1))$ as $\theta \to 0$. Since we can chose β_2 to be as close to 1 as is wished, the theorem follows.

$\square$

A simple example of a game satisfying this theorem is provided by the game with the canonical representation $f(x) = 1/x$, $x \in (0, +\infty)$. Indeed, we have $f'(x) = -1/x^2$ and $f''(x) = 2/x^3$; thus $\frac{f''(x)}{f'(x)} = -\frac{2}{x} \to 0$ as $x \to +\infty$. The theorem implies that $c(\beta) \equiv +\infty$ for this game.

The first example of a game with $c(\beta) \equiv +\infty$ was constructed in [Vov98], Example 6, but the construction was an artificial one and the set of superpredictions of the resulting game was not convex.

Acknowledgement

The authors have been supported by EPSRC through the grants GR/R46670 ('Complexity Approximation Principle and Predictive Complexity: Analysis and Applications') and GR/M16856 ('Comparison of Support Vector Machine and Minimum Message Length methods for induction and prediction'). We would like to thank Volodya Vovk and Graham Farr (whose profound question inspired our research on the topic) for useful discussions. The paper has greatly benefited from the meticulous comments of anonymous COLT reviewers.

References

[CBFH+97] N. Cesa-Bianchi, Y. Freund, D. Haussler, D. P. Helmbold, R. E. Schapire, and M. K. Warmuth. How to use expert advice. *Journal of the ACM*, 44(3):427–485, 1997. 105, 116

[HKW98] D. Haussler, J. Kivinen, and M. K. Warmuth. Sequential prediction of individual sequences under general loss functions. *IEEE Transactions on Information Theory*, 44(5):1906–1925, 1998. 105, 109

[KVV01] Y. Kalnishkan, M. Vyugin, and V. Vovk. Losses, complexities and the Legendre transformation. In *Proceedings of the 12th International Conference on Algorithmic Learning Theory, ALT 2001*, volume 2225 of *Lecture Notes in Artificial Intelligence*. Springer-Verlag, 2001. 109

[LW94] N. Littlestone and M. K. Warmuth. The weighted majority algorithm. *Information and Computation*, 108:212–261, 1994. 105

[Vov90] V. Vovk. Aggregating strategies. In M. Fulk and J. Case, editors, *Proceedings of the 3rd Annual Workshop on Computational Learning Theory*, pages 371–383, San Mateo, CA, 1990. Morgan Kaufmann. 105, 107

[Vov98] V. Vovk. A game of prediction with expert advice. *Journal of Computer and System Sciences*, 56:153–173, 1998. 105, 107, 108, 119

[VW98]   V. Vovk and C. J. H. C. Watkins. Universal portfolio selection. In *Proceedings of the 11th Annual Conference on Computational Learning Theory*, pages 12–23, 1998. 106, 108

[V'y00]   V. V. V'yugin. Sub-optimal measures of predictive complexity for absolute loss function. Technical Report CLRC TR-00-05, Computer Learning Research Centre, Royal Holloway College, University of London, 2000. 116

A Second-Order Perceptron Algorithm

Nicolò Cesa-Bianchi[1], Alex Conconi[1], and Claudio Gentile[2]

[1] Dept. of Information Technologies, Università di Milano, Italy
{cesa-bianchi,conconi}@dti.unimi.it
[2] CRII, Università dell'Insubria, Italy
gentile@dsi.unimi.it

Abstract. We introduce a variant of the Perceptron algorithm called second-order Perceptron algorithm, which is able to exploit certain spectral properties of the data. We analyze the second-order Perceptron algorithm in the mistake bound model of on-line learning and prove bounds in terms of the eigenvalues of the Gram matrix created from the data. The performance of the second-order Perceptron algorithm is affected by the setting of a parameter controlling the sensitivity to the distribution of the eigenvalues of the Gram matrix. Since this information is not preliminarly available to on-line algorithms, we also design a refined version of the second-order Perceptron algorithm which adaptively sets the value of this parameter. For this second algorithm we are able to prove mistake bounds corresponding to a nearly optimal constant setting of the parameter.

1 Introduction

In this paper, we consider on-line learning from binary labeled examples. In each on-line trial the learning algorithm receives an instance and is asked to predict the binary label associated with that instance. Combining the instance with its current internal state, the learner outputs a prediction about the label. The value of the label is then disclosed. We say that the learner has made a mistake when prediction and label disagree. Finally, the learner updates its internal state and a new trial begins. To measure the performance of the learning algorithm, we compare it to the performance of the best predictor in a given class. Within this framework, we introduce a new on-line algorithm called *second-order Perceptron algorithm*. This might be viewed as a variant of the classical (first-order) Perceptron algorithm [26,7,24], and is similar in spirit to an algorithm introduced by Vovk [29], and further studied by Azoury and Warmuth [5], for solving linear regression problems under the square loss. Our second-order Perceptron algorithm is able to exploit certain spectral properties of the data. We analyze the algorithm in the mistake bound model of on-line learning [21,1], by proving bounds in terms of the eigenvalues of the Gram matrix created from the data (Theorem 1). A typical situation where the second-order algorithm outperforms the first-order one is when the data lie on a flat ellipsoid, so that the eigenvalues of the Gram matrix have different magnitude. We performed simple experiments on syntethic data which confirmed our theoretical findings. Once our algorithm

J. Kivinen and R. H. Sloan (Eds.): COLT 2002, LNAI 2375, pp. 121–137, 2002.

is put in dual form, all the operations it performs essentially involve only dot products (Theorem 2). Hence we can replace those dot products by kernel dot products (see, e.g., [27,10]).

In its basic form, the second-order Perceptron algorithm is parameterized by a constant $a > 0$, which rules the extent to which the algorithm adapts to the "warpedness" of the data. In the limit as a goes to infinity our algorithm becomes the (first-order) Perceptron algorithm, so in that limit the bound of the second-order algorithm coincides with that of the first-order algorithm. The value of a affects performance in a significant way. The best choice of a depends on informations about the learning task that are typically not available ahead of time. We develope an adaptive parameter version of our algorithm and prove mistake bounds for it (Theorem 3). Again, such bounds are able to capture the spectral properties of the data.

The next section introduces the main notation used throughout the paper. The basic algorithm is described in Section 3 and analyzed in Section 4. We then show in Section 5 how to formulate our algorithm in dual form, thereby allowing the use of kernel functions. In Section 6 we analyze the second-order Perceptron algorithm with adaptive parameter. Preliminary experiments are reported in Section 7. Section 8 contains conclusions, final remarks and ongoing research.

2   Preliminaries and Notation

In sequential models, prediction proceeds in trials. In each trial $t = 1, 2, \ldots$ the prediction algorithm observes an *instance* vector $\boldsymbol{x}_t \in \mathbb{R}^n$ (all vectors here are understood to be column vectors) and then guesses a binary label $\widehat{y}_t \in \{-1, 1\}$. Before seeing the next vector $\boldsymbol{x}_{t+1}$, the true label $y_t \in \{-1, 1\}$ associated with $\boldsymbol{x}_t$ is revealed and the algorithm knows whether its guess $\widehat{y}_t$ for y_t was correct or not. In the latter case we say that the prediction algorithm has made a *mistake*. We call *example* each pair $(\boldsymbol{x}_t, y_t)$, and *sequence of examples* $\mathcal{S}$ any sequence $\mathcal{S} = ((\boldsymbol{x}_1, y_1), (\boldsymbol{x}_2, y_2), \ldots, (\boldsymbol{x}_T, y_T))$. The formal model we consider is the well-known mistake bound model of on-line learning introduced by Littlestone [21] and Angluin [1], and further investigated by many authors (e.g., [28,22,8,19,2,16,15] and references therein). We do not make any assumption on the mechanism generating the sequence of examples. The goal of the on-line prediction algorithm is to minimize the amount by which its total number of mistakes on an arbitrary sequence $\mathcal{S}$ exceeds some measure of the performance of a fixed predictor (in a given *comparison class* of predictors) on the same sequence $\mathcal{S}$.

The comparison class we consider here is the set of unit norm vectors $\{\boldsymbol{u} \in \mathbb{R}^n : ||\boldsymbol{u}|| = 1\}$. Given an example $(\boldsymbol{x}, y) \in \mathbb{R}^n \times \{-1, +1\}$ and a margin value $\gamma > 0$, we let $D_\gamma(\boldsymbol{u}; (\boldsymbol{x}, y))$ be the hinge loss [13] of vector $\boldsymbol{u}$ at margin γ on example $(\boldsymbol{x}, y)$, that is[1] $D_\gamma(\boldsymbol{u}; (\boldsymbol{x}, y)) = \max\{0, \gamma - y\,\boldsymbol{u}^\top \boldsymbol{x}\}$. Also, for a given sequence of examples $\mathcal{S} = ((\boldsymbol{x}_1, y_1), (\boldsymbol{x}_2, y_2), \ldots, (\boldsymbol{x}_T, y_T))$, we let $D_\gamma(\boldsymbol{u}; \mathcal{S}) = \sum_{t=1}^T D_\gamma(\boldsymbol{u}; (\boldsymbol{x}_t, y_t))$. The quantity $D_\gamma(\boldsymbol{u}; \mathcal{S})$ will measure the performance of

---

[1]   Here and throughout superscript $^\top$ denotes transposition.

u on sequence $\mathcal{S}$. Notice that if u linearly separates $\mathcal{S}$ with margin γ, i.e., if $y_t u^\top x_t \geq \gamma$ for $t = 1, \ldots, T$, then $D_\gamma(u; \mathcal{S}) = 0$.

3   Description of the Algorithm

To introduce the second-order Perceptron algorithm, we start by describing a related algorithm: the "Whitened Perceptron algorithm". Strictly speaking, this is not an on-line algorithm. In fact, it assumes that all the instances $x_1, x_2, \ldots, x_T \in \mathbb{R}^n$ are preliminarily available, and only the labels $y_1, y_2, \ldots, y_T$ are hidden. For the sake of simplicity, assume that these instances span $\mathbb{R}^n$. Therefore $T \geq n$, the correlation matrix $M = \sum_{t=1}^T x_t x_t^\top$ is full-rank and M^{-1} exists. Also, since M is positive definite, $M^{-1/2}$ does exist as well (e.g., [23, Ch. 3]). The Whitened Perceptron algorithm is simply the standard Perceptron algorithm run on the transformed (whitened) sequence $((M^{-1/2}x_1, y_1), (M^{-1/2}x_2, y_2), \ldots, (M^{-1/2}x_T, y_T))$. The transformation $M^{-1/2}$ is called whitening transform (see, e.g., [12]) and has the effect of reducing the correlation matrix of the transformed instances to the identity matrix I_n. In fact,

$$\sum_{t=1}^T \left(M^{-1/2}x_t\right)\left(M^{-1/2}x_t\right)^\top = \sum_{t=1}^T M^{-1/2}x_t \, x_t^\top M^{-1/2}$$
$$= M^{-1/2}M \, M^{-1/2}$$
$$= I_n.$$

Again for the sake of simplicity, suppose the original sequence of examples is linearly separable with margin $\gamma = \min_t y_t \, u^\top x_t > 0$ for some unit norm vector u. Then also the whitened sequence is linearly separable. In fact, hyperplane $z = M^{1/2}u$ separates the whitened sequence with margin $\gamma / \|M^{1/2}u\|$. By the Perceptron convergence theorem [7,24], the number of mistakes made by the Perceptron algorithm on the whitened sequence is thus at most

$$\frac{1}{\gamma^2}\left(\max_t \left\|M^{-1/2}x_t\right\|^2\right)\left\|M^{1/2}u\right\|^2 = \frac{1}{\gamma^2}\max_t \left(x_t^\top M^{-1}x_t\right)\left(u^\top M u\right). \tag{1}$$

To appreciate the potential advantage of whitening the data, notice that when the instance vectors $x_1, \ldots, x_T$ are very correlated the quadratic form $x_t^\top M^{-1}x_t$ tends to be quite small (the expression $\max_t \left(x_t^\top M^{-1}x_t\right)$ might actually be regarded as a measure of correlation of the instance vectors). If the instances look like the ones displayed in the rightmost plot of Figure 3 (Section 7) where the separating hyperplane vector u is strongly correlated with a non-dominant eigenvector of M, then the bound in the right-hand side of (1) can be significantly smaller than the corresponding mistake bound $\max_t \|x_t\|^2 / \gamma^2$ for the classical (non-whitened) Perceptron algorithm.

The second-order Perceptron algorithm might be viewed as an on-line variant of the Whitened Perceptron algorithm; this means that the instances in the data sequence are not assumed to be known beforehand. Besides, the second-order Perceptron algorithm is sparse; that is, the whitening transform applied

Parameter: $a > 0$.
Initialization: $X_0 = \emptyset$; $\boldsymbol{v}_0 = \boldsymbol{0}$; $k = 1$.
Repeat for $t = 1, 2 \ldots, T$:

1. get instance $\boldsymbol{x}_t \in \mathbb{R}^n$;
2. set $S_t = [\, X_{k-1} \; \boldsymbol{x}_t \,]$;
3. predict $\widehat{y}_t = \mathrm{SGN}(\boldsymbol{w}_t^\top \boldsymbol{x}_t) \in \{-1, +1\}$,
   where $\boldsymbol{w}_t = \left(aI_n + S_t\, S_t^\top\right)^{-1} \boldsymbol{v}_{k-1}$;
4. get label $y_t \in \{-1, +1\}$;
5. if $\widehat{y}_t \neq y_t$ then:

$$\boldsymbol{v}_k = \boldsymbol{v}_{k-1} + y_t\, \boldsymbol{x}_t,$$
$$X_k = S_t,$$
$$k \leftarrow k + 1.$$

Fig. 1. The second-order Perceptron algorithm with parameter $a > 0$

to each new incoming instance is based only on a possibly very small subset of the instances observed so far.

In its basic form, the second-order Perceptron algorithm (described in Figure 1) takes an input parameter $a > 0$. To compute its prediction in trial t the algorithm uses an n-row matrix X_{k-1} and an n-dimensional weight vector $\boldsymbol{v}_{k-1}$, where subscript $k - 1$ indicates the number of times matrix X and vector $\boldsymbol{v}$ have been updated in the first $t - 1$ trials. Initially, the algorithm sets $X_0 = \emptyset$ (the empty matrix) and $\boldsymbol{v}_0 = \boldsymbol{0}$. Upon receiving the t-th instance $\boldsymbol{x}_t \in \mathbb{R}^n$, the algorithm builds the augmented matrix $S_t = [\, X_{k-1} \; \boldsymbol{x}_t \,]$ (where $\boldsymbol{x}_t$ is intended to be the last column of S_t) and predicts the label y_t of $\boldsymbol{x}_t$ with $\widehat{y}_t = \mathrm{SGN}\left(\boldsymbol{v}_{k-1}^\top \left(aI_n + S_t\, S_t^\top\right)^{-1} \boldsymbol{x}_t\right)$, with I_n being the $n \times n$ identity matrix (the addition of I_n guarantees that the above inverse always exists). If $\widehat{y}_t \neq y_t$ then a mistake occurs and the algorithm updates both $\boldsymbol{v}_{k-1}$ and X_{k-1}. Vector $\boldsymbol{v}_{k-1}$ is updated using the Perceptron rule $\boldsymbol{v}_k = \boldsymbol{v}_{k-1} + y_t\, \boldsymbol{x}_t$, whereas matrix X_{k-1} is updated using $X_k = S_t = [\, X_{k-1} \; \boldsymbol{x}_t \,]$. The new matrix X_k and the new vector $\boldsymbol{v}_k$ will be used in the next prediction. If $\widehat{y}_t = y_t$ no update takes place, hence the algorithm is mistake driven [21]. Also, just after an update matrix X_k has as many columns as the number of mistakes made by the algorithm so far. Note that, unlike the Perceptron algorithm, here $\boldsymbol{w}_t$ does depend on $\boldsymbol{x}_t$ (through S_t). Therefore the second-order Perceptron algorithm is *not* a linear-threshold predictor.[2]

In a sense, our algorithm might be viewed as a binary classification version of an on-line regression algorithm investigated by Vovk [29] and Azoury and Warmuth [5]. This algorithm is an instance of Vovk's general *aggregating algorithm*, and is called the "forward algorithm" in [5]. Both our algorithm and the forward

---

[2] The reader might wonder whether this nonlinear dependence on the current instance $\boldsymbol{x}_t$ is somehow necessary. As a matter of fact, if in Figure 1 we predicted using X_{k-1} instead of the augmented matrix S_t, then the resulting algorithm would be a linear threshold algorithm. Such an algorithm, however, we have been unable to analyze.

algorithm predict with a weight vector $\boldsymbol{w}_t$ given by the product of the inverse covariance matrix from past trials and a linear combination of past instance vectors. In both cases the current instance $\boldsymbol{x}_t$ is incorporated into the current covariance matrix before prediction. But, unlike the forward algorithm, we only keep track of past trials where the underlying (0-1) loss of the algorithm was nonzero. To complete this qualitative analogy, we notice that the analysis of our algorithm uses tools developed in [5] for the forward algorithm.

4   Analysis

We now claim the theoretical properties of our algorithm. The following theorem is proven in Appendix A.

Theorem 1. *Let the second-order Perceptron algorithm in Figure 1 be run on a sequence of examples* $\mathcal{S} = ((\boldsymbol{x}_1, y_1), (\boldsymbol{x}_2, y_2), \ldots, (\boldsymbol{x}_T, y_T))$. *Then the total number* m *of mistakes satisfies*

$$m \leq \frac{D_\gamma(\boldsymbol{u}; \mathcal{S})}{\gamma} + \sqrt{\frac{\left(a + \boldsymbol{u}^\top X_m X_m^\top \boldsymbol{u}\right) \sum_{i=1}^n \ln\left(1 + \lambda_i/a\right)}{\gamma^2}}$$

for all $\gamma > 0$ *and for all unit norm vectors* $\boldsymbol{u} \in \mathbb{R}^n$, *where* $\lambda_1, \ldots, \lambda_n$ *are the eigenvalues of* $X_m X_m^\top$.

A few remarks are in order.

We observe that the quantity $\boldsymbol{u}^\top X_m X_m^\top \boldsymbol{u}$ in the above bound always lies between $\min_i \lambda_i$ and $\max_i \lambda_i$. In particular, $\boldsymbol{u}^\top X_m X_m^\top \boldsymbol{u} = \lambda_i$ when $\boldsymbol{u}$ is aligned with the eigenvector associated with λ_i. This fact entails a trade-off between the hinge loss term and the square-root term in the bound.

From Figure 1 the reader can see that the larger a the more the "warping" matrix $(aI_n + S_t S_t^\top)^{-1}$ gets similar to the diagonal matrix $a^{-1}I_n$. In fact, in the limit as $a \to \infty$ the second-order Perceptron algorithm becomes the classical Perceptron algorithm and the bound in Theorem 1 takes the form

$$m \leq \frac{D_\gamma(\boldsymbol{u}; \mathcal{S})}{\gamma} + \sqrt{\frac{\sum_{i=1}^n \lambda_i}{\gamma^2}} \ .$$

Now, since the trace of a matrix equals the sum of its eigenvalues and the nonzero eigenvalues of $X_m X_m^\top$ coincide with the nonzero eigenvalues of the Gram matrix $X_m^\top X_m$, we can immediately see that $\sum_{i=1}^n \lambda_i = \operatorname{trace}(X_m^\top X_m) = \sum_{t \in \mathcal{M}} \|\boldsymbol{x}_t\|^2 \leq m\left(\max_{t \in \mathcal{M}} \|\boldsymbol{x}_t\|^2\right)$, where $\mathcal{M} \subseteq \{1, \ldots, T\}$ is the set of mistaken trials. Thus, setting $R^2 = \max_{t \in \mathcal{M}} \|\boldsymbol{x}_t\|^2$, we can solve the resulting bound for m. This gives

$$m \leq \frac{R^2}{2\gamma^2} + \frac{D_\gamma(\boldsymbol{u}; \mathcal{S})}{\gamma} + \frac{R}{\gamma}\sqrt{\frac{D_\gamma(\boldsymbol{u}; \mathcal{S})}{\gamma} + \frac{R^2}{4\gamma^2}},$$

which is the Perceptron bound in the general nonseparable case. In general, the larger a the more the algorithm in Figure 1 resembles the Perceptron algorithm.

In the linearly separable case the mistake bound for the Perceptron algorithm is $(R/\gamma)^2$, whereas the second-order Perceptron algorithm has $\sqrt{(a + \boldsymbol{u}^\top X_m X_m^\top \boldsymbol{u})\sum_{i=1}^{n} \ln(1 + \lambda_i/a)}\,/\,\gamma$. A comparison of these two bounds suggests that data sequences that are linearly separable only by hyperplanes whose normal vectors are aligned with eigenvectors having small eigenvalues should be advantageous for the second-order Perceptron algorithm. The preliminary experimental results we report in Section 7 support this intuition.

We finally observe that the running time per trial of the second-order algorithm is $\Theta(n^2)$, since using the well-known Sherman-Morrison formula (see, e.g., [25]) we can perform matrix inversion incrementally. In particular, the $n \times n$ matrix $\left(aI_n + S_t\, S_t^\top\right)^{-1}$ can be computed from $\left(aI_n + X_{k-1}\, X_{k-1}^\top\right)^{-1}$ in time $\Theta(n^2)$.

5   The Algorithm in Dual Variables

In this section we show that the second-order Perceptron algorithm can be equivalently formulated in dual variables. This formulation allows us to run the algorithm efficiently in any given reproducing kernel Hilbert space (see, e.g., [27,10]). The following theorem is essentially a binary classification version of the dual formulation of the ridge regression algorithm [17]. A proof sketch is given in Appendix B.

Theorem 2. *With the notation of Figure 1, let $\widetilde{\boldsymbol{y}}_t$ be the k component vector whose first $k-1$ components are the labels y_i where the algorithm has made a mistake up to trial $t-1$ and whose last component is 0. Then, for any $\boldsymbol{x}_t \in \mathbb{R}^n$ we have*

$$\boldsymbol{w}_t^\top \boldsymbol{x}_t = \widetilde{\boldsymbol{y}}_t^\top \left(aI_k + G_t\right)^{-1} S_t^\top \boldsymbol{x}_t,$$

where $G_t = S_t^\top S_t$ is a $k \times k$ (Gram) matrix and I_k is the k-dimensional identity matrix.

From a computational standpoint, we remark that the k dimensional matrix $\left(aI_k + G_t\right)^{-1}$ can be computed incrementally from the $k-1$ dimensional matrix $\left(aI_{k-1} + X_{k-1}^\top X_{k-1}\right)^{-1}$ via a known adjustment formula for partitioned matrices (see, e.g., [18]). This adjustment formula requires the calculation of only $\Theta(k^2)$ extra dot products. Hence, sweeping through a sequence of T examples needs only $O(m^2 T)$ dot products, where m is upper bounded as in Theorem 1.

6   Second-Order Perceptron with Adaptive Parameter

A major drawback of the algorithm described in Figure 1 is that its input parameter a is fixed ahead of time. It turns out that in any practical application the value of this parameter significantly affects performance. For instance, a bad choice of a might make the second-order Perceptron algorithm similar to the first-order one, even in cases when the former should perform far better. In this section we refine the arguments of Section 4 by motivating and analyzing an adaptive parameter version of the algorithm in Figure 1. Ideally, we would like the resulting algorithm be able to learn on the fly the "best" a for the given data sequence, such as the value of a that minimizes the bound in Theorem 1. The optimal a clearly depends on unknown quantities, like the spectral structure of data and the unknown target $\boldsymbol{u}$. This ideal choice of a would be able to automatically turn the second-order algorithm into a first-order one when the actual scattering of data has, say, spherical symmetry. This is a typical eigenstructure of data which a second-order algorithm cannot take advantage of.

To make our argument, we first notice that the value of a in Theorem 1 affects the bound only through the quantity

$$(a + \lambda_{\boldsymbol{u}}) \sum_{i=1}^{n} \ln\left(1 + \lambda_i/a\right), \tag{2}$$

where we set for brevity $\lambda_{\boldsymbol{u}} = \boldsymbol{u}^\top X_m X_m^\top \boldsymbol{u}$. In turn, both $\lambda_{\boldsymbol{u}}$ and the $\lambda_i's$ only depend on the examples where the algorithm has made a mistake. Therefore it seems reasonable to let a change only in mistaken trials.

Our second-order algorithm with adaptive parameter is described in Figure 2. The algorithm is the same as the one in Figure 1, except that we now feed the algorithm with an *increasing* sequence of parameter values $\{a_k\}_{k=1,2,\ldots}$, indexed by the current number of mistakes k. The algorithm is analyzed in Theorem 3 below. From the proof of that theorem (given in Appendix C) the reader can see that any strictly increasing sequence $\{a_k\}$ results in a bound on the number of mistakes. In Theorem 3 we actually picked a sequence which grows *linearly* with k. This choice seems best according to the following simple upper bounding argument. Consider again Expression (2). As we noticed in Section 4, $\sum_{i=1}^{n} \lambda_i = \sum_{t \in \mathcal{M}} \|\boldsymbol{x}_t\|^2 \leq R^2 m$, where $R = \max_{t \in \mathcal{M}} \|\boldsymbol{x}_t\|$. Thus

$$(2) \leq \max_{\mu_1,\ldots,\mu_n \,:\, \sum_{i=1}^{n} \mu_i \leq R^2 m} (a + \lambda_{\boldsymbol{u}}) \sum_{i=1}^{n} \ln\left(1 + \mu_i/a\right)$$

$$= (a + \lambda_{\boldsymbol{u}}) \, n \ln\left(1 + \frac{R^2 m}{n \, a}\right), \tag{3}$$

since the maximum is achieved when all μ_j are equal to $R^2 m/n$. Now, from the Cauchy-Schwartz inequality one gets $\lambda_{\boldsymbol{u}} = \boldsymbol{u}^\top X_m X_m^\top \boldsymbol{u} = \boldsymbol{u}^\top \left(\sum_{t \in \mathcal{M}} \boldsymbol{x}_t \boldsymbol{x}_t^\top\right) \boldsymbol{u} = \sum_{t \in \mathcal{M}} (\boldsymbol{u}^\top \boldsymbol{x}_t)^2 \leq R^2 m$. On the other hand, if the data sequence is linearly separable with margin $\gamma > 0$ then $\lambda_{\boldsymbol{u}} = \sum_{t \in \mathcal{M}} (\boldsymbol{u}^\top \boldsymbol{x}_t)^2 \geq \gamma^2 m$. Hence, in any interesting case, $\lambda_{\boldsymbol{u}}$ is linear in m. A further glance at (3) allows us to conclude that, viewed as a function of m, (3) cannot grow less than linearly. Moreover, this minimal growth speed is achieved when a is a linear[3] function of m.

It is important to point out that this qualitative argument does not depend on the number of nonzero eigenvalues of matrix $X_m X_m^\top$. Thus if we could disregard, say, all but the first $r < n$ directions in the instance space $\mathbb{R}^n$ our conclusion would be the same.

---

[3] The reader will notice that if a grows faster than linearly then (3) is still linear in m. However, the resulting (multiplicative) constants in (3) would be larger.

Parameter sequence: $\{a_k\}_{k=1,2,\ldots}, \quad a_{k+1} > a_k > 0, \; k = 1, 2, \ldots.$
Initialization: $X_0 = \emptyset; \; v_0 = 0; \; k = 1.$
Repeat for $t = 1, \ldots, T$:

1. get instance $x_t \in \mathbb{R}^n$;
2. set $S_t = [\, X_{k-1} \; x_t \,]$;
3. predict $\widehat{y}_t = \text{SGN}(w_t^\top x_t) \in \{-1, +1\}$,
   where $w_t = \left(a_k I_n + S_t \, S_t^\top\right)^{-1} v_{k-1}$;
4. get label $y_t \in \{-1, +1\}$;
5. if $\widehat{y}_t \neq y_t$ then
$$v_k = v_{k-1} + y_t \, x_t,$$
$$X_k = S_t,$$
$$k \leftarrow k + 1.$$

Fig. 2. The second-order Perceptron algorithm with increasing parameter sequence $\{a_k\}_{k=1,2,\ldots}$

Theorem 3 below uses[4] $a_k = c R^2 k$, where c is a small positive constant. This tuning captures the "right" order of growth of a_k, up to a multiplicative constant c, whose best choice depends again on unknown quantities.

Theorem 3. *Let the second-order Perceptron algorithm of Figure 2 be run on a sequence of examples* $\mathcal{S} = ((x_1, y_1), (x_2, y_2), \ldots, (x_T, y_T))$, *where* $\|x_t\| \leq R$. *Let the algorithm's parameter sequence be* $a_k = c R^2 k$, *where* $c > 0$. *Then the total number* m *of mistakes satisfies*

$$m \leq \frac{D_\gamma(u; \mathcal{S})}{\gamma} + \sqrt{\frac{\left(a_m + u^\top X_m X_m^\top u\right)\left(B(c, m) + \sum_{i=1}^n \ln\left(1 + \lambda_i / a_m\right)\right)}{\gamma^2}}$$

for all $\gamma > 0$ *and for all unit norm vectors* $u \in \mathbb{R}^n$, *where* $\lambda_1, \ldots, \lambda_n$ *are the eigenvalues of* $X_m X_m^\top$, $a_m = c R^2 m$ *and* $B(c, m) = \frac{1}{c} \ln \frac{m + 1/c}{1 + 1/c}$.

It is useful to compare the bounds in Theorem 1 and Theorem 3. Theorem 3 replaces a with a_m, i.e., with a quantity depending on all (relevant) past examples. The price we pay for this substitution is a further additive term $B(c, m)$ which has a mild (logarithmic) dependence on m. The resulting bound is in implicit form, though (an upper bound on) an explicit solution could be clearly calculated. Details will be given in the full paper.

It is worth pointing out that the total number m of mistakes made by the algorithm conveys relevant information about the specific dataset at hand. Using a parameter that scales with this number allows one to partially exploit this information. Notice, for instance, that if the second-order algorihm in Figure 2 is making "many" mistakes (and c is not too small) then the algorithm tends to behave as a first-order algorithm, since a_k is growing "fast". This approach of parameter tuning is similar to the *self-confident* tuning adopted in [3].

---

[4] The presence of the scaling factor R^2 simplifies the analysis in Appendix C.

We finally notice that, unlike the algorithm with fixed a, here incremental matrix inversion looks a bit more troublesome. In fact, making a change from trial to trial results in a matrix update which is no longer a low-rank adjustment. Therefore the algorithm in Figure 2 (as well as its dual version) does not seem to have an update rule requiring only a quadratic number of operations per trial.

7   Preliminary Experimental Results

We ran our second-order Perceptron algorithm on two sets of linearly separable data with 100 attributes. The correlation matrix of each dataset has a single dominant eigenvalue. In the first dataset (leftmost plot in Figure 3), the separating hyperplane is orthogonal to the eigenvector associated with the dominant eigenvalue. In the second dataset (rightmost plot in Figure 3), the separating hyperplane is orthogonal to the eigenvector associated with the second-largest eigenvalue. According to the remarks following Theorem 1, we expect the Perceptron algorithm to perform similarly on both datasets (as the radius of the enclosing ball and the margin do not change between datasets), whereas the second-order Perceptron algorithm is expected to outperform the Perceptron algorithm on the second dataset.

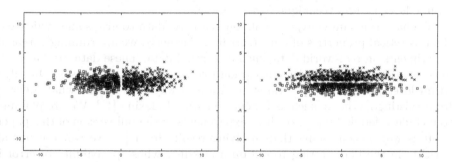

Fig. 3. Projection on the two most relevant coordinates of the 100-dimensional datasets used in our experiments

Algorithm	mistakes 1st dataset	mistakes 2nd dataset
Perceptron	30.20 (6.24)	29.80 (8.16)
2nd-order Perceptron, $a = 1$	9.60 (2.94)	5.60 (2.80)
2nd-order Perceptron, $a = 10$	10.60 (2.58)	3.20 (1.47)
2nd-order Perceptron, $a = 50$	14.00 (4.36)	10.40 (6.05)

Fig. 4. Average number of mistakes and standard deviations (in braces) in the experiments on the two datasets described in the main text

This conjecture is supported by Figure 4, summarizing the number of mistakes made by the Perceptron algorithm and the second-order Perceptron algorithm (for different values of parameter a) on a test set of 3000 examples after training for two epochs on a training set of 9000 examples (the numbers in the table are averaged over 5 random permutations of the training set). Normalizing the instances did not alter significantly Perceptron's performance.

We have not run experiments with the adaptive parameter algorithm yet.

8   Conclusions and Ongoing Research

We have introduced a new on-line binary classification algorithm, called second-order Perceptron algorithm. This algorithm appears to be able to exploit certain spectral properties of the data sequence to improve classification performance. In the absence of such properties, the algorithm can be turned into the (first-order) Perceptron algorithm just by setting its input parameter a to a large number. The optimal tuning of a depends, in general, on the whole training sequence. Since the value of a affects performance significantly, we have also developed a variant of the basic algorithm which is able to adaptively tune this parameter.

Our second-order Perceptron algorithm might be seen as a new on-line classification technology. As such, this technology could be combined with previous techniques, such as the shifting target technique [16,2] and the approximate on-line large margin technique (e.g., [20,14]).

We have run simple experiments on synthetic data to give some evidence of the theoretical properties of our algorithm. Currently, we are running extensive experiments on real-world data, such as textual data. These data are known to have a spectral structure that is exploitable in categorization tasks. Our algorithm leverages on this spectral structure in a way that is somewhat different from existing methods, such as Latent Sematinc Indexing [11]. We are planning to include a detailed report of these experiments in the full version of this paper.

It is worth mentioning that applying results from [9], we can use our algorithm in the i.i.d. setting to obtain a classifier whose probability of error is bounded by a quantity related to the mistake bounds of Theorems 1 and 3. The resulting data-dependent generalization bound is similar in spirit to the bound given in [30] (Theorem 5.2 therein). Both bounds are able to capture the spectral properties of data, though the two bounds are not readily comparable. In fact, the results in [30] are proven through involved covering numbers arguments which consider the Gram matrix G of the *whole* sequence of examples. These results are expressed in terms of all the "large" eigenvalues of G, taken in decreasing order of magnitude up to the "effective number of dimensions".[5] In contrast to that, our result considers only the submatrix of G made up of instances where the algorithm has made a mistake, but the bound is in terms of all the eigenvalues of this submatrix.

The main questions left open in this paper concern the adaptive parameter version of our algorithm. First, we believe more work needs to be done for refining

---

[5] The "effective number of dimensions" depends, for instance, on the margin of the data.

the proof technique used in Theorem 3. The linear growth of a_k is certainly a first step towards on-line parameter adaptation, though it is somewhat unsatisfactory, since it leaves the leading coefficient of a_k unspecified. Second, we are not aware of any incremental updating scheme for this algorithm (neither in primal nor in dual form). In the i.i.d. setting it might actually be possible to get rid of parameter a by projecting onto the subspace of relevant eigenvectors, as is done for the LinRel algorithm in [4]. However, we suspect that this would make the algorithm a bit time-consuming (slower than quadratic).

Acknowledgments

Thanks to Bob Williamson for fruitful conversations. We also thank the COLT program committee members for their helpful comments.

References

1. Angluin, D. (1988). Queries and concept learning. *Machine Learning*, 2(4), 319–342. 121, 122
2. Auer, P., & Warmuth, M. K. (1998). Tracking the best disjunction. *Machine Learning*, 32(2), 127–150. 122, 130
3. Auer, P., Cesa Bianchi, N., & Gentile, C. (2001). Adaptive and self-confident on-line learning algorithms. *Journal of Computer and System Sciences*, to appear. 128
4. Auer, P. (2000). Using Upper Confidence Bounds for Online Learning. In *41st FOCS*, IEEE, pp. 270–279. 131
5. Azoury K. S., & Warmuth, M. K. (2001). Relative loss bounds for on-line density estimation with the exponential familiy of distributions. *Machine Learning*, 43(3), 211–246. 121, 124, 125, 133, 135
6. Ben-Israel, A. & Greville, T. N. E. (1974). *Generalized Inverses: Theory and Applications*. John Wiley and Sons. 134
7. Block, H. D. (1962). The perceptron: A model for brain functioning. *Reviews of Modern Physics*, 34, 123–135. 121, 123
8. Cesa-Bianchi, N., Freund, Y., Haussler, D., Helmbold, D. P., Schapire, R. E., & Warmuth, M. K. (1997). How to use expert advice. *J. ACM*, 44(3), 427–485. 122
9. Cesa-Bianchi, N., Conconi, A., & Gentile, C. (2001). On the generalization ability of on-line learning algorithms. In *NIPS 13*, MIT Press, to appear. 130
10. Cristianini, N. & Shawe-Taylor, J. (2001). *An Introduction to Support Vector Machines*. Cambridge University Press. 122, 126
11. Deerwester, S., Dumais, S. T., Furnas, G. W., Laundauer, T. K., & Harshman, R. A. (1990). Indexing by latent semantic analysis. *Journal of the American Society for Information Science*, 41(6), 391–407. 130
12. Duda, R. O., Hart, P. E., & Stork, D. G. (2000). *Pattern Classification*. John Wiley and Sons. 123
13. Gentile, C. & Warmuth, M. (1998). Linear hinge loss and average margin. In *NIPS 10*, MIT Press, pp. 225–231. 122
14. Gentile, C. (2001). A new approximate maximal margin classification algorithm. *Journal of Machine Learning Research*, 2, 213–242. 130
15. Grove, A. J., Littlestone, N., & Schuurmans, D. (2001). General convergence results for linear discriminant updates. *Machine Learning Journal*, 43(3), 173–210. 122

16. Herbster, M., & Warmuth, M. K. (1998). Tracking the best expert. *Machine Learning Journal*, 32(2), 151–178. 122, 130
17. Hoerl, A., & Kennard, R. (1970). Ridge regression: biased estimation for nonorthogonal problems. *Technometrics*, 12, 55–67. 126
18. Horn, R. A., & Johnson, C. R. (1985). *Matrix Analysis*. Cambridge University Press. 126
19. Kivinen, J., Warmuth, M. K., & Auer, P. (1997). The perceptron algorithm vs. winnow: linear vs. logarithmic mistake bounds when few input variables are relevant. *Artificial Intelligence*, 97, 325–343. 122
20. Li, Y., & Long, P. (2002). The relaxed online maximum margin algorithm. *Machine Learning Journal*, 46(1/3), 361–387. 130
21. Littlestone, N. (1988). Learning quickly when irrelevant attributes abound: a new linear-threshold algorithm. *Machine Learning*, 2(4), 285–318. 121, 122, 124
22. Littlestone, N., & Warmuth, M. K. (1994). The weighted majority algorithm. *Information and Computation*, 108:2, 212–261. 122
23. Marcus, M., & Minc, H. (1965). *Introduction to Linear Algebra*. Dover. 123, 133
24. Novikov, A. B. J. (1962). On convergence proofs on perceptrons. *Proc. of the Symposium on the Mathematical Theory of Automata, vol. XII*, pp. 615–622. 121, 123
25. Press, W. H., Flannery, B. P., Teukolsky, S. A., & Wetterling. W. T. (1989). *Numerical Recipes in Pascal*. Cambridge University Press. 126
26. Rosenblatt, F. (1958). The perceptron: A probabilistic model for information storage and organization in the brain. *Psychological Review*, 65, 386–408. 121
27. Vapnik, V. (1998). *Statistical learning theory*. New York: J. Wiley & Sons. 122, 126
28. Vovk, V. (1990). Aggregating strategies. In *3rd COLT*, Morgan Kaufmann, pp. 371–383. 122
29. Vovk, V. (2001). Competitive on-line statistics. *International Statistical Review*, 69, 213–248. 121, 124
30. Williamson, R. C., Shawe-Taylor, J., Schölkopf, B., & Smola, A. (1999). Sample based generalization bounds. Technical Report NC-TR-99-055, NeuroCOLT. 130

A   Proof of Theorem 1

Fix an arbitrary sequence $\mathcal{S} = ((\boldsymbol{x}_1, y_1), (\boldsymbol{x}_2, y_2), \ldots, (\boldsymbol{x}_T, y_T))$ and let $\mathcal{M} \subseteq \{1, 2, \ldots, T\}$ be the set of trials where the algorithm in Figure 1 made a mistake. Let $A_0 = a I_n$ and $A_k = a I_n + X_k X_k^\top$. We study the evolution of $\boldsymbol{v}_k^\top A_k^{-1} \boldsymbol{v}_k$ over mistaken trials. Let t be the trial where the k-th mistake occurred. We have

$$
\begin{aligned}
\boldsymbol{v}_k^\top A_k^{-1} \boldsymbol{v}_k &= \left(\boldsymbol{v}_{k-1} + y_t \boldsymbol{x}_t\right)^\top A_k^{-1} \left(\boldsymbol{v}_{k-1} + y_t \boldsymbol{x}_t\right) \\
&\qquad (\text{since } \widehat{y}_t \neq y_t \text{ implies } \boldsymbol{v}_k = \boldsymbol{v}_{k-1} + y_t \boldsymbol{x}_t) \\
&= \boldsymbol{v}_{k-1}^\top A_k^{-1} \boldsymbol{v}_{k-1} + 2 y_t \left(A_k^{-1} \boldsymbol{v}_{k-1}\right)^\top \boldsymbol{x}_t + \boldsymbol{x}_t^\top A_k^{-1} \boldsymbol{x}_t \\
&= \boldsymbol{v}_{k-1}^\top A_k^{-1} \boldsymbol{v}_{k-1} + 2 y_t \boldsymbol{w}_t^\top \boldsymbol{x}_t + \boldsymbol{x}_t^\top A_k^{-1} \boldsymbol{x}_t \\
&\qquad (\text{since } \widehat{y}_t \neq y_t \text{ implies } X_k = S_t \text{ and } A_k^{-1} \boldsymbol{v}_{k-1} = \boldsymbol{w}_t) \\
&\leq \boldsymbol{v}_{k-1}^\top A_k^{-1} \boldsymbol{v}_{k-1} + \boldsymbol{x}_t^\top A_k^{-1} \boldsymbol{x}_t \\
&\qquad (\text{since } \widehat{y}_t \neq y_t \text{ implies } y_t \boldsymbol{w}_t^\top \boldsymbol{x}_t \leq 0)
\end{aligned}
$$

Now, note that A_k can be recursively defined using $A_k = A_{k-1} + \boldsymbol{x}_t\boldsymbol{x}_t^\top$. Hence, applying the Sherman-Morrison formula,

$$\boldsymbol{v}_{k-1}^\top A_k^{-1}\boldsymbol{v}_{k-1} = \boldsymbol{v}_{k-1}^\top A_{k-1}^{-1}\boldsymbol{v}_{k-1} - \frac{\left(\boldsymbol{v}_{k-1}^\top A_{k-1}^{-1}\boldsymbol{x}_t\right)^2}{1 + \boldsymbol{x}_t^\top A_{k-1}^{-1}\boldsymbol{x}_t} \leq \boldsymbol{v}_{k-1}^\top A_{k-1}^{-1}\boldsymbol{v}_{k-1},$$

where the inequality holds since A_{k-1}^{-1} is the inverse of a positive definite matrix (and so A_{k-1}^{-1} is positive definite). Thus we get

$$\boldsymbol{v}_k^\top A_k^{-1}\boldsymbol{v}_k \leq \boldsymbol{v}_{k-1}^\top A_{k-1}^{-1}\boldsymbol{v}_{k-1} + \boldsymbol{x}_t^\top A_k^{-1}\boldsymbol{x}_t,$$

holding for all trials $t \in \mathcal{M}$. Summing the last inequality over $k = 1, \ldots, m = |\mathcal{M}|$ (or, equivalently, over $t \in \mathcal{M}$) and using $\boldsymbol{v}_0 = \boldsymbol{0}$ yields

$$\boldsymbol{v}_m^\top A_m^{-1}\boldsymbol{v}_m \leq \sum_{t\in\mathcal{M}} \boldsymbol{x}_t^\top A_k^{-1}\boldsymbol{x}_t$$

$$\leq \sum_{k=1}^{m} \left(1 - \frac{\det(A_{k-1})}{\det(A_k)}\right) \qquad \text{(using Lemma A.1 from [5])}$$

$$\leq \sum_{k=1}^{m} \ln \frac{\det(A_k)}{\det(A_{k-1})} \qquad \text{(since } 1 - x \leq -\ln x \text{ for all } x > 0\text{)}$$

$$= \ln \frac{\det(A_m)}{\det(A_0)}$$

$$= \ln \frac{\det(aI_n + X_m X_m^\top)}{\det(aI_n)}$$

$$= \sum_{i=1}^{n} \ln\left(1 + \frac{\lambda_i}{a}\right), \qquad (4)$$

where $\lambda_1, \ldots, \lambda_n$ are the eigenvalues of $X_m X_m^\top$.

To conclude the proof, note that $A_m^{1/2}$ does exist since A_m is positive definite (e.g., [23, Ch. 3]). Pick any unit norm vector $\boldsymbol{u} \in \mathbb{R}^n$ and let $\boldsymbol{z} = A_m^{1/2}\boldsymbol{u}$. Then, using the Cauchy-Schwartz inequality we have

$$\sqrt{\boldsymbol{v}_m^\top A_m^{-1}\boldsymbol{v}_m} = \left\|A_m^{-1/2}\boldsymbol{v}_m\right\| \geq \frac{\left(A_m^{-1/2}\boldsymbol{v}_m\right)^\top \boldsymbol{z}}{\|\boldsymbol{z}\|} = \frac{\boldsymbol{v}_m^\top\boldsymbol{u}}{\sqrt{\boldsymbol{u}^\top A_m\boldsymbol{u}}} =$$

$$= \frac{\boldsymbol{v}_m^\top\boldsymbol{u}}{\sqrt{a + \boldsymbol{u}^\top X_m X_m^\top\boldsymbol{u}}} \geq \frac{\gamma m - D_\gamma(\boldsymbol{u};\mathcal{S})}{\sqrt{a + \boldsymbol{u}^\top X_m X_m^\top\boldsymbol{u}}}, \qquad (5)$$

where the last inequality follows from the very definition of $D_\gamma(\boldsymbol{u};\mathcal{S})$ and holds for any $\gamma > 0$. Putting together (4) and (5) and solving for m gives the statement of the theorem. □

B   Proof Sketch of Theorem 2

Recalling Figure 1, we have $\boldsymbol{v}_{k-1} = S_t \widetilde{\boldsymbol{y}}_t$. This implies $\boldsymbol{w}_t = \left(aI_n + S_t S_t^\top\right)^{-1} S_t \widetilde{\boldsymbol{y}}_t$ and $\boldsymbol{w}_t^\top \boldsymbol{x}_t = \widetilde{\boldsymbol{y}}_t^\top \left(\left(aI_n + S_t S_t^\top\right)^{-1} S_t\right)^\top \boldsymbol{x}_t$. Thus we only need to prove that $\left(\left(aI_n + S_t S_t^\top\right)^{-1} S_t\right)^\top = (aI_k + G_t)^{-1} S_t^\top$ holds. But this follows from, e.g., part (d) of Exercise 17 in [6]. $\qquad\square$

C   Proof of Theorem 3

The proof is a more refined version of the proof of Theorem 1, and proceeds along the same lines.

Again, we assume that the k-th mistake occurs when processing example $(\boldsymbol{x}_t, y_t)$ and let $\mathcal{M} \subseteq \{1, 2, \ldots, T\}$ be the set of trials where a mistake occurred. Let $A_k = a_k I_n + X_k X_k^\top$, $k = 1, 2, \ldots$, and $A_0 = a_1 I_n$. We have

$$A_k = A_{k-1} + (a_k - a_{k-1})I_n + \boldsymbol{x}_t \boldsymbol{x}_t^\top, \quad k = 1, 2, \ldots, \tag{6}$$

where $a_0 = a_1$. We study the evolution of the quantity $\boldsymbol{v}_k^\top A_k^{-1} \boldsymbol{v}_k$ over mistaken trials. As in the proof of Theorem 1, we have

$$\boldsymbol{v}_k^\top A_k^{-1} \boldsymbol{v}_k \le \boldsymbol{v}_{k-1}^\top A_k^{-1} \boldsymbol{v}_{k-1} + \boldsymbol{x}_t^\top A_k^{-1} \boldsymbol{x}_t . \tag{7}$$

We need to bound $\boldsymbol{v}_{k-1}^\top A_k^{-1} \boldsymbol{v}_{k-1}$ from above. From (6) we see that when $k \ge 2$ the matrix A_k is the sum of the nonsingular matrices A_{k-1} and $(a_k - a_{k-1})I_n + \boldsymbol{x}_t \boldsymbol{x}_t^\top$ (the latter is nonsingular since $a_k > a_{k-1}$). Thus, when $k \ge 2$ computing A_k^{-1} can be done through the general inversion formula

$$(B + C)^{-1} = B^{-1} - B^{-1}(B^{-1} + C^{-1})^{-1}B^{-1}$$

with $B = A_{k-1}$ and $C = (a_k - a_{k-1})I_n + \boldsymbol{x}_t \boldsymbol{x}_t^\top$. Now, since both B and C are positive definite, so is the matrix $B^{-1}(B^{-1}+C^{-1})^{-1}B^{-1}$ (this easily follows from the fact that the inverse of a positive definite matrix is again positive definite and that both the sum and the product of two positive definite matrices give rise to positive definite matrices). Hence if $k \ge 2$ we can write

$$\begin{aligned}
\boldsymbol{v}_{k-1}^\top A_k^{-1} \boldsymbol{v}_{k-1} &= \boldsymbol{v}_{k-1}^\top (B + C)^{-1} \boldsymbol{v}_{k-1} \\
&= \boldsymbol{v}_{k-1}^\top \left(B^{-1} - B^{-1}(B^{-1} + C^{-1})^{-1}B^{-1}\right) \boldsymbol{v}_{k-1} \\
&\le \boldsymbol{v}_{k-1}^\top B^{-1} \boldsymbol{v}_{k-1} = \boldsymbol{v}_{k-1}^\top A_{k-1}^{-1} \boldsymbol{v}_{k-1} .
\end{aligned} \tag{8}$$

On the other hand, when $k = 1$ inequality (8) is trivially true since $\boldsymbol{v}_0 = \boldsymbol{0}$. Thus the inequality holds for all $k \ge 1$. We plug (8) back into (7), sum over $k = 1, \ldots, m = |\mathcal{M}|$ and take into account that $\boldsymbol{v}_0 = \boldsymbol{0}$. We obtain

$$\begin{aligned}
\boldsymbol{v}_m^\top A_m^{-1} \boldsymbol{v}_m &\le \sum_{t \in \mathcal{M}} \boldsymbol{x}_t^\top A_k^{-1} \boldsymbol{x}_t \\
&\le \sum_{k=1}^{m} \left(1 - \frac{\det(A_{k-1} + (a_k - a_{k-1})I_n)}{\det(A_k)}\right)
\end{aligned}$$

(from (6) and Lemma A.1 in [5])

$$\leq \sum_{k=1}^{m} \ln \frac{\det(A_k)}{\det(A_{k-1} + (a_k - a_{k-1})I_n)} \ . \tag{9}$$

The presence of matrix term $(a_k - a_{k-1})I_n$ makes the rest of the proof a bit more involved than the proof of Theorem 1. Willing to obtain bounds in terms of eigenvalues of matrices, we rewrite the rightmost side of (9) as a function of the eigenvalues of matrices $X_k X_k^\top$. Let $\lambda_{k,i}$ be the i-th eigenvalue of matrix $X_k X_k^\top$, with $\lambda_{0,i} = 0$. We can write

$$\ln \frac{\det(A_k)}{\det(A_{k-1} + (a_k - a_{k-1})I_n)} = \sum_{i=1}^{n} \ln \frac{a_k + \lambda_{k,i}}{a_k + \lambda_{k-1,i}} \ .$$

Now, simple manipulations yield

$$\sum_{k-1}^{m} \sum_{i=1}^{n} \ln \frac{a_k + \lambda_{k,i}}{a_k + \lambda_{k-1,i}} = \sum_{k=1}^{m} \sum_{i=1}^{n} \ln \left(\frac{a_k}{a_{k-1}} \frac{a_{k-1} + \lambda_{k-1,i}}{a_k + \lambda_{k,i}} \right)$$

$$+ \sum_{k=1}^{m} \sum_{i=1}^{n} \ln \left(\frac{a_k + \lambda_{k,i}}{a_k + \lambda_{k-1,i}} \right) + \sum_{i=1}^{n} \ln \left(\frac{a_m + \lambda_{m,i}}{a_m} \right)$$

$$= \sum_{k=1}^{m} \sum_{i=1}^{n} \ln \left(\frac{a_k}{a_{k-1}} \frac{a_{k-1} + \lambda_{k-1,i}}{a_k + \lambda_{k-1,i}} \right) + \sum_{i=1}^{n} \ln \left(1 + \frac{\lambda_{m,i}}{a_m} \right) \ .$$

Hence from (9) we have obtained

$$\boldsymbol{v}_m^\top \Lambda_m^{-1} \boldsymbol{v}_m \leq \sum_{k=1}^{m} \sum_{i=1}^{n} \ln \left(\frac{a_k}{a_{k-1}} \frac{a_{k-1} + \lambda_{k-1,i}}{a_k + \lambda_{k-1,i}} \right) + \sum_{i=1}^{n} \ln \left(1 + \frac{\lambda_{m,i}}{a_m} \right). \tag{10}$$

The reader can see that (10) is analogous to (4) but for the presence of a spurious double sum term.

We turn to upper bounding the double sum in (10) as a function of m. We proceed as follows. We first notice that for $k = 1$ the inner sum is zero. Therefore we continue by assuming $k \geq 2$ in the inner sum. Since $X_{k-1} X_{k-1}^\top$ has size $n \times n$ and has rank at most $k - 1$, only $\min\{k - 1, n\}$ among the eigenvalues $\lambda_{k-1,1}, \ldots, \lambda_{k-1,n}$ can be nonzero. Also, as we have observed elsewhere, $X_{k-1} X_{k-1}^\top$ has the same nonzero eigenvalues as the (Gram) matrix $X_{k-1}^\top X_{k-1}$. Since the trace of a matrix equals the sum of its eigenvalues and the trace of $X_{k-1}^\top X_{k-1}$ is at most $(k - 1) R^2$, we have, for $k = 2, \ldots, m$,

$$\sum_{i=1}^{n} \ln \left(\frac{a_k}{a_{k-1}} \frac{a_{k-1} + \lambda_{k-1,i}}{a_k + \lambda_{k-1,i}} \right)$$

$$\leq \max \left\{ \sum_{j=1}^{k'} \ln \left(\frac{a_k}{a_{k-1}} \frac{a_{k-1} + \mu_j}{a_k + \mu_j} \right) : \mu_1, \ldots, \mu_{k'} \geq 0, \ \sum_{j=1}^{k'} \mu_j \leq (k - 1) R^2 \right\},$$

where $k' = \min\{k - 1, n\}$. The maximum is achieved when all μ_j equal $(k-1)$ R^2/k'. Thus

$$\sum_{i=1}^{n} \ln \left(\frac{a_k}{a_{k-1}} \frac{a_{k-1} + \lambda_{k-1,i}}{a_k + \lambda_{k-1,i}} \right) \le k' \ln \left(\frac{a_k}{a_{k-1}} \frac{a_{k-1} + (k-1)R^2/k'}{a_k + (k-1)R^2/k'} \right)$$

$$= k' \ln \left(\frac{k' a_k a_{k-1} + a_k (k-1) R^2}{k' a_k a_{k-1} + a_{k-1} (k-1) R^2} \right), \quad (11)$$

for $k = 2, 3, \ldots, m$.

Now, a derivative argument shows that the function $f(x; \alpha, \beta) = x \ln \left(\frac{x+\alpha}{x+\beta} \right)$ is increasing in $x > 0$ whenever $\alpha > \beta \ge 0$. Therefore we see that

$$(11) = \frac{1}{a_k a_{k-1}} f(a_k a_{k-1} k'; a_k(k-1) R^2, a_{k-1}(k-1) R^2)$$

$$\le \frac{1}{a_k a_{k-1}} f(a_k a_{k-1}(k-1); a_k(k-1) R^2, a_{k-1}(k-1) R^2)$$

$$= (k-1) \ln \left(\frac{a_k}{a_{k-1}} \frac{a_{k-1} + R^2}{a_k + R^2} \right).$$

Hence we can write

$$\sum_{k=1}^{m} \sum_{i=1}^{n} \ln \left(\frac{a_k}{a_{k-1}} \frac{a_{k-1} + \lambda_{k-1,i}}{a_k + \lambda_{k-1,i}} \right) \le \sum_{k=2}^{m} (k-1) \ln \left(\frac{a_k}{a_{k-1}} \frac{a_{k-1} + R^2}{a_k + R^2} \right)$$

$$= \sum_{k=1}^{m-1} k \ln \left(\frac{k+1}{k} \frac{c R^2 k + R^2}{c R^2 (k+1) + R^2} \right)$$

$$\text{(using } a_k = c R^2 k)$$

$$= \sum_{k=1}^{m-1} k \ln \left(1 + \frac{1}{c k^2 + c k + k} \right)$$

$$\le \sum_{k=1}^{m-1} \frac{1}{c k + c + 1} \quad \text{(using } \ln(1 + x) \le x)$$

$$\le \frac{1}{c} \int_{1+1/c}^{m+1/c} \frac{dx}{x}$$

$$= \frac{1}{c} \ln \frac{m + 1/c}{1 + 1/c}$$

$$= B(c, m).$$

To bound $\sqrt{v_m^\top A_m^{-1} v_m}$ from below one can proceed as in the proof of Theorem 1, yielding

$$\sqrt{v_m^\top A_m^{-1} v_m} \ge \frac{\gamma m - D_\gamma(u; \mathcal{S})}{\sqrt{a_m + u^\top X_m X_m^\top u}},$$

where $a_m = c\,R^2 m$. We plug this lower bound back into (10) together with the previous upper bound. After rearranging we obtain

$$\left(\frac{\gamma\,m - D_\gamma(\boldsymbol{u};\mathcal{S})}{\sqrt{a_m + \boldsymbol{u}^\top X_m X_m^\top \boldsymbol{u}}}\right)^2 \leq B(c,m) + \sum_{i=1}^{n} \ln\left(1 + \frac{\lambda_{m,i}}{a_m}\right).$$

Solving for m occurring in the numerator of the left-hand side gives the desired bound.   □

Tracking Linear-Threshold Concepts
with Winnow

Chris Mesterharm

Rutgers Computer Science Department
110 Frelinghuysen Road, Piscataway, NJ 08854
mesterha@paul.rutgers.edu

Abstract. In this paper, we give a mistake-bound for learning arbitrary linear-threshold concepts that are allowed to change over time in the on-line model of learning. We use a standard variation of the Winnow algorithm and show that the bounds for learning shifting linear-threshold functions have many of the same advantages that the traditional Winnow algorithm has on fixed concepts. These benefits include a weak dependence on the number of irrelevant attributes, inexpensive runtime, and robust behavior against noise. In fact, we show that the bound for the tracking version of Winnow has even better performance with respect to irrelevant attributes. Let $X \in [0,1]^n$ be an instance of the learning problem. In the traditional algorithm, the bound depends on $\ln n$. In this paper, the shifting concept bound depends approximately on $\max \ln \left(\|X\|_1 \right)$.

1 Introduction

In this paper, we give a mistake bound for a standard variation of the Winnow algorithm that is used in tracking shifting concepts. We show that this version of Winnow can learn arbitrary linear-threshold functions that are allowed to change in time.

The mistake bound applies to the on-line model of learning [1]. On-line learning is composed of trials where each trial is divided into three steps. First, in trial t, the algorithm receives an instance, $X^t \in [0,1]^n$. Next, the algorithm predicts the label of the instance, $\hat{y}^t \in \{0,1\}$. Last, the environment returns the correct classification, $y^t \in \{0,1\}$. Normally, the correct classification is assumed to come from some fixed target function. In this paper, we will assume the target function is allowed to shift over the course of the trials. The goal of the algorithm is to minimize the total number of prediction mistakes made during the trials.

Winnow is an on-line algorithm that predicts with a linear-threshold function. The algorithm uses the correct classification returned by the environment to update the weights of the linear-threshold function. The update procedure is similar to the Perceptron algorithm[2, 3] except that the updates are multiplicative instead of additive. This results in an algorithm that is relatively insensitive to the behavior of a large number of irrelevant attributes, inexpensive to run, and robust versus noise[4].

J. Kivinen and R. H. Sloan (Eds.): COLT 2002, LNAI 2375, pp. 138–153, 2002.

The only change in the tracking version of Winnow is that the attribute weights are not allowed to go below a given constant, $\epsilon > 0$. Anytime a normal Winnow update attempts to lower a weight below ϵ, the weight is set to ϵ. Intuitively, this modification allows the algorithm to quickly learn a moving concept by not allowing the weights to get too small. When an attribute becomes relevant, its weight only needs to be increased from ϵ to the new value. Therefore the algorithm is able to track moving concepts while still keeping the advantages of the traditional Winnow algorithm.

This weight minimum modification has been used with various Winnow type algorithms. In particular, it has been used to give mistake-bounds for learning changing experts [5, 6] and drifting disjunctions [7]. This paper builds on those results by giving a mistake-bound for arbitrary linear-threshold functions that are allowed to shift. These types of algorithms have been shown to be useful in practice, learning shifting concepts such as predicting disk idle times for mobile applications [8] and solving load balancing problems on a network of computers [9]. The additional knowledge that some of these algorithms have good bounds when learning arbitrary shifting linear-threshold concepts may help justify applying these algorithms to a wider range of tracking problems.

Another contribution of this paper is to show that the tracking version of Winnow eliminates the dependence of the algorithm on the number of attributes. With an appropriate setting of parameters, instead of the algorithm depending on $\ln(n)$, as in the normal Winnow algorithm, the algorithm depends approximately on the maximum value over all trials of $\ln(\|X^t\|_1)$.[1] Therefore the algorithm performs well with sparse instances in ways that are similar to infinite attribute algorithms[10].

Other related work includes [11] which gives a technique to convert a wide range of algorithms that learn fixed linear functions to shifting problems. While learning linear functions is similar to learning linear-threshold functions, at this point, these results have only been extended to cover disjunctions and not arbitrary linear-threshold functions.

The remainder of the paper is organized as follows. In Sect. 2, we give a formal statement of the concept tracking problem and the tracking Winnow algorithm. We then present the mistake bound. In Sect. 3, we give a proof for this mistake bound. In Sect. 4, we compare the mistake bound to previous bounds on certain types of linear-threshold problems. Section 5 contains the conclusion and ideas for future work.

2   Problem Statement and Solution

In this section, we review the concept tracking Winnow algorithm and give the notation that is needed to understand an upper-bound on the number of mistakes.

---

[1] These benefits can most likely be extended to the normal, fixed concept version of Winnow by appropriately setting the parameters.

2.1 Algorithm

Here is the modified Winnow algorithm for learning shifting concepts[5, 7]. The only change in the algorithm, in this paper, is that we force the initial weights to be set to the value of the minimum weight, ϵ.

Initialization

> Weight multiplier, $\alpha > 1$.
> Minimum value of the weights, $0 < \epsilon < 1$.
> Algorithm weights, $w_1^0, \ldots, w_n^0 = \epsilon$.
> Trial number, $t = 0$.

The algorithm proceeds in a series of trials composed of the following three steps.

Instance at trial t

> $X^t = (x_1^t, \ldots, x_n^t) \in [0,1]^n$

Prediction at trial t

> if $\sum_{i=1}^n w_i^t x_i^t \geq 1$
> > predict $\hat{y}^t = 1$
> else
> > predict $\hat{y}^t = 0$

Update at trial t

> correct label $= y^t$
> if $y^t = \hat{y}^t$
> > $\forall i \in \{1, \ldots, n\}\ \ w_i^{t+1} = w_i^t$
> else (mistake)
> > if $y^t = 1$ (promotion step)
> > > $\forall i \in \{1, \ldots, n\}\ \ w_i^{t+1} = \alpha^{x_i^t} w_i^t$
> > else $y^t = 0$ (demotion step)
> > > $\forall i \in \{1, \ldots, n\}\ \ w_i^{t+1} = \max(\epsilon, \alpha^{-x_i^t} w_i^t)$
> $t \leftarrow t + 1$

2.2 Concept

The model of concept on-line tracking we present in this paper is similar to a model defined in [12]. The central element of the mistake bound is a sequence of concepts. Let $C = (C_1, \ldots, C_k)$ be a sequence of concepts where $k \in N$.

An adversary generates the instances and is allowed two operations. The goal of the algorithm is to minimize the number of mistakes for any possible sequence of operations.

Adversary operations

1. The adversary can generate instance (X^t, y^t) if the noise predicate Ω is true.
2. The adversary can step forward in the concept sequence.

The predicate Ω is necessary to limit the amount of noisy instances the adversary can generate. If the adversary was allowed to generate an arbitrary number of noisy instances, the concept would be impossible to learn. For example, we could restrict the adversary so that it is only allowed to generate a fixed amount of noise over all the trials. In this case, $\Omega = \left(\sum_{j=1}^{t} \aleph^j \le K \right)$ where $K \in R$ and $\aleph^j$ is a measure of the noise in trial j. This is similar to the noise model in [1], yet by changing the Ω predicate, it should be possible to extended the results to a more complex noise model such as that found in [13].

We define concept C_j by specifying the weights, $\mathbf{u^j}$, of a linear-threshold function and a separation parameter δ^j. Notice that are using a slightly different notation than that used for the algorithm weights. For the algorithm weights the superscript refers to the trial number; for the target weights the superscript refers to the concept number. The separation parameter specifies a distance from the concept such that any instance that occurs in this region is considered a noisy instance. This is a standard assumption that is needed to prove mistake bounds for these types of algorithms [4, 13, 14]. All other noisy instances come from an instance that is misclassified by the current concept C_j.

Concept C_j parameters

$u_1^j, \ldots, u_n^j \ge 0$ where $u_i^j \in R$
$0 < \delta^j \le 1$ where $\delta^j \in R$

An instance with $\aleph^t = 0$ corresponds an instance of the current concept. An instance with $\aleph^t > 0$ corresponds to a noisy instance, and $\aleph^t$ is a measure of the error in the linear-threshold function.

Concept C_j noise

if $y^t = 1$
$$\aleph^t = \max \left(0, 1 + \delta^j - \sum_{i=1}^{n} (u_i^j x_i^t) \right)$$
if $y^t = 0$
$$\aleph^t = \max \left(0, \sum_{i=1}^{n} (u_i^j x_i^t) - (1 - \delta^j) \right)$$

2.3   Mistake-Bound

The mistake bound uses the following notation. This notation will be explained and motivated in the proof section.

Terms used in the main mistake bound

Let $\lambda \ge \max \left(6.5\delta, \max_{t \in N} \|X^t\|_1 \right)$.
Let $\zeta = \min_{t \in N, \ i \in \{1, \cdots, n\}} \{x_i^t \mid x_i^t > 0\}$.
Let $H(C) = \sum_{i=1}^{n} (u_i^k + \sum_{j=1}^{k-1} \max(0, u_i^j - u_i^{j+1}))$.
Let $\delta \le \min_{j \in \{1, \ldots, k\}} \delta^j$.

Theorem 1. *For instances generated by a concept sequence C with $\sum_{t \in N} \aleph^t$ noise, if $\alpha = 1 + \delta$ and $\epsilon = \frac{\delta}{\lambda \ln(\lambda/\delta)}$ then the number of mistakes is less than*

$$\frac{H(C)(2+\delta)\left(\zeta\delta + \ln\left(\frac{1}{\zeta}\right) + \ln\left(\frac{\lambda}{\delta}\right) + \ln\ln\left(\frac{\lambda}{\delta}\right)\right)}{\delta^2\left(1 - \frac{1}{\ln(\lambda/\delta)}\right)} + \frac{(2+\delta)\sum_{t \in N}\aleph^t}{(\delta+\delta^2)\left(1 - \frac{1}{\ln(\lambda/\delta)}\right)} .$$

Using the fact that $\lambda \geq 6.5\delta$ and $0 < \zeta, \delta \leq 1$, this bound is an element of

$$O\left(H(C)\ln\left(\frac{\lambda}{\zeta\delta}\right)/\delta^2 + \sum_{t \in N}\aleph^t/\delta\right) .$$

3   Proof of Mistake-Bound

The proof in this section closely follows the style of proof given in [4]. While most modern Winnow type proofs use a potential function to bound the number of mistakes[1, 13, 14, 7], the potential function style of proof has been difficult to convert to tracking arbitrary linear-threshold concepts. While the potential function proof has benefits,[2] we have found it fruitful to go back to the old style of proof to deal with tracking linear-threshold functions. It is a topic for future research to understand how this type of proof relates to the potential function techniques.

The purpose of the next four lemmas is to give an upper-bound on the number of demotions as a function of the number of promotions. Remember that a promotion is an update that increases the weights on a mistake where the correct label is 1, and a demotion is an update that decreases the weights on a mistake where the correct label is 0. Intuitively, a bound must exist as long as every demotion removes at least a fixed constant of weight. This is because the algorithm always has positive weights and the only way the weights can increase is through a promotion.

Let $\triangle(f)$ represent the change in function f after a trial is completed. For example, $\triangle\left(\sum_{i=1}^{n} w_i^t\right) = \sum_{i=1}^{n} w_i^{t+1} - \sum_{i=1}^{n} w_i^t$.

Lemma 1. *On a promotion, $\triangle\left(\sum_{i=1}^{n} w_i^t\right) < (\alpha - 1)$.*

Proof. After a promotion,

$$\sum_{i=1}^{n} w_i^{t+1} = \sum_{i=1}^{n} w_i^t\, \alpha^{x_i^t} .$$

Next, we use the fact that $\alpha^{x_i^t} \leq (\alpha - 1)x_i^t + 1$ for all $x_i^t \in [0,1]$. (This is true because $\alpha^{x_i^t}$ is a convex function.) to show that,

$$\sum_{i=1}^{n} w_i^t\, \alpha^{x_i^t} \leq \sum_{i=1}^{n} w_i^t[(\alpha-1)x_i^t + 1] = (\alpha - 1)\sum_{i=1}^{n} w_i^t x_i^t + \sum_{i=1}^{n} w_i^t .$$

---

[2] It is useful for generalization[14] and has slightly better bounds for fixed concepts.

Since we have a promotion, $\sum_{i=1}^{n} w_i^t x_i^t < 1$. This combined with the above facts and remembering that $\alpha > 1$ gives,

$$\sum_{i=1}^{n} w_i^{t+1} < (\alpha - 1) + \sum_{i=1}^{n} w_i^t .$$

Therefore,

$$\triangle \left(\sum_{i=1}^{n} w_i^t \right) = \sum_{i=1}^{n} w_i^{t+1} - \sum_{i=1}^{n} w_i^t < (\alpha - 1) .$$

□

Next we want to prove a similar result about demotions. However, because demotions have the added difficulty of not being able to lower the weight below ϵ, the proof is a little more complex. First we will prove a small lemma that will help with the more difficult proof.

We are going to consider two types of attributes that occur during a demotion. Let $A \subseteq \{1, \ldots, n\}$ be all i such that $w_i \alpha^{-x_i^t} < \epsilon$. These are the indexes of weights that are forced to ϵ since $w_i^{t+1} = \max(\epsilon, \alpha^{-x_i^t} w_i^t)$. Let $B \subseteq \{1, \ldots, n\}$ be the indexes of weights that have a normal demotion. These are the attributes such that $x_i^t > 0$ and $w_i^t \alpha^{-x_i^t} \geq \epsilon$. All the other weights do not change.

Lemma 2. *On a demotion, if* $\sum_{i \in B} w_i^t x_i^t \geq \theta$ *then* $\triangle \left(\sum_{i \in B} w_i^t \right) \leq \frac{1-\alpha}{\alpha} \theta$.

Proof. After a demotion,

$$\sum_{i \in B} w_i^{t+1} = \sum_{i \in B} w_i^t \, \alpha^{-x_i^t} .$$

Next, we use the fact that $\alpha^{-x_i^t} \leq \left(\frac{1}{\alpha} - 1\right) x + 1$ for all $x_i^t \in [0, 1]$ (This fact is true because $\alpha^{-x_i^t}$ is a convex function.) to show that

$$\sum_{i \in B} w_i^t \, \alpha^{-x_i^t} \leq \sum_{i \in B} w_i^t \left[\left(\frac{1}{\alpha} - 1\right) x_i^t + 1 \right] = \frac{1 - \alpha}{\alpha} \sum_{i \in B} w_i^t x_i^t + \sum_{i \in B} w_i^t .$$

Based on the assumption of the lemma, $\sum_{i \in B} w_i^t x_i^t \geq \theta$. This combined with the above facts and remembering that $\alpha > 1$ gives,

$$\sum_{i \in B} w_i^{t+1} \leq \frac{1 - \alpha}{\alpha} \theta + \sum_{i \in B} w_i^t .$$

Therefore,

$$\triangle \left(\sum_{i \in B} w_i^t \right) = \sum_{i \in B} w_i^{t+1} - \sum_{i \in B} w_i^t \leq \frac{1 - \alpha}{\alpha} \theta .$$

□

Here is the main lemma concerning demotions. This lemma gives an upper-bound on how much the weights decrease after a demotion. The amount of decrease will depend on various factors including $\lambda \geq \max\left(6.5\delta, \max_{t \in N} \sum_{i=1}^{n} x_i^t\right)$. (The reason for this condition will become clear latter in the proof.) Also this lemma assumes that $\epsilon \leq 1/\lambda$. This is a reasonable assumption that ensures the algorithm can lower weights during demotions. Otherwise the algorithm could be forced to always make a mistake on certain instances for some linear-threshold concepts.

Lemma 3. *On a demotion, if $\epsilon < 1/\lambda$ then $\triangle\left(\sum_{i=1}^{n} w_i^t\right) < \frac{1-\alpha}{\alpha}(1 - \epsilon\lambda)$.*

Proof. We are going to use the set of attributes A and B defined earlier. We will break the proof into two cases. For the first case assume that there is at least one attribute in B. Since a demotion has occurred we know,

$$\sum_{i \in A} w_i^t x_i^t + \sum_{i \in B} w_i^t x_i^t = \sum_{i=1}^{n} w_i^t x_i^t \geq 1 .$$

From this we can use lemma 2 to derive that

$$\triangle\left(\sum_{i \in B} w_i^t x_i^t\right) \leq \frac{1-\alpha}{\alpha}\left(1 - \sum_{i \in A} w_i^t x_i^t\right) .$$

Now we want to get $\sum_{i \in A} w_i^t x_i^t$ into a more useful form. Let v_i^t represent the amount w_i^t is above ϵ.

$$\sum_{i \in A} w_i^t x_i^t = \sum_{i \in A}(\epsilon + v_i^t)x_i^t = \epsilon\sum_{i \in A} x_i^t + \sum_{i \in A} v_i^t x_i^t < \epsilon\lambda + \sum_{i \in A} v_i^t .$$

Being careful to keep track of what is negative, we can substitute this into the previous formula.

$$\triangle\left(\sum_{i \in B} w_i^t x_i^t\right) < \frac{1-\alpha}{\alpha}\left(1 - \epsilon\lambda - \sum_{i \in A} v_i^t\right) .$$

Next, since all the weights with an index in A get demoted to ϵ, we know that for all $i \in A$, the weight v_i^t will be removed. Therefore $\triangle\left(\sum_{i \in A} w_i^t\right) = -\sum_{i \in A} v_i^t$. Combining this information proves the first case where B has at least one element.

$$\triangle\left(\sum_{i=1}^{n} w_i^t\right) = \triangle\left(\sum_{i \in B} w_i^t\right) + \triangle\left(\sum_{i \in A} w_i^t\right)$$

$$< \frac{1-\alpha}{\alpha}\left(1 - \epsilon\lambda - \sum_{i \in A} v_i^t\right) - \sum_{i \in A} v_i^t \leq \frac{1-\alpha}{\alpha}(1 - \epsilon\lambda) .$$

The second case, where B is empty, is similar. Using some of the same notation,

$$\triangle\left(\sum_{i=1}^{n} w_i^t\right) = \triangle\left(\sum_{i \in A} w_i^t\right) = -\sum_{i \in A} v_i^t .$$

Since a demotion has occurred, we know that $\sum_{i=1}^{n} w_i^t x_i^t \geq 1$, but since the only active attributes are in A,

$$1 \leq \sum_{i=1}^{n} w_i^t x_i^t = \sum_{i \in A}(\epsilon + v_i^t)x_i^t = \epsilon \sum_{i \in A} x_i^t + \sum_{i \in A} v_i^t x_i^t \leq \epsilon \lambda + \sum_{i \in A} v_i^t \ .$$

We can use this to bound $\triangle\left(\sum_{i=1}^{n} w_i^t\right)$.

$$\triangle\left(\sum_{i=1}^{n} w_i^t\right) = -\sum_{i \in A} v_i^t \leq \epsilon \lambda - 1 < \frac{1-\alpha}{\alpha}(1 - \epsilon \lambda) \ .$$

The last step of the inequality is true since we assumed $\epsilon < 1/\lambda$.   □

Now we can combine the lemmas to give an upper-bound on the number of demotions as a function of the number of promotions. Let $P = \{t \mid$ promotion mistake on trial $t\}$, and let $D = \{t \mid$ demotion mistake on trial $t\}$.

Lemma 4. *If $\epsilon < 1/\lambda$ then at any trial, $|D| < \frac{\alpha}{1-\epsilon\lambda}|P|$.*

Proof. We know $\sum_{i=1}^{n} w_i^t$ can never go below ϵn, and we know $\sum_{i=1}^{n} w_i^t$ has a value of ϵn at the beginning of the algorithm. Since the weights can only change during demotions and promotions.

$$\epsilon n \leq \epsilon n + \sum_{t \in P} \triangle\left(\sum_{i=1}^{n} w_i^t\right) + \sum_{t \in D} \triangle\left(\sum_{i=1}^{n} w_i^t\right) \ .$$

Using the upper-bounds from lemma 1 and lemma 3,

$$\epsilon n < \epsilon n + (\alpha - 1)|P| + \frac{1-\alpha}{\alpha}(1 - \epsilon\lambda)|D| \ .$$

Rearranging this inequality proves the lemma.   □

Our goal at this stage is to show how the relevant weights (weights, w_i, where the corresponding target weights have $u_i > 0$) increase in weight during the running of the algorithm. If we can show that they must eventually increase, and that they have a maximum value, we can derive a mistake bound on the algorithm. First we want to give a bound on the maximum value of a weight. To do this, we will use the parameter $\zeta = \min_{t \in N,\ i \in \{1,\cdots,n\}}\{x_i^t \mid x_i^t > 0\}$.

Lemma 5. *if $\alpha < e$ then $\forall i \in \{1,\ldots,n\}\ \forall j \in N\ \ w_i^j < \frac{\alpha^\zeta}{\zeta}$.*

Proof. If a promotion never occurs the maximum weight is ϵ. Otherwise, we need to look at weights that are increased by a promotion, because a weight must reach its maximum value after a promotion. The only time a weight, w_a^j can increase is after a promotion where the attribute $x_a^j > 0$. Promotions can only occur if $\sum_{i=1}^{n} w_i^j x_i^j < 1$. Therefore for any attribute $x_a^j > 0$,

$$w_a^j x_a^j \leq \sum_{i=1}^{n} w_i^j x_i^j < 1 \ .$$

Since the new weight is $\alpha^{x_a^j} w_a^j$, we want to find $\max(\alpha^x w)$ over all x and w where $0 < \zeta \le x \le 1$ and $wx < 1$. Since any feasible solution to the above problem can be changed to increase the maximum by increasing either w or x until $wx = 1$, we can get an upper-bound on the maximum weight by setting $wx = 1$. This transforms the problem to $\max(\alpha^x/x)$ over all x given that $0 < \zeta \le x \le 1$. This can be solved with calculus to show that the maximum must occur at one of the ends of the interval. This gives an upper-bound on any weight of $\max(\epsilon, \alpha, \alpha^\zeta/\zeta)$. Using the assumption that $\epsilon < 1$ and that $\alpha > 1$ shows that $\max(\epsilon, \alpha, \alpha^\zeta/\zeta) = \max(\alpha, \alpha^\zeta/\zeta)$.

To show that $\max(\alpha, \alpha^\zeta/\zeta) = \alpha^\zeta/\zeta$, we need the assumption that $\alpha < e$. Let $f(x) = \alpha x$ and $g(x) = \alpha^x$. Taking derivatives, $f'(x) = \alpha$ and $g'(x) = \ln(\alpha)\alpha^x$. Therefore when $x \in (0,1]$ and $1 < \alpha < e$

$$g'(x) = \ln(\alpha)\alpha^x < \alpha = f'(x) \ .$$

Since the slope of $g(x)$ is always less than the slope of $f(x)$ in the $(0,1]$ interval, the functions can intersect at most once in the interval. (One can prove this with the mean value theorem.) The point they intersect is at $x = 1$. Since $g(0) > f(0)$, it is straightforward to show that for $x \in (0,1]$ and $1 < \alpha < e$ that $g(x) \ge f(x)$, and therefore $\alpha^x/x \ge \alpha$. This shows that $\max(\alpha, \alpha^\zeta/\zeta) = \alpha^\zeta/\zeta$ when $\alpha < e$. $\square$

The next lemma deals with the effects of the demotions and promotions on a sequence of target concepts. Let $H(C) = \sum_{i=1}^{n} \left(u_i^k + \sum_{j=1}^{k-1} \max(0, u_i^j - u_i^{j+1}) \right)$ and let $\delta \le \min_{j \in \{1,\dots,k\}} \delta^j$.

Lemma 6. *If $\alpha < e$ then*

$$\log_\alpha \left(\frac{\alpha^\zeta}{\epsilon\zeta} \right) H(C) + \sum_{t \in N} \aleph^t > (1+\delta)|P| - (1-\delta)|D| \ .$$

Proof. First, we define $s(j) \in N$ as the first trial that has an instance generated from concept j. Let $s(k+1)$ be the final trial in the sequence of instances[3]. The adversary will determine the values of the $s(j)$.

Let $z_i^j = \log_\alpha \left(w_i^{s(j+1)}/\epsilon \right)$ and $z_i^0 = 0$. This is just the amount weight i has been increased by an α factor over the minimum value ϵ after the last trial of concept j. The value of $w_i^{s(j)}$ is ϵ multiplied by α^{x_i} on every promotion and effectively multiplied by a number as small as $\alpha^{-x_i^t}$ on every demotion. Let $P_j = \{t \mid \text{promotion mistake on trial } t \text{ during concept } j\}$. Let $D_j = \{t \mid \text{demotion mistake on trial } t \text{ during concept } j\}$.

$$w_i^{s(j)} \ge \epsilon \exp \left[\ln(\alpha) \left(\sum_{t \in P_1 \cup \cdots \cup P_j} x_i^t - \sum_{t \in D_1 \cup \cdots \cup D_j} x_i^t \right) \right] \ .$$

---

[3] The analysis still works for a potentially infinite number of trials, since the proof does not depend on when this final trial occurs.

Using the definition of z, this gives

$$z_i^j \geq \left(\sum_{t \in P_1 \cup \cdots \cup P_j} x_i^t - \sum_{t \in D_1 \cup \cdots \cup D_j} x_i^t \right) .$$

The value $z_i^j - z_i^{j-1}$ is the change in z_i during concept j. Again on every promotion, we add x_i^t, and on every demotion, we subtract at most x_i^t. Therefore,

$$z_i^j - z_i^{j-1} \geq \left(\sum_{t \in P_j} x_i^t - \sum_{t \in D_j} x_i^t \right) .$$

At this point, we want to weight the change in the z values by u, the target weights. This will allow us to relate the z values to the mistakes on non-noisy instances.

$$\sum_{j=1}^{k} \sum_{i=1}^{n} u_i^j (z_i^j - z_i^{j-1}) \geq \sum_{j=1}^{k} \sum_{i=1}^{n} u_i^j \left(\sum_{t \in P_j} x_i^t - \sum_{t \in D_j} x_i^t \right) .$$

Let $c(t) = j$ where j is the concept that is in effect during trial t. The preceding formula is equal to

$$\sum_{t \in P} \sum_{i=1}^{n} u_i^{c(t)} x_i^t - \sum_{t \in D} \sum_{i=1}^{n} u_i^{c(t)} x_i^t .$$

Let $\hat{P} = \{t \mid t \in P \text{ and } \aleph^t > 0\}$ and $\hat{D} = \{t \mid t \in D \text{ and } \aleph^t > 0\}$. These are the noisy promotion and demotion trials. Using this notation, we can break up the summations. The preceding formula is equal to

$$\sum_{t \in P - \hat{P}} \sum_{i=1}^{n} u_i^{c(t)} x_i^t - \sum_{t \in D - \hat{D}} \sum_{i=1}^{n} u_i^{c(t)} x_i^t + \sum_{t \in \hat{P}} \sum_{i=1}^{n} u_i^{c(t)} x_i^t - \sum_{t \in \hat{D}} \sum_{i=1}^{n} u_i^{c(t)} x_i^t .$$

Since for every non-noisy promotion $\sum_{i=1}^{n} u_i^t x_i^t \geq (1 + \delta)$, and every non-noisy demotion $\sum_{i=1}^{n} u_i^t x_i^t \leq (1 - \delta)$, then the last formula is greater or equal to

$$(1 + \delta)|P - \hat{P}| - (1 - \delta)|D - \hat{D}| + \sum_{t \in \hat{P}} \sum_{i=1}^{n} u_i^{c(t)} x_i^t - \sum_{t \in \hat{D}} \sum_{i=1}^{n} u_i^{c(t)} x_i^t$$

$$= (1+\delta)|P| - (1-\delta)|D| - \sum_{t \in \hat{P}} \left((1+\delta) - \sum_{i=1}^{n} u_i^{c(t)} x_i^t \right) - \sum_{t \in \hat{D}} \left((1-\delta) + \sum_{i=1}^{n} u_i^{c(t)} x_i^t \right) .$$

Using the definitions of noisy promotion and demotion trials, we can use the previous equations to conclude that

$$\sum_{j=1}^{k} \sum_{i=1}^{n} u_i^j (z_i^j - z_i^{j-1}) \geq (1 + \delta)|P| - (1 - \delta)|D| - \sum_{t \in N} \aleph^t .$$

Based on lemma 5, when $\alpha < e$ the maximum value of any weight is less than $\alpha^\varsigma/\varsigma$, therefore, $0 \le z_i^j < \log_\alpha\left(\frac{\alpha^\varsigma}{\epsilon\varsigma}\right)$. We can use this constraint to compute an upper bound. Therefore,

$$(1+\delta)|P| - (1-\delta)|D| - \sum_{t\in N}\aleph^t \le \max\left(\sum_{i=1}^n u_i^1(z_i^1 - z_i^0) + \cdots + u_i^k(z_i^k - z_i^{k-1})\right)$$

$$= \max\left(\sum_{i=1}^n z_i^1(u_i^1 - u_i^2) + \cdots + z_i^{k-1}(u_i^{k-1} - u_i^k) + z_i^k(u_i^k)\right)$$

$$< \log_\alpha\left(\frac{\alpha^\varsigma}{\epsilon\varsigma}\right)\sum_{i=1}^n\left(u_i^k + \sum_{j=1}^{k-1}\max(0, u_i^j - u_i^{j+1})\right) .$$

Rearranging the terms proves the lemma. $\qquad\square$

In its current form, the above lemma is not very intuitive. However, there is another way to look at the bound. Instead of $h(i) = u_i^k + \sum_{j=1}^{k-1}\max(0, u_i^j - u_i^{j+1})$, one can look at the local maxima and minima of the sequence of u_i. The value $h(i)$ is equivalent to summing the local maximums and subtracting the local minimums. For example, if the sequence of a particular u_i is $(.1, .3, .5, .5, .2, .1, .4, .2)$ then $h(i) = .5 - .1 + .4 = .8$.

At this point, we want to prove the main theorem. We have attempted to set the parameters and arrange the inequalities to optimize the bound for small δ.

Theorem 1. *For instances generated by a concept sequence C with $\sum_{t\in N}\aleph^t$ noise, if $\alpha = 1 + \delta$ and $\epsilon = \frac{\delta}{\lambda\ln(\lambda/\delta)}$ then the number of mistakes is less than*

$$\frac{H(C)(2+\delta)\left(\varsigma\delta + \ln\left(\frac{1}{\varsigma}\right) + \ln\left(\frac{\lambda}{\delta}\right) + \ln\ln\left(\frac{\lambda}{\delta}\right)\right)}{\delta^2\left(1 - \frac{1}{\ln(\lambda/\delta)}\right)} + \frac{(2+\delta)\sum_{t\in N}\aleph^t}{(\delta + \delta^2)\left(1 - \frac{1}{\ln(\lambda/\delta)}\right)} .$$

Proof. First we want to show that the algorithm condition $\epsilon < 1$ is satisfied. Using the fact that $\lambda \ge 6.5\delta$, (This is part of the reason we define $\lambda \ge \max\left(6.5\delta, \max_{t\in N}\|X^t\|_1\right)$. Another reason is to minimize the mistake-bound.)

$$\epsilon = \frac{\delta}{\lambda\ln(\lambda/\delta)} \le \frac{\delta}{6.5\delta\ln(6.5)} = \frac{1}{6.5\ln(6.5)} < 1 .$$

Next, we want to substitute lemma 4 into lemma 6 to get an upper-bound on $|P|$. The lemma condition that $\alpha < e$ is satisfied since $\alpha = 1 + \delta \le 2 < e$. The condition that $\epsilon < 1/\lambda$ is satisfied since

$$\epsilon\lambda = \frac{\delta}{\ln(\lambda/\delta)} \le \frac{\delta}{\ln(6.5)} < 1 .$$

Now we can proceed with the substitution.

$$H(C)\log_\alpha\left(\frac{\alpha^\zeta}{\epsilon\zeta}\right) + \sum_{t\in N}\aleph^t > (1+\delta)|P| - (1-\delta)\frac{\alpha}{1-\epsilon\lambda}|P|.$$

Solving for $|P|$ gives,

$$|P| < \frac{H(C)\log_\alpha\left(\frac{\alpha^\zeta}{\epsilon\zeta}\right) + \sum_{t\in N}\aleph^t}{(1+\delta) - (1-\delta)\frac{\alpha}{1-\epsilon\lambda}}.$$

Now we will add $|P|$ to both sides of lemma 4 and substitute in the previous result to get a bound on the number of mistakes.

$$|P| + |D| < \left(1 + \frac{\alpha}{1-\epsilon\lambda}\right)|P| < \left(1 + \frac{\alpha}{1-\epsilon\lambda}\right)\frac{H(C)\log_\alpha\left(\frac{\alpha^\zeta}{\epsilon\zeta}\right) + \sum_{t\in N}\aleph^t}{(1+\delta) - (1-\delta)\frac{\alpha}{1-\epsilon\lambda}}$$

$$= \frac{1-\epsilon\lambda+\alpha}{(1+\delta)(1-\epsilon\lambda) - (1-\delta)\alpha}\left(\frac{H(C)(\zeta\ln(\alpha) + \ln(1/\zeta) + \ln(1/\epsilon))}{\ln(\alpha)} + \sum_{t\in N}\aleph^t\right).$$

Substituting in the values $\alpha = 1 + \delta$ and $\epsilon = \frac{\delta}{\lambda\ln(\lambda/\delta)}$, the preceding equation is equal to

$$\frac{2 + \left(1 - \frac{1}{\ln(\lambda/\delta)}\right)\delta}{(\delta+\delta^2)\left(1 - \frac{1}{\ln(\lambda/\delta)}\right)}\left(\frac{H(C)\left(\zeta\ln(1+\delta) + \ln\left(\frac{1}{\zeta}\right) + \ln\left(\frac{\lambda}{\delta}\right) + \ln\ln\left(\frac{\lambda}{\delta}\right)\right)}{\ln(1+\delta)} + \sum_{t\in N}\aleph^t\right).$$

To make the bound more intuitive use the fact that $\delta - \delta^2/2 \leq \ln(1+\delta) \leq \delta$. (One can prove this using the Taylor formula with a fourth term remainder and a third term remainder.) Therefore the above equation is less than or equal to

$$\frac{2 + \left(1 - \frac{1}{\ln(\lambda/\delta)}\right)\delta}{(\delta+\delta^2)\left(1 - \frac{1}{\ln(\lambda/\delta)}\right)}\left(\frac{H(C)\left(\zeta\delta + \ln\left(\frac{1}{\zeta}\right) + \ln\left(\frac{\lambda}{\delta}\right) + \ln\ln\left(\frac{\lambda}{\delta}\right)\right)}{\delta - \delta^2/2} + \sum_{t\in N}\aleph^t\right)$$

$$< \frac{H(C)(2+\delta)\left(\zeta\delta + \ln\left(\frac{1}{\zeta}\right) + \ln\left(\frac{\lambda}{\delta}\right) + \ln\ln\left(\frac{\lambda}{\delta}\right)\right)}{\delta^2\left(1 - \frac{1}{\ln(\lambda/\delta)}\right)} + \frac{(2+\delta)\sum_{t\in N}\aleph^t}{(\delta+\delta^2)\left(1 - \frac{1}{\ln(\lambda/\delta)}\right)}.$$

$\square$

4   Bounds on Specific Problems

In this section of the paper, we will apply the mistake-bound on tracking arbitrary linear-threshold functions to problems that have published bounds and see how the new bound compares to the previous results.

4.1   Fixed Concept

First we will look at the bound for a fixed concept with no noisy trials. In this case, $C = (C_1)$.

Corollary 1. *When instances are generated from concept C_1, if $\alpha = 1 + \delta$ and $\epsilon = \frac{\delta}{\lambda \ln(\lambda/\delta)}$, then the number of mistakes is less than*

$$\frac{(2 + \delta)\left(\zeta\delta + \ln\left(\frac{1}{\zeta}\right) + \ln\left(\frac{\lambda}{\delta}\right) + \ln\ln\left(\frac{\lambda}{\delta}\right)\right)\sum_{i=1}^{n} u_i^1}{\delta^2\left(1 - \frac{1}{\ln(\lambda/\delta)}\right)}.$$

Proof. We just use theorem 1 with the fact that $H(C_1) = \sum_{i=1}^{n} u_i^1$ and $\aleph = 0$. $\square$

Comparing this bound with the general concept tracking bound, it is clear the main difference is the value of the $H(C)$ function. The $H(C)$ function encodes the extra difficulty of tracking a changing concept.

For the normal Winnow algorithm[15], when $\alpha = 1 + \delta$ and the threshold parameter is set to n, the number of attributes in an instance, the number of mistakes is less than or equal to

$$\frac{(2 + \delta)\left(1 + \sum_{i=1}^{n} u_i^1 \ln u_i^1 + (\ln n - 1)\sum_{i=1}^{n} u_i^1\right)}{\delta^2}.$$

While the two bounds are similar, notice how the preceding Winnow bound depends on $\ln n$. In the target tracking proof, the bound depends on $\ln(\lambda/\delta)$, where λ is roughly equal to $\max \|X\|_1$.

It is possible to get similar benefits with Winnow type algorithms by using an infinite attribute algorithm[10]. Infinite attribute algorithms take advantage of the fact that only attributes that are active ($x_i > 0$) during updates effect the algorithm. Therefore the number of attributes that are involved in the algorithm is just the maximum number of attributes active per trial times the mistake bound. Combining this with the logarithmic nature of the Winnow bounds gives a result that only depends logarithmically on the maximum number of attributes active per trial. However there are certain advantages to the algorithm in this paper. First $\|X\|_1$ may be small, yet the number of active attributes may be large. Second when noise is involved in on-line learning, there cannot be a finite mistake bound, and a large number of attributes could eventually be active during mistakes. Since the analysis in this paper does not depend on the total number of active attributes during mistakes, these problems do not occur for the concept tracking version of Winnow in this paper.

4.2   Tracking Disjunctions

As a second example, we give a bound for shifting disjunctions with boolean attributes. Look at a concept sequence C^d such that each $u_i^j \in \{0, 2\}$ and

$\sum_{i=1}^{n} \sum_{i=1}^{k} u_i^j = 2Z^+$. This corresponds to a sequence where Z^+ is the number of disjunction literals that are added to the concept either at the start of the algorithm or during the trials.

Corollary 2. *When instances $X \in \{0,1\}^n$ are generated from concept C^d with noise $\sum_{t \in N} \aleph^t$, if $\alpha = 2$ and $\epsilon = \frac{1}{\lambda \ln \lambda}$, then the number of mistakes is less than*

$$\frac{6Z^+ \left(1 + \ln(\lambda) + \ln\ln(\lambda)\right)}{\left(1 - \frac{1}{\ln(\lambda)}\right)} + \frac{3 \sum_{t \in N} \aleph^t}{2 \left(1 - \frac{1}{\ln(\lambda)}\right)} .$$

Proof. Concept sequence C^d has $H(C^d) = 2Z^+$ and $\delta = 1$. Substituting these values into theorem 1 gives the result. □

To compare this with the bound given in [7], let Z^- equal to the number of disjunction literals that are removed from the concept and let $Z = Z^+ + Z^-$. For the deterministic disjunction tracking algorithm given in theorem 4 of [7] the number of mistakes is less than or equal to

$$4.32Z(\ln n + 3.89) + 4.32\min(n, Z)(\ln n + 1.34) + 0.232 + 1.2 \sum_{t \in N} \aleph^t .$$

Using the fact that for disjunctions $6.5 \leq \lambda \leq n$, these bounds show that the more general results in this paper compare favorably to the previous bound that deals with the limited case of tracking shifting disjunctions.

5   Conclusions

In this paper, we give a proof for the concept tracking version of Winnow that shows it still has good bounds when tracking arbitrary linear-threshold functions. In particular, we compared the new bounds to the best existing Winnow bounds for fixed concepts and shifting disjunctions, showing that the bounds compare favorably. We also show how the performance of this algorithm does not depend on the number of attributes and instead depends approximately on $\max \|X\|_1$. This is similar to the infinite attribute model but has advantages when dealing with real world constraints such as noise.

One problem with the techniques in this paper is that the mistake bound is allowed to grow arbitrarily large when $\zeta = \min\{x_i^t \mid x_i^t > 0\}$ approaches zero. One solution is to transform the instances such that ζ is not allowed to get arbitrarily small. By making the appropriate assumptions, it is possible to allow the effects of small shifts in the value of attributes to be characterized in the δ and $\sum_{t \in N} \aleph^t$ parameters of the learning problem. However this is not completely satisfactory as the issue with ζ is partially an artifact of the proof technique. An interesting question for future research is to eliminate or mitigate the effect of ζ on the bound.

Additional future work is to extend these results to other Winnow algorithms such as the normalized version of Winnow and Balanced Winnow[1]. Normalized Winnow has various advantages such as simple techniques to generalize from binary prediction to multi-class prediction[16]. This will allow the efficient tracking of multi-class linear-threshold concepts. Another area to explore is the development of lower bounds for the tracking version of Winnow when learning certain types of shifting concepts, such as concepts where all the δ_j are equal. Cases where the δ_j change for the various concepts will most likely be more difficult, but at a minimum, tighter upper-bounds can be made for these types of problems.

Acknowledgments

We would like to thank Haym Hirsh, Sofus Macskassy, and the anonymous reviewers for reading this paper and providing valuable comments and corrections. We would also like to thank Mark Herbster for explaining how the current work on tracking linear functions relates to tracking linear-threshold functions.

References

[1] Littlestone, N.: Mistake bounds and linear-threshold learning algorithms. PhD thesis, University of California, Santa Cruz (1989) Technical Report UCSC-CRL-89-11. 138, 141, 142, 151

[2] Rosenblatt, F.: Principles of Neurodynamics: Perceptrons and the Theory of Brain Mechanisms. Spartan Books, Washington, DC (1962) 138

[3] Minsky, M. L., Papert, S. A.: Perceptrons. MIT Press, Cambridge, MA (1969) 138

[4] Littlestone, N.: Learning quickly when irrelevant attributes abound: A new linear-threshold algorithm. Machine Learning **2** (1988) 285–318 138, 141, 142

[5] Littlestone, N., Warmuth, M. K.: The weighted majority algorithm. Information and Computation **108** (1994) 212–261 139, 140

[6] Herbster, M., Warmuth, M. K.: Tracking the best expert. Machine Learning **32** (1998) 151–178 139

[7] Auer, P., Warmuth, M. K.: Tracking the best disjunction. Machine Learning **32** (1998) 127–150 139, 140, 142, 151

[8] Helmbold, D. P., Long, D. D., Sconyers, T. L., Sherrod, B.: Adaptive disk spin-down for mobile computers. Mobile Networks and Applications **5** (2000) 285–297 139

[9] Blum, A., Burch, C.: On-line learning and the metrical task system problem. Machine Learning **39** (2000) 35–58 139

[10] Blum, A., Hellerstein, L., Littlestone, N.: Learning in the presence of finitely or infinitely many irrelevant attributes. In: COLT-91. (1991) 157–166 139, 150

[11] Herbster, M., Warmuth, M. K.: Tracking the best linear predictor. Journal of Machine Learning Research **1** (2001) 281–309 139

[12] Kuh, A., Petsche, T., Rivest, R. L.: Learning time-varying concepts. In: NIPS-3, Morgan Kaufmann Publishers, Inc. (1991) 183–189 140

[13] Littlestone, N.: Redundant noisy attributes, attribute errors, and linear-threshold learning using winnow. In: COLT-91. (1991) 147–156 141, 142

[14] Grove, A. J., Littlestone, N., Schuurmans, D.: General convergence results for linear discriminant updates. In: COLT-97. (1997) 171–183 141, 142

[15] Littlestone, N.: (1998) Unpublished research that generalizes Winnow algorithm. 150
[16] Mesterharm, C.: A multi-class linear learning algorithm related to winnow. In: NIPS-12, MIT Press (2000) 519–525   152

Learning Tree Languages from Text

Henning Fernau*

Department of Computer Science and Software Engineering, University of Newcastle
University Drive, NSW 2308 Callaghan, Australia
fernau@cs.newcastle.edu.au

Abstract. We study the problem of learning regular tree languages
from text. We show that the framework of function distinguishability
as introduced in our ALT 2000 paper is generalizable from the case of
string languages towards tree languages, hence providing a large source
of identifiable classes of regular tree languages. Each of these classes can
be characterized in various ways. Moreover, we present a generic inference algorithm with polynomial update time and prove its correctness.
In this way, we generalize previous works of Angluin, Sakakibara and
ourselves. Moreover, we show that this way all regular tree languages
can be identified approximately.

1 Introduction

Grammatical inference (GI) mostly focussed on learning *string* languages, although there are many practical motivations for studying formally specified sets
not being comprised of words, as well. For example, linguists are often interested
in the dependencies of different parts of a sentence. This sort of dependencies
is likely to be reflected in the derivation *trees* of a context-free grammar which
captures the main syntactical features of the language in question. So, tree languages are quite important to linguists. Application of GI in this setting is
reported, e.g., in [4,16]. Derivation trees play an important role when studying
the use of GI in connection with programming languages, see [5]. Recently, tree
language inference was proposed as a tool in inductive logic programming [3].
In [14, Chapters 3.2 and 6.4], applications of tree language inference to pattern
recognition can be found. Finally, trees can be interpreted equivalently as terms,
so that the study of the inference of tree languages might also contribute to
the learning of term algebras, a topic touched in [17,18,23]. Hence, the study of
the automatic inference of tree languages is well motivated. Besides [17,18], the
classes of regular tree languages presented in this paper are the first ones which
are characterized by well-defined restrictions on automata, an important issue
in GI [15].

In some sense, the present paper can be seen as a continuation of Sakakibara's
work [26] on the inference of 0-reversible tree languages[1] and of ours on the

---

* Most of the work was done while the author was with Wilhelm-Schickard-Institut
für Informatik, Universität Tübingen, Sand 13, D-72076 Tübingen, Germany.

[1] Ideas similar to Sakakibara's are contained in [6]. The section on approximability
notably supplements Sakakibara's work.

J. Kivinen and R. H. Sloan (Eds.): COLT 2002, LNAI 2375, pp. 153–168, 2002.
© Springer-Verlag Berlin Heidelberg 2002

inference of distinguishable string languages [7,9]: We will explore how to learn —exactly and approximately—function distinguishable regular tree languages from text, a setting introduced by Gold [13]. Both [7] and [26] are based on Angluin's paper [2], which was ground-breaking for the revival of the interest in learning regular languages from text.

In a nutshell, a function distinguishable regular tree language is given by a bottom-up deterministic tree automaton such that any occurring backward nondeterminism can be resolved by means of an "oracle" called distinguishing function. The 0-reversible tree languages considered by Sakakibara [26] are a special case where the oracle gives no information at all.

Note that, from a linguistic point of view, the fact that every context-free language is the yield of a 0-reversible tree language is somewhat misleading, since not all possible syntax trees (which reflect the interesting semantical connections) are 0-reversible. Hence, it is important to go beyond 0-reversible tree languages. As we will see, the tree language classes introduced in this paper are a natural extension of the 0-reversible tree languages.

Let us mention that the inferrability of context-free languages was also studied under different learning paradigms [3,25].

2   Definitions

Let $\mathbb{N}$ be the set of nonnegative integers and let $(\mathbb{N}^*, \cdot, \lambda)$ (or simply $\mathbb{N}^*$) be the free monoid generated by $\mathbb{N}$. For $y, x \in \mathbb{N}^*$, write $y \leq x$ iff there is a $z \in \mathbb{N}^*$ with $x = y \cdot z$; "$y < x$" abbreviates: $y \leq x$ and $y \neq x$. $|x|$ denotes the length of x. We are now giving the necessary definitions for trees and tree automata. More details can be found, e.g., in the chapter written by Gécseg and Steinby in [24].

A *ranked alphabet* V is a finite set of symbols together with a finite *rank relation* $r_V \subset V \times \mathbb{N}$. Define $V_n := \{f \in V \mid (f, n) \in r_V\}$. Since elements in V_n are often considered as *function symbols* (standing for functions of *arity* n), elements in V_0 are also called *constant symbols*. A *tree over* V is a mapping $t : \Delta_t \to V$, where the domain Δ_t is a finite subset of $\mathbb{N}^*$ such that (1) if $x \in \Delta_t$ and $y < x$, then $y \in \Delta_t$; (2) if $y \cdot i \in \Delta_t$, $i \in \mathbb{N}$, then $y \cdot j \in \Delta_t$ for $1 \leq j \leq i$. An element of Δ_t is also called a *node* of t, where the node λ is the *root* of the tree. Then $t(x) \in V_n$ whenever, for $i \in \mathbb{N}$, $x \cdot i \in \Delta_t$ iff $1 \leq i \leq n$. If $t(x) = A$, A is the *label* of x. Let V^t denote the set of all finite trees over V. By this definition, trees are rooted, directed, acyclic graphs in which every node except the root has one predecessor and the direct successors of any node are linearly ordered from left to right. Interpreting V as a set of function symbols, V^t can be identified with the well-formed terms over V. This yields a compact string denotation of trees. A *frontier node* in t is a node $y \in \Delta_t$ such there is no $x \in \Delta_t$ with $y < x$. If $y \in \Delta_t$ is not a frontier node, it is called *interior node*. The *depth* of a tree t is defined as $\text{depth}(t) = \max\{|x| \mid x \in \Delta_t\}$, whereas the *size* of t is given by $|\Delta_t|$. Letters will be viewed as trees of size one and depth zero.

We are now going to define a catenation on trees. Let $\$$ be a new symbol, i.e., $\$ \notin V$, of rank 0. Let $V_\$^t$ denote the set of all trees over $V \cup \{\$\}$ which contain exactly one occurrence of label \$. By definition, only frontier nodes can carry the label \$. For trees $u \in V_{\$}^{t}$ and $t \in (V^{t} \cup V_{\$}^{t})$, we define an operation $\#$ to replace the frontier node labelled with \$ of u by t according to

$$u \# t(x) = \begin{cases} u(x), & \text{if } x \in \Delta_u \wedge u(x) \neq \$, \\ t(y), & \text{if } x = z \cdot y \wedge u(z) = \$ \wedge y \in \Delta_t. \end{cases}$$

If $U \subseteq V_{\$}^{t}$ and $T \subseteq (V^{t} \cup V_{\$}^{t})$, then $U \# T := \{u \# t \mid u \in U \wedge t \in T\}$. For $t \in V^{t}$ and $x \in \Delta_t$, the *subtree* of t at x, denoted by t/x, is defined by $t/x(y) = t(x \cdot y)$ for any $y \in \Delta_{t/x}$, where $\Delta_{t/x} := \{y \mid x \cdot y \in \Delta_t\}$. $\mathrm{ST}(T) := \{t/x \mid t \in T \wedge x \in \Delta_t\}$ is the set of subtrees of trees from $T \subseteq V^{t}$. Furthermore, for any $t \in V^{t}$ and any tree language $T \subseteq V^{t}$, the *quotient* of T and t is defined as:

$$U_T(t) := \begin{cases} \{u \in V_{\$}^{t} \mid u \# t \in T\}, & \text{if } t \in V^{t} \setminus V_0, \\ t, & \text{if } t \in V_0. \end{cases}$$

Let V be a ranked alphabet and m be the maximum rank of the symbols in V. A *(bottom-up) tree automaton* over V is a quadruple $A = (Q, V, \delta, F)$ such that Q is a finite state alphabet (disjoint with V_0),[2] $F \subseteq Q$ is a set of final states, and $\delta = (\delta_0, \ldots, \delta_m)$ is an $m + 1$-tuple of state transition functions, where $\delta_0(a) = \{a\}$ for $a \in V_0$ and $\delta_k : V_k \times (Q \cup V_0)^k \to 2^Q$ for $k = 1, \ldots, m$. In this definition, the constant symbols at the frontier nodes are taken as sort of initial states. Now, a transition relation (also denoted by δ) can be recursively defined on V^{t} by letting

$$\delta(f(t_1, \ldots, t_k)) := \begin{cases} \{f\}, & \text{if } k = 0, \\ \bigcup_{q_i \in \delta(t_i), i=1,\ldots,k} \delta_k(f, q_1, \ldots, q_k), & \text{if } k > 0. \end{cases}$$

A tree t is *accepted* by A iff $\delta(t) \cap F \neq \emptyset$. The tree language accepted by A is denoted by $T(A)$. A is *deterministic* if each of the functions δ_k maps each possible argument to a set of cardinality of at most one. Deterministic tree automata can be viewed as algorithms for labelling the nodes of a tree with states. Analogously to the string case, it can be shown that nondeterministic and deterministic finite tree automata accept the same class of tree languages, namely the *regular tree languages*, at the expense of a possibly exponential state explosion.

The notions of *isomorphic* automata and (state subset induced) *subautomata* can be easily carried over from the well-known string case to the tree case. A state q of a deterministic tree automaton A is *useful* iff there exists a tree t and some node $x \in \Delta_t$ such that $\delta(t/x) = q$ and $\delta(t) \in F$. A deterministic automaton containing only useful states is called *stripped*.

We need four special constructions of tree automata in our treatment:

Firstly, we define the analogue of the well-known prefix-tree acceptor in the string case: Let I_+ be a finite tree language over V. The *base tree automaton* for I_+, denoted by $Bs(I_+) = (Q, V, \delta, F)$, is defined as follows: $Q = \mathrm{ST}(I_+) \setminus V_0$,

---

[2] Observe that there is some sort of arbitrariness in having $Q \cap V_0 = \emptyset$. Other papers on tree languages even enforce $V_0 \subseteq Q$. Fortunately, all basic constructions presented in this paper would work with the indicated different definition(s) of tree automata.

$F = I_+$, $\delta_k(f, u_1, \ldots, u_k) = f(u_1, \ldots, u_k)$ whenever $u_1, \ldots, u_k \in Q \cup V_0$ and $f(u_1, \ldots, u_k) \in Q$. Obviously, $T(Bs(I_+)) = I_+$.

Secondly, we transfer the notion of canonical automaton to the tree case: Let T be a regular tree language over V. The *canonical tree automaton* for T, denoted by $C(T) = (Q, V, \delta, F)$, is defined by: $Q = \{U_T(s) \mid s \in \mathrm{ST}(T) \backslash V_0\}$, $F = \{U_T(t) \mid t \in T\}$, $\delta_k(f, U_T(s_1), \ldots, U_T(s_k)) = U_T(f(s_1, \ldots, s_k))$ if $f(s_1, \ldots, s_k)$ is in $\mathrm{ST}(T)$. Observe that $C(T)$ is a deterministic stripped automaton which is formed completely analogously to the minimal deterministic string automaton.

As in the string case, the notion of a product automaton can be defined.

Finally, we define quotient automata. A *partition* of a set S is a collection of pairwise disjoint nonempty subsets of S whose union is S. If π is a partition of S, then, for any element $s \in S$, there is a unique element of π containing s, which we denote $B(s, \pi)$ and call the *block* of π containing s. A partition π is said to *refine* another partition π' iff every block of π' is a union of blocks of π. If π is any partition of the state set Q of the automaton $A = (Q, V, \delta, F)$, then the *quotient automaton* $\pi^{-1}A = (\pi^{-1}Q, V, \delta', \pi^{-1}F)$ is given by $\pi^{-1}\hat{Q} = \{B(q, \pi) \mid q \in \hat{Q}\}$ (for $\hat{Q} \subseteq Q$) and, for $B_1, \ldots, B_k \in \pi^{-1}Q \cup V_0$, $f \in V_k$, $B \in \delta'_k(f, B_1, \ldots, B_k)$ whenever there exist $q \in B$ and $q_i \in B_i \in \pi^{-1}Q$ or $q_i = B_i \in V_0$ for $1 \leq i \leq k$ such that $q \in \delta_k(f, q_1, \ldots, q_k)$.

3   Function Distinguishability

The main feature of the automata classes which are learnable from text seems to be some sort of "backward determinism" or "reversibility". In the case of string languages, the corresponding notion of reversible languages due to Angluin was generalized in [7] with the aid of distinguishing functions. We will take a similar venue here for the case of tree languages in order to generalize the learnability results of Sakakibara for reversible tree languages.

Let $A_\delta = (Q_\delta, V, \delta, Q_\delta)$ be some deterministic tree automaton; in fact, we only need the functional behaviour of the state transition function δ which we also call a *distinguishing function*, which can be viewed as a partial mapping $V^t \to Q_\delta$. A deterministic tree automaton $A = (Q, V, \bar{\delta}, F)$ is called δ-*distinguishable* if it satisfies the following two properties:

1. For all states $q \in Q$ and all $x, y \in V^t$ with $\bar{\delta}(x) = \bar{\delta}(y) = q$, we have $\delta(x) = \delta(y)$. (In other words, for $q \in Q$, $\delta(q) := \delta(x)$ for some x with $\bar{\delta}(x) = q$ is well-defined.)
2. For all $q_1, q_2 \in Q \cup V_0$, $q_1 \neq q_2$, with either (a) $q_1, q_2 \in F$ or (b) there exist $q_3 \in Q$, $k \geq 1$, $1 \leq i < k$, $p_1, \ldots, p_{k-1} \in Q \cup V_0$ and $f \in V_k$ with $\bar{\delta}_k(f, p_1, \ldots, p_{i-1}, q_1, p_i, \ldots, p_{k-1}) = \bar{\delta}_k(f, p_1, \ldots, p_{i-1}, q_2, p_i, \ldots, p_{k-1}) = q_3$, we have $\delta(q_1) \neq \delta(q_2)$.

In some sense, A is "backward deterministic" with the aid of δ. A regular tree language T over V is called δ-*distinguishable* if it is accepted by a δ-distinguishable tree automaton. Let δ-DT denote the class of δ-distinguishable tree languages.

Observe that trees whose domain is contained in $\{1\}^*$ correspond to usual strings, and the notion of distinguishability obtained in this way is nearly the same as the one introduced in [7][3]. The distinguishing function induced by the trivial tree automaton with just one state leads to a slight generalization of the 0-reversible tree automata studied by Sakakibara [26]; in Sakakibara's model, for each arity $k \geq 1$, there was only one symbol σ_k as label of the interior nodes.

As a further simple example of distinguishing function, consider the function Ter defined by $Ter(a) = \{a\}$ and $Ter_k(f, q_1, \ldots, q_k) = \{f\} \cup \bigcup_{j=1}^{k} q_j$, where 2^V is the state set of A_{Ter}. Ter is the natural tree-analogue of the terminal distinguishing function basically introduced by Radhakrishnan and Nagaraja in [22]. As exhibited in [7] in the string case, several other similar distinguishing functions can be defined which also yield immediate analogues in the tree case.

Inference algorithms for tree languages can be readily used for the inference of context-free string languages, once the structure of the derivation tree is fixed; e.g., if we restrict ourselves to Ter applied to derivation trees of even linear grammars (with trivial labels for interior nodes), we basically arrive at a variant of the terminal distinguishable even linear languages discussed in [8].

Example 1. Consider $A = (\{q_0, q_1\}, V = \{a, *\}, \delta, \{q_1\})$ with

$$\delta_1(*, a) = \delta_2(*, a, a) = q_0$$
$$\delta_3(*, a, q_0, a) = \delta_3(*, a, q_1, a) = q_1$$

A is intended to accept a certain class of derivation trees of context-free grammars. A is not Ter-distinguishable, since it violates the second condition, because $Ter(q_0) = Ter(q_1) = \{*, a\}$. By way of contrast, if we consider an automaton $A' = (\{q_0\}, V, \delta', \{q_0\})$ with the same rank relation r_V and with δ' obtained by merging q_0 and q_1, i.e., $\delta_i' = \delta_i$ for $i = 1, 2$ and $\delta_3'(*, a, q_0, a) = q_0$, then A' is Ter-distinguishable. Obviously, many more trees are accepted by A' than by A, e.g., consider the tree t given by the term $*(*(a, a), *(a, a))$, since $\delta(t) = q_0$.

If we like to keep the property of only accepting the originally intended class of derivation trees of context-free grammars, this is possible by modifying A to cope with larger alphabets. Consider, e.g., $A'' = (\{q_0, q_1\}, V = \{a, *, +\}, \delta'', \{q_1\})$ with $r_V = \{(a, 0), (*, 1), (*, 2), (+, 3)\}$ and

$$\delta_1''(*, a) = \delta_2''(*, a, a) = q_0$$
$$\delta_3''(+, a, q_0, a) = \delta_3''(+, a, q_1, a) = q_1$$

Since $Ter(q_0) = \{a, *\} \neq Ter(q_1) = \{a, *, +\}$, A'' is Ter-distinguishable. Obviously, the automata are constructed for accepting the usual derivation trees of (even-)linear grammars.

Remark 1. Any subautomaton of a δ-distinguishable tree automaton A is δ-distinguishable.   □

---

[3] except from the treatment of the empty word

Lemma 1. *Let $A = (Q, V, \bar{\delta}, F)$ be a δ-distinguishable tree automaton. Let $u \in V_\$^t$, $\{t_1, t_2\} \subseteq V^t$. $\{u\#t_1, u\#t_2\} \subseteq T(A)$ and $\delta(t_1) = \delta(t_2)$ imply $\bar{\delta}(t_1) = \bar{\delta}(t_2)$.*

Proof. [4] Firstly observe that, since $\delta(t_1) = \delta(t_2)$, we have $\delta(u\#t_1) = \delta(u\#t_2)$ for all $u \in V_\$^t$ and $t_1, t_2 \in V^t$. The proof proceeds via induction on the level ℓ of the node with label \$ in u. If $\ell = 0$, then $u = \$$. Consider the final states $q_i = \bar{\delta}(u\#t_i)$ of A for $i = 1, 2$. Since $\delta(q_1) = \delta(u\#t_1) = \delta(u\#t_2) = \delta(q_2)$, condition 2a. for δ-distinguishable tree automata yields $q_1 = q_2$.

Assume the claim holds for $\ell < h$. Consider $u \in V_\$^t$ with label \$ at level h. u can be uniquely represented as $u = u'\#f(s_1, \ldots, s_{i-1}, \$, s_i, \ldots, s_{k-1})$ for some $s_1, \ldots, s_{k-1} \in V^t$ and some $u' \in V_\$^t$ having the node labelled \$ at level $h - 1$. The induction hypothesis yields: if A accepts

$$u\#t_j = u'\#f(s_1, \ldots, s_{i-1}, t_1, s_i, \ldots, s_{k-1}), \quad j = 1, 2,$$

then $\bar{\delta}(f(s_1, \ldots, s_{i-1}, t_1, s_i, \ldots, s_{k-1})) = \bar{\delta}(f(s_1, \ldots, s_{i-1}, t_2, s_i, \ldots, s_{k-1}))$, since $\delta(t_1) = \delta(t_2)$ gives

$$\delta(f(s_1, \ldots, s_{i-1}, t_1, s_i, \ldots, s_{k-1})) = \delta(f(s_1, \ldots, s_{i-1}, t_2, s_i, \ldots, s_{k-1})).$$

Hence, $\bar{\delta}_k(f, \bar{\delta}(s_1), \ldots, \bar{\delta}(s_{i-1}), \bar{\delta}(t_1), \bar{\delta}(s_i), \ldots, \bar{\delta}(s_{k-1}))$
$= \bar{\delta}_k(f, \bar{\delta}(s_1), \ldots, \bar{\delta}(s_{i-1}), \bar{\delta}(t_2), \bar{\delta}(s_i), \ldots, \bar{\delta}(s_{k-1}))$, so that condition 2b. for δ-distinguishable tree automata yields $q_1 = q_2$.   □

With the help of Lemma 1, the following statement is easily shown:

Lemma 2. *Let $A = (Q, V, \bar{\delta}, F)$ be a δ-distinguishable tree automaton. Let $\{u_1, u_2\} \subseteq V_\$^t$ and $\{t, t'\} \subseteq V^t$. If $\{u_1\#t, u_2\#t\} \subseteq T(A)$ and if $\delta(t) = \delta(t')$, then $u_1\#t' \in T(A)$ iff $u_2\#t' \in T(A)$.*   □

Let $T \subseteq V^t$ be a regular tree language. Let $A(T, \delta)$ denote the stripped subautomaton of $C(T) \times A_\delta$. Obviously, $T(A(T, \delta)) = T$. $A(T, \delta)$ is called the *δ-canonical tree automaton* of T. As the following theorem shows, we can take $A(T, \delta)$ as canonical objects describing δ-DT, since $A(T, \delta)$ is a unique object. Moreover, it is proved that the tree language class δ-DT can be characterized in a number of ways.

Theorem 1 (Characterization theorem). *Let $\delta : V^t \to Q_\delta$ be a distinguishing function. Then, the following conditions are equivalent for a regular tree language $T \subseteq V^t$:*

1. $T \in \delta$-DT.

---

[4] We give the proof of this lemma as a sort of representative of proofs of tree language results. The reader comparing the proof with the string analogue will notice that, while the proof ideas are similar, the tree formalism entails more formal complications and care. Due to the similarity to the string case, we will omit most proofs in the following; instead, we refer to [7,10].

2. There is a tree automaton $A = (Q, V, \bar{\delta}, F)$ with $T(A) = T$ satisfying

$$\forall t_1, t_2 \in V^\mathbf{t} \; \forall u \in V_\$^\mathbf{t} : (\{u\#t_1, u\#t_2\} \subseteq T \wedge \delta(t_1) = \delta(t_2)) \Rightarrow \bar{\delta}(t_1) = \bar{\delta}(t_2).$$

3. $\forall t_1, t_2 \in V^\mathbf{t} \; \forall u, v \in V_\$^\mathbf{t} : (\{u\#t_1, v\#t_1\} \subseteq T \wedge \delta(t_1) = \delta(t_2)) \Rightarrow (u\#t_2 \in T \iff v\#t_2 \in T)$.

4. $\forall t_1, t_2 \in V^\mathbf{t} \; \forall u, v \in U_T(t_1) : \delta(t_1) = \delta(t_2) \Rightarrow (u \in U_T(t_2) \iff v \in U_T(t_2))$.

5. $A(T, \delta)$ is δ-distinguishable.

6. $\forall u_1, u_2 \in V^\mathbf{t} \; \forall t \in V_\$^\mathbf{t} : (\{u_1\#t, u_2\#t\} \subseteq T \wedge \delta(t_1) = \delta(t_2)) \Rightarrow U_T(t_1) = U_T(t_2)$.

Proof. 1. $\to$ 2. due to Lemma 1. According to the proof of Lemma 2, 2. $\to$ 3. The implications 3. $\leftrightarrow$ 4., 5. $\to$ 1. and 6. $\to$ 2. are trivial. 5. $\to$ 6. follows with Lemma 1. 4. $\to$ 5. can be shown as in the string case, see [7, Theorem 1].   □

Remark 2. As in the string case [7], we could have added further characterizations of δ-DT by means of grammars or Myhill-Nerode like algebraic formulations. We did not do this here in order to avoid unnecessary technical complications. The interested reader is referred to the chapter written by Gécseg and Steinby in [24] as regards the corresponding formalisms in the tree case.

The following lemma is useful for proving the correctness of our learning algorithms and is, moreover, a simple characterization of our canonical objects.

Lemma 3. *The stripped subautomaton of a δ-distinguishable tree automaton A is isomorphic to $A(T(A), \delta)$.*

Proof. According to Remark 1, the stripped subautomaton A' of A is δ-distinguishable. Let $A = (Q, V, \bar{\delta}, F)$ and $A' = (Q', V, \bar{\delta}', F')$. We have to show that, for all $q_1, q_2 \in Q'$ with $\delta(q_1) = \delta(q_2)$, $\{u \in V_\$^\mathbf{t} \mid \exists t \in V^\mathbf{t} \setminus V_0 : \bar{\delta}'(u\#q_1) \in F'\}$ $= \{u \in V_\$^\mathbf{t} \mid \exists t \in V^\mathbf{t} \setminus V_0 : \bar{\delta}'(u\#q_2) \in F'\}$ implies that $q_1 = q_2$, since then, the mapping $q \mapsto (U_{T(A)}(t), \delta(q))$ for some $t \in V^\mathbf{t}$ with $\bar{\delta}'(t) = q$ will supply the required isomorphism.

Since A' is stripped, there are $t_1, t_2 \in V^\mathbf{t}$ and $u \in V_\$^\mathbf{t}$, $q_1 = \bar{\delta}'(t_1)$, $q_2 = \bar{\delta}'(t_2)$ and $\{u\#t_1, u\#t_2\} \subseteq T(A') = T(A)$. Since A' is δ-distinguishable, $\delta(q_1) = \delta(q_2)$ implies that $\delta(t_1) = \delta(t_2)$. Hence, we can apply Lemma 1 to show the result.   □

4   Inferrability

The learning model we use is *identification in the limit from positive samples* as proposed by Gold [13], sometimes also called *learning from text*. In this well-established model, a language class $\mathcal{L}$ (defined via a class of language describing devices $\mathcal{D}$ as, e.g., grammars or automata) is said to be *identifiable* if there is a so-called *inference machine* I to which as input an arbitrary language $L \in \mathcal{L}$ may be enumerated (possibly with repetitions) in an arbitrary order, i.e., I receives an infinite input stream of words $E(1)$, $E(2)$, ..., where $E : \mathbb{N} \to L$ is an enumeration of L, i.e., a surjection, and I reacts with an output device stream $D_i \in \mathcal{D}$ such that there is an $N(E)$ so that, for all $n \geq N(E)$, we have $D_n = D_{N(E)}$ and, moreover, the language defined by $D_{N(E)}$ equals L.

In order to ensure the convergence of the hypothesis stream output by a Gold-style learner, we need some well-defined canonical output objects. In the case of δ-DT, this will be the δ-canonical automata introduced above.

According to [1, Theorem 1], a class $\mathcal{L}$ (characterized by $\mathcal{D}$) comprised of recursive languages is identifiable iff, for any language description $D \in \mathcal{D}$ a *telltale set* is computable, i.e., a finite subset $\chi(D) \subseteq L$ such that L is a minimal language from $\mathcal{L}$ containing $\chi(D)$.

For the tree language class δ-DT and some language $T \in \delta$-DT, consider the corresponding δ-canonical automaton $A(T, \delta) = (Q, V, \bar{\delta}, F)$ and define

$$\chi(T, \delta) = \{\, u(q)\#t(q) \mid q \in Q \,\}$$
$$\cup \{u(\bar{\delta}_k(f, q_1, \ldots, q_k))\#f(t(q_1), \ldots, t(q_k)) \mid q_1, \ldots, q_k \in Q \cup V_0, f \in V_k\},$$

where $u(q) \in V_{\$}^t$ and $t(q) \in V^t \setminus V_0$ are (arbitrary) trees each of minimal size satisfying $\bar{\delta}(t(q)) = q$ (if $q \in Q$) and $\bar{\delta}(u(q)\#q) \in F$. If $q \in V_0$, we set $t(q) = q$. Naturally, a finite automaton for $\chi(T, \delta)$ may be computed by some Turing machine which is given $C(T)$ and A_δ as input.

Theorem 2 (Telltale property). *For each A_δ and each $T \in \delta$-DT, $\chi(T, \delta)$ is a telltale set of T.*

Proof. Clearly, $\chi(T, \delta) \subseteq T$. Consider some tree language $T' \in \delta$-DT with $\chi(T, \delta) \subseteq T'$. We have to show that $T \subseteq T'$. Let $A(T, \delta) = (Q, V, \bar{\delta}, F)$.

By induction on the height of s, we show

$$(*) \quad U_{T'}(s) = U_{T'}(t(\bar{\delta}(s))) \quad \text{and} \quad \delta(s) = \delta(t(\bar{\delta}(s)))$$

for all $s \in \mathrm{ST}(T)$. Note that $(*)$ implies the following: if $s \in T$, i.e., $q_f = \bar{\delta}(s)$ is a final state of $A(T, \delta)$, then $U_{T'}(t(q_f))$ is a final state of $C(T')$, because $t(q_f) \in \chi(T, \delta) \subseteq T'$. Therefore, $(U_{T'}(t(q_f)), \delta(t(q_f))$ is a final state of $A(T', \delta)$. Due to $(*)$, we conclude that $s \in T'$. Hence, $T \subseteq T'$.

Now, we prove $(*)$. If the height of s is zero, then $s \in V_0$, which means that $s = t(s)$ by definition of $t(\cdot)$. Assume that $(*)$ holds for all trees of depth at most $h \geq 0$. Consider some $s \in \mathrm{ST}(T)$ of depth $h + 1$, i.e., $s = f(s_1, \ldots, s_k)$ for some $f \in V_k$, $s_1, \ldots, s_k \in \mathrm{ST}(T)$; obviously, all s_i are trees of depth at most h. By the induction hypothesis, $U_{T'}(s_i) = U_{T'}(t(\bar{\delta}(s_i)))$ and $\delta(s_i) = \delta(t(\bar{\delta}(s_i)))$, $1 \leq i \leq k$. Hence, $U_{T'}(s) = U_{T'}(f(s_1, \ldots, s_k)) = \bar{\delta}_k(f, U_{T'}(s_1), \ldots, U_{T'}(s_k)) = \bar{\delta}_k(f, U_{T'}(t(\bar{\delta}(s_1))), \ldots, U_{T'}t(\bar{\delta}(s_k))) = U_{T'}(f(t(\bar{\delta}(s_1)), \ldots, t(\bar{\delta}(s_k)))$ and $\delta(s) = \delta(f(s_1, \ldots, s_k)) = \delta(f(t(\bar{\delta}(s_1)), \ldots, t(\bar{\delta}(s_k))))$. Define $q' = \bar{\delta}_k(f, \bar{\delta}(s_1), \ldots, \bar{\delta}(s_k))$. Since by definition of the telltale set $\chi(T, \delta)$, both $u(q')\#f(t(\bar{\delta}(s_1)), \ldots, t(\bar{\delta}(s_k)))$ and $u(q')\#t(q')$ are contained in $\chi(T, \delta) \subseteq T'$, Lemma 1 yields

$$U_{T'}(s) = U_{T'}(f(t(\bar{\delta}(s_1)), \ldots, t(\bar{\delta}(s_k)))) = U_{T'}(t(q')),$$

because $\delta(t(q')) = \delta(\bar{\delta}_k(f, \bar{\delta}(s_1), \ldots, \bar{\delta}(s_k))) = \delta(f(t(\bar{\delta}(s_1)), \ldots, t(\bar{\delta}(s_k))))$. $\qquad\square$

5   Inference Algorithms

For each A_δ, we sketch an algorithm which receives an input sample set $I_+ = \{t_1, \ldots, t_M\}$ (a finite subset of the tree language $T \in \delta$-DT to be identified) and finds a minimal language $T' \in \delta$-DT which contains I_+. Of course, Theorem 2 already guarantees the existence of such an algorithm, but the ad-hoc enumeration algorithm is not very efficient. In contrast, our algorithms will have polynomial update time, but the number of so-called implicit errors of prediction is not polynomially bounded, as explained by Sakakibara for his simpler setting [26].

Our merging state inference algorithm δ-Ident for δ-DT now starts with the automaton $A_0 = Bs(I_+) = (Q = \mathrm{ST}(T) \setminus V_0, V, \bar{\delta}, F = I_+)$ on receiving I_+ as input. Then, it subsequently merges two states which cause a conflict to one of the requirements for δ-distinguishable automata. This way, we get a sequence of automata $A_0, A_1, \ldots, A_f$ each of which can be interpreted as a quotient automaton of A_0 by the partition of the state set of A_0 induced by the corresponding merging operation. Let δ^i denote the transition function of A_i. Observe that each A_i is stripped, since A_0 is stripped. Moreover, A_f is δ-distinguishable, as being the last automaton in this chain. In terms of the partitions inducing the mentioned quotient automata, δ-Ident starts with the trivial partition π_0 of Q and repeatedly merges two distinct blocks B_1 and B_2 at stage i, $i = 0, \ldots, f-1$ if any of the following conditions is satisfied:

final state conflict B_1 and B_2 contain both final states $q_1 \in B_1$, $q_2 \in B_2$ of A_0 with $\delta(q_1) = \delta(q_2)$. This would mean that B_1 and B_2 are both final states (in A_i) with $\delta(B_1) = \delta(B_2)$.

determinism conflict   There exist two states $q_1 \in B_1$, $q_2 \in B_2$ of the form

$$q_1 = f(p_1, \ldots, p_k) \quad \text{and} \quad q_2 = f(p'_1, \ldots, p'_k)$$

such that, for all $1 \leq j \leq k$, either $p_j = p'_j \in V_0$ or $B(p_j, \pi_i) = B(p'_j, \pi_i)$. Namely, if this situation occurred, this would mean that

$$B_i = \delta^i(f, B(p_1, \pi_i), \ldots, B(p_k, \pi_i)) \text{ for } i = 1, 2.$$

backward determinism conflict   There exist two states q_1, q_2 of the form

$$q_1 = f(p_1, \ldots, p_k) \quad \text{and} \quad q_2 = f(p'_1, \ldots, p'_k)$$

with $B(q_1, \pi_i) = B(q_2, \pi_i)$ and an integer $1 \leq \ell \leq k$ such that, for all $1 \leq j \leq k$ with $i \neq \ell$, either $p_j = p'_j \in V_0$ or $B(p_j, \pi_i) = B(p'_j, \pi_i)$. Moreover, $p_\ell \in B_1$, $p'_\ell \in B_2$ and $\delta(p_\ell) = \delta(p'_\ell)$.

To be more concrete, consider the following program fragment:

Algorithm 1 (δ-Ident).
Input: a nonempty positive sample $I_+ \subseteq V^t$.
Output: $A(T, \delta)$, where T is a minimal δ-distinguishable tree language containing I_+.

*** Initialization

Let $A_0 = (Q = \mathrm{ST}(T) \setminus V_0, V, \bar{\delta}, F = I_+) = Bs(I_+)$.

Let π_0 be the trivial partition of Q.

Let LIST contain all unordered pairs $\{q, q'\}$ of final states of Q with $q \neq q'$, $\delta(q) = \delta(q')$.

Let $i := 0$.

*** Merging

While LIST$\neq \emptyset$ do begin

    Remove some element $\{q_1, q_2\}$ from LIST.

    Consider the blocks $B_1 = B(q_1, \pi_i)$ and $B_2 = B(q_2, \pi_i)$.

    If $B_1 \neq B_2$, then begin

        Let π_{i+1} be π_i with B_1 and B_2 merged.

        Resolve newly produced determinism conflicts and update LIST.

        Resolve newly produced backward determinism conflicts and update LIST.

        Increment i by one.

        If $i = |Q| - 1$, then LIST$:= \emptyset$.

    end *** if

end *** while

The conflict resolution can be implemented either by means of an explicit search through all possible conflict situations, which results in an algorithm similar to the one proposed by Sakakibara [26] or by keeping track of the forward and backward transition functions of the automata A_i with the help of union/find techniques, as elaborated in [11] in the case of string language identification. In either case, we obtain algorithms with polynomially bounded update times, see [26] for the definitions.

Example 2. If $I_+ = \{(a, *(a), a), *(a, *(a, a), a), *(a)\}$ is given to *Ter*-Ident, then the automaton A' from Example 1 will result.

Moreover, it is possible to design so-called *incremental versions* of the algorithms, where the input sample is fed to the algorithm in an on-line manner.

We now give the ingredients for showing the correctness of δ-Ident. The following lemma is crucial in this respect:

Lemma 4. *Let $I_+ \subseteq T \in \delta\text{-}DT$ be given. Let π be the partition of $A_0 = Bs(I_+)$ described by: q_1, q_2 belong to the same block if[5] $U_T(q_1) = U_T(q_2)$ and if $\delta(q_1) = \delta(q_2)$. Then, $\pi^{-1}A_0$ is isomorphic to a subautomaton of $A(T, \delta)$.*

Proof. Let $\pi^{-1}A_0 = (\hat{Q}, V, \hat{\delta}, \hat{F})$ and $A(T, \delta) = (Q, V, \bar{\delta}, F)$. By definition, $\hat{Q} = \{B(t, \pi) \mid t \in \mathrm{ST}(I_+) \setminus V_0\}$ and the mapping $h : \hat{Q} \to Q, B(t, \pi) \mapsto (U_T(t), \delta(t))$ is well-defined and injective. If $B_1 \in \hat{F}$, then $B_1 = B(t, \pi)$ for some $t \in I_+ \subseteq T$, and hence, $(U_T(t), \delta(t)) \in F$. Therefore, $h(\hat{F}) \subseteq F$. $\pi^{-1}A_0$ is deterministic, because, if $f(s_1, \ldots, s_k)$, $f(s'_1, \ldots, s'_k) \in \mathrm{ST}(I_+)$, with $B(s_i, \pi) = B(s'_i, \pi)$ if $s_i, s'_i \in \mathrm{ST}(I_+) \setminus V_0$ and $s_i = s'_i$ if $s_i, s'_i \in V_0$, then $B(f(s_1, \ldots, s_k), \pi) = B(f(s'_1, \ldots, s'_k), \pi)$ for any $f \in V_k$. h is an automaton morphism, since

$$h(\hat{\delta}_k(f, q_1, \ldots, q_k)) = h(B(f(t_1, \ldots, t_k), \pi))$$

---

[5] Recall that $q_i \in \mathrm{ST}(I_+) \setminus V_0$.

with $t_i = q_i$ if $q_i \in V_0$ and t_i chosen otherwise to satisfy $B(t_i, \pi) = q_i$. Hence,

$$h(\hat{\delta}_k(f, q_1, \ldots, q_k)) = (U_T(f(t_1, \ldots, t_k)), \delta(f(t_1, \ldots, t_k)))$$
$$= \bar{\delta}_k(f, (U_T(t_1), \delta(t_1)), \ldots, (U_T(t_k), \delta(t_k))).$$

So, h is an isomorphism between $\pi^{-1}A_0$ and a tree subautomaton of $A(T, \delta)$.   □

Theorem 3. *Fix A_δ. Consider a chain of automata $A_0, A_1, \ldots, A_f$ obtained by applying the sketched algorithm δ-Ident on input sample I_+, where $A_0 = Bs(I_+)$. Then, we have: 1. $T(A_0) \subseteq T(A_1) \subseteq \cdots \subseteq T(A_f)$. 2. A_f is δ-distinguishable and stripped. 3. The partition π_f of the state set of A_0 corresponding to A_f is the finest partition π of the state set of A_0 such that the quotient automaton $\pi^{-1}A_0$ is δ-distinguishable.*   □

Theorem 4. *In the notations of the Theorem 3, $T(A_f)$ is a minimal δ-distinguishable language containing I_+.*

Proof. Theorem 3 states that $T(A_f) \in \delta$-DT and $I_+ = T(A_0) \subseteq T(A_f)$. Consider now an arbitrary language $T \in \delta$-DT containing I_+. We consider the quotient automaton $\pi^{-1}A_0$ defined in Lemma 4. This Lemma shows that

$$T(\pi^{-1}A_0) \subseteq T = T(A(T, \delta)).$$

By Remark 1, $\pi^{-1}A_0$ is δ-distinguishable, because $A(T, \delta)$ is δ-distinguishable due to Theorem 1. Theorem 3 yields that π_f refines π, so that

$$T(A_f) = T(\pi_f^{-1}A_0) \subseteq T(\pi^{-1}A_0) \subseteq T.   □$$

Remark 3. Up to now, in accordance with the definition of a telltale set, we always spoke about *a* minimal δ-distinguishable language containing the sample I_+. Considering again the previous proof, one sees that there is actually a *unique* minimal language in δ-DT containing I_+, so that we can talk about *the* smallest language in δ-DT containing I_+ in the following. This means that each telltale is in fact a *characteristic sample* as defined in [2].

Theorem 4 immediately yields:

Corollary 1 (Correctness of δ-Ident). *If $T \in \delta$-DT is enumerated as input to the algorithm δ-Ident, it converges to the δ-canonical automaton $A(T, \delta)$.*   □

6   Approximation

We are going to show that, for any class δ-DT, all regular tree languages may be approximated by some language from δ-DT in a certain sense. Firstly, we give the necessary general definitions due to Kobayashi and Yokomori [19].

Let $\mathcal{L}$ be a language class and L be a language, possibly outside $\mathcal{L}$. An *upper-best approximation* $\bar{\mathcal{L}}L$ of L with respect to $\mathcal{L}$ is defined to be a language $L_* \in \mathcal{L}$ containing L such that for any $L' \in \mathcal{L}$ with $L \subseteq L'$, $L_* \subseteq L'$ holds. If such an L_* does not exist, $\bar{\mathcal{L}}L$ is undefined.

Remark 4. If $\mathcal{L}$ is closed under intersection, then $\bar{\mathcal{L}}L$ is uniquely defined.

Consider an inference machine I to which as input an arbitrary language L may be enumerated (possibly with repetitions) in an arbitrary order, i.e., I receives an infinite input stream of words $E(1)$, $E(2)$, $\ldots$, where $E : \mathbb{N} \to L$ is an enumeration of L. We say that I *identifies an upper-best approximation of L in the limit (from positive data) by* $\mathcal{L}$ if I reacts on an enumeration of L with an output device stream $D_i \in \mathcal{D}$ such that there is an $N(E)$ so that, for all $n \geq N(E)$, we have $D_n = D_{N(E)}$ and, moreover, the language defined by $D_{N(E)}$ equals $\bar{\mathcal{L}}L \in \mathcal{L}$.

Let $\mathcal{L}_1$ and $\mathcal{L}_2$ be two language classes. We say that $\mathcal{L}_1$ has the *upper-best approximation property (u.b.a.p.) with respect to $\mathcal{L}_2$* iff, for every $L \in \mathcal{L}_2$, $\bar{\mathcal{L}}_1 L$ is defined.

A language class $\mathcal{L}_1$ is called *upper-best approximately identifiable in the limit (from positive data) by $\mathcal{L}_2$* iff there exists an inference machine I which identifies an upper-best approximation of each $L \in \mathcal{L}_1$ in the limit (from positive data) by $\mathcal{L}_2$. Observe that this notion of identifiability coincides with Gold's classical notion of learning in the limit in the case when $\mathcal{L}_1 = \mathcal{L}_2$.

Consider a language class $\mathcal{L}$ and a language L from it. A finite subset $F \subseteq L$ is called a *telltale set* of L with respect to $\mathcal{L}$ iff, for any $L' \in \mathcal{L}$, $F \subseteq L'$ implies that $L \subseteq L'$.

Now, let us turn more specifically to the distinguishable languages. Fix some distinguishing function δ. We call a language $T \subseteq V^{\mathbf{t}}$ *pseudo-δ-distinguishable* iff, for all $t_1, t_2 \in V^{\mathbf{t}}$ with $\delta(t_1) = \delta(t_2)$ and for all $u \in V_{\$}^{\mathbf{t}}$, we have $U_T(t_1) = U_T(t_2)$ whenever $\{u\#t_1, u\#t_2\} \subseteq T$. By our characterization theorem, $T \in \delta\text{-DT}$ iff T is a pseudo-δ-distinguishable and regular tree language.

Immediately from the definition, we may conclude:

Proposition 1. *Let $T_1 \subseteq T_2 \subseteq \ldots$ be any ascending sequence of pseudo-δ-distinguishable languages. Then, $\bigcup_{i \geq 1} T_i$ is pseudo-δ-distinguishable.* □

For brevity, we write $t_1 \equiv_{T,\delta} t_2$ iff $U_T(t_1) = U_T(t_2)$ and $\delta(t_1) = \delta(t_2)$.

Remark 5. If $T \subseteq V^{\mathbf{t}}$ is a regular tree language and if $\delta : V^{\mathbf{t}} \to Q_\delta$ is some distinguishing function, then the number of equivalence classes of $\equiv_{T,\delta}$ equals the number of states of $C(T)$ (plus one) times $|Q_\delta|$, and this is just the number of states of $A(T, \delta)$ (plus $|Q_\delta|$).

Let $T \subseteq V^{\mathbf{t}}$. For any integer i, we will define $R_\delta(i, T)$ as follows:

1. $R_\delta(0, T) = T$ and
2. $R_\delta(i, T) = R_\delta(i - 1, T)$
   $\cup \{ u\#t_2 \mid u\#t_1, u'\#t_1, u'\#t_2 \in R_\delta(i - 1, T) \wedge \delta(t_1) = \delta(t_2) \}$ for $i \geq 1$.

Furthermore, set $R_\delta(T) = \bigcup_{i \geq 0} R_\delta(i, T)$.

Since R_δ turns out to be a hull operator, the following statement is obvious.

Proposition 2. *For any tree language T and any distinguishing function δ, $R_\delta(T)$ is the smallest pseudo-δ-distinguishable language containing T.* □

Lemma 5. *Let $T \subseteq V^t$ be any tree language. If t_1 and t_2 are subtrees of T, then $t_1 \equiv_{T,\delta} t_2$ implies that $U_{R_\delta(T)}(t_1) = U_{R_\delta(T)}(t_2)$.*

Proof. Let t_1 and t_2 be subtrees of T with $t_1 \equiv_{T,\delta} t_2$. By definition of $\equiv_{T,\delta}$, $U_T(t_1) = U_T(t_2) \neq \emptyset$. Hence, there is a tree $u \in V_\$^t$ so that $\{u\#t_1, u\#t_2\} \subseteq T \subseteq R_\delta(T)$. Furthermore, by definition of $\equiv_{T,\delta}$, $\delta(t_1) = \delta(t_2)$. Since $R_\delta(T)$ is pseudo-δ-distinguishable due to Proposition 2, $U_{R_\delta(T)}(t_1) = U_{R_\delta(T)}(t_2)$. $\square$

Similarly to the string case [9], we can show:

Lemma 6. *Let $T \subseteq V^t$ be any tree language and let δ be any distinguishing function. Then, for any subtree t_1 of $R_\delta(T)$, there exists a subtree t_2 of T with $U_{R_\delta(T)}(t_1) = U_{R_\delta(T)}(t_2)$.* $\square$

By a reasoning completely analogous to [19], we may conclude:

Theorem 5. *For any distinguishing function δ, the class δ-DT has the u.b.a.p. with respect to the class of regular tree languages.* $\square$

Observe that the number of states of $A_{R_\delta(T)}$ is closely related to the number of states of $A(T, \delta)$, see Remark 5.

Theorem 6. *For any distinguishing function δ, the class of regular languages is upper-best approximately identifiable in the limit from positive data by δ-DT.* $\square$

In addition to the last two theorems, we remark that an upper-best approximation of a regular tree language with respect to each class δ-DT is uniquely defined, since the classical product automaton construction shows that each of these classes is closed under intersection, see Remark 4.

Given some tree automaton A and some distinguishing function δ, an automaton accepting $\overline{\delta\text{-DT}}T(A)$ can be constructed as follows:

1. Compute $C(T(A))$.
2. Construct $A' = A(T(A), \delta)$.
3. Merge "conflicting states" in A' as long as possible.

7   Discussion and Prospects

For a variety of regular tree language classes, we showed in which way they can be inferred efficiently. To this end, we had to define new canonical automata specific to each of these classes. Each of these classes can be characterized in various ways. Moreover, we showed that every regular tree language can be approximated in a well-defined manner by languages from δ-DT for any chosen A_δ.

In the future, we will try to compare our work with other works on the inference of tree languages and of context-free languages, as they are contained, e.g., in [3,12,14,18,20,21,27,28,30,31,32]. Moreover, it would be interesting to extend the work to other, more general classes of tree languages and the corresponding languages of yielded strings, see [29] for a short exposition. Especially, we will employ our results for devising learning algorithms for linear languages. Of course, applications of our learning algorithms in the various domains where tree languages have been successfully applied to would be interesting. One of the nicest resources on the web is `www.informatik.uni-bremen.de/theorie/treebag/`.

An implementation of our tree language inference algorithms is accessible through `www-fs.informatik.uni-tuebingen.de/~fernau/GI.htm` [11].

Acknowledgments

We are grateful for stimulating discussions with S. Kobayashi, A. Radl and J. M. Sempere.

References

1. D. Angluin. Inductive inference of formal languages from positive data. *Information and Control*, 45:117–135, 1980. 160
2. D. Angluin. Inference of reversible languages. *Journal of the Association for Computing Machinery*, 29(3):741–765, 1982. 154, 163
3. M. Bernard and C. de la Higuera. GIFT: Grammatical Inference For Terms. International Conference on Inductive Logic Programming ILP. Late Breaking Paper, 1999. French journal version: Apprentissage de programmes logiques par inférence grammaticale. *Revue d'Intelligence Artificielle*, 14:375–396, 2001. 153, 154, 165
4. J. Besombes and J.-Y. Marion. Identification of reversible dependency tree languages. In L. Popelínský and M. Nepil, editors, *Proceedings of 3rd Workshop on Learning Languages in Logic LLL'01*, pages 11-22, 2001. 153
5. S. Crespi-Reghizzi, M. A. Melkanoff, and L. Lichten. The use of grammatical inference for designing programming languages. *Communications of the ACM*, 16:83–90, 1972. 153
6. L. F. Fass. Learning context-free languages from their structured sentences. *SIGACT News*, 15(3):24–35, 1983. 153
7. H. Fernau. Identification of function distinguishable languages. In H. Arimura, S. Jain, and A. Sharma, editors, *Proceedings of the 11th International Conference Algorithmic Learning Theory ALT*, volume 1968 of *LNCS/LNAI*, pages 116–130. Springer, 2000. 154, 156, 157, 158, 159
8. H. Fernau. Learning of terminal distinguishable languages. In *Proceedings AMAI 2000*, see `http://rutcor.rutgers.edu/~amai/aimath00/AcceptedCont.htm`. 157
9. H. Fernau. Approximative learning of regular languages. In L. Pacholski and P. Ružička, editors, *SOFSEM; Theory and Practice of Informatics*, volume 2234 of *LNCS*, pages 223–232. Springer, 2001. 154, 165
10. H. Fernau. Learning tree languages from text. Technical Report WSI–2001–19, Universität Tübingen (Germany), Wilhelm-Schickard-Institut für Informatik, 2001. 158
11. H. Fernau and A. Radl. Algorithms for learning function distinguishable regular languages. In *Statistical and Syntactical Methods of Pattern Recognition SPR+SSPR*, to appear in the *LNCS* series. Springer, 2002. 162, 166

12. C. C. Florêncio. Consistent identification in the limit of any of the classes k-valued is NP-hard. In *Proceedings of the Conference on Logical Aspects of Computational Linguistics LACL*, volume 2099 of *LNCS/LNAI*, pages 125–138. Springer, 2001. 165

13. E. M. Gold. Language identification in the limit. *Information and Control*, 10:447–474, 1967. 154, 159

14. R. C. Gonzalez and M. G. Thomason. *Syntactic Pattern Recognition; An Introduction*. Addison-Wesley, 1978. 153, 165

15. C. de la Higuera. Current trends in grammatical inference. In F. J. Ferri et al., editors, *Advances in Pattern Recognition, Joint IAPR International Workshops SSPR+SPR*, volume 1876 of *LNCS*, pages 28–31. Springer, 2000. 153

16. M. Kanazawa. Learnable Classes of Categorial Grammars. CSLI, 1998. 153

17. T. Knuutila. How to invent characterizable methods for regular languages. In K. P. Jantke et al., editors, *4th Workshop on Algorithmic Learning Theory ALT*, volume 744 of *LNCS/LNAI*, pages 209–222. Springer, 1993. 153

18. T. Knuutila and M. Steinby. The inference of tree languages from finite samples: an algebraic approach. *Theoretical Computer Science*, 129:337–367, 1994. 153, 165

19. S. Kobayashi and T. Yokomori. Learning approximately regular languages with reversible languages. *Theoretical Computer Science*, 174(1–2):251–257, 1997. 163, 165

20. D. López and S. España. Error correcting tree language inference. *Pattern Recognition Letters*, 23:1–12, 2002. 165

21. D. López and I. Piñaga. Syntactic pattern recognition by error correcting analysis on tree automata. In F. J. Ferri et al., editors, *Advances in Pattern Recognition, Joint IAPR International Workshops SSPR+SPR*, volume 1876 of *LNCS*, pages 133–142. Springer, 2000. 165

22. V. Radhakrishnan and G. Nagaraja. Inference of regular grammars via skeletons. *IEEE Transactions on Systems, Man and Cybernetics*, 17(6):982–992, 1987. 157

23. J. R. Rico-Juan, J. Calera-Rubio, and R. C. Carrasco. Probabilistic k-testable tree languages. In A. L. Oliveira, editor, *Grammatical Inference: Algorithms and Applications, 5th International Colloquium, ICGI*, volume 1891 of *LNCS/LNAI*, pages 221–228. Springer, 2000. 153

24. G. Rozenberg and A. Salomaa, editors. *Handbook of Formal Languages, Volume III*. Berlin: Springer, 1997. 154, 159

25. Y. Sakakibara. Learning context-free grammars from structural data in polynomial time. *Theoretical Computer Science*, 76:223–242, 1990. 154

26. Y. Sakakibara. Efficient learning of context-free grammars from positive structural examples. *Information and Computation*, 97(1):23–60, March 1992. 153, 154, 157, 161, 162

27. Y. Sakakibara and H. Muramatsu. Learning context-free grammars from partially structured examples. In A. L. Oliveira, editor, *Grammatical Inference: Algorithms and Applications, 5th International Colloquium, ICGI*, volume 1891 of *LNCS/LNAI*, pages 229–240. Springer, 2000. 165

28. Y. Takada and T. Y. Nishida. A note on grammatical inference of slender context-free languages. In L. Miclet and C. de la Higuera, editors, *Proceedings of the Third International Colloquium on Grammatical Inference ICGI: Learning Syntax from Sentences*, volume 1147 of *LNCS/LNAI*, pages 117–125. Springer, 1996. 165

29. H. Volger. Grammars with generalized contextfree rules and their tree automata. In *Proceedings of Computational Linguists in the*

Netherlands Meeting CLIN; Selected Papers, pages 223–233. see `http://www-uilots.let.uu.nl/publications/clin1999/papers.html`, 1999. 166

30. T. Yokomori. Inductive inference of context-free languages based on context-free expressions. *International Journal of Computer Mathematics*, 24:115–140, 1988. 165

31. T. Yokomori. Polynomial-time learning of very simple grammars from positive data. In *Proceedings 4th Workshop on Computational Learning Theory COLT*, pages 213–227, San Mateo, CA, 1991. Morgan Kaufmann. 165

32. T. Yokomori. On learning systolic languages. In K. P. Jantke, S. Doshita, K. Furukawa, and T. Nishida, editors, *Proceedings of the 3rd Workshop on Algorithmic Learning Theory ALT*, volume 743 of *LNCS/LNAI*, pages 41–52. Springer, 1992. 165

Polynomial Time Inductive Inference of Ordered Tree Patterns with Internal Structured Variables from Positive Data

Yusuke Suzuki[1], Ryuta Akanuma[1], Takayoshi Shoudai[1], Tetsuhiro Miyahara[2], and Tomoyuki Uchida[2]

[1] Department of Informatics, Kyushu University
Kasuga 816-8580, Japan
{y-suzuki,r-aka,shoudai}@i.kyushu-u.ac.jp
[2] Faculty of Information Sciences, Hiroshima City University
Hiroshima, 731-3194, Japan
{miyahara@its,uchida@cs}.hiroshima-cu.ac.jp

Abstract. Tree structured data such as HTML/XML files are represented by rooted trees with ordered children and edge labels. As a representation of a tree structured pattern in such tree structured data, we propose an ordered tree pattern, called a term tree, which is a rooted tree pattern consisting of ordered children and internal structured variables. A term tree is a generalization of standard tree patterns representing first order terms in formal logic. For a set of edge labels Λ and a term tree t, the term tree language of t, denoted by $L_\Lambda(t)$, is the set of all labeled trees which are obtained from a term tree t by substituting arbitrary labeled trees for all variables in t. In this paper, we propose polynomial time algorithms for the following two problems for two fundamental classes of term trees. The membership problem is, given a term tree t and a tree T, to decide whether or not $L_\Lambda(t)$ includes T. The minimal language problem is, given a set of labeled trees S, to find a term tree t such that $L_\Lambda(t)$ is minimal among all term tree languages which contain all trees in S. Then, by using these two algorithms, we show that the two classes of term trees are polynomial time inductively inferable from positive data.

1 Introduction

Due to rapid growth of Information Technologies, the amount of electronic data has increased rapidly. In the fields of data mining and knowledge discovery, many researchers have developed techniques based on machine learning for analyzing such electronic data. Web documents such as HTML/XML files have tree structures and are called tree structured data. Such tree structured data are represented by rooted trees with ordered children and edge labels [1]. As examples of representations of tree structured data, we give rooted trees T_1, T_2 and T_3 in Fig. 1. As a representation of a tree structured pattern in such tree

J. Kivinen and R. H. Sloan (Eds.): COLT 2002, LNAI 2375, pp. 169–184, 2002.

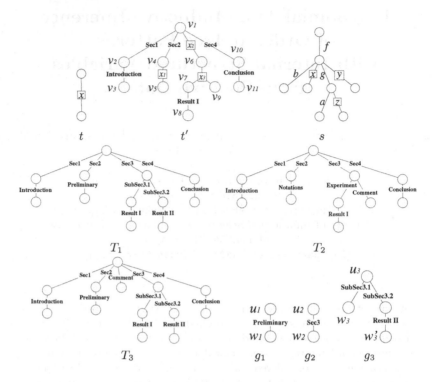

Fig. 1. Term trees t and t' explaining trees T_1, T_2 and T_3. A term tree s represents the tree pattern $f(b, x, g(a, z), y)$. A variable is represented by a box with lines to its elements. The label of a box is the variable label of the variable

structured data, we propose an ordered tree pattern, called a *term tree*, which is a rooted tree pattern with ordered children consisting of tree structures and internal structured variables. A variable in a term tree consists of some number of vertices and it can be substituted by an arbitrary tree. A term tree is more powerful than a standard tree pattern, which is also called a first order term in formal logic, in computational learning theory [2]. For example, in Fig. 1, the tree pattern $f(b, x, g(a, z), y)$ can be represented by the term tree s, but the term tree t' can not be represented by any standard tree pattern because of the existence of internal structured variables represented by x_2 and x_3 in t'. For a set of edge labels Λ, the *term tree language* of a term tree t, denoted by $L_\Lambda(t)$, is the set of all labeled trees which are obtained from t by substituting arbitrary labeled trees for all variables in t. A term tree t is said to be *regular* if all variable labels in t are mutually distinct.

In this paper, we deal with the set $\mathcal{OTT}_\Lambda^{L,K}$ of all regular term trees t with Λ as a set of edge labels such that each variables in t consists of at most $L+1$ vertices for some $L \geq 1$ and any path from the root to a leaf in t has at most K variables for some $K \geq 1$. Let $\mathcal{OTT}_\Lambda^{L,*} = \bigcup_{K \geq 1} \mathcal{OTT}_\Lambda^{L,K}$. Our main result is to show that the two fundamental classes $\mathcal{OTTL}_\Lambda^{1,1} = \{L_\Lambda(t) \mid t \in \mathcal{OTT}_\Lambda^{1,1}\}$ and $\mathcal{OTTL}_\Lambda^{1,*} = \{L_\Lambda(t) \mid t \in \mathcal{OTT}_\Lambda^{1,*}\}$ are polynomial time inductively inferable from positive data. In order to prove this result, we give polynomial time algorithms for the *membership problem* and the *minimal language problem* for $\mathcal{OTT}_\Lambda^{1,*}$ and $\mathcal{OTT}_\Lambda^{1,1}$. Let $\mathcal{R}$ be a set of regular term trees. The membership problem for $\mathcal{R}$ is, given a term tree $t \in \mathcal{R}$ and a tree T, to decide whether or not $T \in L_\Lambda(t)$. Consider the examples of the term tree t' and the tree T_1 in Fig. 1. It holds that $L_\Lambda(t')$ includes T_1, because T_1 is obtained from t' by replacing variables x_1, x_2 and x_3 in t' with the trees g_1, g_2 and g_3 in Fig. 1, respectively. The *minimal language (MINL) problem* for $\mathcal{R}$ is, given a set of labeled trees S, to find a term tree $t \in \mathcal{R}$ such that $L_\Lambda(t)$ is minimal among all languages $L_\Lambda(t')$ for $t' \in \mathcal{R}$ with $S \subseteq L_\Lambda(t')$. That is, the MINL problem is to find one of the least generalized term trees explaining given tree structured data. Our algorithms for the minimal language problem use a set of operations, which are sometimes called refinement operators [5,11]. In Fig. 1, we give examples of term trees t and t' which can explain all trees T_1, T_2 and T_3. But it holds that $L_\Lambda(t) \supsetneq L_\Lambda(t') \supseteq \{T_1, T_2, T_3\}$, since $L_\Lambda(t)$ includes all trees.

As previous works, in [6,12], we gave some sets of *unrooted* regular term trees with *unordered* children whose languages are polynomial time inductive inferable from positive data. In [7,13], we considered the complexities of the membership problem and the MINL problem for a set of rooted regular term trees with unordered children. In [13], we gave a polynomial time algorithm for solving the MINL problem for regular unordered term trees and showed that two MINL problems with optimizing the size of an output term tree are NP-complete. In [8,9], we gave data mining systems having special types of *rooted* regular term trees with unordered children and ordered children as knowledge representations, respectively. As the other related works, the works [2,4] show the learnabilities of extended tree patterns in query learning models.

2 Preliminaries – Ordered Term Trees

Let $T = (V_T, E_T)$ be an ordered tree with a vertex set V_T and an edge set E_T. A list $h = [u_0, u_1, \ldots, u_\ell]$ of vertices in V_T is called a *variable* of T if $u_1, \ldots, u_\ell$ are consecutive children of u_0, i.e., u_0 is the parent of $u_1, \ldots, u_\ell$ and u_{j+1} is the next sibling of u_j for j with any $1 \leq j < \ell$. We call u_0 the *parent port* of the variable h and $u_1, \ldots, u_\ell$ the *child ports* of h. Two variables $h = [u_0, u_1, \ldots, u_\ell]$ and $h' = [u_0', u_1', \ldots, u_{\ell'}']$ are said to be *disjoint* if $u_0 \neq u_0'$ or $\{u_1, \ldots, u_\ell\} \cap \{u_1', \ldots, u_{\ell'}'\} = \emptyset$.

Definition 1. Let $T = (V_T, E_T)$ be an ordered tree and H_T a set of pairwise disjoint variables of T. An *ordered term tree obtained from T and H_T* is a triplet $t = (V_t, E_t, H_t)$ where $V_t = V_T$, $E_t = E_T - \bigcup_{h=[u_0,u_1,\ldots,u_\ell]\in H_T}\{\{u_0, u_i\} \in E_T \mid 1 \leq i \leq \ell\}$, and $H_t = H_T$. For two vertices $u, u' \in V_t$, we say that u is the *parent* of u' in t if u is the parent of u' in T. Similarly we say that u' is a *child* of u in t if u' is a child of u in T. In particular, for a vertex $u \in V_t$ with no child, we call u

a *leaf* of t. We define the order of the children of each vertex u in t as the order of the children of u in T. We often omit the description of the ordered tree T and variable set H_T because we can find them from the triplet $t = (V_t, E_t, H_t)$.

For example, the ordered term tree t' in Fig. 1 is obtained from the tree $T = (V_T, E_T)$ and the set of variables H_T defined as follows. $V_T = \{v_1, \ldots, v_{11}\}$, $E_T = \{\{v_1, v_2\}, \{v_2, v_3\}, \{v_1, v_4\}, \{v_4, v_5\}, \{v_1, v_6\}, \{v_6, v_7\}, \{v_7, v_8\}, \{v_6, v_9\}, \{v_1, v_{10}\}, \{v_{10}, v_{11}\}\}$ with the root v_1 and the sibling relation displayed in Fig. 1. $H_T = \{[v_4, v_5], [v_1, v_6], [v_6, v_7, v_9]\}$.

For any ordered term tree t, a vertex u of t, and two children u' and u'' of u, we write $u' <_u^t u''$ if u' is smaller than u'' in the order of the children of u. We assume that every edges and variables of an ordered term tree are labeled with some words from specified languages. A label of a variable is called a *variable label*. Λ and X denote a set of edge labels and a set of variable labels, respectively, where $\Lambda \cap X = \phi$. An ordered term tree $t = (V_t, E_t, H_t)$ is called *regular* if all variables in H_t have mutually distinct variable labels in X.

Note. In this paper, we treat only regular ordered term trees, and then we call a regular ordered term tree a *term tree*, simply. In particular, an ordered term tree with no variable is called a *ground term tree* and considered to be a tree with ordered children.

For a term tree t and its vertices v_1 and v_i, a *path* from v_1 to v_i is a sequence $v_1, v_2, \ldots, v_i$ of distinct vertices of t such that for any j with any $1 \leq j < i$, v_j is the parent of v_{j+1}. OT_Λ denotes the set of all ground term trees with Λ as a set of edge labels. Let $L \geq 1$ and $K \geq 1$ be integers. Let $OTT_\Lambda^{L,K}$ be the set of all term trees t with Λ as a set of edge labels such that each variable in t has at most L child ports and any path from the root to a leaf in t has at most K variables. Let $OTT_\Lambda^{L,*} = \bigcup_{K \geq 1} OTT_\Lambda^{L,K}$. Let $f = (V_f, E_f, H_f)$ and $g = (V_g, E_g, H_g)$ be term trees. We say that f and g are *isomorphic*, denoted by $f \equiv g$, if there is a bijection φ from V_f to V_g such that (i) the root of f is mapped to the root of g by φ, (ii) $\{u, u'\} \in E_f$ if and only if $\{\varphi(u), \varphi(u')\} \in E_g$ and the two edges have the same edge label, (iii) $[u_0, u_1, \ldots, u_\ell] \in H_f$ if and only if $[\varphi(u_0), \varphi(u_1), \ldots, \varphi(u_\ell)] \in H_g$, and (iv) for any vertex u in f which has more than one child, and for any two children u' and u'' of u, $u' <_u^f u''$ if and only if $\varphi(u') <_{\varphi(u)}^g \varphi(u'')$.

Let f and g be term trees with at least two vertices. Let $h = [v_0, v_1, \ldots, v_\ell]$ be a variable in f with the variable label x and $\sigma = [u_0, u_1, \ldots, u_\ell]$ a list of $\ell + 1$ distinct vertices in g where u is the root of g and $u_1, \ldots, u_\ell$ are leaves of g. The form $x := [g, \sigma]$ is called a *binding* for x. A new term tree $f' = f\{x := [g, \sigma]\}$ is obtained by applying the binding $x := [g, \sigma]$ to f in the following way. For the variable $h = [v_0, v_1, \ldots, v_\ell]$, we attach g to f by removing the variable h from H_f and by identifying the vertices $v_0, v_1, \ldots, v_\ell$ with the vertices $u_0, u_1, \ldots, u_\ell$ of g in this order. We define a new ordering $<_v^{f'}$ on every vertex v in f' in the following natural way. Suppose that v has more than one child and let v' and v'' be two children of v in f'. We note that $v_i = u_i$ for any $0 \leq i \leq \ell$. (1) If $v, v', v'' \in V_g$ and $v' <_v^g v''$, then $v' <_v^{f'} v''$. (2) If $v, v', v'' \in V_f$ and $v' <_v^f v''$, then $v' <_v^{f'} v''$.

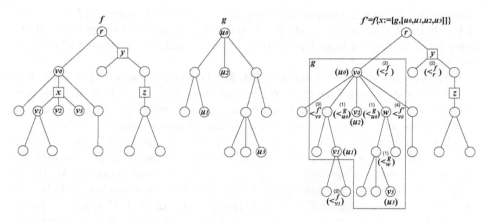

Fig. 2. The new ordering on vertices in the term tree $f' = f\{x := [g, [u_0, u_1, u_2, u_3]]\}$

(3) If $v = v_0(= u_0)$, $v' \in V_f - \{v_1, \ldots, v_\ell\}$, $v'' \in V_g$, and $v' <^f_v v_1$, then $v' <^{f'}_v v''$.
(4) If $v = v_0(= u_0)$, $v' \in V_f - \{v_1, \ldots, v_\ell\}$, $v'' \in V_g$, and $v_\ell <^f_v v'$, then $v'' <^{f'}_v v'$.
In Fig. 2, we give an example of the new ordering on vertices in a term tree.

A *substitution* θ is a finite collection of bindings $\{x_1 := [g_1, \sigma_1], \cdots, x_n := [g_n, \sigma_n]\}$, where x_i's are mutually distinct variable labels in X. The term tree $f\theta$, called the *instance* of f by θ, is obtained by applying the all bindings $x_i := [g_i, \sigma_i]$ on f.Lastly we define the root of the resulting term tree $f\theta$ as the root of f. Consider the examples in Fig. 1. Examples of term trees t and t' are given. Let $\theta = \{x_1 :- [g_1, [u_1, w_1]], x_2 := [g_2, [u_2, w_2]], x_3 := [g_3, [u_3, w_3, w'_3]]\}$ be a substitution, where g_1, g_2, and g_3 are trees. Then the instance $t'\theta$ of the term tree t' by θ is the tree T_1.

Definition 2. Let L and K be positive integers and Λ a set of edge labels. The *term tree language* $L_\Lambda(t)$ of a term tree $t \in \mathcal{OTT}^{L,K}_\Lambda$ is $\{s \in \mathcal{OT}_\Lambda \mid s \equiv t\theta$ for a substitution $\theta\}$. The class $\mathcal{OTTL}^{L,K}_\Lambda$ of term tree languages is defined as $\{L_\Lambda(t) \mid t \in \mathcal{OTT}^{L,K}_\Lambda\}$.

3   Polynomial Time Inductive Inference of Ordered Term Tree Languages from Positive Data

We give the framework of inductive inference from positive data [3,10] and show our main theorem. Let U be a recursively enumerable set to which we refer as a *universal set*. We call $L \subseteq U$ a *concept*. An *indexed family of recursive concepts* or *a class* is a triplet $\mathcal{C} = (C, R, \gamma)$, where C is a family of nonempty concepts, R is a recursively enumerable set, each element in R is called a *representation*, γ is a surjection from R to C, and there exists a recursive function $f : U \times R \to \{0, 1\}$ such that $f(w, r) = 1$ if $w \in \gamma(r)$, 0 otherwise. A class $\mathcal{C} = (C, R, \gamma)$ *has finite thickness* if for any nonempty finite set $T \subseteq U$, the cardinality of $\{L \in C \mid T \subseteq L\}$ is finite. For a class $\mathcal{C} = (C, R, \gamma)$, when the family of concepts C and the surjection γ are clear from the context, we write only the representation R for the class $\mathcal{C}$.

An *inductive inference machine* (IIM, for short) for $\mathcal{C}$ is an effective procedure which requests inputs from time to time and produces elements in R from time to time. The output produced by the machine are called *hypotheses*. A *positive presentation* of a nonempty concept L is an infinite sequence $\rho = w_1, w_2, \ldots$ of elements in L such that $\{w_1, w_2, \ldots\} = L$. We denote by $\rho[n]$ the ρ's initial segment of length $n \geq 0$ and by $M(\rho[n])$ the last hypothesis produced by M which is successively presented $w_1, w_2, \ldots, w_n$ on its input requests. An IIM is said to *converge to a representation* r for a positive presentation ρ, if there is an $n \geq 1$ such that for any $m \geq n$, $M(\rho[m])$ is r. An IIM M *infers a class* $\mathcal{C}$ *in the limit from positive data* if for any $L \in \mathcal{C}$ and any positive presentation ρ of L, M converges to a representation r for ρ such that $L = \gamma(r)$. A class $\mathcal{C}$ is said to be *inferable in the limit from positive data* if there is an IIM which infers $\mathcal{C}$ in the limit from positive data. An IIM M is *consistently working* if for any $L \in C$, any positive presentation $\rho = w_1, w_2, \ldots$ of L and any $n \geq 1$ with $M(\rho[n]) \in R$, we have $\{w_1, \ldots, w_n\} \subseteq \gamma(M(\rho[n]))$. And an IIM M is *responsively working* if for any $L \in C$, any positive presentation ρ of L and any $n \geq 1$, we have $M(\rho[n]) \in R$. Moreover, an IIM is *conservatively working* if for any $L \in \mathcal{C}$, any positive presentation ρ of L and any n, m with $1 \leq n < m$ such that $M(\rho[n]), M(\rho[m]) \in R$ and $M(\rho[n]) \neq M(\rho[m])$, we have $\{w_1, \ldots, w_m\} \not\subseteq \gamma(M(\rho[n]))$. A class $\mathcal{C}$ is *polynomial time inferable from positive data* if there exists a consistently, responsively and conservatively working IIM for $\mathcal{C}$ which outputs hypotheses in polynomial time with respect to the length of the input read so far, and infers $\mathcal{C}$ in the limit from positive data.

For a class $\mathcal{C} = (C, R, \gamma)$, let S be a nonempty finite set of U. We say that a representation $r \in R$ is *minimal for* $(S, \mathcal{C})$ if $S \subseteq \gamma(r)$ and $\gamma(s) \subsetneq \gamma(r)$ implies $S \not\subseteq \gamma(s)$ for any $s \in R$. Then, we define the following problems for $\mathcal{C}$:

Membership Problem for $\mathcal{C}$
  Instance: An element $w \in U$ and a representation $r \in R$.
  Question: Is w included in $\gamma(r)$?

Minimal Language Problem (MINL) for $\mathcal{C}$
  Instance: A nonempty finite subset S of U.
  Question: Find a representation $r \in R$ which is minimal for $(S, \mathcal{C})$.

Angluin [3] and Shinohara [10] showed that if $\mathcal{C}$ has finite thickness, and the membership problem and the minimal language problem for $\mathcal{C}$ are computable in polynomial time then $\mathcal{C}$ is polynomial time inductively inferable from positive data. Let Λ be a finite or infinite alphabet of edge labels. In our setting, the universal set U is the set $\mathcal{OT}_\Lambda$ of all ground term trees, and $\gamma(t)$ is the term tree language $L(t)$ for a term tree $t \in \mathcal{OTT}_\Lambda^{L,K}$. It is easy to see that the classes $\mathcal{OTT}_\Lambda^{L,K}$ have finite thickness for any $L, K \geq 1$. In Section 4, we give a polynomial time algorithm for the membership problem for $\mathcal{OTT}_\Lambda^{1,*}$. Further, in Section 5 and 6, we give polynomial time algorithms for the minimal language problem for $\mathcal{OTT}_\Lambda^{1,1}$ and $\mathcal{OTT}_\Lambda^{1,*}$. Therefore, we show the following main result.

Theorem 1. *For any set of edge labels Λ, the classes $\mathcal{OTT}_\Lambda^{1,1}$ and $\mathcal{OTT}_\Lambda^{1,*}$ are polynomial time inductively inferable from positive data.*

4   A Polynomial Time Algorithm for Solving Membership Problem for $\mathcal{OTT}_\Lambda^{1,*}$

In this section, we give a polynomial time algorithm Matching (Fig.3) for the membership problem for $\mathcal{OTT}_\Lambda^{1,*}$ and any set of edge labels Λ. Let $T = (V, E)$ and $t = (V', E', H')$ be a tree and a term tree, respectively. A term tree t is said to *match* a tree T if T is included in $L_\Lambda(t)$. We assume that all vertices of a term tree are associated with different numbers. The *vertex identifier* of a vertex u' of a term tree t is the associated number of u', and denoted by $I(u')$. A *correspondence-set* of a vertex u of a tree T is a set of vertex identifiers, which are with or without parentheses, of vertices of a term tree t. A vertex identifier in parentheses shows that the vertex is a child port of a variable. The intended meaning of a correspondence-set is stated in the proof of Theorem 2. For a vertex u' of a term tree t, we define the set $Rule(t)$ of all *correspondence-set-attaching rules* of t, as follows. Let $c_1', \cdots, c_{m'}'$ be all ordered children of u' in t. If u' is a child port then $H(u') = (I(u'))$, otherwise $H(u') = I(u')$.

$Rule(t) =$
$\{I(u') \leftarrow I(c_1'), \ldots, I(c_{m'}') \mid$ a vertex u' of t is neither a parent port nor a leaf$\}$
$\cup \{I(u') \Leftarrow H(c_1'), \ldots, H(c_{m'}') \mid u'$ is a vertex of t, and u' is a parent port$\}$
$\cup \{(I(u')) \Leftarrow (I(u')) \mid u'$ is a vertex of t, and u' is a child port$\}$.

We repeatedly attach a correspondence-set to vertices of a tree T from the leaves to the root. In Fig. 4, when the term tree t and the tree T are given, $Rule(t)$ denotes the set of all correspondence-set-attaching rules of t. After the procedure Matching terminates, we can get the resulting correspondence-sets of T.

Procedure Matching (Fig.3) is for the case of $|\Lambda| = 1$. We can easily extend the algorithm for the case of $|\Lambda| \geq 2$ by checking edge labels of a term tree and a tree in applying correspondence-set-attaching rules.

Theorem 2. *Membership Problem for $\mathcal{OTT}_\Lambda^{1,*}$ is computable in polynomial time for any set of edge labels Λ.*

Proof. (Sketch) Let $CS(v)$ be the correspondence-set attached to a vertex v of a tree T, after the procedure Correspondence-Set-Attaching for v terminates. By an induction on applications of correspondence-set-attaching rules, we can show that the following claims. $T[v]$ denotes the subtree which is induced by v and the descendants of v. And $t[v]$ denotes the sub-term tree which is induced by v and the descendants of v. *Claim 1.* $I(u') \in CS(v)$ if and only if $t[u']$ matches $T[v]$. *Claim 2.* $(I(u')) \in CS(v)$ if and only if (i) $t[u']$ matches $T[v]$ or (ii) $t[u']$ matches $T[v']$ for a descendant v' of v. Thus we show that the correspondence-set attached to the root of a tree T contains the vertex identifier of the root of

Procedure Matching(term tree t in $\mathcal{OTT}_\Lambda^{1,*}$ with root r, tree T in $\mathcal{OT}_\Lambda$ with root R);
begin
    Construct the set $Rule(t)$ of all correspondence-set-attaching rules of t;
    For each leaf ℓ of T, attach the correspondence-set $\{I(\ell') \mid \ell'$ is a leaf of $t\}$ to ℓ;
    while there exists a vertex v of T
                such that v is not attached with any correspondence-set and
                all children of v are attached with correspondence-sets
        do Correspondence-Set-Attaching($v, Rule(t)$);
    if the correspondence-set attached to R includes the vertex identifier $I(r)$ of r
    then report that t matches T
    else report that t does not match T
end.

Procedure Correspondence-Set-Attaching
                (vertex v of T, set of correspondence-set-attaching rules $Rule$);
begin
    $C := \emptyset$;
    Let $c_1, \cdots, c_m$ be all ordered children of v in T;
    Let $CS(c_1), \cdots, CS(c_m)$ be the correspondence-sets attached to
        $c_1, \cdots, c_m$, respectively;
    foreach $I(u') \leftarrow I(c_1'), \cdots, I(c_{m'}')$ in $Rule$ **do**
        if $m' = m$ and $I(c_i') \in CS(c_i)$ for all i $(1 \leq i \leq m)$
        then $C := C \cup \{I(u')\}$;
    foreach $I(u') \Leftarrow H(c_1'), \cdots, H(c_{m'}')$ in $Rule$ **do**
        if $m' \leq m$ and the list $[1, 2, \ldots, m]$ can be divided into m' sublists
          $[j(1), \ldots, j(2) - 1], [j(2), \ldots, j(3) - 1], \ldots, [j(m'), \ldots, j(m' + 1)]$
          with $j(1) = 1$ and $j(m' + 1) = m$ satisfying that
             (1) for each $1 \leq i \leq m'$ with $H(c_i') = I(c_i')$, the ith sublist is $[j(i)]$,
                i.e., $j(i) = j(i + 1) - 1$, and $I(c_i') \in CS(c_{j(i)})$, and
             (2) for each $1 \leq i \leq m'$ with $H(c_i') = (I(c_i'))$, the ith sublist is
                $[j(i), \ldots, j(i + 1) - 1]$ and $I(c_i') \in CS(c_{k(i)})$ or $(I(c_i')) \in CS(c_{k(i)})$
                for some $k(i)$ with $j(i) \leq k(i) \leq j(i + 1) - 1$
        then $C := C \cup \{I(u')\}$;
    foreach $(I(u')) \Leftarrow (I(u'))$ in $Rule$ **do**
        if there is a set among $CS(c_1), \cdots, CS(c_m)$ which includes $I(u')$ or $(I(u'))$
        then $C := C \cup \{(I(u'))\}$;
    Attach C to v as its correspondence-set
end.

Fig. 3. Matching: an algorithm for the membership problem for the set $\mathcal{OTT}_\Lambda^{1,*}$ of term trees

a term tree t if and only if t matches T. Let n and s be the numbers of vertices and internal vertices of a term tree t, respectively. Let N and S be the number of vertices and internal vertices of a tree T, respectively. Then Procedure Matching runs in $O(nS + nNs)$ time. $\qquad\qquad\Box$

5 A Polynomial Time Algorithm for MINL for $\mathcal{OTT}_\Lambda^{1,1}$

In this section, we give a polynomial time algorithm MINL1 (Fig. 5) for Minimal Language Problem for $\mathcal{OTT}_\Lambda^{1,1}$ (Theorem 3). Let $S = \{T_1, \ldots, T_m\}$ be a finite set of trees with edge labels from Λ. Let $T_{\min} = (V_{\min}, E_{\min})$ be one of the smallest trees in S with respect to the number of vertices. For a vertex v

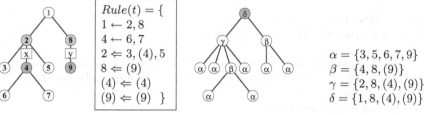

Term Tree t Correspondence-set-   Tree T The resulting correspondence-
attaching rules   sets of a tree T

Fig. 4. The correspondence-set-attaching rules of a term tree t. The resulting correspondence-sets of a tree T after the procedure Matching terminates

of T, $T[v]$ denotes the subtree which is induced by v and the descendants of v. Let $L_S = [T_{\min}[v_1], T_{\min}[v_2], \ldots, T_{\min}[v_{|V_{\min}|}]]$ be the sorted list of all subtrees of $T_{\min}$ for $v_i \in V_{\min}$ with respect to the depth of trees, i.e., for all i, j with $i < j$, the depth of $T_{\min}[v_i]$ is not smaller than that of $T_{\min}[v_j]$. We call this list L_S the *candidate tree list* of S. For $t \in \mathcal{OTT}_\Lambda^{1,K}$, $T(t)$ denotes the ground term tree obtained by replacing all variables with non-labeled edges and labeled edges with non-labeled edges. For $t, t' \in \mathcal{OTT}_\Lambda^{1,K}$, we write $t \approx t'$ if $T(t) \equiv T(t')$.

Lemma 1. *Let S be an input set of trees for* Algorithm MINL1 *(Fig. 5). Let $t = (V_t, E_t, H_t)$ be an output term tree by* Algorithm MINL1 *and $t' = (V_{t'}, E_{t'}, H_{t'})$ a term tree such that $S \subseteq L_\Lambda(t') \subseteq L_\Lambda(t)$. Then $t \equiv t'$.*

Proof. (Sketch) Let $u \in V_t$ (resp. $u' \in V_{t'}$) be the kth vertex of t (resp. t') when we visit the vertices of t (resp. t') in preorder. First we show that the number of children of u is equal to that of u' by induction on k. Hence $t \approx t'$. We omit the proof. Then we have an isomorphism ξ from $T(t')$ to $T(t)$. Let u' be the kth vertex of t' in preorder and v' the ℓth child of u'. Second we show that if $[u', v'] \in H_{t'}$ then $[\xi(u'), \xi(v')] \in H_t$. This is done by induction on k and ℓ. The proof depends on the edges and variables around u' and v'. Let x be the variable label of $[u', v']$. The most cases can be proved by showing that if $[\xi(u'), \xi(v')] \notin H_t$ then $\{t'\theta_A^a, t'\theta_B^a, t'\theta_C^a, t'\theta_D^a\} \not\subseteq L_\Lambda(t)$ for some label $a \in \Lambda$ (these substitutions are described in Fig. 6). When $|\Lambda| = 1$, Fig. 7 shows the only case which possibly satisfies that $\{t'\theta_A, t'\theta_B, t'\theta_C, t'\theta_D\} \subset L_\Lambda(t)$ even if $[\xi(u'), \xi(v')] \notin H_t$. But Algorithm MINL1 does not output a term tree of this type. Since the term tree t is obtained from t'' (Fig. 7) by *Edge-Extension* on $[u, v]$ of t'', if $S \subseteq L_\Lambda(t')$ then *Adding-Ending-Part* chooses the subtree rooted at v' of t' rather than the subtree rooted at v of t''. This is because the subtree rooted at v of t'' does not have the maximum depth with $S \subseteq L_\Lambda(t'')$. □

Theorem 3. *Minimal Language Problem for $\mathcal{OTT}_\Lambda^{1,1}$ is computable in polynomial time.*

Algorithm MINL1;
  input: a set of trees $S = \{T_1, \ldots, T_m\} \subseteq \mathcal{OT}_\Lambda$;
  begin
    Let L_S be the candidate tree list of S; $\Lambda_S := \{a \in \Lambda \mid a$ appears on trees in $S\}$;
    Let $t = (\{u, v\}, \emptyset, \{h = [u, v]\})$ with the root u; Let q be a list initialized to be $[h]$;
    Variable-branching(t, S, q);
    while q is not empty **do begin**
      $t' := Adding\text{-}Ending\text{-}Part(t, S, q[1], L_S)$;
      $t'' := Edge\text{-}Replacing(t', S, q[1])$;
      $t''' := Edge\text{-}Extension(t', S, q[1])$;
      if $t'' \neq t'$ **then begin** $t := t''$ $q := q[2..]$ **end**
      else if $t''' = t'$ **then** $t := t'$; $q := q[2..]$ **end**
      else *Variable-Branching*$(Edge\text{-}Extension(t, q[1]), S, q)$
    end;
    output t
  end.

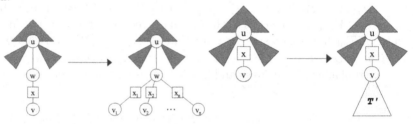

Variable-Branching(t, S, q): Add some new variables to the right of $q[1] = [w, v]$ while $S \subseteq L_\Lambda(t)$, and update the list $q := q[2..]\&[[w, v_1], \ldots, [w, v_n]]$.

Adding-Ending-Part(t, S, h, L_S): Find the first tree T' in the candidate tree list L_S such that the term tree t' made by adding T' to the child port of h satisfies $S \subseteq L_\Lambda(t')$, and return t'.

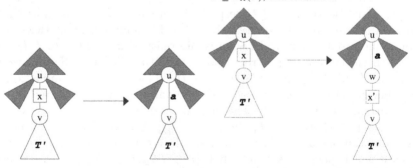

Edge-Replacing(t, S, h): For each edge label a in Λ_S, replace the variable h with the edge labeled with a, and return first new term tree t' with $S \subseteq L_\Lambda(t')$, if there is no such a term tree then return t.

Edge-Extension(t, S, h): For each edge label $h = [u, v]$ in Λ_S, replace the variable $h = [u, v]$ with a labeled edge $\{u, w\}$ and $[w, v]$, and return the first new term tree t' with $S \subseteq L_\Lambda(t')$, if there is no such a term tree then return t.

Fig. 5. Algorithm MINL1. $q[1]$ is the first element of q and $q[2..]$ is the list after removing $q[1]$. "&" denotes the concatenation of two lists

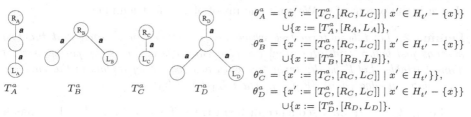

$$\theta_A^a = \{x' := [T_C^a, [R_C, L_C]] \mid x' \in H_{t'} - \{x\}\}$$
$$\cup \{x := [T_A^a, [R_A, L_A]]\},$$
$$\theta_B^a = \{x' := [T_C^a, [R_C, L_C]] \mid x' \in H_{t'} - \{x\}\}$$
$$\cup \{x := [T_B^a, [R_B, L_B]]\},$$
$$\theta_C^a = \{x' := [T_C^a, [R_C, L_C]] \mid x' \in H_{t'}\}\},$$
$$\theta_D^a = \{x' := [T_C^a, [R_C, L_C]] \mid x' \in H_{t'} - \{x\}\}$$
$$\cup \{x := [T_D^a, [R_D, L_D]]\}.$$

Fig. 6. Basic substitutions

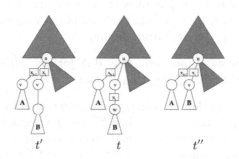

Fig. 7. Possibly $L_\Lambda(t') \subseteq L_\Lambda(t) \subseteq L_\Lambda(t'')$

Proof. The correctness of Algorithm MINL1 follows Lemma 1. Let $S = \{T_1 = (V_1, E_1), \ldots, T_m = (V_m, E_m)\}$. Let $N_{\max} = \max\{|V_i| \mid 1 \le i \le m\}$, $N_{\min} = \min\{|V_i| \mid 1 \le i \le m\}$, and $d_{\min} = \min\{$the number of children of $v \mid v$ is an internal vertex of the trees in $S\}$. Let $\Lambda_S = \{a \in \Lambda \mid a$ appears on trees in $S\}$. Let $\mathrm{MAT}(N, n)$ be the time complexity of *Procedure Matching* for a tree with N vertices and a term tree with n vertices. *Variable-Branching, Adding-Ending-Part, Edge-Replacing*, and *Edge-Extension* call Procedure Matching at most $md_{\min}$, $m|L_S|$, $m|\Lambda_S|$, and $m|\Lambda_S|$ times, respectively. Then one while loop needs $O(m(N_{\min} + |\Lambda_S|)\mathrm{MAT}(N_{\max}, N_{\min}))$ time. Since the number of variables of an output term tree is at most $O(N_{\min})$, totally Algorithm MINL1 runs in $O(mN_{\min}(N_{\min} + |\Lambda_S|)\mathrm{MAT}(N_{\max}, N_{\min}))$ time. $\square$

6 A Polynomial Time Algorithm for MINL for $\mathcal{OTT}_\Lambda^{1,*}$

In this section, we give a polynomial time algorithm for solving the minimal language problem for $\mathcal{OTT}_\Lambda^{1,*}$ with any set of edge labels Λ. Let $S = \{T_1, \ldots, T_n\} \subseteq \mathcal{OT}_\Lambda$ be an input set of trees. Our algorithm *MINL** (Fig. 8) consists of two steps, called *Variable-Extension* and *Edge-Replacing*. We start with a term tree which consists of only one variable. *Variable-Extension* makes bigger a current term tree by increasing the number of variables as many as possible. And then *Edge-Replacing* tries to replace each variable with an edge in the depth decreasing order. An ordered pair $\langle u, v \rangle$ represents either an edge or a variable such that u is the parent of v. We omit the proof of the next lemma.

Lemma 2. *Let t be a term tree which has a variable $[u, v]$ such that the two siblings just before and after $[u, v]$ are also variables and v is the parent port of some variable. Let t' be the term tree obtained from t by replacing the variable $[u, v]$ with an edge $\{u, v\}$ (Fig. 9). Then $L_\Lambda(t') = L_\Lambda(t)$.*

Let $t_0, t_1, \ldots, t_k$ be a sequence of term trees. For $i = 0, \ldots, k - 1$, t_i has a variable h_i such that the two siblings just before and after h_i are also variables and the child port of h_i is the parent port of some variable, and t_{i+1} be the term tree constructed from t_i by replacing the variable h_i with an edge. Then we can easily see that $L_\Lambda(t_0) = L_\Lambda(t_k)$ from Lemma 2.

Lemma 3. *Let t be an output term tree of Algorithm MINL*. If there exists a term tree t' such that $S \subseteq L_\Lambda(t') \subseteq L_\Lambda(t)$ then $t \approx t'$.*

Proof. Let t'' be the regular term tree which is obtained by *Variable-Extension*. Then $L_\Lambda(t) \subseteq L_\Lambda(t'')$ and $t \approx t''$. Let t''' be the regular term tree which is obtained by replacing all edges in t' with variables. Then $t' \approx t'''$ and $L_\Lambda(t') \subseteq L_\Lambda(t''')$. Let θ be a substitution such that $t' \equiv t''\theta$ and θ' a substitution which obtained by replacing all edges appearing in θ with variables. Then $t''' \equiv t''\theta'$. Since $S \subseteq L_\Lambda(t') \subseteq L_\Lambda(t)$, $S \subseteq L_\Lambda(t''\theta')$. Since *Variable-Extension* generates a regular term tree whose language is minimal for $(S, \{g \in \mathcal{OTT}_\Lambda^{1,*} \mid g \text{ has no edge}\})$, $t''\theta' \equiv t''$. Therefore $t''' \equiv t''$, then $t' \approx t$. $\qquad \square$

Lemma 4. *Let S be an input set for Algorithm MINL*. Let $t = (V_t, E_t, H_t)$ be an output term tree by Algorithm MINL* and $t' = (V_{t'}, E_{t'}, H_{t'})$ a term tree such that $S \subseteq L_\Lambda(t') \subseteq L_\Lambda(t)$. Then $t \equiv t'$.*

Proof. (Sketch) From Lemma 3 there exists a bijection ξ from $V_{t'}$ to V_t which realizes $t \approx t'$. Let t_0 be a term tree outputed by *Variable-Extension*. And let t_k be the term tree t just after *Edge-Replacing* tries to replace the kth variable with an edge. We prove this lemma by an induction on k. Suppose that the statement holds for t' and t_{k-1}. We show that for any $u', v' \in V_{t'}$, $[u', v'] \in H_{t'}$ if and only if $[\xi(u'), \xi(v')] \in H_{t_k}$. The proof depends on the edges and variables around u' and v'. Let x be the variable label of $[u', v']$. The most cases can be proved by showing that if $[\xi(u'), \xi(v')] \in H_{t_k}$ then $\{t'\theta_A^a, t'\theta_B^a, t'\theta_C^a, t'\theta_D^a\} \not\subseteq L_\Lambda(t_k)$ (these substitutions are described in Fig. 6). When $|\Lambda| = 1$, the following four cases possibly satisfies that $\{t'\theta_A, t'\theta_B, t'\theta_C, t'\theta_D\} \subset L_\Lambda(t_k)$ even if $[\xi(u'), \xi(v')] \notin H_{t_k}$. Let v'_{i-1} and v'_{i+1} be the previous and the next sibling of v', respectively and v'_{i+2} the next sibling of v'_{i+1}.

1. $[u', v'_{i-1}] \in H_{t'}$, v' has one child w' with $[v', w'] \in H_{t'}$ and $\{u', v'_{i+1}\} \in E_{t'}$.
2. $\{[u', v'_{i-1}], [u', v'_{i+1}]\} \subset H_{t'}$, v' has one child w' with $[v', w'] \in H_{t'}$ and and $\{u', v'_{i+1}\} \in E_{t'}$ (Fig. 10).
3. $\{[u', v'_{i-1}], [u', v'_{i+1}], [u', v'_{i+2}]\} \subset H_{t'}$, v' has one child w' with $[v', w'] \in H_{t'}$, and v'_{i+1} has one child w'_{i+1}, with $[v'_{i+1}, w'_{i+1}] \in H_{t'}$ (Fig. 10).

Algorithm MINL*; /* MINL algorithm for $\mathcal{OTT}_\Lambda^{1,*}$ */
  input: a set of trees $S = \{T_1, \ldots, T_m\} \subseteq \mathcal{OT}_\Lambda$;
  begin
    Let $t = (\{u, v\}, \emptyset, \{h = [u, v]\})$; Let q be a list initialized to be $[h]$;
    Variable-Extension(t, S, q);
    Edge-Replacing(t, S, r_t)
  end.

Procedure Variable-Extension;
  input: a term tree $t = (V_t, E_t, H_t) \in \mathcal{OTT}_\Lambda^{1,*}$, a set of trees S,
       and a queue of variables q;
begin
  while q is not empty **do begin**
    Let $q[1] = [u, v]$; $q := q[2..]$; $u_h := u$; $v_h := v$;
    /* *Step 1* */ Let w be a new vertex;
          $t' := (V_t \cup \{w\}, E_t, H_t \cup \{[u_h, w], [w, v_h]\} - \{[u_h, v_h]\})$;
          if $S \subseteq L_\Lambda(t')$ then begin $t := t'$; $q := q\&[[w, v_h]]$; $v_h := w$; end;
    /* *Step 2* */ Let w be a new vertex which becomes the sibling just before v_h;
          $t' := (V_t \cup \{w\}, E_t, H_t \cup \{[u_h, w]\})$;
          if $S \subseteq L_\Lambda(t')$ then begin $t := t'$; $q := q\&[[u_h, w]]$ end;
    /* *Step 3* */ Let w be a new vertex which becomes the sibling just after v_h;
          $t' := (V_t \cup \{w\}, E_t, H_t \cup \{[u_h, w]\})$;
          if $S \subseteq L_\Lambda(t')$ then begin $t := t'$; $q := q\&[[u_h, w]]$ end
  end
end;

Procedure Edge-Replacing;
  input: a term tree $t = (V_t, E_t, H_t) \in \mathcal{OTT}_\Lambda^{1,*}$, a set of trees S, and a vertex u;
begin
  if u is a leaf **then return**;
  Let $v_1, \ldots, v_k$ be the children of u;
  for $i := 1$ **to** k **do begin** Edge-Replacing(t, S, v_i);
  for $i := 2$ **to** $k - 1$ **do begin**
    if $[u, v_{i-1}] \in H_t$, $[u, v_{i+1}] \in H_t$, and v_i has only one child w with $[v_i, w] \in H_t$ **then**
    begin
      $t' := (V_t, E_t \cup \{\{u, v_i\}, \{u, v_{i+1}\}\}, H_t - \{[u, v_i], [u, v_{i+1}]\})$;
      $t'' := (V_t, E_t \cup \{\{u, v_i\}\}, H_t - \{[u, v_i]\})$;
      $t''' := (V_t, E_t \cup \{\{u, v_{i+1}\}\}, H_t - \{[u, v_{i+1}]\})$;
      if $S \subseteq L_\Lambda(t')$ or $(S \subseteq L_\Lambda(t'')$ and $S \not\subseteq L_\Lambda(t'''))$ then begin $t := t''$; return end
    end else begin
      $t' := (V_t, E_t \cup \{\{u, v_i\}\}, H_t - \{[u, v_i]\})$;
      if $S \subseteq L_\Lambda(t')$ then begin $t := t'$; return end
    end
  end;
  output t
end;

Fig. 8. Algorithm MINL*

182   Yusuke Suzuki et al.

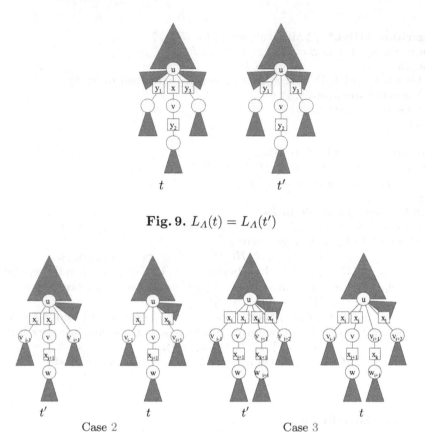

Fig. 9. $L_\Lambda(t) = L_\Lambda(t')$

Case 2   Case 3

Fig. 10. Two important cases

4. $\{[u', v'_{i-1}], [u', v'_{i+1}], [u', v'_{i+2}]\} \subset H_{t'}$, v' has one child w' with $[v', w'] \in H_{t'}$, and v'_{i+1} has one child w'_{i+1} with $\{v'_{i+1}, w'_{i+1}\} \in E_{t'}$ or more than one child.

For the case 1, *Edge-Replacing* tries t' before t_k and replaces with an edge. Therefore $[\xi(u'), \xi(v')]$ is in H_{t_k}. For the other cases, *Edge-Replacing* does not replace $[\xi(u'), \xi(v')]$ with an edge. Then $[\xi(u'), \xi(v')]$ is in H_{t_k}.   □

We can immediately show the next lemma from Lemma 4.

Lemma 5. *Let S be an input set of trees and t an output term tree of Algorithm* MINL*. *Then $L_\Lambda(t)$ is minimal for $(S, \mathcal{OTT}_\Lambda^{1,*})$.*

Theorem 4. *Minimal Language Problem for $\mathcal{OTT}_\Lambda^{1,*}$ is computable in polynomial time.*

Proof. The correctness follows Lemma 5. Let m be the number of trees in S. Let $N_{\max}$ and $N_{\min}$ be the maximum and minimum numbers of vertices of trees in S, respectively. Let $\Lambda_S = \{a \in \Lambda \mid a$ appears on trees in $S\}$. Let $\mathrm{MAT}(N, n)$ be the time complexity of *Procedure Matching* for a tree with N vertices and a term tree with n vertices. *Variable-Extension* computes m membership problems for each variable extension. Since the final term tree has at most $N_{\min}$ vertices, *Variable-Extension* needs $O(mN_{\min}\mathrm{MAT}(N_{\max}, N_{\min}))$ time. *Edge-Replacing* also computes m membership problems for each labeled edge replacement. Then *Edge-Replacing* needs $O(mN_{\min}|\Lambda_S|\mathrm{MAT}(N_{\max}, N_{\min}))$ to find a final term tree. Then the total time complexity of the algorithm $MINL^*$ is $O(mN_{\min}|\Lambda_S|\mathrm{MAT}(N_{\max}, N_{\min}))$. $\qquad\square$

7 Conclusions

From the point of view of data mining, this paper proposes a new extraction method of tree structured patterns from tree structured data. We show that two classes $\mathcal{OTT}_\Lambda^{1,1}$ and $\mathcal{OTT}_\Lambda^{1,*}$ are polynomial time inductively inferable from positive data. In [14], we have proposed a polynomial time algorithm for Membership Problem for $\mathcal{OTT}_\Lambda^{*,*} = \bigcup_{L \geq 1} \mathcal{OTT}_\Lambda^{L,*}$. For any $L \geq 2$, it is still open whether or not $\mathcal{OTT}_\Lambda^{L,*}$ is polynomial time inductively inferable from positive data.

References

1. S. Abiteboul, P. Buneman, and D. Suciu. *Data on the Web: From Relations to Semistructured Data and XML*. Morgan Kaufmann, 2000. 169
2. T. R. Amoth, P. Cull, and P. Tadepalli. Exact learning of unordered tree patterns from queries. *Proc. COLT-99, ACM Press*, pages 323–332, 1999. 170, 171
3. D. Angluin. Finding patterns common to a set of strings. *Journal of Computer and System Science*, 21:46–62, 1980. 173, 174
4. H. Arimura, H. Sakamoto, and S. Arikawa. Efficient learning of semi-structured data from queries. *Proc. ALT-2001, Springer-Verlag, LNAI 2225*, pages 315–331, 2001. 171
5. H. Arimura, T. Shinohara, and S. Otsuki. Finding minimal generalizations for unions of pattern languages and its application to inductive inference from positive data. *Proc. STACS-94, Springer-Verlag, LNCS 775*, pages 649–660, 1994. 171
6. S. Matsumoto, Y. Hayashi, and T. Shoudai. Polynomial time inductive inference of regular term tree languages from positive data. *Proc. ALT-97, Springer-Verlag, LNAI 1316*, pages 212–227, 1997. 171
7. T. Miyahara, T. Shoudai, T. Uchida, K. Takahashi, and H. Ueda. Polynomial time matching algorithms for tree-like structured patterns in knowledge discovery. *Proc. PAKDD-2000, Springer-Verlag, LNAI 1805*, pages 5–16, 2000. 171
8. T. Miyahara, T. Shoudai, T. Uchida, K. Takahashi, and H. Ueda. Discovery of frequent tree structured patterns in semistructured web documents. *Proc. PAKDD-2001, Springer-Verlag, LNAI 2035*, pages 47–52, 2001. 171
9. T. Miyahara, Y. Suzuki, T. Shoudai, T. Uchida, K. Takahashi, and H. Ueda. Discovery of frequent tag tree patterns in semistructured web documents. *Proc. PAKDD-2002, Springer-Verlag, LNAI (to appear)*, 2002. 171
10. T. Shinohara. Polynomial time inference of extended regular pattern languages. In *Springer-Verlag, LNCS 147*, pages 115–127, 1982. 173, 174

11. T. Shinohara and S. Arikawa. Pattern inference. *GOSLER Final Report, Springer-Verlag, LNAI 961*, pages 259–291, 1995. 171

12. T. Shoudai, T. Miyahara, T. Uchida, and S. Matsumoto. Inductive inference of regular term tree languages and its application to knowledge discovery. *Information Modeling and Knowledge Bases XI, IOS Press*, pages 85–102, 2000. 171

13. T. Shoudai, T. Uchida, and T. Miyahara. Polynomial time algorithms for finding unordered tree patterns with internal variables. *Proc. FCT-2001, Springer-Verlag, LNCS 2138*, pages 335–346, 2001. 171

14. Y. Suzuki, T. Shoudai, T. Miyahara, and T. Uchida. Polynomial time inductive inference of ordered tree patterns with internal structured variables from positive data. *Tech. Rep. Japanese Society for Artificial Intelligence, SIG-FAI-A104*, pages 71–78, 2002. 183

Inferring Deterministic Linear Languages

Colin de la Higuera[1]* and Jose Oncina[2]**

[1] EURISE, Université de Saint-Etienne, 23 rue du Docteur Paul Michelon
42023 Saint-Etienne, France
cdlh@univ-st-etienne.fr
http://eurise.univ-st-etienne.fr/~cdlh
[2] Departamento de Lenguajes y Sistemas Informáticos, Universidad de Alicante
Ap.99. E-03080 Alicante, Spain
oncina@dlsi.ua.es
http://www.dlsi.es/~oncina

Abstract. Linearity and determinism seem to be two essential conditions for polynomial language learning to be possible. We compare several
definitions of deterministic linear grammars, and for a reasonable definition prove the existence of a canonical normal form. This enables us
to obtain positive learning results in case of polynomial learning from a
given set of both positive and negative examples. The resulting class is
the largest one for which this type of results has been obtained so far.

1 Introduction

The general problem of learning formal grammars, also known as grammatical
inference has concentrated essentially on the sub-case of deterministic finite automata (*dfa*) or regular inference for which have been obtained positive results
in different learning settings [1], but also negative ones, such as the impossibility
(in polynomial time) to find a small *dfa* consistent with the learning data [2],
or the dependence of being able to approximatively learn *dfa* depending on well
accepted cryptographic assumptions [3].

The harder question of learning context-free grammars has given rise to different approaches over the past few years. A survey on grammatical inference
(with special interest on context-free grammar learning) can be found in [4] and
a specific survey covering a wide range of context-free grammar learning results
can be found in [5]. Main results include:

- Negative results have been provided: the general class of context-free grammars is not learnable [6]. Moreover even though this also holds for the class
  of linear languages, one major problem for the general case is that of expansiveness, *i.e.* the capacity for exponentially long words to be obtained
  through parsing trees of polynomial hight.

---

* This work was done when the first author visited the Departamento de Lenguajes y
Sistemas Informáticos of the University of Alicante, Spain. The visit was sponsored
by the Spanish Ministry of Education.
** The second author thanks the Spanish CICyT for partial support of this work
through project TIC2000-1703-C03-02.

J. Kivinen and R. H. Sloan (Eds.): COLT 2002, LNAI 2375, pp. 185–200, 2002.
© Springer-Verlag Berlin Heidelberg 2002

- Positive results have been obtained in the context of sub-classes of linear grammars. For instance *even linear grammars* have been studied [7] and identification in different contexts established. A generalization of these results (but still to special classes of linear grammars) has been given [8].
- Typical artificial intelligence techniques have been used to search for a small consistent context-free grammar. For instance Sakakibara and Kondo [9] use genetic algorithms to search for a context-free grammar in Chomsky normal form, consistent with the data.
- With the help of additional information (parenthesis, distribution, queries) alternative algorithms have been obtained: structured examples (the strings are given with the unlabelled parse tree) allow to adapt *dfa* learning algorithms to infer context-free grammars [10]. Probabilistic context-free grammars are learned from structured positive strings [11]. A subclass of context-free languages for which the expansiveness problem is an issue is dealt with in [12], but in the context of learning from queries [13].

A close analysis of the positive results for polynomial learning grammars or automata and the negative ones for larger classes shows us the importance of two factors:

- Determinism: the fact that there is just one way of parsing any string, even if it is not in the language, is a much used feature in all greedy algorithms. A rule can be refuted at any one point because it's presence would imply the presence of some undesired string.
- Linearity: this allows a polynomial relationship (in fact linear) between the size of the grammar and that of small, representative strings in the language. Such strings are needed in *characteristic sets* [6].

It is thus reasonable to consider deterministic sub-classes of the linear languages. Moreover it would be interesting that the class could generalize that of the regular languages. A variety of definitions concerning such grammars exist, which we shall discuss in the next section. In section 3 we will give the characteristics of this class and provide a *Nerode* type of theorem, allowing us to consider a canonical form of deterministic linear grammar. In section 4 we make use of this normal form in an algorithm that can identify in the limit deterministic linear grammars from polynomial time and data. We conclude in section 5.

2   Definitions

2.1   Languages and Grammars

An alphabet Σ is a finite nonempty set of symbols. Σ^* denotes the set of all finite strings over Σ, $\Sigma^+ = \Sigma^* \backslash \{\lambda\}$. A language L over Σ is a subset of Σ^*. In the following, unless stated otherwise, symbols are indicated by $a, b, c \ldots$, strings by $u, v, \ldots$, and the empty string by λ. $\mathbb{N}$ is the set of non negative integers. The length of a string u will be denoted $|u|$, so $|\lambda| = 0$. Let S be a finite set of strings, $|S|$ denotes the number of strings in the set and $\|S\|$ denotes the total sum of the lengths of all strings in S.

Let $u, v \in \Sigma^*, u^{-1}v = w$ such that $v = uw$ (undefined if u is not a prefix of v) and $uv^{-1} = w$ such that $u = wv$ (undefined if v is not a suffix of u). Let L be a language and $u \in \Sigma^*$, $u^{-1}L = \{v : uv \in L\}$ and $Lu^{-1} = \{v : vu \in L\}$.

Let L be a language, the *prefix set* is $\mathrm{Pr}(L) = \{x : xy \in L\}$. The symmetrical difference between two languages L_1 and L_2 will be denoted $L_1 \ominus L_2$. The *longest common suffix* ($\mathrm{lcs}(L)$) of L is the longest string u such that $(Lu^{-1})u = L$.

A *context-free grammar* G is a quadruple $< \Sigma, V, P, S >$ where Σ is a finite alphabet (of terminal symbols), V is a finite alphabet (of variables or nonterminals), $P \subset V \times (\Sigma \cup V)^*$ is a finite set of production rules, and $S(\in V)$ is the axiom. We will denote $uTv \rightarrow uwv$ when $(T, w) \in P$. $\xrightarrow{*}$ is the reflexive and transitive closure of $\rightarrow$. If there exists $u_0, \ldots, u_k$ such that $u_0 \rightarrow \cdots \rightarrow u_k$ we will write $u_0 \xrightarrow{k} u_k$. We denote by $L_G(T)$ the language $\{w \in \Sigma^* : T \xrightarrow{*} w\}$. Two grammars are equivalent if they generate the same language. A context-free grammar $G = < \Sigma, V, P, S >$ is *linear* if $P \subset V \times (\Sigma^* V \Sigma^* \cup \Sigma^*)$.

We will be needing to speak of the *size* of a grammar. Without entering into a lengthy discussion, the size has to be a quantity polynomially linked with the number of bits needed to encode a grammar [14]. We will consider here the size of G denoted $\|G\| = \sum_{(T,u) \in P}(|u| + 1)$.

Another way of defining context-free languages is through *pushdown automata* (*pda*). We will not formally define these here. A specific study on these machines can be found in [15].

Informally a *pda* is a one-way finite state machine with a stack. Criteria for recognition can be by empty stack or by accepting states, but in both cases the class of languages is that of the context-free ones. If the machine is deterministic (in a given configuration of the stack, with a certain symbol to be read, only one rule is possible) the class of languages is that of the *deterministic languages*. Given a computation of a *pda*, a *turn* in the computations is a move that decreases the height of the stack and is preceded by a move that did not decrease it. A *pda* is said to be *one-turn* if in any computation there is at most one turn. A language is linear if and only if it is recognized by a one-turn *pda* [15].

2.2   Deterministic Linear Grammars

A variety of definitions have been given capturing the ideas of determinism and linearity. We first give our own formalism:

Definition 1 (Deterministic linear grammars). *A* deterministic linear (DL) *grammar* $G = < \Sigma, V, P, S >$ *is a linear grammar where all rules are of the form* $(T, aT'u)$ *or* (T, λ) *and* $(T, au), (T, av) \in P \Rightarrow u = v$ *with* $u, v \in V\Sigma^*$.

This definition induces the determinism on the first symbol of the right hand of rules (as in [12]). This extends by an easy induction to the derivations: let $T \xrightarrow{*} uT'v$ and $T \xrightarrow{*} uT''w$ then $T' = T''$ and $v = w$.

A more general form of determinism, allowing for less restrictive right hand of rules, is given by the following definition:

Definition 2 (General deterministic grammars). *A general deterministic linear (Gen-DL) grammar is a linear grammar* $G = < \Sigma, V, P, S >$ *where* $\forall u_3 \in \Sigma^+$: $\forall (T, u_1 T_1 v_1), (T, u_2 T_2 v_2), (T, u_3) \in P$, $u_i \notin \mathrm{Pr}(\{u_j\})$ $\forall i \neq j$.

Nasu and Honda [16] defined another class of deterministic linear grammars:

Definition 3 (NH-deterministic grammars). *A* NH-*deterministic linear grammar* $G = < \Sigma, V, P, S >$ *is a linear grammar where all rules in P are of the form* $(T, aT'u)$ *and* (T, a) *and* $\forall u, v \in (\Sigma \cup V)^*$: $(T, au), (T, av) \in P \Rightarrow u = v$.

Ibarra, Jiang and Ravikumar [17] propose another type of grammars:

Definition 4 (IJR-deterministic grammars). *An* IJR-*deterministic linear grammar is a linear grammar* $G = < \Sigma, V, P, S >$ *where* $\forall (T, u_1 T_1 v_1)$, $(T, u_2 T_2 v_2)$, $(T, u_3) \in P$, $u_i \notin \mathrm{Pr}(\{u_j\})$ $\forall i \neq j$.

NH-deterministic linear grammars cannot generate λ, whereas an IJR-deterministic linear grammar can only generate λ when the generated language is exactly $\{\lambda\}$ [18]. The possibility of having λ-rules is what differenciates these models with the one we propose. Another type of grammar, well known in compiler literature is that of the LL-grammars, that we present here adapted to the linear setting [18]:

Definition 5 (Linear LL(1) grammars). *A linear* LL(1) *grammar is a linear grammar* $G = < \Sigma, V, P, S >$ *such that if* $S \xrightarrow{*} uTv \rightarrow uzv \xrightarrow{*} uw$, $S \xrightarrow{*} uTv \rightarrow uz'v \xrightarrow{*} uw'$ *and* $\mathrm{FIRST}_G(w) = \mathrm{FIRST}_G(w')$, *where* $\mathrm{FIRST}_G(w)$ *is the first symbol of w (if* $w = \lambda$, $\mathrm{FIRST}_G(w) = \lambda$*), then* $z = z'$.

Let Det, Lin, DetLin, DL, Gen-DL, NH-DL, IJR-DL, and LinLL(1) be the classes of languages generated respectively by deterministic *pda*, linear grammars or one-turn *pda*, deterministic one-turn *pda*, DL grammars, Gen-DL grammars, NH-deterministic linear grammars, IJR-deterministic linear grammars and linear LL(1) grammars.

2.3   About Deterministic Linear Languages

As described in the previous section there is a variety of definitions that may capture the idea of linearity and determinism in context-free languages. They are not all equivalent, but the following holds:

Theorem 1. DL = Gen-DL.

Proof. Clearly DL $\subseteq$ Gen-DL. Conversely, algorithm 1 transforms any Gen-DL grammar into a DL grammar. Note that the algorithm terminates when a DL grammar is reached (each step decreases the length of some right hand of rule). After each step the grammar remains Gen-DL. Finally the size of the DL grammar we obtain from a Gen-DL grammar $G = < \Sigma, V, P, S >$ is at most $2\|G\|$, so linear in that of G.

Algorithm 1 Transforming a general grammar

Require: G
Ensure: G is DL
  while G not a DL-grammar **do**
    Choose $T \in V, a \in \Sigma$ such that $\exists (T, auT'v) \in P$, with $u \in \Sigma^+, v \in \Sigma^*$
    $U \leftarrow \{v : (T, auT'v) \in P\}$.
    Replace each rule $(T, auT'v)$ by rules $(T, aT''(\mathrm{lcs}(U)))$ and $(T'', uT'v(\mathrm{lcs}(U))^{-1})$
    where T'' is a new non-terminal associated to the pair (a, T)
  end while

We note that LinLL(1) contains only languages with the *prefix*[1] property (so do NH-DL and IJR-DL). Other differences are:

Theorem 2 (Some strict inclusions).

1. DetLin $\subset$ Det $\cap$ Lin
2. DL $\subset$ DetLin
3. LinLL(1) $\subset$ DL
4. IJR-DL $\subset$ LinLL(1)
5. NH-DL $\subset$ IJR-DL

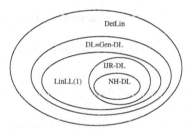

Proof.

1. $\{a^n b^m a^p b^q : n = m$ or $p = q, n, m, p, q > 0\} \in \mathrm{Det} \cap \mathrm{Lin} \setminus \mathrm{DetLin}$ [15]. A deterministic *pda* and a one-turn *pda* can both be designed to generate this language, but no one-turn deterministic *pda* can exist: you have to decide at the beginning of the parse what you want to count.
2. $\{a^n b^n : n > 0\} \cup \{a^n c^n : n > 0\} \in \mathrm{DetLin} \setminus \mathrm{DL}$ based on [15]. Yet the mirror language is in DL.
3. (LinLL(1) $\subset$ DL). Let $G = < \Sigma, V, P, S >$ be a linear LL(1) grammar. Then G has no left recursive variable (*i.e.* T such that $T \xrightarrow{*} Tu$). By standard techniques any rule in P of the form $T \to T'u$ can be replaced by rules $T \to zu$ ($z \in \Sigma^* V \Sigma^* \cup \Sigma^*$) for each rule ($T' \to z$) in P, resulting in a LL(1) linear grammar with no $T \to T'u$ rules. We prove that all rules are either $T \to auT'v$ or $T \to u$, and respect conditions of definition 2: there are 4 cases to consider; we sketch the proof for the 2 main ones:
   - $T \to auT'v \in P$ and $T \to au'T''v' \in P \Rightarrow u = u', T' = T'', v = v'$ since G is linear LL(1).
   - $T \to auT'v \in P$ and $T \to u' \in P \Rightarrow \mathrm{FIRST}(u') \neq a$.
   The inclusion is strict as LinLL(1) only contains languages with the prefix property. A language like $\{a^n b^p, 0 \leqslant n \leqslant p\} \in \mathrm{DL} \setminus \mathrm{LinLL}(1)$.

---

[1] no string in the language is a proper prefix of another string in the language.

4. The stronger NH-DL = λ-free LinLL(1) is proved in [18];
5. One can actually prove the stronger NH-DL = IJR-DL $\setminus \{\lambda\}$ [18].

As we will in the sequel concentrate on DL-languages, here are some examples of such languages: $\{a^n b^n : 0 \leqslant n\}$, $\{a^m b^n : 0 \leqslant m \leqslant n\}$, $\{a^m b^n c^n : 0 \leqslant m, 0 \leqslant n\}$ (a variant of the main example in [9]), the set of all palindromes over some alphabet Σ, any linear LL(1) language. All regular languages are also DL as any regular grammar obtained from a *dfa* is DL.

It should also be noticed that some even linear languages [7] are not DL-languages: $\{a^n b^n, n > 0\} \cup \{a^n c^n, n > 0\}$ for instance.

2.4 Learning and Identifying

A variety of learning paradigms have been examined and used in the literature of machine learning, but in the case of grammatical inference some of these:

- are too hard (no reasonable class can be learned): *PAC*-learning[2] for instance [19];
- are too easy (nearly anything can be learned): identification in the limit [20].

Based on identification in the limit, we will use identification in the limit from polynomial time and data [6] as our learning model. Learning from queries [13] or simple-*PAC* learning [21] are alternative frameworks. It should be noticed that if a class of grammars is identifiable in the limit from polynomial time and data, the simple grammars in this class are also simple-*PAC* learnable [22]. In this setting the learner is asked to learn from a learning *sample*, *i.e.* a finite set of strings, each string labeled by '+' if the string is a positive instance of the language (an element of L), or by '−' if it is a negative instance of the language (an element of $\Sigma^* \setminus L$). Alternatively we will denote $S = (S_+, S_-)$ where S_+ is the sub-sample of positive instances and S_- the sub-sample of negative ones.

Definition 6 (Identification in the limit from polynomial time and data). *A class $\mathcal{G}$ of grammars is identifiable in the limit from polynomial time and data iff there exist two polynomials $p()$ and $q()$ and an algorithm $\mathcal{A}$ such that:*

1. *Given any sample (S_+, S_-), $\mathcal{A}$ returns a grammar G in $\mathcal{G}$ such that $S_+ \subseteq L_G$ and $S_- \cap L_G = \emptyset$ in $O(p(\|S_+\| + \|S_-\|))$ time;*
2. *for each grammar G in $\mathcal{G}$ of size n, there exists a characteristic sample (CS_+, CS_-) such that $\|CS_+\| + \|CS_-\| < q(n)$ for which, if $CS_+ \subseteq S_+$, $CS_- \subseteq S_-$, $\mathcal{A}$ returns a grammar G' equivalent with G.*

With this definition it is known that deterministic finite automata [1] and even linear grammars [7] are identifiable in the limit from polynomial time and data whereas non-deterministic finite automata and linear (and hence context-free) grammars are not [6].

---

[2] Probably Approximatively Correct

3   Deterministic Linear Languages Have Finite Index and Canonical Form

For a class of languages to be identifiable in the limit from polynomial time and data a reasonable assumption is that there exists some small canonical form for any language representable in the class. We prove in this section that such is indeed the case for deterministic linear grammars.

Deterministic linear languages use common suffix properties; in the sequel we are going to denote the *longest common suffix reduction* of a language L by $L \downarrow = L(\text{lcs}(L))^{-1}$.

Definition 7 (Common suffix-free language equivalence). *Given a language L we define recursively the* common suffix-free *languages* $\text{CSF}_L(\cdot)$, *and the associated equivalence relation as follows:*

$$\text{CSF}_L(\lambda) = L$$
$$\text{CSF}_L(xa) = (a^{-1}\,\text{CSF}_L(x)) \downarrow \qquad \qquad x \equiv_L y \iff \text{CSF}_L(x) = \text{CSF}_L(y)$$

We define now another equivalence relation over Σ^*, when given a deterministic linear grammar:

Definition 8. *Let $G = <\Sigma, V, P, S>$ be a DL grammar. With every string x we associate the unique non terminal $[x]_G = T$ such that $S \xrightarrow{*} xTu$; we extend L_G to be a total function by setting $L_G([x]_G) = \emptyset$ when $[x]_G$ is undefined.*

We use this definition to give another equivalence relation over Σ^*, when given a deterministic linear grammar:

Definition 9. *Let $G = <\Sigma, V, P, S>$ be a DL grammar. We define recursively the associated* common suffix-free *languages* $\text{CSF}_G(.)$, *and associated equivalence relation as follows:*

$$\text{CSF}_G(\lambda) = L_G(S)$$
$$\text{CSF}_G(xa) = L_G([xa]_G) \downarrow \qquad \qquad x \equiv_G y \iff \text{CSF}_G(x) = \text{CSF}_G(y)$$

$\equiv_G$ is clearly an equivalence relation, in which all strings x such that $[x]_G$ is undefined are in a unique class. The following lemma establishes that $\equiv_G$ has finite index, when G is a deterministic linear grammar:

Lemma 1. *If $[x]_G = [y]_G$, $x \neq \lambda$ and $y \neq \lambda \Rightarrow x \equiv_G y$. Hence if G contains n non-terminals, $\equiv_G$ has at most $n + 2$ classes.*

The proof is straightforward. There can be at most two possible extra classes corresponding to λ (when it is alone in its class) and the undefined class corresponding to those strings that are prefixes of no string in the language.

Proposition 1. *Let $G = <\Sigma, V, P, S>$ be a DL grammar, and denote $L = L_G(S)$. $\forall x \in \Sigma^*$, either $\text{CSF}_L(x) = \text{CSF}_G(x)$ or $\text{CSF}_L(x) = \emptyset$*

Proof. By induction on the length of x.

Base: $x = \lambda$, then $\mathrm{CSF}_L(x) = L = \mathrm{CSF}_G(x)$.

Suppose: the proposition is true for all strings of length up to k, and consider string xa of length $k + 1$. $\mathrm{CSF}_L(xa) = (a^{-1} \mathrm{CSF}_L(x)) \downarrow$ (by definition 7). If$\mathrm{CSF}_L(x) = \emptyset$, $\mathrm{CSF}_L(xa) = \emptyset$. If not $(\mathrm{CSF}_L(x) = \mathrm{CSF}_G(x))$ by induction hypothesis, $\mathrm{CSF}_L(xa) = (a^{-1} \mathrm{CSF}_L(x)) \downarrow = (a^{-1} \mathrm{CSF}_G(x)) \downarrow$ and there are two sub-cases:

if $x = \lambda$ $\mathrm{CSF}_G(x) = L_G([x]_G)$, so $\mathrm{CSF}_L(xa) = (a^{-1} L_G([x]_G)) \downarrow$

if $x \neq \lambda$ $\mathrm{CSF}_G(x) = L_G([x]_G) \downarrow$, so: $CSF_L(xa) = (a^{-1}(L_G([x]_G) \downarrow)) \downarrow$ (by definition 9), $= (a^{-1}(L_G([x]_G))) \downarrow$

In both cases follows: $CSF_L(xa) = L_G([xa]_G) \downarrow = \mathrm{CSF}_G(xa)$.

The following corollary makes use of lemma 1 and proposition 1:

Corollary 1. *Let $G = < \Sigma, V, P, S >$ be a deterministic linear grammar. So $\equiv_{L_G(S)}$ has finite index.*

The purpose of this section is to reach a computable normal form for DL grammars. For this we first define a normal form for these grammars (called *advanced* as the longest common suffixes appear as soon as possible), and then construct such a grammar from any deterministic linear language.

Definition 10 (Advanced form for deterministic linear grammars). *A linear grammar $G = < \Sigma, V, P, S >$ is deterministic in* advanced *form if:*

1. *all rules are in the form $(T, aT'w)$ or (T, λ);*
2. *$\forall (T, aT'w) \in P, w = \mathrm{lcs}(a^{-1} L_G(T))$;*
3. *all non-terminal symbols are accessible: $\forall T \in V \; \exists u, v \in \Sigma^* : S \xrightarrow{*} uTv$ and usefull: $\forall T \in V, L_G(T) \neq \emptyset$;*
4. *$\forall T, T' \in V, L_G(T) = L_G(T') \Rightarrow T = T'$.*

Definition 11 (A canonical grammar for deterministic linear languages). *Given any linear deterministic language L, the associated canonical grammar is $G_L = < \Sigma, V, P, S_{\mathrm{CSF}_L(\lambda)} >$ where:*

$$V = \{S_{\mathrm{CSF}_L(x)} : \mathrm{CSF}_L(x) \neq \emptyset\}$$
$$P = \{S_{\mathrm{CSF}_L(x)} \to a S_{\mathrm{CSF}_L(xa)} \, \mathrm{lcs}(a^{-1} \mathrm{CSF}_L(x)) : \mathrm{CSF}_L(xa) \neq \emptyset\}$$
$$\cup \{S_{\mathrm{CSF}_L(x)} \to \lambda : \lambda \in \mathrm{CSF}_L(x)\}$$

To avoid extra notations, we will denote (as in definition 8) by $[x]$ the non-terminal corresponding to x in the associated grammar (formally $S_{\mathrm{CSF}_L(x)}$ or $[x]_{G_L}$).

We first prove that G_L generates L: this is established through the following more general result (as the special case where $x = \lambda$):

Proposition 2. $\forall x \in \Sigma^*, L_{G_L}([x]) = \mathrm{CSF}_L(x)$.

Proof. We prove it by double inclusion.

$\forall x \in \Sigma^*,\ \mathrm{CSF}_L(x) \subseteq L_{G_L}([x])$

Proof by induction on the length of all strings in $\mathrm{CSF}_L(x)$.

Base case $|w| = 0 \Rightarrow w = \lambda$. If $\lambda \in \mathrm{CSF}_L(x), [x] \to \lambda$ so $\lambda \in L_{G_L}([x])$

Suppose now (induction hypothesis) that
$$\forall x \in \Sigma^*, \forall w \in \Sigma^{\leqslant k}\colon w \in \mathrm{CSF}_L(x) \Rightarrow w \in L_{G_L}([x]).$$
Let $|w| = k + 1$ and let a be the first symbol of w.
Then $w = auv$, with $u \in \mathrm{CSF}_L(xa)$ and $v = \mathrm{lcs}(a^{-1}\,\mathrm{CSF}_L(x))$.
By induction hypothesis $(|u| \leqslant k)\ u \in L_G([xa])$.
As $[x] \to a[xa]v$ where $v = \mathrm{lcs}(a^{-1}\,\mathrm{CSF}_L(x))$ is a rule in P, $w \in L_G([x])$.

$\forall x \in \Sigma^*,\ L_{G_L}([x]) \subseteq \mathrm{CSF}_L(x)$

Proof by induction on the order (k) of the derivation
$$\forall x \in \Sigma^*, \forall k \in \mathbb{N}, \forall w \in \Sigma^*,\ [x]\overset{k}{\to}w \Rightarrow w \in \mathrm{CSF}_L(x).$$
Base case $[x]\overset{0}{\to}w$. No rule is possible, so clearly
$$\forall x \in \Sigma^*,\ \forall w \in \Sigma^*\colon [x]\overset{0}{\to}w \Rightarrow w \in \mathrm{CSF}_L(x).$$
Suppose now (induction hypothesis) that for any $n \leqslant k$:
$$\forall x \in \Sigma^*,\ \forall w \in \Sigma^*\colon [x]\overset{n}{\to}w \Rightarrow w \in \mathrm{CSF}_L(x)$$

Take $w \in \Sigma^*$ such that $[x]\overset{k+1}{\longrightarrow}w$. There are two cases to consider:

- $[x] \to \lambda\overset{k}{\to}w$ but then $k = 0$, $w = \lambda$, and rule $[x] \to \lambda$ only exists if $\lambda \in \mathrm{CSF}_L(x)$
- $[x] \to a[xa]v\overset{k}{\to}w$.

Necessarily $w = auv$, with $[xa]\overset{k}{\to}u$. And $v = \mathrm{lcs}(a^{-1}\,\mathrm{CSF}_L(x))$
By the induction hypothesis $u \in \mathrm{CSF}_L(xa)$.
Thus $w \in a\,\mathrm{CSF}_L(xa)v \subseteq \mathrm{CSF}_L(x)$.

We turn now to some specificities of the associated canonical grammar:

Proposition 3. *Given any deterministic linear language L, G_L is advanced.*

Proof. We prove that G_L is advanced by showing that conditions 1 to 4 of definition 10 hold:

1. all rules are by construction in the form $(T, aT'w)$ and (T, λ);
2. $\forall (T, aT'w) \in P, w = \mathrm{lcs}(a^{-1}L_G(T))$ by definition 11;
3. only accessible non-terminal symbols are introduced;
4. by definition of G_L if $x \equiv_L y$ then $[x]_{G_L} = [y]_{G_L}$

Lemma 2. *Let G_L be the canonical grammar of a DL language L and let $x \neq \lambda$ such that $\mathrm{CSF}_L(x) \neq \emptyset$, then:*

1. $\mathrm{lcs}(L_{G_L}([x])) = \lambda$
2. $L_{G_L}([x])\!\downarrow\, = L_{G_L}([x])$
3. *let* $w : S \overset{*}{\to} x[x]w$ *then* $w = \mathrm{lcs}(x^{-1}L)$
4. *if* $\mathrm{CSF}_L(xa) \neq \emptyset$ *then* $\mathrm{lcs}(a^{-1}L_{G_L}([x])) = \mathrm{lcs}((ax)^{-1}L)(\mathrm{lcs}(x^{-1}L))^{-1}$

Proof.

1. As $x \neq \lambda$ let $x = ya$. As G_L is advanced and $\mathrm{CSF}_L(ya) \neq \emptyset$, we know that $[y] \to a[ya]w$ with $w = \mathrm{lcs}(a^{-1}L_{G_L}([y]))$. But $a^{-1}L_{G_L}([y]) = L_{G_L}([ya])w$ so $w = \mathrm{lcs}(L_{G_L}([ya])w)$ and then $\mathrm{lcs}(L_{G_L}([ya])) = \lambda$.
2. $L_{G_L}([x])\downarrow = L_{G_L}([x])(\mathrm{lcs}\, L_{G_L}([x]))^{-1} = L_{G_L}([x])$
3. let $S \xrightarrow{*} x[x]w$ then $\mathrm{lcs}(x^{-1}L) = \mathrm{lcs}(L_{G_L}([x])w) = \mathrm{lcs}(L_{G_L}([x]))w = w$
4. As $\mathrm{CSF}_L(xa) \neq \emptyset$ let $S \xrightarrow{*} x[x]v \to xa[xa]uv$. Then $u = (uv)v^{-1}$ and as $u = \mathrm{lcs}(a^{-1}L([x])$, $uv = \mathrm{lcs}((ax)^{-1})$ and $v = \mathrm{lcs}(x^{-1}L)$, so $\mathrm{lcs}(a^{-1}L_{G_L}([x]) = \mathrm{lcs}((ax)^{-1}L))(\mathrm{lcs}(x^{-1}L))^{-1}$.

Lemma 3. *Let G be a DL-grammar,*

$$\forall x \in \Sigma^* : \mathrm{CSF}_L(x) \neq \emptyset \Rightarrow \exists y \in \Sigma^* : L_G([x]_G) = L_{G_L}([x]_{G_L})y.$$

Proof. If $\mathrm{CSF}_L(x) \neq \emptyset$, both $[x]_G$ and $[x]_{G_L}$ are necessarily defined. But by definition 9 $L_G([x]_G) = CSF_G(x)\mathrm{lcs}(L_G([x]_G))$, and in the special case the grammar is canonical $L_{G_L}([x]_{G_L}) = CSF_{G_L}(x)\mathrm{lcs}(L_{G_L}([x]_{G_L}))$. By lemma 2(1) $\mathrm{lcs}(L_{G_L}([x]_{G_L})) = \lambda$. From proposition 1, $CSF_G(x) = CSF_{G_L}(x) = CSF_L(x)$. Hence we have $L_{G_L}([x]_{G_L})\mathrm{lcs}\, L_G([x]_G) = L_G([x]_G)$.

The last theorem of this section tells us that the canonical grammar is at most quadratically larger than any equivalent Gen-DL or DL grammar:

Theorem 3. *Given a Gen-DL grammar $G = <\Sigma, V_G, P_G, S_G>$, let G_L be the canonical grammar that generates $L = L_G(S_G)$, $\|G_L\| \leqslant \|G\|^2$.*

Proof. We denote $L = L_G(S_G)$ in the proof.

- Let G be a Gen-DL grammar, algorithm 1 produces an equivalent DL grammar whose size is at most $2\|G\|$. We thus only have to prove the case where $G = <\Sigma, V_G, P_G, S_G>$ is a DL grammar.
- By proposition 1, V has at least $k-1$ non terminals, where k is the number of classes for $\equiv_L$. We now prove that $\equiv_L$ and $\equiv_{G_L}$ coincide: there are two cases. The case $x = \lambda$ is straightforward and depends uniquely on the definitions 7 and 9. If $x \neq \lambda$, $\mathrm{CSF}_{G_L}(x) = L_{G_L}([x]_{G_L})\downarrow = L_{G_L}([x]_{G_L}) = \mathrm{CSF}_L(x)$ respectively by definition 9, by lemma 2(2) and by proposition 2. It follows that G_L has at most $|V_G| + 1$ non terminals.
- Any rule in the canonical grammar is either $([x]_{G_L}, \lambda)$ or $([x]_{G_L}, a[xa]_{G_L}w)$, with $w = \mathrm{lcs}(a^{-1}L_{G_L}([x]_{G_L}))$. Clearly $|w| \leqslant \min\{|z| : z \in a^{-1}L_{G_L}([x]_{G_L})\}$, so it follows from lemma 3 that $|w| \leqslant \min\{|z| : z \in a^{-1}L_G([x]_G)\}$. Such a string must be derived without repeating non-terminals (if not a shorter string exists), so $|w| \leqslant \sum_{(T,u) \in P_G}(|u|)$.
  From this $\|G_L\| \leqslant \|\Sigma\|(|V| + 1)\sum_{(T,u) \in P_G}(|u|) \leqslant \|G\|^2$.

4 Learning DL Grammars

As DL languages admit a small canonical form it will be sufficient to have an algorithm that can learn this type of canonical form, at least when a characteristic set is provided. In doing so we are following the type of proof used to prove learnability of *dfa* [20,1].

Definition 12. *Let L be a* DL *language, and $\leqslant$ a length lexicographic order relation over Σ^*, the shortest prefix set of L is defined as* $\mathrm{Sp}_L = \{x \in \mathrm{Pr}(L) : \mathrm{CSF}_L(x) \neq \emptyset \wedge y \equiv_L x \Rightarrow x \leqslant y\}$

Note that, in a canonical grammar, we have a one to one relation between strings in Sp and non terminals of the grammar. We shall thus use the strings in Sp as identifiers for the non terminal symbols.

Imagine we have an unlimited oracle that knows language L and to which we can address the following queries:

$$\mathrm{next}(x) = \{xa : \exists xay \in L\} \qquad \mathrm{equiv}(x, y) \iff x \equiv_L y$$
$$\mathrm{right}(xa) = \mathrm{lcs}(a^{-1}\,\mathrm{CSF}_L(x)) \qquad \mathrm{isfinal}(x) \iff \lambda \in \mathrm{CSF}_L(x)$$

Algorithm 2 visits the prefixes of the language L in length lexicographic order, and constructs the canonical grammar responding to definition 11. If a prefix xa is visited and no previous equivalent non terminal has been found (and placed in Sp), this prefix is added to Sp as a new non terminal and the corresponding rule is added to the grammar. If there exists an equivalent non terminal y in Sp then the correponding rule is added but the strings for which x is a prefix will not be visited (they will not be added to W). When the algorithm finishes, Sp contains all the short prefixes of the language.

In order to simplify notations we introduce:

Definition 13.

$$\forall x : CSF(x) \neq \emptyset, \ \mathrm{tail}_L(x) = \begin{cases} \mathrm{lcs}(x^{-1}L) & \text{if } x \neq \lambda \\ \lambda & \text{if } x = \lambda \end{cases}$$

Algorithm 2 Computing G using functions next, right, equiv and isfinal

---

Require: functions next, right, equiv and isfinal, language L
Ensure: $L(G) = L$ with $G = \langle \Sigma, V, P, S_\lambda \rangle$
  $\mathrm{Sp} = \{\lambda\}; V = \{S_\lambda\}$
  $W = \mathrm{next}(\lambda)$
  while $W \neq \emptyset$ **do**
    $xa = \min_\leqslant W$
    $W = W - \{xa\}$
    if $\exists y \in \mathrm{Sp} : \mathrm{equiv}(xa, y)$ **then**
      add $S_x \rightarrow aS_y\,\mathrm{right}(xa)$ to P
    else
      $\mathrm{Sp} = \mathrm{Sp} \cup \{xa\}; V = V \cup \{S_{xa}\}$
      $W = W \cup \mathrm{next}(xa)$
      add $S_x \rightarrow aS_{xa}\,\mathrm{right}(xa)$ to P
    end if
  end while
  for all $x \in \mathrm{Sp} : \mathrm{isfinal}(x)$ **do**
    add $S_x \rightarrow \lambda$ to P
  end for

Lemma 4. *Let $G_L =< \Sigma, V, P, S >$ be the canonical grammar of a DL language L, $\forall x : CSF(x) \neq \emptyset$,*

1. $\mathrm{lcs}(a^{-1} \mathrm{CSF}_L(x)) = (\mathrm{tail}_L(xa))(\mathrm{tail}_L(x))^{-1}$
2. $xv \, \mathrm{tail}_L(x) \in L \iff v \in L_{G_L}([x])$.

In order to use algorithm 2 with a sample $S = (S_+, S_-)$ instead of an oracle with access to the whole language L the 4 functions next, right, equiv and isfinal have to be implemented as functions of $S = (S_+, S_-)$ rather than of L:

$$\mathrm{next}(x) = \{xa : \exists xay \in S_+\}$$
$$\mathrm{right}(xa) = \mathrm{tail}_{S_+}(xa) \, \mathrm{tail}_{S_+}(x)^{-1}$$
$$\mathrm{equiv}(x, y) \iff xv \, \mathrm{tail}_{S_+}(x) \in S_+ \Rightarrow yv \, \mathrm{tail}_{S_+}(y) \notin S_-$$
$$\wedge \, yv \, \mathrm{tail}_{S_+}(y) \in S_+ \Rightarrow xv \, \mathrm{tail}_{S_+}(x) \notin S_-$$
$$\mathrm{isfinal}(x) \iff x \, \mathrm{tail}_{S_+}(x) \in S_+$$

Definition 14 (characteristic sample). *Let $S = (S_+, S_-)$ be a sample of the DL language L. S is a* characteristic sample *(CS) of L if:*

1. $\forall x \in \mathrm{Sp}_L \, \forall a \in \Sigma : xa \in \mathrm{Pr}(L) \Rightarrow \exists xaw \in S_+$
2. $\forall x \in \mathrm{Sp}_L \, \forall a \in \Sigma : \mathrm{CSF}_L(xa) \neq \emptyset \Rightarrow \mathrm{tail}_{S_+}(xa) = \mathrm{tail}_L(xa)$
3. $\forall x, y \in \mathrm{Sp}_L \, \forall a \in \Sigma : \mathrm{CSF}_L(xa) \neq \emptyset \wedge xa \not\equiv_L y \Rightarrow$
   $\exists v : xav \, \mathrm{tail}_L(xa) \in S_+ \wedge yv \, \mathrm{tail}_L(y) \in S_- \vee$
   $\exists v : yv \, \mathrm{tail}_L(y) \in S_+ \wedge xav \, \mathrm{tail}_L(xa) \in S_-$
4. $\forall x \in \mathrm{Sp}_L : x \, \mathrm{tail}_L(x) \in L \Rightarrow x \, \mathrm{tail}_L(x) \in S_+$

Lemma 5. *Let $G_L =< \Sigma, V, P, S >$ be the canonical grammar of a DL language L, and let x, y be such that $\mathrm{CSF}_L(x) \neq \mathrm{CSF}_L(y)$ then $\exists z \in L_{G_L}([x]) \ominus L_{G_L}([y])$ such that $|z| \leq \|G\|^2$.*

Proof. First note that $\forall x \, \exists w : [x] \xrightarrow{*} w, |w| < \|G\|$. There are now 4 cases:

1. $[x] \to \lambda$ but $[y] \not\to \lambda$ (or viceversa), then $z = \lambda$.
2. $[x] \to a[xa]vbu \wedge [y] \to a[ya]v'cu$. Let $w : [x] \to w \wedge |w| < \|G\|$ then $z = awvbu$.
3. $[x] \to a[xa]u \wedge [y] \to a[ya]vbu$ (or viceversa). As G is advanced $L([xa]) \not\subset \Sigma^*b$. So $\exists w \in L([xa]) \setminus \Sigma^*b : |w| < \|G\|$, and $z = awu$.
4. $([x] \to \lambda \iff [y] \to \lambda) \wedge ([x] \to a[xa]u \iff [y] \to a[ya]u)$. As $L([x]) \neq L([y])$ there exists a string w such that for $[xw]$ and $[yw]$ we are in one of the previous cases. Denote by $w_{i,j}$ the substring of w from position i to position j and let $|w| = n$. So $[u] \xrightarrow{k} w_{1,k}[uw_{1,k}] \mathrm{tail}_L(uw_{1,k})$. But if $n > |V|$ it has to exist i, j such that $[xw_{1,i}] = [xw_{1,j}]$ and $[yw_{1,i}] = [yw_{1,j}]$ and then $[xw_{1,i}w_{j+1,n}] = [xw]$ and $[yw_{1,i+1}w_{j,n}] = [yw]$. Then $|w| \leq |V|^2$ and $|\mathrm{tail}_L(uw)| \leq \|G\|^2$

With $O((|\mathrm{Sp}_L| \cdot |\Sigma|)^2)$ strings, a CS can be constructed. Furthermore to comply with conditions 1, 2 and 4 of definition 14, these strings can be linearly bounded. The length of the strings necessary for the third condition can be quadratically bounded by lemma 5. If more correctly labeled strings are added to the sample, the sample remains characteristic for this language.

We will now prove that provided we have a characteristic sample, functions next, right, equiv and isfinal return the same result as when having access to an oracle.

Lemma 6. *Let S be a characteristic sample of a* DL *language L and let $x \in \mathrm{Sp}_L$, then* $\mathrm{next}(x) = \{xa : xay \in L\}$.

Proof. Clear by definition 14(1).

Lemma 7. *Let S be a characteristic sample of a* DL *language L, let $x \in \mathrm{Sp}_L$ and $a \in \Sigma$ such that $\mathrm{CSF}_L(xa) \neq \emptyset$, then* $\mathrm{right}(xa) = \mathrm{lcs}(a^{-1}\mathrm{CSF}_L(x))$.

Proof. $\mathrm{right}(xa) = (\mathrm{tail}_{S_+}(xa))(\mathrm{tail}_{S_+}(x))^{-1} = (\mathrm{tail}_L(xa))(\mathrm{tail}_L(x))^{-1} = \mathrm{lcs}(a^{-1}\mathrm{CSF}_L(x))$ by definition of function right, definition 14(2) and lemma 4(1).

Lemma 8. *Let S be a characteristic sample of a* DL *language L, let $x, y \in \mathrm{Sp}_L$ and $a \in \Sigma$ such that $\mathrm{CSF}_L(xa) \neq \emptyset$, then* $\mathrm{equiv}(xa, y) \iff xa \equiv_L y$.

Proof. Suppose $xa \not\equiv_L y$, by definition 14(3) there is a string v such that:
$xav\,\mathrm{tail}_L(xa) \in S_+ \wedge yv\,\mathrm{tail}_L(y) \in S_- \vee yv\,\mathrm{tail}_L(y) \in S_+ \wedge xav\,\mathrm{tail}_L(xa) \in S_-$
Suppose the first case holds (the second is similar); by definition 14(2) $\exists v :$
$xav\,\mathrm{tail}_{S_+}(xa) \in S_+ \wedge yv\,\mathrm{tail}_{S_+}(y) \in S_-$ and then $\mathrm{equiv}(xa, y)$ evaluates to false.

Conversily suppose $xa \equiv_L y$ ($L_{G_L}([xa]) = L_{G_L}([y])$) and that $\mathrm{equiv}(xa, y)$ evaluates to false. Then there exists $v : xav\,\mathrm{tail}_{S_+}(xa) \in S_+ \wedge yv\,\mathrm{tail}_{S_+}(y) \in S_-$ (the other case is similar). Then, by definition 14(2) we have that $xav\,\mathrm{tail}_L(xa) \in S_+ \subseteq L$, and by lemma 4(2) follows that $v \in L([xa]) = L([y])$. Again by lemma 4(2) $yv\,\mathrm{tail}_L(y) \in L$ and we have a contradiction.

Lemma 9. *Let S be a characteristic sample of a* DL *language L, let $x \in \mathrm{Sp}_L$, then* $\mathrm{isfinal}(x) \iff \lambda \in \mathrm{CSF}_L(x)$

Proof. $\mathrm{isfinal}(x) \iff x\,\mathrm{tail}_{S_+}(x) \in S_+ \iff x\,\mathrm{tail}_L(x) \in S_+ \subseteq L \iff \lambda \in \mathrm{CSF}_L(x)$ respectively by definitions of function isfinal, 14(2) and lemma 4(2).

It is easy to see that the algorithm is going to compute $O(|\mathrm{Sp}|)$ times the function isfinal, $O(|\mathrm{Sp}| \cdot |\Sigma|)$ times the functions next and right, and $O(|\mathrm{Sp}|^2 \cdot |\Sigma|)$ times the function equiv. As all those functions can be calculated in $O(\|S\|)$ and, in the worst case, $|\mathrm{Sp}|$ can be as big as $\|S_+\|$, the whole complexity will be $O(\|S\|^3 \cdot |\Sigma|)$.

When the sample is not characteristic one of three things may happen:

- the obtained grammar may be consistent with the sample;
- the obtained grammar may not be able to parse conveniently all the strings;
- no merge is possible and the results is not even a deterministic linear grammar

Only the first case seems to comply with the first condition of definition 6, *i.e.* that the result is consistent with the sample. Nevertheless, as any finite language is clearly DL, and a trivial DL grammar for such a language can be constructed in polynomial time (for instance a regular grammar), we can call algorithm 2, check if the result is consistent with the sample, and if not, return the trivial DL grammar generating exactly the positive strings in the sample.

By doing so the procedure complies with both conditions of definition 6.

Theorem 4. DL *languages, when represented by* Gen-DL *or* DL *grammars, are identifiable in the limit from polynomial time and data.*

Proof. From theorem 3 we have the fact that any Gen-DL or DL grammar admits an equivalent canonical advanced DL grammar of polynomial size. The corresponding characteristic set is also of polynomial size, and algorithm 2 returns a grammar complying with definition 6. Finally lemmas 6-9 prove that the characteristic set is sufficient for the grammar to be identified.

5   Summary and Open Questions

We have described a type of grammars that generate a large class of language including regular languages, palindrome languages, linear LL(1) languages and other typical linear languages as $\{a^n b^n, 0 \leqslant n\}$. This class is proved to admit a canonical form, that even if not minimal, is at most polynomially larger than any equivalent grammar in the class. By providing an adequate algorithm, we proved that this class was polynomially identifiable in the limit from polynomial tome and data.

Further work should consist in:

– Algorithm 2 is no good when it is given a learning sample that is not characteristic. An obvious extension is for it to return in that case a trivial grammar. This does allow identification in the limit from polynomial time an data, but is not satisfactory. For it to be of practical use, it should also generalize in that case. The proposed extension would be of the same sort as that of *RPNI*[3] [1] on Gold's original algorithm [20].
– Learning in this model is directly linked with learning in the simple-*PAC* setting [22]. Links with active learning are more unclear. It can be proved that there are classes that can be learned through polynomially many membership and equivalence queries and that are not identifiable in the limit from polynomial time and data. Of the converse nothing is known. A polynomial algorithm to learn deterministic linear grammars from a *MAT* [4] seems difficult.
– Our definition of linear deterministic grammars, although less restrictive than that of [16,17], does not fully capture the one by deterministic one turn pda. The learnability of this class of languages (which is also the one of linear LR(1) languages) is a first open problem.

---

[3] Regular Positive and Negative Inference
[4] Minimally Adequate Teacher [13]

– Clearly determinism can be defined from the left (as in this work) or from the right. A natural extension of this work is that linear right-deterministic grammars can be identified in the limit from polynomial time and data. An open problem is that of simultaniously inferring linear right and left deterministic grammars.
– The natural extension of linear languages is that of multilinear languages [23], which correspond to k-turn automata. These languages do not have the expansiveness problem, so would be a natural candidate for non linear languages to be learnable.

References

1. Oncina, J., García, P.: Identifying regular languages in polynomial time. In Bunke, H., ed.: Advances in Structural and Syntactic Pattern Recognition. Volume 5 of Series in Machine Perception and Artificial Intelligence. World Scientific (1992) 99–108   185, 190, 194, 198

2. Pitt, L., Warmuth, M.: The minimum consistent DFA problem cannot be approximated within any polynomial. Journal of the Association for Computing Machinery **40** (1993) 95–142   185

3. Kearns, M., Valiant, L.: Cryptographic limitations on learning boolean formulae and finite automata. In: 21st ACM Symposium on Theory of Computing. (1989) 433–444   185

4. Sakakibara, Y.: Recent advances of grammatical inference. Theoretical Computer Science **185** (1997) 15–45   185

5. Lee, S.: Learning of context-free languages: A survey of the literature (1996)   185

6. de la Higuera, C.: Characteristic sets for polynomial grammatical inference. Machine Learning **27** (1997) 125–138   185, 186, 190

7. Sempere, J., García, P.: A characterisation of even linear languages and its application to the learning problem. In: Grammatical Inference and Applications, ICGI'94. Number 862 in Lecture Notes in Artificial Intelligence, Springer Verlag (1994) 38–44   186, 190

8. Takada, Y.: A hierarchy of language families learnable by regular language learners. In: Grammatical Inference and Applications, ICGI'94. Number 862 in Lecture Notes in Artificial Intelligence, Springer Verlag (1994) 16–24   186

9. Sakakibara, Y., Kondo, M.: Ga-based learning of context-free grammars using tabular representations. In: Proceedings of 16th International Conference on Machine Learning (ICML-99). (1999) 354–360   186, 190

10. Sakakibara, Y.: Learning context-free grammars from structural data in polynomial time. Theoretical Computer Science **76** (1990) 223–242   186

11. Sakakibara, Y., Brown, M., Hughley, R., Mian, I., Sjolander, K., Underwood, R., Haussler, D.: Stochastic context-free grammars for trna modeling. Nuclear Acids Res. **22** (1994) 5112–5120   186

12. Ishizaka, I.: Learning simple deterministic languages. In: Proceedings of COLT 89. (1989)   186, 187

13. Angluin, D.: Learning regular sets from queries and counterexamples. Information and Control **39** (1987) 337–350   186, 190, 198

14. Pitt, L.: Inductive inference, DFA's, and computational complexity. In: Analogical and Inductive Inference. Number 397 in Lecture Notes in Artificial Intelligence. Springer-Verlag, Berlin (1989) 18–44   187

15. Autebert, J., Berstel, J., Boasson, L.: Context-free languages and pushdown automata. In Salomaa, A., Rozenberg, G., eds.: Handbook of Formal Languages. Volume 1, Word Language Grammar. Springer-Verlag, Berlin (1997) 111–174 187, 189

16. Nasu, M., Honda, N.: Mappings induced by pgsm-mappings and some recursively unsolvable problems of finite probabilistic automata. Information and Control **15** (1969) 250–273 188, 198

17. Ibarra, O. H., Jiang, T., Ravikumar, B.: Some subclasses of context-free languages in nc1. Information Processing Letters **29** (1988) 111–117 188, 198

18. Holzer, M., Lange, K. J.: On the complexities of linear $ll(1)$ and $lr(1)$ grammars. In: Proceedings of the 9th International Conference on Fundamentals of Computation Theory. Number 710 in Lecture Notes in Computer Science, Springer Verlag (1993) 299–308 188, 190

19. Valiant, L.: A theory of the learnable. Communications of the Association for Computing Machinery **27** (1984) 1134–1142 190

20. Gold, E.: Complexity of automaton identification from given data. Information and Control **37** (1978) 302–320 190, 194, 198

21. Parekh, R., Honavar, V.: Learning dfa from simple examples. Machine Learning Journal **44** (2001) 9–35 190

22. Parekh, R., Honavar, V.: On the relationship between models for learning in helpful environments. In Oliveira, A., ed.: Proceedings of ICGI 2000. Volume 1891 of Lecture Notes in Artificial Intelligence., Berlin Heidelberg New York, Springer Verlag (2000) 207–220 190, 198

23. Ginsburg, S., Spanier, E.: Finite-turn pushdown automata. SIAM Control **4** (1966) 429–453 199

Merging Uniform Inductive Learners

Sandra Zilles

Fachbereich Informatik, Universität Kaiserslautern
Postfach 3049, D - 67653 Kaiserslautern
zilles@informatik.uni-kl.de

Abstract. The fundamental learning model considered here is identification of recursive functions in the limit as introduced by Gold [8], but the concept is investigated on a meta-level. A set of classes of recursive functions is *uniformly* learnable under an inference criterion I, if there is a single learner, which synthesizes a learner for each of these classes from a corresponding description of the class. The particular question discussed here is how unions of uniformly learnable sets of such classes can still be identified uniformly. Especially unions of classes leading to strong separations of inference criteria in the uniform model are considered. The main result is that for any pair (I, I') of different inference criteria considered here there exists a fixed set of descriptions of learning problems from I, such that its union with any uniformly I-learnable collection is uniformly I'-learnable, but no longer uniformly I-learnable.

1 Introduction

Inductive Inference is concerned with algorithmic learning of programs for recursive functions. In the fundamental model of identification in the limit, cf. [8], a learner successful for a class of recursive functions must eventually find a single correct program for any function in the class from a gradually growing sequence of its values. By modification of the constraints the learner has to satisfy several inference criteria have been defined and compared with respect to the resulting learning power, see for example [2,6,7].

It is a quite natural thought to search for properties that learners in the given abstract model have in common and thus try to find uniform learning methods adequate for the solution of not only one but perhaps infinitely many learning problems. An example for a uniform method is identification by enumeration (cf. [8]). Though this principle does not yield strategies for all learnable classes of recursive functions, it is appropriate for the identification of any recursively enumerable class of recursive functions, if a corresponding enumeration is known. That means, from each enumeration of a set of total recursive functions a program of a learner for the set of functions enumerated can be derived. Another uniform learning method successful in some special hypothesis spaces is temporarily conform identification as defined in [7]. In general uniform learning can be explained as some kind of meta-learning. Instead of considering special strategies each solving a specific learning problem, the aim is to find meta-strategies,

J. Kivinen and R. H. Sloan (Eds.): COLT 2002, LNAI 2375, pp. 201–216, 2002.
© Springer-Verlag Berlin Heidelberg 2002

which synthesize these special learners from a description of the corresponding learning problem. Such meta-learners reveal a common method for learning the classes of functions and thus a common structure in these classes. They might be helpful in explaining the nature of inductive learning, because they represent some kind of general identification method. For literature on uniform learning the reader is especially referred to [1,9,11,10].

In [9] it is verified, that there are classes of rather simple sets of recursive functions which do not allow the synthesis of identification strategies. Also modifications of identification in the limit are considered. Further results of this nature – moreover concerning language learning – can be found in [11] and [10]. Various modifications of uniform language identification in the limit are presented and compared in [1]. They lead to several separations and nice characterizations and thus give insight into general methods of language learning.

The uniform learning model considered here is equivalent to the one defined in [9], but is investigated in three slightly different variants in order to express the specific difficulties in uniform learning in connection with the choice of hypothesis spaces. The scope now is to investigate unions of collections of learning problems. Given two collections which can be identified uniformly under some inference criterion, is the union still uniformly identifiable? If not, is it identifiable with respect to some weaker inference criterion? What properties of learning problems enable the uniform learnability of unions of such classes? Questions of this style are the main concern throughout the following pages. But why are such questions interesting? The idea is the following: suppose you are given a learnable class. If you want to understand the nature of learning and the structure of learnable classes, it seems quite natural to add more and more objects to the class, until you observe that the resulting class can no longer be identified by a single learner. That means you form the union of two classes and try to find out what unions are still learnable and what unions are not. For example the set of classes identifiable in the limit is not closed under union, as has been verified in [2]. Now the same idea is considered in the uniform learning model. A particular issue in the investigation of learnability of unions is the strong separation of learning classes (see below). On the one hand, some simple properties enabling the uniform learnability of the union of two learnable collections are presented here; on the other hand examples are given to show that many collections of very "simple" learning problems do not allow learnability in the union with other collections.

As in the non-uniform inductive inference model, different inference classes have been compared with respect to their learning power also in the context of meta-learning. Most of the hierarchies verified in the classical model (see [2,6,7]) are maintained in the uniform model, see [14]. Hence it might be reasonable to give up certain constraints in the learning model in order to increase the learning power. But still, these separations of inference criteria do not explain, whether any collection of learning problems uniformly identifiable with respect to a criterion I can be *increased* to a superset learnable with respect to some other criterion, but no longer learnable with respect to I. In particular it might give more insight into the structure of inference criteria in uniform learning to find examples of such supersets. Thus an aim might be to transfer *strong separation* results like those in [5] to the meta-learning model. In [5] a strong separation of two inference classes I and I' means that for any object class $U \in I$ there exists some object class $V \in I'$ such that $U \cup V \in I' \setminus I$ (note that this is not a direct consequence of the "weak" separation $I \subset I'$). Still, in the meta-learning model, there might exist a collection of learning problems which is uniformly I-learnable, but no superclass of this collection witnesses to a separation of uniform I'-learning from uniform I-learning. If it were for some reason important to learn at least this collection, then loosening the I-constraints would no longer increase the learning power. Now a strong separation of I and I' ensures that this cannot happen, that means for any collection of learning problems uniformly learnable under the criterion I there exists some collection, such that the union of both is identifiable under I' but not under I. Indeed, such strong separations can be presented for several identification criteria – and even more: for any pair (I, I') of strongly separated criteria there is a *fixed* collection of learning problems which – added to an arbitrary collection uniformly learnable under I – yields a collection appropriate for uniform I'-learning but no longer appropriate for uniform I-learning. Note that this result is much stronger than required before. The proofs of the strong separations moreover provide a method for changing a uniform I-learner into an I'-learner making use of the possible increase of learning power, cf. [5] for similar methods in the non-uniform model.

2   Preliminaries

For notions used here without explicit definition the reader is referred to [12]. $\mathbb{N}$ is used to denote the set of non-negative integers. $\subseteq$ and $\subset$ stand for inclusion and proper inclusion of sets. The cardinality of a set X is denoted by card X. Via some bijective total computable function finite tuples α of integers are identified with elements of $\mathbb{N}$. Given any variable n ranging over $\mathbb{N}$ the quantifier $\forall^{\infty} n$ expresses that the statement quantified is true for all but finitely many $n \in \mathbb{N}$.

Any total or partial function maps elements of $\mathbb{N}$ again to elements of $\mathbb{N}$. Recursion theory in general concentrates on partial-recursive functions, the set of which is denoted by $\mathcal{P}$. Often the subclass $\mathcal{R}$ of all total functions – called recursive functions – is studied. Both notions may also occur with a superscript indicating the number of input values of the functions considered. $\mathcal{P}_{01}$ stands for the set of partial-recursive functions returning only values from $\{0, 1\}$. Given $f \in \mathcal{P}$ and $n \in \mathbb{N}$, the notion $f(n) \downarrow$ expresses that f is defined on input n, the opposite is denoted by $f(n) \uparrow$. Furthermore $f[n]$ is an abbreviation for the tuple $(f(0), \ldots, f(n))$, if all these values are defined. If $f, g \in \mathcal{P}$ and $n \in \mathbb{N}$, then $f =_n g$ means that $\{(x, f(x)) \mid x \leq n \text{ and } f(x) \downarrow\} = \{(x, g(x)) \mid x \leq n \text{ and } g(x) \downarrow\}$. $f =^* g$ expresses that for all but finitely many $n \in \mathbb{N}$ either $f(n)$ and $g(n)$ are both undefined or $f(n) = g(n)$. As functions f, g can be identified with the sequences of their output values, simplified notions might occur, like $f = 0^{\infty}$ for the function constantly zero or $g = 0^5 \uparrow^{\infty}$ for the function which equals zero for all inputs less than 5 and is undefined otherwise. If α, β are tuples of integers,

$\alpha \subseteq f$ ($\alpha \subseteq \beta$) expresses that α is an initial segment of the function f (of β resp.), and $\alpha \uparrow^\infty$ is called an initial function. If $n \in \mathbb{N}$, then $\bar{n} = 1$ in case $n = 0$ and $\bar{n} = 0$ otherwise. If $\psi \in \mathcal{P}^2$ and $i \in \mathbb{N}$, then ψ_i is the function achieved by fixing the first input parameter of ψ by i. Thus ψ enumerates the set $\{\psi_i \mid i \in \mathbb{N}\} \subseteq \mathcal{P}$. From now on $\varphi \in \mathcal{P}^3$ and $\tau \in \mathcal{P}^2$ denote fixed acceptable numberings. Defining $\varphi^b(x,y) := \varphi(b,x,y)$ for all $b, x, y \in \mathbb{N}$ yields an enumeration $(\varphi^b)_{b \in \mathbb{N}}$ of all two-place partial-recursive functions – concomitant with an enumeration of sets $\mathcal{P}_b := \{\varphi_i^b \mid i \in \mathbb{N}\}$. Given $b \in \mathbb{N}$, the subset $\mathcal{R}_b := \mathcal{P}_b \cap \mathcal{R}$ of recursive functions is called the recursive core of φ^b. Assume for example that, for some fixed $b \in \mathbb{N}$ and all $x, y \in \mathbb{N}$, $\varphi(b,x,y) = 0$ if $x = 0$ or $y < x$, $\varphi(b,x,y) \uparrow$, otherwise. Then $\mathcal{P}_b = \{0^\infty\} \cup \{0^i \uparrow^\infty \mid i \geq 1\}$ and $\mathcal{R}_b = \{0^\infty\}$. A Blum complexity measure as in [4] suggests the notion $f(n) \downarrow_{\leq x}$ to indicate that the computation of $f(n)$ terminates within up to x steps (for $f \in \mathcal{P}$, $n, x \in \mathbb{N}$). If the computation does not terminate or takes more than x steps, then $f(n) \uparrow_{\leq x}$.

The basic learning criterion investigated here is identification in the limit, which has first been studied in [8].

Definition 1. *A set $U \subseteq \mathcal{R}$ of recursive functions is called identifiable in the limit iff there is some $\psi \in \mathcal{P}^2$ and a function $S \in \mathcal{P}$ such that for any $f \in U$:*

1. *$S(f[n])$ is defined for all $n \in \mathbb{N}$ ($S(f[n])$ is called hypothesis on $f[n]$),*
2. *there is some $j \in \mathbb{N}$ such that $\psi_j = f$ and $S(f[n]) = j$ for all but finitely many $n \in \mathbb{N}$.*

EX *is the class of all sets U identifiable in the limit. The notion $U \in \mathrm{EX}_\psi(S)$ shall indicate that S and ψ are known to fulfil the conditions above.*

Weakening the constraints concerning convergence yields the model of behaviourally correct learning as defined in [2]. Here the learner may change its output infinitely often, as long as eventually the hypotheses are correct.

Definition 2. *A set $U \subseteq \mathcal{R}$ is BC-identifiable iff there is some $\psi \in \mathcal{P}^2$ and some $S \in \mathcal{P}$ such that any $f \in U$ fulfils $\psi_{S(f[n])} = f$ for all but finitely many n; furthermore $S(f[n])$ is defined for all $f \in U$ and $n \in \mathbb{N}$. BC and $\mathrm{BC}_\psi(S)$ are notions used as explained in Definition 1.*

Defining several learning models always calls for a comparison of the resulting identification power. In [2] EX is proved to be a proper subclass of BC, i.e. there are classes of recursive functions which are BC-identifiable but not EX-identifiable. Case and Smith [6] propose a variant of BC-learning, called BC-learning with finitely many anomalies, in which correct hypotheses are no longer required. The only restriction here is, that eventually all functions suggested by the learner must have an "almost" correct input-output-behaviour.

Definition 3. *A set $U \subseteq \mathcal{R}$ is BC^*-identifiable iff, for some $\psi \in \mathcal{P}^2$ and some $S \in \mathcal{P}$, any $f \in U$ satisfies $\psi_{S(f[n])} =^* f$ for all but finitely many n; additionally $S(f[n])$ is defined for all $f \in U$ and $n \in \mathbb{N}$. BC^* and $\mathrm{BC}_\psi^*(S)$ are defined as usual.*

[6] gives a proof for BC $\subset$ BC* as well as the verification of $\mathcal{R} \in$ BC* (proposed by L. Harrington). In any learning process according to the criteria EX, BC, BC* there is a certain time, after which all hypotheses returned must fulfil certain conditions. But there are no further constraints as to when this time is reached. A restricted learning model with bounds on the number of mind changes is introduced in [6]. In this model the learner is allowed only a certain number of changes in its sequence of hypotheses; in particular, whenever this capacity of mind changes is exhausted, the actual hypothesis must be correct.

Definition 4. *Let $m \in \mathbb{N}$. A set $U \subseteq \mathcal{R}$ is* EX$_m$-*learnable iff some $\psi \in \mathcal{P}^2$ and some $S \in \mathcal{P}$ fulfil the following conditions.*

1. *$U \in$ EX$_\psi(S)$ (where S is additionally permitted to return the sign "?"),*
2. *for all $f \in U$ there is an $n_f \in \mathbb{N}$ such that $S(f[x]) =?$ iff $x < n_f$,*
3. *card$\{n \in \mathbb{N} \mid ? \neq S(f[n]) \neq S(f[n+1])\} \leq m$ for all $f \in U$.*

The sets (EX$_m$)$_\psi(S)$ *and* EX$_m$ *are defined as usual. U is identifiable with a bounded number of mind changes iff there is an $m \in \mathbb{N}$ such that $U \in$ EX$_m$.*

By returning "?" in the initial phase the strategy signals its being hesitant in order not to waste a mind change. For all bounds m the inclusion EX$_m \subset$ EX$_{m+1}$ is verified in [6]. Of course in the study of learning processes not only the mind change complexity is interesting, but also whether the quality of the intermediate hypotheses can be improved in some sense. A quite natural motivation is to demand that any hypothesis returned by the learner has to be consistent with the data seen so far, i. e. it should agree with the known part of the input-output-behaviour of the function to be learned, see for example [8,3,13].

Definition 5. *A class $U \subseteq \mathcal{R}$ is* CONS-*identifiable iff it is in* EX$_\psi(S)$ *for some $\psi \in \mathcal{P}^2$ and some $S \in \mathcal{P}$ satisfying $\psi_{S(f[n])} =_n f$ for all $f \in U$ and $n \in \mathbb{N}$. The corresponding classes* CONS *and* CONS$_\psi(S)$ *are defined in the usual way.*

The demand for consistency results in a loss of learning power, that means CONS $\subset$ EX, cf. [3]. Moreover EX$_0 \subset$ CONS, but EX$_m$ and CONS are incomparable for all $m \geq 1$ (partly verified in [7], the rest follows with similar methods). Note that for all inference criteria defined here – except for CONS – identifiability implies identifiability by a total learner, i. e. whenever there exists a strategy for a class to be learned, then there also exists a strategy $S \in \mathcal{R}$ learning the class. Here consistent learning is an exception, as has been verified in [13].

Throughout the following sections $\mathcal{I}$ denotes the set of inference classes defined above; $\mathcal{I} = \{$EX, BC, BC*, CONS$\} \cup \{$EX$_m \mid m \in \mathbb{N}\}$. Moreover, if $n \in \mathbb{N}$, let $J^n := \{U \subseteq \mathcal{R} \mid \text{card } U \leq n\}$. Obviously $J^n \in I$ for all $n \in \mathbb{N}$ and all $I \in \mathcal{I}$.

3   The Uniform Learning Model

Uniform learning is concerned with methods for deriving successful learners from a description of a learning problem, which first of all requires a tool for describing learning problems. A quite simple way to describe a class U of recursive functions to be identified is to present some index b of a partial-recursive numbering the recursive core of which equals U. Thus any integer $b \in \mathbb{N}$ corresponds to the class $\mathcal{R}_b = \{\varphi_i^b \mid i \in \mathbb{N}\} \cap \mathcal{R}$ of recursive functions, which is interpreted as a class of objects to be learned. Furthermore any set B of integers corresponds to a collection of classes $U \subseteq \mathcal{R}$ to be learned – each one described by some $b \in B$.

Definition 6. *Let $I \in \mathcal{I}$, $J \subseteq I$. A set $B \subseteq \mathbb{N}$ is suitable for uniform learning with respect to (J, I) iff*

1. *$\mathcal{R}_b \in J$ for all $b \in B$,*
2. *there is a learner $S \in \mathcal{P}^2$ such that for any description $b \in B$ there exists some $\psi \in \mathcal{P}^2$ satisfying $\mathcal{R}_b \in I_\psi(\lambda x.S(b, x))$.*

suit(J, I) *denotes the set of all sets B suitable in that sense. The notion $B \in$* suit$(J, I)(S)$ *is used to indicate that S is a learner witnessing to $B \in$ suit(J, I).*

So a set of descriptions is identified uniformly by S under (J, I), if each recursive core described by some $b \in B$ belongs to the class J and is identified by the learner $\lambda x.S(b, x)$ synthesized by S from b. This definition involves some lack of practicability, because only the synthesis of learners but not the synthesis of adequate hypothesis spaces is required. Taking account of this deficiency it is advisable also to consider the following variants of Definition 6.

Definition 7. *Let $I \in \mathcal{I}$, $J \subseteq I$. Then* suit$_\tau(J, I)$ *consists of all sets $B \in$* suit(J, I), *for which there is some learner $S \in \mathcal{P}^2$ such that $\mathcal{R}_b \in I_\tau(\lambda x.S(b, x))$ for all $b \in B$. Furthermore* suit$_\varphi(J, I)$ *is the set of all $B \in$* suit(J, I), *for which there exists some $S \in \mathcal{P}^2$ which fulfils $\mathcal{R}_b \in I_{\varphi^b}(\lambda x.S(b, x))$ for all $b \in B$. The notions* suit$_\tau(J, I)(S)$ *and* suit$_\varphi(J, I)(S)$ *are used by analogy with Definition 6.*

Obviously suit$_\varphi(J, I) \subseteq$ suit$_\tau(J, I) \subseteq$ suit(J, I) for all criteria $I \in \mathcal{I}$, but in general equality of these classes does not hold (suit$_\tau(J, \mathrm{BC}^*) =$ suit(J, BC^*) is an exception for any $J \subseteq \mathrm{BC}^*$, see also [14]). As in the non-uniform model, identifiability implies the existence of total strategies, if consistency is not required.

Proposition 1. *Let $I \in \mathcal{I} \backslash \{\mathrm{CONS}\}$, $J \subseteq I$, $B \subseteq \mathbb{N}$. Assume $B \in$* suit(J, I) *(suit$_\tau(J, I)$, suit$_\varphi(J, I)$). Then there is a total recursive function S such that $B \in$* suit$(J, I)(S)$ *(suit$_\tau(J, I)(S)$, suit$_\varphi(J, I)(S)$ resp.). Moreover, S can be constructed uniformly from a program of a corresponding partial-recursive learner.*

The following example shows that CONS-learning again yields an exception. There even exists a description set suitable for CONS-learning in the most restricted model (suit$_\varphi$-model) but not suitable for uniform learning by a total strategy in the least restricted model (suit-model). The proof is omitted.

Example 1. The description set $B := \{b \in \mathbb{N} \mid \varphi^b \in \mathcal{R}^2\}$ is an element of suit$_\varphi(\mathrm{CONS}, \mathrm{CONS})$, but $B \notin$ suit$(\mathrm{CONS}, \mathrm{CONS})(S)$ for any learner $S \in \mathcal{R}^2$.

4   Results on Unions of Suitable Description Sets

Assume two description sets $B_1, B_2 \in \mathrm{suit}(I, I)$ for a criterion $I \in \mathcal{I}$ are given. The results below concern the question, what properties concerning B_1, B_2 make the union of the two sets suitable for uniform learning with respect to I, i.e. what properties are sufficient for the satisfaction of $B_1 \cup B_2 \in \mathrm{suit}(I, I)$. The same question is considered for suit_τ or suit_φ instead of suit. $\mathrm{suit}(\mathrm{BC}^*, \mathrm{BC}^*)$ and $\mathrm{suit}_\tau(\mathrm{BC}^*, \mathrm{BC}^*)$ are closed under union, as $\mathcal{R} \in \mathrm{BC}^*$, but in general some further condition concerning B_1 and B_2 is needed, as the following example shows.

Example 2. Consider the description sets $B_1 = \{b \in \mathbb{N} \mid \mathcal{R}_b = \{\varphi_0^b\} = \{0^\infty\}\}$ and $B_2 = \{b \in \mathbb{N} \mid \exists m \in \mathbb{N}\,[\mathcal{R}_b = \{\varphi_1^b\} = \{0^m 1^\infty\}]\}$. Both B_1 and B_2 are elements of $\mathrm{suit}_\varphi(J^1, \mathrm{EX}_0)$, but $B_1 \cup B_2 \notin \mathrm{suit}_\tau(J^1, \mathrm{EX}_0)$.

Proof. The learner constantly $i - 1$ yields $B_i \in \mathrm{suit}_\varphi(J^1, \mathrm{EX}_0)$ for $i \in \{1, 2\}$. Assuming $B_1 \cup B_2 \in \mathrm{suit}_\tau(J^1, \mathrm{EX}_0)$ provides a strategy $S \in \mathcal{R}^2$ which fulfils $\mathcal{R}_b \in (\mathrm{EX}_0)_\tau(\lambda x.S(b, x))$ for all $b \in B_1 \cup B_2$. To reveal a contradiction a description $b_0 \subset B_1 \cup B_2$ satisfying $\mathcal{R}_{b_0} \notin (\mathrm{EX}_0)_\tau(\lambda x.S(b_0, x))$ is constructed. For that purpose it is adequate to define numberings ψ^b uniformly in $b \in \mathbb{N}$ and choose b_0 as a fixed point value according to the recursion theorem, such that $\varphi^{b_0} = \psi^{b_0}$.

Construction of b_0. For each $b \in \mathbb{N}$ define a function $\psi^b \in \mathcal{P}^2$ as follows: let $\psi_0^b(0) := 0$. Moreover, let $\psi_0^b(x+1)$ equal 0, if $S(b, 0^{x+1}) =?$ or all $n \le x+1$ such that $S(b, 0^n) \in \mathbb{N}$ fulfil $\tau_{S(b,0^n)}(n) \uparrow_{\le x+1}$ or $\tau_{S(b,0^n)}(n) \ne 0$. Otherwise, $\psi_0^b(x+1)$ is undefined. If $\psi_0^b = 0^k \uparrow^\infty$, there is some minimal integer $n \le k$, such that $S(b, 0^n) \in \mathbb{N}$ and $\tau_{S(b,0^n)}(n) \downarrow_{\le k}$, $\tau_{S(b,0^n)}(n) = 0$. In this case let $\psi_1^b := 0^n 1^\infty$. Otherwise, i.e. if $\psi_0^b = 0^\infty$, let $\psi_1^b := \uparrow^\infty$. In any case, all functions ψ_i^b with $i > 1$ shall be empty.

Since ψ^b is defined uniformly in b, there exists some recursive function g, such that $\varphi^{g(b)} = \psi^b$ for all $b \in \mathbb{N}$. Let $b_0 \in \mathbb{N}$ be a fixed point value of that function g, i.e. $\varphi^{b_0} = \varphi^{g(b_0)} = \psi^{b_0}$.   *End construction of b_0.*

Note that either $\mathcal{R}_{b_0} = \{\varphi_0^{b_0}\} = \{0^\infty\}$ or $\mathcal{R}_{b_0} = \{\varphi_1^{b_0}\} = \{0^m 1^\infty\}$ for some $m \in \mathbb{N}$. Thus $b_0 \in B_1 \cup B_2$. But if $\mathcal{R}_{b_0} = \{0^\infty\}$, then $S(b_0, 0^n) =?$ or $\tau_{S(b_0, 0^n)} \ne 0^\infty$ for all $n \in \mathbb{N}$; if $\mathcal{R}_{b_0} = \{0^m 1^\infty\}$ for some $m \in \mathbb{N}$, then $S(b, 0^m) \in \mathbb{N}$ and $\tau_{S(b, 0^m)}(m) = 0 \ne 1 = \varphi_1^{b_0}(m)$. Therefore $\mathcal{R}_{b_0} \notin (\mathrm{EX}_0)_\tau(\lambda x.S(b_0, x))$, which contradicts the choice of S. Hence $B_1 \cup B_2 \notin \mathrm{suit}_\tau(J^1, \mathrm{EX}_0)$.   □

For other learning classes in $\mathcal{I}$ similar negative results are obtained with recursive cores consisting of one or two elements.

Example 3. Consider the description sets $C = \{b \in \mathbb{N} \mid \mathcal{R}_b = \{\varphi_0^b\}\}$, as well as $B_1 = \{b \in \mathbb{N} \mid \mathrm{card}\,\mathcal{R}_b = \mathrm{card}\{i \mid \varphi_i^b \in \mathcal{R}\} = 2 \,\wedge\, \forall^\infty j\,[\varphi_j^b = \uparrow^\infty]\}$ and $B_2 = \{b \in \mathbb{N} \mid \mathrm{card}\{i \mid \varphi_i^b \in \mathcal{R}\} = 1 \,\wedge\, \forall^\infty j\,[\varphi_j^b = \uparrow^\infty]\}$. Then $C \in \mathrm{suit}_\varphi(J^1, \mathrm{EX}_0)$, $B_1 \in \mathrm{suit}_\varphi(J^2, \mathrm{CONS})$, $B_2 \in \mathrm{suit}_\varphi(J^1, \mathrm{CONS})$, but $C \cup B_1 \notin \mathrm{suit}(J^2, \mathrm{EX})$ and $C \cup B_2 \notin \mathrm{suit}_\tau(J^1, \mathrm{EX})$.

Example 4. Define two sets $B_1 := \{b \in \mathbb{N} \mid \{i \mid \varphi_i^b \text{ not initial}\} = \{0\}\}$ and $B_2 := \{b \in \mathbb{N} \mid \exists k\,[\{i \mid \varphi_i^b \text{ not initial}\} = \{k+1\} \,\wedge\, \forall y > k+1\,[\varphi_y^b = \uparrow^\infty]]\}$. Then $B_1 \in$

$\mathrm{suit}_\varphi(J^1, \mathrm{EX}_0)$, $B_2 \in \mathrm{suit}_\varphi(J^1, \mathrm{CONS})$, but $B_1 \cup B_2 \notin \mathrm{suit}_\tau(J^1, \mathrm{BC})$ and $B_1 \cup B_2 \notin \mathrm{suit}_\varphi(J^1, \mathrm{BC}^*)$.

The proofs use ideas similar to those in the proof of Example 2. As the reasons for the failure of all strategies for the unions in these examples are not obvious, it might be helpful first to collect some simple properties of description sets enabling the learnability of the corresponding unions.

Theorem 1. *Let* $I \in \mathcal{I}$ *and* $B_1, B_2 \in \mathrm{suit}(I, I)$ *(or* $\mathrm{suit}_\tau(I, I)$, $\mathrm{suit}_\varphi(I, I)$ *resp.).*

1. *If* B_1 *is recursive, then* $B_1 \cup B_2 \in \mathrm{suit}(I, I)$ ($\mathrm{suit}_\tau(I, I)$, $\mathrm{suit}_\varphi(I, I)$ *resp.).*
2. *If* B_1, B_2 *are r. e., then* $B_1 \cup B_2 \in \mathrm{suit}(I, I)$ ($\mathrm{suit}_\tau(I, I)$, $\mathrm{suit}_\varphi(I, I)$ *resp.).*
3. *If* $I \in \{\mathrm{EX}, \mathrm{BC}, \mathrm{BC}^*\}$ *and at least one of the sets* $B_1, \mathbb{N} \setminus B_2$ *is r. e., then* $B_1 \cup B_2 \in \mathrm{suit}(I, I)$ ($\mathrm{suit}_\tau(I, I)$, $\mathrm{suit}_\varphi(I, I)$ *resp.).*

Proof (sketch). Fix $I \in \mathcal{I}$, $B_1, B_2 \in \mathrm{suit}(I, I)$. For suit_τ, suit_φ all proofs proceed analogously. Choose $T_1, T_2 \in \mathcal{P}^2$ such that $B_i \in \mathrm{suit}(I, I)(T_i)$ for $i \in \{1, 2\}$.

For the proof of the first claim let a new learner on input $(b, f[n])$ return $T_1(b, f[n])$ if $b \in B_1$, $T_2(b, f[n])$ otherwise. The second claim is shown with a strategy searching for the given b in an enumeration of B_1 and in parallel in an enumeration of B_2. As soon as $b \in B_i$ is verified for some $i \in \{1, 2\}$, the learner simulates T_i. For the third claim, let the new learner simulate T_2 until the given description is proved to belong to B_1 (or $\mathbb{N} \setminus B_2$), then simulate T_1.   □

The second and third claim in Theorem 1 already suggest, that for some learning classes in $\mathcal{I}$ just one r. e. description set is not sufficient for the uniform identifiability of the union of two suitable description sets. Indeed this is true, as Theorem 4 will prove, but first one more special case in which any union of a suitable set with a suitable r. e. set again yields uniform learnability is regarded.

Theorem 2. *Assume* $B_1 \in \mathrm{suit}(\mathrm{CONS}, \mathrm{CONS})$ *and* $B_2 \in \mathrm{suit}_\tau(\mathrm{CONS}, \mathrm{CONS})$. *If* B_1 *(or* $\mathbb{N} \setminus B_2$*) is r. e., then* $B_1 \cup B_2 \in \mathrm{suit}(\mathrm{CONS}, \mathrm{CONS})$. *If* B_1 *(or* $\mathbb{N} \setminus B_2$*) is r. e. and* $B_1 \in \mathrm{suit}_\tau(\mathrm{CONS}, \mathrm{CONS})$, *then also* $B_1 \cup B_2 \in \mathrm{suit}_\tau(\mathrm{CONS}, \mathrm{CONS})$.

Proof (sketch). Let $B_1 \in \mathrm{suit}(\mathrm{CONS}, \mathrm{CONS})$, $B_2 \in \mathrm{suit}_\tau(\mathrm{CONS}, \mathrm{CONS})$, moreover B_1 (or $\mathbb{N} \setminus B_2$) r. e. Then there exist $T_1, T_2 \in \mathcal{P}$ and numberings $\psi^{[b]}$ for $b \in B_1$ with $\mathcal{R}_b \in \mathrm{CONS}_{\psi^{[b]}}(\lambda x. T_1(b, x))$ for $b \in B_1$ and $\mathcal{R}_b \in \mathrm{CONS}_\tau(\lambda x. T_2(b, x))$ for $b \in B_2$. Define a new hypothesis space $\eta^{[b]} \in \mathcal{P}^2$ for each $b \in \mathbb{N}$ as follows.

$$\eta^{[b]}_{2i} = \psi^{[b]}_i \text{ if } b \in B_1, \quad \eta^{[b]}_{2i} = \tau_i \text{ otherwise;} \quad \eta^{[b]}_{2i+1} = \tau_i \text{ for all } i \in \mathbb{N} .$$

If $b \in B_2$, $f \in \mathcal{R}_b$, $n \in \mathbb{N}$, then $T_2(b, f[n])$ is consistent for $f[n]$ with respect to τ. So on input $(b, f[n])$ a meta-strategy for $B_1 \cup B_2$ can test by dove-tailed computation, whether $b \in B_1$ ($\mathbb{N} \setminus B_2$, resp.) or $T_2(b, f[n])$ is defined and consistent for $f[n]$ with respect to τ. As long as the latter property is verified first, the consistent index $2T_2(b, f[n]) + 1$ is returned; as soon as $b \in B_1$ ($b \notin B_2$, resp.) has once been verified, the hypotheses returned by $\lambda x. 2T_1(b, x)$ are used. These are consistent with respect to τ, if $f \in \mathcal{R}_b$. Convergence follows from the choice of T_1, T_2. Proving the second claim does not require new hypothesis spaces.   □

The following result gives an example of how weakening the learning intention can lead to positive results without further demands concerning the two description sets. The proof is omitted.

Theorem 3. *Let $m, k_1, k_2 \in \mathbb{N}$, $m \leq k_1$, $m \leq k_2$. If $B_1 \in \mathrm{suit}(\mathrm{EX}_m, \mathrm{EX}_{k_1})$ and $B_2 \in \mathrm{suit}(\mathrm{EX}_m, \mathrm{EX}_{k_2})$, then $B_1 \cup B_2 \in \mathrm{suit}(\mathrm{EX}_m, \mathrm{EX}_{k_1+k_2+1})$.*

Thus the union of description sets suitable for learning with a bounded number of mind changes is still suitable, if a certain amount of further mind changes is permitted. But unfortunately, if an increasing mind change complexity is forbidden, negative results are obtained, sometimes even if one of the description sets is r. e. (in contrast to Theorems 1 and 2).

Theorem 4. *Let $m \in \mathbb{N}$. There exist two description sets $B_1, B_2 \subseteq \mathbb{N}$ such that*

1. *$B_1, B_2 \in \mathrm{suit}_\varphi(J^2, \mathrm{EX}_m)$ (or $B_1, B_2 \in \mathrm{suit}_\varphi(J^1, \mathrm{EX}_m)$),*
2. *B_1 is r. e., but*
3. *$B_1 \cup B_2 \notin \mathrm{suit}(J^2, \mathrm{EX}_m)$ ($B_1 \cup B_2 \notin \mathrm{suit}_\tau(J^1, \mathrm{EX}_m)$, resp.).*

Proof. Fix $m \in \mathbb{N}$. First B_1, B_2 are defined by constructing functions $\psi \in \mathcal{P}$ and $\mathrm{fp} \in \mathcal{R}$ such that $\varphi^{\mathrm{fp}(i)} = \psi^{(i,\mathrm{fp}(i))}$ for all $i \in \mathbb{N}$. The function fp assigns to each integer i some fixed point value according to the recursion theorem. $B_1 \cup B_2$ will be the value set of fp. Below just the statements concerning descriptions of recursive cores in J^2 are verified, the proof for descriptions of singleton sets works with the same method combined with the ideas in the proof below Example 2.

Definition of B_1, B_2. By Proposition 1 there is a function $\mathrm{rec} \in \mathcal{R}$, such that $\varphi^{\mathrm{rec}(i)} \in \mathcal{R}$ and $\mathrm{suit}(J^2, \mathrm{EX}_m)(\varphi^i) \subseteq \mathrm{suit}(J^2, \mathrm{EX}_m)(\varphi^{\mathrm{rec}(i)})$ for all $i \in \mathbb{N}$. From now on the notion S_i is used instead of $\varphi^{\mathrm{rec}(i)}$. Next the function $\psi \in \mathcal{P}^4$ is defined by constructing a numbering $\psi^i \in \mathcal{P}^3$ for any integer i as follows.

Fix $b \in \mathbb{N}$. Go to stage 0.

Stage 0. $\psi_0^{(i,b)}(0) := 0$. For $x \in \mathbb{N}$ define

$$\psi_0^{(i,b)}(x+1) := \begin{cases} 0 & \text{if } S_i(b, \psi_0^{(i,b)}[y]) =? \text{ for } 0 \leq y \leq x \\ m+2 & \text{if } x \text{ is minimal, such that } S_i(b, \psi_0^{(i,b)}[x]) \in \mathbb{N} \\ \uparrow & \text{otherwise} \end{cases}$$

Then $\psi_0^{(i,b)} = 0^\infty$ iff $S_i(b, 0^n) =?$ for all $n \in \mathbb{N}$. Otherwise, if t is minimal with $S_i(b, 0^t) \in \mathbb{N}$, note $\psi_0^{(i,b)} = 0^t(m+2) \uparrow^\infty$. In the latter case let $\alpha_0^{(i,b)} := 0^t$ and go to stage 1. In the first case $\alpha_0^{(i,b)} \uparrow$ and stage 1 is not reached. *End stage 0.*

Stage k ($1 \leq k \leq m$). If l denotes the length of $\alpha_{k-1}^{(i,b)}$, let $\psi_{2k-1}^{(i,b)}[l-1] = \psi_{2k}^{(i,b)}[l-1] = \alpha_{k-1}^{(i,b)}$. For all $x \geq l$ define

$$\psi_{2k-1}^{(i,b)}(x) := \begin{cases} k-1 & \text{if } S_i(b, \alpha_{k-1}^{(i,b)} r^y) = S_i(b, \alpha_{k-1}^{(i,b)}) \\ & \text{for } 0 \leq y \leq x-l \text{ and for all } r \in \{k-1, k\} \\ m+2 & \text{if } x \text{ is minimal, such that } S_i(b, \alpha_{k-1}^{(i,b)} r^y) \neq S_i(b, \alpha_{k-1}^{(i,b)}) \\ & \text{for } y = x-l \text{ and some } r \in \{k-1, k\} \\ \uparrow & \text{otherwise} \end{cases}$$

$$\psi_{2k}^{(i,b)}(x) := \begin{cases} k & \text{if } \psi_{2k-1}^{(i,b)}(x) = k-1 \\ m+2 & \text{if } \psi_{2k-1}^{(i,b)}(x) = m+2 \\ \uparrow & \text{otherwise} \end{cases}$$

Note that $\psi_{2k-1}^{(i,b)} = \alpha_{k-1}^{(i,b)}(k-1)^\infty$ iff $\psi_{2k}^{(i,b)} = \alpha_{k-1}^{(i,b)}k^\infty$ iff

$$S_i(b, \alpha_{k-1}^{(i,b)}) = S_i(b, \alpha_{k-1}^{(i,b)}(k-1)^n) = S_i(b, \alpha_{k-1}^{(i,b)}k^n) \text{ for all } n \in \mathbb{N}.$$

Otherwise, if t is minimal, such that $S_i(b, \alpha_{k-1}^{(i,b)}) \neq S_i(b, \alpha_{k-1}^{(i,b)}r^t)$ for some $r \in \{k-1, k\}$, then $\psi_{2k-1}^{(i,b)} = \alpha_{k-1}^{(i,b)}(k-1)^t(m+2)\uparrow^\infty$ and $\psi_{2k}^{(i,b)} = \alpha_{k-1}^{(i,b)}k^t(m+2)\uparrow^\infty$. In the latter case let $\alpha_k^{(i,b)} := \alpha_{k-1}^{(i,b)}r^t$ and go to stage $k+1$. In the first case $\alpha_k^{(i,b)}$ is undefined and stage $k+1$ is not reached.   *End stage k.*

Stage $m+1$. $\psi_{2m+1}^{(i,b)} = \alpha_m^{(i,b)}m^\infty$, $\psi_{2m+2}^{(i,b)} = \alpha_m^{(i,b)}(m+1)^\infty$, $\psi_x^{(i,b)} = \uparrow^\infty$ for $x > 2m+2$.   *End stage $m+1$.*

Next let $g \in \mathcal{R}$ be a function satisfying $\varphi^{g(i,b)} = \psi^{(i,b)}$ for all $i, b \in \mathbb{N}$. By the recursion theorem there is a function $\mathrm{fp} \in \mathcal{R}$, such that $\varphi^{\mathrm{fp}(i)} = \varphi^{g(i,\mathrm{fp}(i))} = \psi^{(i,\mathrm{fp}(i))}$ for all $i \in \mathbb{N}$. Define $B := \{\mathrm{fp}(i) \mid i \in \mathbb{N}\}$ and finally let

$$B_1 := \{\mathrm{fp}(i) \mid i \in \mathbb{N} \wedge \exists x \in \mathbb{N} \, [\varphi_0^{\mathrm{fp}(i)}(x) = m+2]\}, \quad B_2 := B \setminus B_1.$$

End definition of B_1, B_2.

It remains to verify the three properties stated in Theorem 4.

Property 1. $B_1, B_2 \in \mathrm{suit}_\varphi(J^2, \mathrm{EX}_m)$.
card $\mathcal{R}_b \leq 2$ for all $b \in B_1 \cup B_2$ follows by construction. The strategy constantly 0 shows $B_2 \in \mathrm{suit}_\varphi(J^2, \mathrm{EX}_m)$. Let a meta-learner for B_1 return "?" as long as the initial segment presented consists of zeros only. Afterwards the minimal consistent index in the numbering described is returned. This yields convergence to a correct program with no more than m mind changes on all relevant inputs.

Property 2. B_1 is r. e.
This property follows obviously by definition of B and B_1.

Property 3. $B_1 \cup B_2 \notin \mathrm{suit}(J^2, \mathrm{EX}_m)$.
Assume $B_1 \cup B_2 \in \mathrm{suit}(J^2, \mathrm{EX}_m)$. Then there exists some $i \in \mathbb{N}$, such that $B \in \mathrm{suit}(J^2, \mathrm{EX}_m)(S_i)$, i. e. for all $b \in B$ there is a numbering $\eta^{[b]} \in \mathcal{P}^2$ satisfying $\mathcal{R}_b \in (\mathrm{EX}_m)_{\eta^{[b]}}(\lambda x.S_i(b, x))$. Now let $b := \mathrm{fp}(i)$. The construction of ψ then implies $\mathcal{R}_b \notin (\mathrm{EX}_m)_{\eta^{[b]}}(\lambda x.S_i(b, x))$ (details are omitted) – a contradiction. □

Corollary 1. *Let $C := \{b \in \mathbb{N} \mid \mathcal{R}_b = \{\varphi_0^b\}\}$. Then $C \in \mathrm{suit}_\varphi(J^1, \mathrm{EX}_0)$ and*

1. *if $I \in \mathcal{I} \setminus \{\mathrm{BC}, \mathrm{BC}^*\}$, there is $B \in \mathrm{suit}_\varphi(J^2, I)$ such that $B \cup C \notin \mathrm{suit}(J^2, I)$,*
2. *if $I \in \mathcal{I} \setminus \{\mathrm{BC}^*\}$, there is $B \in \mathrm{suit}_\varphi(J^1, I)$ such that $B \cup C \notin \mathrm{suit}_\tau(J^1, I)$,*
3. *for all $I \in \mathcal{I}$ there is some $B \in \mathrm{suit}_\varphi(J^1, I)$ such that $B \cup C \notin \mathrm{suit}_\varphi(J^1, I)$.*

Proof. See Examples 2, 3, 4 and the proof of Theorem 4. □

Theorem 1 indicates that regarding the suitability of a union of two description sets it is very promising, if there is a method for separating the two sets algorithmically, that means if a learner can somehow determine which of the two sets a given description belongs to. Since in general such a separability is not attainable, it might be useful to state some properties of appropriate unions more carefully. To merge two meta-learners for two description sets into a successful meta-learner for the union set, it is not really required to find a way of separating the two sets themselves. It is already sufficient to recognize a description, *together* with some initial segment of a function to be learned, as some feasible input corresponding to one determinate description set of the two which are possible. This property can later on be used to prove the strong separations.

Proposition 2. *Let $I \in \mathcal{I}$ and $B_1, B_2 \in \text{suit}(I, I)$ (or $\text{suit}_\tau(I, I)$, $\text{suit}_\varphi(I, I)$ resp.). Assume there is a function $d \in \mathcal{P}_{01}$ satisfying the following two conditions.*

1. *$d(b, f(0)) = 1$ for all descriptions $b \in B_1$ and all functions $f \in \mathcal{R}_b$,*
2. *$d(b, f(0)) = 0$ for all descriptions $b \in B_2 \setminus B_1$ and all functions $f \in \mathcal{R}_b$.*

Then $B_1 \cup B_2 \in \text{suit}(I, I)$ ($\text{suit}_\tau(I, I)$, $\text{suit}_\varphi(I, I)$ resp.).[1]

Proof (sketch). Let $I \in \mathcal{I}$, $B_1, B_2 \in \text{suit}(I, I)$ (the idea is the same for $\text{suit}_\tau(I, I)$ and $\text{suit}_\varphi(I, I)$). Fix two strategies $T_1, T_2 \in \mathcal{P}^2$, such that $B_1 \in \text{suit}(I, I)(T_1)$ and $B_2 \in \text{suit}(I, I)(T_2)$. On input $(b, f[n])$ a learner witnessing to $B_1 \cup B_2 \in \text{suit}(I, I)$ returns $T_1(b, f[n])$ if $d(b, f(0)) = 1$, $T_2(b, f[n])$ if $d(b, f(0)) = 0$. $\square$

Without special requirements concerning the intermediate hypotheses or the mind change complexity, the demands of Proposition 2 can be weakened. For EX- or BC-learning it is not necessary to recognize feasible inputs corresponding to a description set at once. It is enough to determine one of the two sets in the limit from gradually growing feasible information on a function to be learned.

Proposition 3. *Let $I \in \{\text{EX}, \text{BC}, \text{BC}^*\}$ and $B_1, B_2 \in \text{suit}(I, I)$ (or $\text{suit}_\tau(I, I)$, $\text{suit}_\varphi(I, I)$ resp.). Assume some function $d \in \mathcal{P}_{01}$ fulfils the following conditions.*

1. *$\forall^\infty n \ [d(b, f[n]) = 1]$ for all descriptions $b \in B_1$ and all functions $f \in \mathcal{R}_b$,*
2. *$\forall^\infty n \ [d(b, f[n]) = 0]$ for all descriptions $b \in B_2 \setminus B_1$ and all functions $f \in \mathcal{R}_b$.*

Then $B_1 \cup B_2 \in \text{suit}(I, I)$ ($\text{suit}_\tau(I, I)$, $\text{suit}_\varphi(I, I)$ resp.).

For a proof a similar strategy as in the verification of Proposition 2 is adequate. Example 2 witnesses to the fact that Proposition 3 does not hold for $I = \text{EX}_0$. Define a function $d \in \mathcal{P}_{01}$ on input $(b, f[n])$ to equal 1, if $f[n] = 0^{n+1}$, and to equal 0, if $f[n] \neq 0^{n+1}$. This yields the following properties.

- If $b \in B_1$ and $f \in \mathcal{R}_b$ (i.e. $f = 0^\infty$), then $d(b, f[n]) = 1$ for all $n \in \mathbb{N}$.
- If $b \in B_2 \setminus B_1$, $f \in \mathcal{R}_b$ (i.e. $f = 0^m 1^\infty$ for some $m \in \mathbb{N}$), then $d(b, f[n]) = 0$ for all but finitely many $n \in \mathbb{N}$.
- $B_1, B_2 \in \text{suit}_\varphi(\text{EX}_0, \text{EX}_0)$.

If Proposition 3 was also true for the criterion $I = \text{EX}_0$, then $B_1 \cup B_2 \in \text{suit}_\varphi(\text{EX}_0, \text{EX}_0)$ would hold – a contradiction to Example 2.

---

[1] That the decision of the function d, for any $b \in B_1 \cup B_2$ and any $f \in \mathcal{R}_b$, does not depend on the values $f(n)$ for $n > 0$, may seem rather odd. Indeed a stronger version of Proposition 2 holds, yet for the purpose of this paper the actual version suffices.

5 Strong Separations of Criteria for Uniform Learning

In the uniform model now a strong separation of I and I' is expressed in terms of description sets as follows:

$$\forall B_1 \in \text{suit}(I, I) \; \exists B_2 \in \text{suit}(I, I') \; [B_1 \cup B_2 \in \text{suit}(I, I') \setminus \text{suit}(I, I)] \qquad (1)$$

or analogously with suit_τ or suit_φ. Fortunately such strong separations hold for any pair of criteria in which the weak separations have been verified. And it is possible to prove even more; the quantifiers in (1) can be switched. That means for any strongly separated pair (I, I') there is one fixed description set $B \in \text{suit}(I, I')$ such that for any set $B' \in \text{suit}(I, I)$ the union $B \cup B'$ belongs to $\text{suit}(I, I')$, but no longer to $\text{suit}(I, I)$. So there are special fixed description sets, which are in some sense typical for a set not suitable for uniform I-learning, but on the other hand restrictive enough to be suitable for uniform I'-identification in combination with any description set in $\text{suit}(I, I)$. The proof below Theorem 5 just gives an example for the pair (EX, BC), because other results of this style can be achieved by similar methods, even for the suit_τ- and suit_φ-models.

Theorem 5. *Let (I, I') be a pair in $\{(\text{EX}_0, \text{CONS}), (\text{CONS}, \text{EX}), (\text{EX}, \text{BC})\}$ $\cup \{(\text{EX}_m, \text{EX}_{m+1}) \mid m \in \mathbb{N}\}$. Then there is a set $B \subseteq \mathbb{N}$ satisfying*

1. *B is recursively enumerable,*
2. *$\text{card}\,\mathcal{R}_b \leq 2$ for all $b \in B$,*
3. *if $B' \in \text{suit}(I, I)$, then $B \cup B' \in \text{suit}(I, I') \setminus \text{suit}(I, I)$.*

Moreover, this statement holds for suit_τ and suit_φ instead of suit, even if the second condition is strengthened to $\text{card}\,\mathcal{R}_b = 1$ for all $b \in B$.

Proof for $(I, I') = (\text{EX}, \text{BC})$. First the set B is defined via the construction of a partial-recursive function ψ and a recursive function fp such that $\varphi^{\text{fp}(i)} = \psi^{(i, \text{fp}(i))}$ for all $i \in \mathbb{N}$. The function fp assigns to each integer i some fixed point value according to the recursion theorem. B will be the value set of fp.

Definition of B. By Proposition 1 there is some $\text{rec} \in \mathcal{R}$, such that $\varphi^{\text{rec}(i)} \in \mathcal{R}$ and $\text{suit}(\text{EX}, \text{EX})(\varphi^i) \subseteq \text{suit}(\text{EX}, \text{EX})(\varphi^{\text{rec}(i)})$ for all $i \in \mathbb{N}$. From now on the notion S_i is used instead of $\varphi^{\text{rec}(i)}$. Next the function $\psi \in \mathcal{P}^4$ is defined by constructing a numbering $\psi^i \in \mathcal{P}^3$ for any integer i as follows.

Fix $b \in \mathbb{N}$. Let $\alpha_0^{(i,b)} := (i)$, $\psi_0^{(i,b)}(0) = i$ and go to stage 0. In general, the construction in stage k ($k \in \mathbb{N}$) proceeds in the following way:
Look for the minimal integer $m_k^{(i,b)} \in \mathbb{N}$ which fulfils

$$S_i(b, \alpha_k^{(i,b)} 00 m_k^{(i,b)}) \neq S_i(b, \alpha_k^{(i,b)}) \text{ or } S_i(b, \alpha_k^{(i,b)} 10 m_k^{(i,b)}) \neq S_i(b, \alpha_k^{(i,b)}) \,.$$

If such an integer does not exist, $m_k^{(i,b)}$ is undefined. Then let

$$\alpha_{k+1}^{(i,b)} := \begin{cases} \alpha_k^{(i,b)} 00 m_k^{(i,b)} 2 & \text{if } m_k^{(i,b)} \downarrow \text{ and } S_i(b, \alpha_k^{(i,b)} 00 m_k^{(i,b)}) \neq S_i(b, \alpha_k^{(i,b)}) \\ \alpha_k^{(i,b)} 10 m_k^{(i,b)} 2 & \text{if } m_k^{(i,b)} \downarrow \text{ and } S_i(b, \alpha_k^{(i,b)} 00 m_k^{(i,b)}) = S_i(b, \alpha_k^{(i,b)}) \\ \uparrow & \text{if } m_k^{(i,b)} \uparrow \end{cases}$$

In addition $\alpha_{k+1}^{(i,b)}$ becomes an initial segment of $\psi_0^{(i,b)}$, i.e. $\psi_0^{(i,b)}[l-1] := \alpha_{k+1}^{(i,b)}$, if $\alpha_{k+1}^{(i,b)}$ is defined and of length l; $\psi_0^{(i,b)} := \alpha_k^{(i,b)} \uparrow^\infty$ otherwise. Furthermore define

$$
\psi_{2k+1}^{(i,b)} := \begin{cases} \alpha_k^{(i,b)} 00^\infty & \text{if } m_k^{(i,b)} \uparrow \\ \psi_0^{(i,b)} & \text{if } m_k^{(i,b)} \downarrow \text{ and } S_i(b, \alpha_k^{(i,b)} 00^{m_k^{(i,b)}}) \neq S_i(b, \alpha_k^{(i,b)}) \\ \alpha_k^{(i,b)} 00^{m_k^{(i,b)}} \uparrow^\infty & \text{if } m_k^{(i,b)} \downarrow \text{ and } S_i(b, \alpha_k^{(i,b)} 00^{m_k^{(i,b)}}) = S_i(b, \alpha_k^{(i,b)}) \end{cases}
$$

$$
\psi_{2k+2}^{(i,b)} := \begin{cases} \alpha_k^{(i,b)} 10^\infty & \text{if } m_k^{(i,b)} \uparrow \\ \psi_0^{(i,b)} & \text{if } m_k^{(i,b)} \downarrow \text{ and } S_i(b, \alpha_k^{(i,b)} 00^{m_k^{(i,b)}}) = S_i(b, \alpha_k^{(i,b)}) \\ \alpha_k^{(i,b)} 10^{m_k^{(i,b)}} \uparrow^\infty & \text{if } m_k^{(i,b)} \downarrow \text{ and } S_i(b, \alpha_k^{(i,b)} 00^{m_k^{(i,b)}}) \neq S_i(b, \alpha_k^{(i,b)}) \end{cases}
$$

If $m_k^{(i,b)}$ exists, then go to stage $k+1$.   *End stage k.*

Let $g \in \mathcal{R}$ satisfy $\varphi^{g(i,b)} = \psi^{(i,b)}$ for all $i, b \in \mathbb{N}$. By the recursion theorem there is some fp $\in \mathcal{R}$, such that $\varphi^{\text{fp}(i)} = \varphi^{g(i,\text{fp}(i))} = \psi^{(i,\text{fp}(i))}$ for all $i \in \mathbb{N}$. Finally let $B := \{\text{fp}(i) \mid i \in \mathbb{N}\}$.   *End definition of B.*

Claim. Let $b \in B$ and $i \in \mathbb{N}$ such that $\text{fp}(i) = b$. Then

1. $\mathcal{R}_b = \{\varphi_0^b\} \iff m_k^{(i,b)}$ is defined for all $k \in \mathbb{N} \iff$ for all $k \in \mathbb{N}$ some $t_k \in \{0,1\}$ fulfils $\alpha_k^{(i,b)} t_k \subseteq \varphi_0^b$ and $\{\varphi_{2k+1}^b, \varphi_{2k+2}^b\} = \{\varphi_0^b, \alpha_k^{(i,b)} \overline{t_k} 0^{m_k^{(i,b)}} \uparrow^\infty\}$.

2. $\mathcal{R}_b = \{\varphi_{2k+1}^b, \varphi_{2k+2}^b\} = \{\alpha_k^{(i,b)} 00^\infty, \alpha_k^{(i,b)} 10^\infty\} \iff k$ is the minimal integer such that $m_k^{(i,b)}$ is not defined,

3. if $\alpha_k^{(i,b)}$ is defined for some $k \in \mathbb{N}$, then $\text{card}\{r \geq 1 \mid \alpha_k^{(i,b)}(r) = 2\} = k$.

These claims follow immediately from the construction; hence it remains to verify the properties 1 up to 3 stated in the Theorem.

Property 1. B is recursively enumerable.
B is the value set of a recursive function and thus r. e.

Property 2. $\text{card}\,\mathcal{R}_b \leq 2$ for all $b \in B$.
By Claims 1 and 2 either $\mathcal{R}_b = \{\varphi_0^b\}$ or $\mathcal{R}_b = \{\varphi_{2k+1}^b, \varphi_{2k+2}^b\}$ for some $k \in \mathbb{N}$.

Property 3. If $B' \in \text{suit}(\text{EX}, \text{EX})$, then $B \cup B' \in \text{suit}(\text{EX}, \text{BC}) \setminus \text{suit}(\text{EX}, \text{EX})$.
Fix some description set $B' \in \text{suit}(\text{EX}, \text{EX})$. First $B \cup B' \notin \text{suit}(\text{EX}, \text{EX})$ will be verified, afterwards the proof of $B \cup B' \in \text{suit}(\text{EX}, \text{BC})$ follows.

Proof of $B \cup B' \notin \text{suit}(\text{EX}, \text{EX})$. Assume that $B \cup B' \in \text{suit}(\text{EX}, \text{EX})$. Then in particular there exists some total recursive uniform strategy appropriate for EX-identification of the set B; that means, there is some $i \in \mathbb{N}$ such that

$$\text{for all } b \in B \text{ some } \eta^{[b]} \in \mathcal{P}^2 \text{ fulfils } \mathcal{R}_b \in \text{EX}_{\eta^{[b]}}(\lambda x. S_i(b, x)) . \tag{2}$$

Let $b := \text{fp}(i)$, i.e. $\varphi^b = \psi^{(i,b)}$. By Claims 1 and 2 it suffices to consider two cases.

Case (i). $\mathcal{R}_b = \{\varphi_0^b\}$. Then for all $k \in \mathbb{N}$, by Claim 1, $m_k^{(i,b)}$ is defined and the construction yields $\alpha_k^{(i,b)} t_k 0^{m_k^{(i,b)}} \subseteq \varphi_0^b$ and $S_i(b, \alpha_k^{(i,b)}) \neq S_i(b, \alpha_k^{(i,b)} t_k 0^{m_k^{(i,b)}})$ for some $t_k \in \{0, 1\}$. Thus the sequence of hypotheses returned by $\lambda x.S_i(b, x)$ on φ_0^b diverges, which implies $\mathcal{R}_b \notin \mathrm{EX}_{\eta^{[b]}}(\lambda x.S_i(b, x))$ in contradiction to (2).

Case (ii). $\mathcal{R}_b = \{\varphi_{2k+1}^b, \varphi_{2k+2}^b\} = \{\alpha_k^{(i,b)} 00^\infty, \alpha_k^{(i,b)} 10^\infty\}$ for some $k \in \mathbb{N}$. Then by Claim 2 the value $m_k^{(i,b)}$ is not defined. This implies

$$S_i(b, \alpha_k^{(i,b)} 00^m) = S_i(b, \alpha_k^{(i,b)}) = S_i(b, \alpha_k^{(i,b)} 10^m) \text{ for all } m \in \mathbb{N} \ .$$

Thus $S_i(b, \varphi_{2k+1}^b[n]) = S_i(b, \varphi_{2k+2}^b[n])$ for all but finitely many $n \in \mathbb{N}$, although $\varphi_{2k+1}^b \neq \varphi_{2k+2}^b$. Therefore – without influence of the hypothesis space regarded – the sequence of hypotheses returned by $\lambda x.S_i(b, x)$ must converge to an incorrect program for at least one of the two functions in $\mathcal{R}_b$. Hence $\mathcal{R}_b \notin \mathrm{EX}_{\eta^{[b]}}(\lambda x.S_i(b, x))$; again a contradiction to (2).

Both cases lead to a contradiction, so $B \cup B' \notin \mathrm{suit}(\mathrm{EX}, \mathrm{EX})$ is obtained.

Proof of $B \cup B' \in \mathrm{suit}(\mathrm{EX}, \mathrm{BC})$. By definition $B' \in \mathrm{suit}(\mathrm{EX}, \mathrm{BC})$. It is possible to show that $B \in \mathrm{suit}(\mathrm{EX}, \mathrm{BC})$ and afterwards apply Proposition 2. First a strategy $T \in \mathcal{R}$ satisfying $\mathcal{R}_b \in \mathrm{BC}_{\varphi^b}(T)$ for all $b \in B$ is defined as follows: let $f \in \mathcal{R}$. Then $T(f[0]) := 0$ and for any $n > 0$ with $f(n) = 2$, let $T(f[n]) := T(f[n-1])$. If $n > 0$ and $f(n) \neq 2$, let $k := \mathrm{card}\{r \mid 1 \leq r \leq n \wedge f(r) = 2\}$ and define $T(f[n]) := 2k + 1$ in case $f[n] = \alpha 20^x$ for some segment α and some $x > 0$. Otherwise $T(f[n]) := 2k + 2$. $\mathcal{R}_b \in \mathrm{BC}_{\varphi^b}(T)$ for all $b \in B$ can be verified with the help of Claims 1–3. Details are omitted here. So $B \in \mathrm{suit}(\mathrm{EX}, \mathrm{BC})$.

In order to apply Proposition 2 it is necessary to find some $d \in \mathcal{P}_{01}$ satisfying:

1. $d(b, f(0)) = 1$ for all descriptions $b \in B$ and all functions $f \in \mathcal{R}_b$,
2. $d(b, f(0)) = 0$ for all descriptions $b \in B' \setminus B$ and all functions $f \in \mathcal{R}_b$.

For that purpose let $d(b, n) := 1$, if $\mathrm{fp}(n) = b$ and $d(b, n) := 0$, if $\mathrm{fp}(n) \neq b$ $(b, n \in \mathbb{N})$. If $b \in B$, $f \in \mathcal{R}_b$, the construction of ψ implies $\mathrm{fp}(f(0)) = b$, so $d(b, f(0)) = 1$. If $b \notin B = \{\mathrm{fp}(i) \mid i \in \mathbb{N}\}$, then $\mathrm{fp}(n) \neq b$ is obtained for any $n \in \mathbb{N}$; in particular $d(b, n) = 0$. So $B \cup B' \in \mathrm{suit}(\mathrm{EX}, \mathrm{BC})$ by Proposition 2.[2] $\square$

According to Theorem 5 it might in some cases be reasonable to give up certain constraints concerning the inference criterion I, because thus an increase of learning power can be achieved, no matter what description set in $\mathrm{suit}(I, I)$ has to be learned. The proof (together with the proof of Proposition 2) indicates, *how* to modify a uniform I-learner for an arbitrary set in $\mathrm{suit}(I, I)$ into an adequate $\mathrm{suit}(I, I')$-learner for a proper superset, which does no longer belong to $\mathrm{suit}(I, I)$. Hence this result does not only give the advice to sometimes loosen the learning criteria, but furthermore provides a method for designing more powerful learners. The fact that there is a fixed description set, which witnesses to the strong separation for *any* description set in $\mathrm{suit}(I, I)$, indicates that there exists some kind of structure for a somehow characteristic description set corresponding to the class $\mathrm{suit}(I, I') \setminus \mathrm{suit}(I, I)$. The structure of such a characteristic set is on the one hand complex enough to disallow uniform I-learning, but on the other hand

---

[2] Actually Proposition 2 is not needed: since B is r.e., Theorem 1.3 suffices. But in order to provide also the idea for the omitted parts, a universal method is chosen.

simple enough to enable uniform I'-identification of its union with any arbitrary description set in suit(I, I).

Theorem 6. *There is a description set $B \subseteq \mathbb{N}$ satisfying*

1. *B is recursively enumerable,*
2. *card $\mathcal{R}_b = 1$ for all $b \in B$,*
3. *if $B' \in \text{suit}_\tau(\text{BC}, \text{BC})$, then $B \cup B' \in \text{suit}_\tau(\text{BC}, \text{BC}^*) \setminus \text{suit}_\tau(\text{BC}, \text{BC})$ (or analogously for suit_φ instead of suit_τ).*

The proof is omitted. Theorem 6 is formulated separately from Theorem 5, because its statement does not hold for the uniform learning model given by suit(BC, BC) (i. e. without specification of the hypothesis spaces). The reason is that suit(BC, BC) = $\{B \subseteq \mathbb{N} \mid \mathcal{R}_b \in \text{BC for all } b \in B\}$, which implies suit(BC, BC*) = suit(BC, BC) (the proof uses a simple construction of appropriate hypothesis spaces). Note that Theorems 5 and 6 yield strong separations for all pairs (I, I') of learning classes from $\mathcal{I}$, for which $I \subset I'$ holds.

References

1. Baliga, G., Case, J., Jain, S., *The Synthesis of Language Learners*, Information and Computation 152, 16–43 (1999). 202
2. Barzdin, J., *Two Theorems on the Limiting Synthesis of Functions*, Theory of Algorithms and Programs, Latvian State University, Riga 210, 82–88 (1974) (in Russian). 201, 202, 204
3. Barzdin, J., *Inductive Inference of Automata, Functions and Programs*, in Proc. International Congress of Math., Vancouver, 455–460 (1974). 205
4. Blum, M., *A Machine-Independent Theory of the Complexity of Recursive Functions*, Journal of the ACM 14 (2), 322–336 (1967). 204
5. Case, J., Chen, K., Jain, S., *Strong Separation of Learning Classes*, Journal of Experimental and Theoretical Artificial Intelligence 4, 281–293 (1992). 203
6. Case, J., Smith, C., *Comparison of Identification Criteria for Machine Inductive Inference*, Theoretical Computer Science 25, 193–220 (1983). 201, 202, 204, 205
7. Freivalds, R., Kinber, E. B., Wiehagen, R. (1995), *How Inductive Inference Strategies Discover Their Errors*, Information and Computation 118, 208–226. 201, 202, 205
8. Gold, E. M., *Language Identification in the Limit*, Information and Control 10, 447–474 (1967). 201, 204, 205
9. Jantke, K. P., *Natural Properties of Strategies Identifying Recursive Functions*, Elektronische Informationsverarbeitung und Kybernetik 15, 487–496 (1979). 202
10. Kapur, S., Bilardi, G., *On uniform learnability of language families*, Information Processing Letters 44, 35–38 (1992). 202
11. Osherson, D. N., Stob, M., Weinstein, S., *Synthesizing Inductive Expertise*, Information and Computation 77, 138–161 (1988). 202
12. Rogers, H., *Theory of Recursive Functions and Effective Computability*, MIT Press, Cambridge, Massachusetts (1987). 203
13. Wiehagen, R., Zeugmann, T., *Learning and Consistency*, in K. P. Jantke and S. Lange (Eds.): Algorithmic Learning for Knowledge-Based Systems, LNAI 961, 1–24, Springer-Verlag (1995). 205

14. Zilles, S., *On the Comparison of Inductive Inference Criteria for Uniform Learning of Finite Classes*, in N. Abe, R. Khardon, and T. Zeugmann (Eds.): ALT 2001, LNAI 2225, 251–266, Springer-Verlag (2001).   202, 206

The Speed Prior: A New Simplicity Measure Yielding Near-Optimal Computable Predictions[*]

Jürgen Schmidhuber

IDSIA, Galleria 2
6928 Manno (Lugano), Switzerland
juergen@idsia.ch
http://www.idsia.ch/~juergen

Abstract. Solomonoff's optimal but *non*computable method for inductive inference assumes that observation sequences x are drawn from an recursive prior distribution $\mu(x)$. Instead of using the unknown $\mu(x)$ he predicts using the celebrated universal enumerable prior $M(x)$ which for all x exceeds any recursive $\mu(x)$, save for a constant factor independent of x. The simplicity measure $M(x)$ naturally implements "Occam's razor" and is closely related to the Kolmogorov complexity of x. However, M assigns high probability to certain data x that are extremely hard to compute. This does not match our intuitive notion of simplicity. Here we suggest a more plausible measure derived from the fastest way of computing data. In absence of contrarian evidence, we assume that the physical world is generated by a computational process, and that any possibly infinite sequence of observations is therefore computable in the limit (this assumption is more radical and stronger than Solomonoff's). Then we replace M by the novel Speed Prior S, under which the cumulative a priori probability of all data whose computation through an optimal algorithm requires more than $O(n)$ resources is $1/n$. We show that the Speed Prior allows for deriving a *computable* strategy for optimal prediction of future y, given past x. Then we consider the case that the data actually stem from a *non*optimal, unknown computational process, and use Hutter's recent results to derive excellent expected loss bounds for S-based inductive inference. We conclude with several nontraditional predictions concerning the future of our universe.

1   Introduction

How to predict the future from the past? To get a grip on this fundamental question, let us first introduce some notation. B^* denotes the set of finite sequences over the binary alphabet $B = \{0, 1\}$, B^∞ the set of infinite sequences over B, λ the empty string, $B^\sharp = B^* \cup B^\infty$. x, y, z, z^1, z^2 stand for strings in $B^\sharp$. If $x \in B^*$ then xy is the concatenation of x and y (e.g., if $x = 10000$ and $y = 1111$

---

[*] This paper is based on section 6 of TR IDSIA-20-00, Version 2.0:
http://www.idsia.ch/~juergen/toesv2/
http://arXiv.org/abs/quant-ph/0011122 (public physics archive)

J. Kivinen and R. H. Sloan (Eds.): COLT 2002, LNAI 2375, pp. 216–228, 2002.
© Springer-Verlag Berlin Heidelberg 2002

then $xy = 100001111$). For $x \in B^*$, $l(x)$ denotes the number of bits in x, where $l(x) = \infty$ for $x \in B^\infty$; $l(\lambda) = 0$. x_n is the prefix of x consisting of the first n bits, if $l(x) \geq n$, and x otherwise ($x_0 := \lambda$). log denotes the logarithm with basis 2, f, g functions mapping integers to integers. We write $f(n) = O(g(n))$ if there exist positive constants c, n_0 such that $f(n) \leq cg(n)$ for all $n > n_0$. For simplicity let us consider universal Turing Machines (TMs) with input alphabet B and trinary output alphabet including the symbols "0", "1", and " " (blank). For efficiency reasons, the TMs should have several work tapes to avoid potential quadratic slowdowns associated with 1-tape TMs. The remainder of this paper refers assumes a fixed universal reference TM.

Now suppose bitstring x represents the data observed so far. What is its most likely continuation $y \in B^\sharp$? Bayes' theorem yields

$$P(xy \mid x) = \frac{P(x \mid xy)P(xy)}{P(x)} \propto P(xy) \qquad (1)$$

where $P(z^2 \mid z^1)$ is the probability of z^2, given knowledge of z^1, and $P(x) = \int_{z \in B^\sharp} P(xz)dz$ is just a normalizing factor. So the most likely continuation y is determined by $P(xy)$, the *prior probability* of xy. But which prior measure P is plausible? Occam's razor suggests that the "simplest" y should be more probable. But which exactly is the "correct" definition of simplicity?

The next section will offer an alternative to the celebrated but *noncomputable* algorithmic simplicity measure or Solomonoff-Levin measure [24,29,25]. But let us first review Solomonoff's traditional approach.

Roughly fourty years ago Solomonoff started the theory of universal optimal induction based on the apparently harmless simplicity assumption that P is computable [24]. While Equation (1) makes predictions of the entire future, given the past, Solomonoff [25] focuses just on the next bit in a sequence. Although this provokes surprisingly nontrivial problems associated with translating the bitwise approach to alphabets other than the binary one — only recently Hutter managed to do this [8] — it is sufficient for obtaining essential insights. Given an observed bitstring x, Solomonoff assumes the data are drawn according to a recursive measure μ; that is, there is a program for a universal Turing machine that reads $x \in B^*$ and computes $\mu(x)$ and halts. He estimates the probability of the next bit (assuming there will be one), using the remarkable, well-studied, enumerable prior M [24,29,25,6,15]

$$M(x) = \sum_{\substack{program\ prefix\ p\ computes \\ output\ starting\ with\ x}} 2^{-l(p)}. \qquad (2)$$

M is *universal*, dominating the less general recursive measures as follows: For all $x \in B^*$,

$$M(x) \geq c_\mu \mu(x) \qquad (3)$$

where c_μ is a constant depending on μ but not on x. Solomonoff observed that the conditional M-probability of a particular continuation, given previous observations, converges towards the unknown conditional μ as the observation size goes to infinity [25], and that the sum over all observation sizes of the corresponding μ-expected deviations is actually bounded by a constant. Hutter eventually showed that the number of prediction errors made by universal Solomonoff prediction is essentially bounded by the number of errors made by any other predictor, including the optimal scheme based on the true μ [8]. He also derived general loss bounds and showed that the expected loss of the universal scheme does not exceed by much the loss of the optimal scheme [9]. Recent research also generalized Solomonoff's approach to the case of much less restrictive universal nonenumerable priors that are computable in the limit [22,23]. One might say that Solomonoff's restriction of recursiveness leads to a "slightly more computable" approach than the more general case.

However, while M is enumerable, it is not recursive, and thus practically infeasible. This drawback inspired less general yet practically more feasible principles of minimum description length (MDL) [27,17] as well as priors derived from time-bounded restrictions [15] of Kolmogorov complexity [12,24,4]. No particular instance of these approaches, however, is universally accepted or has a general convincing motivation that carries beyond rather specialized application scenarios. For instance, typical efficient MDL approaches require the specification of a class of computable models of the data, say, certain types of neural networks, plus some computable loss function expressing the coding costs of the data relative to the model. This provokes numerous *ad-hoc* choices.

The novel approach pursued here agrees that Solomonoff's assumption of recursive priors without any time and space limitations is too weak, and that we somehow should specify additional resource constraints on the data-generating process to obtain a convincing basis for feasible inductive inference. But which constraints are plausible? Which reflect the "natural" concept of simplicity? Previous resource-oriented priors derived from, say, polynomial time bounds [15] have no obvious and plausible *a priori* justification.

Therefore we will suggest a novel, natural prior reflecting data-independent, optimally efficient use of computational resources. Based on this prior, Section 3 will derive a near-optimal *computable* strategy for making predictions, given past observations.

2   Speed Prior S

Let us assume that the observed data sequence is generated by a computational process, and that any possible sequence of observations is therefore computable in the limit [22].

This assumption is stronger and more radical than the traditional one: Solomonoff just insists that the probability of any sequence prefix is recursively computable, but the (infinite) sequence itself may still be generated probabilistically.

Under our starting assumption that data are deterministically generated by a machine, it seems plausible that the machine suffers from a computational resource problem. Since some things are much harder to compute than others, the resource-oriented point of view suggests the following postulate.

Postulate 1 *The cumulative prior probability measure of all x incomputable within time t is at most inversely proportional to t.*

To add some flesh to this postulate, we introduce the asymptotically fastest way of computing *all* computable data, for our particular universal reference TM:

> **FAST Algorithm** (version 1): For $i = 1, 2, \ldots$ perform PHASE i:
> PHASE i: Execute $2^{i-l(p)}$ instructions of all program prefixes p satisfying $l(p) \leq i$, and sequentially write the outputs on adjacent sections of the output tape, separated by blanks.

Following Levin [14][15, p. 502-505], within 2^{k+1} TM steps **FAST** will generate all prefixes x_n satisfying $Kt(x_n) \leq k$, where x_n's Levin complexity $Kt(x_n)$ is defined as

$$Kt(x_n) = \min_q \{l(q) + \log\ t(q, x_n)\}, \tag{4}$$

where program prefix q computes x_n in $t(q, x_n)$ time steps. The computational complexity of the algorithm is not essentially affected by the fact that PHASE $i = 2, 3, \ldots$, repeats the computation of PHASE $i - 1$ which for large i is approximately half as short (ignoring nonessential speed-ups due to halting programs if there are any).

As noted by Hutter [11], there is an essentially equivalent version of **FAST** which makes very clear just *how* simple the asymptotically optimal method really is:

> **FAST** (version 2): Execute one instruction of the n-th program every 2^n steps on average, using blanks to separate program outputs.

To see how we can obtain universal search [14][15, p. 502-505] from **FAST**, suppose we are seeking the solution y to some inversion problem $\phi(y) = x$. For instance, y might be a path through a maze providing reward $\phi(y) = 1$, while $\phi(z) = 0$ for uneffective paths z. Then we can use **FAST** to work through all programs and check for each whether it generates a path yielding reward. This will identify each reward-generating solution as quickly as the fastest algorithm that generates and tests that particular solution, save for a constant factor (which may be huge). Compare this to Hutter's recent more complex search algorithm for all well-defined problems [11] which reduces the unknown multiplicative constant factor to a remarkably small known value, namely, 5 — at the expense of introducing an unknown, problem class-specific, *additive* constant.

How does the optimal algorithm tie in with Postulate 1? Since the most efficient way of computing all x is embodied by **FAST**, which computes each x as quickly as x's fastest algorithm, save for a constant factor, and since each PHASE of **FAST** (version 1) consumes roughly twice the time and space resources of the previous PHASE, the cumulative prior probability of things first computed in any particular PHASE should be roughly half the one of the previous PHASE; zero probability should be assigned to infinitely resource-consuming PHASEs. Postulate 1 therefore suggests Definition 2 below.

Definition 1 $(p \to x, p \to_i x)$. *Given program prefix p, write $p \to x$ if our TM reads p and computes output starting with $x \in B^*$, while no prefix of p consisting of less than $l(p)$ bits outputs x. Write $p \to_i x$ if $p \to x$ in PHASE i of* **FAST**.

Definition 2 (Speed Prior S). *Define the Speed Prior S on B^* as*

$$S(x) := \sum_{i=1}^{\infty} 2^{-i} S_i(x); \quad where \quad S_i(\lambda) = 1; \; S_i(x) = \sum_{p \to_i x} 2^{-l(p)} \; for \; x \succ \lambda.$$

We observe that $S(x)$ is a semimeasure — compare [15]:

$$S(\lambda) = 1; \; S(x0) + S(x1) \leq S(x).$$

The very fact that a speed prior can be defined in a meaningful way is interesting in itself, and may also be relevant in some practical situations — see Section 5.

3   Speed Prior-Based Inductive Inference

Given S, as we observe an initial segment $x \in B^*$ of some string, which is the most likely continuation? According to Bayes,

$$S(xy \mid x) = \frac{S(x \mid xy)S(xy)}{S(x)} = \frac{S(xy)}{S(x)}, \tag{5}$$

where $S(z^2 \mid z^1)$ is the measure of z^2, given z^1. Having observed x we will predict those y that maximize $S(xy \mid x)$. Which are those? In what follows, we will confirm the intuition that for $n \to \infty$ the only probable continuations of x_n are those with fast programs. The sheer number of "slowly" computable strings cannot balance the speed advantage of "more quickly" computable strings with equal beginnings.

Definition 3 $(p \xrightarrow{<k}_i x$ *etc.*)**.** *Write $p \xrightarrow{<k} x$ if finite program p $(p \to x)$ computes x within less than k steps, and $p \xrightarrow{<k}_i x$ if it does so within PHASE i of* **FAST**. *Similarly for $p \xrightarrow{\leq k} x$ and $p \xrightarrow{\leq k}_i x$ (at most k steps), $p \xrightarrow{=k} x$, (exactly k steps), $p \xrightarrow{\geq k} x$, (at least k steps), $p \xrightarrow{>k} x$ (more than k steps).*

Theorem 1. *Suppose $x \in B^\infty$, $p^x \in B^*$ outputs x_n within at most $f(n)$ steps for all n, and $\lim_{n\to\infty} f(n)/g(n) = 0$. Then*

$$Q(x,g,f) := \lim_{n\to\infty} \frac{\sum_{i=1}^{\infty} 2^{-i} \sum_{p \xrightarrow{\geq g(n)}_i x_n} 2^{-l(p)}}{\sum_{i=1}^{\infty} 2^{-i} \sum_{p \xrightarrow{\leq f(n)}_i x_n} 2^{-l(p)}} = 0.$$

Proof. Since no program that requires at least $g(n)$ steps for producing x_n can compute x_n in a PHASE with number $< \log\ g(n)$, we have

$$Q(x,g,f) \leq \lim_{n\to\infty} \frac{\sum_{i=1}^{\infty} 2^{-\log\ g(n)-i} \sum_{p \xrightarrow{\geq g(n)}_{(i+\log\ g(n))} x_n} 2^{-l(p)}}{\sum_{i=1}^{\infty} 2^{-\log\ f(n)-i} \sum_{p \xrightarrow{=f(n)}_{i} x_n} 2^{-l(p)}}$$

$$\leq \lim_{n\to\infty} \frac{f(n) \sum_{p \to x_n} 2^{-l(p)}}{g(n) \sum_{p \xrightarrow{=f(n)} x_n} 2^{-l(p)}} \leq \lim_{n\to\infty} \frac{f(n)}{g(n)} \frac{1}{2^{-l(p^x)}} = 0.$$

Here we have used the Kraft inequality [13] to obtain a rough upper bound for the enumerator: when no p is prefix of another one, then $\sum_p 2^{-l(p)} \leq 1$. *Q.E.D.*

Hence, if we know a rather fast finite program p^x for x, then Theorem 1 allows for predicting: if we observe some x_n (n sufficiently large) then it is very unlikely that it was produced by an x-computing algorithm much slower than p^x.

  Among the fastest algorithms for x is **FAST** itself, which is at least as fast as p^x, save for a constant factor. It outputs x_n after $O(2^{Kt(x_n)})$ steps.

3.1   Algorithm GUESS

S can be implemented by the following probabilistic algorithm for a universal TM.

  Algorithm **GUESS**:
  1. Toss an unbiased coin until heads is up; let i denote the number of required trials; set $t := 2^i$.
  2. If the number of steps executed so far exceeds t then exit. Execute one step; if this leads to a request for a new input bit (of the growing selfdelimiting program, e.g., [15]), toss the coin to determine the bit, and set $t := t/2$.
  3. Go to **2**.

In the spirit of **FAST**, algorithm **GUESS** makes twice the computation time half as likely, and splits remaining time in half whenever a new input bit is requested, to assign equal runtime to the two resulting sets of possible program continuations. Note that the expected runtime of **GUESS** is unbounded since $\sum_i 2^{-i} 2^i$ does not converge. Still, each invocation of **GUESS** terminates with probability 1.

  Algorithm **GUESS** is almost identical to a probabilistic search algorithm used in previous work on applied inductive inference [19,21]. The programs generated by the previous algorithm, however, were not bitstrings but written in an assembler-like language; their runtimes had an upper bound, and the program outputs were evaluated as to whether they represented solutions to externally given tasks. Using a small set of exemplary training examples, the system discovered the weight matrix of an artificial neural network whose task was to map input data to appropriate target classifications. The network's generalization capability was then tested on a much larger unseen test set. On several toy problems it generalized extremely well in a way unmatchable by traditional neural network learning algorithms.

The previous papers, however, did not explicitly establish the relation mentioned above between "optimal" resource bias and **GUESS**.

3.2   Close Approximation of the Speed Prior

The precise value of $S(x)$ is only computable in the limit. However, within finite time we can compute $S(x)$ with arbitrary precision. There is a halting algorithm **AS** that takes as input x and some $\epsilon > 0$, and outputs an approximation $\bar{S}_\epsilon(x)$ such that

$$| \bar{S}_\epsilon(x) - S(x) | < \epsilon S(x). \tag{6}$$

AS works as follows:

> **Algorithm AS:**
> **1.** Run **FAST** until x is computed for the first time in PHASE $Kt(x)$. Let $n(x)$ denote the size of the smallest program for x found in this PHASE.
> **3.** Set $\bar{S}_\epsilon(x)$ equal to the sum of the contributions to $S(x)$ of all programs of all PHASEs up to the PHASE with number
>
> $$Kt(x) + n(x) + 1 - \log \epsilon.$$

AS halts after step **3** since any additional PHASEs are superfluous in the following sense: even if all their programs computed x, their cumulative contributions to $S(x)$ could not exceed $\epsilon S(x)$.

3.3   Computable Predictions

Given observation x and some $\epsilon > 0$, we use AS to approximate all possibly relevant $S(xy)$ within ϵ accuracy, and predict a continuation y with maximal $\bar{S}_\epsilon(xy)$. This ensures that no $z \neq y$ can yield some $S(xz)$ significantly exceeding $S(xy)$.

That is, with S comes a computable method for predicting optimally within ϵ accuracy. This contrasts with Solomonoff's noncomputable method.

4   Machine Dependence / Suboptimal Computation of the Data: Expected Loss Bounds

So far we have assumed the process computing the data is (asymptotically) optimally efficient, running on a particular universal computer, our reference machine. In general, however, we cannot know the machine used to run this process. Furthermore, the process may be nonoptimal even with respect to its machine. For such reasons we now relax our initial assumption, and show that S-based predictions on our reference machine still work well.

Consider a finite but unknown program p computing $y \in B^\infty$. What if Postulate 1 holds but p is not optimally efficient, and/or computed on a computer that differs from our reference machine? Then we effectively do not sample beginnings y_k from S but from an alternative semimeasure

$$S'(y_k) \leq 1/t$$

for any y_k whose computation through p costs more than $O(t)$ time. Can we still predict well? Yes, because the Speed Prior S dominates S': For all $x \in B^*$,

$$S(x) \geq c_{S'} S'(x), \tag{7}$$

where $c_{S'}$ is a constant depending on S' but not on x, because **FAST** computes y faster than p, and thus $S(y_k) \geq O(1/t)$. This dominance is all we need to apply Hutter's recent loss bounds [9]:

Corollary 1 (Unit loss bound). *Suppose initial sequence prefixes x_n are drawn with true but unknown probability $S'(x_n)$. A system predicts the $k + 1$st sequence element, given x_k, and receives loss $\in [0, 1]$ depending on the true $k+1$st symbol. The $\Lambda_{S'}$-system is optimal in the sense that it predicts as to minimize the S'-expected loss; Λ_S minimizes the S-expected loss. For the first n symbols, the total S'-expected losses $L_{n\Lambda_S}$ of Λ_S and $L_{n\Lambda_{S'}}$ of $\Lambda_{S'}$ are bounded as follows:*

$$0 \leq L_{n\Lambda_S} - L_{n\Lambda_{S'}} = O(\sqrt{L_{n\Lambda_{S'}}}).$$

In practice we have to use $\bar{S}_\epsilon$ instead of S. Does that cost us a lot? Again the answer is no, since for any $\epsilon > 0$,

$$\bar{S}_\epsilon(x) \geq c_S S(x), \tag{8}$$

where c_S is a constant independent of x. That is, in analogy to Corollary 1 (using analogous notation) we obtain

$$0 \leq L_{n\Lambda_{\bar{S}_\epsilon}} - L_{n\Lambda_{S'}} = O(\sqrt{L_{n\Lambda_{S'}}}). \tag{9}$$

To summarize: The loss that we are expected to receive by predicting according to computable $\bar{S}_\epsilon$ instead of the true but unknown S' does not exceed the optimal loss by much.

4.1   Relation to a Popular Classical Approach

It is not hard to show that if we use, say, the Bernoulli model class and the uniform prior and predict using the Bayes predictive distribution (i.e., Laplace's rule of succession), and the data is generated by a process that has indeed a stationary distribution, then with probability 1 our predictions will converge to the predictions that are optimal according to the stationary distribution although strings sampled from the stationary distribution are extremely hard to compute. In addition, the classical approach does not cost much. Hence sometimes (when the assumptions happen to be correct) it is preferrable, and it may also help us to do reasonable (though non-optimal) prediction, no matter whether the true distribution is computable or not. But unlike Laplace's approach the present one also yields asymptotically optimal predictions under the (strong but intriguing) assumption that the data is generated deterministically under certain resource constraints.

It will be of interest to identify the precise set of priors dominated by S.

4.2   Rational Decision Makers Based on Universal Predictors

The sections above treated the case of passive prediction, given the observations. Note, however, that agents interacting with an environment can also use predictions of the future to compute action sequences that maximize expected future reward. Hutter's *AIXI model* [10] does exactly this, by combining Solomonoff's M-based universal prediction scheme with an *expectimax* computation. It can be shown that the conditional M probability of environmental inputs to an AIXI agent, given the agent's earlier inputs and actions, converges with increasing length of interaction against the true, unknown probability [10], as long as the latter is recursively computable, analogously to the passive prediction case.

We can modify the AIXI model such that its predictions are based on the ϵ-approximable Speed Prior S instead of the incomputable M. Thus we obtain the so-called *AIS model*. Using Hutter's approach [10] we can now show that the conditional S probability of environmental inputs to an AIS agent, given the earlier inputs and actions, converges against the true but unknown probability, as long as the latter is dominated by S, such as the S' in subsection 4.

5   Physics

Note: this section can be skipped by readers who are interested in the theoretical framework only, not in its potential implications for the real world.

Virtual realities used for pilot training or video games are rapidly becoming more and more convincing, as each decade computers are getting roughly 1000 times faster per dollar — a consequence of Moore's law first formulated in 1965. At the current pace, however, the Bremermann limit [2] of roughly 10^{51} operations per second, on not more than 10^{32} bits for the "ultimate laptop" [16] with 1 kg of mass and 1 liter of volume, will not be reachable within this century, and there is no obvious reason why Moore's law should break down any time soon. Thus a simple extrapolation has led many to predict that within a few decades computers will match brains in terms of raw computing power, and that soon there will be reasonably complex virtual worlds inhabited by reasonably complex virtual beings.

In the past decades numerous science fiction authors have anticipated this trend in novels about simulated humans living on sufficiently fast digital machines, e.g., [7]. But even serious and reputable computer pioneers have suggested that the universe essentially is just a computer. In particular, the "inventor of the computer" Konrad Zuse not only created the world's first binary machines in the 1930s, the first working programmable computer in 1941, and the first higher-level programming language around 1945, but also introduced the concept of *Computing Space (Rechnender Raum)*, suggesting that all physical events are just results of calculations on a grid of numerous communicating processors [28]. Even earlier, Gottfried Wilhelm von Leibniz (who not only co-invented calculus but also built the first mechanical multiplier in 1670) caused a stir by claiming that everything is computable (compare C. Schmidhuber's concept of the *mathscape* [18]).

So it does not seem entirely ludicrous to study consequences of the idea that we are really living in a "simulation," one that is real enough to make many of its "inhabitants" smile at the mere thought of being computed. In absence of contrarian evidence, let us assume for a moment that the physical world around us is indeed generated by a computational process, and that any possible sequence of observations is therefore computable in the limit [22]. For example, let x be an infinite sequence of finite bitstrings $x^1, x^2, \ldots$ representing the history of some discrete universe, where x^k represents the state of the universe at discrete time step k, and x^1 the "Big Bang" [20]. Suppose there is a finite algorithm A that computes x^{k+1} ($k \geq 1$) from x^k and additional information $noise^k$ (this may require numerous computational steps of A, that is, "local" time of the universe may run comparatively slowly). Assume that $noise^k$ is not truly random but calculated by invoking a finite pseudorandom generator subroutine. Then x has a finite constructive description and is computable in the limit.

Contrary to a widely spread misunderstanding, quantum physics and Heisenberg's uncertainty principle do *not* rule out such pseudorandomness in the apparently random or noisy physical observations — compare reference [26] by 't Hooft (physics Nobel prize 1999).

If our computability assumption holds then in general we cannot know which machine is used to compute the data. But it seems plausible to assume that it does suffer from a computational resource problem, that is, the *a priori* probability of investing resources into any computation tends to decrease with growing computational costs.

To evaluate the plausibility of this, consider that most data generated on your own computer are computable within a few microseconds, some take a few seconds, few take hours, very few take days, etc... Similarly, most files on your machine are small, few are large, very few are very large. Obviously, anybody wishing to become a "God-like Great Programmer" by programming and simulating universes [20] will have a strong built-in bias towards easily computable ones. This provokes the notion of a "Frugal Creator" (Leonid Levin, personal communication, 2001).

The reader will have noticed that this line of thought leads straight to the Speed Prior S discussed in the previous sections. It may even lend some additional motivation to S.

S-based Predictions. Now we are ready for an extreme application. Assuming that the entire history of our universe is sampled from S or a less dominant prior reflecting suboptimal computation of the history, we can immediately predict: **1.** Our universe will not get many times older than it is now [22] — the probability that its history will extend beyond the one computable in the current phase of **FAST** (that is, it will be prolongated into the next phase) is at most 50 %; infinite futures have measure zero. **2.** Any apparent randomness in any physical observation must be due to some yet unknown but *fast* pseudo-random generator PRG [22] which we should try to discover. **2a.** A re-examination of beta decay patterns may reveal that a very simple, fast, but maybe not quite trivial PRG is responsible for the apparently random decays of neutrons into protons, electrons and antineutrinos. **2b.** Whenever there are several possible continuations of our universe corresponding to different Schrödinger wave function collapses — compare Everett's widely accepted many worlds hypothesis [5] — we should be more likely to end up in one computable by a short *and* fast algorithm. A re-examination of split experiment data involving entangled states such as the observations of spins of initially close but soon distant particles with correlated spins might reveil unexpected, nonobvious, nonlocal algorithmic regularity due to a fast PRG. **3.** Large scale quantum computation [1] will not work well, essentially because it would require too many exponentially growing computational resources in interfering "parallel universes" [5].

Prediction **2** is verifiable but not necessarily falsifiable within a fixed time interval given in advance. Still, perhaps the main reason for the current absence of empirical evidence in this vein is that nobody has systematically looked for it yet.

The broader context. The concept of dominance is useful for predicting prediction quality. Let x denote the history of a universe. If x is sampled from an *enumerable* or *recursive* prior then M-based prediction will work well, since M dominates all enumerable priors. If x is sampled from an even more dominant *cumulatively enumerable* measure CEM [22] then we may use the fact that there is a universal CEM μ^E that dominates M and all other CEMs [22,23]. Using Hutter's loss bounds [9] we obtain a good μ^E-based predictor. Certain even more dominant priors [22,23] also allow for nonrecursive optimal predictions computable in the limit. The price to pay for recursive computability of S-based inference is the loss of dominance with respect to M, μ^E, etc.

The computability assumptions embodied by the various priors mentioned above add predictive power to the *anthropic principle* (AP) [3] which essentially just says that the conditional probability of finding oneself in a universe compatible with one's existence will always remain 1 — the AP by itself does not allow for any additional nontrivial predictions.

6 Conclusion

Unlike the traditional universal prior M, the Speed Prior S is recursively approximable with arbitrary precision. This allows for deriving an asymptotically optimal *recursive* way of computing predictions, based on a natural discount of the probability of data that is hard to compute by any method. This markedly contrasts with Solomonoff's traditional *non*computable approach to optimal prediction based on the weaker assumption of recursively computable priors that completely ignore resource limitations [24,25].

Our expected loss bounds building on Hutter's recent work show that S-based prediction is quite accurate as long as the true unknown prior is less dominant than S, reflecting an observation-generating process on some unknown computer that is not optimally efficient.

Assuming that our universe is sampled from a prior that does not dominate S we obtain several nontrivial predictions for physics.

Acknowledgment

The material presented here is based on section 6 of [22]. Thanks to Ray Solomonoff, Leonid Levin, Marcus Hutter, Christof Schmidhuber, and an unknown reviewer, for useful comments.

References

1. C. H. Bennett and D. P. DiVicenzo. Quantum information and computation. *Nature*, 404(6775):256–259, 2000. 226
2. H. J. Bremermann. Minimum energy requirements of information transfer and computing. *International Journal of Theoretical Physics*, 21:203–217, 1982. 224
3. B. Carter. Large number coincidences and the anthropic principle in cosmology. In M. S. Longair, editor, *Proceedings of the IAU Symposium 63*, pages 291–298. Reidel, Dordrecht, 1974. 226
4. G. J. Chaitin. On the length of programs for computing finite binary sequences: statistical considerations. *Journal of the ACM*, 16:145–159, 1969. 218
5. H. Everett III. 'Relative State' formulation of quantum mechanics. *Reviews of Modern Physics*, 29:454–462, 1957. 226
6. P. Gács. On the relation between descriptional complexity and algorithmic probability. *Theoretical Computer Science*, 22:71–93, 1983. 217
7. D. F. Galouye. *Simulacron 3*. Bantam, 1964. 225
8. M. Hutter. Convergence and error bounds of universal prediction for general alphabet. *Proceedings of the 12th European Conference on Machine Learning (ECML-2001)*, (TR IDSIA-07-01, cs.AI/0103015), 2001. 217, 218
9. M. Hutter. General loss bounds for universal sequence prediction. In C. E. Brodley and A. P. Danyluk, editors, *Proceedings of the 18th International Conference on Machine Learning (ICML-2001)*, pages 210–217. Morgan Kaufmann, 2001. TR IDSIA-03-01, IDSIA, Switzerland, Jan 2001, cs.AI/0101019. 218, 223, 226

10. M. Hutter. Towards a universal theory of artificial intelligence based on algorithmic probability and sequential decisions. *Proceedings of the 12th European Conference on Machine Learning (ECML-2001)*, (TR IDSIA-14-00, cs.AI/0012011), 2001. 224
11. M. Hutter. The fastest and shortest algorithm for all well-defined problems. *International Journal of Foundations of Computer Science*, (TR IDSIA-16-00, cs.CC/0102018), 2002. In press. 219
12. A. N. Kolmogorov. Three approaches to the quantitative definition of information. *Problems of Information Transmission*, 1:1–11, 1965. 218
13. L. G. Kraft. A device for quantizing, grouping, and coding amplitude modulated pulses. M.Sc. Thesis, Dept. of Electrical Engineering, MIT, Cambridge, Mass., 1949. 221
14. L. A. Levin. Universal sequential search problems. *Problems of Information Transmission*, 9(3):265–266, 1973. 219
15. M. Li and P. M. B. Vitányi. *An Introduction to Kolmogorov Complexity and its Applications (2nd edition)*. Springer, 1997. 217, 218, 219, 220, 221
16. S. Lloyd. Ultimate physical limits to computation. *Nature*, 406:1047–1054, 2000. 224
17. J. Rissanen. Stochastic complexity and modeling. *The Annals of Statistics*, 14(3):1080–1100, 1986. 218
18. C. Schmidhuber. Strings from logic. Technical Report CERN-TH/2000-316, CERN, Theory Division, 2000. http://xxx.lanl.gov/abs/hep-th/0011065. 225
19. J. Schmidhuber. Discovering solutions with low Kolmogorov complexity and high generalization capability. In A. Prieditis and S. Russell, editors, *Machine Learning: Proceedings of the Twelfth International Conference*, pages 488–496. Morgan Kaufmann Publishers, San Francisco, CA, 1995. 221
20. J. Schmidhuber. A computer scientist's view of life, the universe, and everything. In C. Freksa, M. Jantzen, and R. Valk, editors, *Foundations of Computer Science: Potential - Theory - Cognition*, volume 1337, pages 201–208. Lecture Notes in Computer Science, Springer, Berlin, 1997. 225
21. J. Schmidhuber. Discovering neural nets with low Kolmogorov complexity and high generalization capability. *Neural Networks*, 10(5):857–873, 1997. 221
22. J. Schmidhuber. Algorithmic theories of everything. Technical Report IDSIA-20-00, quant-ph/0011122, IDSIA, Manno (Lugano), Switzerland, 2000. 218, 225, 226, 227
23. J. Schmidhuber. Hierarchies of generalized Kolmogorov complexities and nonenumerable universal measures computable in the limit. *International Journal of Foundations of Computer Science*, 2002. In press. 218, 226
24. R. J. Solomonoff. A formal theory of inductive inference. Part I. *Information and Control*, 7:1–22, 1964. 217, 218, 227
25. R. J. Solomonoff. Complexity-based induction systems. *IEEE Transactions on Information Theory*, IT-24(5):422–432, 1978. 217, 218, 227
26. G. 't Hooft. Quantum gravity as a dissipative deterministic system. Technical Report SPIN-1999/07/gr-gc/9903084, http://xxx.lanl.gov/abs/gr-qc/9903084, Institute for Theoretical Physics, Univ. of Utrecht, and Spinoza Institute, Netherlands, 1999. Also published in *Classical and Quantum Gravity 16*, 3263. 225
27. C. S. Wallace and D. M. Boulton. An information theoretic measure for classification. *Computer Journal*, 11(2):185–194, 1968. 218
28. K. Zuse. *Rechnender Raum*. Friedrich Vieweg & Sohn, Braunschweig, 1969. 225
29. A. K. Zvonkin and L. A. Levin. The complexity of finite objects and the algorithmic concepts of information and randomness. *Russian Math. Surveys*, 25(6):83–124, 1970. 217

New Lower Bounds
for Statistical Query Learning

Ke Yang[*]

Computer Science Department, Carnegie Mellon University
5000 Forbes Ave., Pittsburgh, PA 15213, USA
yangke@cs.cmu.edu
http://www.cs.cmu.edu/~yangke

Abstract. We prove two lower bounds on the Statistical Query (SQ) learning model. The first lower bound is on weak-learning. We prove that for a concept class of SQ-dimension d, a running time of $\Omega(d/\log d)$ is needed. The SQ-dimension of a concept class is defined to be the maximum number of concepts that are "uniformly correlated", in that each pair of them have nearly the same correlation. This lower bound matches the upper bound in [BFJ+94], up to a logarithmic factor. We prove this lower bound against an "honest SQ-oracle", which gives a stronger result than the ones against the more frequently used "adversarial SQ-oracles". The second lower bound is more general. It gives a continuous trade-off between the "advantage" of an algorithm in learning the target function and the number of queries it needs to make, where the advantage of an algorithm is the probability it succeeds in predicting a label minus the probability it doesn't. Both lower bounds extend and/or strengthen previous results, and solved an open problem left in [Y01].

1 Introduction

1.1 The Statistical Query Model

The Statistical Query (SQ) model was first introduced by Kearns [K93]. Unlike the Probably Approximately Correct (PAC)-model [V84], a learning algorithm in the SQ model doesn't see explicit examples or their labels. Instead, the algorithm queries an "SQ-oracle" with boolean questions about a random example with its label. Then the oracle replies with estimates of the probabilities that the answer is "YES" for a random example. An apparent restriction of the PAC model, the SQ model proved to be a very powerful and useful notion. Kearns showed how to efficiently simulate an SQ learning algorithm using a PAC algorithm, even in the presence of noise. He also proved that many PAC algorithms are indeed "SQ-typed", meaning that they can be converted to work in the SQ model. Particularly interesting is the case of noise-tolerant learning, where a random fraction of the examples are labeled wrong. In fact, most of the noise-tolerant

---

[*] Partially supported by the CMU SCS Alumni Fellowship and the NSF Aladdin center, Grant CCR-0122581.

J. Kivinen and R. H. Sloan (Eds.): COLT 2002, LNAI 2375, pp. 229–243, 2002.

PAC learning algorithms are "SQ-typed", due to the noise-tolerant nature inherent in the SQ model.

Given that the SQ model is so useful, it is rather desirable to fully understand its strengths and limits. Right from the moment when SQ model was introduced, people have been interested in the question "which concept classes are SQ-learnable, and which are provably not?". In fact, in the seminal paper on the SQ model, Kearns [K93] proved that PARITY functions are not SQ-learnable. Blum. et. al. [BFJ+94] defined the notion of "SQ-dimension" of a concept class, which is, roughly speaking, the number of "almost uncorrelated" concepts in this class. The SQ-dimension characterizes the weak SQ-learnability very well. In fact, Blum et. al. proved that, to weakly learn a concept class of SQ-dimension d, $O(d)$ queries suffices (though the algorithm might not be efficient), and $\Omega(d^{1/3})$ queries are necessary. However, the upper bound and the lower bound don't match, and their results are only for weak learning. Jackson [J00] proved that for an "SQ-based" algorithm, $\Omega(2^n)$ examples are needed to learning the class of PARITY functions over n bits. An SQ-based algorithm is constructed by first designing an SQ learning algorithm, and then generically simulating each SQ query by sampling and averaging. This lower bound matches the corresponding upper bound. With this very strong result, Jackson was able to show a quadratic gap on learning PARITY functions with a high $(1/2 - 1/\text{poly}(n))$ noise rate by SQ-learning and by PAC-learning. He demonstrated a PAC algorithm that learns noisy PARITY with running time $O(2^{n/2})$, while any SQ-based algorithm needs running time $\Omega(2^n)$.

Along another line of research, Yang [Y01] considered the problem of learning *uniformly correlated* concepts in the SQ model. That paper extended the notion of "SQ-dimension" to the case where each pair of concepts are "correlated in the same way". For correlated concept classes, it could be trivial to weakly learn a concept (in some cases, even without making any query), but it takes exponential time to do strong learning. Yang proved an $\Omega(d^{1/2}S)$ lower bound for learning such a concept class of SQ-dimension d with an "extra advantage" S. This result implies the SQ-unlearnability of the class of Linear Threshold Functions (LTFs) over finite fields. He also showed a PAC algorithm that beats the the best possible SQ algorithms in learning a special class of LTFs. An open problem from [Y01] is to characterize the SQ-learnability of general concept classes where the concepts can be *arbitrarily* correlated.

1.2   Variants of SQ-oracles

Different models of SQ-oracles have been proposed in the literature. Probably the most used one, which we call the "adversarial model", is the one introduced by Kearns in his original paper [K93]. In this model, the algorithm gives the oracle a query function g and an additive "error tolerance" ϵ. The oracle is allowed to reply with *any* real number that is ϵ-close to the expected value of g on a random labelled example. Notice this oracle is adversarial in natural, since it has the freedom to (adversarially) choose which real number to reply. This is a very nice model to prove *upper bounds*, since this gives a *worst-case* guarantee: an algorithm that works with such a adversatial oracle will surely work well with an SQ-oracle simulated by sampling. However, there are problems for proving *lower bounds* for this model. A typical strategy in the lower bound proofs [K93, BFJ+94] is to construct a "bad" oracle. This oracle doesn't commit to any particular target concept. Rather, on each query, the oracle replies with a value that is "consistent" with many "candidate concepts". The argument is that if not enough queries are made, the oracle will always be able to give answers that are consistent with many concepts. In this case, the learning algorithm won't be able to learn very well.

However, one potential problem with this oracle model is: this is not what really happens in practice. In practice, one normally *simulates* an SQ-oracle using a PAC learning algorithm. The simulation is done by repeated sampling and averaging the query function over these examples. There is nothing "adversarial" in the simulation and the simulated SQ-oracle behaves very differently from the adversarial oracle used in the lower bound proofs. Thus, one possibility remains that the lower bounds only hold for an adversarial oracle, but not for the ones simulated by PAC algorithms. In other words, there could be concept classes that are not learnable with an adversarial SQ-oracle but are learnable by an "SQ-style" PAC algorithm. If this "gap" indeed exists, that would imply that this adversarial SQ-oracle is too strong in favor of the adversarial oracle. If this is the case, then a lower bound against an adversarial oracle is a lower bound more for this particular oracle than for the inherent nature of the SQ model.

Several efforts have been made to remedy this problem with the "gap". Jackson [J00] introduced the notion of an "SQ-based PAC algorithm" to prove the $\Omega(2^n)$ lower bound for learning PARITY. Intuitively, an SQ-based PAC algorithm is constructed in the following way. One first designs a learning algorithm in the SQ-model. Then the SQ algorithm is "generically" simulated by a PAC algorithm in the most straightforward way. One important assumption about this generic simulation is that the algorithm cannot use any "internal knowledge" about the query function, nor any "clever tricks" to make the simulation more efficient. This assumption might seem a bit too strong in practice, since clever tricks are normally quite desirable in algorithm design. For example, Aslam and Decatur considered using *relative error* instead of additive error to efficiently simulate an SQ oracle [AS95]. Jackson's result didn't rule out the possibility that algorithms using such a simulation can learning PARITY functions more efficiently. Yang [Y01] introduced the model of "honest SQ-oracles". In this model, the oracle receives a query g and a *sample count* M. Then the oracle independently picks M random labeled examples and returns the average of g on these examples. Intuitively, the honest SQ-oracle model can be regarded as the "SQ-based PAC" model without the "no-clever-trick" assumption. Any lower bound for algorithms using the honest SQ-oracle automatically translates to a lower bound for "SQ-base PAC" algorithms and a lower bound in the adversarial SQ-oracle model. The technique used in [Y01] was to keep track different "scenarios" when different concepts are chosen as targets, and to measure the "all-pair statistical distance" across the scenarios. This technique allows us to work in the new model, but it wasn't powerful enough to yield a tight lower bound.

1.3   Our Contributions

In this paper, we prove two lower bounds for SQ-learning algorithms. The first lower bound considers a concept class that contains a subset of uniformly correlated concepts, where each pair is correlated "in the same way". We define the *SQ-dimension* of a concept class to be the maximum number of such uniformly correlated concepts in this class. We also consider the *total sample count* of an algorithm, which is the sum of the sample counts of all the queries it makes to an honest SQ-oracle. We prove that a learning algorithm must have sample count of $\Omega(d/\log d)$ to learn a concept class of SQ-dimension d. This lower bound almost matches the upper bound given in [BFJ+94] (up to a logarithmic factor), and is strong enough to imply the quadratic separation of SQ- and PAC- learning of the PARITY functions at a high noise rate. Furthermore, this lower bound applies to a wide range of concept classes and uses a different model for SQ-oracles. The proof uses several techniques, some of which could be of independent interests. As in [Y01], we still keep track of the "differences" across the scenarios with different concepts as targets. However, we use a different measure, namely the all-pair KL-divergence. This new measure can yield a very tight bound when the queries are "reasonably unbiased", i.e., when the probability that the query function returns "+1" on a random example is close to $1/2$. But the KL-divergence measure becomes very bad when we have biased queries. In that case, we use an unbiased query to "simulate" a biased one. Combining these 2 techniques together allows us to prove a very tight lower bound.

The second lower bound is for *arbitrary* concept classes. We define a "correlation matrix", whose entries are the correlations of pairs of concepts. We prove that for an algorithm to have ξ advantage in learning by making q queries to an adversarial SQ-oracle with tolerance ξ, then the sum of the $(q+1)$ largest eigenvalues of the correlation matrix must be at least $d \cdot \xi^2$. Here d is the cardinality of the concept class. This result shows a continuous trade-off between the advantage an algorithm can have and the number of queries it needs to make. This trade-off could be useful in designing learning algorithms of certain requirement on the accuracy and confidence. This lower bound is a very general one: as we shall see in Section 4.4, this lower bound almost immediately imply some previous results [BFJ+94, Y01], and sometimes yields even stronger ones. The proof to this lower bound uses the Singular Value Decomposition (SVD). This connection could also be of its independent interests.

1.4   Organization of the Rest of the Paper

We present the notations and definitions used in the paper in Section 2. We prove the 2 lower bounds in Section 3 and Section 4, respectively. We conclude the paper in Section 5. Due to the space constraint, some proofs are omitted and will appear in the full version of this paper.

2   Notations and Definitions

2.1   Mathematical Notations

All logarithms are natural log. All random distributions are over binary strings. We naturally identify a random variable with a probabilistic distribution. For distributions X and Y, we use XY to denote their *direct product*:

$$XY(x, y) = X(x) \cdot Y(y).$$

This definition coincides with that of the *concatenation* of independent random variables X and Y.

2.2   Learning Concepts

We use Ω to denote a finite set of binary strings, and we are interested in learning *concepts* over Ω, i.e., functions that map elements in Ω to $\{-1, +1\}$. Elements in Ω are also called *examples*. A collection of concepts is often denoted by $\mathcal{F} = \{f_1, f_2, ..., f_S\}$, and is called a *concept class*. Each member in $\mathcal{F}$ is a *candidate concept*, and one of them, called a *target concept* is chosen for the learning algorithm to learn.

We fix an arbitrary order for the elements in Ω, and then identify a function over Ω with the vector represented by its truth table. Let D be a (fixed) probabilistic distribution over Ω. There exists an inner product of functions over Ω induced by D, defined as

$$\langle f, g \rangle_D = \sum_{x \in \Omega} D(x) f(x) g(x)$$

When there is no danger of ambiguity, we omit the subscript D. The inner product of f and g is also called the *correlation* between f and g. In the case that both f and g concepts, $\langle f, g \rangle$ is the probability f and g agree on a random input minus the probability they disagree.

The *norm* of function f is defined as $||f|| = \sqrt{\langle f, f \rangle}$. Clearly all concepts have norm 1.

2.3   The Statistical Query Model

We present two different definitions of SQ-oracles.

Definition 2.1 (Adversarial SQ-oracle). *A query to an* adversarial *SQ-oracle for concept f is a pair (g, τ), where $g : \Omega \times \{-1, +1\} \to \{-1, +1\}$ is a boolean function, called the* query function, *and $\tau \in [0, 1]$ is real number, called the* tolerance. *The oracle replies with an (arbitrary) real number s such that*

$$|s - E_D[g(X, f(X))]| \leq \tau$$

This definition, introduced by by Kearns [K93], is used by most literature in the SQ model.

Definition 2.2 (Honest SQ-oracle). *A query to an* honest SQ-oracle *for concept f is a pair (g, M), where $g : \Omega \times \{-1, +1\} \to \{-1, +1\}$ is a boolean function, called the* query function, *and M is a positive integer written in unary, called the* sample count. *The oracle returns a random variable r defined by $r = \frac{1}{M} \sum_{i=1}^{M} g(X_i, f(X_i))$ where each X_i is independently chosen according to D.*

This definition was introduced by Yang [Y01]. It is straightforward to show that one can use an honest SQ-oracle to simulate an adversarial oracle. Intuitively, the honest SQ-oracle describes how a PAC algorithm simulates an SQ algorithm more precisely than the adversarial SQ-oracle. In this sense, the honest SQ-oracle is more "realistic".

3   The First Lower Bound

We prove the first lower bound on learning a concept class where every pair of concepts are "correlated in the same way". Our lower bound is against an honest SQ-oracle. With respect to such an oracle, we define the *total sample count* of an algorithm to be the sum of the sample counts of all the queries it makes. Since we require the sample counts to be written in unary, the total sample count of an algorithm is a lower bound on its running time. We shall prove a lower bound on the total sample count of the learning algorithms.

Our proof strategy is similar to that in [Y01]. Roughly speaking, one considers d different "scenarios": in the j-th scenario, the concept f_j is the target. A quantity Δ, namely the "all-pair L_2 statistical distance" is defined over these scenarios. Three lemmas are then proved:

1. The quantity Δ is initially zero, when no query is performed.
2. Each query increases Δ by a "small" amount.
3. After all the queries are made, Δ much be "large".

Then, from these three lemmas, one concludes that many queries are required.

In this paper, we replace the "all-pair L_2 statistical distance" by another quantity, namely the "all-pair KL-divergence". We shall prove three lemmas similar to that in [Y01].

3.1   KL-divergence

We first present a definition of the KL-divergence, or Kullback-Leibler divergence [KL51].

Definition 3.1 (KL-divergence). *For 2 random variables P, Q with identical support, we define their KL-divergence to be* [1]

$$KL(P||Q) = \sum_{x} P(x) \cdot \log \left(\frac{P(x)}{Q(x)} \right).$$

---

[1] A slight difference for our definition here is that we are using the natural log, instead of log base-2. But the properties will not be affected by the change of the base.

The reader is referred to [KL51, K59, B95] for a comprehensive treatise on the KL-divergence, including the proofs to the properties we state below.

Lemma 3.1 (Identical Distribution). *If P and Q have identical distributions, then $KL(P||Q) = 0$.* □

Lemma 3.2 (Direct Product). *Let P_1, P_2 and Q_1, Q_2 be distributions such that P_i and Q_i have identical support for $i = 1, 2$. We have*

$$KL(P_1 P_2 || Q_1 Q_2) = KL(P_1 || Q_1) + KL(P_2 || Q_2). \tag{1}$$

□

Lemma 3.3 (Monotonicity). *Let P and Q be random variables of identical support and let ϕ be a deterministic function. Then*

$$KL(\phi(P)||\phi(Q)) \le KL(P||Q). \tag{2}$$

□

Lemma 3.4 (Binomial Distribution). *Let P and Q be Bernoulli distributions with parameters p and q, i.e., $P(0) = 1 - p$, $P(1) = p$, $Q(0) = 1 - q$, and $Q(1) = q$. Let P_n and Q_n be binomial distributions with parameters (n, p) and (n, q), respectively, i.e., $P_n(k) = \binom{n}{k} p^k (1-p)^{n-k}$ and $Q_n(k) = \binom{n}{k} q^k (1-q)^{n-k}$. Then we have*

$$KL(P_n || Q_n) = n \cdot KL(P, Q). \tag{3}$$

□

For n distributions $X_1, X_2, ..., X_n$ of identical support, we define their *all-pair KL-divergence* (APKL) to be

$$\mathsf{APKL}(X_1, X_2, ..., X_n) = \sum_{i=1}^{n} \sum_{j=1}^{n} KL(X_i || X_j).$$

3.2 SQ-dimension for Correlated Concept Classes

We adopt the definition of the SQ-dimension of a concept class from [Y01].

Definition 3.2 (SQ-dimension [Y01]). *The SQ-dimension of a concept class $\mathcal{F}$ with respect to D, denoted by $\mathsf{SQ\text{-}DIM}(\mathcal{F}, D)$, is the largest natural number d such that there exists a real number λ, satisfying $0 \le \lambda \le 1/2$, and d concepts $f_1, f_2, ..., f_d \in \mathcal{F}$ with the property that for all $i \ne j$,*

$$|\langle f_i, f_j \rangle - \lambda| \le 1/d^3. \tag{4}$$

We call λ the correlation *of $\mathcal{F}$.*[2]

---

[2] Pedantically, given such a concept class $\mathcal{F}$, there might exist infinitely many λ's satisfying (4), all within a range of size up to $1/d^3$. If this is the case, we choose the *minimal* λ that satisfies (4) as the correlation of $\mathcal{F}$.

Notice that our definition is different from the definition from [BFJ+94]. An important result from [Y01] to be used here is:

Lemma 3.5 (Fourier Analysis for the Query Function, [Y01]). *We follow the notations in Definition 3.2. Let $f_1, f_2, ..., f_d$ be the concepts satisfying $|\langle f_i, f_j \rangle - \lambda| \leq 1/d^3$, and d be the SQ-dimension of $\mathcal{F}$. Let $g(x, y)$ be a query function. There exist real numbers $\beta_1, \beta_2, ..., \beta_d$, such that $\sum_{i=1}^{d} \beta_i^2 \leq 1 + 100/d$ for $d > 100$ and*

$$E_D[g(X, f_i(X))] = C_g + \sqrt{1 - \lambda} \cdot \beta_i \tag{5}$$

for every $i = 1, 2, ..., d$. where C_g is a constant that is independent of the target concept f_i. □

We call C_g the *inherent bias* of g.

3.3   Three Lemmas about the All-Pair KL-divergence

Like in [Y01], we model a learning algorithm A as a randomized Turing Machine. It makes a total of q queries, and at the end of these queries, a random input X is presented to A. Suppose f_j is the target concept, then A must predict $f_j(X)$ with sufficient accuracy.

In the case that f_j is the target concept, we define the *state* of A after the k-th query to be the binary string S_k^j that describes the contents on A's tapes, the position of the heads, the current internal state of A. We define S_0^j to be the state of A before it starts. Notice each S_k^j is a random variable: the randomness comes from both the SQ-oracle and the random tape A uses. The j-th scenario, S^j is simply the concatenation of all the states: $S^j = (S_0^j, S_1^j, ..., S_q^j)$.

We define Δ_k to be the all-pair KL-divergence of $S_k^1, S_k^2, ..., S_k^d$:

$$\Delta_k = \mathsf{APKL}(S_k^1, S_k^2, ..., S_k^d).$$

Intuitively, Δ_k measures how "differently" A behaves with different target concepts. We shall focus on how Δ_k changes with k.

We state the following 3 lemmas:

Lemma 3.6. *The all-pair KL-divergence is initially zero, that is $\Delta_0 = 0$.*

Proof. This is obvious since A hasn't made any queries yet, and the state of A is independent of the target concept. Thus $S_0^1, S_0^2, ..., S_0^d$ have identical distributions. □

We say query function $g(x, y)$ is an *ideal query function*, if

$$| E_D[g(X, f_i(X))] | \leq \frac{1}{2}$$

for $i = 1, 2, ..., d$. Intuitively, if $g(x, y)$ is ideal, then it is not highly biased in any scenario.

Ideal queries are nice since they don't increase the all-pair KL-divergence much, as shown in the following lemma.

Lemma 3.7. *Suppose the k-th query to an honest SQ-oracle by the algorithm is (g, M), where g is an ideal query. then*

$$\Delta_k - \Delta_{k-1} \leq 3Md$$

for $d > 200$.   □

The proof is omitted due to space constraints.

Lemma 3.8. *If the learning algorithm A has accuracy ϵ and confidence δ, satisfying $24(\epsilon + \delta) \leq 1 - \lambda - 1/d^3$, then after all the queries are made, we have*

$$\Delta_q \geq 0.2d^2$$

for $d \geq 3$.   □

The proof is omitted due to space constraints.

Now if we combine Lemma 3.6, Lemma 3.7, and Lemma 3.8, we can already prove an $\Omega(d)$ lower bound on the running time of algorithms that only use ideal queries:

Lemma 3.9. *Suppose $\mathcal{F}$ is a concept class of SQ-dimension $d > 200$ with correlation λ. Let A be a learning algorithm that learns $\mathcal{F}$ with accuracy ϵ and confidence δ with respect to an honest SQ-oracle. If all the queries A makes are ideal queries and $24(\epsilon + \delta) \leq 1 - \lambda - 1/d^3$, then the total sample count of A is at least $d/15$.*

Proof. Suppose the total sample count of algorithm A is T. By Lemma 3.6, Lemma 3.7, and the direct product lemma, we know the all-pair KL-divergence of all the scenarios after all queries are finished is at most $3Td$. Combining this fact with Lemma 3.8, we know that

$$3Td \geq \mathsf{APKL}(S_q^1, S_q^2, ...S_q^d) \geq 0.2d^2$$

which implies our lemma.   □

3.4   Non-ideal Queries

Now we consider the situation where the algorithm A makes non-ideal queries.

Recall that a query function g is ideal, if $| E_D[g(X, f_i(X))] | \leq 1/2$ for all i's. For an ideal query g, the probability that $g(X, f_i(X)) = +1$ is between $1/4$ and $3/4$ for every i, which is "reasonably unbiased". In this case, the KL-divergence is a very nice measure for the "differences" between scenarios. However it doesn't work very well for very biased distributions, since with probabilities close to 0 or 1, even a tiny difference in the probabilities can result in an huge KL-divergence. Therefore we need to treat non-ideal queries differently.

We divide the non-ideal queries into two classes. For a non-ideal query function g, if $|C_g| \leq 1/3$, we call it a *semi-ideal query*; otherwise we call g a *bad query*. We develop different techniques for these 2 classes of non-ideal queries.

Semi-ideal queries We first assume that all non-ideal queries are actually semi-ideal.

For a semi-ideal query function g, if a concept f_i makes $|E_D[g(X, f_i(X))]| > 1/2$, we say f_i is an *abnormal concept for g*. Abnormal concepts are very few, since if f_i is abnormal, then

$$|\beta_i| \geq |\sqrt{1 - \lambda} \cdot \beta_i| = |E_D[g(X, f_i(X))] - C_g| \geq |E_D[g(x, f_i(x))]| - |C_g| \geq \frac{1}{6}.$$

Notice by Lemma 3.5, we have $\sum_{i=1}^d \beta_i^2 \leq 1 + 100/d$. Thus there are at most 40 abnormal concepts for each semi-ideal query for $d > 200$. This is the reason we call such query concepts "semi-ideal": they behave almost like ideal queries, except for very few abnormal concepts.

Now, instead of measuring the all-pair KL-divergence of all the scenarios, we exclude the scenarios for abnormal concepts for each query. Then we measure the all-pair KL-divergence for the remaining scenarios. We obtain the following lemma:

Lemma 3.10. *Suppose $\mathcal{F}$ is a concept class of SQ-dimension $d > 200$ with correlation λ. Let A be a learning algorithm that learns $\mathcal{F}$ with accuracy ϵ and confidence δ with respect to an honest SQ-oracle, and all the queries A makes are semi-ideal queries. If $24(\epsilon + \delta) \leq 1 - \lambda - 1/d^3$, then the total sample count of A is at least $d/60$.* □

The proof is omitted due to space constraints.

Bad Queries Now we extend the lower bound to algorithms that make bad queries as well. Recall that a query function g is bad, if $|C_g| > 1/3$. For a bad g, the probability that $g(X, f_i(X)) = +1$ can be very biased for a lot of target concepts f_i. The KL-divergence won't work very well under this circumstance.

However, intuitively, a highly biased query won't be very efficient since a biased query carries less information than an unbiased one. We shall prove this intuition is correct to some extend. In fact, we show how to efficiently simulate a biased query using an unbiased one.

Theorem 3.1. *Suppose $\mathcal{F}$ is a concept class of SQ-dimension $d > 200$ with correlation λ. Let A be a learning algorithm that learns $\mathcal{F}$ with accuracy ϵ and confidence δ with respect to an honest SQ-oracle. If $24(\epsilon + \delta + 1/d) \leq 1 - \lambda - 1/d^3$, then the total sample count of A is at least $d/(180 \log d)$.* □

The proof is omitted due to space constraints.

Remarks Our result isn't directly comparable with that in [J00]. The lower bound in [J00] is for a slightly different SQ model (the "SQ-based PAC algorithms"), and it doesn't direct translate to a lower bound in our model. Furthermore, Jackson proved that lower bound only for learning PARITY functions, while our lower bound holds for a broader class, namely, the class of "uniformly correlated" concepts. On the other hand, his lower bound is tighter: for PARITY functions over n bits, he proved that an $\Omega(2^n)$ running time is needed, while our result only gives $\Omega(2^n/n)$. However, our lower bound is strong enough to separate the SQ-learning from the PAC-learning of PARITY functions with a high $(1/2 - 1/\text{poly}(n))$ noise rate, as in [J00].

It is also interesting to compare our result to that in [Y01]. We improved the lower bound from $\Omega(\sqrt{d})$ to $\Omega(d/\log d)$. Nevertheless, the result in [Y01] is a "continuous" lower bound in that it shows a continuous trade-off between the number of queries needed and the advantage a learning algorithm has. Our result, on the other hand, is a single lower bound for the running time if a certain accuracy and confidence is needed.

4   The Second Lower Bound

The second lower bound is for classes of concepts that are arbitrarily correlated. This lower bound is against an adversarial SQ-oracle.

4.1   Notations and Definitions

We introduce some notations and definitions to be used in this section, most of which are also used in [Y01].

For a learning algorithm A, we denote its *advantage* in learning a target concept f_i to be the probability it makes a correct prediction on a random example minus the probability that it makes an incorrect prediction. The probability is taken over the randomness from A and the random example.

Notice that after making all the queries, the algorithm is ready to make a prediction on any example x. We can describe the state of this algorithm by its *characteristic function*, which is defined to be a real-valued function over the same domain. $\psi_A : \Omega \to [-1, +1]$, such that $\psi_A(x) = 2 \cdot \Pr[\,A \text{ outputs } +1 \text{ on } x\,] - 1$, where the probability is taken over the randomness A uses and the randomness from the oracles.

It is not hard to see that if the target concept is f_T, then the advantage of A is $\langle f_T, \psi_A \rangle$.

Since we are dealing with a class of concepts that are arbitrarily correlated, we need a means to describe the "correlations" among the concepts.

Definition 4.1 (Correlation Matrix). *Let $\mathcal{F} = \{f_1, f_2, ..., f_d\}$ be a concept class. Its correlation matrix, denoted by $\mathcal{C}^{\mathcal{F}}$ is a $d \times d$ matrix such that $\mathcal{C}_{ij}^{\mathcal{F}} = \langle f_i, f_j \rangle$.*

Clearly $\mathcal{C}^{\mathcal{F}}$ is a semi-positive definite matrix, and it has 1's on the diagonal. When there is no danger of confusion, we omit the superscript $\mathcal{F}$.

4.2   Why the Previous Technique Doesn't Work

The technique of the all-pair KL-divergence from the previous section doesn't work very well here. Here is an intuitive argument. In the case that each pair of concepts has the same correlation, it suffices to upper bound how much "difference" one single query makes. In a sense, no query function is significantly more efficient than others, since the concepts are sort of "uniform". In the case that the concepts are arbitrarily correlated, it is quite possible that there exists some query function that makes a large difference while others don't. In other words, we no longer have the uniformity among the concepts and some queries can be much more efficient than others. So a single upper bound on one query doesn't necessarily scale well to a good upper bound on a sequence of queries.

Here is an example: let Ω be the set of all n-bit strings, and D be the uniform distribution over Ω. Let $\mathcal{F}_0$ be the family of 2^n functions that are PARITY functions if the Least Significant Bit (LSB) of the input is 0 and are constant $+1$ if the LSB is 1. Let $\mathcal{F}_1$ be the family of 2^n functions that are PARITY functions if the LSB of the input is 0 and are constant -1 if the LSB is 1. Let the concept class $\mathcal{F}$ be the union of $\mathcal{F}_0$ and $\mathcal{F}_1$.

It is very easy to tell concepts in $\mathcal{F}_0$ and concepts in $\mathcal{F}_1$ apart, since they have difference biases. Therefore, there exists a very efficient query (just ask for the bias of the target concept) that can learn one bit about the target concept, and there exists a learning algorithm that makes a single query and learns the target concept with accuracy 3/4. If every query were as efficient as this one, then only $O(n)$ queries would have been needed to learn the target function exactly. This is also the best lower bound we can hope for if we use the technique from the previous section.

However, any SQ algorithm needs exponential time to learn the target concept with accuracy higher than 7/8. This is true since in having an accuracy higher than 7/8 implies learning the unique target function, which implies learning a parity function [J00]. This sharp contrast is due to the fact that although the query that distinguishes $\mathcal{F}_0$ from $\mathcal{F}_1$ is very efficient, others are not.

4.3   The Lower Bound

We present a lower bound for the adversarial SQ-oracle model. A part of our proof technique is similar to that of [BFJ+94], but we go further to consider the collective effect of all the queries a learning algorithm makes.

Consider a particular adversarial SQ-oracle that doesn't commit to any target concept. On each query, this oracle returns a special value that is consistent with a large number of concepts. As a result, a small number of "inconsistent" concepts will be "eliminated". So long as there are many concepts remaining (not eliminated), the learning algorithm won't be able to decide which remaining concept is the true target concept. Therefore the learning algorithm will not learn the target concept with high accuracy and high confidence.

Theorem 4.1. *Suppose $\mathcal{F}$ is a concept class with correlation matrix C. Let $\lambda_1 \geq \lambda_2 \geq \cdots \lambda_d$ be the eigenvalues of C. Let A be a learning algorithm that learns $\mathcal{F}$*

with advantage at least ξ using any adversarial SQ-oracle of error tolerance ξ. If A makes q queries, then we have

$$\sum_{i=1}^{q+1} \lambda_i \geq d \cdot \xi^2. \tag{6}$$

$\square$

The proof is omitted due to space constraints.

Immediately from the theorem, we see a continuous trade-off between the advantage an algorithm can achieve and the number of queries it needs to make. This trade-off can be very non-linear: it completely depends on how the eigenvalues of the correlation matrix are distributed. If all eigenvalues are similar, then the advantage of an algorithm will increase almost linearly with the number of queries. If some eigenvalues are much larger than others, then an algorithm might gain a lot of advantage in the first few queries. But after that, it has to make a lot of queries to make a tiny progress — interested readers can verify that this is exactly the case for the example given in Section 4.2.

4.4   Applications

We discuss several applications of Theorem 4.1 by proving 2 corollaries.

Corollary 4.1. *Let $\mathcal{F} = \{f_1, f_2, ..., f_d\}$ be a concept class such that for every pair $i \neq j$, $|\langle f_i, f_j \rangle| \leq 1/d$. Any learning algorithm that makes q queries of tolerance $1/d^{1/3}$ to an adversarial SQ-oracle and has an advantage of $1/d^{1/3}$ in learning $\mathcal{F}$ satisfies that*

$$q \geq d^{1/3}/2 - 1.$$

$\square$

The proof is omitted due to space constraints.

Comparing this corollary to the negative result in [BFJ+94], we used a weaker condition on the SQ-dimension (that $|\langle f_i, f_j \rangle| \leq 1/d$ instead of $1/d^3$) to achieve asymptotically identical bounds, and the proof is simple.

Corollary 4.2. *Let $\mathcal{F} = \{f_1, f_2, ..., f_d\}$ be a concept class such that for every pair $i \neq j$, $|\langle f_i, f_j \rangle - \lambda| \leq 1/d^2$, where λ is a constant. If a learning algorithm doesn't make any queries, it has an advantage of at most $\sqrt{\frac{1+(d-1)\lambda+1/d}{d}}$ in approximating all concepts in $\mathcal{F}$. To achieve an advantage ϵ with tolerance ϵ, an algorithm needs to make $d(\epsilon^2 - \lambda) - 1$ queries to an adversarial SQ-oracle.* $\square$

The proof is omitted due to space constraints.

This result is similar to that in [Y01]. Particularly, in the case that no query is made, the two are almost identical. However, in general they are not directly comparable. In [Y01], a more restricted condition is used: one requires that $|\langle f_i, f_j \rangle - \lambda| \leq 1/d^3$ instead of $1/d^2$. However, their result is against an honest SQ-oracle, which is stronger than one against an adversarial SQ-oracle. Nevertheless, the Theorem 4.1 makes our proof very simple.

5   Conclusion and Future Work

We proved 2 lower bounds for SQ-learning algorithms. The first lower bound is for a uniformly correlated concept class and works against the honest SQ-oracle. This lower bound is almost tight up to a logarithmic factor, and is strong enough to imply the separation of SQ- and PAC- learning of noisy PARITY functions with a high noise rate. This lower bound improves previous results by both extending the range of concept classes and using a stronger SQ-oracle model. The second lower bound is for any concept classes and against an adversarial SQ-oracle. This lower bound applies to a much wider range of concept classes than previous results. It also shows a continuous trade-off between the advantage an algorithm has and the number of queries it needs to make. This trade-off could be useful in designing learning algorithms. As demonstrated in Section 4.4, this lower bound almost immediately implies some previous results in the literature, and sometimes yields even stronger ones.

Some techniques used in the proofs may have independent interests. In proving the first lower bound, a quantity, namely, the all-pair KL-divergence is introduced, which plays a very important role in the proof. Another technique, namely using unbiased queries ("semi-ideal" queries) to simulate biased queries ("bad" queries) was used. In proving the second lower bound, a connection to the Singular Value Decomposition (SVD) was made.

There are still many open problems remaining.

- **Tighter Lower Bounds.**
  The first lower bound we proved in this paper is $\Omega(d/\log d)$, which seems still a logarithmic factor short of being tight. It would be interesting to have a truly tight lower bound. A tight lower bound would directly imply that the "SQ-based PAC algorithm" model is essentially the same as the "honest SQ-oracle" model, at least for certain concept classes. Also a better lower bound translates to a better separation of the SQ model from the PAC model. We conjecture that an $\Omega(d)$ lower bound exists.
- **More General SQ-oracle Model.**
  The second lower bound is only for the adversarial SQ-oracle model. Can we prove a similar result for the honest SQ-oracle model?
- **Complete Characterization of SQ-leaning.**
  The SQ-dimension as defined by Blum et. al. [BFJ+94] characterizes the *weak learnability* of a concept class. If the SQ-dimension is high, then the class is not weakly learnable, and if the dimension is low, then the class is (non-uniformly) weakly learnable. However, it wasn't clear that for strong learning, which characteristics we should consider.

Acknowledgment

Jeff Jackson initiated the (still on-going) quest for a tight lower bound on SQ models, and remains a main driving force behind all the work that lead to the first lower bound in this paper. It is him who first suggested that the KL-divergence could be useful to look at. Many stimulating discussions with him greatly helped the author understand the (quite subtle) differences between various models of SQ-oracle. He proved to be a wonderful error corrector, too.

The author thanks Avrim Blum for his many brilliant suggestions, and in particular, the suggestions of looking into eigenvalues for useful bounds in the arbitrary concept class case. This suggestion contributed significantly to the second lower bound.

The author thanks Ioannis Koutis, Francisco Pereira and Xiaojin Jerry Zhu for useful discussions and comments and Bartosz Przydatek for careful proofreading. Finally we thank the anonymous reviewers for suggestions and comments.

References

[AS95]   Javed A. Aslam and Scott E. Decatur, *Specification and Simulation of Learning Algorithms for Efficiency and Noise-Tolerance*, In COLT 1995, pages 437-446. ACM Press, July 1995. 231

[B95]   Christopher Bishop, *Neural Networks for Pattern Recognition*, Oxford University Press, 1995. 235

[BFJ+94]   Avrim Blum, Merrick Furst, Jeffrey Jackson, Michael Kearns, Yishay Mansour, and Steven Rudich. *Weakly Learning DNF and Characterizing Statistical Query Learning Using Fourier Analysis*. STOC 1994, pages 253–262, 1994. 229, 230, 231, 232, 236, 240, 241, 242

[CC80]   Christopher Chatfield and Alexander Collins, *Introduction to Multivariate Analysis*, Chapman and Hall, 1980.

[HJ85]   Roger Horn and Charles Johnson, *Matrix Analysis*, Cambridge University Press, 1985.

[K59]   S. Kullback, *Information Theory and Statistics*, New York: Dover Publications, 1959. 235

[KL51]   S. Kullback and R. A. Leibler, *On Information and Sufficiency*, Annals of Mathematical Statistics **22**, pp. 79-86, 1951. 234, 235

[J00]   Jeff Jackson *On the Efficiency of Noise-Tolerant PAC Algorithms Derived from Statistical Queries*. In *Proceedings of the 13th Annual Workshop on Computational Learning Theory*, 2000. 230, 231, 238, 239, 240

[K93]   Michael Kearns. *Efficient noise-tolerant learning from statistical queries*. In *Proceedings of the 25th Annual ACM Symposium on Theory of Computing*, pp. 392–401, 1993. 229, 230, 231, 234

[S88]   Gilbert Strang, *Linear Algebra and Its Applications*, third Edition, Harcourt Bruce Jovanovich Inc., 1988.

[V84]   Leslie Valiant, *A theory of the Leanable*. In *Communications of the ACM*, 27(11): 1134–1142, November 1984. 229

[Y01]   Ke Yang, *On Learning Correlated Boolean Concepts Using Statistical Query*, In the Proceedings of the 12th International Conference on Algorithmic Learning Theory (ALT'01), LNAI 2225, pp. 59-76, 2001. 229, 230, 231, 232, 234, 235, 236, 239, 241

Exploring Learnability between Exact and PAC

Nader H. Bshouty[1*], Jeffrey C. Jackson[2**], and Christino Tamon[3]

[1] Technion, Haifa 32000, Israel
bshouty@cs.technion.ac.il
[2] Duquesne University, Pittsburgh, PA 15282-1754, U.S.A.
jackson@mathcs.duq.edu
[3] Clarkson University, Potsdam, NY 13699-5815, U.S.A.
tino@clarkson.edu

Abstract. We study a model of *Probably Exactly Correct* (PExact) learning that can be viewed either as the Exact model (learning from Equivalence Queries only) relaxed so that counterexamples to equivalence queries are distributionally drawn rather than adversarially chosen or as the Probably Approximately Correct (PAC) model strengthened to require a perfect hypothesis. We also introduce a model of Probably Almost Exactly Correct (PAExact) learning that requires a hypothesis with negligible error and thus lies between the PExact and PAC models. Unlike the Exact and PExact models, PAExact learning is applicable to classes of functions defined over infinite instance spaces. We obtain a number of separation results between these models. Of particular note are some positive results for efficient parallel learning in the PAExact model, which stand in stark contrast to earlier negative results for effi-*cient parallel Exact learning.*

1 Introduction

Learning algorithms using membership queries, although theoretically of significant interest, have found relatively little application in applied machine learning. One potential area of application is in circuit design: given some representation of a function, one goal is to create a second representation that is optimized according to some measure, such as DNF size. The initial representation of the function f can be used to simulate a membership oracle for f, and a membership query based learning algorithm producing a representation of f of the appropriate form can be viewed as solving the circuit designer's optimization problem.

Of course, the circuit produced by the learning algorithm must be identical to the original representation and not merely a close approximation to it. So PAC learning algorithms [13] cannot be used for this task. On the other hand, the

---

* Supported by the fund for promotion of research at the Technion, Research no. 120-138.
** This material is based upon work supported by the National Science Foundation under Grant No. CCR-9877079.

traditional model of Exact learning from an equivalence oracle [2] that chooses counterexamples adversarially is probably "harder" than necessary: a choice of counterexamples that is random with respect to some simple probability distribution seems reasonable to expect.

Thus, we consider a model (introduced by Bshouty) that lies between the PAC and Exact models. The *Probably Exactly Correct* (PExact) learning model *(called PEC in [6]) is the PAC model with an added requirement that the hypothesis produced by the learning algorithm must be perfect.* Alternatively, one may view this as a variant of Angluin's Exact model in which each counterexample to an equivalence query is drawn according to a distribution rather than maliciously chosen. In fact, it is more natural to discuss the PExact model from the point of view of the Exact model.

In addition to the potential for applications arising from results in this model, there are significant theoretical reasons for studying it. Strong lower bounds for exact learning in parallel were given by Bshouty [6], who proved that every class that requires $\omega(\log n)$ sequential equivalence queries is not efficiently exactly learnable in parallel. Such classes include monotone conjunctions, monotone DNF formulae, decision trees, and others. Most of these lower bounds rely on adversarial strategies that maliciously choose counterexamples for the equivalence queries. This begs the question of whether these classes are learnable if distributional counterexamples are involved, which led to Bshouty's original interest in the PExact model [6].

In fact, other authors have also considered the PExact model: for example, some results on learning a restricted class of finite automata have previously been obtained [12,8]. Such results further motivate study of the question of how this model compares with existing well-studied models of learning, in particular the PAC model, Exact learning and Online learning [10].

In this paper we provide some initial comparisons between the PExact model and these earlier models. First, we give some simple simulation arguments to formalize the intuition that Exact learnability implies PExact learnability which in turn implies PAC learnability. We also show that if a class is learnable with respect to arbitrary distributions by a deterministic PExact algorithm then that class is in fact Exact learnable.

Next, we turn to some separation results. Making no assumptions, we are able to provide a weak (distribution- and representation-specific) separation between the PExact and PAC models. Also, Blum's well-known separation between Exact and PAC [4], which is based on the standard cryptographic assumption that one-way functions exist, is adapted in order to more strongly separate the PExact and PAC models. Furthermore, we show that there is a (contrived) distribution such that monotone DNF is learnable in the PExact model, which, due to Angluin's hardness result for monotone DNF in Exact [3], separates PExact from Exact.

Finally, we introduce a new model that lies between the PExact and PAC models. This Probably Almost Exactly Correct (PAExact) model requires that the hypothesis produced by the learning algorithm have negligible (smaller than inverse polynomial) error, which is stronger than the PAC requirement and weaker than the PExact requirement. In this model we are able to obtain some positive results for efficient learning in parallel, in marked contrast to Bshouty's profoundly negative results for Exact learning. Figure 1 summarizes the key results of this paper.

It should also be noted that neither the Exact nor the PExact model applies to learning infinite classes of functions defined over infinite instance spaces. As a simple concrete example, note that we cannot exactly learn an arbitrary interval over the reals from counterexamples alone, even if we are allowed constant probability of failure. The PAExact model, on the other hand, can potentially overcome this limitation by allowing for a negligible amount of error in the hypothesis. Thus, the PAExact model appears to be a particularly good analog of Exact learning for use in infinite instance space settings.

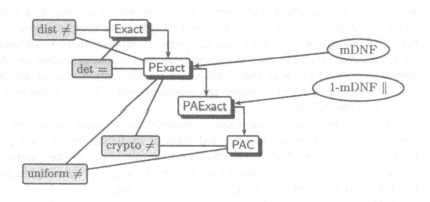

Fig. 1. Summary of Results: (a) Exact $\subseteq$ PExact $\subseteq$ PAExact $\subseteq$ PAC. (b) DPExact = DExact. (c) PAC $\neq$ PExact if one-way functions exist. (d) PAC $\neq$ PExact under the uniform distribution (without assumptions, but representation dependent). (e) Exact $\neq$ PExact since monotone DNF is not properly Exact learnable but is properly PExact learnable under some distribution. (f) monotone Conjunctions are PAExact-learnable (in parallel)

2   Preliminaries

In the following we formally define the PExact learning model. Let D be a probability distribution over a sample space X. The PExact *equivalence oracle* $EQ_{D,f}$ for a target concept f takes an input hypothesis h from the learner and returns a random counterexample a drawn according to the induced distribution of D on $X_{f \triangle h} = \{x \in X \mid f(x) \neq h(x)\}$.

A concept class C is *PExact learnable under distribution* D if there is an algorithm A such that for each $\delta > 0$ and for each $f \in C$, algorithm A queries $EQ_{D,f}$ on at most $poly(n, \delta^{-1}, size(f))$ equivalence queries and then outputs h so that $D(X_{f \triangle h}) = 0$ with probability at least $1 - \delta$. The class C is *efficiently* PExact learnable with respect to distribution D if the running time of A is bounded by $poly(n, \delta^{-1}, size(f))$. We say that C is *(distribution-free) PExact learnable* if, for any distribution D, C is PExact learnable with respect to D. If the algorithm can achieve $D(X_{f \triangle h}) = 1/\omega(poly(n, size(f))$ then we say that C is *PAExact learnable under distribution* D. Here and throughout we assume some parameterization of the instance space and the concept class using n. The size of f is measured with respect to some fixed representation class.

Example 1. Consider the problem of PExact-learning (monotone) conjunctions under the uniform distribution. Using the standard *list-crossoff* technique, the algorithm first queries with the always-0 hypothesis. Each subsequent hypothesis is the conjunction of variables corresponding to 1's in the counterexample received from the oracle in response to the previous hypothesis. Notice that if variable v_i is irrelevant then each counterexample assigns v_i a 0 value with probability $1/2$. Therefore, for any $\delta > 0$, with probability at least $1 - \delta$ variable v_i will not be included in the hypothesis produced by the algorithm after it has seen $\log(\delta^{-1})$ counterexamples. Let ℓ represent the number of irrelevant variables in the target conjunction. Then by the union bound, the hypothesis produced after $\log \ell / \delta \le \log n / \delta$ counterexamples will exactly agree with the target with probability at least $1 - \delta$.

A class C is *efficiently learnable in parallel* if there is a parallel algorithm (on polynomially many processors) learning C in time and sample complexity polynomial in the logarithm of n and the size of the target. As a simple example, consider an algorithm $\mathcal{A}$ such that whenever $\mathcal{A}$ draws an example from its oracle it also draws $t - 1$ more; that is, $\mathcal{A}$ draws examples in batches of size t. Then a parallel version of this algorithm on t processors can be constructed that will have sample complexity $1/t$ that of $\mathcal{A}$.

3   Simulation Results

For a learning model A (*e.g.*, PAC) we use the notation A (*e.g.*, PAC) to represent the set of all function classes that are learnable in model A. Thus, for two learning models A and B, we use A $\subseteq$ B to denote that every class that is learnable in model A is also learnable in model B.

Theorem 1. Exact $\subseteq$ PExact $\subseteq$ PAExact $\subseteq$ PAC.

Proof The relation Exact $\subseteq$ PExact $\subseteq$ PAExact is immediate. The relation PAExact $\subseteq$ PAC is also not hard to see since a PAC simulation of the PAExact algorithm will use the PAC example oracle to provide a random counterexample drawn according to the underlying distribution. This type of rejection sampling will sample according to the induced distribution on the set of counterexamples. Note also that if the PAExact algorithm is efficient then the PAC algorithm will be as well, since failure to find a counterexample after polynomially many examples indicates that with high probability the algorithm has found an adequate hypothesis.   □

In fact, there is a close relationship between the Exact and distribution-free PExact models. Define the Deterministic PExact model DPExact as the PExact model with the provision that the learner is a deterministic algorithm. That is, the confidence parameter δ is provided only to account for uncertainty inherent in accessing examples through the probability distribution D and not to cover any randomness in the algorithm itself. Then we have:

Theorem 2. *Let C be any class for which there exists a nonempty, finite set of deterministic algorithms $\mathcal{A}_1$, $\mathcal{A}_2$, ..., $\mathcal{A}_m$ such that for any distribution D there exists i such that $\mathcal{A}_i$ (efficiently) DPExact learns C with respect to D. Then C is (efficiently) Exact learnable. That is, in the distribution-free setting,*

$$\text{DPExact} = \text{DExact}.$$

Proof First, note that each DPExact algorithm $\mathcal{A}_i$ for C may have knowledge of the class of distributions from which D is chosen. However, we can construct a single master algorithm $\mathcal{M}$ that DPExact learns from unknown distribution D by simply dovetailing the algorithms $\mathcal{A}_i$.

The precise way in which we dovetail the algorithms depends on whether our goal is time or query efficiency. To obtain a time-efficient master algorithm, each $\mathcal{A}_i$ algorithm performs one instruction or query, then relinquishes control to the next algorithm $\mathcal{A}_{(i \bmod m)+1}$. In this case, $\mathcal{M}$ takes only constant more time than the fastest algorithm among the $\mathcal{A}_i$'s. On the other hand, similar query efficiency can be achieved by relinquishing control after each query.

Next, we show that $\mathcal{M}$ can be used to Exact learn C if $\mathcal{M}$ is deterministic. Our claim is that if $\mathcal{M}$ is given an equivalence oracle for C rather than a EQ_D oracle then $\mathcal{M}$ will learn C with the same time and query guarantees it would have given a PExact oracle. Assume otherwise. Then there is some sequence S of counterexamples on which $\mathcal{M}$ always (because it is deterministic) fails to perform as claimed. But then we can construct a "stair step" distribution D that puts a significantly greater weight on the each example s_j in S than on the example s_{j+1} immediately following it. In this way, with high probability $\mathcal{M}$ will also similarly fail under D. But this would imply that C was not distribution-free DPExact learnable.   □

4   Separation Results

In this section we observe a couple of separation results between the PExact and PAC models. The first separation result shows representation-independent hardness for PExact-learning of a cryptographically-based concept class that is PAC-learnable. This is based on Blum's work [4] on separating the PAC model from the exact model.

Theorem 3. *There is a class C that is PAC learnable but not PExact learnable if one-way functions exist.*

Proof (sketch) For completeness, we review and describe the ideas from [4]. Let $g : \{0,1\}^k \to \{0,1\}^{2k}$ be a pseudorandom generator (this exists if one-way functions exist). Denote $g_0(s)$ (resp. $g_1(s)$) as the leftmost (resp. rightmost) k bits of $g(s)$. For an ℓ-bit string x, $g_x(s)$ denotes the $|x|$-fold self-composition of g, i.e., $g_x(s) = g_{x_\ell}(\ldots (g_{x_1}(s))\ldots)$. Based on g, we recall the standard GGM pseudorandom function class $F = \{f_s\}_{s \in \{0,1\}^k}$, where $f_s(x) = g_x(s)$. Then a filtered composition $\tilde{g}_x(s)$ is defined as follows

$$\tilde{g}_x(s) = g_{\tilde{x}_1}(s) \cdot g_{x_1 \tilde{x}_2}(s) \cdot g_{x_1 x_2 \tilde{x}_3}(s) \cdot \ldots \cdot g_{x_1 \ldots x_{k-1} \tilde{x}_k}(s)$$

where $g_{\bar{0}}(s) = g_1(s)$ and $g_{\bar{1}}(s) = \lambda$. Next, a concept class $C = \{c_s\}_{s \in \{0,1\}^k}$ is defined, where

$$c_s = \{x \cdot \tilde{g}_x(s) \mid x \in \{0,1\}^k, \ LSB[g_x(s)] = 1\}$$

The proof in [4] actually showed that if the EQ oracle presents counterexamples in reverse lexicographic order then any algorithm for exactly learning C can be used to invert the one-way function w on which the generator g is based. While in the Exact setting the learning algorithm is deterministic, even the existence of a polynomial-time randomized algorithm for exactly learning C under the given ordering of counterexamples with non-negligible probability would imply that one-way functions do not exist, since it would lead to a polynomial-time (randomized) algorithm that could invert w with non-negligible probability.

Now note that a stair step distribution D_S can be constructed as in Theorem 2 such that there is negligible probability of drawing polynomially many counterexamples under D_S in an order different from reverse lexicographic. Thus, if a randomized algorithm could, with non-negligible probability, exactly learn C in polynomial time under D_S then this would imply that it could learn similarly learn from counterexamples in reverse lexicographic order with non-negligible probability. But, as noted above, this would contradict the existence of one-way functions. So this yields a separation between the PExact and PAC models, since Blum gave a PAC learning algorithm for learning C. □

The second separation result shows—without the need for any unproven assumptions—that the PAC model under the uniform distribution is not identical to the PExact model under the uniform distribution when the output of the algorithm is required to belong to a particular representation class. This result builds on the AC^0 learning algorithm in [11] and a lower bound result in [9].

Theorem 4. *There is a subclass of AC^0 that is efficiently PAC learnable under the uniform distribution but is not PExact learnable under the uniform distribution using the representation of threshold of parities.*

Proof (sketch) Krause and Pudlak [9] proved that there is a collection of functions in AC_4^0 that requires an exponential-sized circuit of threshold of parity gates. In contrast, the Fourier-based learning algorithm of Linial, Mansour, and Nisan [11] (scaled down to polynomial time) outputs a threshold of parities hypothesis that is a PAC approximator to any AC_d^0 function with at most $\exp(\log^{1/O(d)}(n/\epsilon))$ relevant variables.   □

Next, we show that the PExact and Exact models are distinct with respect to distribution-specific proper learning. We do this by showing that there is a distribution under which monotone DNF is properly learnable in the PExact model. That monotone DNF is not Exact properly learnable was shown by Angluin [3].

Theorem 5. *There is a distribution for which monotone DNF is properly PExact learnable.*

Proof (sketch) Define a measure $M : \{0,1\}^n \to R^+$ as follows. Place weight 1 on the point 1^n. Place doubly exponential (in n) weight on each of the points of Hamming weight $n-1$ (01^{n-1}, 101^{n-2}, etc.). Place quadruply-exponential weight on each of the points of Hamming weight $n-2$, and so on. In short, define M such that over the course of learning any monotone DNF expression there will be exponentially more weight on any point of Hamming weight d than on all points of weight more than d combined.

Let D be the probability distribution over $\{0,1\}^n$ corresponding to M. Based on the construction of M, with at least constant probability each of the at most 2^n counterexamples x drawn by EQ_D will have the property that there is no counterexample y such that $|y| < |x|$. We will say in such a case that *the counterexample is drawn from the correct level.*

1. $h \leftarrow$ **false**
2.   **while** $EQ_D(h)$ produces counterexample x
3.   Create term $t_x = \bigwedge_{i \text{ s.t. } x_i=1} v_i$
4.   Add t_x to h
5.   **end while**

Fig. 2. An algorithm for learning monotone DNF from a PExact oracle

Now consider the simple algorithm of Figure 2 for learning monotone DNF from EQ_D. Notice first that every counterexample will be labeled **true**. Assume for the moment that each counterexample x is drawn from the correct level. Then it is not hard to verify that each counterexample causes a term from the target to be added to the hypothesis h. So the algorithm succeeds if each of the examples comes from the correct level, which occurs with at least constant probability. Repeating the algorithm $O(\log 1/\delta)$ times then succeeds with probability at least $1 - \delta$.   □

5   Relaxing Exactness and Parallel Learnability

Consider an algorithm $\mathcal{A}$ that is almost a PExact algorithm for learning a class C with respect to D, but for which we allow the following relaxation: the error in the final hypothesis is guaranteed, with probability at least $1 - \delta$, to be negligible, that is, $o(1/p(n,s))$ for any polynomial p. We will call this model of learning *Probably Almost Exactly Correct* (PAExact).

We obtain several positive results for parallel learnability in this model; for example, immediately below we will show that monotone conjunctions are efficiently learnable in parallel in the PAExact model. On the other hand, Bshouty [6] showed that this class is not efficiently Exact learnable in parallel. In fact, all classes currently known to be Exact learnable are not efficiently learnable in parallel in the Exact model. The PAExact model therefore appears to be much more interesting than the Exact model for purposes of studying parallel learnability.

Input: Oracle EQ_D, confidence δ, number of parallel processors t (assumed polynomial in n)
Output: Monotone conjunction T_k such that with probability at least $1 - \delta$, $\Pr_{x \sim D}[T_k(x) \neq f(x)] < p(n)(1/t)^{\ln n / \ln \ln(n/\delta)}$, where $p(\cdot)$ is a fixed polynomial.

1. $h \leftarrow \mathbf{false}$
2.   Query $EQ_D(h)$ t times producing counterexamples $\{x^j\}_{j \in [1..t]}$
3.   Create term $T_1 = \bigwedge_i \text{ s.t. } \forall_j, x_i^j = 1 \, v_i$
4. $k \leftarrow 1$
5.   **while** $EQ_D(T_k)$ produces counterexample and $k < \ln n / \ln \ln(n/\delta)$
6.   Query $EQ_D(T_k)$ t times producing counterexamples $\{x^j\}_{j \in [1..t]}$
7.   Create term $T_{k+1} = \bigwedge_i \{v_i : v_i \in T_k \text{ and } \forall_j, x_i^j = 1\}$
8. $k \leftarrow k + 1$
9.   **end while**

Fig. 3. An algorithm for PAExact parallel learning of a monotone conjunction

Theorem 6. *The class of monotone conjunctions is efficiently PAExact learnable in parallel.*

Proof Consider the algorithm of Figure 3. Let D be the target distribution and f the target monomial. Then for any $I > 0$, with probability at least $1 - \delta/I$, $\Pr_{x \sim D}[T_1(x) \neq f(x)] < \ln(I/\delta)/t$. To see this, note that this would certainly be an upper bound on the error over the distribution induced by D on positive examples, which is an upper bound on the error with respect to D, if T_1 was fixed before the examples were drawn [2]. But since T_1 is the "worst" hypothesis consistent with the examples (in the sense that any other consistent term must consist of a conjunction of a subset of the variables in T_1 and will therefore predict positive more often), we can in fact say that this is a bound on the error of T_1.

Next, notice that $\Pr_{x \sim D}[T_2(x) \neq f(x)|T_1(x) = f(x)] = 0$, since $T_1 \implies T_2 \implies f$. Therefore, $\Pr_{x \sim D}[T_2(x) \neq f(x)] = \Pr_{x \sim D}[T_2(x) \neq f(x)|T_1(x) \neq$

$f(x)] \cdot \Pr_{x \sim D}[T_1(x) \neq f(x)]$. By an argument as above, the first term of this product is bounded above by $\ln(I/\delta)/t$, and therefore $\Pr_{x \sim D}[T_2(x) \neq f(x)] < (\ln(I/\delta)/t)^2$. It follows that for t a polynomial in n and for $I = \ln n / \ln \ln(n/\delta)$, with probability at least $1 - \delta$, the error in T_k at the end of the algorithm will be superpolynomially small. Finally, since the parallel running time of the algorithm is bounded logarithmically in n, the algorithm is efficient.   □

A composition argument can also be used to show that for any constant k, monotone k-DNF (disjunction of conjunctions of at most k variables) can be learned. A Boolean variable V_i can be defined for each of the $O(n^k)$ conjunctions of at most k of the original variables. A disjunction over this new set of variables V_i is then equivalent to a monotone k-DNF over the original set of variables. Thus, a dual of the above algorithm could be used to learn monotone k-DNF if an oracle over the new set of variables was available. But we can easily simulate such an oracle: given a hypothesis $h(V)$ over the new variables, we simply create a hypothesis $h'(v)$ over the original variables such that for every possible assignment to the original variables v, $h'(v) = h(V)$ and query the original oracle with the hypothesis h'. Thus monotone k-DNF is efficiently parallel PAExact learnable. A similar construction (adding auxiliary variables representing negations of the original literals) can be used to prove that both nonmonotone conjunctions and nonmonotone k-DNF are also efficiently PAExact learnable in parallel.

The above theorem leads naturally to the following more general observation:

Theorem 7. *Let A be an Exact algorithm that learns a class C and has the following property: when learning any function $f \in C$, the sequence $h_1, h_2, \ldots$ of hypotheses made by A are such that for all inputs x, $(h_i(x) = f(x)) \implies (h_{i+1}(x) = f(x))$. Also assume that, given a set of examples S of f, A can be run efficiently in parallel to find a hypothesis h consistent with S. Then C is efficiently PAExact learnable in parallel.*

Proof (sketch) The idea is that we will first determine A's initial hypothesis h_0 and then draw a polynomially large sample S from the given PAExact oracle $EQ_D(h_0)$. Now we run A on S in order to learn a consistent hypothesis h_1 efficiently in parallel. As in the theorem above, the error of our hypothesis over D will be polynomially small for sufficiently large polynomial sample S. Next, we draw a second sample S_2 using oracle $EQ_D(h_1)$ and run A on S_2 to obtain a hypothesis h_2. Notice that, by assumption, if $h_1(x) = f(x)$ then $h_2(x) = f(x)$. It follows by an argument similar to that used in the previous theorem that the probability of error by h_2 is no more than the square of the bound on the probability of error of h_1. Thus a roughly logarithmic number of rounds produces a PAExact error bound.   □

Similarly, we can obtain a relationship between PAExact and PAC learning (in parallel or serially):

Theorem 8. *If a class C is (parallel) PAC learnable with the guarantee that for every target f and distribution D the hypothesis h produced is such that $h \implies f$, then C is (parallel) PAExact learnable.*

Proof (sketch) As above, we first run the PAC algorithm on a set of examples supplied by the EQ_D algorithm run on the always-false hypothesis, producing hypothesis h_1 that has error at most ϵ. Then a sample is drawn from $EQ_D(h_1)$, and as before the hypothesis h_2 produced by running the PAC algorithm on this sample will be at most ϵ^2. Continuing this process roughly logarithmically many times produces the result.   □

As an example of an application of this theorem, consider the class of intervals on the real line mentioned in the Introduction. Since this class is PAC learnable by an algorithm that satisfies the requirements of the theorem (see, *e.g.*, [1]), this class is also PAExact learnable.

6   Further Work

While this paper has begun the exploration of learning models that lie between the PAC and Exact models, a significant number of interesting questions remain open. Two key questions are:

1. Are the Exact and distribution-free, randomized PExact models equivalent?
2. Are the PAC and PAExact models equivalent?

The PAExact model seems to be particularly intriguing. Even if it turns out to be difficult to determine whether or not this model is equivalent to PAC, could we show, for example, that all known PAC learnable classes are also PAExact learnable? In addition to the parallel learning results in this paper, what other classes are efficiently parallel PAExact learnable?

References

1. M. Anthony, A. Biggs. *Computational Learning Theory.* Cambridge University Press, 1992.
2. Dana Angluin. Queries and Concept Learning. *Machine Learning*, 2:319-342, 1988.
3. Dana Angluin. Negative Results for Equivalence Queries. *Machine Learning*, 5:121-150, 1990.
4. Avrim Blum. Separating Distribution-Free and Mistake-Bound Learning Models over the Boolean Domain. *SIAM Journal on Computing*, 23(5):990-1000, 1994.
5. Nader H. Bshouty. Towards the Learnability of DNF Formulae. *Proceedings of the ACM Annual Symposium on Theory of Computing*, 1996.
6. Nader H. Bshouty. Exact Learning of Formulas in Parallel. *Machine Learning*, 26:25-41, 1997.
7. Shai Ben-David, Eyal Kushilevitz, and Yishay Mansour. Online Learning versus Offline Learning. *Machine Learning*, 29:45-63, 1997.
8. Francois Denis. Learning Regular Languages from Simple Positive Examples. *Machine Learning*, 44(1/2):37-66, 2001.
9. Matthias Krause, Pavel Pudlak. On the Computational Power of Depth 2 Circuits with Threshold and Modulo Gates *Proceedings of the ACM Annual Symposium on Theory of Computing*, pages 48-57, 1994.

10. Nick Littlestone. Learning Quickly When Irrelevant Attributes Abound: A New Linear-threshold Algorithm. *Machine Learning*, 2:285-318, 1988.
11. Nathan Linial, Yishay Mansour, Noam Nisan. Constant Depth Circuits, Fourier Transform, and Learnability *Journal of the Association for Computing Machinery*, 40(3):607-620, 1993.
12. Rajesh Parekh and Vasant Honavar. Simple DFA are polynomially probably exactly learnable from simple examples. *Proceedings of the 16th International Conference on Machine Learning*, Morgan Kaufmann, San Francisco, CA, 298–306, 1999.
13. L. G. Valiant. A Theory of the Learnable. *Communications of the ACM*, 27(11):1134-1142, 1984.

PAC Bounds for Multi-armed Bandit and Markov Decision Processes

Eyal Even-Dar[1], Shie Mannor[2], and Yishay Mansour[1]

[1] School of Computer Science, Tel Aviv University
Tel-Aviv 69978, Israel
{evend,mansour}@cs.tau.ac.il
[2] Department of Electrical Engineering, Technion
Haifa 32000, Israel
shie@tx.technion.ac.il

Abstract. The bandit problem is revisited and considered under the PAC model. Our main contribution in this part is to show that given n arms, it suffices to pull the arms $O(\frac{n}{\epsilon^2} \log \frac{1}{\delta})$ times to find an ϵ-optimal arm with probability of at least $1 - \delta$. This is in contrast to the naive bound of $O(\frac{n}{\epsilon^2} \log \frac{n}{\delta})$. We derive another algorithm whose complexity depends on the specific setting of the rewards, rather than the worst case setting. We also provide a matching lower bound.

We show how given an algorithm for the PAC model Multi-armed Bandit problem, one can derive a batch learning algorithm for Markov Decision Processes. This is done essentially by simulating Value Iteration, and in each iteration invoking the multi-armed bandit algorithm. Using our PAC algorithm for the multi-armed bandit problem we improve the dependence on the number of actions.

1 Introduction

The Multi-armed bandit problem is one of the classical problems in decision theory. The problem is very simple to model - there are a number of alternative arms, each with a stochastic reward with initially unknown expectation, and our aim is to maximize the sum of rewards, which in this setting is to choose the arm with the highest expected reward. One of the attractive features of the multi-armed bandit problem, is that although its simplicity, it already encompasses many of important decision theoretic issues, such as the tradeoff between exploration and exploitation.

The multi-armed bandit problem has been widely studied in a variety of setups. The problem was first considered in the 50's in the seminal work of Robbins [18] that derives strategies that asymptotically attain an average reward that converges in the limit to the reward of the best arm. The multi-armed bandit problem was later studied in discounted, Bayesian, Markovian, expected reward, and adversarial setups. (See [4] for a review of the classical results on the multi-armed bandit problem.)

J. Kivinen and R. H. Sloan (Eds.): COLT 2002, LNAI 2375, pp. 255–270, 2002.

Two notable concepts are the Gittins index and efficiency of allocation rules. In the seminal work of Gittins and Jones [12] a simple optimal decision rule was derived, this rule is known as the Gittins Index. The model in question is Bayesian, where the a-priory distribution of each arm is uniform and reward is discounted. The Gittins index is a way to quantify how good is an arm expected to be, and the derived policy is to simply choose the arm with the highest index. For the expected regret model, where the regret is defined as the difference between the optimal return and the online algorithm return, the seminal work of Lai and Robbins [17] provides tight bounds as a function of the Kullback-Leibler divergence between the arms reward distribution, and a logarithmic growth with the number of steps. The bounds of [17] were shown to be efficient, in the sense that the convergence rates are optimal. The adversarial multi-armed bandit problem was considered in [2,3], where it was shown that the expected regret grows proportionally to the square root of the number of steps.

We consider the classical multi-armed bandit problem, but rather than looking at the expected regret, we are concerned with PAC style bounds. Our goal is to find, with high probability, a near optimal arm, namely, with probability at least $1 - \delta$ output an ϵ-optimal arm. This naturally abstracts the case where we need to choose one specific arm, and we are given only limited exploration initially. Our main complexity criterion, in addition to correctness, is the number of steps taken by the algorithm, which can be viewed as pure exploration steps. This is in contrast to most of the results for the multi-armed bandit problem, where the main aim is to maximize the expected cumulative reward while both exploring and exploiting.

Before we start describing our results, we would like to point out that there is a very simple strategy for the PAC multi-armed bandit problem. Namely, sample each arm of the n arms for $O(1/\epsilon^2 \log(n/\delta))$ times, compute the average reward of each arm, and return the arm with the highest average. Our results improve on this simple bound in two different ways, using two different algorithms.

The first algorithm, *Successive Elimination*, has the potential to exhibit an improved behavior in cases where the differences between the expected rewards of the optimal arm and sub-optimal arms are much larger than ϵ. The second algorithm, *Median Elimination*, achieves a better dependence on the number of arms. Namely, the total number of arm trials is $O(n/\epsilon^2 \log(1/\delta))$, which improves the naive bound by a factor of $\log n$. We also show lower bounds, which are tight for $\delta \geq \frac{1}{n}$.

After deriving our PAC algorithm for the multi-armed bandit problem, we establish an interesting connection between learning in Markov Decision Processes (MDPs) and PAC algorithms for multi-armed bandit problem. We show how to use, as a black box, any PAC algorithm for the multi-armed bandit problem, and derive a learning algorithm for MDPs. The derived algorithm is a modification of the Phased Q-Learning algorithm of Kearns and Singh [15]. The basic idea is that we can view each phase of the algorithm as a separate multi-armed bandit problem, at each state. The PAC nature of our algorithm ensures us that a near optimal action is eventuated quickly. Using our general transformation we are able to derive an algorithm with a better dependency on the number of actions, when using our median elimination algorithm.

To put our work in perspective, most of the theoretical work concerning convergence of Reinforcement Learning algorithms concentrated on the performance in the limit. Specifically, it was shown that the popular Q-learning algorithm ([9]) converges in the limit to the optimal Q-function. This result was extended to more general settings in [5,19,6] and other algorithms as well (see [5] for a review). Most of the research is focused on finding the optimal policy (rather than ϵ-optimal policy), and the arguments are usually based on the stochastic approximation algorithm and the Ordinary Differential Equation (ODE) method. Consequently, the results are usually in the limit, and finite sample bounds are not provided (c.f., [6]).

In recent years there has been interest in applying PAC style analysis to MDPs, obtaining PAC style bounds, and deriving provably efficient algorithms. To name some of the contributions along this new research direction: E^3 that efficiently computes an ϵ-optimal policy [15], sparse sampling [16], restricted class of strategies [13], convergence rate for Q-learning [10], average reward games [7], model based learning [14], and adaptive control of linear systems [11]. Our work concentrates on the basic question of how many samples are needed for finding an ϵ-optimal policy with probability $1 - \delta$. In addition, our derived algorithm is computationally efficient.

The paper is organized as follows. Section 2 specifies the multi-armed bandit and the MDP models. Algorithms for finding the almost best arm with high probability are presented and analyzed in Section 3. Lower bounds on the minimal number of samples needed to find an almost optimal arm are provided in Section 4. The phased Q-learning is described in Section 5.

2 The Models

Multi-armed Bandit: The model is comprised of a set of arms A with $n = |A|$. When sampling arm $a \in A$ a reward which is a random variable $R(a)$ is received. We assume that the reward is binary, i.e., for every arm $a \in A$ the reward $R(a) \in \{0, 1\}$ (all the results apply if the reward is bounded in $[0, 1]$). Denote the arms by $a_1, \cdots, a_n$ and $p_i = E[R(a_i)]$. For simplicity of notations we enumerate the arms according to their expected reward $p_1 > p_2 > \ldots > p_n$.

An arm with the highest expected reward is called the *best arm*, and denoted by a^*, and its expected reward r^* is the *optimal reward*. An arm whose expected reward is strictly less than r^*, the expected reward of the best arm, is called a *non-best arm*. An arm a is called an ϵ-*optimal arm* if its expected reward is at most ϵ from the optimal reward, i.e., $E[R(a)] \geq r^* - \epsilon$.

An algorithm for the multi armed bandit problem, at each time step t, samples an arm a_t and receives a reward r_t (distributed according to $R(a_t)$). When making its selection the algorithm may depend on the history (i.e., the actions and rewards) up to time $t - 1$.

An algorithm is a (ϵ, δ)-PAC algorithm for the multi armed bandit if it outputs an ϵ-optimal arm, a', with probability at least $1 - \delta$, when it terminates. The number of time steps the algorithm performs until it terminates is called the *arm sample complexity* of the algorithm.

Markov Decision Processes: We define a Markov Decision process (MDP) as follows.

Definition 1. *A Markov Decision process (MDP) M is a 4-tuple (S, A, P, R), where S is a set of the states, A is a set of actions, $P_{i,j}^a(M)$ is the transition probability from state i to state j when performing action $a \in A$ in state i, and $R_M(s, a)$ is the reward distribution when performing action a in state s.*

A strategy for an MDP assigns, at each time $t+1$, for each state s a probability for performing action $a \in A$, given a history $F_t = \{s_1, a_1, r_1, ..., s_t, a_t, r_t\}$ which includes the states, actions and rewards observed until time t. The action chosen by strategy π, at time t is denoted by a_t. The state at time t is denoted by s_t and similarly the reward obtained at time t is r_t (distributed according to $R_M(s_t, a_t)$), and the next state s_{t+1} (distributed according to $P_{s_t, s_{t+1}}^{a_t}(M)$). We combine the sequence of rewards to a single value called *return*, and our goal is to maximize the return. In this work we focus on *discounted return*, with discount factor $\gamma \in (0, 1)$. The discounted return of policy π is $V_M^\pi = \sum_{t=0}^\infty \gamma^t r_t$, where r_t is the reward observed at time t.

We assume that $R_M(s, a)$ is non-negative and bounded by R_{max}, i.e., $0 \leq R_M(s, a) \leq R_{max}$ for every s and a. This implies that the discounted return is bounded by $V_{max} = \frac{R_{max}}{1-\gamma}$.

We define a value function for each state s, under policy π, as $V_M^\pi(s) = E[\sum_{i=0}^\infty \gamma^i r_i]$, where the expectation is over a run of policy π starting at state s. We further define the Q-function for a state-action pair as the expected reward from state s given that a was played and π is played from that time on $Q_M^\pi(s, a) = E[R_M(s, a)] + \gamma \sum_{s'} P_{s,s'}^a(M) V_M^\pi(s')$.

Let π^* be an optimal policy which maximizes the return from any start state. This implies that for every policy π and every state s we have $V_M^{\pi^*}(s) \geq V_M^\pi(s)$, and $\pi^*(s) = \text{argmax}_a(E[R_M(s, a)] + \gamma(\sum_{s'} P_{s,s'}^a(M) V^*(s')))$. We use V^* for $V_M^{\pi^*}$. We say that a policy π is ϵ-optimal if $\|V_M^* - V_M^\pi\|_\infty \leq \epsilon$.

We use a Sampling Model, which has an invocation $sample(s, a)$ that returns (s', r) where the next state s', distributed according to $P_{s,s'}^a(M)$ and a reward r distributed according to $R_M(s, a)$.

3   PAC Bounds for Multi-armed Bandit Problems

In this section we look for an (ϵ, δ)-PAC algorithms for the multi-armed bandit problem. Such algorithms are required to output with probability $1 - \delta$ an ϵ-optimal arm. A naive solution samples each arm $O(\frac{1}{(\epsilon/2)^2} \log(\frac{n}{\delta}))$, so that with probability $1 - \frac{\delta}{n}$, for every arm we approximate the expected reward within $\epsilon/2$.

Theorem 1. *The algorithm* Naive(ϵ, δ) *is an* (ϵ, δ)-*PAC algorithm with arm sample complexity* $O(\frac{n}{\epsilon^2} \log(\frac{n}{\delta}))$.

Algorithm : **Naive**(ϵ, δ)
1. For every arm $a \in A$: Sample it $\ell = \frac{4}{\epsilon^2} \log(\frac{2n}{\delta})$ times.
2. Let $\hat{p}_a$ be the average reward of arm a.
3. output $a' = \arg\max_{a \in A}\{\hat{p}_a\}$.

Proof. Let a' be an arm for which $E(R(a')) < r^* - \epsilon$. We want to bound the probability of the event $\hat{p}_{a'} > \hat{p}_{a^*}$.

$$P(\hat{p}_{a'} > \hat{p}_{a^*}) \leq P(\hat{p}_{a'} > E(R(a')) + \epsilon/2 \text{ or } \hat{p}_{a^*} < r^* - \epsilon/2)$$
$$\leq P(\hat{p}_{a'} > E(R(a')) + \epsilon/2) + P(\hat{p}_{a^*} < r^* - \epsilon/2)$$
$$\leq 2\exp(-(\epsilon/2)^2\ell),$$

where the last inequality uses the Hoeffding inequality. Choosing $\ell = \frac{4}{\epsilon^2} \log(\frac{2n}{\delta})$ assures that $P(\hat{p}_{a'} > \hat{p}_{a^*}) \leq \frac{\delta}{n}$. The sample complexity is immediate from the definition of the algorithm, which completes the proof. $\square$

3.1 Successive Elimination

To motivate the successive elimination algorithm, suppose that the expected rewards of the arms are known, but the matching of the arms to the expected rewards is unknown. Let $\Delta_i = p_1 - p_i > 0$. Our aim is to sample arm a_i for $\frac{1}{\Delta_i^2} \log(\frac{n}{\delta})$ times, and then eliminate it. This is done in phases. Initially, we sample each arm $\frac{1}{\Delta_n^2} \log(\frac{n}{\delta})$ times. Then we eliminate the arm which has the lowest empirical reward (and never sample it again). At the i-th phase we sample each of the $n - i$ surviving arms $O((\frac{1}{\Delta_{n-i}^2} - \frac{1}{\Delta_{n-i+1}^2})\log(\frac{n}{\delta}))$ times and then eliminate the empirically worst arm.

Theorem 2. *The Successive Elimination with Known Biases algorithm is an* $(0, \delta)$*-PAC algorithm and its arm sample complexity is* $O\left(\log(\frac{n}{\delta})\sum_{i=2}^{n}\frac{1}{\Delta_i^2}\right)$.

Algorithm : **Successive Elimination Known Biases** (δ)
1. Set $S = A$; $t_i = \lceil 4/\Delta_i^2 \log(n/\delta)\rceil$; and $t_{n+1} = 0$.
2. Set for every arm a: $\hat{p}_a = 0$.
3. For $i = 0$ to $n - 2$ DO
   (a) Sample every arm $a \in S$ for $t_{n-i} - t_{n-i+1}$ times.
   (b) Let $\hat{p}_a$ be the average reward of arm a (in all rounds).
   (c) Set $S = S \setminus a_{\min}$, where $a_{\min} = \arg\min_{a \in S}\{\hat{p}_a\}$.
4. output S.

Proof. We claim that this algorithm outputs the best arm with probability $1 - \delta$. This is done by showing that, in each phase, the probability of eliminating the best arm is bounded by $\frac{\delta}{n}$. It is clear that the failure probability at phase i is maximized if all the $i-1$ worst arms have been eliminated in the first $i-1$ phases. Since we eliminate a single arm at each phase of the algorithm, the probability of the best arm being eliminated at phase i is bounded by

$$Pr[\hat{p}_1 < \hat{p}_2, \hat{p}_1 < \hat{p}_3, ..., \hat{p}_1 < \hat{p}_{n-i}] \leq Pr[\hat{p}_1 < \hat{p}_{n-i}]$$

The probability that $\hat{p}_1 < \hat{p}_{n-i}$, after sampling each arm for $O(\frac{1}{\Delta_i^2} \log \frac{n}{\delta})$ times, is bounded by $\frac{\delta}{n}$. Therefore, the total probability of failure is bounded by δ and the arm sample complexity is,

$$O(\log(\frac{n}{\delta}) \sum_{i=2}^{n} \frac{1}{\Delta_i^2}).$$

$\square$

Next, we relax the requirement that the expected rewards of the arms are known in advance, and introduce the **Successive Elimination** algorithm that works with any set of biases.

Algorithm : **Successive Elimination**(δ)
1. Set $t = 1$ and $S = A$
2. Set for every arm a: $\hat{p}_a^1 = 0$.
3. Sample every arm $a \in S$ once and let $\hat{p}_a^t$ be the average reward of arm a by time t.
4. Let $\hat{p}_{max}^t = \max_{a \in S} \hat{p}_a^t$ and $\alpha_t = \sqrt{\frac{\log(cnt^2/\delta)}{t}}$
5. For every arm $a \in S$ such that $\hat{p}_{max}^t - \hat{p}_a^t \geq 2\alpha_t$ set $S = S \setminus a$
6. $t = t + 1$.
7. If $|S| > 1$ Then Go to 3 Else output S.

Theorem 3. *The Successive Elimination algorithm is a $(0, \delta)$-PAC algorithm, and with probability at least $1 - \delta$ its arm sample complexity is bounded by* $O\left(\sum_{i=2}^{n} \frac{\log(\frac{n}{\delta \Delta_i})}{\Delta_i^2}\right)$.

Proof. Our main argument is that the observed probability $\hat{p}_a^t$ is within α_t of the true probability p_a. For any time t and action $a \in S_t$ we have that,

$$Pr[|\hat{p}_a^t - p_a| \geq \alpha_t] \leq e^{-\alpha_t^2 t} \leq \frac{\delta}{cnt^2}.$$

This implies that with probability at least $1 - \delta/n$ for any time t and any action $a \in S_t$, $|\hat{p}_a^t - p_a| \leq \alpha_t$. Therefore, with probability $1 - \delta$, the best arm is never eliminated. Furthermore, since α_t goes to zero as t increases, eventually every non-best arm is eliminated. This completes the proof that the algorithm is $(0, \delta)$-PAC.

It remains to compute the arm sample complexity. To eliminate a non-best arm a_i we need to reach a time t_i such that,

$$\hat{\Delta}_{t_i} = \hat{p}_{a_1}^{t_i} - \hat{p}_{a_i}^{t_i} \geq 2\alpha_{t_i}$$

The definition of α_t combined with the assumption that $|\hat{p}_a^t - p_a| \leq \alpha_t$ yields that

$$\Delta_i - 2\alpha_t = (p_1 - \alpha_t) - (p_i + \alpha_t) \geq \hat{p}_1 - \hat{p}_i \geq 2\alpha_t,$$

which holds with probability at least $1 - \frac{\delta}{n}$ for

$$t_i = O\left(\frac{\log(n/\delta\Delta_i)}{\Delta_i^2}\right).$$

The arm sample complexity is $t_2 + \sum_{i=2}^{n} t_i$, which completes the proof. □

Remark 1. We can improve the dependence on the parameter Δ_i if at the t-th phase we sample each action in S_t for 2^t times rather than once and take $\alpha_t = \sqrt{\frac{\log(cn\log(t)/\delta)}{t}}$. This will give us a bound on the number of samples with a dependency of

$$O\left(\sum_{i=2}^{n} \frac{\log(-\frac{n\log\Delta_i}{\delta})}{\Delta_i^2}\right).$$

Remark 2. One can easily modify the successive elimination algorithm so that it is (ϵ, δ)-PAC. Instead of stopping when only one arm survives the elimination, it is possible to settle for stopping when either only one arm remains or when each of the k surviving arms were sampled $O(\frac{1}{\epsilon^2}\log(\frac{k}{\delta}))$. In the latter case the algorithm returns the best arm so far. In this case it is not hard to show that the algorithm finds an ϵ-optimal arm with probability at least $1 - \delta$ after

$$O\left(\sum_{i:\Delta_i>\epsilon} \frac{\log(\frac{n}{\delta\Delta_i})}{\Delta_i^2} + \frac{N(\Delta, \epsilon)}{\epsilon^2}\log(\frac{N(\Delta, \epsilon)}{\delta})\right),$$

where $N(\Delta, \epsilon) = |\{i \mid \Delta_i < \epsilon\}|$ is the number of arms which are ϵ-optimal.

3.2   Median Elimination

The following algorithm uses a clever trick for substituting $\log(1/\delta)$ for $\log(n/\delta)$ of the naive bound. The idea is to throw the worst half of the arms at each iteration. We do not expect the best arm to be empirically "the best", we only expect an ϵ-optimal arm to be above the median.

Algorithm : **Median Elimination**(ϵ, δ)
1. Set $S = A$.
2. $\epsilon_1 = \epsilon/4$, $\delta_1 = \delta/2$, $\ell = 1$.
3. Sample every arm $a \in S$ for $\frac{1}{(\epsilon_\ell/2)^2} \ln(3/\delta_\ell)$ times, and let $\hat{p}_a^\ell$
   denote its empirical value.
4. Find the median of $\hat{p}_a^\ell$, denoted by m_ℓ.
5. $S_{\ell+1} = S_\ell \setminus \{a : \hat{p}_a^\ell < m_\ell\}$.
6. If $|S_\ell| = 1$ Then output S_ℓ,
   Else $\epsilon_{\ell+1} = \frac{3}{4}\epsilon_\ell$; $\delta_{\ell+1} = \delta_\ell/2$; $\ell = \ell + 1$; Go to 3.

Theorem 4. *The Median Elimination(ϵ, δ) algorithm is an (ϵ, δ)-PAC algorithm and its arm sample complexity is $O(\frac{n \ln(\frac{1}{\delta})}{\epsilon^2})$.*

First we show that in the ℓ-th phase the expected reward of the best arm in S_ℓ drops by at most ϵ_ℓ.

Lemma 1. *For the* Median Elimination(ϵ, δ) *algorithm we have that*

$$Pr[\max_{j \in S_\ell} p_j \leq \max_{i \in S_{\ell+1}} p_i + \epsilon_\ell] \geq 1 - \delta_\ell$$

Proof. Without loss of generality we look at the first round and assume that p_1 is the reward of the best arm. We bound the failure probability by looking at the event $E_1 = \{\hat{p}_1 < p_1 - \epsilon_1/2\}$, which is the case that the empirical estimate of the best arm is pessimistic. By step 3 of the algorithm, we sample sufficiently such that $Pr[E_1] \leq \delta_1/3$.

In case E_1 does not hold, we calculate the probability that an arm which is not an ϵ_1-optimal arm is empirically better than the best arm.

$$Pr[\hat{p}_j \geq \hat{p}_1 \mid \hat{p}_1 \geq p_1 - \epsilon_1/2] \leq Pr[\hat{p}_j \geq p_j + \epsilon_1/2 \mid \hat{p}_1 \geq p_1 - \epsilon_1/2] \leq \delta_1/3$$

Let #bad be the number of arms which are not ϵ_1-optimal but are empirically better than the best arm. We have that $E[\#\text{bad} \mid \hat{p}_1 \geq p_1 - \epsilon_1/2] \leq n\delta_1/3$. Next we apply Markov inequality to obtain,

$$Pr[\#\text{bad} \geq n/2 \mid \hat{p}_1 \geq p_1 - \epsilon_1/2] \leq \frac{n\delta_1/3}{n/2} = 2\delta_1/3.$$

Using the union bound gives us that the probability of failure is bounded by δ_1. $\square$

Next we prove that arm sample complexity is bounded by $O(\frac{n \ln(\frac{1}{\delta})}{\epsilon^2})$.

Lemma 2. *The* Median Elimination(ϵ, δ) *has $O(\frac{n \ln(\frac{1}{\delta})}{\epsilon^2})$ arm sample complexity.*

Proof. The number of arm samples in the ℓ-th round is $\frac{4n_\ell \ln(3/\delta_\ell)}{\epsilon_\ell^2}$. By definition we have that

1. $\delta_1 = \delta/2$; $\delta_\ell = \delta_{\ell-1}/2 = \delta/2^\ell$
2. $n_1 = n$; $n_\ell = n_{\ell-1}/2 = n/2^{\ell-1}$
3. $\epsilon_1 = \epsilon/4$; $\epsilon_\ell = \frac{3}{4}\epsilon_{\ell-1} = \left(\frac{3}{4}\right)^{\ell-1}\epsilon/4$

Therefore we have

$$\sum_{\ell=1}^{\log_2(n)} \frac{n_\ell \ln(3/\delta_\ell)}{(\epsilon_\ell/2)^2} = 4 \sum_{\ell=1}^{\log_2(n)} \frac{n/2^{\ell-1}\ln(2^\ell 3/\delta)}{((\frac{3}{4})^{\ell-1}\epsilon/4)^2}$$

$$= 64 \sum_{\ell=1}^{\log_2(n)} n\left(\frac{8}{9}\right)^{\ell-1}\left(\frac{\ln(1/\delta)}{\epsilon^2} + \frac{\ln(3)}{\epsilon^2} + \frac{\ell \ln(2)}{\epsilon^2}\right)$$

$$\leq 64 \frac{n\ln(1/\delta)}{\epsilon^2} \sum_{\ell=1}^{\infty}\left(\frac{8}{9}\right)^{\ell-1}(\ell C' + C) \leq O\left(\frac{n\ln(1/\delta)}{\epsilon^2}\right)$$

$\square$

Now we can prove Theorem 4.

Proof. From Lemma 2 we have that the sample complexity is bounded by $O(\frac{n\ln(1/\delta)}{\epsilon^2})$. By Lemma 1 we have that the algorithm fails with probability δ_i in each round so that over all rounds the probability of failure is bounded by $\sum_{i=1}^{\log_2(n)} \delta_i \leq \delta$. In each round we reduce the optimal reward of the surviving arms by at most ϵ_i so that the total error is bounded by $\sum_{i=1}^{\log_2(n)} \epsilon_i \leq \epsilon$. $\square$

4 A Lower Bound

In this section we provide a lower bound for the arm sample complexity. We do this by showing that one can convert an algorithm for solving an n-armed bandit problem with sample complexity T, to an algorithm that determines the bias of a single coin in expected time $O(T/n)$. First we define the coin bias problem (e.g., [1]).

Definition 2. *The input to a coin bias problem is a binary random variable X, such that $P[X = 1] \in \{1/2+\epsilon, 1/2-\epsilon\}$. The aim is to determine, with probability at least $1 - \delta$, the correct bias of the coin (i.e., the value of $P[X = 1]$), given access to i.i.d. samples of X. The sample complexity of an (ϵ, δ)-PAC algorithm is the maximum over $P[X = 1] \in \{1/2 + \epsilon, 1/2 - \epsilon\}$ of the expected number of samples of the random variable X that the algorithm makes.*

Lemma 3. *Given an (ϵ, δ)-PAC multi-armed bandit algorithm A for n-armed bandit problem that has expected sample complexity T, there exists an $(\epsilon, 2\delta + 1/n)$-PAC algorithm for the coin bias problem with expected sample complexity $O(T/n)$.*

Proof. Let $C_1, \ldots, C_n$ be i.i.d. $\{0, 1\}$ valued random variables, such that $P(C_i = 1) = 1/2 - \epsilon$. Let $I(X, i)$ represent n random variables, $Y_1, \ldots, Y_n$, where $Y_i = X$ and $Y_k = C_k$, for $k \neq i$.

Given as an input a random variable X, we run two copies of A, the first called min with $I(X, i)$ and the second called max with $I(1 - X, j)$, where i and j are chosen at random uniformly in $\{1, \ldots, n\}$. In both copies of A we seek for the optimal coin, only that in min we have that if $P(X = 1) = 1/2 - \epsilon$ then all coins are identical and in max all coins are identical if $P(X = 1) = 1/2 + \epsilon$. Each time min or max queries X we sample it, and when it queries a different random variable C_k we simulate such a coin. We define our output as follows. We consider only the copy that terminates first. When the min (max) copy returns i (j), which is the index of X, we claim that X has bias $1/2 + \epsilon$ ($1/2 - \epsilon$) and if it returns $k \neq i$ ($k \neq j$) we claim that X has bias $1/2 - \epsilon$ ($1/2 + \epsilon$).

For the correctness, with probability $1 - 2\delta$ both copies of A return the best arm. From now on we assume that each copy that terminates returns the best arm. If X has bias $1/2 - \epsilon$ ($1/2 + \epsilon$) then the min (max) copy has n i.i.d random variables with bias $1/2 - \epsilon$ ($1/2 + \epsilon$). In such a case X and the other random variables are indistinguishable, and the chance X is selected as output is $1/n$ (since its index is chosen initially uniformly at random). Therefore, if $P(X = 1) = 1/2 - \epsilon$ and min terminates first, with probability $1 - 1/n$ another arm is chosen and we have a correct output. But, with probability $1/n$ we have an error, since i is chosen. If $P(X = 1) = 1/2 - \epsilon$ and max terminates first, since A does not err, its output is different from X, and we do not err. (The case when the bias is $1/2 + \epsilon$ is similar.) This implies that our algorithm is $(\epsilon, 2\delta + 1/n)$-PAC. It remains to study our sample complexity.

We now analyze the sample complexity. We assume that the number of samples of X in min and max cannot differ in more than one sample. (Formally, there is a scheduler which schedules the copy that sampled X the least number of times. If they both sampled the same number of times, it chooses an arbitrary one.) Clearly, one of the copies terminates eventually. Since in one of the copies we have n identical random variables, its sample complexity is T/n. This implies that the expected sample complexity is $O(T/n)$.   □

Theorem 5. *Any (ϵ, δ)-PAC multi-armed bandit algorithm has an arm sample complexity of at least $T(\epsilon, \delta, n)$, where*

$$T(\epsilon, \delta, n) = \Omega(\frac{n \log(1/\delta')}{\epsilon^2}),$$

where $\delta' = 2\delta + 1/n$.

Proof. By Lemma 3 we have an (ϵ, δ')-PAC algorithm with sample complexity $O(T(\epsilon, \delta, n)/n)$, where $\delta' = 2\delta + 1/n$. The result follows from the $\Omega(\log(1/\delta')/\epsilon^2)$ lower bound on the expected sample complexity of the biases problem [8].   □

Remark 3. For $\delta < 1/n$, we can give two simple lower bounds. The first is due to [1], which gives us $\Omega(\frac{\log(1/\delta)}{\epsilon^2})$. The second is due to a simple experiment which is composed from $n - 1$ arms with zero expectation and one with ϵ expectation. For this experiment any algorithm should sample $\Omega(\frac{n \log(1/\delta)}{\epsilon})$ times.

5   Markov Decision Processes

In this section we use the techniques developed for multi-armed bandit problems for deriving learning algorithms for MDPs. We show how to use any (ϵ, δ)-PAC multi-armed bandit algorithm to derive an algorithm for learning in an MDP. The learning algorithm in the MDP is based on Phased Q-learning [15]. Using our transformation we are even able to slightly improve the complexity of the Phased Q-Learning, mainly reduce its dependency on the number of action from $O(|A| \log |A|)$ to $O(|A|)$.

5.1   Phased Q-Learning

Phased Q-Learning [15] operates in phases, where in each phase every state action pair is sampled m times, and based on the new sample a new estimate to the Q function is derived.

Algorithm : **Phased Q-Learning**(n, m)
1. For every state-action pair (s, a): $\hat{Q}_0(s, a) = 0$
2. For $k = 1$ to n DO
    (a) For every state action pair invoke $sample(s, a)$ for m times, and let (s_i^k, r_i^k) be the i-th reply.
    (b) Update:

$$\hat{Q}_{k+1}(s, a) = \frac{1}{m} \left(\sum_{i=1}^{m} r_i^k(s, a) + \gamma \hat{V}_k(s_i^k) \right),$$

    (c) $\hat{V}_{k+1}(s) = \max_a \hat{Q}_{k+1}(s, a)$

It is not hard to show that for the appropriate parameters m and n the algorithm is ϵ-optimal with probability at least $1 - \delta$.

Theorem 6 ([15]). *For $n = \frac{\ln(\frac{V_{max}}{2(1-\gamma)\epsilon})}{1-\gamma}$ and $m = O\left(\frac{\ln(|S||A|n/\delta)}{\epsilon^2(1-\gamma)^2}\right)$ the Phased Q-learning(n, m) converges with probability $1 - \delta$ to an ϵ-optimal policy.*

As a consequence from the theorem we have that the sample complexity is:

$$nm|S||A| = O\left(\frac{|S||A|V_{max}^2}{\epsilon^2(1-\gamma)^3}\left(\ln(|S||A|/\delta) + \ln\left(\frac{\ln(V_{max}/\epsilon)}{1-\gamma}\right)\right)\ln\left(\frac{V_{max}}{(1-\gamma)\epsilon}\right)\right)$$

5.2   MAB Phased Q-Learning Algorithm

We like to first establish a simple connection between the multi-armed bandit problem and the Phased Q-learning algorithm. We do this by considering, for each phase and state, the update of the Phased Q-learning as a multi-armed bandit problem.

Note that during phase k of Phased Q-Learning, the value of $V_k(s)$ is fixed. This implies that for every state and action (s, a) we can define a random variable $Y_s(a)$ whose value is $R(s, a) + \gamma V_k(s')$, where $R(s, a)$ is the random variable representing the reward and s' is distributed using $P^a_{s,s'}$.

Our aim is to find, at each state, the action that maximizes the expected reward, and estimate its expected reward, where the rewards are $Y_s(a)$. The Phased Q-Learning can now be viewed as using the Naive algorithm for multi-armed bandit problem in order to find the best arm. In the following we show how, using a more sophisticated multi-armed bandit algorithm, one can improve the convergence rate of the Phased Q-Learning.

Our algorithm uses any (ϵ, δ)-PAC Multi-armed bandit algorithm as a black box to learn an MDP. In order to use the multi-armed bandit algorithm B as, a black box, we define a simple interface, using the following procedures:

- $Init_B(\epsilon, \delta)$ - Initialize the parameters of B.
- $GetArm_B()$ - returns the arm a that B wants to sample next.
- $Update_B(a, r)$ - informs B the latest reward r of arm a.
- $Stop_B(a, v)$ - returns TRUE if B terminates, and in such a case a is the output of B and v is its estimated value. (We assume that on termination, with probability at least $1 - \delta$, the arm a is an ϵ-optimal arm and $|r^* - v| \leq \epsilon$.)

The MAB Phased Q-learning algorithm uses, as a black box, an algorithm B for the multi-armed bandit problem. It receives as input (ϵ, δ) and returns a policy π which is ϵ-optimal with probability at least $1 - \delta$.

Algorithm : **MAB Phased Q-Learning**(ϵ, δ)

1. Let $\hat{\epsilon} = \frac{\epsilon(1-\gamma)}{2}$; $n = \log_\gamma(\hat{\epsilon}/2V_{max}) = O(\ln(\frac{V_{max}}{(1-\gamma)\epsilon})/(1 - \gamma))$;
   $\hat{\delta} = \frac{\delta}{|S|n}$.
2. Initialize for every $s \in S$: $= V_0(s) = 0$,
3. For $i = 1$ to n and for every $s \in S$ Do
   (a) $Init_B(\hat{\epsilon}, \hat{\delta})$
   (b) $a = GetArm_B()$
   (c) $(s', r) = sample(s, a)$
   (d) $r' = r + \gamma V_i(s')$
   (e) $Update_B(a, r')$
   (f) IF $Stop(a, v) = $ FALSE Then Go to (3b)
       ELSE $V_{i+1}(s) = v$; $\pi(s) = a$.
4. output π.

5.3   MAB Phased Q-Learning Analysis

Let B be an (ϵ, δ)-PAC multi-armed bandit algorithm, and assume B has arm sample complexity $T_B(\epsilon, \delta)$. Namely, with probability $1 - \delta$, algorithm B terminates after at most $T_B(\epsilon, \delta)$ and outputs a policy π which is ϵ-optimal. In this subsection we analyze the MAB Phased Q-Learning algorithm, and derive its running time as a function of T_B.

Theorem 7. *Assume B is an $(\hat{\epsilon}, \hat{\delta})$-PAC multi-armed bandit algorithm. MAB Phased Q-Learning(ϵ, δ) algorithm, with probability at least $1-\delta$, outputs a policy π which is an ϵ-optimal policy, and has sample complexity*

$$n|S|T_B(\hat{\epsilon}, \hat{\delta}) = O\left(\frac{|S|}{1 - \gamma}\ln(\frac{V_{max}}{(1 - \gamma)\epsilon})T_B\left(\frac{\epsilon(1 - \gamma)}{2}, \frac{\delta(1 - \gamma)}{|S|\ln(V_{max}/\epsilon)}\right)\right).$$

First we show that in each phase the norm $\|V^* - V\|_\infty$ decreases.

Lemma 4. *Assume B is an $(\hat{\epsilon}, \hat{\delta})$-PAC multi-armed bandit algorithm, and consider the MAB Phased Q-Learning(ϵ, δ) algorithm using B. Then with probability at least $1 - \delta$, for all $k \leq n$, $\|V^* - V_k\|$ is bounded by $\frac{\hat{\epsilon}}{1-\gamma} + V_{max}\gamma^k$.*

Proof. First we bound the probability that B outputs an arm which is not ϵ-optimal. We bound the failure probability by using the union bound on all the invocations of B. There are

$$|S|n = |S|\log_\gamma(\hat{\epsilon}/V_{max}) = O\left(\frac{|S|\ln(\frac{V_{max}}{(1-\gamma)\epsilon})}{1 - \gamma}\right)$$

initializations of algorithm B and for each invocation the failure probability is bounded by $\frac{\delta}{|S|n}$. Thus, the failure probability is at most δ.

Next, we show that the error contracts in every phase. We compare the value vector, V_k, with the standard value iteration value vector $\hat{V}_k$ for the case of a known model (at the end of the k-th step). Formally,

$$\hat{V}_{k+1}(s) = \max_u\{E[R(s, u)] + \gamma E_{s'}[\hat{V}_k(s')]\},$$

where s' is distributed according to $P_{s,s'}^u$ and $\hat{V}_0 = 0$.

We show by induction on the number of phases, that $d_k = \|V_k - \hat{V}_k\|_\infty \leq \frac{\hat{\epsilon}}{1-\gamma}$. The base of the induction, $t = 0$, for every state s we have $d_0 = |V_0(s) - \hat{V}_0(s)| = 0$. We assume that the induction assumption holds for $t < k$ and prove for k. Let $m_{s,a}$ denote the number of times the state action pair (s, a) was sampled in the k-th iteration.

$$\begin{aligned}
|V_k(s) - \hat{V}_k(s)| &= |\max_u [\frac{1}{m_{s,u}} \sum_{i=1}^{m_{s,u}} r(s,u) + \gamma V_{k-1}(s_i')] \\
&\quad - \max_a [E[R(s,a)] + \gamma \sum_{s'} P^a_{s,s'} \hat{V}_{k-1}(s')]| \\
&\leq \max_{\rho \in \{-\hat{\epsilon}, \hat{\epsilon}\}} |\max_u [E[R(s,u)] + \gamma \sum_{s'} P^u_{s,s'} V_{k-1}(s')] + \rho \\
&\quad - \max_a [E[R(s,a)] + \gamma \sum_{s'} P^a_{s,s'} \hat{V}_{k-1}(s')]| \\
&\leq \hat{\epsilon} + \max_a \left| \gamma \sum_{s'} P^a_{s,s'} (V_{k-1}(s') - \hat{V}_{k-1}(s')) \right| \\
&\leq \hat{\epsilon} + \gamma d_{k-1} \\
&\leq \hat{\epsilon} + \gamma (\frac{\hat{\epsilon}}{1-\gamma}) = \frac{\hat{\epsilon}}{1-\gamma}.
\end{aligned}$$

To conclude the proof note that for the value iteration we have that $\|\hat{V}_k - V^*\| \leq \gamma^k V_{max}$, where $\hat{V}_0 = 0$ (see, e.g. [5]). $\quad\square$

Lemma 5. *When the MAB Phased Q-Learning algorithm terminates, with probability at least $1 - \delta$, policy π is an ϵ-optimal policy.*

Proof. By Lemma 4 we have that with probability at least $1 - \delta$ the difference $\|V_k - V^*\| \leq \frac{\hat{\epsilon}}{1-\gamma} + V_{max}\gamma^k$. Since $\hat{\epsilon} = \frac{\epsilon(1-\gamma)}{2}$, we have that $\|V_k - V^*\| \leq \frac{\epsilon}{2} + V_{max}\gamma^k$. The lemma follows from our choice of $n = \log_\gamma(\frac{\hat{\epsilon}}{2V_{max}})$. $\quad\square$

Now we can prove Theorem 7.

Proof. The correctness follows from Lemma 5. We bound the sample complexity as follows. By definition, the MAB Phased Q-Learning algorithm samples at each state and action during every phase $T_B(\hat{\epsilon}, \hat{\delta})$. By definition of the algorithm, the number of phases is $n = O\left(\frac{\ln(V_{max}/\hat{\epsilon})}{1-\gamma}\right)$, and each phase is composed from $|S|$ MAB instances. This completes the bound on the sample complexity. $\quad\square$

Applying the multi-armed bandit algorithms described in the previous sections we derive the following corollary. We show that by using the *median elimination* algorithm, the arm sample complexity can be reduced by a factor of $\log(|A|)$.

Corollary 1. *Let B be the median elimination algorithm. MAB Phased Q-Learning algorithm has sample complexity*

$$O\left(\frac{|S|\,|A|V_{max}^2}{(1-\gamma)^3\epsilon^2} \ln(\frac{V_{max}}{(1-\gamma)\epsilon}) \ln(\frac{|S|\ln(V_{max}/\epsilon)}{\delta(1-\gamma)})\right).$$

Remark 4. One can use the successive elimination algorithm as the basic MAB algorithm. This would result in improved convergence rates if the Q functions at the end of each phase are well separated. We note that by using the successive elimination algorithm with finite stopping time (as suggested in Remark 2) the convergence rate is as good as the rates of [15]. If, however, one is "lucky" and during the process of the phased Q-learning the Q values are well separated in the various rounds, then the convergence rates may improve significantly. It is an open question if properties of the model itself (such as the separation of the optimal Q function) may lead to improved convergence rates.

Acknowledgements

This research was supported in part by a grant from the Israel Science Foundation. S. M. would like to thank Nahum Shimkin for helpful discussions.

References

1. M. Anthony and P. L. Bartlett. *Neural Network Learning; Theoretical Foundations.* Cambridge University Press, 1999. 263, 264
2. P. Auer, N. Cesa-Bianchi, Y. Freund, and R. E. Schapire. Gambling in a rigged casino: The adversarial multi-armed bandit problem. In *Proc. 36th Annual Symposium on Foundations of Computer Science*, pages 322–331. IEEE Computer Society Press, 1995. 256
3. P. Auer, N. Cesa-Bianchi, Y. Freund, and R. E. Schapire. The non-stochastic multi-armed bandit problem. preprint, 2001. 256
4. D. A. Berry and B. Fristedt. *Bandit Problems.* Chapman and Hall, 1985. 255
5. D. P. Bertsekas and J. N. Tsitsiklis. *Neuro-Dynamic Progamming.* Athena Scientific, 1995. 257, 268
6. V. S. Borkar and S.P Meyn. The O. D. E. method for convergence of stochastic approximation and reinforcement learning. *SIAM J. Control,*, 38(2):447–469, 2000. 257
7. R. Brafman and M. Tennenholtz. R-MAX – A General Polynomial Time Algorithm for Near Optimal Reinforcement Learning. In *International Joint Conference on Artificial Intelligence*, 2001. 257
8. H. Chernoff. *Sequential Analysis and Optimal Design.* Society for industrial and Applied Mathematics, Philadelphia, 1972. 264
9. P. Dayan and C. Watkins. Q-learning. *Machine Learning*, 8:279–292, 1992. 257
10. Eyal Even-Dar and Yishay Mansour. Learning rates for q-learning. In *Fourteenth Annual Conference on Computation Learning Theory*, pages 589–604, 2001. 257
11. C. N. Fiechter. PAC adaptive control of linear systems. In *Tenth Annual conference on Computational Learing Theory*, pages 72–80, 1997. 257
12. J. Gittins and D. Jones. A dynamic allocation index for the sequential design of experiments. In J. Gani, K. Sarkadi, and I. Vincze, editors, *Progress in Statistics*, pages 241–266. North-Holland, Amsterdam, 1974. 256
13. M. Kearns, Y. Mansour, and A. Ng. Approximate planning in large POMDPs via reusable trajectories. In *Advances in Neural Information Processing Systems*, 1999. 257

14. M. Kearns and S. Singh. Near-optimal reinforcement learning in polynomial time. In *Proc. of the 15th Int. Conf. on Machine Learning*, pages 260–268. Morgan Kaufmann, 1998. 257
15. M. Kearns and S. Singh. Finite-sample convergence rates for Q-learning and indirect algorithms near-optimal reinforcement learning in polynomial time. In *Neural Information Processing Systems 11*, pages 996–1002. Morgan Kaufmann, 1999. 256, 257, 265, 269
16. Michael J. Kearns, Yishay Mansour, and Andrew Y. Ng. A sparse sampling algorithm for near-optimal planning in large Markov Decision Processes. In *International Joint Conference on AI*, pages 1324–1231, 1999. 257
17. T. L. Lai and H. Robbins. Asymptotically efficient adaptive allocation rules. *Advances in Applied Mathematics*, 6:4–22, 1985. 256
18. H. Robbins. Some aspects of sequential design of experiments. *Bull. Amer. Math. Soc.*, 55:527–535, 1952. 255
19. J. N. Tsitsiklis. Asynchronous stochastic approximation and Q-learning. *Machine Learning*, 16:185–202, 1994. 257

Bounds for the Minimum Disagreement Problem with Applications to Learning Theory

Nader H. Bshouty[1][*] and Lynn Burroughs[2][**]

[1] Department of Computer Science, Technion
Haifa, Israel
bshouty@cs.technion.ac.il
[2] Department of Computer Science, University of Calgary
Calgary, Alberta, Canada
lynnb@cpsc.ucalgary.ca

Abstract. Many studies have been done in the literature on minimum disagreement problems and their connection to Agnostic learning and learning with Malicious errors. We further study these problems and some extensions of them. The classes that are studied in the literature are monomials, monotone monomials, antimonotone monomials, decision lists, halfspaces, neural networks and balls. For some of these classes we improve on the best previously known factors for approximating the minimum disagreement. We also find new bounds for exclusive-or, k-term DNF, k-DNF and multivariate polynomials (Xor of monomials). We then apply the above and some other results from the literature to Agnostic learning and give negative and positive results for Agnostic learning and PAC learning with malicious errors of the above classes.

1 Introduction

In this paper, we study the Minimum Disagreement (MD) problem where the goal is to find a hypothesis h from some class C of hypotheses, such that h minimizes the disagreements with a training sample S. We also study an extension of MD. In the extension, [KSS92, HSV95] we allow h to be from a larger class of hypotheses $H \supset C$ and we ask $h \in H$ to have a disagreement rate within a factor α of the best function in C. We call this C/H-MD.

In [KL93, KSS92, Ha92] it is shown that solving MD for a class C is equivalent to Agnostic learning C. Agnostic learning is a very useful variant of the PAC learning model in which the learning algorithm is required to find the best hypothesis in the class C that agrees with the target concept. In this paper we define α-Agnostic learning of C from H in which we seek a hypothesis $h \in H$

---

[*] This research was supported by the fund for promotion of research at the Technion. Research no. 120-025. Part of this research was done at the University of Calgary, Calgary, Alberta, Canada.

[**] This research was supported by an NSERC PGS-B Scholarship, an Izaak Walton Killam Memorial Scholarship, and an Alberta Informatics Circle of Research Excellence (iCORE) Fellowship.

J. Kivinen and R. H. Sloan (Eds.): COLT 2002, LNAI 2375, pp. 271–286, 2002.
© Springer-Verlag Berlin Heidelberg 2002

that disagrees within a factor α of the best hypothesis in the class C. Then using similar techniques to the ones used in [KL93, KSS92, Ha92] we find a connection between C/H-MD, α-Agnostic learning and PAC learning with malicious errors.

For C/H-MD a few results are known from the literature. In [KL93, ABSS97] and [HSV95] negative results are given for approximating MD for monomials, decision lists and halfspaces. Results for Neural Networks are given in [BB99, K00]. We extend the results to the class of Balls, Xor functions, k-term DNF, k-DNF, multivariate polynomials and other classes. We also show that for boolean classes with VC-dimension d, if the consistent hypothesis problem is solvable in polynomial time then for any constant c there is a $c \cdot poly(d)$-approximation algorithm for MD. This extends results in [KL93] and [BK01]. We then apply the above to α-Agnostic learning and give negative and positive results for α-Agnostic learning and PAC learning with malicious errors, of the above classes.

One of the significant results (our main contribution) in the paper is the negative result for Xor/H-MD problem for a wide class H. We extend the result of Håstad [H97] and show that the Xor/H-MD problem cannot be α-approximated for any constant α even when we extend the hypothesis class H to a "larger" class (unless P=NP). This class H includes all the boolean functions with L_1 norm bounded by $2^{\log^c n}$. This class contains decision trees with Xor nodes of size $2^{\log^c n}$, $O(\log^c n)$-term DNF and $O(\log^c n)$-clause CNF. This result implies that the Xor class of functions is not α-Agnostic learnable for any constant α even with that large class of hypotheses. As a consequence any class $C \subset H$ that contains the XOR functions is not α-Agnostic learnable for any constant α. This is one step further for the conjecture that the set of XOR functions is not Agnostic learnable by *polynomial size* circuits.

The paper is organized as follows. In subsection 1.1 we give results known in the literature and the results in this paper. In section 2 we give preliminary results and definitions. In section 3 we give a general upper bound for approximating MD. In section 4 we give lower bounds for approximating MD of the above classes. In section 5 we give negative results for the MD of the Xor class.

1.1 Results

In this subsection we give the results in the literature and our results for C/H-MD and their connection to Agnostic learning and learning with malicious errors. It is clear that solving C/H-MD implies PAC learnability of C from H. Therefore all the negative results in the literature for PAC learning of classes C from H will give negative results for C/H-MD. Therefore in this paper we will mostly consider classes C that are PAC-learnable. It is also known that there is an α-approximation algorithm for C/H-MD if and only if C is α-Agnostic learnable from H. When $H = C$ we will just write C-MD.

NP-Hardness for Agnostic Learning Angluin and Laird [AL88] showed that Monotone Monomial-MD (MMon-MD) is NP-Hard. Kearns and Li [KL93] showed that Monomial-MD (Mon-MD) is NP-Hard. Höffgen, Simon and Van Horn [HSV95] showed that Halfspace-MD (HS-MD) is NP-Hard. In fact it follows from their result that MMon/HS-MD and DL/HS-MD are NP-Hard. (Here DL is decision list). It follows from the results of Håstad [H97] that Xor-MD is NP-Hard. Those results imply that there is no learning algorithm that Agnostic learns the classes MMon, Mon, DL, HS and Xor.

Bounds for α-Agnostic Learning Combining a reduction by Kearns, Schapire and Sellie [KSS92] and Hoffgen, Simon and Van Horn [HSV95], with the result of Feige [F96] it follows that: If $NP \not\subseteq DTIME(n^{\log\log n})$ then for any $\epsilon > 0$ there is no polynomial time $(1 - \epsilon)\ln n$-approximation algorithm for Mon-MD and for MMon-MD. In fact, from Höffgen, Simon and Van Horn [HSV95] it follows that there is no polynomial time $(1 - \epsilon)\ln n$-approximation algorithm for MMon/HS-MD, DL/HS-MD and HS-MD. Arora, Babai, Stern and Sweedyk [ABSS97] showed that if $NP \not\subseteq DTIME(n^{poly(\log n)})$ then for any $\epsilon > 0$ there is no polynomial time $2^{\log^{0.5-\epsilon} n}$-approximation algorithm for HS-MD and no $2^{\log^{1-\epsilon} n}$-approximation algorithm for Xor-MD and if P$\neq$NP then for any constant c there is no polynomial time c-approximation algorithm for HS-MD. Those results give negative results for α-Agnostic learning of Monomials from Halfspace, decision lists from Halfspace, Halfspace and the class of XOR functions.

In this paper we first show that a constant approximation algorithm for C/H-MD will give a constant approximation algorithm for C/H-Maximum Agreement (C/H-MA) (the problem of finding a hypothesis that maximizes the number of agreements with a training sample). Therefore if C/H-MA has no approximation scheme then C/H-MD has approximation scheme. Since Ball-MA (the class of Balls) has no approximation scheme [BEL00] it follows that Ball-MD has no approximation scheme and therefore is not α-Agnostic learnable for some constant α. We use a reduction from MAX-CUT to achieve a better constant α.

We then investigate other classes. Using the results in [PV88, HSV95, S01] we show that for any α, there is no α-approximation algorithm for MD of the class k-term Monotone DNF with a hypothesis that is $(2k - 3)$-term DNF for any $k \geq 4$. We extend this result to k-term Multivariate Polynomial. That is, there is no α-Agnostic learning algorithm for k-term Multivariate Polynomial for any α. We then consider whether we can restrict the class k-term DNF and get an Agnostic Learning for that restricted class. We restrict the class to k-Same term Monotone DNF where all k terms are the same but on disjoint variables. Functions in this class are read-once, monotone and have a very simple structure. We show that even for this very restricted class it is hard to $O(\ln^k n)$-Agnostic learn even with a hypothesis that is k-term DNF. Since k-term DNF and k-DNF are learnable with k-DNF we also investigate the hardness of α-Agnostic learning k-DNF and show that $O(\ln n)$-Agnostic learning k-DNF is hard.

One of our main contributions in this paper is the negative result for Xor/H-MD problems for a wide class H. We extend the result of Håstad [H97] and show that the Xor/H-MD problems cannot be $(\log n)^c$-approximated for any constant c even when we extend the hypothesis class H to a "larger" class (unless P=NP). This class H includes all the boolean functions with L_1 norm bounded by $2^{\log^c n}$. It contains decision trees with Xor nodes of size $2^{\log^c n}$, $O(\log^c n)$-term DNF and $O(\log^c n)$-clause CNF. This result implies that the Xor class of functions is not $2^{\log^c n}$-Agnostic learnable even with that large class of hypotheses.

2   Preliminary Results and Definitions

2.1   Concept Classes

Let X be a set of *instances* and 2^X be the set of *boolean functions* $f : X \to \{0,1\}$. Let $C \subset \Sigma^\star$ be a class of *formulas* for some alphabet Σ. Each formula $h^\star \in C$ represents a boolean function $h : X \to \{0,1\}$. We will call C the *concept class* over X. The size $|f|_C$ of any boolean function f with respect to C is the minimal length of a formula $h^\star \in C$ such that $h \equiv f$. If no such $h^\star$ exists then we write $|f|_C = \infty$. We will write $|f|$ when C is known from the context. A parametrized class of representations is $C = \bigcup_{n \geq 1} C_n$ where each C_n is a concept class over X_n. For example, $X_n = \{0,1\}^n$ and C_n is the set of all Boolean formulas over n variables with $|f| \leq n^k$ for some fixed constant k. In this case we simply say that C is a concept class over X. For $X_n = \{0,1\}^n$ we define the following classes.

k-Same term MDNF : is a Monotone DNF (MDNF) over the set of variables $x_{j,i}$ where $i = 1, \ldots, n$ and $j = 1, \ldots, k$ and is of the form $T(x^{(1)}) \vee T(x^{(2)}) \vee \cdots \vee T(x^{(k)})$ where T is MMon and $x^{(j)} = (x_{j,1}, \ldots, x_{j,n})$.
XOR : is exclusive-ors of literals over the Boolean variables $\{x_1, \ldots, x_n\}$.
MP : (Multivariate Polynomial) is exclusive-or of Monomials.
MMP : is exclusive-or of Monotone Monomials.
k-term MP : is a MP with k nonconstant monomials.
Ball : is a function $B : \{0, 1, -1\}^n \to \{0,1\}$ of the form

$$B(x_1, \ldots, x_n) = \left[\sqrt{(w_1 - x_1)^2 + (w_2 - x_2)^2 + \cdots + (w_n - x_n)^2} \leq \theta \right]$$

where $w_1, \ldots, w_n, \theta \in \Re$.

A *labeled example* from X is (x, y) where $x \in X$ and $y \in \{0,1\}$. A *labeled sample* from X is a set $S = \{(x_1, y_1), \ldots, (x_m, y_m)\}$ of labeled examples.

2.2   Fourier Transform and the FL_1 Concept Class

In section 5 we will regard the boolean function $f : \{0,1\}^n \to \{0,1\}$ as a function from $\{0,1\}^n$ to $\{-1, +1\}$ where -1 is True (or 1) and 1 is False (or 0). In that case any XOR function can be written as $\chi_a(x) = (-1)^{a \cdot x}$ where $a \cdot x = \sum_{i=1}^n a_i x_i$. The set of all XOR functions forms a basis for the set of all boolean functions and it is known (see [M94] for a good review) that any boolean function f can be written as

$$f = \sum_{a \in \{0,1\}^n} \hat{f}_a \chi_a(x)$$

where $\hat{f}_a = E_{x \in \mathcal{U}\{0,1\}^n}[f(x)\chi_a(x)]$ and $\mathcal{U}$ is the uniform distribution. We define the L_1 norm of a boolean function as $L_1(f) = \sum_a |\hat{f}_a|$. We define the class $FL_1[k]$ to be the set of all boolean functions f with $L_1(f) \leq k$. It is known [M94] that $FL_1[k]$ contains decision trees (with Xor nodes) of size k (size of decision tree is the number of leaves), DNF with $\log k$ terms, CNF with $\log k$ clauses, all the XOR functions and many other functions.

2.3 The Minimum Disagreement and Maximum Agreement Problems

Let $S = \{(x_1, y_1), \ldots, (x_m, y_m)\} \subseteq X \times \{0,1\}$ be a labeled sample and $h \in C$. We say that $(x, y) \in X \times \{0,1\}$ *agrees* with h if $h(x) = y$. Otherwise we say that h *disagrees* with (x, y). We define

$$A(S, h) = \frac{|\{i \mid h(x_i) = y_i\}|}{|S|} = \Pr_{(x,y) \in \mathcal{U} S}[h(x) = y],$$

the ratio of points in S that agree with h. If $A(S, h) = 1$ then we say that h is consistent on S. Define

$$D(S, h) = 1 - A(S, h) = \frac{|\{i \mid h(x_i) \neq y_i\}|}{|S|} = \Pr_{(x,y) \in \mathcal{U} S}[h(x) \neq y],$$

the ratio of points that disagree with h. Define $A(S, C) = \max_{h \in C} A(S, h)$, and $D(S, C) = \min_{h \in C} D(S, h)$. It is clear that $A(S, C) = 1 - D(S, C)$.

Let $C \subseteq H$ be two concept classes over X. Define the *Maximum Agreement* (MA) and *Minimum Disagreement* (MD) problems for C/H as follows.

C/H-MA
Input: A sample $S = \{(x_1, y_1), \ldots, (x_m, y_m)\} \subseteq X \times \{0,1\}$.
Output: A hypothesis h in H where $A(S, h) \geq A(S, C)$.

C/H-MD
Input: A sample $S = \{(x_1, y_1), \ldots, (x_m, y_m)\} \subseteq X \times \{0,1\}$.
Output: A hypothesis h in H where $D(S, h) \leq D(S, C)$.

For all the classes we have in this paper $\{0,1\} \subset C$ and therefore $D(S, C) \leq 1/2$. For $\alpha < 1$, an α-approximation algorithm for C/H-MA is an algorithm $\mathcal{A}_{C/H}$ that on input S outputs a hypothesis $\mathcal{A}_{C/H}(S) \in H$ such that $A(S, \mathcal{A}_{C/H}(S)) \geq \alpha A(S, C)$. For $\alpha > 1$, an α-approximation algorithm for C/H-MD is an algorithm $\mathcal{A}_{C/H}$ that on input S outputs a hypothesis $\mathcal{A}_{C/H}(S) \in H$ such that $D(S, \mathcal{A}_{C/H}(S)) \leq \alpha D(S, C)$.

The *Consistent Hypothesis* (CH) problem for C/H is defined as follows:

C/H-CH
Input: A sample $S = \{(x_1, f(x_1)), \ldots, (x_m, f(x_m))\}$ for some $f \in C$.
Output A hypothesis h in H where $D(S, h) = 0$. That is, an $h \in H$ that
            is consistent with S.

We will write C-CH (resp C-MA, C-MD) for the problem C/C-CH (C/C-MA, C/C-MD).

The next theorem is proved in [BB02].

Theorem 1. *We have*

1. *If there is an α-approximation algorithm for C/H-MD that runs in time T then there is an $\frac{1}{2} + \frac{1}{4\alpha-2}$-approximation algorithm for C/H-MA that runs in time T.*
2. *If there is no β-approximation algorithm for C/H-MA that runs in time T then there is no $\frac{\beta}{2\beta-1}$-approximation algorithm for C/H-MD that runs in time T.*

2.4   Models of Learning

We assume here that the reader is familiar with the standard models of learning. We only define the Agnostic learning Model.

Agnostic PAC [Ha92, KSS92] In the Agnostic PAC learning model we have a distribution P on $X \times \{0,1\}$ and an oracle Ex_P that produces examples according to this distribution. We say that an algorithm $\mathcal{A}$ (of the learner) *Agnostic PAC-learns* the class C if for any distribution P and for any $\epsilon, \delta > 0$ the algorithm $\mathcal{A}(\epsilon, \delta)$ asks queries from Ex_P and, with probability at least $1 - \delta$, outputs a hypothesis $h \in C$ that satisfies

$$\Pr_{(x,y)\in_P X \times \{0,1\}}[h(x) \neq y] \leq \min_{f \in C} \Pr_{(x,y)\in_P X \times \{0,1\}}[f(x) \neq y] + \epsilon.$$

If $\mathcal{A}$ runs in time T in $1/\epsilon, 1/\delta$ and $|f|$ then we say that C is *Agnostic PAC-learnable* in time T. If we allow h to be from a larger class H then we say that C is *Agnostic PAC-learnable* from H in time T. We relax Agnostic PAC-learning and define α-Agnostic PAC-learning. We say that C is α-*Agnostic PAC-learnable* from H in time T if

$$\Pr_{(x,y)\in_P X \times \{0,1\}}[h(x) \neq y] \leq \alpha \min_{f \in C} \Pr_{(x,y)\in_P X \times \{0,1\}}[f(x) \neq y] + \epsilon.$$

See also [HSV95] for some other extensions.

3   General Upper Bounds for MD

In the full paper we derive a general upper bound for MD. The first theorem is implicit in [KL93].

Theorem 2. *If C/H-CH is solvable in time T and H is finite, then for any constant c there is an α-approximation algorithm for C/H-MD that runs in time $poly(T)$ where $\alpha = 1 + \frac{\log |H|}{c \log T}$.*

What if C/H-CH is not solvable? This was observed in [HSV95] and [S01].

Theorem 3. *If C/H-CH is not solvable in time T then α-approximating C/H-MD is not solvable in time T for any α.*

The above theorems give the following.

Corollary 1. *For any constant c there is a polynomial-time $n/(c \log n)$-approximation algorithm for MMon-MD, Mon-MD, DL-MD, Xor-MD and there is a polynomial-time n/c-approximation algorithm for HS-MD.*

In the full paper we prove the following for classes with small VCD dimension.

Theorem 4. *If C/H-CH is solvable in time T then for any constant c there is an α-approximation algorithm for C/H-MD that runs in time $poly(T)$ where*

$$\alpha = 1 + \frac{VCD(H)}{c \log T} \log \frac{m \log m}{VCD(H)}.$$

In particular, there is a $(1 + \epsilon)$-approximation algorithm for C/H-MD that runs in time $m^{VCD(H)}$. For m and T that are polynomial in n (where $X = \{0, 1\}^n$) we have $\alpha = 1 + \frac{VCD(H)}{c}$ for any constant c.

3.1 Connection between MD and α-Agnostic Learning

The next lemma gives the connection between MD and Agnostic learning and PAC learning with malicious errors. The proof is provided in the full version of this paper. Parts are similar to the proofs given in [KL93], [KSS92] and [HSV95]. For PAC learning with malicious error rate β, we define $\epsilon^T_{MAL}(C, \beta)$ to be the minimal possible ϵ such that there exists an algorithm that runs in time $T(1/\delta, |f|, 1/\eta)$ and learns class C with error $\epsilon^T_{MAL}(C, \beta) + \eta$ for any $\eta > 0$.

Lemma 1. *1. If $\epsilon^T_{MAL}(C/H, \beta) \le \alpha\beta$ then there is an $(\alpha + 1)$-approximation algorithm for C/H-MD that runs in time T.*
   2. If there is an α-approximation algorithm for C/H-MD that runs in time T then $\epsilon^T_{MAL}(C/H, \beta) \le (\alpha + 1)\beta$
   3. There is an α-approximation algorithm for C/H-MD that runs in time T if and only if there is an α-Agnostic PAC-learning algorithm for C from H that runs in time T.

4 Lower Bounds for α-Agnostic Learning

4.1 A Negative Result for Balls

Ben-David, Eiron and Long[BEL00] showed that Ball-MA cannot be approximated within $\frac{415}{418} + \epsilon$ unless P = NP. Then by Theorem 1 Ball-MD cannot be approximated within $\frac{421}{418} - \epsilon$ under the same assumption. Using a reduction from MAXCUT, we improve this ratio.

Theorem 5. *For any $\epsilon' > 0$ it is NP-hard to approximate Ball-MD with a ratio less than $\frac{26}{25} - \epsilon'$.*

Proof. Håstad [H97] created instances $G = (V, E)$ of MAXCUT with $|V| = n$ and $|E| = 20m_0 + 22m_1$, where $m_1 \leq m_0$, such that for some small constants $\epsilon, \delta > 0$ it is NP-hard to distinguish graphs with cuts of size at least $(16 - 2\epsilon)m_0 + (18 - 2\epsilon)m_1$, or size at most $(15 + \delta)m_0 + (17 + \delta)m_1$.

For each edge $(u, v) \in E$, we create 6 examples in $\{0, 1, -1\}^n \times \{0, 1\}$. We create one copy of $(z_u, 0)$ where z_u has 0s everywhere except for a 1 in position u. Similarly we make one copy of $(z_v, 0)$. We make two copies of $(z_{uv}, 1)$, where z_{uv} has 0s everywhere except for 1s in positions u and v. Finally, we make two copies of $(z_{uv}^-, 1)$ where z_{uv}^- has 0s everywhere except for -1s in positions u and v. Let X_{uv} denote this multiset of 6 examples. The instance of Ball-MD has $6(20m_0 + 22m_1)$ examples.

It can be shown if $B(x_1, \ldots, x_n) = [\sqrt{(w_1 - x_1)^2 + \cdots + (w_n - x_n)^2} \leq \theta]$ is optimal then w.l.o.g. all $w_i < 0$ are $w_i = -9$, and all $w_i \geq 0$ are $w_i = 4$, while $\theta^2 = 18 + \sum_i (w_i)^2$. Consider X_{uv}. If $\text{sign}(w_u) \neq \text{sign}(w_v)$ then B disagrees with 1 example in X_{uv}. Otherwise it disagrees with two. Define cut S by $u \in S$ iff $w_u = 4$. G has a cut of size k iff some ball disagrees with at most $2(20m_0 + 22m_1 - k) + k$ examples. The result follows from the cut sizes above. $\square$

4.2   Negative Results for k-term DNF, k-term MP and k-DNF

In this section we give negative results for MD of k-term DNF, k-term MP and some other classes.

We first use Theorem 3 with the results in [PV88] to show the following.

Corollary 2. *For $k \geq 2$, it is NP-Hard to α-approximate (k-term MDNF/k-term DNF)- MD for any α. For $k \geq 4$ it is NP-Hard to α-approximate (k-term MDNF/$(2k - 3)$-term DNF)-MD for any α.*

Proof. In [PV88] it is shown that (k-term MDNF/k-term DNF)-CH and (k-term MDNF/$(2k - 3)$-term DNF)-CH are NP-Complete. Now using Theorem 3 the result follows.$\square$

In fact, Pitt and Valiant [PV88] showed that for $k \geq 3$ if coloring a k-colorable graph with $g(n, k)$ colors is hard then (k-term MDNF/$g(n, k)$-term DNF)-CH is hard. The reduction for $k = 2$ is from Set Splitting. There exists algorithms to color 3-colorable graphs with $O(|V|^{1/4} \log |V|)$ colors, and k-colorable graphs with $O(|V|^{1-3/(k+1)} \log |V|)$ colors [KMS94], but unless P = NP, no algorithm can exist that uses fewer than 5 colors to color a 3-colorable graph [KLS93].

We now give a similar result for k-term MMP. We remind the reader that k is the number of nonconstant monomials. Therefore, if $f \in k$-term MP then $f + 1 \in k$-term MP. We first show the following.

Lemma 2. *If $P_k = (k\text{-term MMP}/k\text{-term MP})\text{-CH}$ is not solvable in time T then P_{k+1} is not solvable in time T.*

Proof. We construct a reduction from P_k to P_{k+1}. Suppose $\mathcal{A}$ is an algorithm for P_{k+1} that runs in time T. Let S be an instance of P_k and define instance $S' = \{((x, 0), y), ((x, 1), y + 1) \mid (x, y) \in S\}$. It can be shown that any $(k + 1)$-term MP consistent with S' gives a k-term MP consistent with S. $\square$

Corollary 3. *For $k \geq 2$, it is NP-Hard to α-approximate (k-term MMP/k-term MP)- MD for any α.*

Proof. By Lemma 2 it is enough to prove the result for $k = 2$. The proof is a reduction from the Set Splitting problem and is similar to one in [PV88]. The Set Splitting problem (which is NP-Complete[GJ79]) is defined as follows:

Input: A finite set $X = \{x_1, \ldots, x_n\}$ and a collection $C = \{c_1, \ldots, c_m\}$ of subsets of X.

Output: A partition (X_1, X_2) of X such that for every c_i, $c_i \not\subseteq X_1$ and $c_i \not\subseteq X_2$ (or equivalently, $|c_i \cap X_1| \geq 1$ and $|c_i \cap X_2| \geq 1$).

Let (X, C) be an instance for the Set Splitting problem. First we may assume that $\bigcap_{c \in C} c$ is empty. Otherwise, the solution is trivial. Define

$$I(S) = \{(0_c, 0) \mid c \in C\} \cup \{(0_i, 1) \mid 1 \leq i \leq n\} \cup \{(0^n, 0), (1^n, 0)\},$$

where 1^n is all 1s and 0_c (resp 0_i) has 0s in entries $x \in c$ (resp. entry i) and 1s elsewhere. It is easy to see that if (X_1, X_2) is a solution for the Set Splitting instance (X, C) then $\bigwedge_{x \in X_1} x + \bigwedge_{x \in X_2} x$ is consistent with $I(S)$.

A single term cannot be consistent with $I(S)$. So if f is a 2-term MP consistent with $I(S)$, either $f = T_1 + T_2$ or $f = T_1 + T_2 + 1$. If $f = T_1 + T_2$, it can be shown that both T_1 and T_2 are monotone. Let $X_1 = \{x_i \mid T_1(0_i) = 1\}$ and $X_2 = \{x_i \mid T_2(0_i) = 1\}$. Then (X_1, X_2) is a partition of X and since $f(0_i) = 1$ for all i, it is easy to see that (X_1, X_2) is a solution for the instance (X, C). An analysis of the case $f = T_1 + T_2 + 1$ finds a contradiction. The result follows. $\square$

We now restrict the k-term DNF even more and show that (k-Same term MDNF)-MD is hard to solve. We will make use of the following result.

Theorem 6. *[KSS92, HSV95, F96] For any constant $\epsilon > 0$ there is no $(1 - \epsilon) \ln d$-approximation algorithm for MMon/Mon-MD (with examples of dimension d) unless $NP \subseteq DTIME(n^{O(\log \log n)})$.*

Proof. Feige [F96] gave a reduction mapping some instances of 3SAT with n variables to instances $S = \{S_1, \ldots, S_s\}$, $X = \cup_i S_i = \{1, \ldots, N\}$ of Set Cover, where $N > s$ and $N, s \in n^{O(\log \log n)}$. This proved that for all $\epsilon > 0$, Set Cover cannot be approximated within $(1 - \epsilon) \ln N$ unless $NP \subseteq TIME(n^{O(\log \log n)})$. We give the following reduction from Set Cover. Define

$$I(S) = \{(u_i, 0), (v_j, 1) \mid i = 1, \ldots, N, j = 1, \ldots, s\} \cup \{(1^s, 1)\} \subseteq \{0,1\}^s \times \{0,1\}$$

where $1^s \in \{0,1\}^s$ is the all 1 vector, $u_i = ([i \notin S_1], [i \notin S_2], \ldots, [i \notin S_s])$ and v_j is the vector with all entries 1 except entry j which is equal to 0. The example $(1^s, 1)$ appears s times in $I(S)$. Each $(u_i, 0)$ appears s times in $I(S)$ and each v_j appears once. Therefore, there are $t = s(N + 1)$ examples in $I(S)$.

If T is not monotone then $T(1^s) = 0$ and $t \cdot D(I(S), T) \geq s$. If T is monotone then let $T = x_{j_1} x_{j_2} \cdots x_{j_r}$. Then it can be shown that $t \cdot D(I(S), T) = s |S \setminus (S_{j_1} \cup \cdots \cup S_{j_r})| + r$. Obviously, $D(I(S), T)$ is optimal when T is monotone and $\{S_{j_1}, \ldots, S_{j_r}\}$ is a set cover and therefore, $t \cdot D(I(S), \text{MMon}) = SC(S)$. An α-approximation algorithm for MMon-MD would then give an α-approximation algorithm for Set Cover. The examples have dimension $d = s < N$ and by Feige's [F96] result, MMon-MD does not have a $(1 - \epsilon) \ln d$-approximation algorithm unless NP $\subseteq$ DTIME($n^{O(\log \log n)}$). $\square$

Theorem 7. *Let $k \geq 1$ be a constant. For any constant $\epsilon > 0$ there is no $(1 - \epsilon) \ln^k \frac{d}{k}$-approximation algorithm for (k-Same term MDNF/k-term MDNF)-MD with examples of dimension d unless NP $\subseteq$ DTIME($n^{O(\log \log n)}$).*

Proof. Let S, X be an instance of Set Cover described in the proof of Theorem 6. Define $S_{i+js} = S_i$ for every $1 \leq i \leq s$ and $j = 1, \ldots, k - 1$ and

$$I^k(S) = \{(u_i, 0), (v_{j_1 \ldots, j_k}, 1), (w_\ell, 1) |$$
$$i = 1, \ldots, N, j_\alpha = (\alpha - 1)s + 1, \ldots, \alpha s, \alpha = 1, \ldots, k, \ell = 0, \ldots, k - 1\}$$

where $u_i = ([i \notin S_1], \ldots, [i \notin S_{ks}])$, $v_{j_1, \ldots, j_k} \in \{0, 1\}^{ks}$ has 0s in entries $j_1, \ldots, j_k$ and 1s elsewhere, and $w_\ell \in \{0, 1\}^{sk}$ has 1s in entries $\ell s + 1, \ldots, (\ell + 1)s$ and 0s elsewhere. Each $(u_i, 0)$ and each $(w_\ell, 1)$ appears s^k times in $I^k(S)$. There are $t = Ns^k + s^k + ks^k$ examples in $I^k(S)$. Let $r = SC(S)$ be the size of a minimum Set Cover. We will show that $tD(I^k(S), (k\text{-term MDNF})) = r^k$.
First notice if $S = \{S_{i_1}, \ldots, S_{i_r}\}$ is a minimum set cover then since $\{S_{i_l+js}\}_{l=1}^r = S$ is also a set cover for every j, the function

$$f = \bigvee_{j=0}^{k-1} x_{i_1+js} \cdots x_{i_r+js}$$

is a k-Same term MDNF that disagrees with exactly r^k examples $(v_{j_1, \ldots, j_k}, 1)$. Therefore $tD(I^k(S), (k\text{-term MDNF})) \leq D(I^k(S), f) = r^k$.
For the other direction, let g be any k-term MDNF that disagrees with at most r^k examples. Then $g(w_\ell) = 1$ and $g(u_i) = 0$ for all ℓ and i. For each ℓ, g contains exactly one term $T_\ell = x_{t_1} \cdots x_{t_{\rho_\lambda}}$ such that $\ell s + 1 \leq t_1, \ldots, t_{\rho_\lambda} \leq (\ell + 1)s$, and as in Theorem 6, $\{S_{t_1}, \ldots, S_{t_{\rho_\lambda}}\}$ is a set cover with $t_{\rho_\lambda} \geq r$. The number of $(v_{j_1, \ldots, j_k}, 1)$ examples that disagree with g is $tD(I^k(S), g) = \rho_1 \rho_2 \cdots \rho_k \geq r^k$. So $tD(I^k(S), k\text{-term MDNF}) = r^k$. An α-approximation algorithm for this problem then implies a $\sqrt[k]{\alpha}$-approximation algorithm for Set Cover. Our examples have dimension $d = sk < Nk$. Then by Feige [F96], (k-term MDNF)-MD cannot have a $(1 - \epsilon) \ln^k \frac{d}{k}$-approximation algorithm unless NP $\subseteq$ DTIME($n^{O(\log \log n)}$). $\square$

Theorem 8. *Let $k \geq 1$ be a constant. For any constant $\epsilon < 1$, if NP $\nsubseteq$ DTIME($n^{O(\log \log n)}$) then there is no $(1 - \epsilon) \ln^k \frac{d}{k}$-approximation algorithm for (k-Same term MDNF/k-term DNF)-MD.*

Proof. Let S and X be an instance of Set Cover as described in the proof of Theorem 6, and as before let $S_{i+js} = S_i$ for every $1 \leq i \leq s$ and $j = 1, \ldots, k - 1$. Using the definition of $I^k(S)$ from Theorem 7, define

$$I_2^k(S) = I^k(S) \cup \{(z, 0), (b_{i,\ell}, 1) \mid i = 1, \ldots, N, \ell = 0, \ldots, k - 1\}$$

where z is the zero vector and $b_{i,\ell}$ is the bitwise OR of u_i and w_ℓ. There are s^k copies of each $(u_i, 0)$, each $(w_\ell, 1)$, each $(b_{i,\ell}, 1)$ and of $(z, 0)$, but just one copy of each $(v_{j_1,\ldots,j_k}, 1)$. There are $t = Ns^k + s^k + ks^k + s^k + kNs^k$ examples. In the proof of the previous theorem we gave a k-term MDNF f that agrees with all these examples except r^k of the examples $(v_{j_1,\ldots,j_k}, 1)$. Thus $tD(I_2^k(S), (k\text{-term DNF})) \le r^k$. We now show $tD(I_2^k(S), (k\text{-term DNF})) \ge r^k$.

Let g be any k-term DNF that disagrees with at most r^k examples. Then $g(u_i) = 0$ for all i, $g(w_\ell) = 1$ for all ℓ, $g(z) = 0$, and $g(b_{i,\ell}) = 1$ for all i and ℓ. For each ℓ this implies g contains exactly one term T_ℓ such that $T_\ell(w_\ell) = 1$. If T_ℓ contains a negated literal $\bar{x}_j$, this implies $\{1, \ldots, N\} \in S_j$. For non-trivial instances of Set Cover, each T_ℓ must be monotone.

So an optimal g is a k-term MDNF and $tD(I_2^k(S), (k\text{-term DNF})) = r^k$. The dimension of the examples is $d = sk$. Then it follows from Feige[F96] that unless $NP \subseteq DTIME(n^{O(k \log \log n)})$, $(k\text{-term DNF})$-MD cannot have a $(1 - \epsilon) \ln^k \frac{d}{k}$-approximation algorithm. $\square$

So far we have shown that different subclasses of k-term DNF are hard for MD when the hypothesis is a k-term DNF. Although k-term DNF is hard even for CH from k-term DNF, there is a very simple algorithm for $(k\text{-term DNF}/k\text{-CNF})$-CH and $(k\text{-DNF})$-CH that runs in time $n^{O(k)}$ [KLPV87, PV88]. We now will show that $(k\text{-CNF})$-MD is hard.

Theorem 9. Let $k \ge 1$ be a constant. For any constant $\epsilon > 0$ there is no $(1 - \epsilon) \ln \frac{d}{k}$-approximation algorithm for $(k\text{-CNF})$-MD or $(k\text{-DNF})$-MD over dimension d unless $NP \subseteq DTIME(n^{O(\log \log n)})$.

Proof. Let $S = \{S_1, \ldots, S_s\}$ and $X = \bigcup_{i=1}^s S_i = \{1, \ldots, N\}$ be an instance of Set Cover as described in the proof of Theorem 6. Define $S_{i+js} = S_i$ for every $1 \le i \le s$ and $j = 1, \ldots, k - 1$. Define

$$J^k(S) = \{(v_{j_1,\ldots,j_k}, 1), (u_i, 0) \mid 1 \le j_1 < \cdots < j_k \le N, \ i = 1, \ldots, sk\}$$

where $v_{j_1,\ldots,j_k}$ and u_i are as defined in the proof of theorem 7, each $(v, 1) \in V = \{(v_{j_1,\ldots,j_k}, 1) \mid j_\alpha = (\alpha - 1)s + 1, \ldots, \alpha s, \ \alpha = 1, \ldots, k\}$ appears once in $J^k(S)$ and all the other examples in $J^k(S) \backslash V$ appear s times each. There are $t = s(sk) + s\left(\binom{N}{k} - s^k\right) + s^k \le N^{k+1}$ examples of dimension $d = sk < Nk$.

If $S_{i_1}, \ldots, S_{i_r}$ is a set cover then the k-CNF

$$f = \bigwedge_{j=1,\cdots,r} (x_{i_j} \vee x_{i_j+s} \vee \cdots \vee x_{i_j+(k-1)s})$$

is consistent with all examples in $J^k(S)$ except $\{v_{i_j, i_j+s, i_j+2s, \ldots, i_j+(k-1)s}\}_{j=1,\ldots,r}$. Therefore, $t \cdot D(J^k(S), k - \text{CNF}) \le t \cdot D(J^k(S), f) = r = SC(S)$. We will show now that for any $g \in k\text{-CNF}$, $t \cdot D(J^k(S), g) \ge r$. Let g be any k-CNF. First we may assume that g is consistent with $J^k(S) \backslash V$. Since $g(v_{j_1,\ldots,j_k}) = 1$ for all $v_{j_1,\ldots,j_k} \notin V$, all the clauses in g are monotone and each clause contains exactly one variable from each $X_l = \{x_{(l-1)s+1}, \ldots, x_{ls}\}$. Now suppose

$$g = \bigwedge_{p=1}^{m} \bigvee_{j=1}^{k} x_{q_{p,j}},$$

where $x_{q_{p,j}} \in X_j$. Notice that g disagrees with exactly m samples from V, those that set $\{x_{q_{p,j}}\}_j$ to zero. Let $\phi_j = \bigwedge_{p=1}^{m} x_{q_{p,j}}$. If $\phi_j(u_i) = 1$ for some i then $g(u_i) = 1$. Therefore, $\phi_j(u_i) = 0$ for all i and as in Theorem 6 $\{S_{q_{p,j}} \mid p = 1, \ldots, m\}$ is a set cover. Therefore, $m \geq r$ and $t \cdot D(J^k(S), g) \geq r$. The result for $(k\text{-DNF})$-MD follows from a duality argument. $\square$

5   Results for XOR

In this section we will prove the following.

Theorem 10. *Let* $c_1^\alpha = \left(\frac{1}{3} - \alpha\right) \log \frac{1}{c}$ *and* $c_2^\alpha = \alpha \log \frac{1}{c}$ *for constant* c. *For any* $\alpha < 1/3$, $c_1 < c_1^\alpha$, $c_2 < c_2^\alpha$, *unless* $NP \subset RTIME(n^{O(\log \log n)})$, *there is no poly time* $(\log n)^{c_1}$-*approximation algorithm for* $Xor/FL_1(2^{(\log n)^{c_2}})$-*MD and no poly time* $\frac{1}{2} + \frac{1}{2^{(\log n)^{c_2}}}$-*approximation algorithm for* $Xor/FL_1(2^{(\log n)^{c_2}})$-*MA.*

The class $FL_1(2^{(\log n)^{c_2}})$ was described in section 2.2. The result also implies that for almost all the classes C that we studied in this paper (and many other classes) it is hard to solve $C \cup Xor$-MA and $C \cup Xor$-MD (even, $Xor/C \cup Xor$-MA and $Xor/C \cup Xor$-MD). As mentioned in section 2.2, we assume boolean functions are $f : \{0,1\}^n \to \{-1,1\}$ and XOR functions are $\chi_a(x) = (-1)^{a \cdot x}$.

For XOR-MA, given $S = \{(x^{(1)}, y_1), \ldots, (x^{(m)}, y_m)\} \subseteq \{0,1\}^n \times \{1, -1\}$ we seek a χ_a to maximize $A(S, \chi_a) = \frac{1}{m} \{i \mid \chi_a(x^{(i)}) = y_i\}$. Håstad [H97] reduced a 3SAT5 instance ϕ with n clauses and at most $3n$ variables to an instance $\mathcal{S}^\phi = \{\chi_{\alpha^{(1)}}(x) = \beta_1, \ldots, \chi_{\alpha^{(m)}}(x) = \beta_m\}$ of Lin-2 (equivalent to XOR-MA) where $x = (x_1, \ldots, x_N)$, the number of ones in $\alpha^{(i)}$ is $wt(\alpha^{(i)}) = 3$ for all i,

$$N = O(n^k 2^{2^{3k}}), \quad m = n^{O(k)} 2^{2^{3k}}, \quad 4\epsilon\delta^2 \geq c^k, \tag{1}$$

$c < 1$ is the constant from the Parallel Repetition Theorem of Raz [Raz95, H97], and if ϕ is satisfiable there exists an assignment $a \in \{0,1\}^N$ that satisfies more than $(1 - \epsilon)m$ equations in $\mathcal{S}^\phi$, and if ϕ is not satisfiable, every $a \in \{0,1\}^N$ satisfies at most $\left(\frac{1}{2} + \frac{\delta}{2}\right) m$ equations in $\mathcal{S}^\phi$. This reduction runs in time $poly(N)$.

Claim 1 *There is a randomized* $poly(N)$ *time reduction from a 3SAT5 instance* ϕ *with* n *clauses to a labeled sample* $\hat{\mathcal{S}}_\phi = \{(\alpha^{(1)}, \beta_1), \ldots, (\alpha^{(\hat{m})}, \beta_{\hat{m}})\}$ *where* $\alpha^{(i)} \in \{0,1\}^N$ *and* $\hat{m} = \frac{2}{\epsilon^2}\left(N + \ln \frac{1}{\tau}\right)$ *such that with probability at least* $1 - \tau$,

$$\phi \text{ satisfiable} \Longrightarrow (\exists a) \; A(\hat{\mathcal{S}}_\phi, \chi_a) \geq 1 - \frac{3\epsilon}{2}$$
$$\phi \text{ not satisfiable} \Longrightarrow (\forall a) \; \frac{1}{2} - \frac{\delta + \epsilon}{2} \leq A(\hat{\mathcal{S}}_\phi, \chi_a) \leq \frac{1}{2} + \frac{\delta + \epsilon}{2}$$

Proof. We follow Håstad's reduction, and use the fact that the weight of each assignment is 3. $\square$

Lemma 3. *Suppose for some ϵ and δ there is an algorithm $\mathcal{S}$ such that for any 3SAT5 instance ϕ with n clauses, $\mathcal{S}$ runs in time $T(N)$ and produces XOR-MA instance $\mathcal{S}_\phi = \{(x^{(1)}, y_1), \ldots, (x^{(m)}, y_m)\} \subseteq \{0,1\}^N \times \{-1,1\}$, such that*

$$\phi \text{ satisfiable} \implies (\exists a)\, A(\mathcal{S}_\phi, \chi_a) \geq 1 - \epsilon,$$
$$\phi \text{ not satisfiable} \implies (\forall a)\tfrac{1}{2} - \tfrac{\delta}{2} \leq A(\mathcal{S}_\phi, \chi_a) \leq \tfrac{1}{2} + \tfrac{\delta}{2}.$$

Then there is a randomized reduction $\mathcal{S}^j$ such that for any 3SAT5 instance ϕ with n clauses, $\mathcal{S}^j$ runs in time $T(N) + poly(k, N, 1/\lambda, 1/\tau)$ and produces $\hat{\mathcal{S}}_\phi = \{(x^{(1)}, y_1), \ldots, (x^{(t)}, y_t)\} \subseteq \{0,1\}^N \times \{-1,1\}$ of size $t = \frac{1}{2\lambda^2}\left(N + \ln\frac{1}{\tau}\right)$, an instance of XOR-MA such that with probability at least $1 - \tau$

$$\phi \text{ satisfiable} \implies (\exists a)\, A(\hat{\mathcal{S}}_\phi, \chi_a) \geq 1 - j\epsilon - \lambda$$
$$\phi \text{ not satisfiable} \implies (\forall a)\, \tfrac{1}{2} - \left(\tfrac{\delta^j}{2} + \lambda\right) \leq A(\hat{\mathcal{S}}_\phi, \chi_a) \leq \tfrac{1}{2} + \left(\tfrac{\delta^j}{2} + \lambda\right).$$

Proof. Let $\mathcal{S}_\phi^j = \left\{ \left(\bigoplus_{i \in I} x^{(i)}, \prod_{i \in I} y_i\right) \;\Big|\; (x^{(i)}, y_i) \in \mathcal{S}_\phi, \; I \subseteq \{1, \ldots, m\}, \; |I| = j \right\}$
and choose a random $\hat{\mathcal{S}}_\phi \subseteq \mathcal{S}_\phi^j$ of size t.

If ϕ is satisfiable then there is a χ_a such that $A(\mathcal{S}_\phi, \chi_a) \geq 1 - \epsilon$ which implies $\Pr_{x^{(i)} \in_\mathcal{U} \mathcal{S}_\phi}[y_i \neq \chi_a(x^{(i)})] \leq \epsilon$. Then since $\chi_a(\bigoplus_{i \in I} x^{(i)}) = \prod_{i \in I} \chi_a(x^{(i)})$ we have

$$\Pr_{x^{(i)} \in_\mathcal{U} \mathcal{S}_\phi}\left[\prod_{i \in I} y_i \neq \chi_a(\bigoplus_{i \in I} x^{(i)})\right] \leq \Pr_{x^{(i)} \in_\mathcal{U} \mathcal{S}_\phi}[(\exists i \in I)\, y_i \neq \chi_a(x^{(i)})] \leq j\epsilon.$$

Therefore, by the Chernoff bound,

$$\phi \text{ satisfiable} \implies (\exists a)\, A(\mathcal{S}_\phi{}^j, \chi_a) \geq 1 - j\epsilon \implies (\exists a)\, A(\hat{\mathcal{S}}_\phi, \chi_a) \geq 1 - j\epsilon - \lambda,$$

with probability at least $1 - \tau$. If ϕ is not satisfiable then for every χ_a we have $\left|E_{x^{(i)} \in_\mathcal{U} \mathcal{S}_\phi}[y_i \chi_a(x^{(i)})]\right| \leq \delta$. This follows because

$$E_{x^{(i)} \in_\mathcal{U} \mathcal{S}_\phi}[y_i \chi_a(x^{(i)})] = 2\Pr_{x^{(i)} \in_\mathcal{U} \mathcal{S}_\phi}[y_i = \chi_a(x^{(i)})] - 1 = 2A(\mathcal{S}_\phi, \chi_a) - 1. \quad (2)$$

Now for every a we have

$$\left|E_{x^{(i)} \in_\mathcal{U} \mathcal{S}_\phi}\left[\left(\prod_{i \in I} y_i\right) \chi_a\left(\bigoplus_{i \in I} x^{(i)}\right)\right]\right| = \left|E_{x^{(i)} \in_\mathcal{U} \mathcal{S}_\phi}\left[\prod_{i \in I} y_i \chi_a(x^{(i)})\right]\right|$$

$$= \left|\prod_{i \in I} E_{x^{(i)} \in_\mathcal{U} \mathcal{S}_\phi}[y_i \chi_a(x^{(i)})]\right| \leq \delta^j$$

which implies

$$\phi \text{ not satisfiable} \implies (\forall a)\, \frac{1}{2} - \frac{\delta^j}{2} \leq A(\mathcal{S}_\phi{}^j, \chi_a) \leq \frac{1}{2} + \frac{\delta^j}{2}$$
$$\implies (\forall a)\, \frac{1}{2} - \left(\frac{\delta^j}{2} + \lambda\right) \leq A(\hat{\mathcal{S}}_\phi, \chi_a) \leq \frac{1}{2} + \left(\frac{\delta^j}{2} + \lambda\right).$$

with probability at least $1 - \tau$. This proves the Lemma. □

We now give the key Lemma for our main result in this section.

Lemma 4. *For any constant $\alpha < \frac{1}{3}$ there is a randomized $n^{O(\log \log n)}$ time reduction from 3SAT5 with n clauses to a labeled sample $S_\phi \subseteq \{0,1\}^N \times \{-1,1\}$, with $N = O\left(n^{\frac{1}{3} \log \log n + 1}\right)$ of size $|S_\phi| = n^{O(\log \log n)} poly(1/\tau)$ such that with probability at least $1 - \tau$*

$$\phi \ satisfiable \Longrightarrow (\exists a) \ A(\hat{S}_\phi, \chi_a) \geq 1 - \frac{1}{(\log N)^{c_1^\alpha}}$$

$$\phi \ not \ satisfiable \Longrightarrow (\forall a) \ \frac{1}{2} - \frac{1}{O\left(2^{(\log N)^{c_2^\alpha}}\right)} \leq A(\hat{S}_\phi, \chi_a) \leq \frac{1}{2} + \frac{1}{O\left(2^{(\log N)^{c_2^\alpha}}\right)}.$$

where $c_1^\alpha = \left(\frac{1}{3} - \alpha\right) \log \frac{1}{c} - o(1), \quad c_2^\alpha = \alpha \log \frac{1}{c}.$

Proof. By Claim 1 and Lemma 3 there is a randomized reduction S such that for any 3SAT5 instance ϕ with n clauses, S runs in time $poly(N, 1/\epsilon, 1/\delta, 1/\tau)$ and produces an instance $S_\phi = \{(x^{(1)}, y_1), \ldots, (x^{(t)}, y_t)\} \subset \{0,1\}^N \times \{-1,1\}$ of size $t = poly(N, 1/\epsilon^j, 1/\delta, 1/\tau)$ such that with probability at least $1 - \tau$

$$\phi \ \text{satisfiable} \Longrightarrow (\exists a) \ A(\hat{S}_\phi, \chi_a) \geq 1 - \frac{3(j+1)}{2}\epsilon$$

$$\phi \ \text{not satisfiable} \Longrightarrow (\forall a) \ \frac{1}{2} - \frac{(\delta + \epsilon)^j}{2} \leq A(\hat{S}_\phi, \chi_a) \leq \frac{1}{2} + \frac{(\delta + \epsilon)^j}{2}.$$

We now choose $k = \frac{1}{3} \log \log n$, $\delta = \frac{1}{2}$, $j = (\log N)^{\alpha \log \frac{1}{c}}$ and $\epsilon = (\log n)^{\frac{1}{3} \log c}$. See (1). Then

$$N = O\left(n^k 2^{2^{3k}}\right) = O\left(n^{\frac{1}{3} \log \log n + 1}\right), \qquad \log N = (\log n)^{1 + o(1)},$$

$$\epsilon = (\log N)^{\frac{1}{3} \log c + o(1)}, \qquad 4\epsilon\delta^2 = (\log n)^{\frac{1}{3} \log c} = c^{\frac{1}{3} \log \log n} \geq c^k,$$

$$\frac{3(j+1)\epsilon}{2} = (\log N)^{\left(\frac{1}{3} - \alpha\right) \log c + o(1)} \quad \text{and} \quad \frac{(\delta + \epsilon)^j}{2} = \frac{1}{O\left(2^{(\log N)^{\alpha \log \frac{1}{c}}}\right)}.$$

The result follows. $\square$

We are now ready to prove our main theorem.

Proof of Theorem 10. Suppose for some constants $c_1 < c_1^\alpha$ and $c_2 < c_2^\alpha$ there is a $(\log n)^{c_1}$-approximation algorithm $\mathcal{A}$ for $Xor/FL_1(2^{(\log n)^{c_2}})$-MD that runs in polynomial time. Let ϕ be a 3SAT5 instance. We use the reduction from Lemma 4 to create an instance S_ϕ for $Xor/FL_1(2^{(\log n)^{c_2}})$-MD such that

$$\phi \ satisfiable \Rightarrow (\exists a) \ D(\hat{S}_\phi, \chi_a) \leq \frac{1}{(\log N)^{c_1^\alpha}}$$

$$\phi \ not \ satisfiable \Rightarrow (\forall a) \ \frac{1}{2} - \frac{1}{O\left(2^{(\log N)^{c_2^\alpha}}\right)} \leq D(\hat{S}_\phi, \chi_a) \leq \frac{1}{2} + \frac{1}{O\left(2^{(\log N)^{c_2^\alpha}}\right)}.$$

Let $f \in FL_1(2^{(\log N)^{c_2}})$. By lemma 4 if ϕ is not satisfiable $|E_{x^{(i)} \in_U \hat{S}_\phi}[y_i \chi_a(x_i)]|$
$\leq \frac{1}{O(2^{(\log N)^{\frac{\alpha}{2}}})}$, and therefore $|E_{\hat{S}_\phi}[y_i f(x_i)] = |E_{\hat{S}_\phi}[\sum_a \hat{f}_a \chi_a(x_i) y_i]|$

$$= |\sum_a \hat{f}_a E_{\hat{S}_\phi}[y_i \chi_a(x_i)]| \leq \left(\sum_a |\hat{f}_a|\right) \max_a |E_{\hat{S}_\phi}[y_i \chi_a(x_i)]| \leq \frac{1}{O\left(2^{(\log N)^{\frac{c_2^\alpha}{2}}}\right)}.$$

Therefore,

$$\phi \text{ satisfiable} \implies (\exists \chi_a \in Xor) \; D(\hat{S}_\phi, \chi_a) \leq \frac{1}{(\log N)^{c_1^\alpha}}$$

$$\phi \text{ not satisfiable} \implies (\forall f \in FL_1(2^{(\log N)^{\frac{c_2^\alpha}{2}}}))$$
$$\frac{1}{2} - \frac{1}{O\left(2^{(\log N)^{\frac{c_2^\alpha}{2}}}\right)} \leq D(\hat{S}_\phi, f) \leq \frac{1}{2} + \frac{1}{O\left(2^{(\log N)^{\frac{c_2^\alpha}{2}}}\right)}.$$

We run algorithm $\mathcal{A}$ on $\hat{S}_\phi$ to get $h \in FL_1(2^{(\log N)^{c_2}})$. If ϕ is satisfiable then

$$D(\hat{S}_\phi, h) \leq (\log N)^{c_1} D(\hat{S}_\phi, Xor) \leq (\log N)^{c_1} D(\hat{S}_\phi, \chi_a) \leq \frac{1}{(\log N)^{c_1^\alpha}}.$$

On the other hand, if ϕ is not satisfiable then $D(\hat{S}_\phi, h) \geq \frac{1}{O\left(2^{(\log N)^{\frac{c_2^\alpha}{2}}}\right)}.$ $\square$

References

[AL88]   D. Angluin and P. D. Laird, Learning from noisy examples, *Machine Learning*, 2:343-370,1988. 272

[ABSS97]   S. Arora, L. Babai, J. Stern and Z. Sweedyk, Hardness of approximate optima in lattices, codes, and systems of linear equations, *JCSS* 54(2): 317-331, 1997. 272, 273

[BB99]   P. L. Barlett, S. Ben-David. Hardness results for neural network approximation problems. *4th Euro-COLT*, 50-62, 1999. 272

[BEL00]   S. Ben-David, N. Eiron, P. M. Long. On the difficulty of approximately maximizing agreement. *13th COLT*, 266-274, 2000. 273, 277

[BK01]   P. Berman and M. Karpinski. Approximating minimal unsatisfiability of linear equations, Manuscript. From ECCC reports 2001, TR01-025. 272

[BB02]   N. H. Bshouty and L. Burroughs. Maximizing Agreements, CoAgnostic Learning and Weak Agnostic Learning. Manuscript, 2002. 276

[F96]   U. Feige, A threshold of $\log n$ for approximating set cover, *28th STOC*, 314-318, 1996. 273, 279, 280, 281

[GJ79]   M. R. Garey, D. S. Johnson, Computers and Intractability: A Guide to the theory of NP-Completeness. W. H. Freeman, 1979. 279

[H97]   J. Håstad, Some optimal inapproximability results, *29th STOC*, 1-10, 1997. 272, 273, 278, 282

[Ha92]   D. Haussler, Decision theoretic generalization of the PAC model for neural net and other learning applications. *Inform. Comput.*, 100(1):78-150, Sept. 1992. 271, 272, 276

[HSV95]   Klaus-U Höffgen, Hans-U. Simon and Kevin S. Van Horn, Robust train-
            ability of single neurons, *J. of Comput. Syst. Sci.*, 50(1): 114-125, 1995.
            271, 272, 273, 276, 277, 279
[KMS94]   D. Karger, R. Motwani, and M. Sudan, Approximate graph coloring by
            semidefinite programming. *35th FOCS*, 2–13, 1994. 278
[KL93]   M. Kearns and M. Li, Learning in the presence of malicious errors, *SIAM
            Journal on Computing*, 22(4): 807-837, 1993. 271, 272, 276, 277
[KLPV87]   M. Kearns, M. Li, L. Pitt and L. Valiant. On the learnability of Boolean
            formulae, *19th STOC*, 285–295, 1987. 281
[KSS92]   M. Kearns, R. E. Schapire and L. M. Sellie. Toward efficient agnostic learn-
            ing. *5th COLT*, 341-352, 1992. 271, 272, 273, 276, 277, 279
[KLS93]   S. Khanna, N. Linial and S. Safra. On the hardness of approximating the
            chromatic number, *Proc. 2nd Israel Symp. on Theory of Computing and
            Systems*, 250–260, 1993. 278
[K00]   C. Kuhlmann. Harness Results for General Two-Layer Neural Networks.
            13th COLT, 275–285, 2000. 272
[M94]   Y. Mansour, Learning Boolean Functions via the Fourier Transform. In
            Theoretical Advances in Neural Computation and Learning, (V. P. Roy-
            chodhury, K-Y. Siu and A. Orlitsky, ed), 391-424 (1994). 274, 275
[PV88]   L. Pitt and L. G. Valiant, Computational Limitation on Learning from
            Examples. *JACM*, 35, (4): 965-984, 1988. 273, 278, 279, 281
[Raz95]   R. Raz, A parallel repetition theorem. *27th STOC*, 447-456, 1995. 282
[S01]   H. U. Simon, private communication, 2001. 273, 276

On the Proper Learning
of Axis Parallel Concepts

Nader H. Bshouty[1*] and Lynn Burroughs[2**]

[1] Department of Computer Science, Technion
Haifa, Israel
bshouty@cs.technion.ac.il
[2] Department of Computer Science, University of Calgary
Calgary, Alberta, Canada
lynnb@cpsc.ucalgary.ca

Abstract. We study the proper learnability of axis parallel concept classes in the PAC learning model and in the exact learning model with membership and equivalence queries. These classes include union of boxes, DNF, decision trees and multivariate polynomials.

For the *constant* dimensional axis parallel concepts C we show that the following problems have the same time complexity

1. C is α-properly exactly learnable (with hypotheses of size at most α times the target size) from membership and equivalence queries.
2. C is α-properly PAC learnable (without membership queries) under any product distribution.
3. There is an α-approximation algorithm for the MINEQUI C problem. (given a $g \in C$ find a minimal size $f \in C$ that is equivalent to g).

In particular, C is α-properly learnable in poly time from membership and equivalence queries **if and only if** C is α-properly PAC learnable in poly time under the product distribution **if and only if** MINEQUI C has a poly time α-approximation algorithm. Using this result we give the first proper learning algorithm of decision trees over the constant dimensional domain and the first negative results in proper learning from membership and equivalence queries for many classes.

For the non-constant dimensional axis parallel concepts we show that with the equivalence oracle (1) $\Rightarrow$ (3). We use this to show that (binary) decision trees are not properly learnable in polynomial time (assuming P$\neq$NP) and DNF is not s^ϵ-properly learnable ($\epsilon < 1$) in polynomial time even with an NP-oracle (assuming $\Sigma_2^p \neq P^{NP}$).

1 Introduction

We study the proper learnability of axis parallel concept classes in the PAC-learning model and in the exact learning model with membership and equivalence

* This research was supported by the fund for promotion of research at the Technion. Research no. 120-025. Part of this research was done at the University of Calgary, Calgary, Alberta, Canada and supported by NSERC of Canada.
** This research was supported by an NSERC PGS-B Scholarship, an Izaak Walton Killam Memorial Scholarship, and an Alberta Informatics Circle of Research Excellence (iCORE) Fellowship.

J. Kivinen and R. H. Sloan (Eds.): COLT 2002, LNAI 2375, pp. 287–302, 2002.
© Springer-Verlag Berlin Heidelberg 2002

queries. A class $\mathcal{N}\text{-}\mathcal{P}\Phi$ of axis parallel concepts is a class of boolean formulas $\phi(T_1, T_2, \ldots, T_t)$ where ϕ is from a class of boolean formulas Φ (such as DNF, decision tree, etc.) and $\{T_i\}$ are boxes in $\mathcal{N}_m^n$, where $\mathcal{N}_m = \{0, \ldots, m-1\}$, that satisfy a certain property $\mathcal{P}$ (such as disjointness, squares, etc.). These classes include union of boxes, union of disjoint boxes, exclusive or of boxes, decision tree partition, and for the boolean case $\mathcal{N}_2^n$, they include DNF, decision trees, disjoint DNF and multivariate polynomials.

The term α-proper learning refers to learning where the intermediate hypotheses used by the learner (in the equivalence queries) and the final hypothesis have size (number of boxes T_i) at most α times the size of the target formula. A class is properly learnable if it 1-learnable. The following table summarizes the results for the n-dimensional boolean case.

	Upper for	Complexity	Source	Lower	Condition	Source
DNF	Nonproper	$2^{\tilde{O}(n^{1/3})}$	[KS01]	Proper	$P \neq NP$	[PR96]
	Nonproper	NP-oracle	[BCG96]	$n^{\frac{1}{2}-\epsilon}$-Proper		[HR02]
	Proper	Σ_p^4-oracle	OPEN	s^ϵ-Proper	$\Sigma_p^2 \neq P^{NP}$	[ours]
CDNF	Nonproper	$poly(n)$	[Bs95]			
	Proper	Σ_p^4-oracle	[HPRW96]			
	Proper	$poly(n)$	OPEN			
Disj-DNF	Nonproper	$poly(n)$	[BCV96]	Proper	$P \neq NP$	OPEN
	Proper	Σ_p^4-oracle	OPEN			
DT	Nonproper	$poly(n)$	[Bs95]	Proper	$P \neq NP$	[ours]
	Proper	Σ_p^4-oracle	OPEN			
MP	Nonproper	$poly(n)$	[BCV96]	Proper	$P \neq NP$	OPEN
	Proper	Σ_p^4-oracle	OPEN			
MMP	Proper	$poly(n)$	[SS93]			

Hellerstein et al. [HPRW96] show that proper learnability of a class C from membership and equivalence queries is possible in a machine with unlimited computational power if and only if C has *polynomial certificates*. They also show that if C has a polynomial certificate then C is properly learnable using an oracle for Σ_4^p. They then give a polynomial size certificate for CDNF (a polynomial size DNF that has a polynomial size CNF). This implies that CDNF is properly learnable using an oracle for Σ_4^p. For decision trees (DT), Disjoint DNF (DNF where the conjunction of every two terms is 0) and multivariate polynomials (with nonmonotone terms (MP)) it is not known whether they have polynomial certificates. Therefore it is not known if they are properly learnable. Pillaipakkamnatt and Raghavan [PR96] show that if DNF is properly learnable then P=NP. On the other hand, Bshouty et al. [BCG96] show that any circuit is (nonproperly) learnable with equivalence queries only and the aid of NP-oracle. The best algorithm today for learning DNF runs in time $2^{\tilde{O}(n^{1/3})}$ [KS01]. Recently in [HR02], Hellerstein and Raghavan show that DNF has no polynomial certificate and is not $f(n)$-properly learnable for any $f(n) = o(\sqrt{n}/\log n)$.

CDNF, Decision trees, disjoint DNF and multivariate polynomials are (nonproperly) learnable in polynomial time from membership and equivalence queries

[Bs95, BCV96, BBBKV00]. Multivariate polynomials with monotone terms (denoted MMP) are properly learnable [SS93].

In this paper we use a new technique for finding negative results for learning from membership queries (see Theorem 2). We use Theorem 2 and the result of Zantema and Bodlaender [ZB00] to show that if a decision tree is properly learnable from membership and equivalence queries then P=NP. We then use a result of Umans [U99] and show that if DNF is s^ϵ-properly learnable with an NP-oracle, where s is the size of the DNF, then $\Sigma_2^p = P^{NP}$. We show our results are still true even if the learner can use other oracles such as Subset, Superset, Disjointness, etc. Therefore, if P$\neq$NP then decision trees and DNF are not properly learnable from membership and equivalence queries (and all the other oracles defined in subsection 2.3).

The following table summarizes our results for axis parallel classes over a constant dimension.

	Positive results poly(n)	Negative results iff P=NP
Union of t Boxes	log t-Proper	Proper
Disjoint Union Boxes	dim=2 Proper	dim>2 Proper
Decision tree	Proper	
Xor of Boxes	α-Proper	OPEN

For axis parallel classes over a constant dimension we show that these classes have polynomial certificates. Therefore by [HPRW96], they are properly learnable from membership and equivalence queries using the Σ_4^p oracle. We further investigate the learnability of these classes and show that an NP-oracle is sufficient for proper learnability. We also show that the following problems have the same time complexity.

1. C is α-properly exactly learnable from membership and equivalence queries.
2. C is α-properly PAC learnable (without membership queries) under any product distribution.
3. There is an α-approximation algorithm for the MINEQUI C problem (given a $g \in C$ find a minimal size $f \in C$ that is equivalent to g).
4. C is exactly learnable with a learning algorithm that uses all the queries (membership and nonproper equivalence, subset, superset, etc.) and outputs a hypothesis that has size at most α times the target size.

Some surprising results follow from this. The first is (1)$\Rightarrow$(2). It is known that (proper) learnability from equivalence and membership queries implies (proper) learnability in the PAC model with membership queries [A88]. Here we show that in the case of finite dimensional space and for the product distribution we can change a weak learner (that learns with membership queries) to a strong learner (that learns without membership queries). Another surprising result that we show from this is: a decision tree over any constant dimension is *properly learnable* from membership and equivalence queries. We also show that decision tree is proper PAC-learnable under any distribution.

We also show that union of disjoint DNF in dimension 2 has a polynomial time proper learning algorithm. On the other hand, union of boxes and disjoint union of boxes over dimensions greater than 2 are properly learnable if and only if P=NP. Union of boxes is $\log t$-properly learnable where t is the number of boxes and Xor of boxes is α-properly learnable for some constant α.

All results in the literature for the constant dimensional domain give non-proper learning of the above classes in the exact learning model and there were no negative results for proper learning of these classes from membership and equivalence queries.

In [CM94] Chen and Maass give a proper exact learning of one box from equivalence queries. Beimel and Kushilevitz [BK98] show that $\mathcal{N}_m^n$-Disjoint DNF is (nonproperly) learnable from membership and equivalence queries. This result is also true for the nonconstant dimensional domain. The output hypothesis is represented as a $\mathcal{N}_m^n$-Multiplicity Automaton.[1] Since $\mathcal{N}_m^n$-Multiplicity Automaton contains the class of $\mathcal{N}_m^n$-Multivariate Polynomials [BBBKV00], the class of $\mathcal{N}_m^n$-Multivariate Polynomials is (nonproperly) learnable in polynomial time from membership and equivalence queries. In [BGGM99] Bshouty et al. give an $O(d \log t)$-proper learning algorithm that learns a union of t boxes in d-dimensional space. The algorithm in this paper is $\log t$-proper.

Many algorithms in the literature learn the union of boxes in the constant dimensional space [CH96, MW98] (and even any combination of thresholds in the constant dimensional space from equivalence queries only [BBK97, B98]). All of these algorithms are nonproper and return hypotheses of large size.

2   Preliminaries

2.1   Learning Models

The learning criteria we consider are *exact learning* and *PAC-learning*.

In the exact learning model there is a function f called the *target function* $f : \mathcal{N}_m^n \to \{0,1\}$ (where $\mathcal{N}_m = \{0,1,\ldots,m-1\}$), which has a formula representation in a class C of formulas defined over the variable set $V_n = \{x_1,\ldots,x_n\}$. The goal of the learning algorithm is to halt and output a formula $h \in C$ that is equivalent to f.

The learning algorithm performs a *membership query* by supplying an assignment a to the variables in V_n as input to a *membership oracle* and receives in return the value of $f(a)$.

The learning algorithm performs an *equivalence query* by supplying a formula $h \in C$ as input to an *equivalence oracle* with the oracle returning either "YES", signifying that h is equivalent to f, or a *counterexample*, which is an assignment b such that $h(b) \neq f(b)$.

---

[1] One can also define $\mathcal{N}_m^n$-Multiplicity Automaton. Using the algorithm from that paper, $\mathcal{N}_m^n$-Multiplicity Automaton is properly learnable from membership and equivalence queries.

We say that a class C of boolean functions is α-*properly exactly learnable* from membership and equivalence queries in polynomial time if there is an algorithm that for any $f \in C$ over V_n runs in polynomial time, asks a polynomial number (polynomial in n, $\log m$ and in the size of the target function) of membership and equivalence queries with hypothesis $h \in C$ of size at most α times the size of the target, and outputs a hypothesis $h \in C$ that is equivalent to f. The size of h is at most α times the size of the target. We say that C is *properly exactly learnable* if it is 1-properly exactly learnable.

The PAC learning model is as follows. There is a distribution D defined over the domain $\mathcal{N}_m^n$. The goal of the learning algorithm is to halt and output a formula h that is ϵ-close to f with respect to the distribution D, that is,

$$\Pr_D[f(x) = h(x)] \geq 1 - \epsilon.$$

We say that h is an ϵ-approximation of f with respect to the distribution D. In the PAC or *example query* model, the learning algorithm asks for an example from the *example oracle*, and receives an example $(a, f(a))$ where a is chosen from $\mathcal{N}_m^n$ according to the distribution D.

We say that a class of boolean functions C is α-*properly PAC learnable* under the distribution D in polynomial time if there is an algorithm A, such that for any $f \in C$ over V_n and any ϵ and δ, algorithm A runs in polynomial time, asks a polynomial number of queries (polynomial in n, $\log m$, $1/\epsilon$, $1/\delta$ and the size of the target function) and with probability at least $1 - \delta$ outputs a hypothesis $h \in C$ that is an ϵ-approximation of f with respect to the distribution D. The size of h is at most α times the size of f. It is known from [A88] that if a class C is α-properly exactly learnable in polynomial time from equivalence queries (and membership queries) then it is α-properly PAC learnable (with membership queries) in polynomial time under any distribution D.

We say that a distribution D is a *product* distribution if $D(x_1, \ldots, x_n) = D_1(x_1)D_2(x_2)\cdots D_n(x_n)$ where each D_i is a distribution over $\mathcal{N}_m$.

2.2   Axis Parallel Concept Classes

A boolean function over $\mathcal{N}_m^n$ is a function $f : \mathcal{N}_m^n \to \{0, 1\}$. The elements of $\mathcal{N}_m^n$ are called *assignments*. We will consider the set of variables $V_n = \{x_1, \ldots, x_n\}$ where x_i will describe the value of the i-projection of the assignment in the domain $\mathcal{N}_m^n$ of f. For an assignment a, the i-th entry of a will be denoted by a_i.

An $\mathcal{N}_m^n$-*literal* is a function $[x_i \geq a]$ or $[x_i < a]$ where $i \leq n$ and $a \in \mathcal{N}_m \cup \{m\}$. Here $[x_i \geq a] = 1$ if $x_i \geq a$ and 0 otherwise. An $\mathcal{N}_m^n$-*monotone literal* is $[x_i \geq a]$. An $\mathcal{N}_m^n$-*term* is a product (conjunction) of literals. An $\mathcal{N}_m^n$-*monotone term* is a product (conjunction) of monotone literals. An $\mathcal{N}_m^n$-*DNF* is a disjunction of terms. An $\mathcal{N}_m^n$-*Monotone DNF* is a disjunction of monotone terms. An $\mathcal{N}_m^n$-*multivariate polynomial* is a sum of terms (mod 2). An $\mathcal{N}_m^n$-*disjoint DNF* is an $\mathcal{N}_m^n$-DNF where the conjunction of every two terms is 0.

An $\mathcal{N}_m^n$-*decision tree* ($\mathcal{N}_m^n$-DT) over V_n is a binary tree whose nodes are labeled with $\mathcal{N}_m^n$-literals and whose leaves are labeled with constants from $\{0, 1\}$. Each decision tree T represents a function $f_T : \mathcal{N}_m^n \to \{0, 1\}$. To compute $f_T(a)$

we start from the root of the tree T: if the root is labeled with the literal l and $l(a) = 1$ (resp. $l(a) = 0$), then $f_T(a) = f_{T_R}(a)$ $(f_T(a) = f_{T_L}(a))$ where T_R (T_L) is the right (left) subtree of the root (i.e., the subtree of the right (left) child of the root). If T is a leaf then $f_T(a)$ is the label of this leaf.

Sometimes we write $\mathcal{N}_m$-DNF when we do not want to specify the dimension. A DNF (multivariate polynomial, decision tree) is an $\mathcal{N}_2$-DNF (respectively, $\mathcal{N}_2$-multivariate polynomial, $\mathcal{N}_2$-decision tree).

In general, for every set of boolean functions Φ (e.g., exclusive or, or, etc.) and polynomial-time computable *property* function $\mathcal{P}_t : (\mathcal{N}_m^n\text{-}term)^t \to \{0,1\}$, (e.g., $\mathcal{P}_t(T_1, \ldots, T_t) = 1$ if $T_1, \ldots, T_t$ are pairwise disjoint) we can build a concept over $\mathcal{N}_m^n$ as follows. Define the concept class $\mathcal{P}\Phi[\mathcal{N}_m^n]$ (or $\mathcal{N}_m^n$-$\mathcal{P}\Phi$) to be the set of all $\phi(T_1, \ldots, T_t)$ where $\phi \in \Phi$ and $\{T_i\}$ are $\mathcal{N}_m^n$-terms with $\mathcal{P}_t(T_1, \ldots, T_t) = 1$. The property $\mathcal{P}$ is always computable in polynomial time and independent of m and thus can be defined for $\mathcal{N}_m^n$-terms for any m. These classes are called *axis parallel concept classes*. When $\mathcal{P}_t \equiv 1$ then we write $\Phi[\mathcal{N}_m^n]$ (or $\mathcal{N}_m^n$-Φ).

For an $f \in \mathcal{P}\Phi[\mathcal{N}_m^n]$ we define $size_{\mathcal{P}\Phi}(f)$ to be the minimal number of $\mathcal{N}_m^n$ terms $T_1, \ldots, T_t$ with property $\mathcal{P}_t$ such that some $h \in \Phi$ has $f \equiv h(T_1, \ldots, T_t)$. For a decision tree f the size is the minimal number of non-leaf nodes in an $\mathcal{N}_m^n$-decision tree equivalent to f. Similarly one can define the class $\mathcal{P}\Phi[\mathcal{N}_{m_1} \times \cdots \times \mathcal{N}_{m_n}]$. All the results of this paper are also true for that class.

A *monotone projection* from $\mathcal{N}_{m'}$ to $\mathcal{N}_m$ is a function $M : \mathcal{N}_{m'} \cup \{m'\} \to \mathcal{N}_m \cup \{m\}$ such that for every $i, j \in \mathcal{N}_{m'}$ where $i < j$ we have $M(i) \leq M(j)$ and $M(m') = m$. A monotone projection $\mathcal{M} : (\mathcal{N}_{m'} \cup \{m'\})^n \to (\mathcal{N}_m \cup \{m\})^n$ is $\mathcal{M} = (M_1, \ldots, M_n)$ where each $M_i : \mathcal{N}_{m'} \cup \{m'\} \to \mathcal{N}_m \cup \{m\}$ is a monotone projection. We say that $C = \mathcal{P}\Phi[\mathcal{N}_m^n]$ is *closed under monotone projection* if whenever $\mathcal{P}(T_1, \ldots, T_t) = 1$ we also have $\mathcal{P}(T_1\mathcal{M}, \ldots, T_t\mathcal{M}) = 1$. Notice that if $f = \phi(T_1, \ldots, T_t) \in \Phi[\mathcal{N}_m^n]$ then $f\mathcal{M} = \phi(T_1\mathcal{M}, \ldots, T_t\mathcal{M}) \in \Phi[\mathcal{N}_{m'}^n]$. When the class $C = \mathcal{P}\Phi[\mathcal{N}_m^n]$ is closed under monotone projection then $f\mathcal{M} \in \mathcal{P}\Phi[\mathcal{N}_{m'}^n]$.

For a monotone projection M define the *dual monotone projection* $M^\star$ where $M^\star(y)$ is the minimal x such that $M(x) \geq y$. It is then easy to see that if $T = \wedge_{k=1}^n [a_{i,k} \leq x_k < b_{i,k}]$ then

$$T\mathcal{M} = \bigwedge_{k=1}^n [a_{i,k} \leq M_k(x_k) < b_{i,k}] = \bigwedge_{k=1}^n [M_k^\star(a_{i,k}) \leq x_k < M_k^\star(b_{i,k})].$$

and therefore $T\mathcal{M}$ is again an $\mathcal{N}^n$-term. Now the proof of the following Lemma is straightforward.

Lemma 1. *If C is closed under monotone projection and $f \in C$, then $f\mathcal{M} \in C$ for any monotone projection $\mathcal{M}$. Also, $size_{\mathcal{P}\Phi}(f\mathcal{M}) \leq size_{\mathcal{P}\Phi}(f)$.*

It follows that all classes in this paper are closed under monotone projection.

Constructiveness Assumption: We assume that there is an algorithm "Construct" such that for any function $\psi : \mathcal{N}_{m_1} \times \cdots \times \mathcal{N}_{m_n} \to \{0,1\}$ that is computable in polynomial time, Construct(ψ) runs in time $poly(\prod m_i)$ and returns some formula $f \in \mathcal{P}\Phi[\mathcal{N}_{m_1} \times \cdots \times \mathcal{N}_{m_n}]$ that is equivalent to ψ, if there exist such a formula, and returns "error" otherwise. Such algorithms exist (and are in fact very trivial) for all the classes presented in this paper.

2.3 Oracles

The other oracles we will consider in this paper are the Subset oracle, Superset oracle, Disjointness oracle and Exhaustiveness oracle defined in [A88]. Given a set of oracles $\mathcal{O}$, we say that $\mathcal{O}$ is *easy* (resp. NP-easy) for C if every oracle in $\mathcal{O}$ can be computed in polynomial time for C (resp. using an NP-oracle).

Lemma 2. *Let Φ be a set of boolean functions. For a constant dimension d, membership and equivalence oracles and all the above oracles (subset, superset, etc.) are easy for $\Phi[\mathcal{N}_m^d]$.*

Proof. Let $R_f(h)$ be an oracle asked for the target f. We take all the literals $[x_i Q a]$ for $Q \in \{\geq, <\}$ in the terms of the target f and of the function h in the oracle. Let A be the set of all the a's in those terms and the two constants 0 and m. Suppose $A = \{0 \leq a_1 < a_2 < \cdots < a_t \leq m\}$. Notice that $t \leq 2d(s_h + s_f)$ where s_h and s_f are the number of terms in h and f, respectively. It is easy to see that the functions h and f are constant functions 0 or 1 in each subdomain $[a_{i_1}, a_{i_1+1}) \times \cdots \times [a_{i_d}, a_{i_d+1})$. We check the oracle R_f for every such subdomain. The number of subdomains is $(t+1)^d$ which is polynomial for any constant d.□

2.4 Lattice Projection

In this section we will give the definition of the *lattice projection* of functions and prove some Lemmas. This will be the main tool used in this paper. Since this technique is used for constant dimension we will use d for the dimension n.

A *lattice* in $\mathcal{N}_m^d$ is $L = L_1 \times \cdots \times L_d$ where $L_i \subseteq \mathcal{N}_m$. Let $f = \phi(T_1, \ldots, T_t) \in \Phi[\mathcal{N}_m^d]$ where $\phi \in \Phi$ and

$$T_i = \bigwedge_{k=1}^{d} [a_{i,k} \leq x_k < b_{i,k}].$$

Let $L = L_1 \times \cdots \times L_d$ be a lattice in $\mathcal{N}_m^d$. For $a, b \in \mathcal{N}_m$ define

$$\lfloor a \rfloor_{L_i} = \max\{x \in L_i \mid x \leq a\} \cup \{0\}, \quad \lceil b \rceil_{L_i} = \min\{x \in L_i \mid x \geq b\} \cup \{m\}.$$

For an assignment $v \in \mathcal{N}_m^d$ we define $\lfloor v \rfloor_L = (\lfloor v_1 \rfloor_{L_1}, \ldots, \lfloor v_d \rfloor_{L_d})$. Define

$$T_i^L = \bigwedge_{k=1}^{d} [\lceil a_{i,k} \rceil_{L_k} \leq x_k < \lceil b_{i,k} \rceil_{L_k}]$$

and $f^L = \phi(T_1^L, \cdots, T_t^L)$. We call f^L the *lattice projection* of f on L.

Lemma 3. *For every u we have $f^L(u) = f(\lfloor u \rfloor_L) = f^L(\lfloor u \rfloor_L)$.*

Proof. Notice that the lattice projection is a monotone projection with $M_i(x_i) = \lfloor x_i \rfloor_{L_i}$. Also, $M_i^\star(x_i) = \lceil x_i \rceil$. Let $\mathcal{M} = (M_1, M_2, \ldots, M_d)$. Then $\mathcal{M}(x) = \lfloor x \rfloor_L$ is a monotone projection and $\mathcal{M}^\star(x) = \lceil x \rceil_L$. We also have $\mathcal{M}\mathcal{M} = \mathcal{M}$. Therefore,

$$f^L(\lfloor u \rfloor_L) = f\mathcal{M}(\mathcal{M}u) = f(\mathcal{M}\mathcal{M}u) = f(\mathcal{M}u) = f^L(u) = f(\mathcal{M}u) = f(\lfloor u \rfloor_L).\square$$

Lemma 4. *Let $\mathcal{P}\Phi[\mathcal{N}_m^d]$ be closed under monotone projection. For any function $f \in \mathcal{P}\Phi[\mathcal{N}_m^d]$ and lattice L we have $f^L \in \mathcal{P}\Phi[\mathcal{N}_m^d]$.*

Proof. Since $\mathcal{M}(x) = \lfloor x \rfloor_L$ is a monotone projection and $\mathcal{P}\Phi[\mathcal{N}_m^d]$ is closed under monotone projection, the result follows.$\square$

Lemma 5. *Let $f = \phi(T_1, \ldots, T_t)$ where $\phi \in \Phi$ and $T_i = \bigwedge_{k=1}^d [a_{i,k} \leq x_k < b_{i,k}]$. If for every i and k we have $a_{i,k}, b_{i,k} \in L_k$ then $f^L \equiv f$.*

Proof. If $a_{i,k}, b_{i,k} \in L_i$ then $\lceil a_{i,k} \rceil_{L_k} = a_{i,k}$, $\lceil b_{i,k} \rceil_{L_k} = b_{i,k}$, $T_i^L = T_i$ and $f^L = \phi(T_1^L, \ldots, T_t^L) = \phi(T_1, \ldots, T_t) = f.\square$

2.5   Polynomial Certificates

Following the definition of [HPRW96], the class $C = \mathcal{P}\Phi[\mathcal{N}_m^n]$ has polynomial certificates if for every $f \in C$ of size t there are $q = poly(t, n)$ assignments $A = \{a_1^f, \ldots, a_q^f\}$ such that for every $g \in C$ of size less than t, g is not consistent with f on A.

Theorem 1. *Let d be constant. If $C = \mathcal{P}\Phi[\mathcal{N}_m^d]$ is closed under monotone projection then it has polynomial certificates.*

Proof. Let $f = \phi(T_1, \ldots, T_t)$ where $\phi \in \Phi$ and $T_i = \bigwedge_{k=1}^d [a_{i,k} \leq x_k < b_{i,k}]$. Let $L_k = \{a_{i,k}, b_{i,k} \mid i = 1, \ldots, t\}$ and $L = L_1 \times \cdots \times L_d$. Notice that $|L| \leq (2t)^d = poly(t)$ for constant d. We now show that if $g \in \mathcal{P}\Phi[\mathcal{N}_m^d]$ is consistent with f on L then $size_{\mathcal{P}\Phi}(g) \geq t$.

Since g is consistent with f on L, by Lemmas 3 and 5 we have $g^L(x) = g(\lfloor x \rfloor_L) = f(\lfloor x \rfloor_L) = f^L(x) = f(x)$. By Lemma 4 we have $g^L \in \mathcal{P}\Phi[\mathcal{N}_m^d]$. Therefore, $size_{\mathcal{P}\Phi}(g) \geq size_{\mathcal{P}\Phi}(g^L) = size_{\mathcal{P}\Phi}(f).\square$

It follows from [HPRW96] that if $C = \mathcal{P}\Phi[\mathcal{N}_m^d]$ is closed under monotone projection then C is learnable from membership and equivalence queries using an oracle for Σ_4^p. We will show that an NP oracle is sufficient.

2.6   Approximation Algorithms

We assume the reader is familiar with α-approximation algorithms and some of the basic concepts in theory of approximation algorithms, and complexity theory. Given a class $C = \mathcal{P}\Phi[\mathcal{N}_m^n]$, we define the optimization problem Minimal Equivalent Formula (MINEQUI C) to be the following problem:

MINEQUI C

Given a formula $f \in C = \mathcal{P}\Phi[\mathcal{N}_m^n]$.
Find a minimal size $h \in C$ that is equivalent to f.

We expect the algorithm to run in time polynomial in n and the size of f. In some cases the function is given as an n-dimensional $m_1 \times m_2 \times \cdots \times m_n$ matrix and the time is expected to be polynomial in $\prod m_i$. We call this the *unary representation* of the input. The problem is defined as follows.

MINEQUI C_U
Given an $m_1 \times \cdots \times m_n$ matrix A representing a formula in $\mathcal{P}\Phi[\mathcal{N}_{m_1} \times \cdots \times \mathcal{N}_{m_n}]$.
Find a minimal size $h \in C$ that represents A.

A generalization of this problem is the MINEQUI$^\star C_U$ problem. In this problem the input is given in its unary representation. The matrix may contain $\star$ entries which denote unspecified values.

MINEQUI$^\star C_U$
Given an $m_1 \times \cdots \times m_n$ matrix A with entries $0, 1$ and $\star$, representing a function in $\mathcal{P}\Phi[\mathcal{N}_{m_1} \times \cdots \times \mathcal{N}_{m_n}]$.
Find a minimal size $h \in C$ that is equivalent to f on the specified values.

Another problem that is related to the latter problem is the minimal size consistency problem.

MINEQUI$^\star C$
Given a set $S = \{(a_1, f(a_1)), \cdots, (a_t, f(a_t))\}$ where $f \in \mathcal{P}\Phi[\mathcal{N}_m^n]$.
Find a minimal size $h \in C$ that is consistent with S. That is, $h(a_i) = f(a_i)$ for all i.

Some of these problems appear in the literature. For example, MINEQUI $\mathcal{N}_m^2$-DNF$_U$ is the task of covering orthogonal polygons by rectangles. MINEQUI $\mathcal{N}_m^2$-Disj-DNF$_U$ is the problem of partitioning orthogonal polygons into rectangles.

It turns out that MINEQUI C and MINEQUI C_U are equivalent for the constant dimensional domain.

Lemma 6. *Let $C = \mathcal{P}\Phi[\mathcal{N}_m^d]$ for a constant d, be closed under monotone projection. Then*

1. *MINEQUI C has a polynomial time α-approximation algorithm if and only if MINEQUI C_U has a polynomial time α-approximation algorithm.*

2. *MINEQUI$^\star C$ has a polynomial time α-approximation algorithm if and only if MINEQUI$^\star C_U$ has a polynomial time α-approximation algorithm.*

Proof. We prove (1). The proof of (2) is similar. Let $\mathcal{A}$ be a polynomial time α-approximation algorithm for MINEQUI C_U. Let $f \in C$ be represented as $\hat{\phi}(\hat{T}_1, \ldots, \hat{T}_{t'})$ where $\hat{\phi} \in \Phi$ and $\hat{T}_i = \bigwedge_{k=1}^{d}[a_{i,k} \leq x_k < b_{i,k}]$. We build an approximation algorithm $\mathcal{B}$ for MINEQUI$^\star C$. Let $L_k = \{a_{i,k}, b_{i,k} \mid i = 1, \ldots, t'\}$ and suppose $L_k = \{c_{1,k}, \ldots, c_{m_k,k}\}$ where $c_{1,k} < c_{2,k} < \cdots < c_{m_k,k}$. Algorithm $\mathcal{B}$ defines $L = L_1 \times \cdots \times L_d$. By Lemma 5 we have $f^L(x) = f(x) = f(\lfloor x \rfloor_L)$. Let A be $m_1 \times \cdots \times m_d$ matrix where $A[i_1, \ldots, i_d] = f(c_{i_1,1}, \cdots, c_{i_d,d})$. This matrix represents the function $f\mathcal{M}$ where $\mathcal{M}(i_1,\ldots,i_d) = (c_{i_1,1},\cdots,c_{i_d,d})$. Notice that the size of this matrix is at most $\prod m_i \leq (2t')^d$ which is polynomial for a constant d. Define the inverse function $\mathcal{M}^{-1} : L \rightarrow \mathcal{N}_{m_1} \times \cdots \times \mathcal{N}_{m_d}$ where $\mathcal{M}^{-1}(c_{i_1,1},\cdots,c_{i_d,d}) = (i_1,\ldots,i_d)$ and let $\mathcal{M}^-(x) = \mathcal{M}^{-1}(\lfloor x \rfloor_L)$. Notice that $\mathcal{M}^-$ is a monotone projection. Since C is closed under monotone projection we have $f\mathcal{M} \in \mathcal{P}\Phi[\mathcal{N}_{m_1} \times \cdots \times \mathcal{N}_{m_d}]$. $\mathcal{B}$ now runs algorithm $\mathcal{A}$ to find $\phi \in \Phi$ and $T_1,\ldots,T_t$ such that $\mathcal{P}_t(T_1,\ldots,T_t) = 1$, $f\mathcal{M} = \phi(T_1,\ldots,T_t)$ and $t \leq \alpha \cdot size_{\mathcal{P}\Phi}(f\mathcal{M})$. Consider the function $g = \phi(T_1\mathcal{M}^-,\ldots,T_t\mathcal{M}^-)$. Since C is closed under monotone projection and $\mathcal{M}^-$ is a monotone projection we have $\mathcal{P}_t(T_1\mathcal{M}^-,\ldots,T_t\mathcal{M}^-) = 1$. Therefore, $g \in \mathcal{P}\Phi[\mathcal{N}_m^d]$. We also have by Lemma 1,

$$size_{\mathcal{P}\Phi}(g) \leq t \leq \alpha size_{\mathcal{P}\Phi}(f\mathcal{M}) \leq \alpha \cdot size_{\mathcal{P}\Phi}(f).$$

Finally, we have $g(x) = \phi(T_1\mathcal{M}^-,\ldots,T_t\mathcal{M}^-) = (f\mathcal{M})(\mathcal{M}^-(x))$

$$= (f\mathcal{M})(\mathcal{M}^{-1}(\lfloor x \rfloor_L)) = f(\lfloor x \rfloor_L) = f(x).$$

The algorithm returns $g = \phi(T_1\mathcal{M}^-,\ldots,T_t\mathcal{M}^-)$.

For the other direction, suppose that we have an algorithm for $\textsc{MinEqui}\,C$. Given an $m_1 \times \cdots \times m_d$ matrix A, by the constructiveness assumption we can build a formula $f \in \mathcal{P}\Phi[\mathcal{N}_{m_1} \times \cdots \times \mathcal{N}_{m_d}]$ that represents A in time $poly(\prod m_i)$ and then using the algorithm for $\textsc{MinEqui}\,C$ we get the desired representation. $\square$

3   Approximation Algorithms and Learning

In this section we show the connection between approximation and learning.

Theorem 2. *If C is α-properly exactly learnable from a set $\mathcal{O}$ of oracles and $\mathcal{O}$ is easy (resp., NP-easy) for C then $\textsc{MinEqui}\,C$ has an α-approximation algorithm (resp., with the aid of an NP-oracle).*

Proof. Let $\mathcal{A}$ be a learning algorithm that uses the oracles in $\mathcal{O}$ to learn a hypothesis of size less than α times the size of the target. Since $\mathcal{O}$ is easy for C, all the oracles in $\mathcal{O}$ can be simulated in polynomial time for C. So we can run algorithm $\mathcal{A}$ and simulate all the oracles in polynomial time. Since the learning is α-proper, the output hypothesis has size less than α times the size of the target. $\square$

The next Theorem follows from Lemma 6 and the Consistence Theorem [PV88].

Theorem 3. *Let $C = \mathcal{P}\Phi[\mathcal{N}_m^d]$ for a constant d be closed under monotone projection. The following three problems have the same time complexity.*

1. *C is α-properly PAC-learnable.*

2. *There is an α-approximation algorithm for $\textsc{MinEqui}^\star\,C$.*

3. *There is an α-approximation algorithm for $\textsc{MinEqui}^\star\,C_U$.*

Theorem 4. *Let $C = \mathcal{P}\Phi[\mathcal{N}_m^d]$ for a constant d be closed under monotone projection. The following problems have the same time complexity.*

1. *C is α-properly exactly learnable from membership and equivalence queries.*
2. *C is α-properly PAC learnable (without membership queries) under any product distribution.*
3. *There is an α-approximation algorithm for the MINEQUI C problem.*

Proof Sketch. We first show (1) $\equiv$ (3). By Theorem 2 we have (1) $\Rightarrow$ (3). Now we show (3) $\Rightarrow$ (1). Let $\mathcal{A}$ be an α-approximation algorithm for MINEQUIC. Let $f = \phi(T_1, \ldots, T_t)$ be the target function where $\phi \in \Phi$, $f \in \mathcal{P}\Phi[\mathcal{N}_m^d]$ and

$$T_i = \bigwedge_{k=1}^{d} [a_{i,k} \le x_k < b_{i,k}].$$

The learning algorithm works as follows. At each stage it holds d sets $L_1, \ldots, L_d$ where $L_k \subseteq \{a_{i,k}, b_{i,k} \mid i = 1, \ldots, t\} \cup \{0\}$. L_k is initially $\{0\}$. The elements of L_k are sorted in an increasing order:

$$L_k = \{c_{1,k} < c_{2,k} < \cdots < c_{i_k,k}\}.$$

The learning algorithm then builds the function f^L. It saves a table A of size $\prod_{k=1}^{d}(i_k + 1)$ where $A[j_1, \ldots, j_d] = f(c_{j_1,1}, \ldots, c_{j_d,d})$. This can be done using the membership oracle. Now, f^L can be defined using this table by $f^L(u) = f(\lfloor u \rfloor_L) = A[j_1, \ldots, j_d]$ where $\lfloor u_i \rfloor_{L_i} = c_{j_i}$ for $i = 1, \ldots, d$. Since $f^L \in \mathcal{P}\Phi[\mathcal{N}_m^d]$ (the class is closed under monotone projection), we can use algorithm $\mathcal{A}$ and construct a formula h that is equivalent to f^L and has size at most α times the size of f^L. Since the size of f^L is at most the size of f, the size of h is at most α times the size of f.

After we construct $h \equiv f^L(x)$, we make an equivalence query with hypothesis h. Let v be the counterexample. That is, $f^L(v) = h(v) \ne f(v)$. Then $f(\lfloor v \rfloor_L) = f^L(\lfloor v \rfloor_L) = f^L(v) \ne f(v)$. Intuitively, since $f(\lfloor v \rfloor_L) \ne f(v)$, the straight line that connects the two points v and $\lfloor v \rfloor_L$ hits the "boundary" of f. Now we give an algorithm to find a point close to this boundary and using this point we will add a new point to the lattice L that is equal to one new $a_{i,j}$ or $b_{i,j}$.

The algorithm works as follows. It first finds the smallest value k (or some k using binary search) such that $f(\lfloor v_1 \rfloor_{L_1}, \ldots, \lfloor v_{k-1} \rfloor_{L_{k-1}}, v_k, v_{k+1}, \ldots, v_d) \ne f(\lfloor v_1 \rfloor_{L_1}, \ldots, \lfloor v_{k-1} \rfloor_{L_{k-1}}, \lfloor v_k \rfloor_{L_k}, v_{k+1}, \ldots, v_d)$. Such a k exists since $f(\lfloor v \rfloor_L) \ne f(v)$. Then (again with a binary search) the algorithm finds an integer c such that $\lfloor v_k \rfloor_{L_k} < c \le v_k$ where $f(\lfloor v_1 \rfloor_{L_1}, \ldots, \lfloor v_{k-1} \rfloor_{L_{k-1}}, c - 1, v_{k+1}, \ldots, v_d) \ne f(\lfloor v_1 \rfloor_{L_1}, \ldots, \lfloor v_{k-1} \rfloor_{L_{k-1}}, c, v_{k+1}, \ldots, v_d)$.

We prove the following Lemma in the full paper.

Lemma 7. *We have $c \in \{a_{i,k}, b_{i,k}\}$ for some i, and $c \notin L_k$.*

We add c to L_k and update the table by adding all the missing values $f(v)$ where $v \in L_1 \times \cdots \times L_d$. We now show that this algorithm runs in polynomial time. Notice that the number of equivalence queries is at most

$$\sum_{k=1}^{d} |\{a_{i,k}, b_{i,k} \mid i = 1, \ldots, t\} \cup \{0\}| \le (2t + 1)d,$$

and the number of membership queries is at most the size of the table which is $(2t + 1)^d$ plus the number of membership queries needed for the binary search. We do one binary search for each equivalence query. Therefore the algorithm uses at most $(2t + 1)^d + (2t + 1)d^2 \log m$ membership queries.

We now sketch the proof that (2) is equivalent to (3). We show (2) $\Rightarrow$ (3) in the full paper. To prove (3) $\Rightarrow$ (2), let $\mathcal{A}$ be an α-approximation algorithm for MinEqui C. Let $r(1/\epsilon, 1/\delta)$ be the number of examples needed to learn C, given unlimited computational power. This r is polynomial and can be upper bounded by the VCdimension Theorem. Let $\mathcal{B}$ be a polynomial time (nonproper) PAC-learning algorithm for C under any distribution D. We define the following algorithm to learn f.

Proper_Learning

1. Run $\mathcal{B}$ with $\hat{\epsilon} = 1/(8r^d)$ where $r = r(1/\epsilon, 8)$ and $\hat{\delta} = 1/8$. Let $\hat{h}$ be the output hypothesis.

2. Get $r = r(1/\epsilon, 8)$ examples $(x^{(1)}, f(x^{(1)})), \ldots, (x^{(r)}, f(x^{(r)}))$.

3. Define $L_i = \{x_i^{(j)} \mid j = 1, \ldots, r\}$ and $L = L_1 \times \cdots \times L_d$.

4. Define the $\hat{m}_1 \times \cdots \times \hat{m}_d$ matrix A, where $\hat{m}_i = |L_i|$, and $A[i_1, \ldots, i_d] = \hat{h}(x_1^{(i_1)}, \ldots, x_d^{(i_d)})$.

5. Run $\mathcal{A}$ on A and let $h : \mathcal{N}_{\hat{m}_1} \times \cdots \times \mathcal{N}_{\hat{m}_d} \to \{0, 1\}$ be the output.

6. Define $g = h\mathcal{M}^\star$ where $\mathcal{M}^\star(x) = \mathcal{M}^{-1}(\lfloor x \rfloor_L)$, and $\mathcal{M}^{-1}(x_1^{(i_1)}, \ldots, x_d^{(i_d)}) = (i_1, \ldots, i_d)$.

7. Output (g)

In algorithm **Proper_Learning**, step 1 learns some function $\hat{h}$. Steps 2-3 take examples and build a lattice L. Since we do not have membership queries to find the value of the target on this lattice we use instead $\hat{h}$ to find the values. Steps 4-6 build a consistent hypothesis.

We now show that with probability 7/8 all of the membership queries that are simulated by $\hat{h}$ give a correct answer. Notice that since the distribution is the product distribution, $x_1^{(i_1)}, \ldots, x_d^{(i_d)}$ are chosen independently. Therefore,

$$\Pr[\hat{h}(x_1^{(i_1)}, \ldots, x_d^{(i_d)}) \neq f(x_1^{(i_1)}, \ldots, x_d^{(i_d)})] \leq \hat{\epsilon}$$

and

$$\Pr[\exists x \in L : \hat{h}(x) \neq f(x)] \leq \hat{\epsilon}|L| \leq \hat{\epsilon}r^d = \tfrac{1}{8}.$$

Since the learning algorithms $\mathcal{B}$ and $\mathcal{A}$ also have failure probability 1/8, algorithm **Proper_Learning** succeeds with probability at least $1 - (3/8) > 1/2$. We can run the above algorithm many times to achieve success $1 - \delta$. This completes the proof of Theorem 4.$\square$

Corollary 1. *Let $C = \mathcal{P}\Phi[\mathcal{N}_m^d]$ for a constant d be closed under monotone projection. Then C is properly learnable from membership and equivalence queries using an oracle for NP.*

Proof. Since $\textsc{MinEqui}\,C_U$ can be solved in polynomial time using an NP-oracle, by Theorem 4, C is properly learnable from membership and equivalence queries using an oracle for NP.$\square$

Let $C = \mathcal{P}\Phi[\mathcal{N}_m^d]$ for a constant d be closed under monotone projection. Consider these problems:

1. C is exactly learnable with a learning algorithm that uses oracles that are easy for C, and outputs a hypothesis of size at most α times the target size.
2. C is exactly learnable with a learning algorithm that uses equivalence queries only. The hypotheses may not be of small size but the output hypothesis has size at most α times the target size.

Since all the oracles for $C = \mathcal{P}\Phi[\mathcal{N}_m^d]$ are easy, both problems give an α-approximation algorithm for $\textsc{MinEqui}\,C$. Therefore they are equivalent to the problems in Theorem 4.

This shows that a negative result for the α-approximation of $\textsc{MinEqui}\,C$ will give a negative result for the α-proper learnability of C from all of the oracles mentioned in section 2.3.

4   Positive and Negative Results for Proper Learning

In this section we will prove positive and negative results for the α-proper learning of different axis parallel classes.

4.1   Decision Trees

The first Lemma is proved in the full version of this paper.

Lemma 8. *The class of Decision Trees is easy for all the oracles.*

Theorem 5. *If there is a proper learning algorithm for $\mathcal{N}_2^n$-decision trees from membership and equivalence queries (and other oracles) then $P = NP$.*

Proof. This follows from Theorem 2 because $\textsc{MinEqui}\,\mathcal{N}_2^n$-Decision Tree is NP-complete [ZB00].$\square$

Theorem 6. *There is a proper learning algorithm from membership and equivalence queries for $\mathcal{N}_m^d$-decision tree for constant dimension d.*

Proof. In the full paper we give a dynamic programming algorithm to partition a matrix into a minimum number of monochrome blocks. $\square$

Theorem 7. *There is a proper PAC-learning algorithm for $\mathcal{N}_m^d$-decision trees for constant d.*

Proof. The same algorithm above will also solve $\textsc{MinEqui}^*\,C_U$. By Theorem 3 the result follows.$\square$

4.2   DNF and Union of Boxes

Theorem 8. *There is an $\epsilon < 1$ such that: If the class $\mathcal{N}_m^n$-DNF is s^ϵ-properly learnable with membership and equivalence oracles (and all the other oracles) where s is the size of the DNF, then $\Sigma_2^p = P^{NP}$.*

Proof. The oracles are NP-easy for $\mathcal{N}_2^n$-DNF and approximating $\mathrm{MINEQUI}\,\mathcal{N}_2^n$-DNF within s^ϵ is Σ_2^p-hard [U99]. Then the result follows from Theorem 2. □

Theorem 9. *For union of boxes over dimension 2 ($\mathcal{N}_m^2$-DNF) we have*

1. *There is a $\log t$-proper learning algorithm for union of boxes over dimension 2 from membership and equivalence queries, where t is the optimal number of boxes required.*
2. *There is an α such that there is an α-proper learning algorithm for union of boxes over dimension 2 from any set of oracles if and only if $P = NP$.*

Proof. Part 1 uses the fact that $\mathrm{MINEQUI}\,\mathcal{N}_m^2$-DNF$_U$ has a $\log t$-approximation algorithm [Fr89]. Part 2 uses the result that $\mathrm{MINEQUI}\,\mathcal{N}_m^2$-DNF$_U$ is NP-complete and does not admit an approximation scheme unless P=NP [BD92]. Then both parts follow from Theorem 4 and Lemma 6. □

For union of disjoint boxes ($\mathcal{N}_m^n$-disjoint DNF) we have

Theorem 10. *1. There is a proper learning algorithm for union of disjoint boxes over dimension 2 from membership and equivalence queries.*

2. *There is a proper learning algorithm for union of disjoint boxes over dimension 3 from membership and equivalence queries if and only if $P = NP$.*

Proof. This follows from Theorem 4 and Lemma 6, and the fact that problem $\mathrm{MINEQUI}\;\mathcal{N}_m$-disjoint DNF$_U$ is the same as the problem of partitioning a (set of) orthogonal polygons into a minimum number of boxes. This problem is in P for dimension 2 [LLLMP79], and NP-complete for dimension 3 [DK91]. □

4.3   Multivariate Polynomials and Xor of Boxes

We prove the following Theorems in the full paper.

Theorem 11. *There is a proper learning algorithm for $\mathcal{N}_m^d$-Monotone Multivariate Polynomial from membership and equivalence queries.*

Theorem 12. *There is a proper learning algorithm for $\mathcal{N}_m^d$-Almost-Monotone Multivariate Polynomial from membership and equivalence queries, where $\mathcal{N}_m^d$-Almost-Monotone Polynomial is a sum of terms that contain literals of the form $[x_i \geq a]$ for $i = 1, \ldots, d$ and $[x_1 < b]$ (only x_1 may be negated).*

Theorem 13. *There is a 2^{d-1}-proper learning algorithm for $\mathcal{N}_m^d$-Multivariate Polynomial from membership and equivalence queries.*

References

[A88]   D. Angluin. Queries and concept learning. *Machine Learning*, 319–342, 1988. 289, 293

[ABSS97]   S. Arora, L. Babai, J. Stern, Z. Sweedyk. The hardness of approximate optima in lattices, codes, and systems of linear equations. *JCSS*, 43, 317-331, 1997.

[BBBKV00]   A. Beimel, F. Bergadano, N. H. Bshouty, E. Kushilevitz, S. Varricchio. Learning functions represented as multiplicity automata. *JACM* 47(3): 506-530, 2000. 289, 290

[BK98]   A. Beimel and E. Kushilevitz. Learning boxes in high dimension. *Algorithmica*, 22(1/2):76-90, 1998. 290

[BBK97]   S. Ben-David, N. H. Bshouty, E. Kushilevitz. A composition theorem for learning algorithms with applications to geometric concept classes. *29th STOC*, 1997. 290

[BCV96]   F. Bergadano, D. Catalano, S. Varricchio. Learning sat-k-DNF formulas from membership queries. In *28th STOC*, pp 126–130, 1996. 288, 289

[BD92]   P. Berman, B. DasGupta. Approximating the rectilinear polygon cover problems. In *Proceedings of the 4th Canadian Conference on Computational Geometry*, pages 229–235, 1992. 300

[Bs95]   N. H. Bshouty, Exact learning of boolean functions via the monotone theory. *Information and Computation*, **123**, pp. 146-153, 1995. 288, 289

[B95a]   N. H. Bshouty. Simple learning algorithms using divide and conquer. In *Proceedings of the Annual ACM Workshop on Computational Learning Theory*, 1995.

[B98]   N. H. Bshouty. A new composition theorem for learning algorithms. *Proceedings of the 30th annual ACM Symposium on Theory of Computing (STOC)*, May 1998. 290

[BCG96]   N. H. Bshouty, R. Cleve, R. Gavalda, S. Kannan, C. Tamon. Oracles and queries that are sufficient for exact learning. *JCSS* 52(3): pp. 421-433, 1996. 288

[BGGM99]   N. H. Bshouty, P. W. Goldberg, S. A. Goldman, D. H. Mathias. Exact learning of discretized geometric concepts. *SIAM J. of Comput.* 28(2), 678-699, 1999. 290

[CH96]   Z. Chen and W. Homer. The bounded injury priority method and the learnability of unions of rectangles. *Annals of Pure and Applied Logic* 77(2):143-168, 1996. 290

[CM94]   Z. Chen, W. Maass. On-line learning of rectangles and unions of rectangles, *Machine Learning*, 17(1/2), pages 201-223, 1994. 290

[DK91]   V. J. Dielissen, A. Kaldewaij. Rectangular partition is polynomial in two dimensions but NP-complete in three. In *IPL*, pages 1–6, 1991. 300

[Fr89]   D. Franzblau. Performance guarantees on a sweep-line heuristic for covering rectilinear polygons with rectangles. *SIAM J. on Discrete Math 2*, 307-321, 1989. 300

[HPRW96]   L. Hellerstein, K. Pillaipakkamnatt, V. Raghavan, D. Wilkins. How many queries are needed to learn? *JACM*, 43(5), pages 840-862, 1996. 288, 289, 294

[HR02]   L. Hellerstein and V. Raghavan. Exact learning of DNF formulas using DNF hypotheses. In *34rd Annual Symposium on Theory of Computing (STOC)*, 2002. 288

[KS01]   A. Klivans and R. Servedio. Learning DNF in Time $2^{O(n^{1/3})}$. In 33rd
             Annual Symposium on Theory of Computing (STOC), 2001, pp. 258-
             265. 288

[LLLMP79]   W. Lipski, Jr., E. Lodi, F. Luccio, C. Mugnai and L. Pagli. On two-
             dimensional data organization II. In *Fund. Inform.* 2, pages 245-260,
             1979. 300

[MW98]   W. Maass and M. K. Warmuth Efficient learning with virtual threshold
             gates *Information and Computation*, 141(1): 66-83, 1998. 290

[PR96]   K. Pillaipakkamntt, V. Raghavan, On the limits of proper learnability of
             subclasses of DNF formulas, *Machine Learning*, 25(2/3), pages 237-263,
             1996. 288

[PV88]   L. Pitt and L. G. Valiant. Computational Limitations on Learning from
             Examples. *Journal of the ACM*, 35(4):965–984, October 1988. 296

[SS93]   R. E. Schapire, L. M. Sellie. Learning sparse multivariate polynomial
             over a field with queries and counterexamples. In *Proceedings of the Sixth
             Annual ACM Workshop on Computational Learning Theory*. July, 1993.
             288, 289

[U99]   C. Umans. Hardness of approximating Σ_2^p minimization problems. In
             Proceedings of the 40th Symposium on Foundations of Computer Science,
             1999. 289, 300

[Val84]   L. Valiant. A theory of the learnable. *Communications of the ACM*,
             27(11):1134–1142, November 1984.

[ZB00]   H. Zantema, H. Bodlaender. Finding small equivalent decision trees is
             hard. In *International Journal of Foundations of Computer Science*,
             11(2): 343–354, 2000. 289, 299

A Consistent Strategy for Boosting Algorithms

Gábor Lugosi* and Nicolas Vayatis**

Department of Economics, Pompeu Fabra University
Ramon Trias Fargas 25-27, 08 005 Barcelona, Spain
lugosi@upf.es
nicolas.vayatis@econ.upf.es

Abstract. The probability of error of classification methods based on convex combinations of simple base classifiers by "boosting" algorithms is investigated. The main result of the paper is that certain regularized boosting algorithms provide Bayes-risk consistent classifiers under the only assumption that the Bayes classifier may be approximated by a convex combination of the base classifiers. Non-asymptotic distribution-free bounds are also developed which offer interesting new insight into how boosting works and help explain their success in practical classification problems.

1 Introduction

One of the most important recent developments in the practice of classification has been the introduction of *boosting* algorithms which have had a remarkable performance on a large variety of classification problems. These algorithms aim at producing a combined classifier from a given class of *weak* (or *base*) classifiers. While the corpus of empirical studies has reached impressive proportions, there are still few theoretical results to explain their efficiency. Originally (see, e.g., Schapire [29], Freund [15], Freund and Schapire [17]), boosting was considered as an iterative procedure which, given the training data, would at each step: (i) select a classifier from a given class of base classifiers, (ii) evaluate a weight for this classifier, (iii) output the weighted majority vote of the selected classifiers up to this step. The main idea in the updating rule of this procedure is to put a probability distribution on the sample points, starting with the uniform distribution at the initial step, and then to change this distribution at every step according to some rule reinforcing the probability associated to misclassified points along the process. This heuristic generated numerous variations on the choice of the initial pool of weak learners and on the way to perform the weight update. Generally speaking, the derived algorithms perform very well on most of the usual benchmark data sets in the sense that the generalization error decreases as successive iterations are run. However, the resistance to overfitting of the family of boosting

---

* The work of the first author was supported by DGI grant BMF2000-0807
** The work of the second author was supported by a Marie Curie Fellowship of the European Community "Improving Human Potential" programme under contract number HPMFCT-2000-00667.

J. Kivinen and R. H. Sloan (Eds.): COLT 2002, LNAI 2375, pp. 303–319, 2002.

methods have not found a fully satisfactory explanation so far (see Breiman [9], Freund, Mansour, Schapire [16]). One of the most interesting attempts to explain the success of boosting methods points out that they tend to maximize the margin of the correctly classified points. These arguments are based on margin-based bounds for the probability of misclassification, see Schapire, Freund, Bartlett, and Lee [30], Koltchinskii and Panchenko [24]. However, as it was pointed out by Breiman [7], these bounds alone do not completely explain the efficiency of these methods (see also Freund and Schapire [20]). Boosting algorithms have also been explicitly connected with additive logistic regression by Friedman, Hastie, and Tibshirani [21] and Bühlmann and Yu [10]. This connection points out that boosting methods effectively minimize an empirical loss functional (different from the probability of misclassification). This property has also been pointed out in slightly different contexts by Breiman [8], Mason, Baxter, Bartlett, and Frean [28], and Collins, Schapire, and Singer [12]. The last observation places boosting into a much wider perspective and this is the one we adopt along the present paper. It is now common knowledge that minimization of the empirical probability of misclassification is subject to overfitting and is computationally unfeasible, while replacing the empirical probability of misclassification by an appropriate smooth loss functional avoids overfitting and becomes computationally feasible in many cases. However, this leaves open the issue of consistency because it is not clear to what extent solving the approximated problem of the empirical functional minimization is equivalent to minimizing the generalization error. This paper attempts to fill in the theoretical vacuum about consistency of boosting methods, and proposes elements of explanation for their efficiency in practice. We combine known techniques for deriving margin-based bounds with some new results to explain under which conditions minimizing a cost functional conducts to the Bayes risk, at least asymptotically. For previous work on Bayes risk consistency, we refer to Breiman [9], Bühlmann and Yu [11], Jiang [22], [23], Mannor and Meir [26], Mannor, Meir and Mendelson [27]. The rest of the paper is organized as follows. The next section introduces the formal setting and the notations. In Section 3 the simplest version of the method is defined and the consistency results are presented. In Section 4 the effect of the cost function is studied. Section 5 discusses variants of the main results based on data-dependent regularized choices of the loss function. In Section 6 we point out that some of the bounds developed here show that the proposed regularized boosting algorithm minimizes the best Chernoff bound on the probability of error.

2 Setup and Notation

In this paper, we consider binary classification problems described as follows. Let $\mathcal{X}$ be a measurable feature space and let (X, Y) be a pair of random variables taking values in $\mathcal{X} \times \{-1, 1\}$. The random variable X models some observation and Y its unknown binary label. In the standard classification problem, the statistician is asked to construct a classifier $g_n : \mathcal{X} \to \{-1, 1\}$ which assigns a label to each possible value of the observation. The statistician has access to training data consisting of n independent, identically distributed observation/label pairs $D_n = (X_1, Y_1), \ldots, (X_n, Y_n)$, having the same distribution as (X, Y). The quality of g_n is measured by the loss

$$L(g_n) = \mathbb{P}\left\{g_n(X) \neq Y | D_n\right\} .$$

Ideally, $L(g_n)$ should be close, with large probability, to the Bayes risk, that is, to the minimal possible probability of error

$$L^* = \inf_g L(g) = \mathbb{E}\left\{\min(\eta(X), 1 - \eta(X))\right\}$$

where the infimum is taken over all classifiers $g : \mathcal{X} \to \{-1, 1\}$ and $\eta(x) = \mathbb{P}\{Y = 1 | X = x\}$ denotes the regression function. Note that the infimum is achieved by the Bayes classifier[1] $g^*(x) = \mathbb{I}_{[\eta(x)>1/2]} - \mathbb{I}_{[\eta(x)\leq 1/2]}$ (where $\mathbb{I}$ denotes the indicator function).

In recent years, a large part of research has been focused on classifiers which base their decision on a certain combination of very simple rules. Such rules include different versions of "boosting", "bagging", and "arcing" methods, see, e.g., Breiman [3,4,6,8], Freund and Schapire [15,18,19,29]. To describe such averaging methods, consider a class of classifiers $\mathcal{C}$, where elements $g : \mathcal{X} \to \{-1, 1\}$ of $\mathcal{C}$ will be called the *base classifiers*. We usually think of $\mathcal{C}$ as a class of simple rules such as all "decision stumps", or all binary trees with $d+1$ terminal nodes, but our results hold for more general families. In the general framework defined here we only assume that the VC dimension of $\mathcal{C}$ is finite.

Define $\mathcal{F}$ as the class of functions $f : \mathcal{X} \to [-1, 1]$ obtained as convex combinations of the classifiers in $\mathcal{C}$:

$$\mathcal{F} = \left\{f(x) = \sum_{j=1}^{N} w_j g_j(x) \, : \, N \in \mathbb{N}, \, w_1, \ldots, w_N \geq 0, \, \sum_{j=1}^{N} w_j = 1\right\}.$$

Each estimator $f \in \mathcal{F}$ defines a classifier g_f, in a natural way, by

$$g_f(x) = \begin{cases} 1 & \text{if } f(x) > 0 \\ -1 & \text{otherwise.} \end{cases}$$

To simplify notation, we write $L(f)$ for the probability of error $L(g_f)$ of the corresponding classifier. Similarly, introduce the empirical error by

$$\widehat{L}_n(f) = \frac{1}{n}\sum_{i=1}^{n} \mathbb{I}_{[Y_i g_f(X_i)<0]}$$

To shorten notation, we define $Z(f) = -f(X)Y$ and $Z_i(f) = -f(X_i)Y_i$. Thus, minimization of the probability of error $L(f)$ over $f \in \mathcal{F}$ is approximately equivalent to the minimization of the expected value of the "cost function" $\mathbb{I}_{[\cdot > 0]}$

---

[1] Note that, with this convention, ties are broken in favor of -1, and this has no consequence on the value of the Bayes error.

of $Z(f)$. Since the expected value cannot be evaluated in the absence of the knowledge of the joint distribution of (X, Y), minimization of the empirical cost $\frac{1}{n} \sum_{i=1}^{n} \mathbb{I}_{[Z_i(f)>0]}$ may be attempted as an approximation. However, the class $\mathcal{F}$ of estimators is too large in the sense that minimization of the empirical cost over the whole class overfits the data and may yield a classifier with large probability of error. Indeed, even in the simplest cases the class of all g_f is easily seen to have an infinite VC dimension.

The estimators studied in this paper minimize a criterion which replaces the natural cost function (i.e., the indicator of misclassification $\mathbb{I}_{[-f(X)Y>0]}$) by a smooth convex cost function of the random variable $Z = -f(X)Y$. Indeed, various versions of boosting algorithms have been shown to minimize such cost functions, see, for example, Mason, Baxter, Bartlett, and Frean [28], Friedman, Hastie, and Tibshirani [21], Collins, Schapire, and Singer [12]. The usual choice of the cost function is the exponential, though other choices have also been proposed. The advantage of introducing such cost functions is twofold. First, the empirical optimization problem becomes tractable, since the objective function becomes convex. The second advantage is that the probability of error of the resulting classifier may be bounded nontrivially, something that cannot be done for the direct minimizer of the empirical probability of error. The first such result was pointed out by Schapire, Freund, Bartlett, and Lee [30] (interesting extensions are given by Blanchard [2]) and more explicitly by Koltchinskii and Panchenko [24], who showed that meaningful confidence bounds may be derived for the probability of error of the classifier minimizing a smooth upper bound. Even though, as Breiman [8] argues, the bounds in [30] alone do not explain the spectacular practical success of these algorithms, in this paper we show how these bounds may be used to prove Bayes-risk consistency.

In this paper all we assume about the classification algorithm is that the method at hand minimizes a smooth convex cost function, and we do not investigate the specific ways such algorithms are realized. For example, minimization based on gradient-descent methods leads to some standard versions of boosting algorithms, see Mason, Baxter, Bartlett, and Frean [28].

More specifically, let $\phi : [-1, 1] \to \mathbb{R}^+$ be a nondecreasing convex function such that $\phi(0) = 1$ and for all $x \in [-1, 1]$, $\mathbb{I}_{[x>0]} \le \phi(x)$. Introduce the notations

$$A(f) = \mathbb{E}\phi(Z(f)) \quad \text{and} \quad A_n(f) = \frac{1}{n} \sum_{i=1}^{n} \phi(Z_i(f)).$$

Then clearly, since $\mathbb{I}_{[x>0]} \le \phi(x)$, we have $L(f) \le A(f)$ for all $f \in \mathcal{F}$. It is also clear that the empirical cost $A_n(f)$ is a convex function of the parameters $w_1, w_2, \ldots$ and therefore efficient algorithms are available for minimizing $A_n(f)$ over $f \in \mathcal{F}$. (In fact, some versions of boosting, e.g., the so-called L_1-boosting method in [28] minimize $A_n(f)$ using gradient descent algorithms.)

The purpose of this paper is to investigate the probability of error $L(g_n)$ of classifiers $g_n = g_{\widehat{f}_n}$, where $\widehat{f}_n$ is obtained by minimizing a convex cost functional $A_n(f)$ over $f \in \mathcal{F}$. The performance, of course, depends on the choice of

ϕ. The first main result of this paper (Theorem 1) shows that ϕ may be chosen such that the probability of error $L(\widehat{f}_n)$ of the corresponding minimizer $\widehat{f}_n$ converges, almost surely, as $n \to \infty$, to the Bayes risk L^* for all distributions under the sole assumption that the class of all constant multiples of elements in $\mathcal{F}$ is dense in the class of all measurable functions which is easily seen to hold for some simple choices of the base class $\mathcal{C}$. The cost function ϕ is chosen from a one-dimensional family. We offer several possible choices. The simplest choice selects the cost function before seeing the data, as a function of the sample size. For better performance, data-dependent regularization may be performed, which is detailed in Section 5.

We also derive some distribution-free non-asymptotic upper bounds for the probability of error of the classifier obtained by a regularized choice of the cost function. These bounds offer a new and interesting interpretation of what boosting methods do: instead of minimizing the probability of error, they minimize the best Chernoff bound on this probability (see Section 6).

3   Consistency

As indicated in the introduction, the main focus of this paper is on classifiers $g_{\widehat{f}_n}$ where the estimator $\widehat{f}_n$ minimizes the empirical quantity $A_n(f)$ based on some convex cost function ϕ. We begin this section by defining a prototype regularization procedure for the choice of the cost function and prove that the resulting classifier has a probability of error converging to the Bayes risk, almost surely.

To this end, let $\phi : \mathbb{R} \to \mathbb{R}^+$ be a differentiable strictly increasing strictly convex function such that $\phi(x) \geq \mathbb{I}_{[x>0]}$ for all $x \in \mathbb{R}$, $\phi(0) = 1$, $\lim_{x \to -\infty} \phi(x) = 0$, and introduce, for all $\lambda > 0$,

$$\phi_\lambda(x) = \phi(\lambda x) .$$

Denote the empirical and expected loss functional associated with the cost function ϕ_λ by A_n^λ and A^λ, that is,

$$A_n^\lambda(f) = \frac{1}{n} \sum_{i=1}^n \phi_\lambda(Z_i(f)) \quad \text{and} \quad A^\lambda(f) = \mathbb{E}\phi_\lambda(Z(f)) .$$

Note that on $[-1, 1]$ the function ϕ_λ is Lipschitz with constant $\lambda \phi'(\lambda)$. If $\lambda = 1$, we simply write $A_n(f)$ and $A(f)$ instead of $A_n^\lambda(f)$ and $A_n^\lambda(f)$. Observe that

$$A_n^\lambda(f) = A_n(\lambda f) \qquad A^\lambda(f) = A(\lambda f) .$$

REMARK. This simple observation highlights the two different interpretations of the scale parameter λ. One way of viewing λ reveals it as a parameter of the cost function we minimize. However, minimizing $A^\lambda(f)$ over $\mathcal{F}$ is equivalent to minimizing $A(f)$ over the scaled class $\lambda \cdot \mathcal{F}$. Though scaling the estimator f has no effect on the corresponding decision function (performance is unchanged since $L(f) = L(\lambda f)$ for all $\lambda > 0$), the introduction of the parameter λ is indeed a decisive step to design consistent strategies in boosting. As the analysis below reveals it, large values of λ offer more flexibility of approximation at the price of making the estimation problem more difficult. It is worth noting at this point that the original AdaBoost algorithm attempts to minimize the functional A in the linear span of $\mathcal{C}$. In contrast to this, here we consider a family of optimization problems (minimizing various functionals A^λ) over the convex hull of $\mathcal{C}$.

Now let $\widehat{f}_n^\lambda$ denote a function in $\mathcal{F}$ which minimizes the empirical loss

$$A_n^\lambda(f) = \frac{1}{n} \sum_{i=1}^n \phi_\lambda(Z_i(f))$$

over $f \in \mathcal{F}$.

The simplest version of the main consistency result of the paper is the following. The only assumption for the class $\mathcal{C}$ of base classifiers (apart from having a finite VC dimension) is that the union, for all $\lambda > 0$, of the classes of functions $\lambda \cdot \mathcal{F} = \{\lambda f : f \in \mathcal{F}\}$ is sufficiently rich to approximate the function f^* minimizing $A(f)$.

For the cost function ϕ we need the properties listed in Assumption 1 below. To this end, let

$$f^*(x) = \arg\min_{\alpha \in \mathbb{R}} \{\eta(x)\phi(-\alpha) + (1 - \eta(x))\phi(\alpha)\} .$$

We will see in Lemma 3 below that f^* is well-defined for all x with $\eta(x) \in (0, 1)$.

Assumption 1. *Let ϕ be a convex, nonnegative, increasing cost function with $\phi(x) \geq \mathbb{I}_{[x>0]}$ for all $x \in \mathbb{R}$, $\phi(0) = 1$, $\lim_{x \to -\infty} \phi(x) = 0$, such that*
(i) ϕ is three times differentiable with an increasing third derivative;
(ii) $\eta(x)\phi''(-f^*(x)) + (1 - \eta(x))\phi''(f^*(x))$ is bounded away from zero if η is bounded away from 0 and 1.
(iii) $(-\eta(x)\phi^{(3)}(-f^*(x)) + (1 - \eta(x))\phi^{(3)}(f^*(x))) \cdot f^*(x) \leq 0$ for all x with $\eta(x) \in (0, 1)$.

An alternative assumption on the cost function ϕ is the one proposed by Zhang [31]:

Assumption 2. *Let ϕ be a convex, nonnegative, increasing cost function with $\phi(x) \geq \mathbb{I}_{[x>0]}$ for all $x \in \mathbb{R}$, $\phi(0) = 1$, $\lim_{x \to -\infty} \phi(x) = 0$, such that there exists a constant c and $s \geq 1$ satisfying, for any $\eta \in [0, 1]$,*

$$\left| \frac{1}{2} - \eta \right|^s \leq c^s(1 - H(\eta))$$

where $H(\eta) = \inf_{\alpha \in \mathbb{R}} \{\eta\phi(-\alpha) + (1 - \eta)\phi(\alpha)\}$.

Theorem 1. *Assume that the cost function ϕ satisfies Assumption 1 or 2 and that the distribution of (X, Y) and the class $\mathcal{C}$ are such that*

$$\lim_{\lambda \to \infty} \inf_{f \in \lambda \cdot \mathcal{F}} A(f) = A^*,$$

where $A^* = \inf A(f)$ over all measurable functions $f : \mathcal{X} \longrightarrow \mathbb{R}$. Assume that $\mathcal{C}$ has a finite VC dimension. Let $(\lambda_n)_n$ be a sequence of positive numbers satisfying

$$\lambda_n \to \infty \quad and \quad \lambda_n \phi'(\lambda_n) \sqrt{\frac{\ln n}{n}} \to 0 \quad as \; n \to \infty$$

and define the estimator $f_n = \widehat{f}_n^{\lambda_n} \in \mathcal{F}$. Then g_{f_n} is strongly Bayes-risk consistent, that is,

$$\lim_{n \to \infty} L(g_{f_n}) = L^* \quad almost \; surely.$$

REMARK. (UNIVERSAL CONSISTENCY.) For many base classes $\mathcal{C}$, the first condition of the theorem is satisfied for all possible distributions of (X, Y). In Lemma 1 below we provide a simple sufficient condition for such a universal approximation property. In such cases, the classifier g_{f_n} is *strongly universally consistent*.

REMARK. (ASSUMPTIONS ON THE COST FUNCTION.) It is easy to see that the cost function most widely used in practice, the exponential function, satisfies Assumptions 1 and 2. Indeed, it is easy to see that for $\phi(x) = e^x$,

$$f^*(x) = \frac{1}{2} \ln \left(\frac{\eta(x)}{1 - \eta(x)} \right)$$

and both (ii) and (iii) are easily seen to hold. Another important cost functions such as the logit function $\log_2(1 + e^x)$ meets only the condition of Assumption 2. The relationship between Assumptions 1 & 2 is not clear though Assumption 2 seems to cover most of the classical settings. For some discussion, we refer to Section 4.

REMARK. (DENSENESS ASSUMPTION.) The assumption on the class $\mathcal{C}$ given by $\lim_{\lambda \to \infty} \inf_{f \in \lambda \cdot \mathcal{F}} A(f) = A^*$ may be replaced by a simpler completeness condition such as in the argument of Breiman in [9]. Examples satisfying this condition are the class of indicators of all rectangles, or the class of binary trees with a number of terminal nodes equal to the dimension d plus one (see [9]). We offer the following lemma to emphasize this remark:

Lemma 1. *Let the class $\mathcal{C}$ be such that its convex hull contains all the indicators of elements of $\mathcal{B}_0$, a subalgebra of the Borel σ-algebra of $\mathbb{R}^d$, denoted by $\mathcal{B}(\mathbb{R}^d)$, with $\mathcal{B}_0$ generating $\mathcal{B}(\mathbb{R}^d)$. Then,*

$$\lim_{\lambda \to \infty} \inf_{f \in \lambda \cdot \mathcal{F}} A(f) = A^*,$$

where $A^* = \inf A(f)$ over all measurable functions $f : \mathbb{R}^d \longrightarrow \mathbb{R}$.

The proof relies on some properties of the minimizer of the functional A described in Lemma 3.

REMARK. (λ AS A SMOOTHING PARAMETER.) The theorem requires that the cost function ϕ_λ become steeper as the sample size grows, but this steepness should grow at a controlled fashion. One may think about λ as a smoothing parameter. Small values of λ mean smooth estimators, while a large λ allows more rigged estimators. As is always the case in nonparametric curve estimation, a data-dependent choice of the smoothing parameter is desirable for better performance. This may be performed in several different ways, one of which is discussed in Section 5.

The proof of Theorem 1 is based on a few simple lemmas. One of the main ingredients is a variation of a result of Koltchinskii and Panchenko [24] which we provide below. It summarizes the "probabilistic" part of the argument.

Lemma 2. *For any n and $\lambda > 0$,*

$$\mathbb{E}\sup_{f \in \mathcal{F}} \left| A^\lambda(f) - A_n^\lambda(f) \right| \leq 4\lambda\phi'(\lambda)\sqrt{\frac{2V\ln(4n+2)}{n}}.$$

Also, for any $\delta > 0$, with probability at least $1 - \delta$,

$$\sup_{f \in \mathcal{F}} \left| A^\lambda(f) - A_n^\lambda(f) \right| \leq 4\lambda\phi'(\lambda)\sqrt{\frac{2V\ln(4n+2)}{n}} + \lambda\phi'(\lambda)\sqrt{\frac{\ln(1/\delta)}{2n}}.$$

Some basic properties of the minimizer are summarized in the following lemma.

Lemma 3. *Let ϕ be a convex, nonnegative, increasing cost function with $\phi(0) = 1$, $\lim_{x \to -\infty} \phi(x) = 0$. Consider either one of the following two cases:*

− *If $\eta(X) \notin \{0,1\}$ almost surely then, for each λ, there exists a unique measurable function f_λ^*, such that*

$$A^\lambda(f_\lambda^*) \leq A^\lambda(f) \quad \text{for all functions } f.$$

Then the classifier

$$\begin{cases} 1 \text{ if } f_\lambda^*(x) > 0 \\ -1 \text{ otherwise} \end{cases}$$

is just the Bayes classifier g^*. Also, if f^* denotes f_1^*, then $f^* = \lambda f_\lambda^*$.

− *If $\eta(X) \in \{0,1\}$ almost surely then, for each λ, we have*

$$\inf_f A^\lambda(f) = 0.$$

Also, for any sequence of measurable functions f_n such that

$$\lim_{n \to \infty} A^\lambda(f_n) = 0,$$

there exists some n_0 such that, for $n \geq n_0$, the classifiers

$$\begin{cases} 1 & \text{if } f_n(x) > 0 \\ -1 & \text{otherwise} \end{cases}$$

are all equal to the Bayes classifier g^*.

The proof is based on simple properties of the cost function and we provide it in the Appendix.

Now, before considering the fundamental Lemma 5, we need an auxiliary result which characterizes the pointwise minimum of the cost functional as a function of the regression function η. This quantity can be understood as an entropy measure (see Section 4).

Lemma 4. *Let ϕ be a convex, nonnegative, increasing cost function with $\phi(0) = 1$, $\lim_{x \to -\infty} \phi(x) = 0$. Then the function*

$$H(\eta) = \inf_{\alpha \in \mathbb{R}} (\eta \phi(-\alpha) + (1 - \eta)\phi(\alpha)) ,$$

defined for $\eta \in [0, 1]$, is concave, symmetric around $1/2$, and $H(0) = H(1) = 0$, $H(1/2) = 1$.

PROOF. Concavity follows from the fact that the infimum of concave functions is concave. By the convexity of ϕ, $(1/2)\phi(-\alpha) + (1/2)\phi(\alpha) \geq \phi(0)$ with equality achieved at $\alpha = 0$, which implies $H(1/2) = 1$. The rest of the properties are obvious. □

Our last key lemma before turning to the proof of Theorem 1 shows that near optimization of the functional A yields nearly optimal classifiers.

Lemma 5. *Let ϕ be a cost function satisfying Assumption 1. Let f_n be an arbitrary sequence of functions such that $\lim_{n \to \infty} A(f_n) = A^*$. Then the classifier*

$$g_{f_n}(x) = \begin{cases} 1 & \text{if } f_n(x) > 0 \\ -1 & \text{otherwise} \end{cases}$$

has a probability of error converging to L^*.

Note that our Lemma 5 can be proved also under Assumption 2 thanks to the following result due to Zhang in [31].

Lemma 6. *Under Assumption 2, for any estimator f,*

$$L(f) - L^* \leq 2c(A(f) - A^*)^{1/s} .$$

PROOF OF THEOREM 1. Denote by $\overline{f}_\lambda$ an element of $\mathcal{F}$ which minimizes A^λ. Then we may write

$$A(\lambda_n f_n) - A^* = \left(A(\lambda_n f_n) - A(\lambda_n \overline{f}_{\lambda_n})\right) + \left(A(\lambda_n \overline{f}_{\lambda_n}) - A^*\right)$$

$$= \left(A^{\lambda_n}(\widehat{f}_n^{\lambda_n}) - A^{\lambda_n}(\overline{f}_{\lambda_n})\right) + \left(\inf_{f \in \lambda_n \cdot \mathcal{F}} A(f) - A^*\right) .$$

clearly, the second term on the right-hand side converges to zero by the assumption on $\mathcal{F}$ and since $\lambda_n \to \infty$. To bound the first term, simply note that

$$A^{\lambda_n}(\widehat{f}_n^{\lambda_n}) - A^{\lambda_n}(\overline{f}_{\lambda_n}) \leq 2 \sup_{f \in \mathcal{F}} \left| A^{\lambda_n}(f) - A_n^{\lambda_n}(f) \right| ,$$

see, e.g., [13, Lemma 8.2]. But by Lemma 2 this converges to zero with probability one, by the choice of λ_n.

Thus, we have that $A(\lambda_n f_n) \to A^*$ with probability one. The consistency result now follows by Lemma 5 or Lemma 6. □

4   Cost Functions

The choice of the cost function $\phi : \mathbb{R} \to \mathbb{R}^+$ may influence the performance of the obtained classifier. The inequality of Lemma 2 offers a guide for choosing ϕ: the smaller the quantity $\phi'(\lambda)$, the tighter the bound is. On the other hand, the choice is restricted by the requirement that ϕ is convex. In addition, Assumption 1 (resp. Assumption 2), especially the first part of it, poses further restrictions on the growth of ϕ. The reason these restrictions are present is Lemma 5 (resp. Lemma 6), the rest of the arguments remain valid for any strictly convex, non-negative, increasing cost functions. A glance at the proof of Lemma 5 reveals that, for any such cost function, if $\eta(x)$ is guaranteed to be sufficiently far from $1/2$ (i.e., in low-noise problems), the proof remains valid. In particular, we obtain the following result:

Theorem 2. *Let ϕ be a convex, nonnegative, increasing cost function with $\phi(0) = 1$, $\lim_{x \to -\infty} \phi(x) = 0$. Assume that the distribution of (X, Y) is such that[2]*

$$\operatorname*{ess\,inf}_{x \in \mathcal{X}} (1 - \eta(x) - H(\eta(x))) > 0$$

where H is the function defined in Lemma 4, and $\lim_{\lambda \to \infty} \inf_{f \in \lambda \cdot \mathcal{F}} A(f) = A^*$. Assume also that $\mathcal{C}$ has a finite VC dimension. If

$$\lambda_n \to \infty \quad \text{and} \quad \lambda_n \phi'(\lambda_n) \sqrt{\frac{\ln n}{n}} \to 0 \quad \text{as } n \to \infty$$

then $f_n = \widehat{f}_n^{\lambda_n} \in \mathcal{F}$ is strongly Bayes-risk consistent.

Below we consider some specific choices of the cost function.

EXAMPLE 1. The standard choice in most boosting algorithms is $\phi(x) = \exp(x)$. This function, as indicated above, satisfies Assumption 1, and therefore consistency holds without any restriction on the distribution. Note that in this case $f^*(x) = \frac{1}{2} \ln \left(\frac{\eta(x)}{1 - \eta(x)} \right)$ and $H(\eta) = 2\sqrt{\eta(1 - \eta)}$.

---

[2] The essential infimum $\operatorname{ess\,inf}_S f$ of a function f over a measurable set S is the infimum of constants c for which $\{f \leq c\}$ has non-zero measure.

EXAMPLE 2: Another important example is

$$\phi(x) = \text{logit}(x) := \log_2(1 + \exp(x))$$

considered in [21]. This cost function does not satisfy Assumption 1 but it fulfills Assumption 2 with $s = 2$. Observe that $f^*(x) = \ln\left(\frac{\eta(x)}{1-\eta(x)}\right)$ and $H(\eta) = -\eta \log_2 \eta - (1-\eta)\log_2(1-\eta)$ is the binary entropy function.

EXAMPLE 3: Another interesting alternative is

$$\phi(x) = \psi(x) := \begin{cases} \exp(x) \text{ , if } x < 0 \\ x+1 \text{ , if } x \geq 0 \end{cases}$$

Here $f^*(x) = \ln\left(\frac{\eta(x)}{1-\eta(x)}\right)$ and $H(\eta) = \eta(2 + \ln((1-\eta)/\eta))$ for $\eta \leq 1/2$. Even though the function ψ is not strictly convex, it is easy to see that the proof of Lemma 3 remains valid for this function as well, and consistency for low-noise distributions may be established similarly to the previous example.

5 Penalized Model Selection

In Section 3, we established the existence of a consistent strategy based on boosting methods. In these results, the sequence of estimators $f_n = f_n^{\lambda_n}$ requires for each n to minimize the functional $A_n^{\lambda_n}$ over $\mathcal{F}$, for a predetermined sequence $(\lambda_n)_n$. Of course, it would be much more practical to handle the choice of λ on the basis of the sample. The following theorem shows that consistency remains true for a data-dependent regularized choice of the smoothing parameter λ:

Theorem 3. *Assume that the cost function ϕ satisfies Assumption 1 or 2 and that the distribution of (X, Y) and the class C are such that $\lim_{\lambda \to \infty} \inf_{f \in \lambda \cdot \mathcal{F}} A(f) = A^*$, where $A^* = \inf A(f)$ over all measurable functions $f : \mathcal{X} \longrightarrow \mathbb{R}$. Let V denote the VC dimension of the base class C. For any divergent sequence $(\lambda_k)_k$ of positive numbers, let*

$$f_n = \arg\min_{k \geq 1} \tilde{A}_n^{\lambda_k}(\widehat{f}_n^{\lambda_k}) ,$$

where

$$\tilde{A}_n^{\lambda_k}(f) = A_n^{\lambda_k}(f) + 4\lambda_k \phi'(\lambda_k)\sqrt{\frac{2V \ln(4n+2)}{n}} + \lambda_k \phi'(\lambda_k)\sqrt{\frac{\ln(6n^2 k^2/\pi^2)}{n}} ,$$

and

$$\widehat{f}_n^{\lambda_k} = \arg\min_{f \in \mathcal{F}} A_n^{\lambda_k}(f) .$$

Then f_n is strongly Bayes-risk consistent, that is,

$$\lim_{n \to \infty} L(f_n) = L^* \quad \text{almost surely.}$$

The outline of the proof is the same as before. We provide some clues in the Appendix.

6   Boosting Minimizes Chernoff Bounds

The idea of combining simple classifiers via voting methods is often motivated by the argument that if one happens to find several "independent" classifiers such that all of them have a probability of error slightly better than random guessing, then taking a majority vote will radically decrease the probability of error. The improvement may easily be quantified by Chernoff bounds. The discussion we develop here was mainly inspired by [1] and [2].

We say that the classifiers $g_1, \ldots, g_N$ are independent if the events $[g(X) = Y]$ are independent. If a combined estimator f is obtained as the convex combination $f = \frac{1}{N} \sum_{j=1}^{N} g_j$ where g_j are independent classifiers with error $L(g_j) \leq p < 1/2$, then by a classical Chernoff bound,

$$L(f) \leq \inf_{\lambda > 0} (p \exp(\lambda/N) + (1 - p) \exp(-\lambda/N))^N .$$

A straightforward computation shows that the optimal value of λ corresponds to

$$\lambda^* = \frac{N}{2} \log \left(\frac{1 - p}{p} \right) .$$

yielding

$$L(f) \leq \left(2\sqrt{p(1 - p)} \right)^N .$$

The difficulty, of course, is to find, in a data-based manner, independent classifiers with a sufficiently small probability of error. The point of this section is that the regularized boosting method of Section 5 effectively finds such classifiers, provided that they exist in the convex hull of the base class $\mathcal{C}$.

In order to support this point, recall that, assuming that the exponential cost function is used, Theorem 4 shows that the probability of error of the classifier obtained with f_n minimizing the penalized cost function satisfies

$$L(f_n) \leq \inf_{k \geq 1} \left\{ \inf_{f \in \mathcal{F}} \mathbb{E} \exp(-\lambda_k f(X)Y) + \epsilon_{n,k} \right\}$$

where $\lim_{n \to +\infty} \epsilon_{n,k} = 0$. Now it is clear that, if the sequence λ_k covers sufficiently densely the set of positive numbers, the upper bound is close to the best Chernoff bound on the generalization error which is given by

$$\inf_{\lambda > 0} \inf_{f \in \mathcal{F}} \mathbb{E} \exp(-\lambda f(X)Y) .$$

In particular, if the class $\mathcal{F}$ contains N independent classifiers with probability of error bounded by $p < 1/2$, then the quantity above is bounded by $\left(2\sqrt{p(1 - p)} \right)^N$, an exponentially small quantity.

Note, however, that the assumption of the presence of such independent classifiers is very strong and it is more realistic to consider weaker concepts of independence as in [1].

Moreover, when $L(f) \neq 0$, there is no hope to obtain tight upper bounds with this method. For instance, assuming that $f(X) \in \{-1, +1\}$, we have, for a general cost function ϕ,

$$L(f) \leq \mathbb{E}\phi(-\lambda f(X)Y) = (1 - L(f))\phi(-\lambda) + L(f)\phi(\lambda) .$$

Indeed, this upper bound is clearly suboptimal in the case when $L(f) \neq 0$, for all choices of λ.

References

1. Y. Amit and G. Blanchard and K. Wilder. *Multiple Randomized Classifiers*. Submitted, 2001. 314
2. G. Blanchard. *Méthodes de mélange et d'agrégation en reconnaissance de formes. Application aux arbres de décision*. PhD thesis, Université Paris XIII, 2001. In English. 306, 314
3. L. Breiman. Bagging predictors. *Machine Learning*, 26(2):123–140, 1996. 305
4. L. Breiman. Bias, variance, and arcing classifiers. Technical Report 460, Statistics Department, University of California, April 1996. 305
5. L. Breiman. Arcing the edge. Technical Report 486, Statistics Department, University of California, June 1997.
6. L. Breiman. Pasting bites together for prediction in large data sets. Technical report, Statistics Department, University of California, July 1997. 305
7. L. Breiman. Prediction games and arcing algorithms. Technical Report 504, Statistics Department, University of California, December 1997. 304
8. L. Breiman. Arcing classifiers. *Annals of Statistics*, 26:801–849, 1998. 304, 305, 306
9. L. Breiman. Some infinite theory for predictor ensembles. Technical Report 577, Statistics Department, UC Berkeley, August 2000. 304, 309
10. P. Bühlmann and B. Yu. Discussion of the paper "Additive Logistic Regression" by Jerome Friedman, Trevor Hastie and Robert Tibshirani. *The Annals of Statistics*, 28:377–386, 2000. 304
11. P. Bühlmann and B. Yu. Boosting with the L_2-Loss: Regression and Classification Manuscript, August 2001. 304
12. M. Collins, R. E. Schapire, and Y. Singer. Logistic regression, AdaBoost and Bregman distances. In *Proceedings of the Thirteenth Annual Conference on Computational Learning Theory*, 2000. 304, 306
13. L. Devroye, L. Györfi, and G. Lugosi. *A Probabilistic Theory of Pattern Recognition*. Springer-Verlag, New York, 1996. 312, 317
14. L. Devroye and G. Lugosi. *Combinatorial Methods in Density Estimation*. Springer-Verlag, New York, 2000.
15. Y. Freund. Boosting a weak learning algorithm by majority. *Information and Computation*, 121(2):256–285, September 1995. 303, 305
16. Y. Freund, Y. Mansour, and R. E. Schapire. Why averaging classifiers can protect against overfitting. In *Proceedings of the Eighth International Workshop on Artificial Intelligence and Statistics*, 2001. 304
17. Y. Freund and R. E. Schapire. Experiments with a new boosting algorithm. In *Proc. 13th International Conference on Machine Learning*, pages 148–146. Morgan Kaufmann, 1996. 303

18. Y. Freund and R. E. Schapire. Game theory, on-line prediction and boosting. In *Proc. 9th Annu. Conf. on Comput. Learning Theory*, pages 325–332. ACM Press, New York, NY, 1996. 305

19. Y. Freund and R. E. Schapire. A decision-theoretic generalization of on-line learning and an application to boosting. *Journal of Computer and System Sciences*, 55(1):119–139, August 1997. 305

20. Y. Freund and R. E. Schapire. Discussion of the paper "additive logistic regression: a statistical view of boosting" by J. Friedman, T. Hastie and R. Tibshirani. *The Annals of Statistics*, 38(2):391–393, 2000. 304

21. J. Friedman, T. Hastie, and R. Tibshirani. Additive logistic regression: a statistical view of boosting. Technical report, Department of Statistics, Sequoia Hall, Stanford University, July 1998. 304, 306, 313

22. W. Jiang. Process consistency for adaboost. Technical Report 00-05, Department of Statistics, Northwestern University, November 2000. 304

23. W. Jiang. Some theoretical aspects of boosting in the presence of noisy data. In Proceedings of The Eighteenth International Conference on Machine Learning (ICML-2001), June 2001, Morgan Kaufmann. 304

24. V. Koltchinskii and D. Panchenko. Empirical margin distributions and bounding the generalization error of combined classifiers. Submitted, 2000. 304, 306, 310

25. M. Ledoux and M. Talagrand. *Probability in Banach Space*. Springer-Verlag, New York, 1991.

26. S. Mannor and R. Meir. Weak learners and improved convergence rate in boosting. In *Advances in Neural Information Processing Systems 13: Proc. NIPS'2000*, 2001. 304

27. S. Mannor, R. Meir, and S. Mendelson. On the consistency of boosting algorithms. Manuscript, June 2001. 304

28. L. Mason, J. Baxter, P. L. Bartlett, and M. Frean. Functional gradient techniques for combining hypotheses. In A. J. Smola, P. L. Bartlett, B. Schölkopf, and D. Schuurmans, editors, *Advances in Large Margin Classifiers*, pages 221–247. MIT Press, Cambridge, MA, 1999. 304, 306

29. R. E. Schapire. The strength of weak learnability. *Machine Learning*, 5(2):197–227, 1990. 303, 305

30. R. E. Schapire, Y. Freund, P. Bartlett, and W. S. Lee. Boosting the margin: A new explanation for the effectiveness of voting methods. *The Annals of Statistics*, 26(5):1651–1686, October 1998. 304, 306

31. T. Zhang Statistical Behavior and Consistency of Classification Methods based on Convex Risk Minimization. Manuscript, 2001. 308, 311

Proofs

A. Proof of Lemma 3

The function f_λ^* defined, for all x, by

$$f_\lambda^*(x) = \arg\min_{\alpha \in \mathbb{R}} \{\eta(x)\phi_\lambda(-\alpha) + (1 - \eta(x))\phi_\lambda(\alpha)\}$$

minimizes A^λ.

We provide the proof in the case where $\eta(x) \notin \{0, 1\}$. Then, since ϕ is increasing and strictly convex, the function $h(\alpha) = \eta(x)\phi_\lambda(-\alpha) + (1 - \eta(x))\phi_\lambda(\alpha)$ has a unique minimum, and therefore $f_\lambda^*(x)$ is well-defined.

Since ϕ is differentiable, the derivative of h is zero at $f_\lambda^*(x)$, and so

$$\frac{\phi_\lambda'(-f_\lambda^*(x))}{\phi_\lambda'(f_\lambda^*(x))} = \frac{1 - \eta(x)}{\eta(x)} .$$

Clearly, $\eta(x) < 1/2$ if and only if $\phi_\lambda'(-f_\lambda^*(x)) > \phi_\lambda'(f_\lambda^*(x))$ and thus $f_\lambda^*(x) < 0$, by the strict convexity of ϕ_λ, proving the second statement.

B. Proof of Lemma 5

In the proof we use the notation $g_n = g_{f_n}$. Recall that

$$L(g_n) - L^* = \mathbb{E} |2\eta(X) - 1| \, \mathbb{I}_{[g_n(X) \neq g^*(X)]}$$

(see, e.g., [13]). Fix $\delta > 0$ and define $S_\delta = \{x : \eta(x) \in [1/2 - \delta, 1/2 + \delta]\}$. Then clearly,

$$L(g_n) - L^* \leq 2\delta + \mathbb{P}\{X \notin S_\delta \text{ and } g_n(X) \neq g^*(X)\},$$

and therefore it suffices to show that $\mathbb{P}\{X \notin S_\delta \text{ and } g_n(X) \neq g^*(X)\} \to 0$ as $n \to \infty$. Proceeding by contradiction, assume that this statement is false. Then there exists a sequence of sets $K_n \subset S_\delta$ with $\liminf_{n\to\infty} \mathbb{P}\{X \in K_n\} > 0$ such that the estimators f_n and f^* lead to a different prediction. By symmetry, we may assume that on K_n, $f_n(x) > 0$ and $f^*(x) < 0$. Note that $f^*(x) < 0$ implies that $\eta < 1/2 - \delta$.

By Lemma 4, there exists an $\alpha \in (0, 1/2)$ such that for all $\inf_{\eta<\alpha}(1 - \eta - H(\eta)) > 0$. We decompose K_n into two subsets: $K_n' = K_n \cap \{x : \eta(x) < \alpha\}$ and $K_n'' = K_n \cap \{x : \eta(x) \geq \alpha\}$. Then either $\liminf_{n\to\infty} \mathbb{P}\{X \in K_n'\} > 0$ or $\liminf_{n\to\infty} \mathbb{P}\{X \in K_n''\} > 0$. Below we show that both assumptions lead to a contradiction.

CASE 1: $\liminf_{n\to\infty} \mathbb{P}\{X \in K_n'\} > 0$. Note that $A(f_n) - A^*$ can be written as the expectation of a positive function since, by definition, the optimal $f^*(x)$ is the pointwise minimizer of the quantity $h(\alpha) = \eta(x)\phi(-\alpha) + (1 - \eta(x))\phi(\alpha)$. Now write, for any set $B \subset \mathcal{X}$,

$$A|_B(f_n) = \mathbb{E} \{\mathbb{I}_B(X) (\eta(X)\phi(-f_n(X)) + (1 - \eta(X))\phi(f_n(X)))\} .$$

We then have, for any B, $A(f_n) - A^* \geq A|_B(f_n) - A|_B(f^*)$.

On the one hand, since the function H defined in Lemma 4 is increasing in $[0, 1/2]$,

$$A|_{K_n'}(f^*) = \mathbb{E} \{\mathbb{I}_{K_n'}(X)H(\eta(X))\} \leq H(\alpha) \mathbb{P}\{K_n'\} .$$

On the other hand, since $f_n(x) > 0$ on K_n',

$$A|_{K_n'}(f_n) = \mathbb{E} \{\mathbb{I}_{K_n'}(X) (\eta(X)\phi(-f_n(X)) + (1 - \eta(X))\phi(f_n(X)))\}$$
$$\geq (1 - \alpha) \mathbb{P}\{K_n'\} .$$

Thus,

$$A(f_n) - A^* \geq A|_{K'_n}(f_n) - A|_{K'_n}(f^*) \geq (1 - \alpha - H(\alpha))\,\mathbb{P}\{K'_n\}\ ,$$

implying $\liminf_{n\to\infty} A(f_n) - A^* > 0$, which is a contradiction.

CASE 2: $\liminf_{n\to\infty} \mathbb{P}\{X \in K''_n\} > 0$. We set the notation

$$\Delta_n(x) = \eta(x)\left(\phi(-f_n(x)) - \phi(-f^*(x))\right) + (1 - \eta(x))\left(\phi(f_n(x)) - \phi(f^*(x))\right)$$

and we attempt to lower bound $\mathbb{E}\left\{\mathbb{I}_{K''_n}(X)\Delta_n(X)\right\}$.

Using that $\phi^{(3)}$ is increasing, the fact that the first-order terms cancel (by the definition of f^*), and by Assumption 1 (iii), we obtain

$$\Delta_n(x) \geq (\eta(x)\phi''(-f^*(x)) + (1 - \eta(x))\phi''(f^*(x)))\,\frac{(f_n(x) - f^*(x))^2}{2}\ .$$

Thus, by Assumption 1 (ii), and since, for $x \in K''_n$, $\eta(x) \geq \alpha$, there exists a $\gamma > 0$ such that

$$\mathbb{E}\left\{\mathbb{I}_{K''_n}(X)\Delta_n(X)\right\} \geq \mathbb{E}\left\{\mathbb{I}_{K''_n}(X)\gamma(f_n(X) - f^*(X))^2\right\}\ .$$

Since $\eta(x) < 1/2 - \delta$ on K''_n, then $f^*(x) < -\epsilon_\delta$ for some $\epsilon_\delta > 0$. This is because f^* is a continuous function of η under the conditions over ϕ in Assumption 1. Therefore, we have reached a contradiction since $A|_{K''_n}(f_n) - A|_{K''_n}(f^*) \geq \gamma\epsilon_\delta^2\mathbb{P}\{K''_n\}$.
□

C. Proof of Theorem 3

The next result replaces here Lemma 2 and provides an oracle inequality with respect to a family of penalized criteria.

Theorem 4. *For any sequence* $(\lambda_k)_k$ *of positive numbers, let*
$f_n = \arg\min_{k\geq 1} \tilde{A}_n^{\lambda_k}(\hat{f}_n^{\lambda_k})$, *where*

$$\tilde{A}_n^{\lambda_k}(f) = A_n^{\lambda_k}(f) + 4\lambda_k\phi'(\lambda_k)\sqrt{\frac{2V\log(4n+2)}{n}} + \lambda_k\phi'(\lambda_k)\sqrt{\frac{\log(6n^2k^2/\pi^2)}{n}}\ .$$

Then, for some constant c, *with probability at least* $1 - \frac{1}{n^2}$,

$$\inf_{k\geq 1} A^{\lambda_k}(f_n) \leq \inf_{k\geq 1}\left\{A^{\lambda_k}(\overline{f}_{\lambda_k}) + c\lambda_k\phi'(\lambda_k)\left(\sqrt{\frac{V\log n}{n}} + \sqrt{\frac{\log(nk)}{n}}\right)\right\}\ .$$

PROOF OF THEOREM 3. By definition of $\overline{f}_{\lambda_k}$, we have that

$$A^{\lambda_k}(\overline{f}_{\lambda_k}) \leq A^{\lambda_k}(f_n)\ .$$

As a consequence, taking the limit as n goes to infinity, in this inequality and the one in Theorem 4, by the Borel-Cantelli lemma we obtain

$$\lim_{n \to \infty} \inf_k A^{\lambda_k}(f_n) = \inf_k A^{\lambda_k}(\overline{f}_{\lambda_k}) \quad \text{almost surely.}$$

Since, by assumption,

$$\inf_k A^{\lambda_k}(\overline{f}_{\lambda_k}) = A^* ,$$

for some subsequence $(\lambda_{k_n})_n$, we have that $A(\lambda_{k_n} f_n) \to A^*$ with probability one. The consistency result now follows by Lemma 5. □

The Consistency of Greedy Algorithms for Classification

Shie Mannor[1], Ron Meir[1], and Tong Zhang[2]

[1] Department of Electrical Engineering, Technion
Haifa 32000, Israel
{shie,rmeir}@{tx,ee}.technion.ac.il
[2] IBM T. J. Watson Research Center
Yorktown Heights, NY, 10598, USA
tzhang@watson.ibm.com

Abstract. We consider a class of algorithms for classification, which are based on sequential greedy minimization of a convex upper bound on the $0 - 1$ loss function. A large class of recently popular algorithms falls within the scope of this approach, including many variants of Boosting algorithms. The basic question addressed in this paper relates to the statistical consistency of such approaches. We provide precise conditions which guarantee that sequential greedy procedures are consistent, and establish rates of convergence under the assumption that the Bayes decision boundary belongs to a certain class of smooth functions. The results are established using a form of regularization which constrains the search space at each iteration of the algorithm. In addition to providing general consistency results, we provide rates of convergence for smooth decision boundaries. A particularly interesting conclusion of our work is that Logistic function based Boosting provides faster rates of convergence than Boosting based on the exponential function used in AdaBoost.

1 Introduction

The Boosting [16] algorithm for classification, particularly AdaBoost [5] and its many variants, provides the Pattern Recognition practitioner with a large repertoire of useful algorithms. Following the successful application of Boosting across a broad spectrum of problems, it was realized that in spite of initial expectations, Boosting algorithms may overfit, and often badly so, under noisy conditions. Several authors suggested various approaches aimed at regularizing Boosting algorithms in order to prevent overfitting. A particularly interesting algorithm, termed LogitBoost, based on the logistic loss rather than the exponential loss used in AdaBoost, was proposed by Hastie *et al.* [6], who argued for its advantage over AdaBoost under noisy circumstances. Moreover, they provided an interpretation of Boosting in terms of additive models widely studied within the Statistics literature.

The present work considers a large class of algorithms, based on greedily minimizing a smooth convex loss function which upper bounds the $0 - 1$ loss

J. Kivinen and R. H. Sloan (Eds.): COLT 2002, LNAI 2375, pp. 319–333, 2002.
© Springer-Verlag Berlin Heidelberg 2002

function used in classification. The utilization of a convex loss function serves two purposes. First, it greatly reduces the computational burden, as minimization of the $0 - 1$ loss is known to be intractable even for very simple (e.g., linear) classifiers. Second, the smoothness of the minimized loss function helps in forming a natural regularization procedure, which prevents overfitting. Since many recent approaches to Boosting and its variants are based on greedy algorithms of the above type (e.g., [4,6,13]), our results provide rigorous performance bounds for a large class of widely used learning algorithms.

The learning framework considered here is the standard supervised learning setup, where a learner attempts to select a hypothesis h from some space of hypotheses $\mathcal{H}$, based on a finite data set, generated according to some unknown probability distribution. The original work within the PAC framework, assumed that the 'true' hypothesis space was known, the only objective being to identify the correct hypothesis. Later work, extending this framework to the so-called *agnostic setup*, attempted to select an optimal hypothesis from the class $\mathcal{H}$ without making any assumptions about the true target. In this work we make rather general regularity assumptions about the data generating mechanism, but require that the algorithm produces an optimal hypothesis, where optimality is measured with respect to a large class of functions, as opposed to the relatively small classes of hypotheses considered within the agnostic framework.

Let $\mathcal{P}$ be a class of probability distributions, and denote by $\hat{f}_m$ a hypothesis produced by a learning algorithm based on m examples. Denoting the expected $0 - 1$ loss of a hypothesis f by $L(f)$, and by L^* the minimal loss attainable (assuming knowledge of the underlying law generating the data), we investigate conditions under which $L(\hat{f}_m)$ converges to L^* (in a well defined probabilistic sense), with increasing sample size m. Algorithms for which this occurs, without any assumptions on $\mathcal{P}$, are termed *universally consistent*. In general, we refer to algorithms for which $L(\hat{f}_m) \to L^*$ for all distributions in a class $\mathcal{P}$, as *consistent with respect to $\mathcal{P}$*.

For the class of greedy algorithms mentioned above, we provide conditions for consistency for large classes of probability distributions $\mathcal{P}$. Moreover, we establish finite sample bounds under certain smoothness conditions on $\mathcal{P}$.

Before moving to the detailed derivation of the results, we discuss some previous work related to the issues studied here. The question of the consistency of Boosting algorithms has attracted some attention in recent years. Jiang raised the questions of whether AdaBoost is consistent and whether regularization is needed. It was shown in [8] that AdaBoost is consistent at some point in the process of boosting. Since no stopping conditions were provided, this result essentially does not determine whether boosting forever is consistent or not. A one dimensional example was provided in [7], where it was shown that AdaBoost is not consistent in general since it tends to a Nearest neighbor rule. Furthermore, it was shown in the example that for noiseless situations AdaBoost is in fact consistent. The conclusion from this series of papers is that boosting forever for AdaBoost is not consistent and that sometimes along the boosting process a good classifier may be found.

In a recent paper Lugosi and Vayatis [10] also presented an approach to establishing consistency based on the minimization of a convex upper bound on the $0 - 1$ loss. According to this approach the convex cost function, is modified depending on the sample size. By making the convex cost function sharper as the number of samples increases, it was shown that the solution to the convex optimization problem yields a consistent classifier. Finite sample bounds are also provided in [10]. The issue of greedy algorithms, which is one of the main foci of this paper, was not considered in [10].

A different kind of consistency result was established by Mannor and Meir ([11,12]). In this work geometric conditions needed to establish the consistency of boosting with linear weak learners were established. It was shown that if the Bayes error is zero (and the oppositely labelled points are well separated) then AdaBoost is consistent.

We summarize our main findings. We consider general two-category classification problems, where the classes may overlap. We find that for rather general smooth decision boundaries, running the greedy algorithm until convergence (termed 'Boosting forever' in [8]) leads to the best results, leading to universal consistency. Regularization is achieved by restricting certain parameters during the optimization process. In particular, we show that AdaBoost-type algorithms, based on linear classifiers as weak learners, are consistent if the Bayes decision boundary is smooth. However, approaches based on loss functions other than the exponential loss used in AdaBoost lead to improved upper bounds on the rates of convergence. It remains an open question to see whether the upper bounds we provide are indicative of the true behavior. These results lend theoretical support to the experimentally observed superiority of algorithms such as LogitBoost over AdaBoost in noisy situations.

2   Background and Preliminary Results

We begin with the standard formal setup for supervised learning. Let $(\mathcal{Z}, \mathcal{A}, P)$ be a probability space and let $\mathcal{F}$ be a class of $\mathcal{A}$ measurable functions from $\mathcal{Z}$ to $\mathbb{R}$. In the context of learning one takes $\mathcal{Z} = \mathcal{X} \times \mathcal{Y}$ where $\mathcal{X}$ is the input space and $\mathcal{Y}$ is the output space. We let $D_m = \{(X_1, Y_1), \ldots, (X_m, Y_m)\}$ denote a sample generated independently at random according to the probability distribution $P = P_{X,Y}$; in the sequel we drop subscripts (such as X, Y) from P, as the argument of P will suffice to specify the particular probability. In this paper we consider the problem of classification where $\mathcal{Y} = \{-1, +1\}$ and $\mathcal{X} = \mathbb{R}^d$, and where the decision is made by taking the sign of a real-valued function $f(x)$. Consider the $0 - 1$ loss function given by

$$\ell(y, f(x)) = I[yf(x) \leq 0], \tag{1}$$

where $I[E]$ is the indicator function of the event E. Using the notation $\eta(x) \stackrel{\triangle}{=} P(Y = 1 | X = x)$, it is well known that L^*, the minimum of $L(f) = \mathbf{E}\ell(Y, f(X))$, can be achieved by setting $f(x) = 2\eta(x) - 1$. Note that the decision choice at the point $f(x) = 0$ is not essential in the analysis. In this paper we simply assume that $I[0] = 1/2$, so that the decision rule $2\eta(x) - 1$ is Bayes optimal at $\eta(x) = 1/2$.

We consider a learning algorithm which, based on the sample D_m, selects a hypothesis $\hat{f}_m$ from some class of functions $\mathcal{F}$. The following definition is the standard definition of strong consistency for this setup.

Definition 1. *A classification algorithm is strongly consistent with respect to a class of distributions $\mathcal{P}$ if*

$$\lim_{m \to \infty} L(\hat{f}_m) = L^* ,$$

with probability one for any $P \in \mathcal{P}$. If $\mathcal{P}$ contains all Borel probability measures, we say that the algorithm is universally consistent.

In this work we show that algorithms based on greedily minimizing a convex upper bound on the $0 - 1$ loss are consistent with respect to the class of distributions $\mathcal{P}$, where certain regularity assumptions will be made concerning the conditional distribution $\eta(x) = P(y = 1|x)$. Denote the class of functions to which $\eta(x)$ belongs by $\mathcal{T}$ (the 'target' class). We start by proving universal consistency under certain conditions. We then refine our results, and impose certain smoothness conditions on the class of conditional densities. In this case, bounds on the convergence rates will be established.

We begin with a few useful results. Let $\{\epsilon_i\}_{i=1}^m$ be a sequence of binary random variables such that $\epsilon_i = \pm 1$ with probability $1/2$. The *Rademacher complexity* of $\mathcal{F}$ is given by

$$R_m(\mathcal{F}) \overset{\triangle}{=} \mathbf{E} \sup_{f \in \mathcal{F}} \left| \frac{1}{m} \sum_{i=1}^m \epsilon_i f(X_i) \right| ,$$

where the expectation is over $\{\epsilon_i\}$ and $\{X_i\}$, see [3] for some properties of $R_m(\mathcal{F})$.

The following theorem can be obtained by a slight modification of the proof of Theorem 1 in [9].

Theorem 1. (Adapted from Theorem 1 in [9])
Let $\{X_1, X_2, \ldots, X_m\} \in \mathcal{X}$ be a sequence of points generated independently at random according to a probability distribution P, and let $\mathcal{F}$ be a class of measurable functions from $\mathcal{X}$ to $\mathbb{R}$. Furthermore, let ϕ be a non-negative Lipschitz function with Lipschitz constant κ, such that $\phi \circ f$ is uniformly bounded by a constant M. Then with probability at least $1 - \delta$

$$\mathbf{E}\phi(f(X)) - \frac{1}{m} \sum_{i=1}^m \phi(f(X_i)) \leq 4\kappa R_m(\mathcal{F}) + M\sqrt{\frac{\log(1/\delta)}{2m}}$$

for all $f \in \mathcal{F}$.

For many function classes, $R_m(\mathcal{F})$ can be estimated directly. Results summarized in [3] are useful for bounding this quantity for algebraic composition of function classes. We can also relate the Rademacher complexity, $R_m(\mathcal{F})$, to the ℓ_2^m covering number of $\mathcal{F}$. Let ℓ_2^m be the empirical ℓ_2 norm with respect to the data $\{X_1, X_2, \ldots, X_m\}$, namely $\ell_2^m(f,g) = \left(\frac{1}{m}\sum_{i=1}^m |f(X_i) - g(X_i)|^2\right)^{1/2}$. If $\mathcal{F}$ contains 0, then there exists a constant C such that (see Corollary 2.2.8 in [17])

$$R_m(\mathcal{F}) \leq \left(\mathbf{E}\int_0^\infty \sqrt{\log \mathcal{N}(\epsilon, \mathcal{F}, \ell_2^m)}\, d\epsilon\right)\frac{C}{\sqrt{m}}, \tag{2}$$

where $\mathcal{N}(\epsilon, \mathcal{F}, \ell_2^m)$ is the covering number of the class $\mathcal{F}$ at a scale of ϵ with respect to the ℓ_2^m norm, and the expectation is taken with respect to the choice of m points. We note that the approach of using Rademacher complexity and the ℓ_2^m covering number of a function class can often result in tighter bounds than some of the earlier studies that employed the ℓ_1^m covering number (for example, in [15]).

3   Consistency of Methods Based on Greedy Minimization of a Convex Upper Bound

Consider a class of so-called *weak learners* $\mathcal{H}$, and assume that it is closed under negation. We define the order t convex hull of $\mathcal{H}$ as

$$\mathrm{co}_t(\mathcal{H}) = \left\{f: \ f(x) = \sum_{i=1}^t \alpha_i h_i(x),\ \alpha_i \geq 0,\ \sum_{i=1}^t \alpha_i \leq 1,\ h_i \in \mathcal{H}\right\}.$$

The convex hull of $\mathcal{H}$, denoted by $\mathrm{co}(\mathcal{H})$, is given by taking the limit $t \to \infty$. We are interested in algorithms that sequentially select a hypothesis from $\beta\mathcal{H}$, where β is a constant which will be specified at a later stage. We use the notation $\beta\mathcal{H} = \{\beta f : f \in \mathcal{H}\}$.

We assume throughout that functions in $\mathcal{H}$ take values in $[-1, 1]$. This implies that functions in $\beta\mathrm{co}(\mathcal{H})$ take values in $[-\beta, \beta]$. Since the space $\beta\mathrm{co}(\mathcal{H})$ may be huge, we consider algorithms that sequentially and greedily select a hypothesis from $\beta\mathcal{H}$. Moreover, since minimizing the $0-1$ loss is often intractable, we consider approaches which are based on minimizing a convex upper bound on the $0-1$ loss. The main contribution of this work is the demonstration of the consistency of such a procedure.

To describe the algorithm, let $\phi(x)$ be a strictly convex function, which upper bounds the $0-1$ loss, namely $\phi(yf(x)) \geq I[yf(x) \leq 0]$. Specific examples for ϕ are given in Section 3.1. Consider the empirical and true losses incurred by a function f based on the loss ϕ,

$$\hat{A}(f) \triangleq \frac{1}{m}\sum_{i=1}^m \phi(y_i f(x_i)),$$

$$A(f) \triangleq \mathbf{E}_{X,Y}\phi(Yf(X)),$$
$$= \mathbf{E}_X\{\eta(X)\phi(f(X)) + (1 - \eta(X))\phi(-f(X))\}.$$

Input: A sample D_m; a stopping time t; a constant β
Algorithm:
 1. Set $\hat{f}^0_{\beta,m} = 0$
 2. For $\tau = 1, 2, \ldots, t$

$$\hat{h}_\tau, \hat{\alpha}_\tau, \hat{\beta}_\tau = \underset{h \in \mathcal{H}, 0 \le \alpha \le 1, 0 \le \beta' \le \beta}{\operatorname{argmin}} \hat{A}((1-\alpha)\hat{f}^{\tau-1}_{\beta,m} + \alpha\beta'h)$$

$$\hat{f}^\tau_{\beta,m} = (1 - \hat{\alpha}_\tau)\hat{f}^{\tau-1}_{\beta,m} + \hat{\alpha}_\tau\hat{\beta}_\tau\hat{h}_\tau$$

Output: Classifier $\hat{f}^t_{\beta,m}$

Fig. 1. A sequential greedy algorithm based on the convex empirical loss function $\hat{A}$

Where $E_{X,Y}$ is the expectation operator with respect to the measure P and E_X is the expectation with respect to the marginal on X.

Based on a finite sample D_m, we cannot hope to minimize $A(f)$ directly, but rather minimize its empirical counterpart $\hat{A}(f)$. Instead of minimizing $\hat{A}(f)$ directly, we consider a sequential greedy algorithm, which is described in Figure 1.

We observe that many recent approaches to Boosting-type algorithms (e.g., [4,6,13]) are based on algorithms similar to the one presented in Figure 1. Two points are worth noting. First, at each step τ, the value of the previous composite hypothesis $\hat{f}^{\tau-1}_{\beta,m}$ is multiplied by $(1-\alpha)$, a procedure which is usually not followed in other Boosting-type algorithms; this ensures that the composite function at every step is in $\beta\mathrm{co}(\mathcal{H})$. Second, the parameters α and β are constrained at every stage; this serves as a regularization measure and prevents overfitting.

It is clear from the description of the algorithm that $\hat{f}^t_{\beta,m} \in \beta\mathrm{co}_t(\mathcal{H})$ for every t. Note that for fixed α and β, the function $\hat{A}((1-\alpha)\hat{f}^{\tau-1}_{\beta,m} + \alpha\beta h)$ is convex in h.

In order to analyze the behavior of the algorithm, we need several definitions. For $\eta \in [0,1]$ and $f \in \mathbb{R}$ let

$$G(\eta, f) = \eta\phi(f) + (1 - \eta)\phi(-f).$$

Let $\mathbb{R}^*$ denote the extended real line ($\mathbb{R}^* = \mathbb{R} \cup \{-\infty, +\infty\}$). We extend a convex function $g : \mathbb{R} \to \mathbb{R}$ to a function $g : \mathbb{R}^* \to \mathbb{R}^*$ by defining $g(\infty) = \lim_{x \to \infty} g(x)$ and $g(-\infty) = \lim_{x \to -\infty} g(x)$. Note that this extension is merely for notational convenience. It ensures that the optimal minimizer $f_G(\eta)$ given below is well-defined at $\eta = 0$ or 1 for certain loss functions. For every value of $\eta \in [0,1]$ let

$$f_G(\eta) \overset{\triangle}{=} \underset{f \in \mathbb{R}^*}{\operatorname{argmin}} G(\eta, f) \quad ; \quad G^*(\eta) \overset{\triangle}{=} G(\eta, f_G(\eta)) = \inf_{f \in \mathbb{R}^*} G(\eta, f).$$

It can be shown [19] that in many cases of interest, including the examples given in Section 3.1, $f_G(\eta) > 0$ when $\eta > 1/2$. We begin with a result from [19]. For completeness, we duplicate the proof in the appendix. Let f_β^* minimize $A(f)$ over $\beta\mathrm{co}(\mathcal{H})$, and denote by f_{opt} the minimizer of $A(f)$ over all Borel measurable functions f.

Theorem 2. (Theorem 2.1 from [19]) *Assume that* $f_G(\eta) > 0$ *when* $\eta > 1/2$, *and that there exist* $c > 0$ *and* $s \geq 1$ *such that for all* $\eta \in [0, 1]$,

$$|\eta - 1/2|^s \leq c^s (G(\eta, 0) - G^*(\eta)).$$

Then for all Borel measurable functions $f(x)$

$$L(f) - L^* \leq 2c \left(A(f) - A(f_{\mathrm{opt}}) \right)^{1/s}, \tag{3}$$

where the Bayes error is given by $L^* = L(2\eta(\cdot) - 1)$.

The condition that $f_G(\eta) > 0$ when $\eta > 1/2$ in Theorem 2 ensures that the optimal minimizer f_{opt} achieves the Bayes error. This condition can be satisfied by assuming that $\phi(f) < \phi(-f)$ for all $f > 0$. The parameters c and s depend only on the loss ϕ. In general, if ϕ is second order differentiable, then one can take $s = 2$. Examples of the values of c and s are given in Section 3.1. The bound (3) allows one to work directly with the function A rather than with the less wieldy $0 - 1$ loss L.

We are interested in bounding the loss $L(f)$ of the empirical estimator $\hat{f}_{\beta,m}^t$ obtained after t steps of the sequential greedy algorithm described in Figure 1. Substitute $\hat{f}_{\beta,m}^t$ in (3), and consider bounding the r.h.s. as follows (ignoring the $1/s$ exponent for the moment):

$$A(\hat{f}_{\beta,m}^t) - A(f_{\mathrm{opt}}) = \left[A(\hat{f}_{\beta,m}^t) - \hat{A}(\hat{f}_{\beta,m}^t) \right] + \left[\hat{A}(\hat{f}_{\beta,m}^t) - \hat{A}(f_\beta^*) \right]$$
$$+ \left[\hat{A}(f_\beta^*) - A(f_\beta^*) \right] + \left[A(f_\beta^*) - A(f_{\mathrm{opt}}) \right]. \tag{4}$$

Next, we bound each of the terms separately.

The first term can be bounded using Theorem 1. In particular, since $A(f) = \mathbf{E}\phi(Yf(X))$, where ϕ is assumed to be convex, and since $\hat{f}_{\beta,m}^t \in \beta\mathrm{co}(H)$ then $f(x) \in [-\beta, \beta]$ for every x. It follows that on its (bounded) domain the Lipschitz constant of ϕ is finite and can be written as κ_β (see explicit examples in Section 3.1). We have that with probability at least $1 - \delta$,

$$A(\hat{f}_{\beta,m}^t) - \hat{A}(\hat{f}_{\beta,m}^t) \leq 4\beta\kappa_\beta R_m(\mathcal{H}) + \phi_\beta \sqrt{\frac{\log(1/\delta)}{2m}},$$

where $\phi_\beta \triangleq \sup_{f \in [-\beta, \beta]} \phi(f)$. Recall that $\hat{f}_{\beta,m}^t \in \beta\mathrm{co}(\mathcal{H})$, and note that we have used the fact that $R_m(\beta\mathrm{co}(\mathcal{H})) = \beta R_m(\mathcal{H})$ (e.g., [3]). The third term on the r.h.s. of (4) can be estimated directly from the Chernoff bound. We have with probability at least $1 - \delta$:

$$\hat{A}(f_\beta^*) - A(f_\beta^*) \leq \phi_\beta \sqrt{\frac{\log(1/\delta)}{2m}}.$$

Note that f^* is fixed (independent on the sample), and therefore a simple Chernoff bound suffices here. In order to bound the second term in (4) we assume that

$$\sup_{v \in [-\beta,\beta]} \phi''(v) \leq M_\beta < \infty, \tag{5}$$

where $\phi''(u)$ is the second derivative of $\phi(u)$.

From Theorem 4.2 in [20] we know that for a fixed sample

$$\hat{A}(\hat{f}_{\beta,m}^t) - \hat{A}(f_\beta^*) \leq \frac{8\beta^2 M_\beta}{t}.$$

This result holds for every convex ϕ and fixed β.

The fourth term in (4) is a purely approximation theoretic term. An appropriate assumption will need to be made concerning the Bayes boundary for this term to vanish.

In summary, for every t, with probability at least $1 - 2\delta$,

$$A(\hat{f}_{\beta,m}^t) - A(f_{\text{opt}}) \leq 4\beta\kappa_\beta R_m(\mathcal{H}) + \frac{8\beta^2 M_\beta}{t} + \phi_\beta \sqrt{\frac{2\log(1/\delta)}{m}} + (A(f_\beta^*) - A(f_{\text{opt}})). \tag{6}$$

The final term in (6) can be bounded using the Lipschitz property of ϕ. In particular,

$$
\begin{aligned}
A(f_\beta^*) - A(f_{\text{opt}}) &= \mathbf{E}_X \left\{ \eta(X)\phi(f_\beta^*(X)) + (1-\eta(X))\phi(-f_\beta^*(X)) \right\} \\
&\quad - \mathbf{E}_X \left\{ \eta(X)\phi(f_{\text{opt}}(X)) + (1-\eta(X))\phi(-f_{\text{opt}}(X)) \right\} \\
&= \mathbf{E}_X \left\{ \eta(X)[\phi(f_\beta^*(X)) - \phi(f_{\text{opt}}(X))] \right\} \\
&\quad + \mathbf{E}_X \left\{ (1-\eta(X))[\phi(-f_\beta^*(X)) - \phi(-f_{\text{opt}}(X))] \right\} \\
&\leq \kappa_\beta \mathbf{E}_X |f_\beta^*(X) - f_{\beta,\text{opt}}(X)| + \Delta_\beta,
\end{aligned} \tag{7}
$$

where the triangle inequality and the Lipschitz property were used in the final inequality. Here $f_{\beta,\text{opt}}(X) = \max(-\beta, \min(\beta, f_{\text{opt}}(X)))$ is the projection of f_{opt} onto $[-\beta, \beta]$, and

$$\Delta_\beta \stackrel{\triangle}{=} \sup_{\eta \in [1/2,1]} \left\{ I(f_G(\eta) > \beta)[G(\eta, \beta) - G(\eta, f_G(\eta))] \right\}.$$

Note that $\Delta_\beta \to 0$ when $\beta \to \infty$ since Δ_β represents the tail behavior $G(\eta, \beta)$. See examples in the next section.

3.1   Examples for ϕ

We consider three commonly used choices for the convex function ϕ.

$\exp(-x)$	Exponential
$\log(1 + \exp(-x))/\log 2$	Logistic loss
$(x-1)^2$	Least squares

In this paper, the natural logarithm is used in the definition of logistic loss. The division by $\log 2$ sets the scale so that the loss function equals 1 at $x = 0$. For each one of these cases we provide in Table 1 the values of the constants M_β, ϕ_β, κ_β, and Δ_β defined above. We also include the values of c and s from Theorem 2, as well as the optimal minimizer $f_G(\eta)$. Note that the values of Δ_β and κ_β listed in Table 1 are upper bounds (see [19]).

Table 1. Parameter values for several popular choices of ϕ

$\phi(x)$	$\exp(-x)$	$\log(1 + \exp(-x))/\log 2$	$(x - 1)^2$
M_β	$\exp(\beta)$	$1/(4\log 2)$	2
ϕ_β	$\exp(\beta)$	$\log(1 + \exp(\beta))/\log 2$	$(\beta + 1)^2$
κ_β	$\exp(\beta)$	$1/\log 2$	$2\beta + 2$
Δ_β	$\exp(-\beta)$	$\exp(-\beta)/\log 2$	$\max(0, 1 - \beta)^2$
$f_G(\eta)$	$\frac{1}{2}\log\frac{\eta}{1-\eta}$	$\log\frac{\eta}{1-\eta}$	$2\eta - 1$
c	$1/\sqrt{2}$	$\sqrt{\log 2}/2$	$1/2$
s	2	2	2

3.2   Universal Consistency

We assume that $h \in \mathcal{H}$ implies $-h \in \mathcal{H}$, which in turn implies that $0 \in \text{CO}(\mathcal{H})$. This implies that $\beta_1\text{CO}(\mathcal{H}) \subset \beta_2\text{CO}(\mathcal{H})$ when $\beta_1 \leq \beta_2$. Therefore, using a larger β always gives us more approximation power.

We define $\text{SPAN}(\mathcal{H}) = \cup_{\beta>0}\beta\text{CO}(\mathcal{H})$, which is the largest function class that can be reached in the greedy algorithm by increasing β.

In order to establish universal consistency, we may assume initially that the class of functions $\text{SPAN}(\mathcal{H})$ is dense in $C(K)$ — the class of continuous functions over a domain $K \subseteq \mathbb{R}^d$ under the uniform norm topology. ¿From Theorem 4.1 in [19], we know that for all ϕ considered in this paper, and all Borel measures, $\inf_{f \in \text{SPAN}(\mathcal{H})} A(f) = A(f_{\text{opt}})$. Since $\text{SPAN}(\mathcal{H}) = \cup_{\beta>0}\beta\text{CO}(\mathcal{H})$, we obtain $\lim_{\beta\to\infty} A(f_\beta^*) - A(f_{\text{opt}}) = 0$, leading to the vanishing of the final term in (6) when $\beta \to \infty$.

Theorem 3. *Assume that the class of functions* $\text{SPAN}(\mathcal{H})$ *is dense in* $C(K)$ *over a domain* $K \subseteq \mathbb{R}^d$. *Assume further that* ϕ *is convex and Lipschitz and that (5) holds. Choose* β *such that as* $m \to \infty$, *we have* $\beta \to \infty$, $\phi_\beta^2 \log m/m \to 0$, *and* $\beta\kappa_\beta R_m(\mathcal{H}) \to 0$. *Then the greedy algorithm of Figure 1, applied for t steps where* $(\beta^2 M_\beta)/t \to 0$ *as* $m \to \infty$, *is strongly universally consistent.*

Proof. Let $\delta_m = \frac{1}{m^2}$. It follows from (6) that with probability smaller than $2\delta_m$

$$A(\hat{f}_{\beta,m}^{t_m}) - A(f_{\text{opt}}) > 4\beta_m\kappa_{\beta_m}R_m(\mathcal{H}) + \frac{8\beta_m^2 M_{\beta_m}}{t_m} + 2\phi_\beta\sqrt{\frac{\log m}{m}} + \Delta A_\beta,$$

where $\Delta A_\beta = A(f_\beta^*) - A(f_{\text{opt}}) \to 0$ as $\beta \to \infty$. Using the Borel Cantelli Lemma this happens finitely many times, so there is a (random) number of samples m_1 after which the above inequality is always reversed. Since all terms (6) converge to 0, it follows that for every $\epsilon > 0$ from some time on $A(\hat{f}_{\beta,m}^t) - A(f_{\text{opt}}) < \epsilon$ with probability 1. Using (3) concludes the proof.   □

Unfortunately, no convergence rate can be established in the general setting of universal consistency. Convergence rates for particular functional classes can be derived by applying appropriate assumptions on the classes $\mathcal{H}$ and $\mathcal{T}$.

3.3   Consistency and Convergence Rates for Smooth Decision Boundaries

We consider a special case here, where $\mathcal{H}$ is the class of ridge functions

$$\mathcal{H} = \left\{ f : f(x) = \alpha\sigma(w^T x + w_0),\ w \in \mathbb{R}^d, w_0 \in \mathbb{R}, \alpha \in [-1,1] \right\}, \qquad (8)$$

often used in Neural Networks research. We assume that $\sigma(\cdot)$ is a non-decreasing bounded function taking values in $[-1,+1]$. Since it is well known that $\text{SPAN}(\mathcal{H})$ is dense in $C(K)$ for any compact set K, Theorem 3 implies that the greedy algorithm of Figure 1 is strongly universally consistent, when β is selected as in Theorem 3.

We show that a bound on the rate of convergence can be obtained under certain assumptions. In order to define the target class, we define smoothness of functions in terms of the integrability of high order derivatives. In particular, for a d-dimensional function $f(x)$, define

$$D^k f(x) = \frac{\partial^{|k|} f(x)}{\partial x_1^{k_1} \cdots \partial x_d^{k_d}},$$

where $|k| = k_1 + \cdots + k_d$. The Sobolev class (e.g., [1]) over a domain K is then defined for any natural number r as

$$W_p^r(K) = \left\{ f\ :\ \|f\|_{W_p^r(K)} = \max_{0 \le |k| \le r} \|D^k f\|_{L_p(K)} < \infty,\ r \in \mathbb{N} \right\}, \qquad (9)$$

where the maximum is over all partitions of k, $|k| = k_1 + \cdots + k_d$, $k_i \ge 0$. In this work we assume $f_G(\mathcal{T}) = \{f_G(\eta) : \eta \in \mathcal{T}\}$ belongs to the Sobolev ball $B_2^r(K)$ characterized by $\|f\|_{W_2^r(K)} \le 1$ (any constant replacing 1 would lead to similar results). Furthermore, let $(u)_+ = \max(0, u)$. We quote a slightly revised version of a result from [14]. Observe that this result requires that the domain K is compact.

Theorem 4. (Adapted from Theorem 4.2 of [14]) *There exists a positive number $\bar{\beta}$ such that for all $\beta \ge \bar{\beta}$ and $f \in B_2^r(K)$, where $K \subset \mathbb{R}^d$ is a compact domain, and for every $\eta > 0$,*

$$\inf_{g \in \beta CO(\mathcal{H})} \|g - f\|_{L_2(K)} \le c\beta^{-a_r}, \qquad (10)$$

where $a_r = \frac{1}{(d/2r-1)_+} + \eta$ and c is a constant depending on r, d and K.

Observe that $a_r = \infty$ if $r \geq d/2$, implying that if the target space $B_2^r(K)$ is characterized by highly smooth functions, i.e. $r \geq d/2$, then

$$\inf_{g \in \bar{\beta}\mathrm{CO}(\mathcal{H})} \|g - f\|_{L_2(K)} = 0, \tag{11}$$

for some finite number $\bar{\beta}$. Thus, functions belonging to $B_2^r(K)$, $r \geq d/2$, can be represented *exactly* by functions from the closure of $\bar{\beta}\mathrm{CO}(\mathcal{H})$ for some *finite* value of $\bar{\beta}$. We note in passing (see [1]) that the condition $r \geq d/2$ implies boundedness of functions in $B_2^r(K)$ in the supremum norm. Finally, if we assume that the underlying probability distribution can be represented as a probability density $P(x, y) = P(y|x)\mu(x)$, then it follows from the Cauchy-Schwartz inequality, assuming that $\int_K \mu(x)^2 dx$ is finite, that $E_X|g - f_{\beta,\mathrm{opt}}| \leq c\beta^{-a_r}$.

In order to establish rates we need to bound the Rademacher complexity of the class $\mathcal{H}$. First, let $\mathcal{F}$ be a class of bounded functions such that $f(x) \in [-1, +1]$ for every $f \in \mathcal{F}$ and $x \in K$. Assume further that $d_p = \mathrm{Pdim}(\mathcal{F})$ is finite, where $\mathrm{Pdim}(\mathcal{F})$ is the pseudo-dimension of $\mathcal{F}$. Then Theorem 2.6.7 in [17] implies that there is a universal constant K such that

$$\log \mathcal{N}(\epsilon, \mathcal{F}, \ell_2^m) \leq K + \log d_p + d_p \log(16e) + 2(d_p - 1) \log \frac{1}{\epsilon}, \tag{12}$$

where $0 < \epsilon < 1$. Consider the class of linear functions $\mathcal{L} = \{w^T x + w_0 : w \in \mathbb{R}^d, w_0 \in \mathbb{R}\}$, for which it is known that $\mathrm{Pdim}(\mathcal{L}) = d+1$, where d is the Euclidean dimension of x. Since σ is monotonic, it follows from Theorem 11.3 in [2] that $\mathrm{Pdim}(\sigma(\mathcal{L})) \leq \mathrm{Pdim}(\mathcal{L})$. Since $\sigma(\cdot)$ is bounded, we conclude that (12) applies to the class of functions $\mathcal{H}$ given in (8). Using (2) and (12), and the observation that $\int_0^1 \sqrt{\log(1/\epsilon)}d\epsilon$ is finite, it follows that

$$R_m(\mathcal{H}) \leq C\sqrt{\frac{d}{m}}, \tag{13}$$

for some constant C. Combining our results we have from (4),(6),(10) and (13) that for β large enough with probability at least $1 - 2\delta$

$$A(\hat{f}_{\beta,m}^t) - A(f_{\mathrm{opt}}) \leq 4C\beta\kappa_\beta\sqrt{\frac{d}{m}} + \frac{8\beta^2 M_\beta}{t} + \phi_\beta\sqrt{\frac{2\log(1/\delta)}{m}} + c\kappa_\beta\beta^{-a_r} + \Delta_\beta. \tag{14}$$

It is interesting to observe the trade-off implicit in (14). First, in the case where $r \geq d/2$, the final approximation terms are absent from the bound. In this case, simply set $\beta_m = \bar{\beta}$, and the bound is minimized. In the general case where $r < d/2$, a trade-off in the choice of β_m is evident. In order for the first term to vanish, we require that β_m increase slowly, while the final, approximation terms, require that β_m increase rapidly. The balance between the two terms determines the optimal rates. An additional consequence of (14) is that it is always best to choose the number of iterations t to be as large as possible. Regularization is incorporated through the proper selection of the value of β_m, rather than through the number of iterations.

Let $\beta = \beta_m$ be a monotonically increasing function of m, and let the number of iterations of the algorithm in Figure 1 be given by $t = t_m$. Select β_m and t_m as in Theorem 3, keeping (13) in mind. From Theorem 3 we immediately conclude that strong consistency holds with respect to the class $B_2^r(K)$.

Finally, we provide an explicit selection of β_m and t_m for which strong consistency holds, and for which convergence rates can be established for the three examples given in Section 3.1. In order to obtain bounds on the $0 - 1$ loss, we compute an upper bound on $\mathbf{E}L(\hat{f}_{\beta,m}^t) - L^*$. To do so, let X be a random variable satisfying $\mathbf{P}\{X > A + B\sqrt{\log(1/\delta)}\} < \delta$ for every $\delta > 0$. It can be shown that in this case $\mathbf{E}X \le A + cB$ where $c \le 2\sqrt{\log 2}$. The proof can be found in the appendix. Substituting the value of a from (14), recalling (3) and using Jensen's inequality $\mathbf{E}X^{1/s} \le (\mathbf{E}X)^{1/s}$, $s \ge 1$, we have that

$$\mathbf{E}L(\hat{f}_{\beta,m}^t) - L^* \le c_1 \left(\beta \kappa_\beta \sqrt{\frac{d}{m}}\right)^{1/s} + c_2 \left(\frac{\beta^2 M_\beta}{t}\right)^{1/s} + c_3 \left(\kappa_\beta \beta^{-a_r}\right)^{1/s} + c_4 \Delta_\beta^{1/s},$$

(15)

for some constants c_1, c_2, c_3 and c_4, where we have used the inequality $(x+y)^\rho \le (1/2)^\rho (x^\rho + y^\rho)$ for $x, y, \rho \ge 0$.

First, observe that for the exponential loss, because of the exponential dependence of κ_β on β, the third term in (15) can only vanish if $r \ge d/2$, implying that a fast convergence rate for the exponential loss can only be obtained in our setting if the boundary is sufficiently smooth. In the least squares case, the factor of κ_β in the penultimate term in (15) can be eliminated by noting that Theorem 4 applies directly to the L_2 loss, and using the results from Section 3.1 in [19]. For the logistic loss, since $\kappa_\beta = O(1)$, we find that the approximation term vanishes for every r.

Theorem 5. *Let K be a compact subset of $\mathbb{R}^d$ and suppose that $\int_K \mu(x)^2 dx < \infty$. Then the algorithm of Figure 1 is strongly consistent for $f_G(\mathcal{T}) = \{f_G(\eta) : \eta \in \mathcal{T}\} \subseteq B_2^r(K)$ under the conditions specified in Table 2, where $\beta_m \to \infty$ and $t_m \to \infty$ is assumed. The asymptotic convergence rates obtained from (15) are also given in Table 2. We use the notation $\tilde{O}(\cdot)$ in order to disregard logarithmic factors in m.*

Table 2. Rate bounds for popular choices of ϕ and Sobolev Bayes boundary

Loss	Smoothness	β_m	$\mathbf{E}L(\hat{f}_{\beta,m}^t) - L^*$
Exponential	$r \ge d/2$	$\log m^\alpha$, $(\alpha < 1/4)$	$\tilde{O}(1/m^{1/4-\alpha})$
LS	$r \ge d/2$	$\log m$	$\tilde{O}(1/m^{1/4})$
LS	$r < d/2$	$m^{(d-2r)/2d}$	$\tilde{O}(1/m^{r/2d})$
Logistic	$r \ge d/2$	$\log m$	$\tilde{O}(1/m^{1/4})$
Logistic	$r < d/2$	$m^{(d-2r)/2d}$	$\tilde{O}(1/m^{r/2d})$

Proof. The proof is a direct application of (15) where we select β_m so as to minimize the bound, and recall that $s = 2$ for all the loss functions considered.

$\square$

4 Discussion

We have considered a class of sequential greedy algorithms, similar to AdaBoost, but differing in some implementation details. Our conclusions concerning the consistency of these algorithms can be described as follows. In all cases we have shown that "boosting forever", namely letting the number of Boosting iterations be infinite, is advantageous and does not lead to overfitting. Overfitting is prevented by regularization through the proper choice of the value of β in Figure 1. The upper bounds on the rates of convergence provided in Theorem 5 indicate faster rates of convergence for the logistic and least squares losses over that of the exponential loss. Note that the choice of β is Table 2 requires knowledge of the smoothness parameter r. It would be nice to extend the algorithm so that it is fully adaptive, not requiring knowledge of r. A further open question at this point is whether the bounds derived are indicative of the true behavior, a conclusion which can only be drawn if the asymptotic tightness of the bounds is established. In this context it would be particularly interesting to see whether the recently derived minimax rates for nonparametric classification [18] can be established for the algorithms analyzed in this paper.

A Appendix

Proof of Theorem 2

The classification error of f can be expressed as

$$L(f(\cdot)) = \mathbf{E}(1 - \eta(x))I(f(x) \geq 0) + \mathbf{E}(\eta(x))I(f(x) \leq 0),$$

where the expectation is with respect to the input variable x. We thus have

$$\begin{aligned}
L(f(\cdot)) - L^* &= L(f(\cdot)) - L(2\eta(\cdot) - 1) \\
&= \mathbf{E}_{2\eta(x)-1)f(x)\leq 0}|2\eta(x) - 1| \\
&\leq 2(\mathbf{E}_{(\eta(x)-1)f(x)\leq 0}|\eta(x) - 0.5|^s)^{1/s}.
\end{aligned}$$

The last inequality follows from Jensen's inequality. Using the assumption of the theorem, we obtain

$$L(f(\cdot)) - L^* \leq 2c[\mathbf{E}_{(2\eta(x)-1)f(x)\leq 0}(G(\eta, 0) - G^*(\eta))]^{1/s}. \tag{16}$$

If we can further show that $(2\eta - 1)f \leq 0$ implies $G(\eta, 0) \leq G(\eta, f)$, then

$$\mathbf{E}_{(2\eta(x)-1)f(x)\leq 0}(G(\eta, 0) - G^*(\eta)) \leq \mathbf{E}(G(\eta(x), f(x)) - G^*(\eta)) = A(f) - A(f_{\text{opt}}).$$

Combining this inequality with (16), we obtain the theorem. Therefore in the following we only need to prove the fact that $(2\eta - 1)f \leq 0$ implies $G(\eta, 0) \leq G(\eta, f)$. To see this, we consider the following three cases:

- $\eta > 0.5$: By assumption, we have $f_G(\eta) > 0$. Now $(2\eta - 1)f \leq 0$ implies $f \leq 0$. Using $0 \in [f, f_G(\eta)]$, and the convexity of $G(\eta, f)$ with respect to f, we obtain $G(\eta, 0) \leq \max(G(\eta, f), G(\eta, f_G(\eta))) = G(\eta, f)$.
- $\eta < 0.5$: Due to the symmetry, we can set $f_G(\eta) = -f_G(1 - \eta)$. Therefore $f_G(\eta) < 0$. Since $(2\eta-1)f \leq 0$ implies that $f \geq 0$, we have $0 \in [f_G(\eta), f]$, which implies that $G(\eta, 0) \leq \max(G(\eta, f), G(\eta, f_G(\eta))) = G(\eta, f)$.
- $\eta = 0.5$: Note that we can take $f_G(\eta) = 0$ which implies $G(\eta, 0) \leq G(\eta, f)$ for all values f.

This completes the proof.

An Auxiliary Lemma

Lemma 1. *Let X be a non-negative scalar random variable for which $\mathbf{P}\{X > A + B\sqrt{\log(1/\delta)}\} < \delta$ for every $\delta > 0$. Then $\mathbf{E}X \leq A + cB$ where $c \leq 2\sqrt{\log 2}$.*

Proof. Recall that $\mathbf{E}X = \int_0^\infty P(X > x)dx$. Since $P(X > x)$ is a decreasing function of x we can bound the expectation as follows. Let $x_0 = 0$, and $x_i = A + B\sqrt{\log 2^i}$ for $i = 1, 2, \ldots$. Obviously $x_i \nearrow \infty$. Bounding the integral one gets that

$$\mathbf{E}X \leq \sum_{i=0}^\infty P(X > x_i)(x_{i+1} - x_i)$$

$$= A + B\sqrt{\log 2} + \sum_{i=1}^\infty P(X > x_i)(x_{i+1} - x_i)$$

$$= A + B\sqrt{\log 2} + B\sqrt{\log 2} \sum_{i=1}^\infty \frac{1}{2^i}(\sqrt{i+1} - \sqrt{i})$$

$$\leq A + (2\sqrt{\log 2})B.$$

$\square$

Acknowledgements

The authors are grateful to Shahar Mendelson for helpful discussions, and to Gabor Lugosi for sending them a copy of his work prior to publication. The work of R.M. was partially supported by the Technion fund for promotion of research. Support from the Ollendorff foundation at the Technion is also gratefully acknowledged.

References

1. R. A. Adams. *Sobolev Spaces.* Academic Press, New York, 1975. 328, 329
2. M. Anthony and P. L. Bartlett. *Neural Network Learning; Theoretical Foundations.* Cambridge University Press, 1999. 329

3. P. Bartlett and S. Mendelson. Rademacher and Gaussian complexities: risk bounds and structural results. In *Proceedings of the Fourteenth Annual Conference on Computational Learning Theory*, pages 224–240, 2001. 322, 325
4. L. Breiman. Arcing classifiers. *The Annals of Statistics*, 26(3):801–824, 1998. 320, 324
5. Y. Freund and R. E. Schapire. A decision theoretic generalization of on-line learning and application to boosting. *Comput. Syst. Sci.*, 55(1):119–139, 1997. 319
6. J. Friedman, T. Hastie, and R. Tibshirani. Additive logistic regression: a statistical view of boosting. *The Annals of Statistics*, 38(2):337–374, 2000. 319, 320, 324
7. W. Jiang. Does boosting overfit: Views from an exact solution. Technical Report 00-03, Department of Statistics, Northwestern University, 2000. 320
8. W. Jiang. Process consistency for adaboost. Technical Report 00-05, Department of Statistics, Northwestern University, 2000. 320, 321
9. V. Koltchinksii and D. Panchenko. Empirical margin distributions and bounding the generalization error of combined classifiers. *Ann. Statis.*, 30(1), 2002. 322
10. G. Lugosi and N. Vayatis. On the bayes-risk consistency of bosting methods. Technical report, Pompeu Fabra University, 2001. 321
11. S. Mannor and R. Meir. Geometric bounds for generlization in boosting. In *Proceedings of the Fourteenth Annual Conference on Computational Learning Theory*, pages 461–472, 2001. 321
12. S. Mannor and R. Meir. On the existence of weak learners and applications to boosting. *Machine Learning*, 2002. To appear. 321
13. L. Mason, P. Bartlett, J. Baxter, and M. Frean. Functional gradient techniques for combining hypotheses. In B. Schölkopf A. Smola, P. Bartlett and D. Schuurmans, editors, *Advances in Large Margin Classifiers*. MIT Press, 2000. 320, 324
14. R. Meir and V. Maiorov. On the optimality of neural network approximation using incremental algorithms. *IEEE Trans. Neural Networks*, 11(2):323–337, 2000. 328
15. D. Pollard. *Convergence of Empirical Processes*. Springer Verlag, New York, 1984. 323
16. R. Schapire. The strength of weak learnability. *Machine Learning*, 5(2):197–227, 1990. 319
17. A. W. van der Vaart and J. A. Wellner. *Weak Convergence and EmpiricalProcesses*. Springer Verlag, New York, 1996. 323, 329
18. Y. Yang. Minimax nonparametric classification - patr i: rates of convergence. *IEEE Trans. Inf. Theory*, 45(7):2271–2284, 1999. 331
19. T. Zhang. Statistical behavior and consistency of classification methods based on convex risk minimization. Technical Report RC22155, IBM T. J. Watson Research Center, Yorktown Heights, 2001. 324, 325, 327, 330
20. T. Zhang. Sequential greedy approximation for certain convex optimization problems. Technical Report RC22309, IBM T. J. Watson Research Center, Yorktown Heights, 2002. 326

Maximizing the Margin with Boosting[*]

Gunnar Rätsch[1] and Manfred K. Warmuth[2]

[1] RSISE, Australian National University
Canberra, ACT 0200, Australia
Gunnar.Raetsch@anu.edu.au
[2] University of California at Santa Cruz
Santa Cruz, CA 95060, USA
manfred@cse.ucsc.edu

Abstract. AdaBoost produces a linear combination of weak hypotheses. It has been observed that the generalization error of the algorithm continues to improve even after all examples are classified correctly by the current linear combination, i.e. by a *hyperplane* in feature space spanned by the weak hypotheses. The improvement is attributed to the experimental observation that the distances (margins) of the examples to the separating hyperplane are increasing even when the training error is already zero, that is all examples are on the correct side of the hyperplane. We give an iterative version of AdaBoost that explicitly maximizes the minimum margin of the examples. We bound the number of iterations and the number of hypotheses used in the final linear combination which approximates the maximum margin hyperplane with a certain precision. Our modified algorithm essentially retains the exponential convergence properties of AdaBoost and our result does not depend on the size of the hypothesis class.

1 Introduction

In the most common version of boosting the algorithm is given a fixed set of labeled training examples. In each stage the algorithm produces a probability weighting on the examples. It then is given a *weak* hypothesis whose error (probability of wrong classification) is slightly below 50%. The weak hypothesis is used to update the distribution. Intuitively, the hard examples receive high weights. At the end of each stage the weak hypothesis is added to the linear combination, which forms the current hypothesis of the boosting algorithm.

The most well known boosting algorithm is AdaBoost [5,]. It is "adaptive" in that the linear coefficient of the weak hypothesis depends on error of the weak hypothesis. Earlier work on boosting includes [18,3]. AdaBoost has two

---

[*] This work was done while G. Rätsch was at Fraunhofer FIRST Berlin and at UC Santa Cruz. G. Rätsch was partially funded by DFG under contract JA 379/91, JA 379/71, MU 987/1-1 and by EU in the NeuroColt II project. M.K. Warmuth and visits of G. Rätsch to UC Santa Cruz were partially funded by the NSF grant CCR-9821087. G. Rätsch thanks S. Mika, S. Lemm and K.-R. Müller for discussions.

interesting properties. First, along with earlier boosting algorithms [18,], it has the property that its training error converges exponentially fast to zero. More precisely, if the training error of the t-th weak learner is $\epsilon_t = \frac{1}{2} - \frac{1}{2}\gamma_t$, then an upper bound on the training error of the linear combination is reduced by a factor of $1 - \frac{1}{2}\gamma_t^2$ at stage t. Second, it has been observed experimentally that AdaBoost continues to "learn" even after the training error of the linear combination is zero [19,]; in experiments the generalization error is continuing to improve. When the training error is zero, then all examples are on the "right side" of the linear combination (viewed as a *hyperplane* in a feature space, where each base hypothesis is one feature/dimension). The *margin* of an example is the signed distance to the hyperplane times its $\pm$ label. As soon as the training error is zero, the examples are on the right side and have positive margin. It has also been observed that the margins of the examples continue to increase even after the training error is zero. There are theoretical bounds on the generalization error of linear classifiers e. g. [19,2,10] that improve with the size of the minimum margin of the examples. So the fact that the margins improve experimentally seems to explain why AdaBoost still learns after the training error is zero.

There is one shortfall in this argument. AdaBoost has not been proven to maximize the minimum margin of the examples. In fact, in our experiments in Section 4 we observe that AdaBoost does not seem to maximize the margin. [2] proposed a modified algorithm – Arc-GV (**Arcing-Game Value**) – suitable for this task and showed that it *asymptotically* maximizes the margin (similar results are shown in [7] and [1]). In this paper we give an algorithm that produces a final hypothesis whose margin lies in $[\varrho^* - \nu, \varrho^*]$, where ϱ^* is the maximum margin and ν a precision parameter. The final stage of the algorithm produces a linear combination of at most $2 \log N / \nu^2$ weak learners. The algorithm requires a guess of the margin in the interval $[\varrho^* - \nu, \varrho^*]$ and up $\log_2(2/\nu)$ stages are needed before finding a guess in that interval.

To our knowlegde, this is the first result on the fast convergence of a boosting algorithm to the maximum margin solution that works for all $\varrho^* \in [-1, 1]$. Using previous results one can only show that AdaBoost *assymptically* converges to a final hypothesis with margin at least $\varrho^*/2$ (cf. Corollary 2) if $\varrho^* > 0$ and if other subtle conditions on the base learner are satisfied.

AdaBoost was designed to find a final hypothesis of margin at least zero. Our algorithm maximizes the margin for all values of ϱ^*. This includes the inseparable case ($\varrho^* < 0$), where one minimizes the overlap between the two classes. Our algorithm is also useful when the hypotheses given to the Boosting algorithm are *strong* in the sense that they already separate the data and have margin greater than zero, but less than one. In this case $0 < \varrho^* < 1$ and AdaBoost aborts immediately because the linear coefficients for such hypotheses are unbounded. Our new algorithm also maximizes the margin by combining strong learners.

The paper is structured as follows: In Section 2 we first extend the original AdaBoost algorithm leading to *AdaBoost$_\varrho$*. Then we propose *Marginal AdaBoost*, which uses AdaBoost$_\varrho$ as a subroutine. In Section 3 we give a more detailed analysis of both algorithms. First, we prove that if the training error of the t-th weak learner is $\epsilon_t = \frac{1}{2} - \frac{1}{2}\gamma_t$, then an upper bound on the fraction of examples with margin smaller than ϱ is reduced by a factor of $1 - \frac{1}{2}(\varrho - \gamma_t)^2$ at stage t of AdaBoost$_\varrho$ (cf. Section 3.2). To achieve a large margin, however, one needs to assume that the guess ϱ is at most ϱ^*. Exploiting this property, we prove the exponential convergence rate of our algorithm (cf. Theorem 2) if $\varrho \le \rho^*$. A good guess at most ν below ϱ^* can be found in essentially $\log_2(2/\nu)$ stages. We complete the paper with experiments confirming our theoretical analysis (Section 4) and a conclusion.

2 Marginal Boosting

Boosting algorithms form linear combinations of weak hypothesis. In iteration t the weak hypothesis $h_t(\mathbf{x})$ is added to the linear combination. For AdaBoost it has been shown it generates a combined hypothesis

$$f_{\boldsymbol\alpha}(\mathbf{x}) = \sum_t \frac{\alpha_t}{\sum_r \alpha_r} h_t(\mathbf{x})$$

that is consistent with the training set in a small number of iterations [5,]. This is desirable for the analysis in the PAC setting [18,21,]. Consistency on the training set means that the margin[1] of each training example is greater than zero, i.e. $\min_{n=1,\dots,N} y_n f(\mathbf{x}_n) > 0$.

We start with a slight modification of AdaBoost, which does not only aim to find a hypothesis with margin of at least zero, but with at least margin ϱ, where ϱ is pre-specified (cf. Algorithm 1).[2]

We call this algorithm AdaBoost$_\varrho$, as it naturally generalizes AdaBoost for the case when the *target margin* is ϱ. The original AdaBoost algorithm now becomes *AdaBoost$_0$*, as it targets $\varrho = 0$.

The algorithm AdaBoost$_\varrho$ is already known as *unnormalized Arcing* [2,] or *AdaBoost-type Algorithm* [17,]. Moreover, it is related to a algorithms proposed in [6] and [23]. The only difference to AdaBoost is the choice of the hypothesis coefficients α_t: An additional term $-\frac{1}{2}\log\frac{1+\varrho}{1-\varrho}$ appears in the expression for α_t. This term is zero for AdaBoost$_0$. The constant ϱ might be seen as a *guess* of the maximum margin ϱ^*. If ϱ is chosen properly (slightly below ϱ^*), then AdaBoost$_\varrho$ will converge exponentially fast to a combined hypothesis with a near maximum margin. See Section 3.2 for details.

The following example illustrates how AdaBoost$_\varrho$ works. Assume the base

---

[1] If $\|\boldsymbol\alpha\|_1 = 1$, then a result by [11] shows that the dot product $\mathbf{x} \cdot \boldsymbol\alpha$ is equal to the signed distance of the point $\mathbf{x}$ to the closest point on the plane with normal vector $\boldsymbol\alpha$ through the origin, where the distance is measured with the ℓ_∞-norm. This explains why we can use $y_n f(\mathbf{x}_n)$ instead of the ℓ_∞-norm distance to the separating hyperplane.

[2] The original AdaBoost algorithm was formulated in terms of weighted training error ϵ_t of a weak hypothesis. Here we use an equivalent formulation in terms of the edge γ, where $\epsilon_t = \frac{1}{2} - \frac{1}{2}\gamma_t$ (cf. Section 3.1), since it is more convenient [2,].

Algorithm 1 – The AdaBoost$_\varrho$ algorithm

---

1. **Input:** $S = \langle (\mathbf{x}_1, y_1), \ldots, (\mathbf{x}_N, y_N) \rangle$, No. of Iterations T, margin target ϱ
2. **Initialize:** $d_n^1 = 1/N$ for all $n = 1 \ldots N$
3. **Do for** $t = 1, \ldots, T$,
   (a) Train classifier on $\{S, \mathbf{d}^t\}$ and obtain hypothesis $h_t : \mathbf{x} \mapsto [-1, 1]$
   (b) Calculate the edge γ_t of h_t: $\gamma_t = \sum\limits_{n=1}^{N} d_n^t y_n h_t(\mathbf{x}_n)$.
   (c) **if** $\gamma_t \leq \varrho$ or $\gamma_t = 1$, **then break**
   (d) Set $\alpha_t = \dfrac{1}{2} \log \dfrac{1 + \gamma_t}{1 - \gamma_t} - \dfrac{1}{2} \log \dfrac{1 + \varrho}{1 - \varrho}$.
   (e) Update weights: $d_n^{t+1} = d_n^t \exp\{-\alpha_t y_n h_t(\mathbf{x}_n)\} / Z_t$, s.t. $\sum\limits_{n=1}^{N} d_n^{t+1} = 1$.

4. **Output:** $f(\mathbf{x}) = \sum\limits_{t=1}^{T} \dfrac{\alpha_t}{\sum_r \alpha_r} h_t(\mathbf{x})$, $\gamma = \min\limits_{t=1,\ldots,T} \gamma_t$, and $\rho = \max\limits_{n=1,\ldots,N} y_n f(\mathbf{x}_n)$

---

learner returns the constant hypothesis $h_t(\mathbf{x}) \equiv 1$. The error of this hypothesis is the sum of all negative weights, i.e. $\epsilon_t = \sum_{y_n = -1} d_n^t$, its edge is $\gamma_t = 1 - 2\epsilon_t$. If $\gamma_t > \rho$, then the new distribution $\mathbf{d}^{t+1}$ is computed (otherwise the algorithm stops). The parameter α_t is chosen so that the edge of h_t with respect to the new distribution is exactly ϱ (instead of 0 as in AdaBoost). Actually, the edge is ϱ for any ± 1-valued base hypotheses or more generally, if one chooses α_t s.t. $Z_t(\alpha_t)$ is minimized. In [9] the standard boosting algorithms are interpreted as approximate solutions to the following optimization problem: choose distribution $\mathbf{d}$ subject to the constraints that the edges of the previous hypotheses are *equal* zero. In this paper we use the *inequality* constraints that the edges of the previous hypotheses are at most ϱ. The α_t's are the Lagrange multipliers for these inequality constraints, which are always positive.

Since one does not know the value of ϱ^* beforehand, one also needs to find ϱ^*. We propose an algorithm that constructs a sequence $\{\varrho_r\}_{r=1}^{R}$ converging to ϱ^*: A fast way to find a real value up to a certain accuracy ν on the interval $[-1, 1]$ is to use a *binary search* – one needs only $\log_2(2/\nu)$ search steps.[3] AdaBoost$_\varrho$, (Algorithm 1) is used to decide whether the current guess ϱ is *larger* or *smaller* than ϱ^*. This leads to the *Marginal AdaBoost* algorithm (cf. Algorithm 2).

The algorithm proceeds in R steps, where R is determined by the accuracy ν that we would like to reach: In each iteration r it calls AdaBoost$_{\varrho_r}$ (cf. step 3b in Marginal AdaBoost), where ϱ_r is chosen to be in the middle of an interval $[l_r, u_r]$ (cf. step 3a). Based on the success of AdaBoost$_{\varrho_r}$ to achieve a large enough margin, the interval is updated (cf. step 3c). We can show that the interval is chosen such that it always contains ϱ^*, the *unknown* maximal margin, while the length of the interval is almost reduced by a factor of two. Finally, in the last step of the algorithm, one has reached a good estimate ϱ_R of ϱ^* and calls AdaBoost$_\varrho$ for $\varrho = l_{R+1} - \nu$ generating a combined hypothesis with margin at least $\varrho^* - 4\nu$ (as we will show later). In the next section we will give a detailed analysis of

---

[3] If one knows that $\varrho^* \in [a, b]$, one needs only $\log_2((b - a)/\nu)$ steps.

how the algorithm works and how many calls to the base learner are needed to approximate ϱ^*: in the worst case one needs about $\log_2(2/\nu)$ times more iterations than for the case when ϱ^* is known.

Since AdaBoost$_\varrho$ is used as a sub-routine and starts from the beginning in each round, one can think of several speed-ups, which might help to reduce the computation time. For instance, one could store the base hypotheses of previous iterations and instead of calling the base learner, one first sifts through these previously used hypotheses. Furthermore, one may stop AdaBoost$_\varrho$, when the combined hypothesis has reached a margin of ϱ or the base learner returns a hypothesis with edge lower than ϱ.

Algorithm 2 – The Marginal AdaBoost algorithm

1. **Input:** $S = \langle (\mathbf{x}_1, y_1), \ldots, (\mathbf{x}_N, y_N) \rangle$, Accuracy ν
2. **Initialize:** $\varrho_1 = 0$, $l_1 = -1$, $u_1 = 1$, $R = \lceil \log_2(1/\nu) \rceil$, $T = \lceil 2\log(N)/\nu^2 \rceil + 1$.
3. **Do for** $r = 1, \ldots R$,
   (a) $\varrho_r = \frac{l_r + u_r}{2}$
   (b) $[f_r, \gamma_r, \rho_r] = \text{AdaBoost}_{\varrho_r}(S, T)$
   (c) **if** $\rho_r \geq \varrho_r$, **then** $l_{r+1} = \max(\rho_r, l_r)$, $u_{r+1} = \min(\gamma_r, u_r)$
       else $l_{r+1} = \max(\rho_r, l_r)$, $u_{r+1} = \min(\gamma_r, \varrho_r + \nu, u_r)$
   (d) **if** $u_{r+1} - l_{r+1} \leq 3\nu$, **then** break
4. **Output:** $f = \text{AdaBoost}_{l_{r+1} - \nu}(S, 2\log(N)/\nu^2)$

Constraining the edges of the previous hypotheses to equal zero (as done in the *totally corrective algorithm* of [9]) leads to a problem if there is no solution satisfying these constraints. Because of duality, the maximal edge over all base hypotheses is always greater than the minimal margin of the examples. Thus, if there is a separation with margin greater than 0, then the equality constraints on the edges are not satisfyable. In Marginal AdaBoost we consider a system of *inequality constraints* $\sum_{n=1}^{N} y_n d_n h_t(\mathbf{x}_n) \leq \varrho$, where ϱ is adapted. Again, if there is a separation with margin greater than ϱ, then the system of inequalities has no solution (and the Lagrange multipliers diverge to infinity). However, in this case our algorithm stops and increases ϱ, which increases the size of the feasible set. Finally, if $\varrho = \varrho^*$, then there is presumably only one point left, which is then the dual solution of the maximum margin solution.

3   Detailed Analysis

3.1   Weak Learning and Margins

The standard assumption made on the base learning algorithm in the PAC-Boosting setting is that it returns a hypothesis h from a fixed set H that is slightly better than random guessing on any training set.[4] More formally this

---

[4] In the PAC setting, the base learner is allowed to fail with probability δ. Since we are seeking for simple presentation, we ignore this fact here. Our algorithm can be extended to this case.

means that the error rate ϵ is consistently smaller than $\frac{1}{2} - \frac{1}{2}\gamma$ for some $\gamma > 0$. Note that the error rate of $\frac{1}{2}$ (i.e. $\gamma = 0$) could easily be reached by a fair coin, assuming both classes have the same prior probabilities. Thus, this requirement is the least we can expect from a learning algorithm [5,].

The error rate ϵ is defined as the fraction of points that are misclassified. In Boosting this is extended to weighted example sets and one defines

$$\epsilon_h(\mathbf{d}) = \sum_{n=1}^{N} d_n \, \mathbf{I}(y_n \neq \text{sign}(h(\mathbf{x}_n))),$$

where h is the hypothesis returned by the base learner and $\mathbf{I}$ is the indicator function with $\mathbf{I}(\text{true}) = 1$ and $\mathbf{I}(\text{false}) = 0$. The weighting $\mathbf{d} = [d_1, \ldots, d_N]$ of the examples is such that $d_n \geq 0$ and $\sum_{n=1}^{N} d_n = 1$. A more convenient quantity to measure the quality of the hypothesis h is the edge $\gamma_h(\mathbf{d}) = \sum_{n=1}^{N} d_n y_n h(\mathbf{x}_n)$, which is an affine transformation of $\epsilon_h(\mathbf{d})$ in the case when $h(\mathbf{x}) \in \{-1, +1\}$: $\epsilon_h(\mathbf{d}) = \frac{1}{2} - \frac{1}{2}\gamma_h(\mathbf{d})$. Recalling from Section 1, the margin of a given example $(\mathbf{x}_n, y_n)$ is defined by $y f_\alpha(\mathbf{x})$.

Suppose we would combine all possible hypotheses from H (assuming H is finite), then the following well-known theorem establishes the connection between margins and edges first seen in connection with Boosting in [4,2]:

Theorem 1 (Min-Max-Theorem, [22]).

$$\gamma^* = \min_{\mathbf{d}} \max_{h \in H} \sum_{n=1}^{N} d_n y_n h(\mathbf{x}_n) = \max_{\alpha} \min_{n=1,\ldots,N} y_n \sum_{k=1}^{|H|} \alpha_k h_k(\mathbf{x}_n) = \varrho^*, \quad (1)$$

where $\mathbf{d} \in \mathcal{P}^N$, $\alpha \in \mathcal{P}^{|H|}$ and $\mathcal{P}^k$ is the k-dimensional probability simplex.

Thus, the minimal edge γ^* that can be achieved over all possible weightings $\mathbf{d}$ of the training set is equal to the maximal margin ϱ^* of a combined hypothesis from H. Also, for any non-optimal weightings $\mathbf{d}$ and α we always have $\max_{h \in H} \gamma_h(\mathbf{d}) \geq \gamma^* = \varrho^* \geq \min_{n=1,\ldots,N} y_n f_\alpha(\mathbf{x}_n)$. If the base learning algorithm guarantees to return a hypothesis with edge at least γ for any weighting, there exists a combined hypothesis with margin at least γ. If $\gamma = \gamma^*$, i.e. the lower bound γ is largest possible, then there exists a combined hypothesis with margin exactly $\gamma = \varrho^*$ (only using hypotheses that are actually returned by the base learner). From this discussion we can derive a sufficient condition on the base learning algorithm to reach the maximal margin: If it returns hypotheses whos edges are at least γ^*, there exists a linear combination of these hypotheses that has margin $\gamma^* = \varrho^*$. This explains the termination condition (cf. step 3c in AdaBoost$_\varrho$). We will prove later that our Marginal AdaBoost algorithm is able to compute the coefficients of the combination efficiently (cf. Theorem 2).

3.2   Convergence Properties of AdaBoost$_\varrho$

We now analyze a slightly generalized version of AdaBoost$_\varrho$, where ϱ is not fixed but could be adapted in each iteration. We therefore consider sequences $\{\varrho_t\}_{t=1}^{T}$, which might either be specified before running the algorithm or computed based on results during the algorithm. For instance, the idea proposed by [2] is to compute ϱ_t by $\min\limits_{n=1,\ldots,N} y_n f_{\boldsymbol{\alpha}_{t-1}}(\mathbf{x}_n)$, which leads to Arc-GV *asymptotically* converging to the maximum margin solution.

In the following we are answering the question how good AdaBoost$_{\{\varrho_t\}}$ is able to increase the margin and bound the fraction of examples, which have a margin smaller than say θ. We start with the following useful lemma similar to a lemma shown in [19,20]:

Lemma 1. *Assume that in a run of AdaBoost$_\varrho$ holds $\alpha_t \geq 0$ for all t. Then we have*

$$\frac{1}{N}\sum_{n=1}^{N}\mathbf{I}\left(y_n f_{\boldsymbol{\alpha}}(\mathbf{x}_n) \leq \theta\right) \leq \left(\prod_{t=1}^{T} Z_t\right)\exp\left\{\sum_{t=1}^{T}\theta\alpha_t\right\} = \prod_{t=1}^{T}\exp\left\{\theta\alpha_t + \log Z_t\right\} \quad (2)$$

where Z_t is as in AdaBoost$_\varrho$, step (3e).

This leads to a result generalizing Theorem 5 in [5,] for the case $\varrho \neq 0$:

Proposition 1 ([17]). *Let γ_t be the edge of h_t in the t-th step of AdaBoost$_\varrho$. Assume $-1 \leq \varrho_t \leq \gamma_t$. Then holds for all $\theta \in [-1, 1]$*

$$\exp\left\{\theta\alpha_t + \log Z_t\right\} \leq \exp\left(-\frac{1+\theta}{2}\log\left(\frac{1+\varrho_t}{1+\gamma_t}\right) - \frac{1-\theta}{2}\log\left(\frac{1-\varrho_t}{1-\gamma_t}\right)\right). \quad (3)$$

The algorithm makes progress, if the right hand side of (3) is smaller than one. Suppose we would like the reach a margin θ on all training examples, where we obviously need to assume $\theta \leq \varrho^*$. Then the question arises, which sequence of $\{\varrho_t\}_{t=1}^{T}$ one should use to find such combined hypothesis in as few iterations as possible. Since the right hand side (rhs.) of (3) is minimized for $\varrho_t = \theta$, one should always use this choice, independent of how the base learner performs.

We therefore assume for the rest of the paper that ϱ is held constant in a run of AdaBoost$_\varrho$. Let us reconsider (3) of Proposition 1 for the special case $\varrho_t = \varrho \equiv \theta$:

$$\exp\left\{\varrho\alpha_t + \log Z_t\right\} \leq \exp\left\{-\Delta_2(\varrho, \gamma_t)\right\}, \quad (4)$$

where $\Delta_2(\varrho, \gamma_t) := \frac{1+\varrho}{2}\log\frac{1+\varrho}{1+\gamma_t} + \frac{1-\varrho}{2}\log\frac{1-\varrho}{1-\gamma_t}$ is the binary relative entropy. This means that the right hand side of (2) is reduced by a factor exactly $\exp(-\Delta_2(\varrho, \gamma_t))$, which can be bounded from above by using Taylor expansion and the convexity in the second argument of $\exp(-\Delta_2(\cdot, \cdot))$:

$$\exp(-\Delta_2(\varrho, \gamma_t)) \leq 1 - \frac{1}{2}\frac{(\varrho - \gamma_t)^2}{1 - \varrho^2} \quad (5)$$

where we need to assume[5] $\gamma_t \geq \varrho$ and $0 \leq \varrho \leq 1$. Note that this is the same form of bound one also obtains for original AdaBoost (i.e. $\varrho = 0$), where the fraction

---

[5] For the case $\varrho < 0$ one gets a slightly worse bound: $1 - \frac{3}{14}(\varrho - \gamma_t)^2$.

of points with margin smaller than zero is reduced by at least $1 - \frac{1}{2}\gamma_t^2$, if $\gamma_t > 0$. Note that one yields a factor $\frac{1}{1-\varrho^2}$ in (5), which makes the convergence faster, if $\varrho > 0$.

Now we determine an upper bound on the number of iterations needed by AdaBoost$_\varrho$ for achieving a margin of ϱ on all examples, given that the maximum margin is ϱ^*:

Corollary 1. *Assume the base learner always achieves an edge $\gamma_t \geq \varrho^*$. If $0 \leq \varrho \leq \varrho^* - \nu$, $\nu > 0$, then AdaBoost$_\varrho$ will converge to a solution with margin of at least ϱ on all examples in at most $\lceil \frac{2\log(N)(1-\varrho^2)}{\nu^2} \rceil + 1$ steps.*

Proof. We use Lemma 1 and (5) and can bound

$$\frac{1}{N} \sum_{n=1}^{N} \mathbf{I}\left(y_n f(\mathbf{x}_n) \leq \varrho\right) \leq \prod_{t=1}^{T}\left(1 - \frac{1}{2}\frac{(\varrho - \gamma_t)^2}{1-\varrho^2}\right) \leq \left(1 - \frac{1}{2}\frac{\nu^2}{1-\varrho^2}\right)^T.$$

The margin is at least ϱ for all examples, if the right hand side is smaller than $\frac{1}{N}$, hence after at most $\left\lceil \frac{\log(N)}{-\log\left(1 - \frac{1}{2}\frac{\nu^2}{1-\varrho^2}\right)} \right\rceil + 1 \leq \left\lceil \frac{2\log(N)(1-\varrho^2)}{\nu^2} \right\rceil + 1$ iterations, which proves the statement. $\qquad\square$

A similar result is found for $\varrho < 0$ in [15], but without the additional factor $1 - \varrho^2$; in that case the number of iterations is bounded by $\lceil 2\log(N)/\nu^2 \rceil + 1$.

3.3   Asymptotical Margin of AdaBoost$_\varrho$

With the methods shown so far, we can also analyse to what value the maximum margin of the original AdaBoost algorithm converges to asymptotically. First, we state a lower bound on the margin that is achieved by AdaBoost$_\varrho$. We find, that the size of the margin is not as large as it could be theoretically (by considering Theorem 1). In a second part we consider an experiment that shows that depending on some subtle properties of the base learner, the margin of combined hypotheses generated by AdaBoost can converge to quite different values (while the maximum margin is kept constant). We observe that the previously lower bound on the margin is almost tight in empirical cases.

As long each factor in Eq. (3) is smaller than 1, the right hand side of the bound reduces. If it is bounded away from 1,[6] then the rhs. converges exponentially fast to zero. The following corollary considers the asymptotical case and gives a lower bound on the margin.

Corollary 2 ([15]). *Assume AdaBoost$_\varrho$ generates hypothesis $h_1, h_2, \ldots$ with edges $\gamma_1, \gamma_2, \ldots$ and coefficients $\alpha_1, \alpha_2, \ldots$. Let $\gamma = \inf_{t=1,2,\ldots} \gamma_t$ and assume*

---

[6] This means that there exists a constant $\mu > 0$ such that the square-root term is *always* smaller than $1 - \mu$. Otherwise, the sequence of square-root terms might converge to 1 and the product of them might not converge to zero (this case is analyzed in greater detail in [15].

$\gamma > \varrho$. Then the asymptotically $(t \to \infty)$ smallest margin $\hat{\rho}$ of the combined hypothesis is bounded from below by

$$\hat{\rho} \geq \frac{\log(1 - \varrho^2) - \log(1 - \gamma^2)}{\log\left(\frac{1+\gamma}{1-\gamma}\right) - \log\left(\frac{1+\varrho}{1-\varrho}\right)}. \tag{6}$$

From (6) one can understand the interaction between ϱ and γ: if the difference between γ and ϱ is small, then the right hand side of (6) is small. Thus, if ϱ with $\varrho \leq \gamma$ is large, then $\hat{\rho}$ must be large, i.e. choosing a larger ϱ results in a larger margin on the training examples. Note that (6) implies the weaker bound $\hat{\rho} \geq \frac{\gamma+\varrho}{2}$. Previously it was only known that $\hat{\rho} \geq \varrho$ [2, Theorem 7.2].

However, in the Section 3.1 we have shown that the maximal achievable margin is at least γ. Thus if ϱ is chosen too small, then we guarantee only a *suboptimal asymptotical margin*. In the original formulation of AdaBoost we have $\varrho = 0$ and we guarantee only that AdaBoost$_0$ achieves a margin of at least $\frac{1}{2}\gamma + \frac{1}{12}\gamma^3$. *This gap in the theory motivates our Marginal AdaBoost algorithm.*

Experimental Illustration of Corollary 2:   To illustrate that the above-mentioned gap, we perform an experiment showing how tight (6) can be. We analyze two different settings: the base learner selects (i) the hypothesis with largest edge over all hypotheses and (ii) the hypothesis with minimal edge among all hypothesis with edge larger than ϱ^*. This is the best and the worst case, respectively. Note that Corollary 2 holds in particular for the *worst case*, where the base learner is allowed to return any hypothesis with edge larger than ϱ^* (the maximal achievable margin). In practice, however, the base learner may perform better.

We use random data with N training examples, where N is drawn uniformly between 10 and 200. The labels are drawn at random from a binomial distribution with equal probability. We use a hypothesis set with 10^4 hypotheses. The output of every hypothesis is either -1 or $+1$ and is chosen such that with probability p it is equal to the previously generated label.[7] First we compute the solution of the margin-LP problem (left hand side of (1)) and determine ϱ^*. Then we compute the combined hypothesis generated by AdaBoost$_\varrho$ after 10^4 iterations for $\varrho = 0$ and $\varrho = \frac{1}{3}$ using the best and the worst selection strategy, respectively. The latter depends on ϱ^*. This procedure is repeated for 300 random draws of p from an uniform distribution. The parameter p ensures that there are cases with small and large optimal margins.

The resulting margins computed by the three algorithms are plotted in Figure 1. On the abscissa is the maximal achievable margin ϱ^* for a particular data realization. On the ordinate is the margin of AdaBoost$_\varrho$ using the best and the worst strategy. We observe a great difference between both selection strategies. Whereas the margin of the worst strategy is *tightly lower bounded* by (6), the best strategy has near maximal margin.

---

[7] With low probability, the output of an hypothesis is equal to all labels. These cases are excluded.

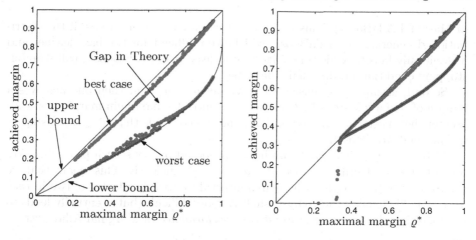

Fig. 1. Achieved margins of AdaBoost$_\varrho$ using the best (green) and the worst (red) selection on random data for $\varrho = 0$ [left] and $\varrho = \frac{1}{3}$ [right]: On the abscissa is the maximal achievable margin ϱ^* and on the ordinate the margin achieved by AdaBoost$_\varrho$ for one data realization. For comparison the line $y = x$ ("upper bound") and the bound (6) ("lower bound") are plotted. On the interval $[\varrho, 1]$, Eq. (6) lower bounds the achieved margin of the worst strategy tightly. The optimal strategy almost achieves the maximal margin. There is a clear gap between best and worst performance of the selection scheme, which we cannot explain by theory. If ϱ is chosen appropriately, then this gap is reduced to 0

These experiments show that one obtains different results by changing some properties of the base learning algorithm. These properties are not used for computing the bound (only the minimal edge is used). This is indeed a problem, as one is not able to predict where AdaBoost$_\varrho$ is converging to.[8] We therefore propose Marginal AdaBoost, which solves this problem. Roughly speaking, by choosing ϱ near ϱ^*, one can make the difference between worst and best case performance of the base learner arbitrary small (cf. Figure 1). This is exploited in the next section.

3.4 Convergence of Marginal AdaBoost

So far we have always considered the case where we already know some proper value of ϱ. Let us now assume the case that the maximum achievable margin is ϱ^* and we would like to achieve a margin of $\varrho^* - \nu$. Our algorithm *guesses* a value of ϱ^* starting with 0. We need to understand what happens if our guess is too high, i.e. $\varrho > \varrho^*$, or too low, i.e. $\varrho < \varrho^*$?

First, if $\varrho > \varrho^*$, then one cannot reach the margin of ϱ since the maximum achievable margin is ϱ^*. By Corollary 1, if AdaBoost$_\varrho$ has not reached a margin of at least ϱ in $2\log(N)/\nu^2$ steps, we can conclude that $\varrho > \varrho^* - \nu$ (cf. step 3c

---

[8] One might even be able to construct cases where the outputs are not at all converging.

in Marginal AdaBoost). This is the worst case. The better case is, if the distribution $\mathbf{d}$ generated by AdaBoost$_\varrho$ will be too difficult for the base learner and it eventually fails to achieve an edge γ of at least ϱ and AdaBoost$_\varrho$ will stop (cf. stopping condition in Marginal AdaBoost).

Second, assume ϱ is chosen too low, say $\varrho < \varrho^* - \nu$, then one achieves a margin of ϱ in a few steps by Corollary 1 . Since the maximum margin is always greater that a certain achieved margin, one can conclude that $\varrho^* \geq \varrho$ (cf. step 3c in Marginal AdaBoost).

Note that there is a *small gap* in the proposed binary search procedure: We are not able to identify the case $\varrho^* - \nu \leq \varrho \leq \varrho^*$ efficiently. This means that we cannot reduce the length of the search interval by *exactly* a factor of two in *each* iteration. This makes the analysis slightly more difficult, but eventually leads to the following theorem on the *worst case performance* of Marginal AdaBoost:

Theorem 2. *Assume the base learner always achieves an edge $\gamma_t \geq \varrho^*$. Then Marginal AdaBoost (Algorithm 2) will find a combined hypothesis f that maximizes the margin up to accuracy 4ν in at most $\lceil \frac{2\log(N)}{\nu^2} + 1\rceil \lceil \log_2(2/\nu)\rceil$ calls of the base learner. The final hypothesis combines at most $\lceil \frac{2\log(N)}{\nu^2} + 1\rceil$ base hypotheses.*

Proof. See Algorithm 2 for definitions of $u_r, l_r, \gamma_r, \rho_r$.

We claim that in any iteration $u_r \geq \varrho^* \geq l_r$. We show, if $u_{r-1} \geq \varrho^* \geq l_{r-1}$, then $u_r \geq \varrho^* \geq l_r$ for all $r = 1, \ldots, R$. It holds $l_1 \geq \varrho^* \geq u_1$ (induction start). By assumption $\gamma_{t,r} \geq \varrho^*$ and we may set $u_{r+1} = \min_{r_0=1,\ldots,r} \min_{t=1,\ldots,T} \gamma_{t,r}$. By Theorem 1 holds $\varrho^* \geq \rho_r$ for all $r = 1, 2, \ldots$ and, hence, we may set $l_{r+1} = \max_{r_0=1,\ldots,r} \rho_{r_0}$. We have to consider two cases. (a) $\rho_r \geq \varrho_r$ and (b) $\rho_r < \varrho_r$. In case (b) we have an additional term in u_{r+1}, which follows from $\varrho_r + \nu \geq \varrho^*$, justified by $\rho_r < \varrho_r$ and Proposition 1.

By construction, the length of interval $[l_r, u_r]$ is (almost) decreased in each iteration by a factor of two. We show $u_r - l_r \leq 2^{-r+1} + 2\nu$. In case (a) the interval is reduced by at least a factor of two. The worst case is if always (b) happens:

$$u_r - l_r \leq \varrho_r + \nu - l_r$$
$$= \frac{\varrho_{r-1} + \nu + l_{r-1}}{2} + \nu - l_r$$
$$= \frac{\varrho_{r-1} + \nu + l_{r-1} + 2\nu - 2l_r}{2}$$

$$= \frac{\varrho_{r-j} + \nu \sum_{i=0}^{j} 2^j + \sum_{i=1}^{j} 2^{j-i} l_{r-i} - 2^j l_r}{2^j}$$
$$= \frac{\varrho_{r-j} + (2^{j+1} - 1)\nu + \sum_{i=1}^{j} 2^{j-i} l_{r-i} - 2^j l_r}{2^j}$$
$$= \frac{\varrho_1 + (2^r - 1)\nu + \sum_{i=1}^{r-1} 2^{r-1-i} l_{r-i} - 2^{r-1} l_r}{2^{r-1}}.$$

Since l_r is non-decreasing, $\sum_{i=1}^{j} 2^{r-1-i} l_{r-i} - 2^{r-1} l_r$ is maximized for $l_r = \text{const}$, i.e. $\sum_{i=1}^{j} 2^{r-1-i} l_{r-i} - 2^{r-1} l_r \leq l_r \sum_{i=0}^{r-2} 2^i - 2^{r-1} l_r = l_r(2^{r-1} - 1 - 2^{r-1}) = -l_r$. We continue by using $\varrho_1 = 0$ and $\min_r l_r = -1$:

$$\leq \frac{(2^r - 1)\nu - l_r}{2^{r-1}}$$

$$\leq \frac{1}{2^{r-1}} + 2\nu.$$

Thus after $R = \lceil \log_2(1/\nu) \rceil$ steps we have $u_{R+1} - l_{R+1} \leq 3\nu$ and $\varrho^* - l_{R+1} \leq 3\nu$.[9]

Now we run AdaBoost $l_{R+1-\nu}(S, 2\log(N)/\nu^2)$ and achieve a margin of at least $l_{R+1} - \nu$ by Corollary 1. This can only be 4ν away from ϱ^*.

We called $R+1 = \lceil \log_2(1/\nu) + 1 \rceil$ times AdaBoost$_\varrho$, each time calling at most $\lceil 2\log(N)/\nu^2 + 1 \rceil$ times the base learning algorithm. Marginal AdaBoost returns only the last hypothesis, combining only $\lceil 2\log(N)/\nu^2 + 1 \rceil$ base hypotheses. $\square$ The bound could be improved by a factor $1 - \varrho^{*2}$, if $\varrho \geq 0$, since we have not exploited the additional factor $(1 - \varrho^2)$ as in Proposition 1.

3.5   Infinite Hypothesis Sets

So far we have implicitly assumed that the hypothesis space is finite. In this section we will show that this assumption is (often) not necessary. Also note, if the output of the hypotheses is discrete, the hypothesis space is effectively finite [16,]. For *infinite hypothesis sets*, Theorem 1 can be restated in a weaker form as:

Theorem 3 (Weak Min-Max, e.g. [12]).

$$\gamma^* := \min_{\mathbf{d}} \sup_{h \in H} \sum_{n=1}^{N} y_n h(\mathbf{x}_n) d_n \geq \sup_{\alpha} \min_{n=1,\ldots,N} y_n \sum_{t:\alpha_t > 0} \alpha_t h_t(\mathbf{x}_n) =: \varrho^*, \qquad (7)$$

where $\mathbf{d} \in \mathcal{P}^N$, $\alpha \in \mathcal{P}^{|H|}$ *with finite support. We call* $\Gamma = \gamma^* - \varrho^*$ *the "duality gap".*

In particular for any $\mathbf{d} \in P^N$: $\sup_{h \in H} \sum_{n=1}^{N} y_n h(\mathbf{x}_n) d_n \geq \gamma^*$ and for any $\alpha \in P^{|H|}$ with finite support: $\min_{n=1,\ldots,N} y_n \sum_{t:\alpha_t \geq 0} \alpha_t h_t(\mathbf{x}_n) \leq \varrho^*$.

In theory the duality gap may be nonzero. However, Proposition 1 and Theorem 2 do not assume finite hypothesis sets and show that the margin will converge arbitrarily close to ϱ^*, as long as the base learning algorithm can return *a single* hypothesis that has an edge not smaller than ϱ^*.

In other words, the duality gap may result from the fact that the sup on the left side can not be replaced by a max, i.e. there might not exists a *single* hypothesis h with edge larger or equal to ϱ^*. By assuming that the base learner is always able to pick good enough hypotheses ($\geq \varrho^*$) one automatically gets that $\Gamma = 0$ (by Proposition 1).

---

[9] Note, if one chooses ϱ_r not exactly in the middle of the interval $[l_r, u_r]$, one can balance the influence of ν and obtain a slightly better constant for the worst case performance.

Under certain conditions on H this maximum always exists and strong duality holds (see e.g. [16,15,8,12] for details):

Theorem 4 (Strong Min-Max). *If the set $\{[h(\mathbf{x}_1), \ldots, h(\mathbf{x}_N)] \mid h \in H\}$ is compact, then $\Gamma = 0$.*

In general this requirement can be fulfilled by base learning algorithms whose outputs continuously depend on the distribution $\mathbf{d}$. Furthermore, the outputs of the hypotheses need to be bounded (cf. step 3a in AdaBoost$_\varrho$). The first requirement might be a problem with base learning algorithms such as some variants of decision stumps or decision trees. However, there is a simple trick to avoid this problem: Roughly speaking, at each point with discontinuity $\hat{\mathbf{d}}$, one adds all hypotheses to H that are limit points of $L(S, \mathbf{d}^s)$, where $\{\mathbf{d}^s\}_{s=1}^\infty$ is an arbitrary sequence converging to $\hat{\mathbf{d}}$ and $L(S, \mathbf{d})$ denotes the hypothesis returned by the base learning algorithm for weighting $\mathbf{d}$ and training sample S [15,].

4   Experimental Illustration of Marginal AdaBoost

First of all, we would like to note that we are aware of the fact that maximizing the margin of the ensemble does not lead in all cases to an improved generalization performance. For fairly noisy data sets even the opposite has been reported cf. [14,2,7,17]. Also, Breiman once reported an example where the margins of all examples are larger in one ensemble than another and the latter generalized considerably better.

However, at least for well separable data the theory applies for *hard margins* and for larger margins one can prove better generalization error bounds. We expect that one should be able to measure differences in the generalization error, if one function approximately maximizes the margin while another function does

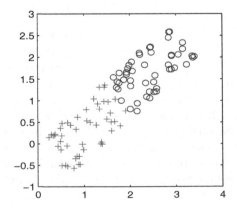

Fig. 2. The two *discriminative dimensions* of our separable one hundred dimensional data set

not, as similar results have been obtained in [19] on a multi-class optical character recognition problem.

Here we report experiments on artificial data to (a) illustrate how our algorithm works and (b) how it compares to AdaBoost. Our data is 100 dimensional and contains 98 nuisance dimensions with uniform noise. The other two dimensions are plotted exemplary in Figure 2. For training we use only 100 examples and there is obviously the need to carefully control the capacity of the ensemble.

As base learning algorithm we use C4.5 decision trees provided by Ross Quinlan [13, cf.] using an option to control the number of nodes in the tree. We have set it such that C4.5 generates trees with about three nodes. Otherwise, the base learner often classifies all training examples correctly and over-fits the data already. Furthermore, since in this case the margin is already maximal (equal to 1), both algorithms would stop since $\gamma = 1$. We therefore need to limit the complexity of the base learner, in good agreement with the bounds on the generalization error [19,].

In Figure 3 (left) we see a typical run of Marginal AdaBoost for $\nu = 0.1$. It calls AdaBoost$_\varrho$ three times. The first call of AdaBoost$_\varrho$ for $\gamma = 0$ already stops after four iterations, since it has generated a consistent combined hypothesis. The lower bound l on ϱ^* as computed by our algorithm is $l = 0.07$ and the upper bound u is 0.94 (cf. step 3c in Marginal AdaBoost). The second time ϱ is chosen to be in the middle of the interval $[l, u]$ and AdaBoost$_\varrho$ reaches the margin of $\varrho = 0.51$ after 80 iterations. The interval is now $[0.51, 0.77]$. Since the length of the interval $u - l = 0.27$ is small enough, Marginal AdaBoost leaves the loop through exit condition 3d, calls AdaBoost$_\varrho$ the last time for $\varrho = u - \nu = 0.41$ and finally achieves a margin of $\rho = 0.55$. For comparison we also plot the margins of the hypotheses generated by AdaBoost (cf. Figure 3 (right)). One observes that it is not able to achieve a large margin efficiently ($\rho = 0.37$ after 1000 iterations).

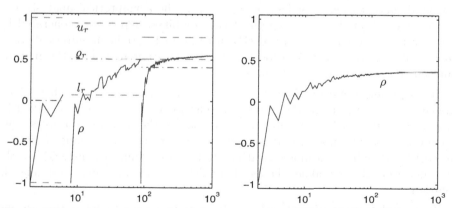

Fig. 3. Illustration of the achieved margin of Marginal AdaBoost (upper) and AdaBoost$_0$ (lower) at each iteration. Our algorithm calls AdaBoost$_\varrho$ three times while adapting ϱ (dash-dotted). We also plot the values for l and u as in Marginal AdaBoost (dashed) (For details see text.)

Table 1. Estimated generalization performances and margins with confidence intervals for decision trees (C4.5), AdaBoost (AB) and Marginal AB on the toy data. The last row shows the number of times the algorithm had the smallest error. All numbers are averaged over 200 splits into 100 training and 19900 test examples

	C4.5	AB	Marginal AB
E_{gen}	$7.4 \pm 0.11\%$	$4.0 \pm 0.11\%$	$3.6 \pm 0.10\%$
ϱ	—	0.31 ± 0.01	0.58 ± 0.01
wins	$1/200$	$59/200$	$140/200$

In Table 1 we see the average performance of the three classifiers. For Ada-Boost we combined 200 hypotheses for the final prediction. For Marginal Ada-Boost we use $\nu = 0.1$ and let the algorithm combine only 200 hypotheses for the final prediction to get a fair comparison. We see a large improvement of both ensemble methods compared to the single classifier. There is also a slight, but – according to a T-test with confidence level 98% – significant difference between the generalization performances of both boosting algorithms. Note also that the margins of the combined hypothesis achieved by Marginal AdaBoost are on average almost twice as large as for AdaBoost.

5   Conclusion

We have analyzed a generalized version of AdaBoost in the context of large margin algorithms. From von Neumann's Min-Max theorem the maximal achievable margin ϱ^* is at least γ, if the base learner always returns a hypothesis with weighted classification error less than $\frac{1}{2} - \frac{1}{2}\gamma$. The asymptotical analysis lead us to a lower bound on the margin of the combined hypotheses generated by AdaBoost$_\varrho$ in the limit, which was shown to be rather tight in empirical cases. Our results indicate that AdaBoost generally does not maximize the margin, but achieves a reasonable large margin.

To overcome these problems we proposed an algorithm for which we have shown the convergence to the maximum margin solution. This is achieved by increasing ϱ iteratively, such that the gap between the best and the worst case becomes arbitrarily small. In our analysis we did not need to assume additional properties of the base learning algorithm. To the best of our knowledge this is the first algorithm that combines the merits of Boosting with the maximum margin solution.

In a simulation experiment we have illustrated the validity of our analysis and also that a larger margin can improve the generalization ability when learning on high dimensional data with a few informative dimensions.

References

1. K.P. Bennett, A. Demiriz, and J. Shawe-Taylor. A column generation algorithm for boosting. In P. Langley, editor, *Proceedings, 17th ICML*, pages 65–72, San Francisco, 2000. 335
2. L. Breiman. Prediction games and arcing algorithms. *Neural Computation*, 11(7):1493–1518, 1999. Also Technical Report 504, Statistics Dept., University of California Berkeley. 335, 336, 339, 340, 342, 346
3. Y. Freund. Boosting a weak learning algorithm by majority. *Information and Computation*, 121(2):256–285, September 1995. 334
4. Y. Freund and R.E. Schapire. Experiments with a new boosting algorithm. In *Proc. 13th International Conference on Machine Learning*, pages 148–146. Morgan Kaufmann, 1996. 339
5. Y. Freund and R.E. Schapire. A decision-theoretic generalization of on-line learning and an application to boosting. *Journal of Computer and System Sciences*, 55(1):119–139, 1997. 334, 336, 339, 340
6. Y. Freund and R.E. Schapire. Adaptive game playing using multiplicative weights. *Games and Economic Behavior*, 29:79–103, 1999. 336
7. A.J. Grove and D. Schuurmans. Boosting in the limit: Maximizing the margin of learned ensembles. In *Proc. of the Fifteenth National Conference on Artifical Intelligence*, 1998. 335, 346
8. R. Hettich and K.O. Kortanek. Semi-infinite programming: Theory, methods and applications. *SIAM Review*, 3:380–429, September 1993. 346
9. J. Kivinen and M. Warmuth. Boosting as entropy projection. In *Proc. 12th Annu. Conference on Comput. Learning Theory*, pages 134–144. ACM Press, New York, NY, 1999. 337, 338
10. V. Koltchinskii, D. Panchenko, and F. Lozano. Some new bounds on the generalization error of combined classifiers. In *Advances in Neural Inf. Proc. Systems*, volume 13, 2001. 335
11. O.L. Mangasarian. Arbitrary-norm separating plane. *Op. Res. Letters*, 24(1):15–23, 1999. 336
12. S. Nash and A. Sofer. *Linear and Nonlinear Programming*. McGraw-Hill, New York, 1996. 345, 346
13. J.R. Quinlan. *C4.5: Programs for Machine Learning*. Morgan Kaufmann, 1992. 347
14. J.R. Quinlan. Boosting first-order learning. *Lecture Notes in Comp. Sci.*, 1160:143, 1996. 346
15. G. Rätsch. *Robust Boosting via Convex Optimization*. PhD thesis, University of Potsdam, October 2001. http://mlg.anu.edu.au/~raetsch/thesis.ps.gz. 341, 346
16. G. Rätsch, A. Demiriz, and K. Bennett. Sparse regression ensembles in infinite and finite hypothesis spaces. *Machine Learning*, 48(1-3):193–221, 2002. Special Issue on New Methods for Model Selection and Model Combination. Also NeuroCOLT2 Technical Report 2000-085. 345, 346
17. G. Rätsch, T. Onoda, and K.-R. Müller. Soft margins for AdaBoost. *Machine Learning*, 42(3):287–320, March 2001. also NeuroCOLT Technical Report NC-TR-1998-021. 336, 340, 346
18. R.E. Schapire. *The Design and Analysis of Efficient Learning Algorithms*. PhD thesis, MIT Press, 1992. 334, 335, 336
19. R.E. Schapire, Y. Freund, P.L. Bartlett, and W. S. Lee. Boosting the margin: A new explanation for the effectiveness of voting methods. *Annals of Statistics*, 26(5):1651 ff., 1998. 335, 340, 347

20. R.E. Schapire and Y. Singer. Improved boosting algorithms using confidence-rated predictions. *Machine Learning*, 37(3):297–336, December 1999. also Proceedings of the 14th Workshop on Computational Learning Theory 1998, pages 80–91. 340
21. L.G. Valiant. A theory of the learnable. *Comm. of the ACM*, 27(11):1134–1142, 1984. 336
22. J. von Neumann. Zur Theorie der Gesellschaftsspiele. *Math. Ann.*, 100:295–320, 1928. 339
23. T. Zhang. Sequential greedy approximation for certain convex optimization problems. Technical report, IBM T.J. Watson Research Center, 2002. 336

Performance Guarantees
for Hierarchical Clustering

Sanjoy Dasgupta

University of California, Berkeley
dasgupta@cs.berkeley.edu

Abstract. We show that for any data set in any metric space, it is
possible to construct a hierarchical clustering with the guarantee that
for *every* k, the induced k-clustering has cost at most eight times that of
the optimal k-clustering. Here the cost of a clustering is taken to be the
maximum radius of its clusters. Our algorithm is similar in simplicity
and efficiency to common heuristics for hierarchical clustering, and we
show that these heuristics have poorer approximation factors.

1 Introduction

A *hierarchical clustering* of n data points is a recursive partitioning of the data
into $2, 3, 4, \ldots$ and finally n, clusters. Each intermediate clustering is made more
fine-grained by dividing one of its clusters. Figure 1 shows one possible hierarchical clustering of a five-point data set.

Such hierarchical representations of data have long been a staple of biologists
and social scientists, and since the sixties or seventies they have been a standard
part of the statistician's toolbox. They require no prior specification of the number of clusters, they permit the data to be understood simultaneously at many
levels of granularity, and there are some very simple greedy heuristics which can
be used to construct them.

The wide popularity of this kind of data analysis has fueled, and been re-
inforced by, a large body of theoretical work (e.g., Hartigan, 1985, and the references therein). However, there is still a fundamental and nontrivial existence
question which needs to be addressed: must there always exist a hierarchical

Fig. 1. A hierarchical clustering of five points

J. Kivinen and R. H. Sloan (Eds.): COLT 2002, LNAI 2375, pp. 351–363, 2002.

clustering in which, for *every* k, the induced k-clustering (grouping into k clusters) is close to the optimal k-clustering under some reasonable cost function? After all, it could be that the optimal cost-based k-clustering cannot be obtained by merging clusters of the optimal $(k + 1)$-clustering, and that in fact the two are so far removed that they cannot be reconciled even approximately into a hierarchical structure. The conventional wisdom is that a hierarchical clustering cannot be optimal at *every* level, and this is true; however, we show that the story is quite different if approximate optimality is sufficient.

Theorem 1. *Take the cost of a clustering to be the largest radius of its clusters. Then, any data set in any metric space has a hierarchical clustering in which, for each k, the induced k-clustering has cost at most eight times that of the optimal k-clustering.*

We present an algorithm for constructing such a hierarchy which is similar in simplicity and efficiency to standard heuristics for hierarchical clustering. It is based upon the *farthest-first traversal* of a set of points, introduced by Hochbaum and Shmoys (1985) as an approximation algorithm for the closely-related k-*center* problem. Their use of this traversal for clustering is ingenious, and in fact just a cursory examination of its properties is necessary for their result. For hierarchical clustering, we examine it in far greater detail and need to built upon it. Specifically, the farthest-first traversal of n data points yields a sequence of "centers" $\mu_1, \ldots, \mu_n$ such that for any k, the first k of these centers define a k-clustering which is within a factor two of optimal. However, the n clusterings created in this way are not hierarchical. Our main contribution is to demonstrate a simple and elegant way of using the information found by the traversal to create a hierarchical clustering. The approximation factor we achieve might not be optimal; however, it is possible to construct cases showing that a factor of at least two is inevitable.

Unlike our algorithm, common heuristics for hierarchical clustering work *bottom-up*, starting with a separate cluster for each point, and then progressively merging the two "closest" clusters until only a single cluster remains. The different schemes are distinguished by their notion of closeness. In *single-linkage* clustering, the distance between two clusters is the distance between their closest pair of points. In *complete-linkage* clustering, it is the distance between their farthest pair of points (and thus complete-linkage is explicitly trying to minimize our cost function). *Average-linkage* has many variants; in the one we consider, the distance between clusters is the distance between their means (Hartigan, 1985; Eisen *et al.*, 1998).

We analyze the worst-case behavior of these three heuristics, and find that their approximation ratios are unbounded.

Theorem 2. *For any k, single-linkage can produce induced k-clusterings which are a multiplicative factor k from optimal, while average- and complete-linkage can be off by a multiplicative factor of $\log_2 k$.*

The problems of single-linkage clustering are already well understood by statisticians; our lower bound on its performance can be seen as a convenient quantification of this common knowledge. On the other hand, our bad cases for the other two heuristics yield new insights into their behavior.

For an illustrative application of hierarchical clustering, the reader is directed to recent analyses of gene expression data (for instance, Alizadeh *et al.*, 2000, and Eisen *et al.*, 1998). These high-dimensional data sets contain well-separated groups at various levels of detail, and the use of hierarchical clustering allows the data, and the cluster information, to be displayed with stunning clarity.

2   Some Background on Clustering

2.1   Approximation Algorithms for Clustering

The most widely-used clustering algorithms – k-means, EM, and (hierarchical) agglomerative clustering – have received almost no attention from theoretical computer scientists. Some exceptions include work by Kearns, Mansour, and Ng (1997), and by Dasgupta and Schulman (2000). On the other hand, there has been a lot of theoretical work on the k-center and k-medians problems. In either case, the input consists of points in Euclidean space (or more generally, in a metric space) as well as a preordained number of clusters k, and the goal is to find a partition of the points into clusters $C_1, \ldots, C_k$, and also cluster centers $\mu_1, \ldots, \mu_k$, so as to minimize some cost function which is related to the radius of the clusters.

(a) *(geometric) k-center*: Maximum radius of clusters

$$\max_j \ \max_{x \in C_j} \ \|x - \mu_j\|$$

(b) *(geometric) k-medians*: Average radius of clusters

$$\sum_j \sum_{x \in C_j} \|x - \mu_j\|$$

Both problems are NP-hard but have simple constant-factor approximation algorithms. For k-center, a 2-approximation was found by González (1985) and by Hochbaum and Shmoys (1985), and this is the best approximation factor possible (Feder and Green, 1985). For k-medians there has been a series of results, of which the most recent (Charikar and Guha, 1999) achieves an approximation ratio of eight on this geometric version of the problem.

What does a constant-factor approximation mean for a clustering problem? Consider the scenario of Figure 2. The solid lines show the real clusters, and the three dots represent the centers of a bad 3-clustering whose cost (in either measure) exceeds that of the true solution by a factor of at least ten. This clustering would therefore not be returned by the approximation algorithms we mentioned. However, EM and k-means regularly fall into local optima of this kind, and practitioners have to take great pains to try to avoid them. In this sense, constant-factor approximations avoid the worst, and might provide good starting points for local search procedures (like EM) which can then fine-tune the solution.

Fig. 2. The circles represent an optimal 3-clustering; all the data points lie within them. The dots are centers of a really bad clustering

2.2   Previous Work on Hierarchical Clustering

There has been a lot of work on hierarchical clustering in the theoretical statistics community, and we will describe just one typical kind of analysis (Hartigan, 1975). Fix some underlying distribution P, and from it define some "natural" hierarchical clustering T (based, say, on level sets of P). Also fix an algorithm, and let the random variable T_n denote the hierarchical clustering returned by this algorithm when it is given as input n i.i.d. points from P. Is it true that as n approaches infinity, T_n approaches T almost surely? And if so, what is the variance of this estimator, asymptotically?

3   An Approximation Algorithm for Hierarchical Clustering

3.1   Farthest-First Traversals

Hochbaum and Shmoys (1985) introduced the *farthest-first traversal* of a data set as an approximation algorithm for what is sometimes called the *k-center* problem, that of finding an optimal k-clustering under our cost function, maximum cluster radius. The idea is to pick any data point to start with, then choose the point furthest from it, then the point furthest from the first two (the distance of a point x from a set S is the usual $\min\{d(x, y) : y \in S\}$), and so on until k points are obtained. These points are taken as cluster centers and each remaining point is assigned to the closest center. If the distance function is a metric, the resulting clustering is within a factor two of optimal. For hierarchical clustering, we will study the farthest-first traversal in detail, and will need to build upon it.

Starting with n points in a metric space, number the points in it using a farthest-first traversal (Figure 3). For any point i, describe its closest neighbor among $1, 2, \ldots, i-1$ as its *parent*, $\pi(i)$. Let R_i be its distance to this parent,

$$R_i = d(i, \pi(i)) = d(i, \{1, 2, \ldots, i-1\}).$$

The Hochbaum-Shmoys algorithm uses points $1, 2, \ldots, k$ as centers for a k-clustering. Let $\mathbb{C}_k$ be this clustering.

We begin by showing that the distances R_i are decreasing, and that the cost of each k-clustering $\mathbb{C}_k$ is exactly R_{k+1}.

Lemma 1. *Adopt the convention that $R_1 = \infty$ and $R_{n+1} = 0$.*

Input: n data points with a distance *metric* $d(\cdot, \cdot)$.

> Pick a point and label it 1.
> For $i = 2, 3, \ldots, n$
>> Find the unlabeled point furthest from $\{1, 2, \ldots, i-1\}$, and label it i. Use the standard notion of distance from a point to a set: $d(x, S) = \min_{y \in S} d(x, y)$.
>> Let $\pi(i) = \arg\min_{j < i} d(i, j)$.
>> Let $R_i = d(i, \pi(i))$.

Fig. 3. Farthest-first traversal of a data set

(1) For all i, $\pi(i) < i$.
(2) $R_1 \geq R_2 \geq R_3 \geq \cdots \geq R_n$.
(3) For all k, $cost(\mathbb{C}_k) = R_{k+1}$.

Proof. By the manner in which any point i is chosen, we know that for all $j > i$,

$$
\begin{aligned}
R_j &= d(j, \pi(j)) \\
&= d(j, \{1, 2, \ldots, j-1\}) \\
&\leq d(j, \{1, 2, \ldots, i-1\}) \\
&\leq d(i, \{1, 2, \ldots, i-1\}) \\
&= R_i.
\end{aligned}
$$

This immediately gives us (2). To see (3), notice that for all $i > k$,

$$
d(i, \{1, 2, \ldots, k\}) \leq d(k+1, \{1, 2, \ldots, k\}) = R_{k+1}.
$$

$\square$

For easy reference, and to illustrate our notation, we repeat here the result of Hochbaum and Shmoys.

Lemma 2 (Hochbaum-Shmoys). *For any k,*

$$
cost(\mathbb{C}_k) \leq 2 \cdot cost(\text{optimal } k\text{-clustering}).
$$

Proof. Let $S_1, \ldots, S_k$ denote the clusters of the optimal k-clustering. Suppose one of these clusters contains two or more of the points $\{1, 2, \ldots, k\}$. These points are at distance at least R_k from each other. Therefore the clusters must have radius at least $\frac{1}{2} R_k \geq \frac{1}{2} R_{k+1} = \frac{1}{2} cost(\mathbb{C}_k)$.

On the other hand, if each optimal cluster S_j contains exactly one of the points $\{1, 2, \ldots, k\}$, then (for any j) every point in S_j is within $2 \cdot \text{radius}(S_j)$ of $\{1, 2, \ldots, k\}$. Therefore

$$
cost(\mathbb{C}_k) = R_{k+1} = d(k+1, \{1, 2, \ldots, k\}) \leq 2 \cdot \max_j \text{radius}(S_j),
$$

and again we're done.

$\square$

3.2   Constructing a Hierarchical Clustering

The Hochbaum-Shmoys result gives us an ordering of the points such that for any k, the first k points constitute the centers of a near-optimal k-clustering $\mathbb{C}_k$. Unfortunately, the n clusterings defined in this manner are not hierarchical.

We will stick with the same choice of centers, but we will no longer be able to assign each remaining point to the closest center. As a first try at a hierarchical clustering,

- construct a tree T^π on nodes $\{1, 2, \ldots, n\}$, rooted at 1, and with an edge between each point i and its parent $\pi(i)$ (see Figure 4 for an example); and
- for any k, let $\mathbb{C}_k^\pi$ be the clustering with centers $1, 2, \ldots, k$, in which each remaining point is associated with the center which is its closest ancestor in T^π.

These clusterings $\{\mathbb{C}_1^\pi, \mathbb{C}_2^\pi, \ldots, \mathbb{C}_n^\pi\}$ *are* hierarchical; the $(k+1)$-clustering $\mathbb{C}_{k+1}^\pi$ is obtained from the k-clustering $\mathbb{C}_k^\pi$ by splitting the cluster centered at point $\pi(k+1)$. However, if the tree T^π is very deep (taking distances into account), then the cost of an induced k-clustering could be a lot larger than $\mathrm{cost}(\mathbb{C}_k)$. We therefore need to shrink the tree somehow. We will do so by adjusting the parent function $\pi(\cdot)$ to get a $\pi'(\cdot)$ for which $\mathrm{cost}(\mathbb{C}_k^{\pi'}) \leq 4\mathrm{cost}(\mathbb{C}_k)$.

The parent function $\pi(\cdot)$ has two salient properties:

- $\pi(i) < i$; and
- $d(i, \pi(i)) = d(i, \{1, 2, \ldots, i-1\})$.

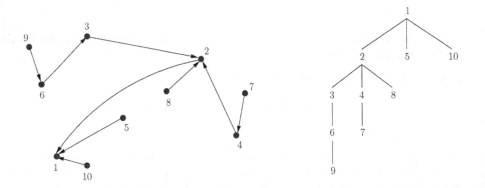

Fig. 4. A first try at a hierarchical clustering of ten points in $\mathbf{R}^2$, under the Euclidean metric. The graph on the left has been numbered by a farthest-first traversal, and has an edge from each point i to its parent $\pi(i)$. The tree on the right is T^π. The numbering and the tree are completely determined by the choice of point number one (and by the method of breaking any ties that arise)

Input: n data points with a distance metric $d(\cdot, \cdot)$.

By a farthest-first traversal, number the points and obtain parent function $\pi(\cdot)$.
For each $i = 2, 3, \ldots, n$
$\qquad \pi'(i) = \min\{j < i : d(i, j) \le 2 \cdot d(i, \pi(i))\}.$
Return the hierarchical clustering corresponding to tree $T^{\pi'}$.

Fig. 5. A hierarchical clustering procedure

We will now consider parent functions π' in which the second property is relaxed somewhat. We will require only that

$$d(i, \pi'(i)) \;\le\; 2 \cdot d(i, \{1, 2, \ldots, i-1\})$$

and this will enable us to shrink the tree. The resulting hierarchical clustering algorithm is shown in Figure 5, and its effect on our earlier example is shown in Figure 6.

3.3   A Performance Guarantee

We now show a strong guarantee for the hierarchical clustering induced by π'. To this end, fix any k, and define the sequence $k_0, k_1, k_2, \ldots, k_J$ by

- $k_0 = k + 1$
- if $R_{k_j} > 0$ then $k_{j+1} = \min\{i : R_i < \frac{1}{2} R_{k_j}\}$ (note $k_{j+1} > k_j$);
  $\qquad$ otherwise end the sequence, that is, $J = j$.

For the last element k_J we know $R_{k_J} = 0$; recall our convention that $R_{n+1} = 0$. The sequence definition ensures that R_{k_j} decreases geometrically (or faster).

Lemma 3. *For the sequence k_j defined above,*

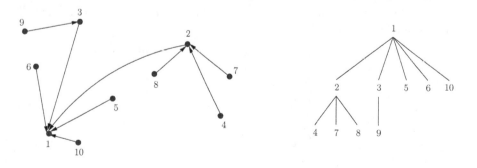

Fig. 6. A continuation of the example of Figure 4. On the left is the new parent function π'; on the right, the new tree $T^{\pi'}$, which defines the final hierarchical clustering

(1) If $k_j \le i < k_{j+1}$, then

$$R_{k_j} \ge R_i \ge \tfrac{1}{2} R_{k_j} > R_{k_{j+1}}.$$

(2) $R_{k_j} < R_{k_0} \cdot \frac{1}{2^j}$.

We will next see that for any point i in the interval $[k_j, k_{j+1})$, its new parent $\pi'(i)$ must lie in $[1, k_j)$. Therefore, tree $T^{\pi'}$ has height at most J.

Lemma 4. *For any i in the range $k_j \le i < k_{j+1}$, we have*

1. $\pi'(i) < k_j$, *and*
2. $d(i, \pi'(i)) \le 2R_{k_j}$.

Proof. Let's start with (1). Pick such an i; then
   (i) In the farthest-first traversal, since $i \ge k_j$, we know

$$d(i, \{1, 2, \ldots, k_j - 1\}) \; \le \; d(k_j, \{1, 2, \ldots, k_j - 1\}) \; = \; R_{k_j}.$$

   (ii) As observed in Lemma 3, $R_{k_j} \le 2R_i = 2d(i, \pi(i))$.
Combining these two gives

$$d(i, \{1, 2, \ldots, k_j - 1\}) \le 2d(i, \pi(i)),$$

whereupon $\pi'(i) < k_j$.
   Now for (2): $d(i, \pi'(i)) \le 2d(i, \pi(i)) = 2R_i \le 2R_{k_j}$.   □

Lemma 5. *If $d(\cdot, \cdot)$ is a metric, then the cost of the k-clustering induced by π' is at most four times that of $\mathbb{C}_k$,*

$$cost(\mathbb{C}_k^{\pi'}) \; \le \; 4\,cost(\mathbb{C}_k).$$

Proof. Pick any point x_0, and say it gets associated with center $i \le k$ in clustering $\mathbb{C}_k^{\pi'}$. That is, of the points $\{1, 2, \ldots, k\}$, i is the closest ancestor of x_0 in $T^{\pi'}$. Consider the path in this tree which ascends from x_0 to i:

$$x_0 - x_1 - \cdots - x_{l-1} - x_l = i,$$

where each $x_j = \pi'(x_{j-1})$, and $x_0 > x_1 > \cdots > x_{l-1} > k$. By the previous lemma, these points $x_0, \ldots, x_{l-1}$ touch each interval $[k_j, k_{j+1})$ at most once, and for any x in such an interval, $d(x, \pi'(x)) \le 2R_{k_j}$. Therefore, since $d(\cdot, \cdot)$ obeys the triangle inequality,

$$d(x_0, i) \le d(x_0, x_1) + d(x_1, x_2) + \cdots + d(x_{l-1}, x_l)$$

$$\le \sum_{j=0}^{\infty} 2R_{k_j}$$

$$\le \sum_{j=0}^{\infty} 2R_{k_0} \cdot \frac{1}{2^j}$$

$$= 4R_{k_0} \; = \; 4R_{k+1}.$$

where the third step uses Lemma 3. We finish up the proof with $R_{k+1} = cost(\mathbb{C}_k)$ (Lemma 1).   □

This holds for all k; with Lemma 2 we can then clinch Theorem 1.

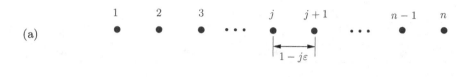

Fig. 7. (a) Data points on a line. (b) The k-clustering induced by a single-linkage heuristic

4 Worst-Case Performance of Standard Agglomerative Clustering Heuristics

4.1 Single Linkage

Single-linkage clustering has a performance ratio of at least k for intermediate k-clusterings, even in the simple case when the data points lie on a line. This particular kind of bad behavior is known to statisticians as "chaining" (Hartigan, 1985).

Consider the set of points shown in Figure 7(a). Let the distance between any two adjacent points j and $j + 1$ be $1 - j\varepsilon$, for some tiny $\varepsilon > 0$. Then the intermediate k-clustering found by single linkage is as shown in the bottom half of the figure. It consists of one large cluster containing $n - k + 1$ points, and $k - 1$ singleton clusters. The diameter of the big cluster can be made arbitrarily close to $n - k$ by setting ε small enough. On the other hand, the optimal k-clustering has clusters of diameter at most $\lceil \frac{n}{k} \rceil - 1$, for vanishingly small ε. Therefore the approximation ratio is at least k.

4.2 Average Linkage

The average-linkage heuristic can create intermediate k-clusterings of cost $\log k$ times optimal. Fix any k which is a power of two. Our bad example in this case involves points in $(\log k)$-dimensional space under an L_1 metric. Again we will make use of a tiny constant $\varepsilon > 0$.

- For $j = 1, 2, \ldots, \log k$, define $B_j = (1 - \varepsilon j) \cdot \{-1, +1\} = \{-(1 - \varepsilon j), +(1 - \varepsilon j)\}$.
- Let $S = B_1 \times B_2 \times \cdots \times B_{\log k}$ be the set of vertices of a $(\log k)$-dimensional cube whose side lengths are just slightly less than two.
- Arbitrarily label the points of S as $x_1, \ldots, x_k$. Now define points $S' = \{x'_1, \ldots, x'_k\}$ as follows. For $j = 1, 2, \ldots, k$,
  - if x_j has a positive first coordinate, then let x'_j be identical to x_j, but with first coordinate $+3 + j \cdot 2\varepsilon \log k$;

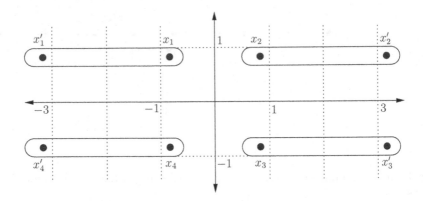

Fig. 8. A two-dimensional bad case for average-linkage clustering. The optimal 4-clustering is shown, and has clusters of diameter ≈ 2. Average-linkage will put the central four points together; these have diameter ≈ 4. By increasing the dimension to $\log k$, we find that average-linkage can return k-clusterings whose component clusters have diameter $\log k$ times optimal

- if x_j has a negative first coordinate, then let x'_j be identical to x_j, but with first coordinate $-3 - j \cdot 2\varepsilon \log k$.
  - The data set so far consists of $S \cup S'$, a total of $2k$ points. Duplicate points as necessary to get the count up to n. Figure 8 shows this data set for $k = 4$.

Lemma 6. *For the data set just defined, under the L_1 metric,*

(1) The distance between any two distinct points of S' is at least two.
(2) The distance from any point in S' to $[-1, +1]^{\log k}$ is more than two.
(3) Any two points in S which disagree on the jth coordinate have distance at least $2(1 - \varepsilon j)$ between them.

Proof.

(1) Pick distinct $x'_a, x'_b \in S'$. If x_a, x_b disagree on the first coordinate then x'_a, x'_b differ by at least six on the first coordinate. If x_a, x_b differ on the jth coordinate, then x'_a, x'_b differ by at least $2\varepsilon \log k$ on the first coordinate, and by $2(1 - \varepsilon j)$ on the jth coordinate, giving a total of at least two.
(2) This can be seen by considering the first coordinate alone.   □

The closest pairs of points (once duplicates get merged) are therefore those pairs in S which disagree only on the last coordinate. The distance between such pairs is $2(1 - \varepsilon \log k)$. They get merged, and in this way S is reduced to just $k/2$ clusters, with means $B_1 \times B_2 \times \cdots \times B_{\log k - 1} \times \{0\}$. Continuing in this way, eventually all the points in S get merged into one cluster centered at the origin, while the points of S' remain untouched. During this phase, clusters getting merged always have means which are within distance two of each other, and which lie in $[-1, +1]^{\log k}$.

The k-clustering therefore includes a large cluster containing all of S. The diameter of the cluster is at least the diameter of S, namely $2 \log k - \varepsilon \log k - \varepsilon \log^2 k$.

There is a better k-clustering: $\{x_1, x_1'\}, \{x_2, x_2'\}, \ldots, \{x_k, x_k'\}$. These clusters have diameter at most $2 + 2\varepsilon k \log k + \varepsilon \log k$. Letting ε go to zero, we get an approximation ratio of $\log k$.

4.3 Complete Linkage

Our negative result for complete linkage requires an unusual (non-L_p) metric. The data lie in $\mathbf{R} \times \mathbf{R}$, and the distance between two points (x, y) and (x', y') is defined as

$$d((x, y), (x', y')) = 1(x \neq x') + \log_2(1 + |y - y'|).$$

It can quickly be confirmed that this is a metric.

Assume k is a power of two for convenience. The data set consists of k clusters $S_1, S_2, \ldots, S_k$, each with k points (points can be duplicated to get the total up to n). Within each cluster, all points have the same y-coordinate, and have x-coordinates (say) $\{1, 2, \ldots, k\}$ (it doesn't matter what they are, as long as they are the same across clusters). Therefore the clusters all have diameter one. The y-spacing between clusters is shown in Figure 9 for the case $k = 4$. The y-distance between S_j and S_{j+1} is $1 - \varepsilon(\log_2 k - q)$, where 2^q is the largest power of two dividing j.

This example is set up so that the k-clustering found by complete linkage will have clusters which (each) touch every S_j, and which therefore have diameter $\log_2 k$, as ε goes to zero.

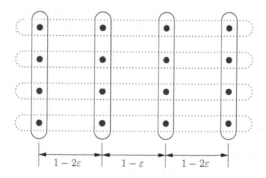

Fig. 9. A bad case for complete-linkage clustering. The norm here is unusual; see the definition. The optimal 4-clustering is shown in bold and the 4-clustering found by complete-linkage is delineated by dots

5   Practical Issues and Open Questions

5.1   Small Values of k

It is often sufficient to guarantee good k-clusterings just for small values of k, say in the hundreds or so. Therefore it would be quite heartening if it turned out that our $\Omega(\log k)$ lower bound on the approximation ratio of average- and complete-linkage were actually an upper bound as well.

5.2   Other Cost Functions

Can similar performance guarantees be obtained under other commonly-used cost functions, for instance that of k-means (average squared distance to nearest cluster center) or k-medians (average distance to nearest cluster center)?

5.3   Efficiency

Can our algorithm, or any of the standard heuristics we have considered, be implemented in $o(n^2)$ time for data sets of size n? Results of Borodin et al. (1999) and Thorup (2001) offer some hope here.

Acknowledgements

The author thanks Phil Long for suggesting this problem.

References

1. Alizadeh, A. A., et al. (2000) Distinct types of diffuse large B-cell lymphoma identified by gene expression profiling. *Nature*, 403:503-511.
2. Borodin, A., Ostrovsky, R., & Rabani Y. (1999) Subquadratic approximation algorithms for clustering problems in high dimensional spaces. *ACM Symposium on Theory of Computing*.
3. Charikar, M. & Guha, S. (1999) Improved combinatorial algorithms for facility location and k-median problems. *IEEE Foundations of Computer Science*.
4. Dasgupta, S. & Schulman, L. J. (2000) A two-round variant of EM for Gaussian mixtures. *Uncertainty in Artificial Intelligence*.
5. Eisen, M. B., Spellman, P. T., Brown, P. O., & Botstein, D. (1998) Cluster analysis and display of genome-wide expression patterns. *Proceedings of the National Academy of Sciences*, 95:14863-14868.
6. Feder, T. & Greene, D. (1988) Optimal algorithms for approximate clustering. *ACM Symposium on Theory of Computing*.
7. González, T. F. (1985) Clustering to minimize the maximum intercluster distance. *Theoretical Computer Science*, 38:293-306.
8. Hartigan, J. A. (1985) Statistical theory in clustering. *Journal of Classification*, 2:63-76.
9. Hochbaum, D. & Shmoys, D. (1985) A best possible heuristic for the k-center problem. *Mathematics of Operations Research*, 10(2):180-184.

10. Kearns, M., Mansour, Y. & Ng, A. (1997) An information-theoretic analysis of hard and soft assignment methods for clustering. *Uncertainty in Artificial Intelligence.*
11. Thorup, M. (2001) Quick k-median, k-center, and facility location for sparse graphs. *International Colloquium on Automata, Languages, and Programming.*

Self-Optimizing and Pareto-Optimal Policies in General Environments Based on Bayes-Mixtures

Marcus Hutter

IDSIA, Galleria 2, CH-6928 Manno-Lugano, Switzerland *
marcus@idsia.ch
http://www.idsia.ch/~marcus

Abstract. The problem of making sequential decisions in unknown probabilistic environments is studied. In cycle t action y_t results in perception x_t and reward r_t, where all quantities in general may depend on the complete history. The perception x_t and reward r_t are sampled from the (reactive) environmental probability distribution μ. This very general setting includes, but is not limited to, (partial observable, k-th order) Markov decision processes. Sequential decision theory tells us how to act in order to maximize the total expected reward, called value, if μ is known. Reinforcement learning is usually used if μ is unknown. In the Bayesian approach one defines a mixture distribution ξ as a weighted sum of distributions $\nu \in \mathcal{M}$, where $\mathcal{M}$ is any class of distributions including the true environment μ. We show that the Bayes-optimal policy p^ξ based on the mixture ξ is self-optimizing in the sense that the average value converges asymptotically for all $\mu \in \mathcal{M}$ to the optimal value achieved by the (infeasible) Bayes-optimal policy p^μ which knows μ in advance. We show that the necessary condition that $\mathcal{M}$ admits self-optimizing policies at all, is also sufficient. No other structural assumptions are made on $\mathcal{M}$. As an example application, we discuss ergodic Markov decision processes, which allow for self-optimizing policies. Furthermore, we show that p^ξ is Pareto-optimal in the sense that there is no other policy yielding higher or equal value in *all* environments $\nu \in \mathcal{M}$ and a strictly higher value in at least one.

1 Introduction

Reinforcement Learning: There exists a well developed theory for reinforcement learning agents in known probabilistic environments (like Blackjack) called sequential decision theory [Bel57, Ber95]. The optimal agent is the one which maximizes the future expected reward sum. This setup also includes deterministic environments (like static mazes). Even adversarial environments (like Chess or Backgammon) may be seen as special cases in some sense [Hut00, ch.6] (the reverse is also true [BT00]). Sequential decision theory deals with a wide range of problems, and provides a general formal solution in the sense that it is mathematically rigorous and (uniquely) specifies the optimal solution (leaving aside

---

* This work was supported by SNF grant 2000-61847.00 to Jürgen Schmidhuber.

J. Kivinen and R. H. Sloan (Eds.): COLT 2002, LNAI 2375, pp. 364–379, 2002.

computational issues). The theory breaks down when the environment is unknown (like when driving a car in the real world). Reinforcement learning algorithms exist for unknown Markov decision processes (MDPs) with small state space, and for other restricted classes [KLM96, SB98, Ber95, KV86], but even in these cases their learning rate is usually far from optimum.

Performance Measures: In this work we are interested in general (probabilistic) environmental classes $\mathcal{M}$. We assume $\mathcal{M}$ is given, and that the true environment μ is in $\mathcal{M}$, but is otherwise unknown. The expected reward sum (value) V_μ^p when following policy p is of central interest. We are interested in policies $\tilde{p}$ which perform well (have high value) independent of what the true environment $\mu \in \mathcal{M}$ is. A natural demand from an optimal policy is that there is no other policy yielding higher or equal value in *all* environments $\nu \in \mathcal{M}$ and a strictly higher value in one $\nu \in \mathcal{M}$. We call such a property *Pareto-optimality*. The other quantity of interest is how close $V_\mu^{\tilde{p}}$ is to the value V_μ^* of the optimal (but infeasible) policy p^μ which knows μ in advance. We call a policy whose average value converges asymptotically for all $\mu \in \mathcal{M}$ to the optimal value V_μ^* if μ is the true environment, *self-optimizing*.

Main New Results for Bayes-Mixtures: We define the Bayes-mixture ξ as a weighted average of the environments $\nu \in \mathcal{M}$ and analyze the properties of the Bayes-optimal policy p^ξ which maximizes the mixture value V_ξ. One can show that not all environmental classes $\mathcal{M}$ admit self-optimizing policies. One way to proceed is to search for and prove weaker properties than self-optimizingness [Hut00]. Here we follow a different approach: Obviously, the least we must demand from $\mathcal{M}$ to have a chance of finding a self-optimizing policy is that there exists some self-optimizing policy $\tilde{p}$ at all. The main new result of this work is that this necessary condition is also sufficient for p^ξ to be self-optimizing. No other properties need to be imposed on $\mathcal{M}$. The other new result is that p^ξ is always Pareto-optimal, with no conditions at all imposed on $\mathcal{M}$.

Contents: Section 2 defines the model of agents acting in general probabilistic environments and defines the finite horizon value of a policy and the optimal value-maximizing policy. Furthermore, the mixture-distribution is introduced and the fundamental linearity and convexity properties of the mixture-values is stated. Section 3 defines and proves Pareto-optimality of p^ξ. The concept is refined to balanced Pareto-optimality, showing that a small increase of the value for some environments only leaves room for a small decrease in others. Section 4 shows that p^ξ is self-optimizing if $\mathcal{M}$ admits self-optimizing policies, and also gives the speed of convergence in the case of finite $\mathcal{M}$. The finite horizon model has several disadvantages. For this reason Section 5 defines the discounted (infinite horizon) future value function, and the corresponding optimal value-maximizing policy. Pareto-optimality and self-optimizingness of p^ξ are shown shown for this model. As an application we show in Section 6 that the class of ergodic MDPs admits self-optimizing policies w.r.t. the undiscounted model and w.r.t. the discounted model if the effective horizon tends to infinity. Together with the results from the previous sections this shows that p^ξ is self-optimizing for erdodic MDPs. Conclusions and outlook can be found in Section 7.

2 Rational Agents in Probabilistic Environments

The Agent Model: A very general framework for intelligent systems is that of rational agents [RN95]. In cycle k, an agent performs *action* $y_k \in \mathcal{Y}$ (output) which results in a *perception* or *observation* $x_k \in \mathcal{X}$ (input), followed by cycle $k+1$ and so on. We assume that the action and perception spaces $\mathcal{X}$ and $\mathcal{Y}$ are finite. We write $p(x_{<k}) = y_{1:k}$ to denote the output $y_{1:k} \equiv y_1 \dots y_k$ of the agents policy p on input $x_{<k} \equiv x_1 \dots x_{k-1}$ and similarly $q(y_{1:k}) = x_{1:k}$ for the environment q in the case of deterministic environments. We call policy p and environment q behaving in this way *chronological*. Note that policy and environment are allowed to depend on the complete history. We do not make any MDP or POMDP assumption here, and we don't talk about states of the environment, only about observations. In the more general case of a *probabilistic environment*, given the history $yx_{<k}y_k \equiv yx_1 \dots yx_{k-1}y_k \equiv y_1 x_1 \dots y_{k-1} x_{k-1} y_k$, the probability that the environment leads to perception x_k in cycle k is (by definition) $\rho(yx_{<k}\underline{yx}_k)$. The underlined argument $\underline{x}_k$ in ρ is a random variable and the other non-underlined arguments $yx_{<k}y_k$ represent conditions.[1] We call probability distributions like ρ *chronological*. Since value optimizing policies can always be chosen deterministic, there is no real need to generalize the setting to probabilistic policies. Arbitrarily we formalize Sections 3 and 4 in terms of deterministic policies and Section 5 in terms of probabilistic policies.

Value Functions and Optimal Policies: The goal of the agent is to maximize future *rewards*, which are provided by the environment through the inputs x_k. The inputs $x_k \equiv x'_k r_k$ are divided into a regular part x'_k and some (possibly empty or delayed) reward $r_k \in [0, r_{max}]$.[2] We use the abbreviation

$$\rho(yx_{<k}\underline{yx}_{k:m}) = \rho(yx_{<k}\underline{yx}_k) \cdot \rho(yx_{1:k}\underline{yx}_{k+1}) \cdot \dots \cdot \rho(yx_{<m}\underline{yx}_m), \tag{1}$$

which is essentially Bayes rules, and $\varepsilon = yx_{<1}$ for the empty string. The ρ-expected reward sum (value) of future cycles k to m with outputs $y_{k:m}$ generated by the agent's policy p, the optimal policy p^ρ which maximizes the value, its action y_k and the corresponding value can formally be defined as follows.

---

[1] The standard notation $\rho(x_k | yx_{<k}y_k)$ for conditional probabilities destroys the chronological order and would become quite confusing in later expressions.

[2] In the reinforcement learning literature when dealing with (PO)MDPs the reward is usually considered to be a function of the environmental state. The zero-assumption analogue here is that the reward r_k is some probabilistic function ρ' depending on the complete history. It is very convenient to integrate r_k into x_k and ρ' into ρ.

Definition 1 (Value function and optimal policy). *We define the value of policy p in environment ρ given history $y\!x_{<k}$, or shorter, the ρ-value of p given $y\!x_{<k}$, as*

$$V_{km}^{p\rho}(y\!x_{<k}) := \sum_{x_{k:m}} (r_k + \ldots + r_m)\rho(y\!x_{<k}\underline{y\!x}_{k:m})|_{y_{1:m}=p(x_{<m})}. \qquad (2)$$

m is the lifespan or initial horizon of the agent. The ρ-optimal policy p^ρ which maximizes the (total) value $V_\rho^p := V_{1m}^{p\rho}(\varepsilon)$ is

$$p^\rho := \arg\max_p V_\rho^p, \quad V_{km}^{*\rho}(y\!x_{<k}) := V_{km}^{p^\rho\rho}(y\!x_{<k}). \qquad (3)$$

Explicit expressions for the action y_k in cycle k of the ρ-optimal policy p^ρ and their value $V_{km}^{*\rho}(y\!x_{<k})$ are

$$y_k = \arg\max_{y_k}\sum_{x_k}\max_{y_{k+1}}\sum_{x_{k+1}}\ldots\max_{y_m}\sum_{x_m}(r_k+\ldots+r_m)\cdot\rho(y\!x_{<k}\underline{y\!x}_{k:m}), \qquad (4)$$

$$V_{km}^{*\rho}(y\!x_{<k}) = \max_{y_k}\sum_{x_k}\max_{y_{k+1}}\sum_{x_{k+1}}\ldots\max_{y_m}\sum_{x_m}(r_k+\ldots+r_m)\cdot\rho(y\!x_{<k}\underline{y\!x}_{k:m}). \qquad (5)$$

where $y\!x_{<k}$ is the actual history.

One can show [Hut00] that these definitions are consistent and correctly capture our intention. For instance, consider the expectimax expression (5): The best expected reward is obtained by averaging over possible perceptions x_i and by maximizing over the possible actions y_i. This has to be done in chronological order $y_k x_k \ldots y_m x_m$ to correctly incorporate the dependency of x_i and y_i on the history. Obviously

$$V_{km}^{*\rho}(y\!x_{<k}) \geq V_{km}^{p\rho}(y\!x_{<k}) \;\forall p, \quad \text{especially} \quad V_\rho^* \geq V_\rho^p \;\forall p. \qquad (6)$$

Known Environment μ: Let us now make a change in conventions and assume that μ is the true environment in which the agent operates and that we know μ (like in Blackjack).[3] Then, policy p^μ is optimal in the sense that no other policy for an agent leads to higher μ-expected reward. This setting includes as special cases deterministic environments, Markov decision processes (MDPs), and even adversarial environments for special choices of μ [Hut00]. There is no principle problem in determining the optimal action y_k as long as μ is known and computable and $\mathcal{X}$, $\mathcal{Y}$ and m are finite.

The Mixture Distribution ξ: Things drastically change if μ is unknown. For (parameterized) MDPs with small state (parameter) space, suboptimal reinforcement learning algorithms may be used to learn the unknown μ [KLM96, SB98],

---

[3] If the existence of true objective probabilities violates the philosophical attitude of the reader he may assume a deterministic environment μ.

[Ber95, KV86]. In the Bayesian approach the true probability distribution μ is not learned directly, but is replaced by a Bayes-mixture ξ. Let us assume that we know that the true environment μ is contained in some known set $\mathcal{M}$ of environments. For convenience we assume that $\mathcal{M}$ is finite or countable. The Bayes-mixture ξ is defined as

$$\xi(\underline{yx}_{1:m}) = \sum_{\nu \in \mathcal{M}} w_\nu \nu(\underline{yx}_{1:m}) \quad \text{with} \quad \sum_{\nu \in \mathcal{M}} w_\nu = 1, \quad w_\nu > 0 \quad \forall \nu \in \mathcal{M} \qquad (7)$$

The weights w_ν may be interpreted as the prior degree of belief that the true environment is ν. Then $\xi(\underline{yx}_{1:m})$ could be interpreted as the prior subjective belief probability in observing $x_{1:m}$, given actions $y_{1:m}$. It is, hence, natural to follow the policy p^ξ which maximizes V_ξ^p. If μ is the true environment the expected reward when following policy p^ξ will be $V_\mu^{p^\xi}$. The optimal (but infeasible) policy p^μ yields reward $V_\mu^{p^\mu} \equiv V_\mu^*$. It is now of interest (a) whether there are policies with uniformly larger value than $V_\mu^{p^\xi}$ and (b) how close $V_\mu^{p^\xi}$ is to V_μ^*. These are the main issues of the remainder of this work.

A Universal Choice of ξ and $\mathcal{M}$: One may also ask what the most general class $\mathcal{M}$ and weights w_ν could be. Without any prior knowledge we should include *all* environments in $\mathcal{M}$. In this generality this approach leads at best to negative results. More useful is the assumption that the environment possesses some structure, we just don't know which. From a computational point of view we can only unravel effective structures which are describable by (semi)computable probability distributions. So we may include *all* (semi)computable (semi)distributions in $\mathcal{M}$. Occam's razor tells us to assign high prior belief to simple environments. Using Kolmogorov's universal complexity measure $K(\nu)$ for environments ν one should set $w_\nu \sim 2^{-K(\nu)}$, where $K(\nu)$ is the length of the shortest program on a universal Turing machine computing ν. The resulting policy p^ξ has been developed and intensively discussed in [Hut00]. It is a unification of sequential decision theory [Bel57, Ber95] and Solomonoff's celebrated universal induction scheme [Sol78, LV97]. In the following we consider generic $\mathcal{M}$ and w_ν. The following property of V_ρ is crucial.

Theorem 1 (Linearity and convexity of V_ρ in ρ). V_ρ^p *is a linear function in ρ and V_ρ^* is a convex function in ρ in the sense that*

$$V_\xi^p = \sum_{\nu \in \mathcal{M}} w_\nu V_\nu^p \quad and \quad V_\xi^* \leq \sum_{\nu \in \mathcal{M}} w_\nu V_\nu^* \quad where \quad \xi(\underline{yx}_{1:m}) = \sum_{\nu \in \mathcal{M}} w_\nu \nu(\underline{yx}_{1:m})$$

Proof: Linearity is obvious from the definition of V_ρ^p. Convexity follows from $V_\xi^* \equiv V_\xi^{p^\xi} = \sum_\nu w_\nu V_\nu^{p^\xi} \leq \sum_\nu w_\nu V_\nu^*$, where the identity is definition (3), the equality uses linearity of $V_\rho^{p^\xi}$ just proven, and the last inequality follows from the dominance (6) and non-negativity of the weights w_ν. $\square$

One loose interpretation of the convexity is that a mixture can never increase performance. In the remainder of this work μ denotes the true environment, ρ any distribution, and ξ the Bayes-mixture of distributions $\nu \in \mathcal{M}$.

3   Pareto Optimality of Policy p^ξ

The total μ-expected reward $V_\mu^{p^\xi}$ of policy p^ξ is of central interest in judging the performance of policy p^ξ. We know that there *are* policies (e.g. p^μ) with higher μ-value ($V_\mu^* \geq V_\mu^{p^\xi}$). In general, every policy based on an estimate ρ of μ which is closer to μ than ξ is, outperforms p^ξ in environment μ, simply because it is more taylored toward μ. On the other hand, such a system probably performs worse than p^ξ in other environments. Since we do not know μ in advance we may ask whether there exists a policy p with better or equal performance than p^ξ in *all* environments $\nu \in \mathcal{M}$ and a strictly better performance for one $\nu \in \mathcal{M}$. This would clearly render p^ξ suboptimal. We show that there is no such p.

Theorem 2 (Pareto optimality). *Policy p^ξ is Pareto-optimal in the sense that there is no other policy p with $V_\nu^p \geq V_\nu^{p^\xi}$ for all $\nu \in \mathcal{M}$ and strict inequality for at least one ν.*

Proof: We want to arrive at a contradiction by assuming that p^ξ is not Pareto-optimal, i.e. by assuming the existence of a policy p with $V_\nu^p \geq V_\nu^{p^\xi}$ for all $\nu \in \mathcal{M}$ and strict inequality for at least one ν:

$$V_\xi^p = \sum_\nu w_\nu V_\nu^p > \sum_\nu w_\nu V_\nu^{p^\xi} = V_\xi^{p^\xi} \equiv V_\xi^* \geq V_\xi^p$$

The two equalities follow from linearity of V_ρ (Theorem 1). The strict inequality follows from the assumption and from $w_\nu > 0$. The identity is just Definition 1(3). The last inequality follows from the fact that p^ξ maximizes by definition the universal value (6). The contradiction $V_\xi^p > V_\xi^p$ proves Pareto-optimality of policy p^ξ.$\square$

Pareto-optimality should be regarded as a necessary condition for an agent aiming to be optimal. From a practical point of view a significant increase of V for many environments ν may be desirable even if this causes a small decrease of V for a few other ν. The impossibility of such a "balanced" improvement is a more demanding condition on p^ξ than pure Pareto-optimality. The next theorem shows that p^ξ is also balanced-Pareto-optimal in the following sense:

Theorem 3 (Balanced Pareto optimality).

$$\Delta_\nu := V_\nu^{p^\xi} - V_\nu^{\tilde{p}}, \quad \Delta := \sum_{\nu \in \mathcal{M}} w_\nu \Delta_\nu \quad \Rightarrow \quad \Delta \geq 0.$$

This implies the following: Assume $\tilde{p}$ has lower value than p^ξ on environments $\mathcal{L}$ by a total weighted amount of $\Delta_\mathcal{L} := \sum_{\lambda \in \mathcal{L}} w_\lambda \Delta_\lambda$. Then $\tilde{p}$ can have higher value on $\eta \in \mathcal{H} := \mathcal{M} \setminus \mathcal{L}$, but the improvement is bounded by $\Delta_\mathcal{H} := |\sum_{\eta \in \mathcal{H}} w_\eta \Delta_\eta| \leq \Delta_\mathcal{L}$. Especially $|\Delta_\eta| \leq w_\eta^{-1} \max_{\lambda \in \mathcal{L}} \Delta_\lambda$.

This means that a weighted value increase $\Delta_\mathcal{H}$ by using $\tilde{p}$ instead of p^ξ is compensated by an at least as large weighted decrease $\Delta_\mathcal{L}$ on other environments. If the decrease is small, the increase can also only be small. In the special case of only a single environment with decreased value Δ_λ, the increase is bound by $\Delta_\eta \leq \frac{w_\lambda}{w_\eta}|\Delta_\lambda|$, i.e. a decrease by an amount Δ_λ can only cause an increase by at most the same amount times a factor $\frac{w_\lambda}{w_\eta}$. For the choice of the weights $w_\nu \sim 2^{-K(\nu)}$, a decrease can only cause a smaller increase in simpler environments, but a scaled increase in more complex environments. Finally note that pure Pareto-optimality (Theorem 2) follows from balanced Pareto-optimality in the special case of no decrease $\Delta_\mathcal{L} \equiv 0$.

Proof: $\Delta \geq 0$ follows from $\Delta = \sum_\nu w_\nu [V_\nu^{p^\xi} - V_\nu^{\tilde{p}}] = V_\xi^{p^\xi} - V_\xi^{\tilde{p}} \geq 0$, where we have used linearity of V_ρ (Theorem 1) and dominance $V_\xi^{p^\xi} \geq V_\xi^p$ (6). The remainder of Theorem 3 is obvious from $0 \leq \Delta = \Delta_\mathcal{L} - \Delta_\mathcal{H}$ and by bounding the weighted average Δ_η by its maximum. $\square$

4   Self-Optimizing Policy p^ξ w.r.t. Average Value

In the following we study under which circumstances[4]

$$\tfrac{1}{m} V_{1m}^{p^\xi \nu} \to \tfrac{1}{m} V_{1m}^{*\nu} \quad \text{for} \quad m \to \infty \quad \text{for } all \quad \nu \in \mathcal{M}. \tag{8}$$

The least we must demand from $\mathcal{M}$ to have a chance that (8) is true is that there exists some policy $\tilde{p}$ at all with this property, i.e.

$$\exists \tilde{p} : \tfrac{1}{m} V_{1m}^{\tilde{p}\nu} \to \tfrac{1}{m} V_{1m}^{*\nu} \quad \text{for} \quad m \to \infty \quad \text{for } all \quad \nu \in \mathcal{M}. \tag{9}$$

Luckily, this necessary condition will also be sufficient. This is another (asymptotic) optimality property of policy p^ξ. *If* universal convergence in the sense of (9) is possible at all in a class of environments $\mathcal{M}$, then policy p^ξ converges in the sense of (8). We will call policies $\tilde{p}$ with a property like (9) *self-optimizing* [KV86]. The following two Lemmas pave the way for proving the convergence Theorem.

Lemma 1 (Value difference relation).

$$0 \leq V_\nu^* - V_\nu^{\tilde{p}} =: \Delta_\nu \quad \Rightarrow \quad 0 \leq V_\nu^* - V_\nu^{p^\xi} \leq \tfrac{1}{w_\nu}\Delta \quad with \quad \Delta := \sum_{\nu \in \mathcal{M}} w_\nu \Delta_\nu$$

Proof: The following sequence of inequalities proves the lemma:

$$0 \leq w_\nu[V_\nu^* - V_\nu^{p^\xi}] \leq \sum_\nu w_\nu[V_\nu^* - V_\nu^{p^\xi}] \leq \sum_\nu w_\nu[V_\nu^* - V_\nu^{\tilde{p}}] = \sum_\nu w_\nu \Delta_\nu \equiv \Delta$$

In the first and second inequality we used $w_\nu \geq 0$ and $V_\nu^* - V_\nu^{p^\xi} \geq 0$. The last inequality follows from $\sum_\nu w_\nu V_\nu^{p^\xi} = V_\xi^{p^\xi} \equiv V_\xi^* \geq V_\xi^{\tilde{p}} = \sum_\nu w_\nu V_\nu^{\tilde{p}}$. $\square$

We also need some results for averages of functions $\delta_\nu(m) \geq 0$ converging to zero.

---

[4] Here and elsewhere we interpret $a_m \to b_m$ as an abbreviation for $a_m - b_m \to 0$. $\lim_{m \to \infty} b_m$ may not exist.

Lemma 2 (Convergence of averages). *For $\delta(m) := \sum_{\nu \in \mathcal{M}} w_\nu \delta_\nu(m)$ the following holds (we only need $\sum_\nu w_\nu \leq 1$):*

> *i) $\delta_\nu(m) \leq f(m) \; \forall \nu$ implies $\delta(m) \leq f(m)$.*
>
> *ii) $\delta_\nu(m) \overset{m\to\infty}{\longrightarrow} 0 \; \forall \nu$ implies $\delta(m) \overset{m\to\infty}{\longrightarrow} 0 \;$ if $0 \leq \delta_\nu(m) \leq c$.*

Proof: (i) immediately follows from $\delta(m) = \sum_\nu w_\nu \delta_\nu(m) \leq \sum_\nu w_\nu f(m) \leq f(m)$. For (ii) we choose some order on $\mathcal{M}$ and some $\nu_0 \in \mathcal{M}$ large enough such that $\sum_{\nu \geq \nu_0} w_\nu \leq \frac{\varepsilon}{c}$. Using $\delta_\nu(m) \leq c$ this implies

$$\sum_{\nu \geq \nu_0} w_\nu \delta_\nu(m) \; \leq \; \sum_{\nu \geq \nu_0} w_\nu c \; \leq \; \varepsilon.$$

Furthermore, the assumption $\delta_\nu(m) \to 0$ means that there is an $m_{\nu\varepsilon}$ depending on ν and ε such that $\delta_\nu(m) \leq \varepsilon$ for all $m \geq m_{\nu\varepsilon}$. This implies

$$\sum_{\nu \leq \nu_0} w_\nu \delta_\nu(m) \; \leq \; \sum_{\nu \leq \nu_0} w_\nu \varepsilon \; \leq \; \varepsilon \quad \text{for all} \quad m \; \geq \; \max_{\nu \leq \nu_0}\{m_{\nu\varepsilon}\} \; =: m_\varepsilon.$$

$m_\varepsilon < \infty$, since the maximum is over a finite set. Together we have

$$\delta(m) \equiv \sum_{\nu \in \mathcal{M}} w_\nu \delta_\nu(m) \; \leq \; 2\varepsilon \quad \text{for} \quad m \geq m_\varepsilon \quad \Rightarrow \quad \delta(m) \to 0 \quad \text{for} \quad m \to \infty$$

since ε was arbitrary and $\delta(m) \geq 0$. $\square$

Theorem 4 (Self-optimizing policy p^ξ w.r.t. average value). *There exists a sequence of policies $\tilde{p}_m$, $m = 1,2,3,\ldots$ with value within $\Delta(m)$ to optimum for all environments $\nu \in \mathcal{M}$, then, save for a constant factor, this also holds for the sequence of universal policies p_m^ξ, i.e.*

> *i) If $\exists \tilde{p}_m \forall \nu : V_{1m}^{*\nu} - V_{1m}^{\tilde{p}_m \nu} \leq \Delta(m) \implies V_{1m}^{*\mu} - V_{1m}^{p_m^\xi \mu} \leq \frac{1}{w_\mu}\Delta(m)$.*

If there exists a sequence of self-optimizing policies $\tilde{p}_m$ in the sense that their expected average reward $\frac{1}{m}V_{1m}^{\tilde{p}_m \nu}$ converges to the optimal average $\frac{1}{m}V_{1m}^{*\nu}$ for all environments $\nu \in \mathcal{M}$, then this also holds for the sequence of universal policies p_m^ξ, i.e.

> *ii) If $\exists \tilde{p}_m \forall \nu : \frac{1}{m}V_{1m}^{\tilde{p}_m \nu} \overset{m\to\infty}{\longrightarrow} \frac{1}{m}V_{1m}^{*\nu} \implies \frac{1}{m}V_{1m}^{p_m^\xi \mu} \overset{m\to\infty}{\longrightarrow} \frac{1}{m}V_{1m}^{*\mu}$.*

The beauty of this theorem is that if universal convergence in the sense of (9) is possible at all in a class of environments $\mathcal{M}$, then policy p^ξ converges (in the sense of (8)). The necessary condition of convergence is also sufficient. The unattractive point is that this is not an asymptotic convergence statement for $V_{km}^{p^\xi \mu}$ of a single policy p^ξ for $k \to \infty$ for some fixed m, and in fact no such theorem could be true, since always $k \leq m$. The theorem merely says that under the stated conditions the average value of p_m^ξ can be arbitrarily close to optimum for sufficiently large (pre-chosen) horizon m. This weakness will be resolved in the next subsection.

Proof: (i) $\Delta_\nu(m) = f(m)$ implies $\Delta(m) = f(m)$ by Lemma $2(i)$. Inserting this in Lemma 1 proves Theorem $4(i)$ (recovering the m dependence and finally renaming $f \leadsto \Delta$).

(ii) We define $\delta_\nu(m) := \frac{1}{m}\Delta_\nu(m) = \frac{1}{m}[V_\nu^* - V_\nu^{\tilde{p}}]$. Since we assumed bounded rewards $0 \le r \le r_{max}$ we have

$$V_\nu^* \le m r_{max} \quad \text{and} \quad V_\nu^{\tilde{p}} \ge 0 \quad \Rightarrow \quad \Delta_\nu \le m r_{max} \quad \Rightarrow \quad 0 \le \delta_\nu(m) \le c := r_{max}.$$

The premise in Theorem $4(ii)$ is that $\delta_\nu(m) = \frac{1}{m}[V_{1m}^{*\nu} - V_{1m}^{\tilde{p}\nu}] \to 0$ which implies

$$0 \le \frac{1}{m}[V_{1m}^{*\nu} - V_{1m}^{p^\xi\nu}] \le \frac{1}{w_\nu}\frac{\Delta(m)}{m} = \frac{1}{w_\nu}\delta(m) \to 0.$$

The inequalities follow from Lemma 1 and convergence to zero from Lemma $2(ii)$. This proves Theorem $4(ii)$. $\square$

In Section 6 we show that a converging $\tilde{p}$ exists for ergodic MDPs, and hence p^ξ converges in this environmental class too (in the sense of Theorem 4).

5   Discounted Future Value Function

We now shift our focus from the total value V_{1m}, $m \to \infty$ to the future value (value-to-go) $V_{k?}$, $k \to \infty$. The main reason is that we want to get rid of the horizon parameter m. In the last subsection we have shown a convergence theorem for $m \to \infty$, but a specific policy p^ξ is defined for all times relative to a fixed horizon m. Current time k is moving, but m is fixed[5]. Actually, to use $k \to \infty$ arguments we *have* to get rid of m, since $k \le m$. This is the reason for the question mark in $V_{k?}$ above.

We eliminate the horizon by discounting the rewards $r_k \leadsto \gamma_k r_k$ with $\sum_{i=1}^\infty \gamma_i < \infty$ and letting $m \to \infty$. The analogue of m is now an effective horizon h_k^{eff} which may be defined by $\sum_{i=k}^{k+h_k^{eff}} \gamma_k \sim \sum_{i=k+h_k^{eff}}^\infty \gamma_k$. See [Hut00, Ch.4] for a detailed discussion of the horizon problem. Furthermore, we renormalize $V_{k\infty}$ by $\sum_{i=k}^\infty \gamma_i$ and denote it by $V_{k\gamma}$. It can be interpreted as a future expected weighted-average reward. Furthermore we extend the definition to probabilistic policies π.

Definition 2 (Discounted value function and optimal policy). *We define the γ discounted weighted-average future value of (probabilistic) policy π in environment ρ given history $y x_{<k}$, or shorter, the ρ-value of π given $y x_{<k}$, as*

$$V_{k\gamma}^{\pi\rho}(y x_{<k}) := \frac{1}{\Gamma_k}\lim_{m\to\infty}\sum_{y x_{k:m}}(\gamma_k r_k + \ldots + \gamma_m r_m)\rho(y x_{<k}\underline{y x}_{k:m})\pi(y x_{<k}\underline{y x}_{k:m})$$

with $\Gamma_k := \sum_{i=k}^\infty \gamma_i$. The policy p^ρ is defined as to maximize the future value $V_{k\gamma}^{\pi\rho}$:

$$p^\rho := \arg\max_\pi V_{k\gamma}^{\pi\rho}, \qquad V_{k\gamma}^{*\rho} := V_{k\gamma}^{p^\rho\rho} = \max_\pi V_{k\gamma}^{\pi\rho} \ge V_{k\gamma}^{\pi\rho} \forall \pi.$$

---

[5] A dynamic horizon like $m \leadsto m_k = k^2$ can lead to policies with very poor performance [Hut00, Ch.4].

Remarks:

- $\pi(y x_{<k} y x_{k:m})$ is actually independent of x_m, since π is chronological.
- Normalization of $V_{k\gamma}$ by Γ_k does not affect the policy p^ρ.
- The definition of p^ρ is independent of k.
- Without normalization by Γ_k the future values would converge to zero for $k \to \infty$ in every environment for every policy.
- For an MDP environment, a stationary policy, and geometric discounting $\gamma_k \sim \gamma^k$, the future value is independent of k and reduces to the well-known MDP value function.
- There is always a deterministic optimizing policy p^ρ (which we use).
- For a deterministic policy there is exactly one $y_{k:m}$ for each $x_{k:m}$ with $\pi \neq 0$. The sum over $y_{k:m}$ drops in this case.
- An iterative representation as in Definition 1 is possible.
- Setting $\gamma_k = 1$ for $k \leq m$ and $\gamma_k = 0$ for $k > m$ gives back the undiscounted model (1) with $V_{1\gamma}^{p\rho} = \frac{1}{m} V_{1m}^{p\rho}$.
- $V_{k\gamma}$ (and w_k^ν defined below) depend on the realized history $y x_{<k}$.

Similarly to the previous sections one can prove the following properties:

Theorem 5 (Linearity and convexity of V_ρ in ρ). $V_{k\gamma}^{\pi\rho}$ is a linear function in ρ and $V_{k\gamma}^{*\rho}$ is a convex function in ρ in the sense that

$$V_{k\gamma}^{\pi\xi} = \sum_{\nu \in \mathcal{M}} w_k^\nu V_{k\gamma}^{\pi\nu} \quad and \quad V_{k\gamma}^{*\xi} \leq \sum_{\nu \in \mathcal{M}} w_k^\nu V_{k\gamma}^{*\nu}$$

$$where \quad \xi(y x_{<k} y x_{k:m}) = \sum_{\nu \in \mathcal{M}} w_k^\nu \nu(y x_{<k} y x_{k:m}) \quad with \quad w_k^\nu := w_\nu \frac{\nu(y x_{<k})}{\xi(y x_{<k})}$$

The conditional representation of ξ can be proven by dividing the definition (7) of $\xi(y x_{1:m})$ by $\xi(y x_{<k})$ and by using Bayes rules (1). The posterior weight w_k^ν may be interpreted as the posterior belief in ν and is related to learning aspects of policy p^ξ.

Theorem 6 (Pareto optimality). *For every k and history $y x_{<k}$ the following holds: p^ξ is Pareto-optimal in the sense that there is no other policy π with $V_{k\gamma}^{\pi\nu} \geq V_{k\gamma}^{p^\xi\nu}$ for all $\nu \in \mathcal{M}$ and strict inequality for at least one ν.*

Lemma 3 (Value difference relation).

$$0 \leq V_{k\gamma}^{*\nu} - V_{k\gamma}^{\tilde{\pi}_k\nu} =: \Delta_k^\nu \quad \Rightarrow \quad 0 \leq V_{k\gamma}^{*\nu} - V_{k\gamma}^{p^\xi\nu} \leq \frac{1}{w_k^\nu} \Delta_k \quad with \quad \Delta_k := \sum_{\nu \in \mathcal{M}} w_k^\nu \Delta_k^\nu$$

The proof of Theorem 6 and Lemma 3 follows the same steps as for Theorem 2 and Lemma 1 with appropriate replacements. The proof of the analogue of the convergence Theorem 4 involves one additional step. We abbreviate "with μ probability 1" by w.μ.p.1.

Theorem 7 (Self-optimizing policy p^ξ w.r.t. discounted value). *For any* $\mathcal{M}$, *if there exists a sequence of self-optimizing policies* $\tilde{\pi}_k$ $k = 1,2,3,...$ *in the sense that their expected weighted-average reward* $V_{k\gamma}^{\tilde{\pi}_k\nu}$ *converges for* $k \to \infty$ *with* ν-*probability one to the optimal value* $V_{k\gamma}^{*\nu}$ *for all environments* $\nu \in \mathcal{M}$, *then this also holds for the universal policy* p^ξ *in the true* μ-*environment, i.e.*

$$\text{If } \exists\tilde{\pi}_k\forall\nu : V_{k\gamma}^{\tilde{\pi}_k\nu} \overset{k\to\infty}{\longrightarrow} V_{k\gamma}^{*\nu} \quad w.\nu.p.1 \quad \Longrightarrow \quad V_{k\gamma}^{p^\xi\mu} \overset{k\to\infty}{\longrightarrow} V_{k\gamma}^{*\mu} \quad w.\mu.p.1.$$

The probability qualifier refers to the historic perceptions $x_{<k}$. *The historic actions* $y_{<k}$ *are arbitrary.*

The conclusion is valid for action histories $y_{<k}$ if the condition is satisfied for this action history. Since we usually need the conclusion for the p^ξ-action history, which is hard to characterize, we usually need to prove the condition for *all* action histories. Theorem 7 is a powerful result: An (inconsistent) sequence of probabilistic policies $\tilde{\pi}_k$ suffices to prove the existence of a (consistent) deterministic policy p^ξ. A result similar to Theorem 4(i) also holds for the discounted case, roughly saying that $V^{\tilde{\pi}} - V^* = O(\Delta(k))$ implies $V^{p^\xi} - V^* = \frac{1}{\varepsilon}O(\Delta(k))$ with μ probability $1 - \varepsilon$ for finite $\mathcal{M}$.

Proof: We define $\delta_\nu(k) := \Delta_k^\nu = V_{k\gamma}^{*\nu} - V_{k\gamma}^{\tilde{\pi}\nu}$. Since we assumed bounded rewards $0 \le r \le r_{max}$ and $V_{k\gamma}^{*\nu}$ is a weighted average of rewards we have

$$V_{k\gamma}^{*\mu} \le r_{max} \quad \text{and} \quad V_{k\gamma}^{\tilde{\pi}\mu} \ge 0 \quad \Rightarrow \quad 0 \le \delta_\nu(k) = \Delta_k^\nu \le c := r_{max}.$$

The following inequalities follow from Lemma 3:

$$0 \le V_{k\gamma}^{*\mu} - V_{k\gamma}^{p^\xi\mu} \le \tfrac{1}{w_k^\mu}\Delta_k = \tfrac{1}{w_k^\mu}\delta(k) \overset{?}{\to} 0 \tag{10}$$

The premise in Theorem 7 is that $\delta_\nu(k) = V_{k\gamma}^{*\nu} - V_{k\gamma}^{\tilde{\pi}\nu} \to 0$ for $k \to \infty$ which implies $\delta(k) \to 0$ (w.μ.p.1) by Lemma 2(ii). What is new and what remains to be shown is that w_k^μ is bounded from below in order to have convergence of (10) to zero. We show that $z_{k-1} := \frac{w_\mu}{w_k^\mu} = \frac{\xi(y x_{<k})}{\mu(y x_{<k})} \ge 0$ converges to a finite value, which completes the proof. Let **E** denote the μ expectation. Then

$$\mathbf{E}[z_k|x_{<k}] = \sum_{x_k}{}' \mu(y x_{<k} y x_k) \frac{\xi(y x_{1:k})}{\mu(y x_{1:k})}$$

$$= \frac{\sum_{x_k}' \xi(y x_{<k} y x_k)\xi(y x_{<k})}{\mu(y x_{<k})} \le \frac{\xi(y x_{<k})}{\mu(y x_{<k})} = z_{k-1}$$

$\sum_{x_k}'$ runs over all x_k with $\mu(y x_{1:k}) \ne 0$. The first equality holds w.μ.p.1. In the second equality we have used Bayes rule twice. $\mathbf{E}[z_k|x_{<k}] \le z_{k-1}$ shows that $-z_k$ is a semi-martingale. Since $-z_k$ is non-positive, [Doo53, Th.4.1s(i),p324] implies that $-z_k$ converges for $k \to \infty$ to a finite value w.μ.p.1. $\qquad\square$

6   Markov Decision Processes

From all possible environments, Markov (decision) processes are probably the most intensively studied ones. To give an example, we apply Theorems 4 and 7 to ergodic Markov decision processes, but we will be very brief.

Definition 3 (Ergodic Markov Decision Processes). *We call μ a (stationary) Markov Decision Process (MDP) if the probability of observing $x_k \in \mathcal{X}$, given history $yx_{<k}y_k$ does only depend on the last action $y_k \in \mathcal{Y}$ and the last observation x_{k-1}, i.e. if $\mu(yx_{<k}y_k\underline{x}_k) = \mu(yx_{k-1}\underline{x}_k)$. In this case x_k is called a state, $\mathcal{X}$ the state space, and $\mu(yx_{k-1}\underline{x}_k)$ the transition matrix. An MDP μ is called ergodic if there exists a policy under which every state is visited infinitely often with probability 1. Let $\mathcal{M}_{MDP}$ be the set of MDPs and $\mathcal{M}_{MDP1}$ be the set of ergodic MDPs. If an MDP $\mu(yx_{k-1}\underline{x}_k)$ is independent of the action y_{k-1} it is a Markov process, if it is independent of the last observation x_{k-1} it is an i.i.d. process.*

Stationary MDPs μ have stationary optimal policies p^μ mapping the same state / observation x_t always to the same action y_t. On the other hand a mixture ξ of MDPs is itself not an MDP, i.e. $\xi \notin \mathcal{M}_{MDP}$, which implies that p^ξ is, in general, not a stationary policy. The definition of ergodicity given here is least demanding, since it only demands on the existence of a single policy under which the Markov process is ergodic. Often, stronger assumptions, e.g. that every policy is ergodic or that a stationary distribution exists, are made. We now show that there are self-optimizing policies for the class of ergodic MDPs in the following sense.

Theorem 8 (Self-optimizing policies for ergodic MDPs). *There exist self-optimizing policies $\tilde{p}_m$ for the class of ergodic MDPs in the sense that*

$$i) \quad \exists \tilde{p}_m \forall \nu \in \mathcal{M}_{MDP1} : \tfrac{1}{m}V_{1m}^{*\nu} - \tfrac{1}{m}V_{1m}^{\tilde{p}_m\nu} \leq c_\nu m^{-1/3} \stackrel{m\to\infty}{\longrightarrow} 0,$$

where c_ν are some constants. In the discounted case, if the discount sequence γ_k has unbounded effective horizon $h_k^{eff} \stackrel{k\to\infty}{\longrightarrow} \infty$, then there exist self-optimizing policies $\tilde{\pi}_k$ for the class of ergodic MDPs in the sense that

$$ii) \quad \exists \tilde{\pi}_k \forall \nu \in \mathcal{M}_{MDP1} : V_{k\gamma}^{\tilde{\pi}_k\nu} \stackrel{k\to\infty}{\longrightarrow} V_{k\gamma}^{*\nu} \quad if \ \tfrac{\gamma_{k+1}}{\gamma_k} \to 1.$$

There is much literature on constructing and analyzing self-optimizing learning algorithms in MDP environments. The assumptions on the structure of the MDPs vary, all include some form of ergodicity, often stronger than Definition 3, demanding that the Markov process is ergodic under *every* policy. See, for instance, [KV86, Ber95]. We will only briefly outline one algorithm satisfying Theorem 8 without trying to optimize performance.

Proof idea: For (i) one can choose a policy $\tilde{p}_m$ which performs (uniformly) random actions in cycles $1...k_0-1$ with $1 \ll k_0 \ll m$ and which follows thereafter the optimal policy based on an estimate of the transition matrix $T_{ss'}^a \equiv \nu(as\underline{s}')$ from the initial $k_0 - 1$ cycles. The existence of an ergodic policy implies that for every pair of states $s_{start}, s \in \mathcal{X}$ there is a sequence of actions and transitions of length at most $|\mathcal{X}| - 1$ such that state s is reached from state s_{start}. The probability that the "right" transition occurs is at least T_{min} with T_{min} being the smallest non-zero transition probability in T. The probability that a random action is the "right" action is at least $|\mathcal{Y}|^{-1}$. So the probability of reaching a state s in $|\mathcal{X}| - 1$ cycles via a random policy is at least $(T_{min}/|\mathcal{Y}|)^{|\mathcal{X}|-1}$. In state s action a is taken with probability $|\mathcal{Y}|^{-1}$ and leads to state s' with probability $T_{ss'}^a \geq T_{min}$. Hence, the expected number of transitions $s \xrightarrow{a} s'$ to occur in the first k_0 cycles is $\geq \frac{k_0}{|\mathcal{X}|}(T_{min}/|\mathcal{Y}|)^{|\mathcal{X}|} \sim k_0$.[6] The accuracy of the frequency estimate $\hat{T}_{ss'}^a$ of $T_{ss'}^a$ hence is $\sim k_0^{-1/2}$. Similar MDPs lead to "similar" optimal policies, which lead to similar values. More precisely, one can show that $\hat{T} - T \sim k_0^{-1/2}$ implies the same accuracy in the average value, i.e. $|\frac{1}{m}V_{k_0 m}^{\tilde{p}_m \nu} - \frac{1}{m}V_{k_0 m}^{*\nu}| \sim k_0^{-1/2}$, where $\tilde{p}_m$ is the optimal policy based on $\hat{T}$ and $*$ is the optimal policy based on $T(=\nu)$. Since $\frac{1}{m}V_{1k_0} \sim \frac{k_0}{m}$, (i) follows (with probability 1) by setting $k_0 \sim m^{2/3}$. The policy $\tilde{p}_m$ can be derandomized, showing (i) for sure.

The discounted case (ii) can be proven similarly. The history $y x_{<k}$ is simply ignored and the analogue to $m \to \infty$ is $h_k^{eff} \to \infty$ for $k \to \infty$, which is ensured by $\frac{\gamma_{k+1}}{\gamma_k} \to \infty$. Let $\tilde{\pi}_k$ be the policy which performs (uniformly) random actions in cycles $k...k_0 - 1$ with $k \ll k_0 \ll h_k^{eff}$ and which follows thereafter the optimal policy[7] based on an estimate $\hat{T}$ of the transition matrix T from cycles $k...k_0 - 1$. The existence of an ergodic policy, again, ensures that the expected number of transitions $s \xrightarrow{a} s'$ occurring in cycles $k...k_0 - 1$ is proportional to $\Delta := k_0 - k$. The accuracy of the frequency estimate $\hat{T}$ of T is $\sim \Delta^{-1/2}$ which implies

$$V_{k_0\gamma}^{\tilde{\pi}_k \nu} \to V_{k_0\gamma}^{*\nu} \quad \text{for} \quad \Delta = k_0 - k \to \infty, \tag{11}$$

where $\tilde{\pi}_k$ is the optimal policy based on $\hat{T}$ and $*$ is the optimal policy based on $T(=\nu)$. It remains to show that the achieved reward in the random phase $k...k_0 - 1$ gives a negligible contribution to $V_{k\gamma}$. The following implications for $k \to \infty$ are easy to show:

$$\frac{\gamma_{k+1}}{\gamma_k} \to 1 \Rightarrow \frac{\gamma_{k+\Delta}}{\gamma_k} \to 1 \Rightarrow \frac{\Gamma_{k+\Delta}}{\Gamma_k} \to 1 \Rightarrow \frac{1}{\Gamma_k}\sum_{i=k}^{k_0-1}\gamma_i r_i \leq \frac{r_{max}}{\Gamma_k}[\Gamma_{k+\Delta} - \Gamma_k] \to 0.$$

Since convergence to zero is true for all fixed finite Δ it is also true for sufficiently slowly increasing $\Delta(k) \to \infty$. This shows that the contribution of the first Δ rewards $r_k + ... + r_{k_0-1}$ to $V_{k\gamma}$ is negligible. Together with (11) this shows $V_{k\gamma}^{\tilde{\pi}_k \nu} \to V_{k\gamma}^{*\nu}$ for $k_0 := k + \Delta(k)$. $\square$

The conditions $\Gamma_k < \infty$ and $\frac{\gamma_{k+1}}{\gamma_k} \to 1$ on the discount sequence are, for instance, satisfied for $\gamma_k = 1/k^2$, so the Theorem is not vacuous. The popular

---

[6] For $T_{ss'}^a = 0$ the estimate $\hat{T}_{ss'}^a = 0$ is exact.

[7] For non-geometric discounts as here, optimal policies are, in general, *not* stationary.

geometric discount $\gamma_k = \gamma^k$ fails the latter condition; it has finite effective horizon. [Hut00] gives a detailed account on discount and horizon issues, and motivates $h_k^{eff} \to \infty$ philosophically.

Together with Theorems 4 and 7, Theorem 8 immediately implies that policy p^ξ is self-optimizing for the class of to ergodic MDPs.

Corollary 1 (Policy p^ξ is self-optimizing for ergodic MDPs). *If $\mathcal{M}$ is a finite or countable class of ergodic MDPs, and $\xi() := \sum_{\nu \in \mathcal{M}} w_\nu \nu()$, then policies p_m^ξ maximizing $V_{1m}^{p\xi}$ and p^ξ maximizing $V_{k\gamma}^{\pi\xi}$ are self-optimizing in the sense that*

$$\forall \nu \in \mathcal{M} : \frac{1}{m} V_{1m}^{p_m^\xi \nu} \overset{m\to\infty}{\longrightarrow} \frac{1}{m} V_{1m}^{*\nu} \quad and \quad V_{k\gamma}^{p^\xi \nu} \overset{k\to\infty}{\longrightarrow} V_{k\gamma}^{*\nu} \quad if \quad \frac{\gamma_{k+1}}{\gamma_k} \to 1.$$

If $\mathcal{M}$ is finite, then the speed of the first convergence is at least $O(m^{-1/3})$.

7   Conclusions

Summary: We studied agents acting in general probabilistic environments with reinforcement feedback. We only assumed that the true environment μ belongs to a known class of environments $\mathcal{M}$, but is otherwise unknown. We showed that the Bayes-optimal policy p^ξ based on the Bayes-mixture $\xi = \sum_{\nu \in \mathcal{M}} w_\nu \nu$ is Pareto-optimal and self-optimizing if $\mathcal{M}$ admits self-optimizing policies. The class of ergodic MDPs admitted self-optimizing policies w.r.t. the average value and w.r.t. the discounted value if the effective horizon grew indefinitely.

Continuous Classes $\mathcal{M}$: There are uncountably many (ergodic) MDPs. Since we have restricted our development to countable classes $\mathcal{M}$ we had to give the Corollary for a countable subset of $\mathcal{M}_{MDP1}$. We may choose $\mathcal{M}$ as the set of all ergodic MDPs with rational (or computable) transition probabilities. In this case $\mathcal{M}$ is a dense subset of $\mathcal{M}_{MDP1}$ which is, from a practical point of view, sufficiently rich. On the other hand, it is possible to extend the theory to continuously parameterized families of environments μ_θ and $\xi = \int w_\theta \mu_\theta \, d\theta$. Under some mild (differentiability and existence) conditions, most results of this work remain valid in some form, especially Corollary 1 for *all* ergodic MDPs.

Bayesian Self-Optimizing Policy: Policy p^ξ with unbounded effective horizon for ergodic MDPs is the first purely Bayesian self-optimizing consistent policy for ergodic MDPs. The policies of all previous approaches were either hand crafted, like the ones in the proof of Theorem 8, or were Bayesian with a pre-chosen horizon m, or with geometric discounting γ with finite effective horizon (which does not allow self-optimizing policies) [KV86, Ber95]. The combined conditions $\Gamma_k < \infty$ and $\frac{\gamma_{k+1}}{\gamma_k} \to 1$ allow a consistent self-optimizing Bayes-optimal policy based on mixtures.

Bandits: Bandits are a special subclass of ergodic MDPs. In a two-armed bandit problem you pull repeatedly one of two levers resulting in a gain of A\$1 with probability p_i for arm number i. The game can be described as an MDP with parameters p_i. If the p_i are unknown, Corollary 1 shows that policy p^ξ yields asymptotically optimal payoff. The discounted unbounded horizon approach and result is, to the best of our knowledge, even new when restricted to Bandits.

Other Environmental Classes: Bandits, i.i.d. processes, classification tasks, and many more are all special (degenerate) cases of ergodic MDPs, for which Corollary 1 shows that p^ξ is self-optimizing. But the existence of self-optimizing policies is not limited to (subclasses of ergodic) MDPs. Certain classes of POMDPs, k^{th} order ergodic MDPs, factorizable environments, repeated games, and prediction problems are not MDPs, but nevertheless admit self-optimizing policies (to be shown elsewhere), and hence the corresponding Bayes-optimal mixture policy p^ξ is self-optimizing by Theorems 4 and 7.

Outlook: Future research could be the derivation of non-asymptotic bounds, possibly along the lines of [Hut01]. To get good bounds one may have to exploit extra properties of the environments, like the mixing rate of MDPs [KS98]. Another possibility is to search for other performance criteria along the lines of [Hut00, Ch.6], especially for the universal prior [Sol78] and for the Speed prior [Sch02]. Finally, instead of convergence of the expected reward sum, studying convergence with high probability of the actual reward sum would be interesting.

References

[Bel57]   R. Bellman. *Dynamic Programming*. Princeton University Press, New Jersey, 1957. 364, 368

[Ber95]   D. P. Bertsekas. *Dynamic Programming and Optimal Control, Vol. (I) and (II)*. Athena Scientific, Belmont, Massachusetts, 1995. Volumes 1 and 2. 364, 365, 368, 375, 377

[BT00]   R. I. Brafman and M. Tennenholtz. A near-optimal polynomial time algorithm for learning in certain classes of stochastic games. *Artificial Intelligence*, 121(1–2):31–47, 2000. 364

[Doo53]   J. L. Doob. *Stochastic Processes*. John Wiley & Sons, New York, 1953. 374

[Hut00]   M. Hutter. A theory of universal artificial intelligence based on algorithmic complexity. Technical Report cs.AI/0004001, 62 pages, 2000. http://arxiv.org/abs/cs.AI/0004001. 364, 365, 367, 368, 372, 377, 378

[Hut01]   M. Hutter. General loss bounds for universal sequence prediction. *Proceedings of the 18th International Conference on Machine Learning (ICML-2001)*, pages 210–217, 2001. 378

[KLM96]   L. P. Kaelbling, M. L. Littman, and A. W. Moore. Reinforcement learning: a survey. *Journal of AI research*, 4:237–285, 1996. 365, 367

[KS98]   M. Kearns and S. Singh. Near-optimal reinforcement learning in polynomial time. In *Proc. 15th International Conf. on Machine Learning*, pages 260–268. Morgan Kaufmann, San Francisco, CA, 1998. 378

[KV86]   P. R. Kumar and P. P. Varaiya. *Stochastic Systems: Estimation, Identification, and Adaptive Control.* Prentice Hall, Englewood Cliffs, NJ, 1986. 365, 368, 370, 375, 377

[LV97]   M. Li and P. M. B. Vitányi. *An introduction to Kolmogorov complexity and its applications.* Springer, 2nd edition, 1997. 368

[RN95]   S. J. Russell and P. Norvig. *Artificial Intelligence. A Modern Approach.* Prentice-Hall, Englewood Cliffs, 1995. 366

[SB98]   R. Sutton and A. Barto. *Reinforcement learning: An introduction.* Cambridge, MA, MIT Press, 1998. 365, 367

[Sch02]   J. Schmidhuber. The Speed Prior: a new simplicity measure yielding near-optimal computable predictions. *Proceedings of the 15th Annual Conference on Computational Learning Theory (COLT 2002)*, 2002. 378

[Sol78]   R. J. Solomonoff. Complexity-based induction systems: comparisons and convergence theorems. *IEEE Trans. Inform. Theory*, IT-24:422–432, 1978. 368, 378

Prediction and Dimension

Lance Fortnow[1] and Jack H. Lutz[2]*

[1] NEC Research Institute
4 Independence Way, Princeton, NJ 08540
[2] Department of Computer Science, Iowa State University
Ames, IA 50010

Abstract. Given a set X of sequences over a finite alphabet, we investigate the following three quantities.

(i) The *feasible predictability* of X is the highest success ratio that a polynomial-time randomized predictor can achieve on all sequences in X.

(ii) The *deterministic feasible predictability* of X is the highest success ratio that a polynomial-time deterministic predictor can achieve on all sequences in X.

(iii) The *feasible dimension* of X is the polynomial-time effectivization of the classical Hausdorff dimension ("fractal dimension") of X.

Predictability is known to be *stable* in the sense that the feasible predictability of $X \cup Y$ is always the minimum of the feasible predictabilities of X and Y. We show that deterministic predictability also has this property if X and Y are computably presentable. We show that deterministic predictability coincides with predictability on singleton sets. Our main theorem states that the feasible dimension of X is bounded above by the maximum entropy of the predictability of X and bounded below by the segmented self-information of the predictability of X, and that these bounds are tight.

1 Introduction

The relationship between prediction and gambling has been investigated for decades. In the 1950s, Shannon [21] and Kelly [10] studied prediction and gambling, respectively, as alternative means of characterizing information. In the 1960s, Kolmogorov [11] and Loveland [12] introduced a strong notion of unpredictability of infinite binary sequences, now known as *Kolmogorov-Loveland stochasticity*. In the early 1970s, Schnorr [19,20] proved that an infinite binary sequence is *random* (in the sense of Martin-Löf [15]) if and only if no constructive gambling strategy (martingale) can accrue unbounded winnings betting on the successive bits of the sequence. It was immediately evident that every random sequence is Kolmogorov-Loveland stochastic, but the converse question remained open until the late 1980s, when Shen' [22] established the existence of

---

* This author's research was supported in part by National Science Foundation Grant CCR-9988483. Much of the work was done while this author was on sabbatical at NEC Research Institute.

J. Kivinen and R. H. Sloan (Eds.): COLT 2002, LNAI 2375, pp. 380–395, 2002.

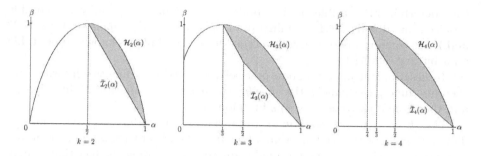

Fig. 1. Prediction-dimension diagrams for $k = 2, 3, 4$

Kolmogorov-Loveland stochastic sequences that are not random, i.e., sequences that are unpredictable but on which a constructive gambling strategy can accrue unbounded winnings. This result gave a clear qualitative separation between unpredictability and randomness, and hence between prediction and gambling. However, the precise quantitative relationship between these processes has not been elucidated. Given the obvious significance of prediction and gambling for computational learning [2,3,25] and information theory [7,8] this situation should be remedied.

Recently, Lutz [13,14] has defined computational effectivizations of classical Hausdorff dimension ("fractal dimension") and used these to investigate questions in computational complexity and algorithmic information theory. These effectivizations are based not on Hausdorff's 1919 definition of dimension [9,6], but rather on an equivalent formulation in terms of gambling strategies called *gales* [13]. These gales (defined precisely in section 4 below) give a convenient way of quantifying the discount rate against which a gambling strategy can succeed. (Ryabko [16,17,18] and Staiger [23,24]) have conducted related investigations of classical Hausdorff dimension in equivalent terms of the rate at which a gambling strategy can succeed in the absence of discounting.) The *feasible dimension* $\dim_p(X)$ of a set X of sequences is then defined in terms of the maximum discount rate against which a feasible gambling strategy can succeed.

In this paper we use feasible dimension as a model of feasible gambling, and we compare $\dim_p(X)$ quantitatively with the *feasible predictability* $\operatorname{pred}_p(X)$ of X, which is the highest success ratio that a polynomial-time randomized predictor (defined precisely in section 3 below) can achieve on all sequences in X. Our main theorem, described after this paragraph, gives precise bounds on the relationship between $\operatorname{pred}_p(X)$ and $\dim_p(X)$. We also investigate the *deterministic feasible predictability* $\operatorname{dpred}_p(X)$, in which the predictor is required to commit to a single outcome. We use the probabilistic method to prove that $\operatorname{dpred}_p(X) = \operatorname{pred}_p(X)$ whenever X consists of a single sequence, and we show that deterministic feasible predictability is *stable* on computably presentable sets, i.e., that $\mathrm{dpred_p}(X \cup Y) = \min\{\mathrm{dpred_p}(X), \mathrm{dpred_p}(Y)\}$ whenever the sets X and Y are computably presentable. (Feasible predictability is known to be stable on arbitrary sets [2].)

To describe our main theorem precisely, we need to define two information-theoretic functions, namely, the k-*adic segmented self-information* function $\overline{\mathcal{I}_k}$ and the k-*adic maximum entropy* function $\mathcal{H}_k$.

The k-*adic self-information* of a real number $\alpha \in (0,1]$ is $\mathcal{I}_k(\alpha) = \log_k \frac{1}{\alpha}$. This is the number of symbols from a k-element alphabet that would be required to represent each of $\frac{1}{\alpha}$ equally probable outcomes (ignoring the fact that $\frac{1}{\alpha}$ may not be an integer). The k-*adic segmented self-information* function $\overline{\mathcal{I}_k} : [\frac{1}{k}, 1] \rightarrow [0, 1]$ is defined by setting $\overline{\mathcal{I}_k}(\frac{1}{j}) = \mathcal{I}_k(\frac{1}{j})$ for $1 \le j \le k$ and interpolating linearly between these points.

Recall [4] that the k-*adic entropy* of a probability measure p on a discrete sample space X is

$$H_k(p) = \sum_{x \in X} p(x) \log_k \frac{1}{p(x)}.$$

This is the expected value of $\mathcal{I}_k(p(x))$, i.e., the average number of symbols from a k-element alphabet that is required to represent outcomes of the experiment (X, p) reliably. The k-*adic maximum entropy* function $\mathcal{H}_k : [0, 1] \rightarrow [0, 1]$ is defined by

$$\mathcal{H}_k(\alpha) = \max_p H_k(p),$$

where the maximum is taken over all probability measures p on a k-element alphabet Σ such that $p(a) = \alpha$ for some $a \in \Sigma$. This maximum is achieved when the other $k - 1$ elements of Σ are equally probable, so

$$\mathcal{H}_k(\alpha) = \alpha \log_k \frac{1}{\alpha} + (1 - \alpha) \log_k \frac{k - 1}{1 - \alpha}.$$

Our main theorem says that for every set $X \subseteq \Sigma^\infty$,

$$\overline{\mathcal{I}_k}(\mathrm{pred_p}(X)) \le \dim_p(X) \le \mathcal{H}_k(\mathrm{pred_p}(X)).$$

That is, the feasible dimension of any set of sequences is bounded below by the k-adic segmented self-information of its feasible predictability and bounded above by the k-adic maximum entropy of its feasible predictability. Graphically, this says that for every set X of sequences, the ordered pair $(\mathrm{pred_p}(X), \dim_p(X))$ lies in the region R_k bounded by the graphs of $\overline{\mathcal{I}_k}$ and $\mathcal{H}_k$. The regions R_2, R_3, and R_4 are depicted in Figure 1. In fact, these bounds are tight in the strong sense that for every $k \ge 2$ and every point $(\alpha, \beta) \in R_k$, there is a set X of sequences over a k-element alphabet such that $\mathrm{pred_p}(X) = \alpha$ and $\dim_p(X) = \beta$. Our main theorem is thus a precise statement of the quantitative relationship between feasible predictability and feasible dimension. Since dimension is defined in terms of the achievable success rates of gambling strategies, this can also be regarded as a precise statement of the quantitative relationship between prediction and gambling.

For brevity and clarity in this conference paper, our results are stated in terms of feasible (i.e., polynomial-time) prediction and dimension. However, our results generalize to other levels of complexity, ranging from finite-state computation through polynomial-space and unrestricted algorithmic computation and beyond to prediction by arbitrary mathematical functions and classical Hausdorff dimension. At the finite-state level, Feder, Merhav, and Gutman [8] have derived a graph comparing predictability to compressibility for binary sequences. This graph (Figure 3 in [8]) is equivalent to the finite-state version of our $k = 2$ graph in Figure 1. (This equivalence follows from the recent proof by Dai, Lathrop, Lutz, and Mayordomo [5] of the equivalence of finite-state dimension and finite-state compressibility.)

2   Preliminaries

We work in an arbitrary finite alphabet Σ with cardinality $|\Sigma| \geq 2$. When convenient, we assume that Σ has the form $\Sigma = \{0, 1, \ldots, k - 1\}$. A *sequence* is an element of Σ^∞, i.e., an infinite sequence of elements of Σ. Given a sequence $S \in \Sigma^\infty$ and natural numbers $i, j \in \mathbb{N}$ with $i \leq j$, we write $S[i..j]$ for the string consisting of the ith through j^{th} symbols of S and $S[i]$ for the ith symbol in S. (The leftmost symbol of S is $S[0]$.) We say that a string $w \in \Sigma^*$ is a *prefix* of S and we write $w \sqsubseteq S$, if $w = S[0..|w| - 1]$.

Given a time bound $t : \mathbb{N} \to \mathbb{N}$, we define the complexity class $\text{DTIME}_\Sigma(t(n))$ to consist of all sequences $S \in \Sigma^\infty$ such that the nth symbol in S can be computed in $O(t(\log n))$ steps. We are especially interested in the classes $\text{DTIME}_\Sigma(2^{cn})$ for fixed $c \in \mathbb{N}$ and the class $\text{E}_\Sigma = \cup_{c \in \mathbb{N}} \text{DTIME}_\Sigma(2^{cn})$. Note that if $S \in \text{E}_\Sigma$, then the time required to compute the nth symbol of S is exponential in the length of the binary representation of n and polynomial in the number n itself.

If D is a discrete domain, then a real-valued function $f : D \to \mathbb{R}$ is *polynomial-time computable* if there is a polynomial-time computable, rational-valued function $\hat{f} : D \times \mathbb{N} \to \mathbb{Q}$ such that for all $x \in D$ and $r \in \mathbb{N}$, $|\hat{f}(x, r) - f(x)| \leq 2^{-r}$.

3   Prediction

Our models of deterministic and randomized prediction are very simple. In both cases, there is a given alphabet Σ containing two or more symbols. Having seen a string $w \in \Sigma^*$ of symbols, a predictor's task is to predict the next symbol.

Definition. A *deterministic predictor* on an alphabet Σ is a function

$$\pi : \Sigma^* \to \Sigma.$$

Intuitively, $\pi(w)$ is the symbol that π predicts will follow the string w. This prediction is well-defined and unambiguous, and it is either correct or incorrect. In contrast, a randomized predictor is allowed to simply state the probabilities with which it will predict the various symbols in Σ.

Notation. We write $\mathcal{M}(\Sigma)$ for the set of all probability measures on Σ, i.e., all functions $p : \Sigma \to [0, 1]$ satisfying $\sum_{a \in \Sigma} p(a) = 1$.

Definition. A *(randomized) predictor* on an alphabet Σ is a function

$$\pi : \Sigma^* \to \mathcal{M}(\Sigma).$$

Intuitively, having seen the string $w \in \Sigma^*$, a randomized predictor π performs a random experiment in which each symbol $a \in \Sigma$ occurs with probability $\pi(w)(a)$. The outcome of this experiment is the symbol that π predicts will follow w. It is evident that π will be correct with probability $\pi(w)(a)$, where a is the symbol that does in fact follow w.

It is natural to identify each deterministic predictor π on Σ with the randomized predictor $\pi' : \Sigma^* \to \mathcal{M}(\Sigma)$ defined by

$$\pi'(w)(a) = \begin{cases} 1 & \text{if } a = \pi(w) \\ 0 & \text{if } a \neq \pi(w). \end{cases}$$

Using this identification, a deterministic predictor is merely a special type of randomized predictor. Thus, in our terminology, a *predictor* is a randomized predictor, and a predictor π is *deterministic* if $\pi(w)(a) \in \{0, 1\}$ for all $w \in \Sigma^*$ and $a \in \Sigma$.

Definition. Let π be a predictor on Σ.

1. The *success rate* of π on a nonempty string $w \in \Sigma^+$ is $\pi^+(w) = \frac{1}{|w|} \sum_{i=0}^{|w|-1} \pi(w[0..i-1])(w[i])$.
2. The *success rate* of π on a sequence $S \in \Sigma^\infty$ is $\pi^+(S) = \limsup_{n \to \infty} \pi^+(S[0..n-1])$.
3. The *(worst-case) success rate* of π on a set $X \subseteq \Sigma^\infty$ is $\pi^+(X) = \inf_{S \in X} \pi^+(S)$.

Note that $\pi^+(w)$ is the expected fraction of symbols in w that π predicts correctly. In particular, if π is deterministic, then $\pi^+(w)$ is the fraction of symbols in w that π predicts correctly.

We say that a predictor $\pi : \Sigma^* \to \mathcal{M}(\Sigma)$ is *feasible* provided that the associated function $\pi' : \Sigma^* \times \Sigma \to [0, 1]$ defined by $\pi'(w, a) = \pi(w)(a)$ is computable in polynomial time. We say that π is *exactly feasible* if the values of π' are rational and can be computed exactly in polynomial time.

Definition. Let Σ be an alphabet, and let $X \subseteq \Sigma^\infty$.

1. The *(randomized feasible) predictability* of X is

$$\text{pred}_p(X) = \sup\{\pi^+(X) | \pi \text{ is a feasible predictor on } \Sigma\}.$$

2. The *deterministic (feasible) predictability* of X is

$$\text{dpred}_p(X) = \sup\{\pi^+(X) | \pi \text{ is a deterministic feasible predictor on } \Sigma\}.$$

It is clear that

$$0 \leq \operatorname{dpred}_p(X) \leq \operatorname{pred}_p(X)$$

and

$$\frac{1}{|\Sigma|} \leq \operatorname{pred}_p(X) \leq 1$$

for all $X \subseteq \Sigma^\infty$. As the following example shows, all these inequalities can be proper.

Example 3.1. If

$$X = \left\{ S \in \{0,1\}^\infty \,\big|\, (\forall n)\big[S[2n] = 1 \text{ or } S[2n+1] = 1\big] \right\},$$

then the reader may verify that

$$\operatorname{dpred}_p(X) = \frac{1}{2} < \frac{5}{8} = \operatorname{pred}_p(X).$$

It is clear that predictability is *monotone* in the sense that

$$X \subseteq Y \Rightarrow \operatorname{pred}_p(X) \geq \operatorname{pred}_p(Y)$$

and

$$X \subseteq Y \Rightarrow \operatorname{dpred}_p(X) \geq \operatorname{dpred}_p(Y)$$

for all $X, Y \subseteq \Sigma^\infty$. Very roughly speaking, the smaller a set of sequences is, the more predictable it is. The following theorem shows that, for fixed $c \in \mathbb{N}$, the set $\operatorname{DTIME}_\Sigma(2^{cn})$ is "completely predictable," while the set E_Σ is "completely unpredictable." From now on, Σ is an alphabet with $|\Sigma| \geq 2$.

Theorem 3.2.

1. For each $c \in \mathbb{N}$, $\operatorname{dpred}_p(\operatorname{DTIME}_\Sigma(2^{cn})) = \operatorname{pred}_p(\operatorname{DTIME}_\Sigma(2^{cn})) = 1$.
2. $\operatorname{dpred}_p(E_\Sigma) = 0$, and $\operatorname{pred}_p(E_\Sigma) = \frac{1}{|\Sigma|}$.

Proof. (Sketch.)

1. For fixed c, there is an n^{c+1}-time-computable function $g : \mathbb{N} \times \Sigma^* \to \Sigma$ such that $\operatorname{DTIME}_\Sigma(2^{cn}) = \{S_0, S_1, \ldots\}$, where $g(k, S_k[0..n-1]) = S_k[n]$ for all $k, n \in \mathbb{N}$. The deterministic predictor $\pi : \Sigma^* \to \Sigma$ defined by $\pi(w) = g(k_w, w)$, where

   $$k_w = \min\{k \in \mathbb{N} | (\forall n < |w|) g(k, w[0..n-1]) = w[n]\},$$

   is then computable in polynomial time and satisfies $\pi^+(\operatorname{DTIME}_\Sigma(2^{cn})) = 1$.
2. For any feasible predictor π there is an adversary sequence $S \in E_\Sigma$ that minimizes the value of $\pi^+(S[0..n])$ at every step n. If π is deterministic, then $\pi^+(S) = 0$. In any case, $\pi^+(S) \leq \frac{1}{|\Sigma|}$.

$\square$

Definition. If π_1 and π_2 are predictors on Σ, then the *distance* between π_1 and π_2 is

$$d(\pi_1, \pi_2) = \sup_{w \in \Sigma^*} \max_{a \in \Sigma} |\pi_1(w)(a) - \pi_2(w)(a)|.$$

Observation 3.3. *If π_1 and π_2 are predictors on Σ, then for all $S \in \Sigma^\infty$, $|\pi_1^+(S) - \pi_2^+(S)| \leq d(\pi_1, \pi_2)$.*

Definition. Let π be a predictor on Σ, and let $l \in \mathbb{N}$. Then π is *l-coarse* if $2^l \pi(w)(a) \in \mathbb{N}$ for all $w \in \Sigma^*$ and $a \in \Sigma$.

That is, a predictor π is l-coarse if every probability $\pi(w)(a)$ is of the form $\frac{m}{2^l}$ for some $m \in \mathbb{N}$. Note that every l-coarse predictor is $(l+1)$-coarse and that a predictor is deterministic if and only if it is 0-coarse.

Lemma 3.4. (Coarse Approximation Lemma) *For every feasible predictor π on Σ and every $l \in \mathbb{N}$, there is an exactly feasible l-coarse predictor π' such that $d(\pi, \pi') \leq 3 \cdot 2^{-l}$.*

We now use the probabilistic method to show that deterministic predictability coincides with predictability on singleton sets.

Theorem 3.5. *For all $S \in \Sigma^\infty$, $\mathrm{dpred}_p(\{S\}) = \mathrm{pred}_p(\{S\})$.*

Proof. Let $S \in \Sigma^\infty$, and let $\alpha < \mathrm{pred}_p(\{S\})$. It suffices to show that $\mathrm{dpred}_p(\{S\}) > \alpha$.

Let $\epsilon = \frac{\mathrm{pred}_p(\{S\}) - \alpha}{2}$, and choose $l \in \mathbb{N}$ such that $3 \cdot 2^{-l} < \epsilon$. Since $\alpha + \epsilon < \mathrm{pred}_p(\{S\})$, there is a feasible predictor π' such that $\pi'^+(S) > \alpha + \epsilon$. By the Coarse Approximation Lemma, there is an exactly feasible l-coarse predictor π such that $d(\pi, \pi') \leq 3 \cdot 2^{-l} < \epsilon$. It follows by Observation 3.3 that $\pi^+(S) > \alpha$.

For each $w \in \Sigma^*$ and $a \in \Sigma$, define an interval $I(w, a) = [x_a, x_{a+1}) \subseteq [0, 1)$ by the recursion

$$x_a = 0, \quad x_{a+1} = x_a + \pi(w)(a).$$

Given $\rho \in [0, 1)$, define a deterministic predictor π_ρ on Σ by

$$\pi_\rho(w)(a) = \begin{cases} 1 & \text{if } \rho \in I(w, a) \\ 0 & \text{if } \rho \notin I(w, a). \end{cases}$$

Since π is l-coarse, we have

$$d\lfloor 2^l \rho \rfloor = \lfloor 2^l \rho' \rfloor \Rightarrow \pi_\rho = \pi_{\rho'} \tag{1}$$

for all $\rho \in [0, 1)$. If we choose ρ probabilistically according to the uniform probability measure on $[0,1)$ and E_ρ denotes the expectation with respect to this experiment, then Fatou's lemma tells us that (writing $w_i = S[0..i - 1]$)

$$\begin{aligned}
\mathrm{E}_\rho \pi_\rho^+(S) &= \mathrm{E}_\rho \limsup_{n\to\infty} \pi_\rho^+(w_n) \\
&\geq \limsup_{n\to\infty} \mathrm{E}_\rho \pi_\rho^+(w_n) \\
&= \limsup_{n\to\infty} \frac{1}{n} \sum_{i=0}^{n-1} \mathrm{E}_\rho \pi_\rho(w_i)(S[i]) \\
&= \limsup_{n\to\infty} \frac{1}{n} \sum_{i=0}^{n-1} \mathrm{Pr}_\rho[\pi_\rho(w_i)(S[i]) = 1] \\
&= \limsup_{n\to\infty} \frac{1}{n} \sum_{i=0}^{n-1} \mathrm{length}(I(w_i, S[i])) \\
&= \limsup_{n\to\infty} \frac{1}{n} \sum_{i=0}^{n-1} \pi(w_i)(S[i]) \\
&= \limsup_{n\to\infty} \pi^+(w_n) \\
&= \pi^+(S).
\end{aligned}$$

It follows that there exists $\rho \in [0, 1)$ such that $\pi_\rho^+(S) \geq \pi^+(S) > \alpha$. Hence by (1) there is a rational $\rho' \in [0, 1)$ for which $\pi_{\rho'}^+(S) > \alpha$. Since $\pi_{\rho'}$ is a feasible deterministic predictor, this implies that $\mathrm{dpred}_\mathrm{p}(\{S\}) > \alpha$. $\qquad\square$

An important property of predictability is its *stability*, which is the fact that the predictability of a union of two sets is always the minimum of the predictabilities of the sets. (The term "stability" here is taken from the analogous property of dimension [6].) The stability of predictability follows from the (much stronger) main theorem of Cesa-Bianchi, Freund, Helmhold, Haussler, Schapire, and Warmuth [2]. For deterministic predictability, we have the following partial result.

Recall [1] that a set $X \subseteq \Sigma^\infty$ is *computably presentable* if $X = \emptyset$ or there is a computable function $f : \mathbb{N} \to \mathbb{N}$ such that $X = \{L(M_{f(i)}) | i \in \mathbb{N}\}$, where $M_0, M_1, \ldots$ is a standard enumeration of all Turing machines over the alphabet Σ and $M_{f(i)}$ halts on all inputs for all $i \in \mathbb{N}$. Deterministic predictability is stable on sets that are recursively presentable.

Theorem 3.6. *For all computably presentable sets* $X, Y \subseteq \Sigma^\infty$,

$$\mathrm{dpred}_\mathrm{p}(X \cup Y) = \min\{\mathrm{dpred}_\mathrm{p}(X), \mathrm{dpred}_\mathrm{p}(Y)\}.$$

At the time of this writing we do not know whether deterministic predictability is stable on arbitrary sets. We conjecture that it is not.

4 Dimension

In this section we sketch the elements of feasible dimension in Σ^∞, where Σ is a finite alphabet. Without loss of generality, we let $\Sigma = \{0, 1, \ldots, k - 1\}$, where $k \geq 2$.

Definition. Let $s \in [0, \infty)$.

1. An *s-gale* over Σ is a function $d : \Sigma^* \to [0, \infty)$ that satisfies the condition

$$d(w) = k^{-s} \sum_{a \in \Sigma} d(wa) \tag{2}$$

for all $w \in \Sigma^*$.

2. An s-gale d *succeeds* on a sequence $S \in \Sigma^\infty$, and we write $S \in S^\infty[d]$, if

$$\limsup_{n \to \infty} d(S[0..n-1]) = \infty.$$

3. An s-gale is *feasible* if it is computable in polynomial time.
4. An s-gale is *exactly feasible* if its values are rational and can be computed exactly in polynomial time.
5. For $X \subseteq \Sigma^\infty$, we let

$$\mathcal{G}(X) = \left\{ s \;\middle|\; \begin{array}{l} \text{there is an } s\text{-gale } d \\ \text{such that } X \subseteq S^\infty[d] \end{array} \right\},$$

$$\mathcal{G}_p(X) = \left\{ s \;\middle|\; \begin{array}{l} \text{there is a feasible } s\text{-gale } d \\ \text{such that } X \subseteq S^\infty[d] \end{array} \right\}.$$

The gale characterization of classical Hausdorff dimension [13] shows that the classical Hausdorff dimension $\dim_H(X)$ of a set $X \subseteq \Sigma^\infty$ is given by the equation

$$\dim_H(X) = \inf \mathcal{G}(X).$$

This motivates the following.

Definition. The *feasible dimension* of a set $X \subseteq \Sigma^\infty$ is

$$\dim_p(X) = \inf \mathcal{G}_p(X).$$

It is easy to see that $0 \le \dim_H(X) \le \dim_p(X) \le 1$ for all $X \subseteq \Sigma^\infty$ and that feasible dimension is *monotone* in the sense that $X \subseteq Y$ implies $\dim_p(X) \subseteq \dim_p(Y)$ for all $X, Y \subseteq \Sigma^\infty$. It is shown in [13] that feasible dimension is *stable* in the sense that

$$\dim_p(X \cup Y) = \max\{\dim_p(X), \dim_p(Y)\}$$

for all $X, Y \subseteq \Sigma^\infty$. The following result is the dimension-theoretic analog of Theorem 3.2.

Theorem 4.1. ([13])

1. *For each $c \in \mathbb{N}$, $\dim_p(\mathrm{DTIME}_\Sigma(2^{cn})) = 0$.*
2. *$\dim_p(\mathrm{E}_\Sigma) = 1$*

The following example establishes the existence of sets of arbitrary feasible dimension between 0 and 1.

Example 4.2. ([13]) Let q be a feasible probability measure on Σ, and let $\mathrm{FREQ}(q)$ be the set of all sequences $S \in \Sigma^\infty$ such that each $a \in \Sigma$ has asymptotic frequency $q(a)$ in S. Then

$$\dim_p(\mathrm{FREQ}(q)) = H_k(q).$$

5   Prediction versus Dimension

This section develops our main theorem, which gives precise quantitative bounds on the relationship between predictability and dimension. As before, let $\Sigma = \{0, 1, \ldots, k-1\}$ be an alphabet with $k \geq 2$. Recall the k-adic segmented self-information function $\overline{\mathcal{I}_k}$ and the k-adic maximum entropy function $\mathcal{H}_k$ defined in section 1.

Theorem 5.1. (Main Theorem) *For all $X \subseteq \Sigma^\infty$,*

$$\overline{\mathcal{I}_k}(\mathrm{pred}_{\mathrm{p}}(X)) \leq \dim_{\mathrm{p}}(X) \leq \mathcal{H}_k(\mathrm{pred}_{\mathrm{p}}(X)).$$

The rest of this section is devoted to proving Theorem 5.1.

Construction 5.2. Given an alphabet Σ with $|\Sigma| = k \geq 2$, a predictor π on Σ, and rational numbers $\beta, s \in (0, 1)$, we define an s-gale

$$d = d(\pi, \beta, s) : \Sigma^* \to [0, \infty)$$

by the recursion

$$d(\lambda) = 1,$$

$$d(wa) = k^s \mathrm{bet}_w(a) d(w),$$

where $\mathrm{bet}_w(a)$, the amount that d bets on a having seen w, is defined as follows. If π were to deterministically predict b (i.e., $\pi(w)(b) = 1$), then the amount that d would bet on a is

$$\gamma(a, b) = \begin{cases} \beta & \text{if } a = b \\ \frac{1-\beta}{k-1} & \text{if } a \neq b. \end{cases}$$

However, π is a randomized predictor that predicts various b according to the probability distribution $\pi(w)$, so d instead uses the quantity

$$\gamma_w(a) = \prod_{b \in \Sigma} \gamma(a, b)^{\pi(w)(b)}$$

$$= \beta^{\pi(w)(a)} \left(\frac{1-\beta}{k-1} \right)^{1-\pi(w)(a)},$$

which is the geometric mean of the bets $\gamma(a, b)$, weighted according to the probability distribution $\pi(w)$. The amount that d bets on a is then the normalization

$$\mathrm{bet}_w(a) = \frac{\gamma_w(a)}{\sigma_w},$$

where

$$\sigma_w = \sum_{a \in \Sigma} \gamma_w(a).$$

Observation 5.3. *In Construction 5.2, $0 < \sigma_w \leq 1$ for all $w \in \Sigma^*$.*

Observation 5.4. *In Construction 5.2, d is an s-gale, and d is p-computable if π is feasible.*

Lemma 5.5. *In Construction 5.2,*

$$\log_k d(w) \geq |w| \left(s + \log_k \frac{1-\beta}{k-1} + \pi^+(w) \log_k \frac{\beta(k-1)}{1-\beta} \right)$$

for all $w \in \Sigma^*$.

Proof. Let $w \in \Sigma^*$, and let $n = |w|$. For each $0 \leq i < n$, write $\pi_i = \pi(w[0..i-1])(w[i])$. By the construction of d and Observation 5.3,

$$d(w) = k^{sn} \prod_{i=0}^{n-1} \mathrm{bet}_{w[0..i-1]}(w[i])$$

$$= k^{sn} \prod_{i=0}^{n-1} \frac{\gamma_{w[0..i-1]}(w[i])}{\sigma_{w[0..i-1]}}$$

$$\geq k^{sn} \prod_{i=0}^{n-1} \gamma_{w[0..i-1]}(w[i])$$

$$= k^{sn} \prod_{i=0}^{n-1} \beta^{\pi_i} \left(\frac{1-\beta}{k-1} \right)^{1-\pi_i}.$$

It follows that

$$\log_k d(w) \geq sn + \sum_{i=0}^{n-1} \left[\pi_i \log_k \beta + (1-\pi_i) \log_k \frac{1-\beta}{k-1} \right]$$

$$= n \left(s + \log_k \frac{1-\beta}{k-1} \right) + \log_k \frac{\beta(k-1)}{1-\beta} \sum_{i=0}^{n-1} \pi_i$$

$$= n \left(s + \log_k \frac{1-\beta}{k-1} + \pi^+(w) \log_k \frac{\beta(k-1)}{1-\beta} \right).$$

$\square$

We can now prove an upper bound on dimension in terms of predictability.

Theorem 5.6. *If Σ is an alphabet with $|\Sigma| = k \geq 2$, then for all $X \subseteq \Sigma^\infty$,*

$$\dim_p(X) \leq \mathcal{H}_k(\mathrm{pred}_p(X)).$$

Proof. Let $X \subseteq \Sigma^\infty$, and let $\alpha = \mathrm{pred}_p(X)$. If $\mathcal{H}_k(\alpha) = 1$ then the result holds trivially, so assume that $\mathcal{H}_k(\alpha) < 1$, i.e., $\alpha \in \left(\frac{1}{k}, 1 \right]$. Choose a rational number $s \in (\mathcal{H}_k(\alpha), 1]$. It suffices to show that $\dim_p(X) \leq s$.

By our choice of s, there is a rational number $\beta \in \left(\frac{1}{k}, \alpha\right)$ such that $\mathcal{H}_k(\beta) \in (\mathcal{H}_k(\alpha), s)$. Since $\beta < \alpha$, there is a feasible predictor π such that $\pi^+(X) > \beta$. Let $d = d(\pi, \beta, s)$ be the s-gale of Construction 5.2. By Observation 5.4, it suffices to show that $X \subseteq S^\infty[d]$. To this end, let $S \in X$. For each $n \in \mathbb{N}$, let $w_n = S[0..n-1]$. Then the set

$$J = \{n \in \mathbb{Z}^+ \mid \pi^+(w_n) \geq \beta n\}$$

is infinite, and Lemma 5.5 tells us that for each $n \in J$,

$$\log_k d(w_n) \geq n \left(s + \log_k \frac{1-\beta}{k-1} + \pi^+(w_n) \log_k \frac{\beta(k-1)}{1-\beta} \right)$$

$$\geq n \left(s + \log_k \frac{1-\beta}{k-1} + \beta \log_k \frac{\beta(k-1)}{1-\beta} \right)$$

$$= n(s - \mathcal{H}_k(\beta)).$$

Since $s > \mathcal{H}_k(\beta)$, this implies that $S \in S^\infty[d]$. $\square$

The lower bound on dimension is a function of predictability whose graph is not a smooth curve. It is thus instructive to *derive* this bound rather than to simply assert and prove it. As before, let Σ be an alphabet with $|\Sigma| \geq 2$.

It is easiest to first derive a lower bound on predictability in terms of dimension, since this can be achieved by using an s-gale to construct a predictor. So let s be a positive rational, and let d be a p-computable s-gale over Σ with $d(\lambda) > 0$. The most natural predictor to construct from d is the function $\pi_0 : \Sigma^* \to \mathcal{M}(\Sigma)$ defined by

$$\pi_0(w)(a) = \text{bet}_d(wa) \tag{3}$$

for all $w \in \Sigma^*$ and $a \in \Sigma$. This is indeed a predictor, and it is clearly feasible. For all $w \in \Sigma^*$, we have

$$d(w) = d(\lambda)k^{s|w|} \prod_{i=0}^{|w|-1} \text{bet}_d(wa)$$

$$\leq d(\lambda)k^{s|w|} \left(\frac{1}{|w|} \sum_{i=0}^{|w|-1} \text{bet}_d(wa) \right)^{|w|}$$

$$= d(\lambda) \left(k^s \pi_0^+(w) \right)^{|w|}$$

(because the geometric mean is at most the arithmetic mean), so if $S \in S^\infty[d]$ there must be infinitely many prefixes $w \sqsubseteq S$ for which $\pi_0^+(w) > k^{-s}$. Thus this very simple predictor π_0 testifies that

$$\text{pred}_p(S^\infty[d]) \geq k^{-s}. \tag{4}$$

This establishes the following preliminary bound.

Lemma 5.7. *For all* $X \subseteq \Sigma^\infty$,

$$\dim_p(X) \geq \mathcal{I}_k(\text{pred}_p(X)).$$

Proof. The above argument shows that

$$\text{pred}_p(X) \geq k^{-\dim_p(X)},$$

whence the lemma follows immediately. □

If we suspect that Lemma 5.7 can be improved, how might we proceed? One approach is as follows. The predictor π_0 achieved (4) via the prediction probability (3), which is equivalent to

$$\pi_0(w)(a) = k^{-\mathcal{I}_k(\text{bet}_d(wa))}. \tag{5}$$

To improve on (4), let $f(s) = u - vs$ be a function whose graph is a line intersecting k^{-s} at two points given by $s_0, s_1 \in [0, 1]$. We would like to improve (4) to

$$\text{pred}_p(S^\infty[d]) \geq f(s). \tag{6}$$

For what values of s_0 and s_1 can we establish (6)?

Guided by (5), we set

$$\pi_1(w)(a) = \max\{0, f(\mathcal{I}_k(\text{bet}_d(wa)))\}$$

for all $w \in \Sigma^*$ and $a \in \Sigma$. The function π_1 may not be a predictor because the function $\sigma : \Sigma^* \to [0, \infty)$ defined by

$$\sigma(w) = \sum_{a \in \Sigma} \pi_1(w)(a)$$

may not be identically 1. However, it is clear that $\sigma(w) > 0$ for all $w \in \Sigma^*$, so if we set

$$\pi(w)(a) = \frac{\pi_1(w)(a)}{\sigma(w)}$$

for all $w \in \Sigma^*$ and $a \in \Sigma$, then π is a predictor. For all $w \in \Sigma^+$ we have

$$\pi_1^+(w) \geq \frac{1}{|w|} \sum_{i=0}^{|w|-1} (u - v\mathcal{I}_k(\text{bet}_d(w[0..i])))$$

$$= u + \frac{v}{|w|} \sum_{i=0}^{|w|-1} \log_k(\text{bet}_d(w[0..i]))$$

$$= u + \frac{v}{|w|} \log_k \prod_{i=0}^{|w|-1} \text{bet}_d(w[0..i])$$

$$= u + \frac{v}{|w|} \log_k \left(\frac{d(w)}{k^{s|w|}d(\lambda)} \right)$$

$$= u - vs + \frac{1}{|w|} \log_k \frac{d(w)}{d(\lambda)},$$

so if $\sigma(w) \le 1$ and $d(w) > d(\lambda)$, then

$$\pi^+(w) > u - vs = f(s).$$

Thus if s_0 and s_1 are chosen so that $\sigma(w) \le 1$ for all $w \in \Sigma^*$, then for all $S \in S^\infty[d]$ there exist infinitely many prefixes $w \sqsubseteq S$ for which $\pi^+(w) > f(s)$. This implies that (6) holds (provided that π is feasible). Thus the question is how to choose s_0 and s_1 so that $\sigma(w) \le 1$ for all $w \in \Sigma^*$.

If we let

$$B_w = \{a | f(\mathcal{I}_k(\mathrm{bet}_d(wa))) > 0\},$$

then for all $w \in \Sigma^*$,

$$\sigma(w) = \sum_{a \in B_w} f(\mathcal{I}_k(\mathrm{bet}_d(wa)))$$

$$= u|B_w| + v \sum_{a \in B_w} \log_k \mathrm{bet}_d(wa)$$

$$= u|B_w| + v \log_k \prod_{a \in B_w} \mathrm{bet}_d(wa)$$

$$\le u|B_w| + v \log_k \left(\frac{1}{|B_w|} \sum_{a \in B_w} \mathrm{bet}_d(wa) \right)^{|B_w|}$$

$$\le |B_w|(u - v \log_k |B_w|)$$

$$= g(|B_w|),$$

where

$$g(x) = x f(\log_k(x)).$$

Since $|B_w| \le k$ for all $w \in \Sigma^*$, it thus suffices to choose s_0 and s_1 so that

$$g(j) \le 1 \tag{7}$$

for all $1 \le j \le k$. Of course we want our lower bound f, and hence the function g, to be as large as possible while satisfying (7). Since

$$g'(x) = u - v \left(\frac{1}{\ln k} + \log_k x \right)$$

is positive to the left of some point (namely, $x = \frac{k^{\frac{u}{v}}}{e}$) and negative to the right of this point, (7) can be achieved by arranging things so that

$$g(i) = g(i+1) = 1 \tag{8}$$

for some (any!) $1 \le i < k$. Now (8) is equivalent to the conditions

$$f(\log_k i) = \frac{1}{i}, \quad f(\log_k(i+1)) = \frac{1}{i+1},$$

which simply say that

$$s_0 = \log_k i, \quad s_1 = \log_k(i+1). \tag{9}$$

For $1 \le i < k$, the predictor π determined by the choice of (9) is feasible and thus establishes (6). This argument yields the following improvement of Lemma 5.7.

Theorem 5.8. *For all $X \subseteq \Sigma^\infty$,*

$$\dim_p(X) \ge \overline{\mathcal{I}_k}(\mathrm{pred}_p(X)).$$

Proof. For each $1 \le i < k$, if we let $f_i(s) = u_i - v_i s$ be the function that agrees with k^{-s} at $\log_k i$ and $\log_k(i+1)$, then the above argument shows that

$$\mathrm{pred}_p(X) \ge f_i(\dim_p(X)),$$

whence

$$\dim_p(X) \ge f_i^{-1}(\mathrm{pred}_p(X)).$$

Since $\mathrm{pred}_p(X) \ge \frac{1}{k}$ in any case and f_i^{-1} agrees with $\overline{\mathcal{I}_k}$ on $[\frac{1}{i+1}, \frac{1}{i}]$, this establishes the theorem. $\qquad\square$

For each $k \ge 2$, let R_k be the set of all $\alpha, \beta \in [0,1]$ satisfying $\alpha \ge \frac{1}{k}$ and $\overline{\mathcal{I}_k}(\alpha) \le \beta \le \mathcal{H}_k(\alpha)$. Thus R_2, R_3, and R_4 are the shaded regions depicted in Figure 1, and Theorem 5.1 says that $(\mathrm{pred}_p(X), \dim_p(X)) \in R_k$ for all $k \ge 2$ and $X \subseteq \Sigma^\infty$. It can in fact be shown that Theorem 5.1 is tight in the strong sense that for each $(\alpha, \beta) \in R_k$ there is a set $X \subseteq \mathrm{E}\Sigma$ such that $\mathrm{pred}_p(X) = \alpha$ and $\dim_p(X) = \beta$. Thus R_k is precisely the set of all points of the form $(\mathrm{pred}_p(X), \dim_p(X))$ for $X \subseteq \Sigma^\infty$ (or, equivalently, for $X \subseteq \mathrm{E}\Sigma$).

Let R_∞ be the limit of the regions R_k, in the sense that R_∞ consists of all $(\alpha, \beta) \in [0,1]^2$ such that for every $\epsilon > 0$, for every sufficiently large k, there exists $(\alpha', \beta') \in R_k$ such that $(\alpha - \alpha')^2 + (\beta - \beta')^2 < \epsilon$. Then it is interesting to note that R_∞ is the triangular region given by the inequalities $\alpha \ge 0, \beta \ge 0, \alpha + \beta \le 1$. Thus if the alphabet Σ is very large, then the primary constraint is simply that a set's predictability cannot be significantly greater than 1 minus its dimension.

References

1. J. L. Balcázar, J. Díaz, and J. Gabarró. *Structural Complexity I (second edition)*. Springer-Verlag, Berlin, 1995. 387
2. N. Cesa-Bianchi, Y. Freund, D. Haussler, D. P. Helmbold, R. E. Schapire, and M. K. Warmuth. How to use expert advice. *Journal of the ACM*, 44(3):427–485, May 1997. 381, 382, 387
3. N. Cesa-Bianchi and G. Lugosi. On prediction of individual sequences. *Annals of Statistics*, 27(6):1865–1895, 1999. 381
4. T. M. Cover and J. A. Thomas. *Elements of Information Theory*. John Wiley & Sons, Inc., New York, N.Y., 1991. 382

5. J. J. Dai, J. I. Lathrop, J. H. Lutz, and E. Mayordomo. Finite-state dimension. In *Proceedings of the Twenty-Eighth International Colloquium on Automata, Languages, and Programming*, pages 1028–1039. Springer-Verlag, 2001. 383

6. K. Falconer. *Fractal Geometry: Mathematical Foundations and Applications*. John Wiley & Sons, 1990. 381, 387

7. M. Feder. Gambling using a finite state machine. *IEEE Transactions on Information Theory*, 37:1459–1461, 1991. 381

8. M. Feder, N. Merhav, and M. Gutman. Universal prediction of individual sequences. *IEEE Transations on Information Theory*, 38:1258–1270, 1992. 381, 383

9. F. Hausdorff. Dimension und äusseres Mass. *Math. Ann.*, 79:157–179, 1919. 381

10. J. Kelly. A new interpretation of information rate. *Bell Systems Technical Journal*, 35:917–926, 1956. 380

11. A. N. Kolmogorov. On tables of random numbers. *Sankhyā, Series A*, 25:369–376, 1963. 380

12. D. W. Loveland. A new interpretation of von Mises' concept of a random sequence. *Zeitschrift für Mathematische Logik und Grundlagen der Mathematik*, 12:279–294, 1966. 380

13. J. H. Lutz. Dimension in complexity classes. In *Proceedings of the Fifteenth Annual IEEE Conference on Computational Complexity*, pages 158–169. IEEE Computer Society Press, 2000. Updated version appears as Technical report cs.CC/0203016, ACM Computing Research Repository, 2002. 381, 388

14. J. H. Lutz. Gales and the constructive dimension of individual sequences. In *Proceedings of the Twenty-Seventh International Colloquium on Automata, Languages, and Programming*, pages 902–913. Springer-Verlag, 2000. Updated version appears as Technical report cs.CC/0203017, ACM Computing Research Repository, 2002. 381

15. D. A. Martin. Classes of recursively enumerable sets and degrees of unsolvability. *Zeitschrift für Mathematische Logik und Grundlagen der Mathematik*, 12:295–310, 1966. 380

16. B. Ya. Ryabko. Noiseless coding of combinatorial sources. *Problems of Information Transmission*, 22:170–179, 1986. 381

17. B. Ya. Ryabko. Algorithmic approach to the prediction problem. *Problems of Information Transmission*, 29:186–193, 1993. 381

18. B. Ya. Ryabko. The complexity and effectiveness of prediction problems. *Journal of Complexity*, 10:281–295, 1994. 381

19. C. P. Schnorr. A unified approach to the definition of random sequences. *Mathematical Systems Theory*, 5:246–258, 1971. 380

20. C. P. Schnorr. Zufälligkeit und Wahrscheinlichkeit. *Lecture Notes in Mathematics*, 218, 1971. 380

21. C. E. Shannon. Certain results in coding theory for noisy channels. *Bell Systems Technical Journal*, 30:50–64, 1951. 380

22. A. Kh. Shen'. On relations between different algorithmic definitions of randomness. *Soviet Mathematics Doklady*, 38:316–319, 1989. 380

23. L. Staiger. Kolmogorov complexity and Hausdorff dimension. *Information and Control*, 103:159–94, 1993. 381

24. L. Staiger. A tight upper bound on Kolmogorov complexity and uniformly optimal prediction. *Theory of Computing Systems*, 31:215–29, 1998. 381

25. V. Vovk. A game of prediction with expert advice. *Journal of Computer and System Sciences*, pages 153–173, 1998. 381

Learning the Internet

Christos Papadimitriou*

UC Berkeley, USA
http://www.cs.berkeley.edu/~christos

Abstract. The Internet is arguably the most important, complex, interesting, and intellectually challenging computational artifact of our time, and it is therefore worthy of the research community's attention. The most novel and defining characteristic of the Internet is its nature as an artifact that was not designed by a single entity, but emerged from the complex interaction of many economic agents (network operators, service providers, users, etc.), in various and varying degrees of collaboration and competition. There is a nascent research area that combines algorithmic thinking with concepts from Game Theory, as well as the realities of the Internet, in order to better understand it. This line of research may actually bring back to the fore certain foundational aspects of Game Theory (namely, the nature of equilibria as well as their relationship to repeated play and evolution) in which the methodology of Learning Theory has much to contribute.

The Internet is also an information repository of unprecedented extent, diversity, availability, and lack of structure, and it has therefore become an arena for the development of a new generation of sophisticated techniques for information retrieval and data mining (and to which Learning Theory has obviously much to offer). It has been suggested that economic considerations are crucial in formulating problems also in this environment, and can shed new light on important topics such as clustering and privacy.

Because of its spontaneous emergence, the Internet is the first computational artifact that must be studied as a mysterious object (akin to matter, market, and intelligence) whose laws we must derive by observation, experiment, and the development of falsifiable theories. Recently, a plausible explanation of the skewed degree distributions one observes in the Internet topology was based on simple models of network creation, in which arriving nodes choose connections that achieve a favorable tradeoff among criteria such as last-mile distance and communication delays. These topics will be illustrated in terms of recent models and results by the speaker and co-authors, generally available at the speaker's web page.

* Research supported by two NSF ITR grants, and an IBM award.

J. Kivinen and R. H. Sloan (Eds.): COLT 2002, LNAI 2375, p. 396, 2002.

Author Index

Lecture Notes in Artificial Intelligence (LNAI)

Lecture Notes in Computer Science